THE
COMPLETE GUIDE

TO THE BIBLE

THE
COMPLETE GUIDE
TO THE BIBLE

STEPHEN M. MILLER

BARBOUR BOOKS
An Imprint of Barbour Publishing, Inc

Member of the
Evangelical Christian
Publishers Association

I spent a year working full-time on this book—with occasional workday breaks to look out the window.

No, I wasn't bird-watching, goofing off, or giving my mind a place to wander. Just the opposite. I was trying to keep my head focused.

How does looking out the window do that?

Well, sometimes I get stumped over what words to type. I've been a Christian since I was a little boy. I'm used to church jargon, pulpit clichés, and Bible scholar lingo—which I call academese (ACK-uh-duh-MEEZE). Rhymes with *sneeze*.

So it's easy for me to use the Christian tech talk I grew up with. Trouble is, it's a foreign language to the people I want to see reading this book.

I didn't write this for folks who understand Christian jargon. I wrote it for curious people who have more questions about the Bible than answers.

That's a tough crowd.

But I figure if I can get them to read this book, maybe the Bible old-timers will read it, too. Who knows, maybe both groups will enjoy seeing ancient ideas all dressed up in fresh words that make sense today.

So when I was writing, I looked out the window to remind myself who I was writing for.

I work out of a home office. When I look out the window, I see a cul-de-sac of neighbors—most of whom I know, and most of whom are not Christians. When I back my car down the driveway on Sunday mornings to go to church, there's no rush hour going on. More like a hush hour. Dead silence. No movement but me and my family disturbing the peace while my neighbors obey at least one Sabbath Day commandment: rest.

I write for people in bed on Sunday mornings.

I'm hoping that once they get vertical they'll come across this book somewhere. Maybe as a curiosity that catches their eye while they're trolling aisles in a store. Or surfing Web sites. Or maybe it'll come in the mail as a gift.

I'm hoping they'll take a peek inside to discover an easy-reading Bible reference book that

- looks like a magazine,
- treats the Bible with the respect due a 2,000-year-old, and
- explores different opinions about what the Bible is saying.

If you're one of those Sunday morning, sleepy-eyed readers curious about the Bible and the God behind it, I have a confession. I thought I was donating a year of my life to you—a sacrifice of sorts. Boy, was I wrong. No one spends a year in the Bible only to come out on the short end of the deal.

If this book I've written leads you into the Bible—and I sure hope it does—you'll see what I mean.

A word of thanks

Lots of people helped bring this book to daylight. From midnight to dawn, here are a few.

Steve Laube, my agent. He believed in the idea enough to risk his time and money pitching it to publishers.

Paul K. Muckley, Barbour editor. He liked the idea enough to pitch it to his publishing board committee.

Linda A. Miller, my wife and first-round proofreader. She catches most of my mistakes and happily tells me about them. I smile and thank her. Well, usually.

Jason Rovenstine, design director. He envisioned this book as something colorful and gorgeous—then he found the folks to bring his vision to life.

Catherine Thompson, book designer. She created a fresh canvas of art with each turn of the page. With such a design-intensive book, she and her colleague (below) had to pull some overtime. So I'd like to thank them both at time and a half.

Ashley Schrock, design associate and map czar. Okay, I made up that second title because she worked so hard refining the maps. She did the same with other art in the book, too.

George Knight, Kelly Williams, Connie Troyer, and Annie Tipton, who all contributed to the editing and production process.

Shalyn Hooker, marketing manager. She spread the word that this is a book worth reading.

God bless each one of these people.

And God bless you as you read this book, and more importantly as you read *his* Book.

Steve

Stephen M. Miller
stephenmillerbooks.com

CONTENTS

Paul's Bible. Credited with writing nearly half the books in the New Testament, Apostle Paul had this to say about the only Bible he used—the Old Testament: "All Scripture is inspired by God and is useful to teach us what is true and to make us realize what is wrong in our lives" (2 Timothy 3:16).

OLD TESTAMENT

Some Christians hate this title almost as much as Jews do. They prefer First Testament.

Old Testament suggests "out of date." Yet many of the New Testament's favorite teachings come from the Old Testament—the first two-thirds of the Bible.

Take Jesus' commandment to love our neighbors as ourselves. He quoted that from Leviticus 19:18, a law written in Moses' time.

HOW WE GOT THE OLD TESTAMENT

Many of the oldest and most memorable stories—like those about Moses and Abraham—were passed along by word of mouth from one generation to the next. At least that's what Bible experts guess. The Hebrews didn't develop an alphabet until later, when they settled in Israel after Moses led them out of Egypt. Before that, Jews would have written with other alphabets, such as those from Egypt or Phoenicia, in modern-day Lebanon.

In King David's day, about a thousand years before Jesus, Jewish writers and editors started compiling the stories. They did it to preserve a record of their people and the new nation they started. As the centuries rolled on, this cherished library grew, adding stories, genealogies, laws, prophecy, poetry, and songs. Some books were lost, and survive only as titles that Bible writers mention in passing, such as *"The Record of Samuel the Seer, The Record of Nathan the Prophet,* and *The Record of Gad the Seer"* (1 Chronicles 29:29).

In time, Jews began to cherish certain books—treating them as sacred. First, the laws and stories of Moses in the first five books of the Bible. Then the books of the prophets. And finally the rest of the books in Old Testament—a diverse assortment of writings such as Psalms, Proverbs, and Job.

It's unclear when the Jews settled on the 39 books we now have. But many guess that Jewish leaders finalized their Bible shortly after Romans destroyed the last Jewish temple in AD 70. That's when Jewish faith started to spin around sacred words instead of a sacred place—since the Jerusalem temple was gone.

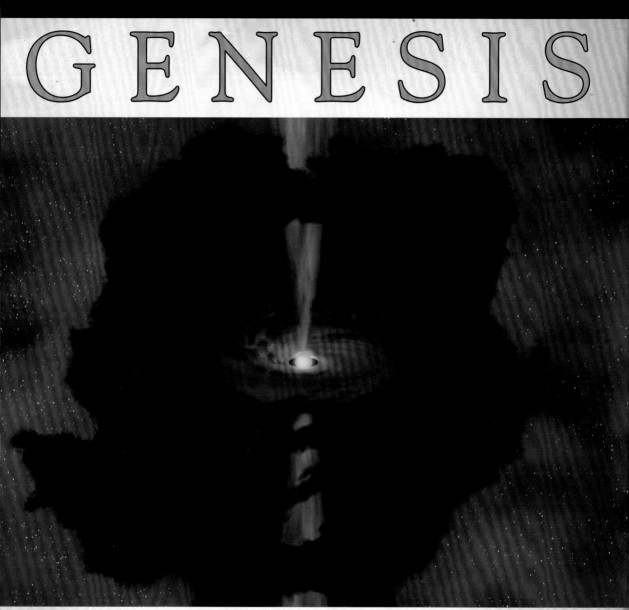

GENESIS

A star is born. Astronomers theorize that a star develops inside a dense cloud of gas and dust. Gravity from the newborn star draws in the dust, which forms a swirling disk. Jets of some kind of material seem to spray out at both poles, based on evidence gathered from peering into these clouds with NASA's Spitzer Space Telescope. Genesis doesn't answer questions about exactly how the universe was created. Instead, it answers the question of *who* created it.

WHEN A PERFECTLY GOOD WORLD GOES BAD

God creates a wonderful universe, with the perfect world for humans. But it doesn't stay perfect for long.

If God's to blame, it's for giving humans the freedom to make their own decisions. The Bible, however, teaches that humans are the ones responsible because they misused that freedom.

God creates the first couple, Adam and Eve. He gives them the run of the planet and only one rule to obey. It's one rule too many. They aren't supposed to eat fruit from a particular tree. But they eat it anyway.

This sin not only hurts their intimate relationship with God. It somehow contaminates the entire world—like a spiritual toxin that breaks into the physical dimension. Paradise is lost.

The rest of the Bible is the story of God working to rebuild his relationship with humanity, to get rid of sin, and to restore his perfect creation.

Genesis tells about the beginning of God's restoration plan. God starts with one man who trusts him completely: Abraham. God promises to produce from Abraham a race of descendants who will be devoted to the Lord—a chosen people who will teach the world the value of choosing obedience to God over disobedience.

Abraham has two sons, Ishmael and Isaac. But only Isaac will continue the family line that produces the chosen people. Isaac also has two sons, Esau and Jacob. But only Jacob's family grows into the nation devoted to God. Jacob has 12 sons, and they become the founding fathers of Israel's 12 tribes.

By the end of Genesis, Jacob's extended family has fled a drought in what is now Israel. They are living as welcome refugees in Egypt. Unfortunately, they will wear out their welcome. But that's the story of Moses and the Exodus.

MAIN POINT:

God created and sustains everything that exists. Though sin damaged God's creation and his relationship with humanity, God is at work in the world restoring both.

WRITER:

The book doesn't name the writer. An old Jewish tradition says Moses wrote the first five books in the Bible—Genesis through Deuteronomy. But Abraham, the book's starring character, lived at least 700 years before Moses, and perhaps almost 1,000 years. Many Bible experts say Genesis is a collection of stories passed down by word of mouth from one generation to the next. They say Jewish scholars assembled these stories into a book hundreds of years after Moses, during the time when kings ruled Israel.

DATE:

Genesis begins at the beginning of time and continues into the lifetime of Abraham's great-grandson, Joseph, who lived in about 1800 BC.

LOCATION:

The stories cover a lot of Middle Eastern territory, including what are now the countries of Iraq, Syria, Turkey, Israel, and Egypt.

LOTS OF BEGINNINGS

There are plenty of good reasons to call this book *Genesis*. That name comes from a Greek word. It means "origin," "birth," or "beginning." And this is a book full of beginnings:

- the universe
- humanity
- sin
- civilization
- the Jewish nation

CREATOR at work

In the beginning God created the heavens and the earth. The earth was formless and empty, and darkness covered the deep waters. And the Spirit of God was hovering over the surface of the waters.

GENESIS 1:1–2

God creates the physical universe, from the most distant stars to the starlight reflected in human eyes. In the creation story, God's work extends over seven days.

Day one. "Let there be light," God commands.

Day two. God separates the sky from water on the earth.

Day three. God separates the land from the water. Then he creates plants.

Day four. God creates the sun, moon, and stars.

Day five. Fish and birds fill the oceans and sky.

Day six. God creates land animals and human beings.

Day seven. God rests and declares Creation excellent.

BIBLE BOOKS OUT OF ORDER

Creation starts the Bible, in the book of Genesis. The end of the world finishes it, in Revelation. That could lead us to think the Bible is printed in chronological order. But it's not.

If it were, Job would likely come after Genesis. That's because Job seems to have lived in about the time of Abraham, whose story appears in Genesis. Instead, Job's story comes after Esther, though this Persian queen wasn't born for at least 1,500 years after Abraham and Job.

The Bible is a library of 66 books written in many genres and over a span of more than a thousand years. How the books ended up in the order we find them in our Bibles today is complicated—so complicated that it leaves Bible experts guessing.

In Old Testament times, the books in the Jewish Bible were divided into several sections: Law, Prophets, and Writings. And the first section—the first five books in the Bible—seems to have been the earliest material the Jews considered sacred. Next came the Prophets. And then the Writings, which include books like Psalms, Job, and Esther.

The New Testament also falls into several categories. There are the four Gospels about Jesus. Next comes the story of how the church got started (Acts). Then there's a stack of letters, generally arranged from the longest to the shortest. That's why Paul's 16-chapter letter to the Romans comes first and Jude's one-chapter letter comes last. The prophecy in Revelation wraps up the Bible, turning all eyes to the future that God has in store for his people.

Some people read this creation story as a myth. Others read it like a science book, searching for clues about how the universe unfolded—some insisting that the story took place over seven 24-hour days.

Many Bible experts say both approaches are too extreme. The story is no more a myth than God is, because the point of the story is to show that God created everything. In ancient times, there were many creation stories and many gods who got the credit. But the Bible writer wants to make sure the credit goes to where the credit belongs.

Many experts say there's also a problem reading this story like science. It was, after all, written some 2,500 years before Galileo launched the scientific revolution. That happened in the 1500s, when Galileo and others declared that the earth revolves around the sun. Scientists reading Genesis today might wonder how plants could grow (day three) before the sun was created (day four). They might also wonder why some Christians insist that the story took place over seven 24-hour days when the sun that is used to measure 24 hours wasn't created until day four.

In the Hebrew language, as in English, *day* can mean 24 hours, or something much longer: "In Abraham's day." That's part of the reason many Christians have no trouble with the idea that God may have taken eons to create the universe.

Yet Christians who prefer the literal six-day approach to creation offer a few questions of their own. If God created the world over a period of eons instead of 24-hour days, how could fruit trees have survived that long? Genesis says God created trees with seed-bearing fruit on day three. Yet it wasn't until the next day—or eon as some Christians would argue—that he created the insects necessary to pollinate those fruit trees.

The creation story has a finale—humanity: "Let us make human beings in our image, to be like us" (Genesis 1:26). Earlier, God had declared his work "good." But after creating humans, he upped his evaluation: "He saw that it was very good!" (Genesis 1:31).

ONE RULE too many

"You may freely eat the fruit of every tree in the garden—except the tree of the knowledge of good and evil. If you eat its fruit, you are sure to die."

GENESIS 2:16–17

WHY ARE WE HERE?

That's the big question. Why in the world did God create human beings?

Was he lonely? Did he have the same desire for children that many adults have today? Did he want someone to love—and to love him back?

Though Genesis doesn't directly answer those questions, it does provide at least one line of a job description for humans—a purpose for life: "They will reign over the fish in the sea, the birds in the sky, the livestock, all the wild animals on the earth, and the small animals that scurry along the ground" (Genesis 1:26).

There may be many reasons why God put human beings on this planet. But one of the reasons is to take care of his creation—to "tend and watch over it" (Genesis 2:15).

Before there are 10 Commandments, there's just one. Adam and Eve aren't supposed to eat fruit from a particular tree in the Garden of Eden.

Why the fruit is off-limits is anyone's guess. Perhaps Adam and Eve aren't mature enough to eat fruit that gives insight about good and evil. Maybe God intends to give them that knowledge later.

A talking snake, described later in the Bible as "the ancient serpent called the devil, or Satan" (Revelation 12:9), convinces Eve to eat the fruit.

"You won't die!" the serpent tells her. "Your eyes will be opened as soon as you eat it, and you will be like God, knowing both good and evil" (Genesis 3:4–5).

Eve eats. She convinces Adam to do the same.

That single act of disobedience somehow changes life on this planet—for the worse. The rest of the Bible is the story of God working to correct the damage and to defeat sin.

Decimated. That's a fair word to describe what happens to the intimate relationship between God and humanity. Once upon a time, Adam and Eve had recognized the sound of God's footsteps, apparently because he spent time "walking in the garden" (Genesis 3:10). But now God orders the couple out of his garden, forever.

Some Bible readers speculate that:
- Adam and Eve were created to live forever;
- animals were vegetarians living in peace with each other; and
- crops grew in the wild.

If so, all that changes. Adam and Eve will eventually die. In the meantime, their survival will depend on Adam's hard work at battling weeds, weather, and critters to grow enough food to survive. Humanity will survive only through painful childbirth.

THE ORIGINAL SIN

Some Bible experts, especially in past centuries, have speculated that the world's first sin somehow changed God's creation in a physical way—even to the point of genetically altering humans. In other words, those experts are speculating that it's like Eden's forbidden fruit contained a chemical that tripped our DNA sin switch—and that ever since, humans have suffered from the effects of what theologians call "original sin" or the "sinful nature."

The effects are this: Given the choice of taking a walk on the sinfully wild side or the righteously mild side, we'll generally go wild.

Most Bible experts today reject this physics-bound theory about original sin, as though the idea is a few loony birds shy of a flock. They argue—with what certainly seems like solid logic—that if sin's a physical problem, we'll one day find a cure. And once we do, future generations can spend their free time debating whose sins Jesus died for. That,

of course, doesn't track with the New Testament, which teaches that it's Jesus who saves us.

This much is clear, both in Bible teaching and in the personal observations of most people: "Everyone has sinned" (Romans 3:23).

How sin got a grip on people remains a mystery. But the Bible does tell us *when* it started: "When Adam sinned, sin entered the world. Adam's sin brought death, so death spread to everyone, for everyone sinned" (Romans 5:12).

The Bible also tells us how to break sin's grip: "Who will free me from this life that is dominated by sin and death? Thank God! The answer is in Jesus Christ our Lord. . .because you belong to him, the power of the life-giving Spirit has freed you from the power of sin that leads to death" (Romans 7:24–25; 8:2). (See also "Sinful Nature: The Short Course," page 382.)

WHAT "SONS OF GOD" married human women?

The sons of God saw the beautiful women and took any they wanted as their wives.

GENESIS 6:2

The Bible adds that children of these matches became the heroes and famous warriors of ancient times.

This puzzles Bible experts. They offer three theories about who the "sons of God" were.

- **Angels or some other kind of spirit beings.** In Job's ancient story, "sons of God" refers to angels. Yet Jesus said, "When the dead rise, they will neither marry nor be given in marriage. In this respect they will be like the angels in heaven" (Matthew 22:30).
- **Kings, princes, or other rulers.** The Bible sometimes calls kings and other leaders "sons of God." "You are gods," one writer said of court judges, "children of the Most High" (Psalm 82:6).
- **Godly men.** These sons of God are the descendants of Seth instead of the murderer Cain, who killed his brother, Abel. Abraham and the Jews came from Seth's family. And the Bible calls the Jewish people "God's children": "This is what the LORD says: Israel is my firstborn son" (Exodus 4:22).

An angel of a husband.
Angels were the "sons of God" that Genesis says married human women. That's the oldest theory about who those mysterious figures were. But other theories point to national leaders and to holy men.

NOAH and the flood

"I am about to cover the earth with a flood that will destroy every living thing that breathes."

GENESIS 6:17

Within 10 generations, people have become so sinful that "the LORD was sorry he had ever made them and put them on the earth. It broke his heart" (Genesis 6:6).

He decides to start over. He starts with the family of the only good human on earth: Noah. God decides to wash away the sin—and the sinners—with a massive flood. At God's instruction, Noah and his three sons build a floating warehouse that's longer than a football field, half as wide, and about four stories high.

The boat has the storage capacity of about 370 railroad boxcars, minus whatever interior space is used for support beams and walls. Noah loads the boat with supplies and with pairs of land animals, male and female.

For 40 days—perhaps a round number that simply means a long time—rain thunders down and geysers spray up from wells deep underground. By then, even the mountain peaks are entertaining curious fish.

Five months later, Noah's boat scrapes to a halt, running aground on a mountain in the Ararat range. That's somewhere on the border of what is now Turkey, Iran, and Armenia. But Noah and his passengers have to wait inside a little over a year. That's how long it takes for the land to dry out enough for Noah's family and the animals to leave the boat and begin repopulating the region.

God fills the sky with a rainbow. It's the seal on a promise he makes: "Never again will the floodwaters destroy all life" (Genesis 9:15).

A WORLDWIDE FLOOD?

Bible experts debate whether the flood covered the entire world as we know it, or the entire world as the ancients knew it—perhaps just the region where civilization started.

The first known Middle Eastern cities sprang up in the fertile river valleys of the Tigris and Euphrates rivers, in what is now Iraq and Iran. These rivers provided water for the people, animals, and crops. And they served as riverboat highways. Archaeologists have found evidence of massive floods that wiped out cities along the rivers.

But there was another flood farther north in about 4500 BC, geologists estimate. This flood took place about 200 miles north of Mount Ararat—the highest peak in the Ararat range. A whopper of a deluge, this flood turned the Black Sea from a freshwater lake to an ocean. It happened when the ocean broke through a narrow strip of land at what became the Bosporus Strait. Salt water rushed into the lake basin with the force of many Niagara Falls, pushing back the shoreline many miles.

Whether or not Noah's flood covered the entire earth, flood stories certainly do. They're woven into about 70 cultures—from Middle Easterners, to the American Indians, to the Chinese, to the South Pacific islanders.

The Epic of Gilgamesh, an ancient story from what is now Iraq, even tells of a Babylonian man who survived a flood by building a huge boat for his family and animals. Like Noah, he released a dove after the flood to see if it would find a resting place. The dove came back, just as it did for Noah.

ABRAHAM: Iraqi father of the Jews

"I am giving all this land, as far as you can see, to you and your descendants as a permanent possession. And I will give you so many descendants that, like the dust of the earth, they cannot be counted."

GENESIS 13:15–16

Abraham grows up in the Euphrates River town of Ur, in what is now southern Iraq. It's the New York City of its day—busy, wealthy, and bursting with culture: art, crafts, and the oldest written language on record, called cuneiform. Instead of using an alphabet, ink, and paper, writers use reed sticks to press pictures into soft clay.

For reasons unknown, Abraham's father, Terah, decides to move his entire extended family to the boonies of Canaan. That's a bit like a New Yorker moving to the cornfields of Des Moines—both in distance and in culture shock. Perhaps Terah has a feeling in the 2100s BC that Ur is ripe for invasion. In fact, invaders arrive about a century later.

Terah stops halfway to Canaan. He settles some 600 miles upriver in the busy caravan town of Haran, on Turkey's side of the border with Syria. After Terah dies, God tells Abraham to finish the trip to Canaan. That's when God promises to grow Abraham's family into a great nation.

Quite a promise for a childless 75-year-old man with a 66-year-old wife.

But Abraham obeys God. So he packs up and moves his household entourage and his herds south to what is now Israel.

A decade later—and still no kids—Abraham's wife, Sarah, decides it's time to call in a surrogate mother. Ancient Middle Eastern custom allows it. By law, this child will belong to Sarah and Abraham. Sarah chooses her Egyptian-born servant, Hagar, as the substitute mother. Hagar gives birth to Abraham's first son, Ishmael.

But God says the son he has in mind for Abraham will come from Sarah. God actually shows up as a traveler in Abraham's camp and says so. Sarah overhears this. She's 91 at the time—way too old to have kids, she thinks, but not too old to laugh. God hears the laugh and assures her, in his gentle way, that he'll get the last laugh.

Within the year, Sarah gives birth to a boy. She names him Isaac, Hebrew for "laughter." Seems appropriate given the history, as well as the future. Isaac would fill the tent of his parents with joy.

Sarah doesn't want Isaac to grow up having to split Abraham's wealth with Ishmael. In these days, the oldest son usually gets a double share of the inheritance and becomes leader of the extended family. So Sarah convinces Abraham to send Hagar and her son away. God approves, promising to

DID PEOPLE REALLY LIVE HUNDREDS OF YEARS?

Before the devastating flood, people generally lived for centuries, according to the Bible. Some lived almost 1,000 years.

Methuselah lived longest: 969 years. If people lived that long today, Richard the Lionheart might still be telling his war stories—from the Crusades.

As high as these numbers are, they're dwarfed by those in other ancient records. A clay prism from the world's first known civilization, Sumer, in what is now Iraq, says only eight kings ruled the land up until the flood—and those eight ruled for a total of 241,200 years. That's an average of 30,000 years per king. The shortest reign was 18,600 years.

Maybe the ancients measured time differently than we do, some history experts guess. Or maybe these are polite exaggerations, a way of honoring beloved leaders—perhaps a bit like giving some folks today honorary doctorates even though they didn't spend a day in college.

Others wonder if the numbers might be accurate. Perhaps the flood somehow changed the world in a way that drastically cut life spans. Maybe constant cloud cover before the flood gave way to blue skies and harmful sun rays. Or maybe the geysers released toxins previously buried deep in the earth.

Quarter-million empire. Inscribed almost 4,000 years ago, this Sumerian clay prism says eight kings ruled the empire before the flood.

take care of both sons and to make them each into great nations.

Isaac's descendants become the Jewish people. Ishmael is considered father of the Arab people. Ishmael has a dozen sons who start a dozen tribes scattered from Egypt to Saudi Arabia.

THEORIES on the toasting of Sodom

The LORD rained down fire and burning sulfur from the sky on Sodom and Gomorrah. He utterly destroyed them, along with the other cities and villages of the plain, wiping out all the people and every bit of vegetation.

GENESIS 19:24–25

The twin sin cities of Sodom and Gomorrah, along with their satellite villages, were notorious in Bible times for "pride, gluttony, and laziness, while the poor and needy suffered outside her door" (Ezekiel 16:49). And because some men in Sodom tried to gang-rape angels sent to escort Lot out of town, this city also earned a reputation for rape and homosexuality. *Sodomy,* which is homosexual sex, takes its name from the city.

Bible experts don't know exactly where Sodom and the other cities were, or how God seared them off the planet.

As for the location, one of the most persistent theories puts them in or near the shallow water on the Dead Sea's south end. The idea is that in Bible times, this area was a fertile plain—not flooded as it is today.

Snow-capped Mount Ararat, with Little Ararat behind.

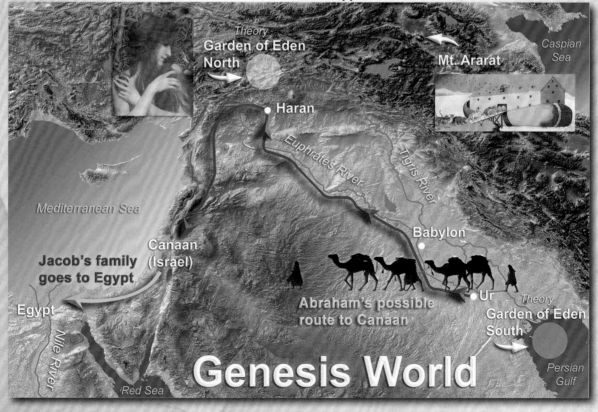

Theory
Garden of Eden North

Caspian Sea

Mt. Ararat

Haran

Euphrates River

Tigris River

Mediterranean Sea

Babylon

Canaan (Israel)

Jacob's family goes to Egypt

Abraham's possible route to Canaan

Ur

Theory
Garden of Eden South

Egypt

Nile River

Red Sea

Persian Gulf

Genesis World

Dead Sea chemical mining. Floating on nature's abstract canvas, chemicals await collection by miners. The chemicals rise from the water and dry in evaporation beds of the Dead Sea's southern shallows. Some Bible experts say Sodom and Gomorrah once thrived here—until an earthquake set off a chain of disasters: explosions, chemical fires, and the flooding of a once-fertile plain now covered by the southern Dead Sea.

At the moment, there are a couple of intriguing theories about *how* God destroyed the cities. Both depend on two facts. First, the entire area sits on a massive rip in the earth's crust, called the Great Rift Valley. Second, the region is rich in natural gas and minerals such as sulfur and salt. Israel and Jordan mine these resources today.

- **Big boom theory.** An earthquake ripped apart pockets of natural gas, which were ignited by predawn lamps in the cities. Explosions propelled ground minerals high into the air, and they rained back down in a firestorm.
- **Surfing turf theory.** Built on sand beside the sea, the cities were shaken by an earthquake. For a moment, the landscape floated on the groundwater beneath, like quicksand. Then pulled by gravity, the entire area slid down into the sea, the cities aflame from natural gas fires. This theory was suggested by a retired geologist, Graham H. Harris, writing in the *Quarterly Journal of Engineering Geology and Hydrogeology*, November 1995.

GOD TO ABRAHAM: "Kill your son"

"Take your son, your only son—yes, Isaac, whom you love so much. . . . Go and sacrifice him as a burnt offering."

GENESIS 22:2

God orders Abraham to slaughter Isaac, hack his corpse into manageable pieces, and burn it to ashes. That's Abraham's son—the son God had promised would produce a nation of descendants who would inherit Israel.

What sense could that possibly make? Yet Abraham agrees. Some wonder if Abraham is expecting God to raise Isaac from the dead, piece by piece.

The Bible doesn't say how old Isaac is at the time. But Jewish legend says he's 37—and that the news of Abraham's plan shocks Sarah to death at age 127.

Father and son walk about three days north to Mount Moriah, the hill where Jews a thousand years later will build the Jerusalem temple. There, Abraham piles up stones to make a simple altar. He arranges wood on top. Then he ties up his son, lays him on the altar, and picks up a knife to slice his boy's throat for a quick death.

"Don't lay a hand on the boy!" says an angel—who may actually be the Lord himself. "Now I know that you truly fear God. You have not withheld from me even your son, your only son" (Genesis 22:12).

As if an all-knowing God needed to test Abraham's faith.

New Testament writers will later see in this story a foreshadowing of another Father-Son sacrifice. What Abraham was willing to do—sacrifice his son—God did.

Perhaps Abraham's story is to help people understand how much God suffered because of humanity's sin. Though it seems impossible for us to understand why Jesus had to die for the sins of human beings, the Bible teaches this is what happened. And it was God who sent Jesus to die. When the Roman soldier raised his hammer to drive in the nails on that Friday morning, no angel came to stop him.

But angels were there at dawn on Sunday.

JACOB AND ESAU, twins at war

Rebekah became pregnant with twins. But the two children struggled with each other in her womb.

GENESIS 25:21–22

Isaac marries Rebekah, who becomes pregnant with twin sons: Jacob and Esau. They wrestle so much in the uterus that Rebekah asks God, "Why is this happening to me?"

"The sons in your womb will become two nations," God answers. "From the very beginning, the two nations will be rivals. One nation will be stronger than the other; and your older son will serve your younger son."

Perhaps that's why the number two son, Jacob—who was born one moment after Esau—becomes her favorite. Papa Isaac prefers Esau, the red-haired hunter who brings home savory meat.

Jacob cheats Esau out of two of the most valuable things in ancient life:

- an inheritance; and
- the deathbed blessing of the father.

Esau, in what reads like one of the dumbest acts in the Bible, willingly trades his rich inheritance for a bowl of hot soup. As the oldest son, he gets a double share of the family estate. So perhaps what he trades is only his rights as the oldest son, while retaining a single share. In either case, the soup is overpriced. And the story reads like a set-up—as though Jacob waited for just the right time, when Esau came home from a hunt exhausted and starving.

Later, Isaac intends to give his deathbed blessing to Esau. This blessing will put Esau in charge of the family. And it will call on God to bless Esau with power, prestige, and wealth. Isaac thinks of this blessing as more than a prayer. It's a promise that he expects God to bring to life for Esau.

It's not to happen.

Rebekah helps Jacob trick the blind, old Isaac into thinking Jacob is Esau. Convinced, Isaac blesses the wrong son with words he can't take back. When Esau shows up later, the only words left for him sound more like a curse than a blessing. "You will live away from the richness of the earth, and away from the dew of the heaven above" (Genesis 27:39).

Esau vows to kill Jacob as soon as their father dies. So Jacob leaves the country and heads north to the home of his mother's brother, Laban. Uncle Laban lives along the border of what is now Turkey and Syria.

THE FAMILY TREE OF THE BIBLICAL PATRIARCHS

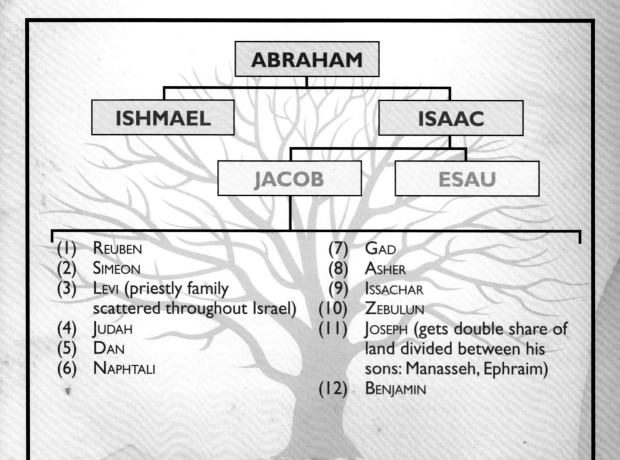

ABRAHAM

ISHMAEL   **ISAAC**

JACOB   **ESAU**

(1) REUBEN
(2) SIMEON
(3) LEVI (priestly family scattered throughout Israel)
(4) JUDAH
(5) DAN
(6) NAPHTALI
(7) GAD
(8) ASHER
(9) ISSACHAR
(10) ZEBULUN
(11) JOSEPH (gets double share of land divided between his sons: Manasseh, Ephraim)
(12) BENJAMIN

JACOB'S surprise wife

There was no sparkle in Leah's eyes, but Rachel had a beautiful figure and a lovely face. Since Jacob was in love with Rachel, he told her father, "I'll work for you for seven years if you'll give me Rachel, your younger daughter, as my wife."

GENESIS 29:17–18

Women are property in Jacob's world. They pass from father to husband in a business transaction. The father loses a household worker, so he expects some compensation for his loss.

Jacob falls in love with the gorgeous Rachel. She's his first cousin and Laban's number two daughter. Unfortunately, Jacob had left home in a hurry without any of his father's substantial assets—most of which had four legs and ate grass. So Jacob offers to work seven years for Laban, as payment for Rachel.

It's a deal.

Seven years later Jacob gets the surprise of his life—the surprise of his wife. On the morning of the first day of the rest of his life as a married man, Jacob wakes up in bed with the wrong woman: Leah.

How Jacob manages to get through the wedding ceremony, the dinner party, and the night of lovemaking without taking a look at his surprise bride is a wonder. This might suggest a nighttime ceremony, a thick veil over the bride, and a lot of wine inside the groom.

Sober by sunrise, Jacob storms off to Laban, the cheat who cheated a cheater. Laban simply explains it's the custom to marry off the oldest daughter first. But apparently it's not the custom to mention the custom ahead of time.

Jacob agrees to finish out the traditional week of wedding celebrations. It's out of respect for Leah, who must have felt horribly used. At week's end, Jacob marries Rachel, but only after committing to another seven years of labor for Laban—the only winner in this deal.

Mrs. Beauty and Mrs. Beast. Jacob works seven years for the privilege of marrying Rachel, a "beautiful" young woman. But Rachel's father pulls a wedding-day switcheroo. Jacob wakes up the next morning with Rachel's older sister, Leah. She has "weak" or "glazed-over" eyes, though scholars aren't sure what to make of that. Whatever it means, it seems intended as the flip side of Rachel's description. If Rachel's the beauty, Leah's the beast.

GOOD-BYE LABAN, hello Esau

Jacob put his wives and children on camels, and he drove all his livestock in front of him. He packed all the belongings he had acquired. . .and set out for the land of Canaan, where his father, Isaac, lived.

GENESIS 31:17–18

Working as a shepherd, Jacob not only manages to make Laban rich. Jacob gets rich, too. Not only in herds, but in children—13 of them. Wealth in ancient times is measured partly by the size of the family. The bigger the family, the more workers you have. And when they grow up, the more security you have in your old age.

Jacob ends up with this many children because of his dueling wives. They compete for his affection by trying to give him sons. God takes pity on Leah because Jacob doesn't love her like he does Rachel. So God allows her to have six sons and a daughter. Leah also gives Jacob her maid as a surrogate mother, who provides two more sons. Rachel, infertile for years, offers her maid, as well—and gets two sons. In time, Rachel has two sons of her own—Jacob's favorite boys: Joseph first and then Benjamin, who is born on the road trip back to Canaan.

With his 14 years served and another six used to build his own flocks, Jacob heads for home. But he's terrified of Esau. The night before crossing into Canaan, he sends his family ahead, intending to spend some time alone. A mysterious man arrives. Somehow Jacob seems to recognize this man as a being with the power to influence the future.

Jacob grabs hold of the man, whom many Bible experts say is either an angel or God in human form. Jacob says, "I will not let you go unless you bless me" (Genesis 32:26).

After an all-night struggle, the man finally blesses Jacob and gives him a new name: Israel. It means "God struggles" or "one who struggles with God." Centuries later, Jacob's descendants will take this name for their nation.

With Esau ahead, Jacob sends wave after wave of gifts for his brother: hundreds of prime livestock delivered by a corps of herders. The herders return with news that Esau is coming—with an army of 400 men. Jacob arranges his family in a column, putting his beloved Rachel and young Joseph at the very back. Benjamin isn't born yet.

Jacob walks ahead of his entire family and bows to his brother. "Esau ran to meet him and embraced him, threw his arms around his neck, and kissed him. And they both wept" (Genesis 33:4).

Jacob settles in Canaan, where he had grown up. Esau moves into what is now Jordan. And the land takes his nickname: Edom, which means "red."

SELLING little brother Joseph

When Joseph arrived, his brothers ripped off the beautiful robe he was wearing. Then they grabbed him and threw him into the cistern.

GENESIS 37:23–24

Jacob plays favorites with his dozen sons. Normally, it's the oldest son who gets special attention—and that would be Reuben, son of Leah. But Jacob preferred the oldest son of his dear Rachel: Joseph—number 11 in line of the dozen boys. Rachel had died en route to Canaan while giving birth to her second son, Benjamin. So these two boys are all Jacob has to remember the only woman he truly loved.

Joseph grows into a spoiled, braggadocious, tattletale teen. And his big brothers grow to hate him for it.

A dream is what turns his brothers violent. Joseph, age 17, tells his family he had a dream that the sun, moon, and 11 stars bowed before him. Even old Jacob gets upset about that because he sees the symbolism.

"Will your mother and I and your brothers actually come and bow to the ground before you?" Jacob scolded (Genesis 37:10).

Soon afterward, perhaps within a few weeks, Jacob's 10 oldest sons are out grazing the sheep about 60 miles north of the Hebron home. That's about a hard three-day walk. Jacob sends Joseph to check on them. So Joseph puts on the beautiful robe his father had given him, and he heads out.

"Here comes the dreamer!" one of his brothers says. They rip off Joseph's robe and throw him into a dry cistern, which is a deep pit that's built to store water. While they argue over whether or not to kill him, a traders' caravan stops. The caravan is headed to Egypt, and one of the merchants agrees to buy Joseph and sell him in Egypt as a slave. Selling price: eight ounces of silver. On today's market, that's about $80 when silver sells for $10 an ounce.

With Joseph gone, the brothers smear his torn robe in goat's blood. Then they take it

DADDY IS MY GRANDPA

Judah, one of Jacob's dozen sons, fathered twin boys—with his daughter-in-law. In fairness to Judah, he thought she was a prostitute.

The woman's name was Tamar. She married Judah's son, Er, but he died before the couple had any children. Custom called for Er's brother to marry the widow. That way, Tamar could have a son in Er's name, to inherit Er's property. (Women couldn't inherit property—since they were property.) Younger brother Onan married Tamar and had sex with her, but he refused to release semen inside her. He wanted his children to inherit all the property. For that, God killed him.

With two sons down, Judah refused to give Tamar his next son, Shelah.

So Tamar dressed as a prostitute, covered her face with a veil, and put herself in Judah's path. He propositioned her, had sex with her, and gave her his walking stick as collateral for payment. She kept the stick—which turned out to be a good thing for her.

When Judah found out Tamar was pregnant, he ordered her burned to death. That's when she brought out the walking stick. Humiliated, Judah replied, "She is more righteous than I am because I didn't arrange for her to marry my son Shelah." (Genesis 38:26).

Tamar's twins, Perez and Zerah, became the legal sons of Er. Judah never slept with Tamar again.

home and tell their father they found it, convincing old Jacob that a wild animal ate his son. There's no consoling Jacob. The love of his life is gone, and so is her first son.

BOWING to Joseph

Since Joseph was governor of all Egypt and in charge of selling grain to all the people, it was to him that his brothers came. When they arrived, they bowed before him with their faces to the ground.

GENESIS 42:6

From a slave to a ruler—Joseph's step up into high society is one that his brothers never anticipate.

Joseph begins his life in Egypt as a household slave for Potiphar, captain of the palace guard. Potiphar takes a liking to the hardworking boy and eventually puts him in charge of all his household affairs. Potiphar's wife takes a liking to the handsome boy, as well. And she wants to become one of those household affairs.

Sexual harassment continues day after day. It finally ends when Potiphar's wife grabs Joseph's cloak one day and says, "Come and sleep with me" (Genesis 39:7). Joseph sprints away, leaving her holding the cloak. Furious, she screams rape. This acts like a trumpet call that rallies all the servants in range of her blast.

Potiphar apparently doubts her story about a good-looking, well-built teenager who wants her body. Law allows the slave owner to instantly execute a violent slave. Instead, Potiphar just sends Joseph to prison.

Governor Joseph. Promoted from slave to governor of Egypt, Joseph hears a report about the grain reserves the king assigned him to manage during a seven-year drought.

That's a good thing for Joseph. There, he interprets dreams for two of the king's recently jailed servants, correctly predicting what will happen to the men. The baker is executed. The wine server gets his job back.

Two years later the king has some troubling dreams, and the wine server tells him about Joseph. In one dream, seven starving cows eat seven fat cows. And in another, seven withered heads of grain gobble up seven plump grain heads.

"The next seven years will be a period of great prosperity throughout the land of Egypt," Joseph tells the king, interpreting the dream. "But afterward there will be seven years of famine so great that all the prosperity will be forgotten in Egypt. Famine will destroy the land" (Genesis 41:29–30).

The king not only believes Joseph's interpretation, he believes God has given Joseph special insight and wisdom. So he puts Joseph in charge of managing the grain reserves to get the nation through the coming famine.

Drought spreads at least as far north as modern-day Israel. There, elderly Jacob hears about the grain reserves in Egypt. So he sends his 10 oldest sons to buy some. He keeps with him Benjamin, which is all he has left to remind him of Rachel.

The men bow before their brother, who's about 20 years older than when they saw him last. They don't recognize him. But he recognizes them. And he hatches a scheme to see if they regret what they did to him.

"You are spies!" he tells them. And he orders them to bring their younger brother, Benjamin, before him to prove they're not lying about who they are. In the meantime, Joseph holds one of his brothers hostage. It's Simeon, the second oldest. Perhaps Joseph skips Reuben, the oldest, because it was Reuben who talked the others out of killing Joseph on the day slave traders bought him.

With Joseph listening, the brothers admit they're getting what they deserve. "Clearly we are being punished because of what we did to Joseph long ago," they say. "We saw his anguish when he pleaded for his life, but we wouldn't listen. That's why we're in this trouble" (Genesis 42:21). Joseph weeps, realizing they're sorry for what they had done to him.

The men return to Canaan. But old Jacob refuses to let Benjamin go. He holds out as long as he can, until the family needs more grain. Then he reluctantly sends all of his sons to Egypt, Benjamin included.

JOSEPH'S family reunion

"Hurry back to my father and tell him, 'This is what your son Joseph says: God has made me master over all the land of Egypt. So come down to me immediately! You can live in the region of Goshen, where you can be near me with all your children and grandchildren, your flocks and herds, and everything you own.'"

GENESIS 45:9–10

With his brothers again at his mercy, Joseph concocts one more test. He loads them up with grain. Then he has a servant stuff one of his silver cups into Benjamin's sack. Later Joseph arrests Benjamin for stealing. Joseph wants to see if the older brothers will abandon their little brother, just as they had once done to him.

But the brothers plead for Benjamin. Judah confesses what they had done to Benjamin's brother, and how it broke their father's heart. It was Judah who talked his brothers into selling Joseph to the slave traders. But now it's Judah who offers to take Benjamin's place and stay in Egypt as a slave.

Joseph can't hold back the surge of emotion any longer. "I am Joseph!" he cries. "Is my father still alive?"

Stunned silent, the older brothers expect retaliation. Instead, they get forgiveness.

"Don't be upset, and don't be angry with yourselves for selling me to this place," Joseph assures them. "It was God who sent me here ahead of you to preserve your lives" (Genesis 45:5).

With the king's blessing, Joseph invites his entire extended family to move down to the lush Goshen grasslands of northern Egypt to weather out the remaining five years of the famine. Jacob, ecstatic at discovering his son is still alive, happily agrees. And the descendents of Abraham, Isaac, and Jacob—all 70 of them—move to Egypt.

EXODUS

Good-bye Egypt. Freed from Egyptian slavery, Israelites hurriedly pack everything they can carry and start their long journey home.

SLAVES FOLLOW MOSES OUT OF EGYPT

A seven-year drought blisters Canaan, a region today known as Israel. So Jacob packs up his extended family—all 70 souls—and moves to Egypt.

There's plenty of water along the Nile River. And Egypt's king has invited the family down since Jacob's son Joseph is one of the king's favorite officials.

Four hundred and thirty years later, Jacob's descendants are still there. Somewhere along the way a new king has turned them into a slave race. They build cities.

God sends Moses to free them. But Egypt's king, identified only by his title—Pharaoh—

MAIN POINT:

In a series of dramatic miracles, God steps into human history and rescues the Israelites from slavery. Then he organizes them into a nation, complete with laws to govern them as his people.

WRITER:

The book doesn't name the writer. An old Jewish tradition says Moses wrote it. Clue #1: God told Moses to "write down all these instructions, for they represent the terms of the covenant I am making with you and with Israel" (Exodus 34:27). Clue #2: Jesus called Exodus "the writings of Moses" (Mark 12:26). But many scholars say the stories were probably passed along by word of mouth for many centuries before Jewish writers finally wrote them down as part of the nation's history.

DATE:

The Exodus may have taken place in the mid-1400s BC or 200 years later. The early date of about 1440 BC is based on 1 Kings 6:1, which says that Solomon's earliest construction of the temple (about 960 BC) took place 480 years after the Exodus. The later date of the 1200s BC is based partly on Exodus 1:11, which says the slaves built the city of Rameses. The famed builder-king of Egypt, Rameses II, ruled from 1279–1212 BC.

LOCATION:

Egypt

insists on keeping his slave labor. He releases them only after God, acting through Moses, hammers the Egyptians with 10 plagues, decimating their crops, herds, and families.

Moses leads the Israelites out of Egypt on what becomes a 40-year journey home. During that time, God organizes the people into a nation. He gives them hundreds of laws—religious, civil, and criminal. These laws set up a system for worship and for running the country, with God as king.

GUESTS become slaves

The Egyptians worked the people of Israel without mercy. They made their lives bitter, forcing them to mix mortar and make bricks and do all the work in the fields.

EXODUS 1:13–14

Jacob's extended family of 70 children and grandchildren overstay their welcome in Egypt. The drought in Canaan ends. But Jacob's family doesn't go home. Instead, they keep grazing their flocks in Egypt's lush, northeast pastures. Jacob dies, and so do all of his 12 sons. But they leave behind a fast-growing family.

In time, perhaps after a century or more, a new Egyptian king realizes there are so many immigrants that they could take over his country. So he herds them into a slave labor force. They build at least two cities: Rameses and Pithom. The king hopes that the brutal labor will wear them down and slow their surging birthrate. The original language describes the Israelites with a dramatic word that translates as a "swarm."

Plan A for population control fails. Hard work does nothing to stop the baby boom.

So the king moves to Plan B: self-inflicted genocide. He orders Israelite midwives to kill all newborn Israelite boys. But they can't bring themselves to do it.

The king announces Plan C. It's his final solution for the Israelite problem. When the Egyptians see an Israelite baby boy, they are to express their patriotism by throwing him into the Nile River. Since Egyptian cities rest along the banks of the Nile, this is a convenient way to kill a baby. One toss and the life is gone. No cleanup or burial needed.

MOSES floats

The woman became pregnant and gave birth to a son. . . . When she could no longer hide him, she got a basket made of papyrus reeds and waterproofed it with tar and pitch. She put the baby in the basket and laid it among the reeds along the bank of the Nile River.

EXODUS 2:2–3

Slave brick makers

"Make bricks!" (Exodus 5:16). That's what Egyptians demanded of their Israelite slaves—mud bricks reinforced with straw.

Pictures on Egyptian tombs from Bible times show slaves called "foreigners" making bricks. One is from the tomb of a government official for Thutmose III, Egyptian king who started ruling about 1450 BC. A caption quotes the slave driver: "The club is in my hand. Don't rest."

One painting describes the life of a slave brick maker: "He is dirtier than vines or pigs from working in the mud. . . . He is simply miserable."

An Egyptian scroll from the time of Rameses II, the builder-king from the 1200s BC, reports the quota for a work gang of 10 brick makers: 2,000 handmade bricks every day.

The woman is Jochebed, mother of Moses. In a way, she obeys the king. She puts her son in the Nile River. However, she makes sure he floats. And she puts him near where the king's daughter bathes.

Hiding nearby, watching, is the baby's big sister—Miriam. As expected, the princess finds the baby basket, opens it, and realizes the boy must be an Israelite. Still, her heart melts.

Miriam walks over and says she knows a woman who can breastfeed the boy and take care of him. Jochebed gets the job. She actually gets paid to be a mother to her own son.

The princess adopts the boy and names him Moses—probably for two reasons. She drew him out of the water, and *Moses* sounds like a Hebrew word meaning "draw out." Also, in Egyptian the name simply means "boy." It's a name often used in various forms among Egyptian royalty: Ahmose I and II, along with Thutmose I through IV. Thutmose I (ruling from 1524–1518 BC) may have been the Israelite-hating king on the throne when Moses was born. If so, it's a tad funny that the Israelite-hating king ends up with an adopted Israelite grandson named after him.

As an adult, Moses becomes emotionally attached to his people. When he sees an Egyptian beating a slave, Moses kills the Egyptian slave driver and then buries the corpse under the sand. But when Moses finds out that some Israelites saw the murder, he flees the country—because he believes the king will order him executed.

Moses travels east—in the same direction he will later lead his people. He settles east of the Sinai Peninsula, along what is now the border of Jordan and Saudi Arabia. There he meets a shepherd, marries one of the man's daughters, has a son, and works as a shepherd until he's 80 years old.

Baby in a basket, to go. Riding high, baby Moses accompanies his new guardian—the princess of Egypt. While bathing in the Nile River, she discovered him floating in a basket among the riverbank reeds.

GOD in the bushes

The angel of the Lord appeared to him in a blazing fire from the middle of a bush.

EXODUS 3:2

Elderly Moses is grazing his father-in-law's sheep in a field near Mount Sinai. A bush erupts in fire but doesn't burn up. Some folks say this might have been a natural phenomenon involving *fraxinella*, commonly called the "gas plant." Native to the Middle East, this plant emits gas vapor that can ignite under a scorching sun—and burn without destroying the plant.

But even if the fire is natural, the talking bush isn't.

"Take off your sandals, for you are standing on holy ground." The voice comes from inside the fire. It's either an angel or God himself, since the divine being is later described as the Lord. In either case, the message comes from God.

"You will lead my people, the Israelites, out of Egypt."

Moses isn't so sure. He makes three excuses for not going back to Egypt.

Excuse number one: "Who am I to appear before Pharaoh?"

God answers, "I will be with you."

Excuse number two: "They won't believe me."

God promises to give Moses miracle-working power that will convince everyone—Israelites and Egyptians alike—that God has sent him.

Excuse number three: "I'm clumsy with words."

God answers with a question: "Who makes mouths?"

Reluctantly, Moses heads for Egypt, accompanied by his wife and son.

MEETING the god-king

"Let my people go."

EXODUS 5:1

This is probably their book's most famous line. It's the message God told Moses and his older brother, Aaron, to deliver to Pharaoh.

The king is underwhelmed.

"Who is the Lord that I should listen to him?" the king asks.

That's a good question.

Egyptians consider their king a god: the son of Ra, who is the powerful sun god in this desert land. The king certainly knows of many gods, since Egyptians worship a packed gallery of them. But he has apparently heard little or nothing about the Israelite God. Even if he has, what's to impress him about a god who allows his worshippers to languish in slavery for generations? A god like that would seem wimpy.

Pharaoh decides to teach Moses and the Israelites who's boss. He orders the Israelites to start gathering their own straw—while making just as many bricks as before.

The Israelites complain to Moses. "May the Lord judge you for getting us into this terrible situation with Pharaoh."

In response, Moses complains to God. "Why did you send me?"

"You will see what I will do to Pharaoh," God answers. "When he feels my powerful hand upon him, he will let the people go."

Modern plague of locusts. A swarm of locusts devours its way across Egypt, northern Africa, and Spain in November 2004. That's in spite of seasonal pest-control spraying in the region, to keep the infestation numbers down. (For more pictures and information about locust plagues, see pages 236 and 238.)

TEN plagues

"If you refuse to let them go, I will send a plague of frogs across your entire land."

EXODUS 8:2

The Egyptians suffer through 10 catastrophic plagues before their stubborn king agrees to free the Israelites.

It's possible that most of the plagues follow a cycle of natural disasters, with each disaster triggering the next. At least that's what scientists in various specialties have said—including experts in infectious diseases, tropical health, botany, marine life, and amphibians.

Here's a list of the 10 plagues, and the possible natural causes that God may have intensified to cause panic among the Egyptians. It starts with autumn floods. And it ends after springtime crop failure.

1. Nile River turns to blood. This may have been caused by something like the modern-day Red Tide algae that turns water red and kills fish—more than 21 million off the Texas coast in 1998–99. The Red Tide normally happens at sea but can occur near where rivers meet the sea. Flooding and storms stir up the sediment in central African swamps where the Nile begins. This releases cells that develop into toxic algae. The algae blooms red and spits out chemicals that paralyze fish gills as it passes through.

An ancient Egyptian document from about the time of the exodus seems to confirm this Bible story by reporting a similar incident: "The river is blood. People refuse to drink it, and thirst for water." This is from *The Admonitions of Ipuwer*, a story about a nationwide disaster recorded during the Nineteenth Dynasty (about 1300–1200 BC).

2. Frogs. Without fish to eat the frog eggs, the frog population takes a giant leap. Frogs flee the toxic river and infest the Egyptian communities—most of which are built along the fertile riverbanks. Eventually the frogs die, perhaps from river toxin.

3. Swarms of flying insects. The general Hebrew term could refer to gnats, mosquitoes, tiny mosquito-like flies called midges, or some other insect. Any of these could have bred in swampy pools left after the floodwater receded.

4. Swarms of flies. The stable fly—a worldwide pest—can lay several hundred eggs during its month-long lifespan. The fly usually lays its eggs in manure, wet straw, or some other decaying substance—such as dead frogs. This quarter-inch fly that looks much like a housefly has a flesh-piercing bite, feeds on blood, and can transmit many diseases. Health specialists are looking into the possibility that they might even be able to transmit AIDS.

5. Diseased livestock. Anthrax has been suggested as a possibility. One of the oldest known diseases, it is often transmitted to animals through contaminated drinking water. Other possible diseases, carried by insects such as midges or mosquitoes, include viruses called African horse sickness (70–95 percent fatal in horses) and bluetongue virus, which can be deadly to sheep and cattle.

6. Boils. The stable fly can carry various diseases that produce blisters or boils. Again, anthrax is a possible culprit. Often transmitted to animals through contaminated drinking water, it moves up the food chain when the infected animals are eaten. And it produces burning, pus-filled blisters. Glanders is another bacterial infection that can be carried by the stable fly and produce boils. Both anthrax and glanders can be fatal.

7. Hail. Still common in Egypt today, hail can devastate crops.

8. Locusts. This destroys even more crops. Swarms still threaten the region but are monitored carefully and are usually controlled with widespread spraying of pesticides. Millions descended on Northern Africa—Egypt included—in 2004.

9. Three days of darkness. In the spring, a hot wind that Egyptians call a *Khamsin* (Arabic for "50 days") can blast in from the Sahara Desert. It's possible anytime from March through May. Filling the air with sand, this wind sometimes blocks the sun for days.

10. Death of firstborn. There may have been nothing natural about this, since it selectively took the lives of the firstborn Egyptian sons and their firstborn male animals. One theory is that in the rush to harvest what few crops they could, the Egyptians gathered the grain when it was wet and covered in locust droppings. The bacterial contamination could have made people deathly sick—and doubly so for the firstborn. That's because it was a common Middle East custom to give the oldest boy a double portion of food. This, however, wouldn't explain why the firstborn animals died.

In a separate theory about these disasters, some scientists say the trigger may have been the eruption of a volcano on the island of Thera, north of Egypt. The quaking ground could have released gasses that turned the Nile River red. In 1986, gasses released below Lake Nyos in Cameroon did just that. Oxygen and iron particles produced a rust color.

No scientific theory about the plagues has generated widespread support.

GOD VS. EGYPTIAN GODS

Some specialists in Egyptian religion wonder if God targeted Egyptian gods when he sent the 10 plagues.

Each plague seems to step on the turf of at least one Egyptian god. So maybe this was God's way of showing that he was the only true God.

Turning the Nile River to blood, for instance, showed God's power over Sobek—a god of the Nile who is portrayed in Egyptian art as a man with a crocodile head. Turning the sky dark showed God's power over Ra, god of the sun, who was considered Egypt's strongest god. Killing the oldest Egyptian children—including the king's son—showed God's power over Pharaoh, considered a divine son of Ra.

Son of the sun. Egypt's king, considered the divine son of Egypt's most powerful god—the sun god—offers a sacrifice to his heavenly father.

THE FIRST Passover

"I will pass through the land of Egypt and strike down every firstborn son and firstborn male animal in the land of Egypt."

EXODUS 12:12

Before the last and most heartbreaking of the 10 plagues, God tells Moses to have the Israelites prepare a special meal. It will be their last supper in slavery. And it will become a ritual meal that Jews more than 3,000 years later still celebrate every spring.

It's called *Passover*. The name comes from the fact that a divine being passes over the Israelites but strikes the Egyptian households, killing the oldest sons.

Each Israelite family butchers a lamb and smears some of its blood on the outside door-posts of their home—a sign for God to pass over this house.

Shortly after the Egyptian sons die—that very night—Pharaoh sends for Moses. "Leave us!" he cries. "Go away, all of you!"

The Israelites are gone before sunrise.

God tells Moses to make sure the Israelites commemorate this day each spring by eating a Passover meal. It's a meal full of symbolism.

On the menu for many Jews today celebrating Passover:

- Lamb, which was the main course for the first Passover;
- Bitter herbs such as raw horseradish, representing the bitterness of slavery;
- A vegetable such as parsley dipped in salt. The vegetable represents the lowly beginnings of the Jews in slavery. The salt represents tears of slavery;
- A dip made of mixed nuts, apples, cinnamon, and wine. The mixture represents mortar used to construct brick buildings;
- Bread made without yeast. This reminds Jews that their ancestors left in a hurry and didn't have time for bread dough to rise.

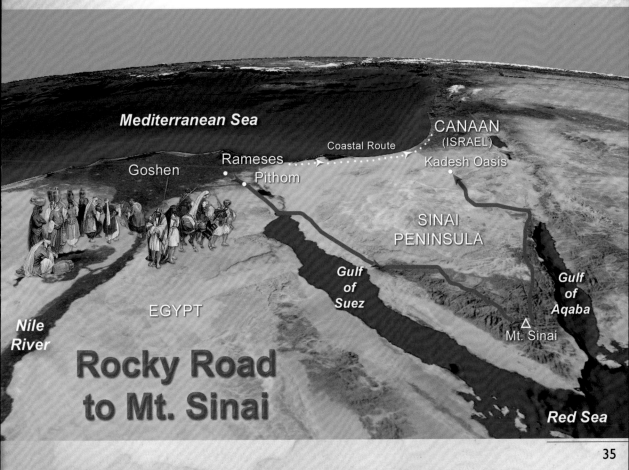

Mediterranean Sea

CANAAN
(ISRAEL)

Coastal Route

Goshen

Rameses

Kadesh Oasis

Pithom

SINAI
PENINSULA

Gulf
of
Suez

Gulf
of
Aqaba

EGYPT

Nile
River

Mt. Sinai

Rocky Road
to Mt. Sinai

Red Sea

CROSSING the Red Sea

The people of Israel walked through the middle of the sea on dry ground, with walls of water on each side!

EXODUS 14:22

A travel agent mapping the quickest route to Israel would have steered Moses to the caravan road that parallels the Mediterranean coastline. But archaeologists confirm that Egyptian forts guarded this road. The Bible says God didn't want the fleeing refugees to fight any battles that soon.

So Moses turns south, taking one of the roads less traveled. A mysterious, hovering pillar guides the Israelites. By day it looks like a cloud. At night it glows.

Meanwhile, Pharaoh changes his mind. He wants his slaves back, so he sends his chariot corps to get them. As the Egyptian army advances, the heavenly pillar moves behind the crowd of fleeing Israelite refugees and stops the Egyptians. But the Israelites have no place to go. They are blocked by a large body of water.

It may not have been the Red Sea.

The Hebrew words sometimes translated that way are *yam sup*. *Yam* means "sea." But *sup* can mean "reeds"—as in Sea of Reeds. Or it can mean "far away"—as in the Faraway Sea. Maybe the body of water in their way was one of the large lakes in the area. Or maybe it was the northern tip of the Red Sea, at the narrow Gulf of Suez.

Scientists specializing in meteorology and oceanography have theorized that a wind blowing about 45 mph for 10 hours could temporarily lower the depth of the Red Sea 10 feet or more, pushing back the shallow northern shoreline for about a mile. This report appeared in the March 1992 issue of the *Bulletin of the American Meteorological Society*. If the Israelites crossed on a raised sandbar, there could have been water on both sides of them.

Two Russian scientists reached a similar conclusion, which they published in the *Bulletin of the Russian Academy of Sciences* in 2004. After studying a four-mile-long reef at the north end of the Gulf of Suez, they said an all-night wind could have pushed back the 10-foot-deep water. And once the wind stopped, the ocean would have roared back in place within 30 minutes.

Yet neither of these theories fully tracks with the Bible description, which has the Israelites walking through a path "with walls of water on each side!" (Exodus 14:22). For this reason, many Christians prefer the more traditional approach to the story. The one that has God dramatically pushing aside the laws of physics along with the water—and making a path through the middle of the sea. They figure if Cecil B. DeMille can do it on film for *The Ten Commandments*, God can do it for real.

But many Bible experts say that speculating about the where or the how misses the point—which is the *who*. Wherever and however it happened, it was God who saved the Israelites by creating an escape route through the water. Then he ended the Egyptian threat by drowning the soldiers when they continued their chase into the sea.

FAST FOOD from heaven

"Look, I'm going to rain down food from heaven for you."

EXODUS 16:4

A month into their trip, about May, the refugees start running out of food. They're in the Sinai Peninsula badlands at the time.

God responds with a sweetly flavored bread substitute and fresh meat: manna and quail.

Manna means "what is it?" The Israelites don't have a clue. Each morning except on the Saturday Sabbath, it covers the ground like a white frost. The Israelites use it like flour, grinding it up and making flat bread that tastes like honey-flavored cakes.

Some scholars today wonder if the manna was insect droppings. Late in the spring, manna scale insects draw sap from tamarisk trees in the area. They secrete what they can't digest. And the pea-sized liquid balls dry into white flakes that nomadic herders today still call *manna*, using it as a sweetener.

The problem with this theory is that the manna season extends only from May to June. And the Bible says the Israelites had manna year-round.

The quail may have been the stubby game bird that migrates back toward Europe each

HOW MANY REFUGEES WERE THERE?

There were about 600,000 men, plus all the women and children.
EXODUS 12:37

Adding an average of one woman and two children for each man, there would have been about 2.5 million Israelites on this desert trek. That's enough to fill more than 30 large football stadiums.

That would explain why Pharaoh was worried about the Israelites taking over Egypt. But to some Christians, 2.5 million seems far too many to feed on the sparse badland pickings.

Many Christians wonder if there's something wrong with the head count—which brings us to a few theories suggested by Bible experts.

- **Wrong translation.** Maybe the Hebrew word translated "thousand" means something else, like "groups." So "600,000" men could mean "600 groups"—such as extended families known as clans. In that case, the total number could have been about 20,000 people.
- **Confused secretaries.** Perhaps scribes who wrote the numbers onto scrolls didn't understand the ancient numbering system. So they made their best guess, sometimes combining categories. For example, Judah's

tribe of 74,600 might have had 70 warriors and 4,600 others. If scribes incorrectly add 70 to the thousands category, the total becomes 74,600 instead of 4,670 (Numbers 2:4).

- **Symbolic numbers.** Hebrew letters have numerical equivalents, a bit like A=1 and B=2. Moses later took a census that tallied 603,551 men. That's just one person higher than the sum you get from "sons of Israel," a common biblical phrase describing the Israelites. And if you add Moses to those "sons," you get exactly 603,551. Maybe the writer's point was that Moses led out all the Israelites, whatever the number.
- **Exaggeration.** Some scholars say the numbers may simply have been exaggerated, as was common in ancient times.

Many scholars aren't satisfied with any of these theories. Yet some doubt that Moses led an exodus of 2.5 million souls. Others say they have no problem with the numbers. They argue that the God who created the universe could easily feed that many people.

spring, from its winter home in Africa. They fly low and slow—the Bible puts their altitude at three feet after flying through an exhausting windstorm. Ancient Egyptian art shows hunters throwing nets over them in springtime grain fields.

MOSES LEARNS to delegate

"You're going to wear yourself out—and the people, too. This job is too heavy a burden for you to handle all by yourself."

EXODUS 18:18

That's Jethro talking, the father-in-law of Moses. Jethro has come to visit. And he's disturbed when he sees his son-in-law's daily routine. From morning to night Moses settles disputes among the refugees. Even tiny disputes. It's exhausting for Moses—and for the people waiting in line all day.

Jethro has a word of advice: delegate.

"Select from all the people some capable, honest men who fear God and hate bribes," Jethro says. "Appoint them as leaders over groups of one thousand, one hundred, fifty, and ten. They should always be available to solve the people's common disputes, but have them bring the major cases to you" (Exodus 18:21–22).

That's fatherly advice Moses decides to take.

Breaking commandments. Moses climbs down from Mount Sinai carrying the 10 Commandments that God inscribed on stone slabs. Already the Israelites are breaking the first two commandments. They've made a calf idol—and they're worshipping it. Moses angrily breaks the slabs. Egyptians worshipped a bull-like god named Apis—painted as a man with a bull's head. He was a fertility god who promised large herds and harvests.

THE 10 Commandments

They came to the wilderness of Sinai and set up camp there at the base of Mount Sinai.

EXODUS 19:2

This is the same location where, many months earlier, God had appeared to Moses in a burning bush. Perhaps Moses expects to hear from him again. If so, he isn't disappointed.

The Israelites camp here for about a year. During that time, God organizes them into a nation of 12 tribes governed by a new set of laws—hundreds of laws.

Every law is based on a short collection of laws known as the 10 Commandments. Before God gives Moses the hundreds of laws that fill many of the pages in Exodus, Leviticus, Numbers, and Deuteronomy, God starts with 10 foundational laws:

1. Don't worship any god but the Lord.
2. Don't make idols or worship them.
3. Don't treat God's name disrespectfully.
4. Rest and worship every seventh day.
5. Honor your parents.
6. Don't murder.
7. Don't commit adultery.
8. Don't steal.
9. Don't lie.
10. Don't envy what other people have.

PROMISED LAND ahead

"I am sending an angel before you to protect you on your journey and lead you safely to the place I have prepared for you."

EXODUS 23:20

The place God's talking about is what will become Israel.

Actually, the boundaries exceed modern-day Israel. God promises the Israelites land from the Red Sea to the Mediterranean Sea, and from the Negev badlands in the south to the Euphrates River in what is now northern Syria.

God makes good on his promise. During the reign of Solomon, Israel's influence extends clear up to the Euphrates River—and well into what is now Jordan. That territory is about double the size of Israel today.

God promises that his angel will gradually drive out the people living in the area. It won't happen in a short time, God says, because the Israelites wouldn't be able to maintain the evacuated cities. And wild animals would take over.

But in time, if the Israelites obey him, God vows to cleanse the land of all the idol-worshipping residents. God doesn't want any of them left alive, any more than a surgeon today would want to leave a single cancer cell in one of his patients. Idolatry grows like cancer. And God wants all the idol worshippers gone.

So he tells the Israelites not to make peace treaties with the people there. "They must not live in your land, or they will cause you to sin against me," God explains. "If you serve their gods, you will be caught in the trap of idolatry" (Exodus 23:33).

And if that happens, God says he will have to cleanse the land again—this time of idol-worshipping Israelites.

Unfortunately, this is exactly what will happen.

The Israelites won't drive out all the people. Instead, they'll make peace treaties with them and learn to live with them as neighbors. The Israelites will also learn to worship their false gods.

MOBILE WORSHIP center

"Have the people of Israel build me a holy sanctuary so I can live among them. You must make this Tabernacle and its furnishings exactly according to the pattern I will show you."

EXODUS 25:8–9

Many of the new laws that God gives to Moses deal with how to worship him. Within a few centuries, the Israelites will be worshipping at a Jerusalem temple—which they consider God's earthly home among them. But for now, while on the road, God tells them to build a tent tabernacle 15 yards long and 5 yards wide. They'll pitch this sacred tent in the center of their camp whenever they stop for any length of time. And they'll surround the tent with a curtain-walled courtyard 50 yards long and 25 yards wide.

Inside the tent, they'll place holy furnishings such as menorah lampstands and a gold-covered chest that holds the 10 Commandments written on stone. This chest is called the Ark of the Covenant. Nothing the Jews own is more precious to them. They consider this chest God's earthly footstool.

Outside the tent, in the courtyard, Israelites will burn animal and grain sacrifices on a portable altar—as offerings of repentance and thanks.

God in a tent. On their trip out of Egypt, Israelites worshipped at a tent sanctuary, depicted in this replica near the Dead Sea badlands. A wall of curtains separated the holy courtyard from Israel's camp. Priests burned animal sacrifices on the bronze altar in front of the tent.

Moses tells the people that craftsmen need a lot of building supplies: cloth, leather hides, gold, silver, and wood. Egyptians had given the Israelites parting gifts—anything the Israelites requested—as payment for leaving right away. So the people have plenty of supplies, which they generously donate. They bring so much that Moses has to put a stop to it. "Bring no more materials! You have already given more than enough."

FAMILY of priests

"Aaron, and his sons. . . .may minister to me and be my priests."

EXODUS 28:1

To manage the worship center and to lead worship rituals including animal sacrifices, God picks the older brother of Moses—Aaron—as Israel's first high priest. Aaron's four sons will work under his authority as priests.

Aaron is fitted for an elegant uniform, including a chest covering that's embedded with a dozen gemstones. Each stone represents one of the 12 tribes of Israel. This vest is intended as a reminder of the people Aaron represents when he stands before God at the worship center. Attached to the forehead part of Aaron's turban is a solid gold medallion inscribed with the words: "Holy to the Lord."

Aaron's sons are fitted for robe-covering tunics, belts, and turbans "to give them dignity and respect."

In an ordination service that extends for a week, Aaron and his sons become Israel's first priests. Future priests will come from Aaron's descendants. So this ordination begins a family dynasty that will survive more than 1,000 years. It will die after the Romans tear down the last Jerusalem temple in AD 70, forever ending the Jewish sacrificial system. Without a worship center to offer sacrifices, the priesthood becomes extinct—gradually replaced by rabbis in synagogues scattered throughout the world.

Holy uniforms. A family affair, Israel's priests descend from their first high priest, Aaron. As high priest, Aaron wears elegant garments featuring a breastplate with a dozen jewels representing the 12 tribes of Israel. Aaron's sons, as lower priests, wear plain robes.

TRACKING GENES OF JEWISH PRIESTS TO AARON

Exodus says that all of Israel's priests descended from Aaron's family.

Genetic scientists have found shared markers in the Y chromosomes of Jewish men who say they are descendants of Jewish priests—markers not found in other Jewish men. *Cohanim* is Hebrew for "priest." Jews who have last names like it—such as Cohen, Coen, Kohn, or Kahn—may be descended from Aaron, the study suggests.

The study, reported in the British science journal *Nature*, July 1998, says that the Cohen markers are about 3,000 years old—from around the time of Aaron.

LEVITICUS

Sacrificial lamb. Sheep and goats were the most common animals that the Israelites sacrificed. Rich people could afford to sacrifice bulls. Poor people were allowed to sacrifice birds.

ISRAEL'S GUIDE TO HOLY LIVING

Camped at the foot of Mount Sinai, the Israelite refugees find out what God expects of them.

"Consecrate yourselves and be holy, because I am holy" (Leviticus 11:44).

God isn't asking for perfect behavior. If he were, he could have skipped the sacrificial rituals he set up so people could get forgiveness when they sinned.

Instead, he's asking for devotion. Then he shows the Israelites how he wants them to express that devotion.

God gives them an assortment of laws and worship rituals that will distinguish them as a holy nation—a race of people devoted to him.

Leviticus is a how-to book. How to live in the presence of a holy God by obeying him in matters such as:

- sacrificing animals;
- eating only kosher food;
- observing holy days; and
- getting rid of ritual impurities before worshipping.

By obeying these rules, the Israelites express their devotion to God. This is what he wants from them. In return, he promises to protect and bless them. "You will eat your fill and live securely in your own land" (Leviticus 26:5).

AN ANIMAL DIES
for a person's sin

"If the animal you present as a burnt offering is from the herd, it must be a male with no defects. . . . Lay your hand on the animal's head, and the LORD *will accept its death in your place to purify you, making you right with him."*

LEVITICUS 1:3–4

Leviticus begins by explaining the most important ancient Jewish ritual: sacrifice. It's through animal and grain sacrifices that the Israelites express to God their gratitude for blessings and their remorse for sin.

In the eyes of a holy God, sin is a capital offense. It has been that way from the beginning. God warned Adam and Eve they would die if they ate the forbidden fruit. They ate it anyway. And sin entered God's creation, dragging along death as the consequence.

During the exodus, God sets up a sacrificial system. He offers to accept the death of animals as a substitute for sinful human beings.

"The life of the body is in its blood," God explains. "I have given you the blood on the

MAIN POINT:

God is holy. And he expects the Israelites to live holy lives, devoted to him. He gives them rules to live by as a way for them to express their devotion and to maintain their holiness.

WRITER:

The book doesn't identify the writer. Jewish and Christian tradition says Moses wrote it. Most of the book is a collection of instructions God gave Moses. But many scholars argue that these could have been passed along as spoken words long before anyone wrote them down.

DATE:

Some Bible experts say the story is set in about 1440 BC. Others say about 200 years later. For more see page 28.

LOCATION:

Camped at the foot of Mount Sinai, in Egypt's rugged Sinai Peninsula

The first animals to die for human sin

Since the world's first sin, animals have been dying for humanity's sins.

Eyes wide open with guilt, Adam and Eve suddenly became embarrassed about their nakedness. "And the LORD God made clothing from animal skins for Adam and his wife" (Genesis 3:21).

altar to purify you, making you right with the LORD. It is the blood, given in exchange for a life, that makes purification possible" (Leviticus 17:11). The bloody ritual also serves as a graphic reminder of how serious sin is—serious enough to warrant the death penalty.

God sets up several kinds of offerings.

Burnt offering. This is Israel's most common sacrifice. The worshipper kills and burns an animal on the altar. This purifies the worshipper of sin. Rich people kill a bull. Most others kill a male goat or sheep. Poorer people kill a dove or pigeon.

Grain offering. Grain from the harvest is brought as thanks to God. Worshippers can present it as flour, baked goods, or roasted kernels. The priest burns some of it and keeps the rest as part of his salary.

Peace offering. A worshipper burns part of an animal as an expression of thanks to God. He eats the rest of it, often with family and friends.

Sin and guilt offerings. These animal sacrifices purify a person who has committed specific types of sins such as stealing, lying, and unintentional sins such as making a rash promise that's impossible to keep.

Where Leviticus gets its name

People in ancient times called this book the "priest's manual." That's because a lot of the book covers the job description of Israelite priests—including step-by-step procedures for animal sacrifices.

Even today's name points in that direction. *Leviticus* means "about the Levites."

Levites were the people in Aaron's tribe—an extended family descended from one of Jacob's 12 sons: Levi. God appointed the Levites to serve as Israel's worship leaders. Aaron's family provided the priests. All other Levite men worked as associates, helping with the sacrifices and maintaining the worship center.

THE FIRST ordination

Moses took the anointing oil and anointed the Tabernacle and everything in it, making them holy. . . . Then he poured some of the anointing oil on Aaron's head, anointing him and making him holy for his work.

LEVITICUS 8:10, 12

Before Israelites start worshipping at the tent Tabernacle under the direction of high priest Aaron and his four sons, God instructs Moses to dedicate the men and the worship center.

What follows is a week of ordination rituals intended to consecrate the men and the tabernacle as holy—devoted to serving God. At God's instruction, Moses washes the priests and dresses them in their priestly uniforms. Then he sprinkles olive oil on the worship center furnishings and on the priests. Centuries later, Israel's kings also will be anointed with oil to commission them for their life's work.

Three animal sacrifices come next.

- A bull is slaughtered and burned, purifying the altar for its future work.
- A ram is killed and burned, but only after the priests place their hands on it. This might be a symbol showing their complete devotion to God, as expressed in the death of the ram.
- A "ram of ordination" is killed and eaten by the priests. Some of this ram's blood is

dabbed on the priests' right ear, right thumb, and right big toe—perhaps to symbolize that God considers them holy from head to toe and fit for service.

On the eighth day, the priests begin their ministry of leading Israel's worship rituals. This is a ministry that their descendants will continue for more than a millennium—until Romans destroy the Jerusalem temple in AD 70, ending the Jewish practice of animal sacrifice.

Gone fishing. An Orthodox Jew bargains for a good price at a fish market in New York City. God told the Israelites they could eat only sea creatures that have scales and fins. Many Jews still observe the ancient food laws.

KOSHER menu

"You may eat any animal that has completely split hooves and chews the cud."

LEVITICUS 11:3

God gives Moses a list of animals the Israelites are allowed to eat. Cattle, sheep, and goats make the menu. It's because those animals either have split hooves or they chew the cud, meaning they swallow their food and bring it up later to chew again. Off the menu—with no split hooves or cud chewing—are pigs, rabbits, and camels.

Fish on the menu must have scales and fins. No shellfish such as lobster, crab, or oyster.

Birds aren't sorted by any physical traits. Instead, God simply gives a list of birds that don't make the menu. These include vultures, bats, ravens, and seagulls.

Most insects are off the menu, too. But there are a few kosher bugs: locusts, crickets, and grasshoppers.

God doesn't explain why gag-inducing crickets are kosher and delicious lobsters are not. Many Bible experts guess that God wasn't especially concerned about the meat, but that he simply wanted to teach the Israelites how to obey him. The kosher laws, unique to Israel, also helped distinguish the Israelites as God's people. It became the sign of a nation devoted to God, and blessed for it.

The later arrival of Jesus will mark the beginning of God's new covenant with humanity—an agreement less concerned with outward rules and more concerned with what's going on inside a person's heart or mind. The food laws become obsolete. What goes into a person doesn't make him unclean, Jesus explains. "It is what comes from inside that defiles you. . .evil thoughts, sexual immorality, theft, murder, adultery, greed. . .they are what defile you" (Mark 7:20–23).

PURE ENOUGH to worship God

"If a woman becomes pregnant and gives birth to a son, she will be ceremonially unclean for seven days, just as she is unclean during her menstrual period."

LEVITICUS 12:2

Ritually unclean, the mother of a newborn isn't allowed to take part in any worship ceremonies. She has to be ritually clean to approach the holy God. Not only is she unclean, but so is anyone who touches her.

God identifies several situations beyond childbirth and menstruation that can make a person unclean: skin disease, touching a corpse, mildew on clothing or in the house, and even wet dreams.

Getting rid of ritual impurity usually involves a waiting period and washing. In the case of skin disease or mildew, a priest has to make an examination and declare the problem resolved.

HOW TO LIVE the holy life

"You must be holy because I, the LORD your God, am holy."

LEVITICUS 19:2

The first half of Leviticus deals with sacrifices and other religious rituals. But the last half is a guidebook about daily behavior and holy living.

God doesn't expect perfection. But he does expect that the behavior of the Israelites will serve as a testimony to the world that they are devoted to God—set apart and reserved for his use.

The Israelites are holy in much the same way that furnishings in the worship center are holy. A lampstand could be ritually cleansed and then devoted for use only in the worship tent. It couldn't be used for secular purposes, such as lighting a family supper.

There are certain things the Israelites aren't allowed to do, as well. No incest or homosexual acts. No child sacrifices. No work on the Sabbath day of rest. No lying or cheating.

There are also certain responsibilities the Israelites have to fulfill. Among them:

- Respect their parents.
- Generously help the poor and strangers in the land.

And one duty Jesus made famous: "Love your neighbor as yourself" (Leviticus 19:18). By observing these rules for holy living, the Israelites maintained their sacred relationship with God. And when they sinned, rituals of sacrifice provided forgiveness for those who were genuinely repentant.

SEVEN JEWISH HOLY DAYS

"These are the LORD's appointed festivals. Celebrate them each year."
LEVITICUS 23:37

In addition to the Sabbath day of rest and worship, from sunset on Friday to sunset on Saturday, the Israelites observed seven religious holidays. Many Jews today still observe these festivals, which stretch from March through October.

Passover. One day each spring. At a family meal, Israelites retold the story of God freeing the Israelite slaves in Egypt.

Bread with no yeast. One week, beginning the day after Passover. This recalled the Israelite slaves leaving Egypt in such a hurry that they didn't have time to let the bread dough rise.

First fruits. One day. Israelites thanked God for the first of the springtime barley harvest.

Pentecost (also called Harvest or Weeks). One day. Held 50 days after the Festival of First Fruits, to thank God for the continued harvest.

Trumpets (*Rosh Hashanah* in Hebrew). One day each fall. Musicians blew trumpets to mark the beginning of the Jewish New Year.

Day of Atonement (*Yom Kippur* in Hebrew). One day each fall. A nationwide day of repentance.

Shelters (also called Booths or Tabernacles). One week. Jews camped out in huts and lean-tos. It was to remember how God protected the Israelites during the Exodus.

Passover lamb on a stick. Passover lambs grill above a pit fire in Israel. Jews stopped sacrificing animals after Romans tore down the Jerusalem temple in AD 70. But Samaritans—a religious group that observes the laws of Moses—didn't worship in Jerusalem. A small community of Samaritans still sacrifice lambs each Passover.

47

NUMBERS

Refugee census. Along the shores of the Red Sea—before turning north to Canaan—Moses orders a census of men old enough to fight in battle.

ISRAEL'S SENTENCE: 40 YEARS

This should be the story of the Israelites marching back into their homeland. But it's the story of them marching to the border—and then waiting for an entire generation of Israelites to die off.

They've been camped at the foot of Mount Sinai for nearly a year. Finally, Moses tells them to break camp. They trudge north toward Canaan, modern-day Israel—complaining as they go. Not enough water. Not enough meat. And manna after all these months has become mundane.

Months later, as the crowd of refugees approaches Canaan's southern border, Moses sends scouts to explore the land. They come back with a report that terrorizes the Israelites. Walls, armies, and giants defend the cities in Canaan.

With that, the Exodus stops. The Israelites refuse to go any farther.

For failing to trust God in spite of all the miracles they have seen him do for them, the Israelites are sentenced to 40 years in the badlands. That's long enough for most of the cowardly generation to die.

The Israelite homeland will wait for a new and improved generation—braver and more obedient.

Sentence served, a new generation breaks camp, led by a 120-year-old Moses. He takes them east into what is now Jordan. Near the banks of the Jordan River, the Israelites are finally ready and willing to reclaim the land God has promised them.

Where Numbers gets its name

The book starts with a census. And it ends with another census 40 years later.

As the Israelites left Mount Sinai to continue their long trip home, Moses wanted to know how many men were available to fight the battles they would face. He repeated the census after the Israelites had served their 40-year sentence in the badlands.

GOOD-BYE Sinai

In the second year after Israel's departure from Egypt—on the twentieth day of the second month—the cloud lifted from the Tabernacle of the Covenant. So the Israelites set out from the wilderness of Sinai and traveled on from place to place.

NUMBERS 10:11–12

After camping at the foot of Mount Sinai for about a year, it's time for the Israelites to move on. They've organized themselves into a nation of 12 extended families called tribes. God has given them the 10 Commandments and hundreds of other laws to guide them in religious and civil matters. And they now have an elaborate worship system, complete with a tent as a traveling worship center—the tabernacle.

The mysterious pillar that guided them to Mount Sinai and that parked above the worship tent is now on the move again. Where it leads, the Israelites follow.

MAIN POINT:

God punishes sin. It's a fact he dramatically illustrates when he sentences the Israelites to 40 years in the badlands—punishment for failing to trust and obey him.

WRITER:

The book doesn't identify the writer. Ancient Jewish and Christian tradition points to Moses. But many Bible experts today say ancient Jewish leaders compiled Genesis through Deuteronomy from a variety of sources. Moses may have provided material for at least some of those sources. But it would have been out of character for him to write that he was "more humble than any other person on earth" (Numbers 12:3). If he did, he wasn't particularly humble.

DATE:

About 1400 BC or 200 years later. For more see page 28.

LOCATION:

The story starts in the rugged Sinai Peninsula in what is now Egypt, south of Israel. It ends in a country called Moab, in what is now Jordan.

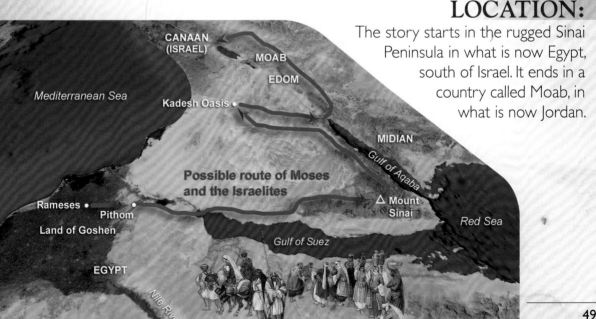

CANAAN (ISRAEL)
MOAB
EDOM
Mediterranean Sea
Kadesh Oasis •
MIDIAN
Gulf of Aqaba
Possible route of Moses and the Israelites
△ Mount Sinai
Red Sea
Rameses •
Pithom
Land of Goshen
Gulf of Suez
EGYPT
Nile River

DEAD end

"You will all drop dead in this wilderness! Because you complained against me, every one of you who is twenty years old or older and was included in the registration will die. You will not enter and occupy the land I swore to give you."

NUMBERS 14:29–30

The Sinai Peninsula is not a hiker's paradise. It's blistering. It's brown. And it's a sand-littered wedge of rocks. Looking less like a desert, it seems more like Mars—or the Dakota badlands. So it should come as no surprise that the Israelite refugees start complaining to Moses—and never really stop.

FINDING WATER IN ROCKS

Moses tapped a desert rock with his walking staff, "and water gushed out" (Numbers 20:11).

Savvy desert travelers can do the same if they know what to look for: moisture in the cracks of rock. Many of the desert rocks are a type of soft sandstone. Rainwater filters through them and into pockets inside.

Sometimes there's enough for a gulp or two. But in Moses' case, "the entire community and their livestock drank their fill."

Snakebit. Snake poison surging through their veins from fresh bites, the Israelites look up for a cure. God had sent the snakes to punish the people for complaining. But when the people repented, he sent a cure. He told Moses to attach a snake replica to a pole. "All who are bitten will live if they simply look at it!" (Numbers 21:8).

The distance from Mount Sinai to the Kadesh-barnea oasis near Canaan's southern border is roughly 200 miles. It takes the Israelites perhaps a couple of months to get there—leaving Sinai in the spring and arriving at Canaan's border well into summer.

Moses sends a dozen scouts into Canaan—one man from each tribe. They spend 40 days exploring the land. Then they return with a taster's choice of crops harvested at the end of summer: pomegranates, figs, and grapes.

"It is indeed a bountiful country—a land flowing with milk and honey," the scouts report (Numbers 13:27).

But there's bad news, too. "The people living there are powerful, and their towns are large and fortified. We even saw giants there. . . . Next to them we felt like grasshoppers" (Numbers 13:28, 33). Only two scouts recommend going farther: Joshua and Caleb.

The Israelites cry and complain all night. Then they plot to choose another leader and go back to Egypt. Only the intercession of Moses keeps God from killing them all. But a disease kills the 10 rebellious scouts. And God sentences everyone else to 40 years in the badland wilderness—a year for each day the scouts explored Canaan.

Habitually rebellious, the Israelites have second thoughts about their aborted invasion. And against God's order, they attack the Canaanites who meet and greet them with swords, and send them scurrying back to Moses.

The Israelites spend most of the next 40 years planted right where they are, in an oasis that seems to contain the largest source of freshwater in the region. The greenery of Kadesh-barnea is fed by a spring that pumps a quarter of a million gallons of water a day.

REBELS IN THE FAMILY

Even Moses' own brother and sister, Aaron and Miriam, turned against him.

Their gripes:

• **Moses married a Cushite.** She was from a race of people descended from Noah's grandson Cush and living in what is now southern Egypt, Sudan, and Ethiopia. This may refer to Zipporah or to a second wife the Bible doesn't name.

• **Moses was the prophet in charge.** "Has the LORD spoken only through Moses?" they complain. "Hasn't he spoken through us, too?" (Numbers 12:2).

God answers for Moses, saying he speaks to Aaron, Miriam, and other prophets only in dreams and visions. "But not with my servant Moses. Of all my house, he is the one I trust. I speak to him face to face" (Numbers 12:7–8).

God turned Miriam's skin white with disease, forcing her to live outside the camp for a week.

Moses pleaded for mercy, which God granted.

INSURRECTION

One day Korah. . .incited a rebellion against Moses, along with 250 other leaders of the community, all prominent members of the assembly.

NUMBERS 16:1–2

Even after God levies a 40-year sentence on them, the Israelites keep doing what they seem to do best: gripe, bicker, and stir up trouble. One man named Korah insists that God has chosen the Israelites as his special people. He says Moses has gone too far in acting like God's favorite son.

"What right do you have to act as though you are greater than the rest of the LORD's people?" Korah asks (Numbers 16:3).

"What's more," some of Korah's supporters add, "You haven't brought us into another land flowing with milk and honey. You haven't given us a new homeland with fields and vineyards" (Numbers 16:14).

Furious, Moses tells the rebel group to come back the next day and present themselves to God. The Lord will decide who should lead the people.

God's decision becomes obvious when the ground cracks open in this earthquake-prone region today called the Great Rift Valley. The earth swallows the entire rebel group and then its rock jaws slam shut. All the would-be leaders and their entire families disappear.

BOUND for the Promised Land

Then the people of Israel traveled to the plains of Moab and camped east of the Jordan River, across from Jericho.

NUMBERS 22:1

A new generation of Israelites heads toward Canaan. Miriam, older sister of Moses, is dead. She died at the oasis. Aaron, the older brother, is dead, as well. He died shortly after the group started to travel.

Moses won't make it to Canaan, either. He and Aaron committed some unidentified sin when they called water out of a rock. Maybe they took credit for the miracle. Or maybe they behaved improperly—perhaps by hitting the rock instead of simply speaking to it as God had instructed. For whatever reason, God tells them both, "Because you did not trust me enough to demonstrate my holiness to the people of Israel, you will not lead them into the land I am giving them!" (Numbers 20:12).

The shortest route into Canaan is north. But Moses isn't famous for taking short routes. Perhaps God points the Israelites east so they won't worry about the earlier defeat they faced in south Canaan.

Moses hopes to travel into what is now Jordan, turn north, and then tell the Israelites to cross the Jordan

The traveler's upgrade. Traveling first class a century ago, this Bethlehem man rides a donkey down a rocky slope. It beats walking. Centuries earlier, a sorcerer named Balaam traveled hundreds of miles by donkey, on a mission to stop an Israelite invasion. Moab's king hired him to put a curse on the invaders. Instead, Balaam blessed them, as an angel told him to do. Balaam's donkey saw the angel first—and talked about it.

River into Canaan. But the people of Edom refuse to grant them safe passage. God warns the Israelites not to fight Edom because the two nations are related. The Israelites descended from Jacob, and the Edomites came from Jacob's brother, Esau. So Moses turns the refugees south, on a long bypass around Edom. Then he takes them north to Moab, another ancient country in what is now Jordan.

Along the way, several armies attack. But Israelite warriors led by Joshua prove unstoppable.

God-given women's rights

Before the Israelites arrived in Canaan, Moses set up a system for dividing the land among the 12 tribes. He wanted the tribal boundaries to last. So he told fathers to pass their land inheritance on to their sons. That way the land stayed in the family.

If a father would give the land to a daughter and she married into another tribe, the land would become her husband's property—and the property of his tribe. The Bible says God didn't want that.

"What about us?" That's the question Moses got from five daughters of Zelophehad, a man who had died without a son. In this man's world of Old Testament times, it wasn't customary for Middle Eastern women to inherit property. But Moses took the problem to God.

God replied, "If a man dies and has no son, then give his inheritance to his daughters" (Numbers 27:8). There was just one condition: "Let them marry anyone they like, as long as it is within their own ancestral tribe" (Numbers 36:6).

Mount Sinai, with St. Catherine's Monastery below in this painting from the mid 1800s, where the Israelites were said to have camped for a year.

DEUTERONOMY

Promised Land ahead. Travelers descend into the Jordan River Valley, in this painting from the early 1800s. The valley separates the hills of modern-day Jordan from those of Israel. The Israelites camped in Jordan before invading the land God promised them.

LAST WORDS OF MOSES

Home is just across the river. Standing on the highland plateau in what is now Jordan, the Israelites can finally see their green river valley below and the hills beyond.

It's certainly an emotional sight for this band of refugees. They and their ancestors have just endured 430 years in Egypt followed by another 40 in the Egyptian badlands.

It's probably emotional for Moses, too, but for another reason. He has to say good-bye. He will die before the river crossing.

Deuteronomy is a record of his last speeches to the Israelites.

Moses does three things in these speeches.

1. He gives the people a history lesson. Many of the Israelites are too young to remember the miracles God did for them in Egypt and during the Exodus. So Moses carefully reviews them and assures the people that more miracles are coming.

2. He renews the agreement between God and the Israelites. Moses reminds the people that God expects them to obey his laws. Only then will God continue to bless this emerging nation. So Moses reviews those laws. Afterward, he leads the group in a ritual of renewing the contractual agreement, or covenant, which God made with the previous generation.

3. He appoints Joshua as his replacement. God chooses Joshua, a warrior, to lead the Israelites in taking back their homeland. Moses installs him as the nation's new leader.

With his work finished, Moses dies.

AN OLD MAN teaches history

These are the words that Moses spoke to all the people of Israel while they were in the wilderness east of the Jordan River.

DEUTERONOMY 1:1

Of all the adults age 20 and above who left Egypt, only three are still alive: Moses, Joshua, and Caleb. The rest died while serving a 40-year sentence in the badlands.

God imposed that sentence after the Israelites refused to invade Canaan. They were terrified by scouting reports of walled cities, strong armies, and giants. Even after they saw what God had done to the Egyptian army and how he gave the Israelites an escape route by parting a large body of water, these first-generation exodus Israelites apparently figured that Canaan's defenses were too strong for God. So God ordered the Israelites to stop in their tracks. And he waited for a new and braver generation to grow up.

Trouble is, the new generation hasn't lived the dramatic history that would seem to inspire steely faith in God—though the drama certainly didn't have that effect on Generation One.

But God knows that Generation Two will respond differently.

MAIN POINT:

If the Israelites obey God, they can expect protection, blessing, and a good life in their promised homeland. If they don't, they might as well pack their bags and move on—before God sends disaster, disease, and invaders to drive them out.

WRITER:

The book doesn't name the writer. But Jewish and Christian tradition says Moses wrote the first five books of the Bible, ending with Deuteronomy. Most of Deuteronomy is a collection of speeches Moses gave to the Israelites. And most of those speeches review the laws and instructions God gave the Israelites. "Moses wrote this entire body of instruction in a book and gave it to the priests" (Deuteronomy 31:9).

DATE:

About 1400 BC or 200 years later. For more see page 28.

LOCATION:

East of the Jordan River, in what is now the country of Jordan. Canaan, now called Israel, is within view, westward across the river.

So he has Moses tell them the exodus story—only part of which may be preserved in Deuteronomy.

In chapters 1–4, Moses tells Generation Two about:
- organizing the group of refugees into a nation of 12 tribes;
- scouts exploring Canaan, but Generation One refusing to invade; and
- waiting in the Egyptian badlands for 40 years.

Then he reminds them of what they've experienced for themselves. They've seen the battle victories during their final march to Canaan—including the collapse of 60 walled cities in the kingdom of Og, a giant who slept in a bed "more than thirteen feet long and six feet wide" (Deuteronomy 3:11).

They've also seen the first of the land change hands to the Israelites. Moses has already divided the conquered land east of the Jordan River, in what is now Jordan. He gave it to the tribes of Reuben and Gad, and to half the tribe of Manasseh.

History established, Moses moves on to talk about the laws that the Israelites need to follow to ensure a happy future.

"Listen carefully to these decrees and regulations that I am about to teach you," Moses says. "Obey them so that you may live, so you may enter and occupy the land that the LORD, the God of your ancestors, is giving you" (Deuteronomy 4:1).

Laws chiseled in stone. At the Louvre Museum in Paris, you can see the world's oldest surviving set of laws: the Code of Hammurabi. Chiseled onto this stone pillar several hundred years before Moses are 282 laws—some similar to laws Moses gave the Israelites.

LAWS OF MOSES, in Iraq

"What great nation has decrees and regulations as righteous and fair as this body of instructions that I am giving you today?"
DEUTERONOMY 4:8

That's Moses talking to the Israelites. Many of the laws he's referring to are unique to Israel—but not all of them. Some show up in the law codes of other ancient nations.

A few appear in the Code of Hammurabi, named after a Babylonian king in what is now Iraq. Like Jewish laws, these Babylonian laws cover civil and criminal cases such as divorce, remarriage, slavery, injury, and property rights.

Some Babylonian laws are similar to the Jewish laws:

Law of Moses

"Punishment must match the injury; a life for a life, an eye for an eye" (Exodus 21:23–24).

"Suppose a pregnant woman suffers a miscarriage as the result of an injury caused by someone who is fighting. If she isn't badly hurt, the one who injured her must pay whatever fine her husband demands and the judges approve" (Exodus 21:22 CEV).

Hammurabi's Code

"If a man put out the eye of another man, his eye shall be put out" (Law 196).

"If a man strikes a free-born woman so that she loses her unborn child, he shall pay ten shekels for her loss" (Law 209).

Despite the similarities, the laws of Moses are different from Hammurabi's Code in two important ways. Laws in the Bible

- cover spiritual matters, such as how to worship, and
- are more just when it comes to dishing out punishment.

The "eye for an eye" law in Hammurabi's Code, for example, favors the rich. If a noble accidentally blinded a peasant, the noble got off with just a fine. Yet if the peasant blinded the noble, that peasant would end up with the depth perception of a Cyclops.

Hammurabi's Code also punishes the innocent in some cases. If a house caved in and killed a son living there, "the son of the builder shall be put to death" (Law 230). That's a son for a son. And the laws of Moses have none of that.

The Bible in a head box. "Wear them on your forehead," Moses told the Israelites, speaking of the laws God gave them. Some Jews, like this man in a Los Angeles synagogue, take that instruction literally. They wear selected Bible verses from Deuteronomy in boxes strapped to their heads.

THE JEWISH creed

"Listen, O Israel! The LORD is our God, the Lord alone. And you must love the LORD your God with all your heart, all your soul, and all your strength. And you must commit yourselves wholeheartedly to these commands that I am giving you today. Repeat them again and again to your children."

DEUTERONOMY 6:4–7

Moses begins to review all the laws God has given the Israelites—laws that distinguish the people as unique, marking them as God's chosen people. Only the Israelites observe this collection of laws. After reviewing the 10 Commandments, which are the rock-solid base on which all the other laws are built, Moses launches into a section that has become as important to Jews as the Apostles' Creed is to Christians.

Many churches ask their people to recite the Apostles' Creed each Sunday, to remind them of their most basic beliefs. "I believe in God, the Father Almighty, the Creator of heaven and earth, and in Jesus Christ, His only Son, our Lord." That's how the Apostles' Creed begins.

Where Deuteronomy gets its name

"Deuteronomy" comes from a Greek word: *deuteronomion*. It means "repeated law."

Before Moses died, he wanted to make sure this new generation of Israelites understood the laws God gave them. So he carefully reviewed them.

Jews call the book by a different name: "Words." It's a short version of the fuller name that comes from the book's first phrase: "These are the words."

Jews don't have any creed that their scholars wrote to condense the Jewish Bible into a paragraph of key beliefs. But Jews don't need one. Moses wrote a creed for them. It's a collection of three passages, which many Jews recite each morning and evening: Deuteronomy 6:4–9; 11:13–21; Numbers 15:37–41.

Jews call it the *Shema* (shuh-MAH). That's the Hebrew word for "hear" or "listen." It comes from the first word in the passage: "Hear, O Israel!"

Moses tells the Israelites there is only one God—the God they serve. And serving God is their purpose in life. So Moses urges the Israelites to memorize the laws of God. "Tie them to your hands and wear them on your forehead as reminders," Moses says. "Write them on the doorposts of your house and on your gates" (Deuteronomy 6:8–9).

Moses with horns. Artists long ago often portrayed Moses with horns. The idea came from an incorrect Bible translation. The first Latin version of the Bible said that after Moses met with God the head of Moses "became horned." It should have said "became radiant." Light rays, not horns, sprang from him.

GOD ORDERS A HOLOCAUST

"In those towns that the LORD your God is giving you as a special possession, destroy every living thing."
DEUTERONOMY 20:16

Ethnic cleansing. That's what it looks like God is ordering. A holocaust—not conducted against the Jews, but *by* them.

Moses is telling the Israelites that once they invade Canaan, they are to kill everyone living there.

All the explanation we get comes in one sentence from Moses: "This will prevent the people of the land from teaching you to imitate their detestable customs in the worship of their gods, which would cause you to sin deeply against the LORD your God" (Deuteronomy 20:18).

Canaanite worship features some ugly practices, including infant sacrifice and sex rituals between worshippers and worship leaders.

The cleansing that God orders is more spiritual than ethnic. There are lots of races in Canaan. The cleansing will be a bit like the washing away of sin in the flood and the burning off of sin at Sodom and Gomorrah. In ages past, God purged the land of sin and sinners. And now he's planning to do it again, this time through warfare.

Israel will fail on the follow-through. They'll kill many Canaanites. But they'll learn to live as neighbors with many others. And as Moses predicts, Israel will gradually start worshipping Canaanite gods.

In time, God will have to cleanse the land once again—this time of Jews. Invaders will arrive in 586 BC, slaughtering the Jews, driving off the survivors, and erasing the sovereign nation of Israel from the world map.

Many Jews today do that literally. They'll write parts of the Shema on tiny pieces of paper and wear them in *tefillin* boxes strapped to their foreheads and hands. And some Jews put those verses in tiny *mezuzah* boxes nailed near the entrance of their homes. And as they come and go, the Jews brush those boxes with their fingers—a daily reminder to devote themselves to the God who is devoted to them.

CONTRACT with God

"Today I have given you the choice between life and death, between blessings and curses. . . . Oh, that you would choose life, so that you and your descendants might live!"

DEUTERONOMY 30:19

God and Israel have an agreement. It's a contract or covenant that reads a lot like ancient treaties between rulers and peasants. Like those ancient treaties, God's covenant with Israel includes a section of blessings and curses.

If the Israelites maintain their allegiance to God by obeying the laws he gave them in this contract, he will bless them with "many children, numerous livestock, and abundant crops" (Deuteronomy 28:11). He'll also protect them, conquering their enemies.

But if they break their contract and disobey him, they can expect one disaster after another. In the end, God will send invaders to "scatter you among all the nations from one end of the earth to the other" (Deuteronomy 28:64).

Moses urges the Israelites to choose a life of blessing by obeying God's laws.

GOOD-BYE MOSES, hello Joshua

Then the Lord said to Moses, "The time has come for you to die. Call Joshua and present yourselves at the Tabernacle, so that I may commission him there."

DEUTERONOMY 31:14

Moses brings Joshua to the worship center, where God commissions him as Israel's new leader. Moses recites a song praising God. Then he sets off to climb nearby Mount Nebo. From the peak, he's able to see the Promised Land across the Jordan River Valley in the west. It's the last thing he sees, as far as the Bible tells.

At age 120, Moses dies. Some ancient copies of the story say "he"—implying God—buried Moses. Other copies say "they"—implying the Israelites. The people mourn him for 30 days. From that time on, the Jews have honored him as one of a kind. "There has never been another prophet in Israel like Moses, whom the LORD knew face to face" (Deuteronomy 34:10).

One last look. Moses climbs Mount Nebo and surveys the Promised Land that will become the nation of Israel. It's as close as he gets to the Jewish homeland. He dies in what is now Jordan and is buried there.

Israel gets a new leader. Joshua and Israel's high priest bow before God's earthly footstool—the gold-covered Ark of the Covenant that holds the 10 Commandments. It's part of a ritual ceremony to commission Joshua as Moses' successor.

JOSHUA

Conquering Canaan. Joshua and his lightly armed militia surprise a Canaanite force. Joshua carefully picks his fights, targeting Canaan's highlands. There, his militia's swift mobility gives him an incredible advantage over heavily armed forces such as chariot corps.

GOD GOES TO WAR

The time has come for God to deliver on his promise to Abraham some 700 years earlier.

God had told Abraham, "I am giving all this land, as far as you can see, to you and your descendants as a permanent possession" (Genesis 13:15). God was talking about Canaan, roughly the area now called Israel.

Yet Abraham's grandson, Jacob, moved the entire extended family to Egypt. He did that to survive—to escape a seven-year drought. The Israelites ended up staying there 430 years—first as guests, then as slaves.

In the meantime, settlers were building cities all over Canaan. Even as the Israelites approach from the east, a powerful group of people called Philistines is arriving on the west coast and building towns there.

Moses is dead. Joshua's in charge. And the Israelites are getting ready to invade from the east bank of the Jordan River.

God speaks to Joshua, perhaps in a dream, telling him not to fear. "No one will be able to stand against you as long as you live," God says. "For I will be with you as I was with Moses.

I will not fail you or abandon you" (Joshua 1:5).

The invasion begins. A border town is the first to fall: Jericho. From there, Joshua moves his army into the southern highlands, conquering Canaanite cities. Then he sweeps north, with nothing but success.

Major cities defeated, Joshua divides the land among the 12 tribes. Then he assigns them the job of mopping up the resistance in their own territories.

The Israelites are home.

MAIN POINT:

The conquest of Canaan has little to do with Israelite military savvy. Canaan is God's gift to his people. Even before the invasion starts, God speaks of the victory in past tense: "Wherever you set foot, you will be on land I have given you" (Joshua 1:3).

WRITER:

Unknown. Because of his starring role in the stories, Joshua has traditionally been considered the writer.

DATE:

The conquest of Canaan may have taken place in the 1400s BC or the 1200s BC. For more see page 28.

LOCATION:

The story begins east of the Jordan River, in what is now the country of Jordan. Then the Israelites cross the river, invading Canaan—which is today called Israel.

FINAL PREP for invasion

"Tell the people to get their provisions ready. In three days you will cross the Jordan River and take possession of the land the LORD *your God is giving you."*

Joshua 1:11

After a month of mourning Moses, it's time for the Israelites to move on with Joshua in the lead.

Joshua certainly must be worried. Not only is he suddenly in charge of a nation of refugees, he's about to lead them into war against a country full of cities protected by walls and seasoned soldiers. Invaders out in the open almost always suffer more casualties than defenders behind walls.

God calms Joshua, perhaps speaking to him in a dream or a vision. That's how the Bible says God typically communicated to prophets and other leaders.

"Strength! Courage!" God says. "You are going to lead this people to inherit the land that I promised to give their ancestors. Give it everything you have. . . . GOD, your God, is with you every step you take" (Joshua 1:6–7, 9 THE MESSAGE).

Joshua passes this encouragement on to the Israelites as he orders them to get ready to break camp and cross the river.

While the Israelites prepare, Joshua sends two spies into the border town of Jericho, six miles across the river. Once inside the city they go to the house of a prostitute named Rahab.

Why go to a prostitute?

The Bible doesn't say. Perhaps because it wouldn't have looked especially suspicious for traveling strangers to go there. Or maybe they go there for the same reason other men in the Bible go to prostitutes.

For whatever reason, they do go there. And they apparently talk too much, apparently bragging about their attack force. Rookie spies.

Someone—maybe a customer of Rahab's—overhears it and passes the news along to the king. He's horrified to hear the Israelites are scouting his city for an

RED LIGHT DISTRICT

Prostitutes in the United States started putting red lights in their windows around 1890. It was a signal light. It identified them as working women on the night shift, and open for business.

Some say railroad workers started the practice by parking their red lights outside while visiting inside.

Others say the inspiration came from the Bible's most famous prostitute: Rahab. She helped Israelite spies escape by sending them down a red rope that she dangled from a window of her house. The spies told her to hang the rope back in the window when they returned with the Israelite army. This signal would help them know which house to spare.

attack. He knows that these are the invaders who have just captured the land east of the river.

He sends officers to arrest the scouts. But Rahab hides the men under piles of flax stalks drying on her roof. She tells the king's men that the Israelites have left. As soon as the officers head for the river to run down the spies, Rahab uncovers her guests and asks a favor.

"I know that God has given you the land. We're all afraid. Everyone in the country feels hopeless," Rahab says. "I showed you mercy; now show my family mercy."

The spies promise to spare Rahab and her family.

Welcome to Jericho. A Jericho prostitute named Rahab invites Israelite spies into her home, perhaps thinking they're customers. When she learns they're scouting the city for an invasion, she hides them from the authorities. She has heard about this advancing army—and she fears the Israelite God more than she fears her king.

Crossing the Jordan. Without bridges, people cross the Jordan River at shallow fords, as shown in this painting from the 1840s.

CROSSING THE RIVER in flood season

The Jordan was overflowing its banks. But as soon as the feet of the priests who were carrying the Ark touched the water at the river's edge, the water above that point began backing up a great distance away at a town called Adam. . .until the riverbed was dry.

JOSHUA 3:15–16

Spring is a horrible time to cross the Jordan River. The tag team of rain along with snowmelt from Mount Hermon generally ensures that the Jordan overflows its banks throughout the harvest (Joshua 3:15), surging about 10 feet deep.

There are no bridges. Travelers usually wade across on underwater sandbars called fords. But not these travelers.

Priests carrying Israel's sacred chest that holds the 10 Commandments lead the march. And as soon as they step onto the river's edge, something dramatic happens. The rushing flow of floodwater quickly wanes to a trickle—then stops. No more river. Just a damp riverbed.

It doesn't take a theologian to make the connection between this miracle and God's most amazing miracle of the Exodus: parting the sea. Certainly some of the Israelites realize right away that God is doing it again. He's paving a way before them, just as he did for their parents a generation earlier. He's still as real as he ever was.

Once across, Joshua orders one man from each of the 12 tribes to gather a stone from the riverbed.

"We will use these stones to build a memorial," Joshua explains. "In the future your children will ask you, 'What do these stones mean?' Then you can tell them, 'They remind us that the Jordan River stopped flowing when the Ark of the LORD's Covenant went across' " (Joshua 4:6–7).

Did a quake block the Jordan River?

Earthquakes have dammed up the Jordan River plenty of times.

Once the river stopped at the very spot the Bible says it backed up in Joshua's day: the city of Adam, 20 miles upstream from Jericho.

The Jordan River snakes through the Great Rift Valley, a rock seam between two shifting plates of the earth's crust. Clay cliffs tower above the river in some areas. And cliffs have come crashing down, blocking the river several times in recorded history: 1267, 1546, 1834, 1907, 1927, and 1956.

It's the 1927 date that's most remarkable. A killer quake shook loose the 150-foot cliffs near the ruins of Adam, now a Jordanian ghost town called by its Arabic name: *Damiya*. This dirt wall plugged the river, damming it for more than 21 hours while people downstream explored the dry riverbed.

Cliffs come tumblin' down, too. Clay cliffs rise high above the Jordan River. Earthquakes sometimes shake them loose, and big chunks crash into the river, damming it for hours.

WALLS COME tumblin' down

When the people heard the sound of the rams' horns, they shouted as loud as they could. Suddenly, the walls of Jericho collapsed, and the Israelites charged straight into the town and captured it.

JOSHUA 6:20

Jericho is the first Canaanite city in the path of Joshua's army. Located in a lush and sprawling oasis near the Jordan River, it's the oldest settlement ever discovered—established at least 7,000 years before Joshua.

Based on descriptions of archaeologists, Jericho must have looked impregnable. It rested on top of a 10-acre sloped mound of earth about 70 feet high. Three walls surrounded it. One held the sides of the mound in place, as a retaining wall. Another sat on top of this wall, bulging six feet thick and perhaps a dozen feet high. Farther up the slope, near the top of the mound, towered the main wall.

One ancient strategy for taking a town like this would have been to build a mountainous ramp up and over the walls. But for the Israelites, there's no need. God is about to build a ramp for them.

Israelites march around the city once a day for six days, led by priests carrying the sacred chest that holds the 10 Commandments. On day seven, they march in absolute silence. But this time they circle Jericho seven times. Suddenly, priests blow rams' horns. At that signal the people scream with lungs at full force. The mighty walls of Jericho collapse. Conveniently, the walls fall outward. This creates a ramp that the Israelites use to charge up and into the city.

Some Bible experts wonder if this was a miracle of timing. They wonder if God crumbled Jericho with an earthquake or aftershocks from an earlier quake that had dammed up the Jordan River. But the Bible doesn't say how God did it.

Israelite soldiers kill everyone except Rahab's family. And they're instructed not to take anything for themselves. In fact, archaeologist John Garstang, digging in the ruins of what is now Jericho, found pots filled with grain—a valuable commodity for an invading army. It's not something most invaders would have left, unless ordered to do so.

Jericho, resting in pieces. This bump in the Jericho oasis is all that's left of the ancient city. Jericho City sat on top, surrounded by three walls. Holes carved into the mound are the work of archaeologists. Most of the experts agree the city fell suddenly and violently. But they can't agree when. Some say in Joshua's day. Others insist Jericho was a ghost town at least a century before Joshua got there.

ONE BATTLE THE ISRAELITES LOSE

The men of Ai chased the Israelites from the town gate as far as the quarries....
The Israelites were paralyzed with fear at this turn of events, and their courage melted away.
JOSHUA 7:4–5

Right after wiping Jericho off the map, the seemingly unstoppable Israelites were stopped by a tiny contingent of militia, from a tiny town, with a tiny name: Ai. Archaeologists estimate that no more than 300 people lived there at the time.

Joshua sent 3,000 fighters to take the city. But 10 to 1 odds in Israel's favor weren't good enough. Shocked at the defeat, Joshua asked God for an explanation. It's punishment, God said. An Israelite had taken some goods from Jericho, against God's orders. Joshua found the man—Achan—and executed him and his entire family.

It was a harsh lesson in obedience. But the Israelites seemed to learn it. There's no report of Israel losing another battle during Joshua's entire campaign.

JOSHUA'S MILITARY STRATEGY

Red Sea

SINAI PENINSULA

EGYPT

Debir
Hebron
Dead Sea
Lachish
Lebnah
Eglon
Jericho
Aijalon
Bethel, Ai
Gibeon

Sea of Galilee
Merom
Hazor

Mediterranean Sea

Conquering Canaan. Israelites didn't manage to capture all the cities of Canaan in Joshua's lifetime, according to the Bible. Instead, they concentrated on cities where they had a strategic military advantage: the highlands.

The Israelites were lightly armed foot soldiers who could maneuver swiftly in rough terrain. Often, they faced heavily armed infantry, cavalry, and chariot corps, which fought best on flat fields. That may be why Joshua avoided the coastal plains.

From Jericho, the Israelites drove deeper into central Canaan, taking one highland city after another. Next they swept south. Then they charged north, beyond the Sea of Galilee. Armies of many cities united to stop them. But there was no stopping God or his people. By the end of Joshua's campaign west of the Jordan, he had defeated the armies of 31 kings.

With this captured strip of land slicing all the way through Canaan's core, Joshua apparently decided the rest of the work was a mopping-up action. So he told Israel's tribal leaders to finish the conquering in their own territories.

It's an order they would not fully execute.

Many tribes found it easier to get along with the Canaanites than to get rid of them. Canaanite religion would stay, too. And that was bad news for the Israelites.

THE DAY the earth stopped

The sun stood still and the moon stayed in place until the nation of Israel had defeated its enemies.

JOSHUA 10:13

God has told Joshua not to make peace treaties with any Canaanite kingdoms. But one city kingdom, Gibeon, shrewdly tricks Joshua into a treaty.

They send ambassadors to his camp at Gilgal, near the Jordan River. The ambassadors lie and say they're from a faraway land. They even have the tattered clothes, patched sandals, and moldy bread to prove it.

Three days after the done deal, Joshua discovers that the ambassadors came from a Canaanite city only 20 miles away—a one-day march. But lie or no lie, Joshua feels bound by his agreement.

Gibeon's neighbors aren't happy. They feel betrayed. So they send a coalition army from five cities to surround Gibeon and to kill the people living there.

Immediately, Gibeon rushes messengers to Joshua with an urgent call for help. Joshua responds by mustering his army, leading them on an all-night march up into the hills, and taking the coalition forces by surprise.

That morning, Joshua prays a bizarre prayer. "Let the sun stand still over Gibeon, and the moon over the valley of Aijalon" (Joshua 10:12). That's exactly what happens, according to the Bible. God stops the sun and moon in the sky.

Some Christians say they believe that God literally stopped the earth's rotation, which would have given the illusion that the sun and moon froze in the sky. As scientific evidence, some say NASA has calculated that the calendar is missing one day. But this is a claim NASA denies on its Web site. They say it would be impossible to calculate a lost day.

Others say the writer admits to pulling the story from *The Book of Jashar*, a lost book of Hebrew poetry. And they argue that readers today should give the writer some poetic license.

Perhaps Joshua wanted God to help the Israelites finish the battle before the day's end. Or maybe Joshua was asking for cloud cover, so the sun wouldn't burn the energy out of his soldiers who were already weary from the all-night climb some 3,300 feet up from the river valley. The Hebrew word that says the sun "stood still" is *damam*, and it can also mean the sun "stopped shining."

In fact, the Bible says thick storm clouds did roll in. "Hail killed more of the enemy than the Israelites killed with the sword" (Joshua 10:11).

"Let the sun stand still." Joshua prays for the sun and moon to stand still so his soldiers can finish a battle against a coalition of five armies.

CARVING UP the Promised Land

"Give this land to Israel as a special possession, just as I have commanded you."

JOSHUA 13:6

With many of the Canaanite armies defeated, Joshua divides the land among the 12 Israelite tribes. It's a bit like dividing a state into a dozen counties. And Canaan—on the west side of Jordan River—was about the size of New Jersey.

Each tribe is descended from one of Jacob's 12 sons. So each tribe takes its name from one of those sons. Every tribe gets a plot of ground in the Promised Land, with the exception of the tribe of Levi. The Levites are worship leaders, so Joshua scatters them into 48 Levite cities throughout the country. That way, no Israelite is too far from their spiritual leaders.

But even without Levite territory, the land is divided into a dozen regions. The Israelites pick up the extra tribe by giving Joseph's family a double share. Joseph's father, Jacob, had predicted as much centuries earlier. When he blessed Joseph's two sons, Jacob elevated them from the status of grandsons to sons: "I am claiming as my own sons these two boys of yours, Ephraim and Manasseh" (Genesis 48:5). Jacob said they would inherit their own sections of the Promised Land. That's why there's no tribe of Joseph, but tribes of Ephraim and Manasseh instead.

CITIES OF REFUGE and justice

"Anyone who kills another person accidentally and unintentionally can run to one of these cities."

JOSHUA 20:3

Accidents happen. And sometimes people die because of them. In Joshua's day, it's an eye for an eye and a life for a life. That's a common law throughout the Middle East.

There's a problem. Some people don't distinguish between murder and accidental manslaughter. Accident or not, the killer has to die. Without law enforcement officers, it's usually up to angry relatives of the victim to hunt down and execute the killer.

Unlike such laws of the day, God's law distinguishes between murder and manslaughter—and makes provision for a fair trial. God names six of 48 Levite cities as cities of refuge. He scatters these half dozen cities throughout the land so a killer on the run doesn't have too far to go.

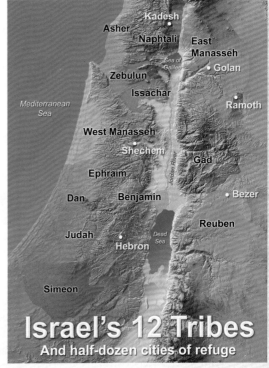

Israel's 12 Tribes
And half-dozen cities of refuge

Once inside the city, the killer gets asylum and a trial. If the killer is found guilty of murder, city elders turn the killer over to the victim's relatives. If found innocent, the killer gets to live—but must stay inside the city. Only when the nation's high priest dies is the killer allowed to safely return home.

The idea behind this may be that according to the laws God gave Moses, it takes a life to atone for killing someone—even if the death is accidental. "The life of the body is in its blood," God told Moses. "It is the blood, given in exchange for a life, that makes purification possible" (Leviticus 17:11). The death of the priest apparently atones for the manslaughter. And this death is supposed to satisfy even the victim's relatives.

LAST WORDS of Joshua

"Choose today whom you will serve. . . . But as for me and my family, we will serve the LORD."

JOSHUA 24:15

Years pass and Joshua grows old. He's 110, and he knows he'll die soon. So he calls together the tribal leaders one last time.

As Moses had done in his last days with the people, Joshua speaks with the compassion of a father, urging the Israelites to renew their agreement with God.

Joshua sees one serious problem. The Israelites have failed to drive out all the Canaanites. So he offers a stern warning.

"If you turn away from him [God] and cling to the customs of the survivors of these nations remaining among you, and if you intermarry with them, then know for certain that the LORD your God will no longer drive them out of your land. Instead, they will be a snare and a trap to you. . .and you will vanish from this good land the LORD your God has given you" (Joshua 23:12–13).

Israel's leaders pledge their allegiance to God, vowing "We will serve the LORD our God. We will obey him alone" (Joshua 24:24).

Joshua dies soon afterward. And for the first time in their life as a nation that's only two generations old, the Israelites have no central, charismatic person to lead them.

A prostitute in Jesus' family tree

Israelites not only spared Rahab, the prostitute who helped their spies in Jericho, they accepted her as a convert. Then Joshua married her—at least that's what some ancient Jewish stories say.

But the New Testament, dangling her from the family tree of Jesus, says she married a man named Salmon and became the great-grandmother of King David (Matthew 1:5–6).

It's possible Matthew was talking about another Rahab. But there's only one famous Rahab in the Bible—the former prostitute who has a tainted background that tracks well with three other women listed as Jesus' ancestors. There was Tamar, who slept with her father-in-law; Bathsheba, who committed adultery with David; and Ruth, a foreigner from Moab in what is now Jordan.

Some Bible experts guess that Matthew included these women to show that women with questionable backgrounds—like Mary, the unwed mother of Jesus—were mothers of Israel's greatest kings, and worthy of respect.

JUDGES

SEND IN THE HEROES

Joshua is dead. But he has left the Israelites with a commission: Finish conquering Canaan and honor the agreement they made with God, to obey his laws in return for his continued protection and blessing.

They do neither.

They decide it's easier to live as neighbors with the Canaanites than to fight them. Before long, they've abandoned God's laws. Instead, they start picking up Canaanite culture and religion—just as Moses and Joshua warned would happen if they didn't clear the land of the Canaanites.

What follows is a bit like watching a rerun over and over. The Israelites get locked into a cycle they can't seem to break. It goes like this:

- They sin, usually by worshipping idols of Canaan.
- God punishes them, usually by sending an oppressor such as raiders or a bully nation that forces the Israelites to do as they're told.
- The Israelites repent and ask God to help them.

After the haircut. Beneath a Philistine prod, the once-mighty Samson does the work of an animal: powering a mill that grinds grain into flour. Samson is one of a dozen heroes God raised up to protect Israel from hostile neighbors. But like several of the heroes, his story ends tragically.

- God forgives them and sends a hero who stops the oppression.

This happens over and over—at least a dozen times. It's as though the Israelite race has lost its genetic code for memory.

By the end of this exhausting trip through one of the saddest slices of Israel's history, anarchy has taken over. The Israelites are killing each other in their first civil war.

MAIN POINT:

God never gives up on his people. When they sin—as they repeatedly do throughout the book of Judges—he punishes them by sending oppressors. But every time the Israelites repent and ask God for help, he delivers.

WRITER:

The book doesn't name the writer. But it does say Jebusites lived in an unconquered Jerusalem "to this day" (Judges 1:21). So at least part of the book was written before King David took Jerusalem. Some experts guess that Samuel—a prophet who anointed David as king and whom many consider Israel's last judge—compiled the stories that were passed down from one generation to the next. Others guess that Jewish editors recorded the stories sometime after Samuel, perhaps to let this tragic history show why Israel needed kings.

DATE:

The stories begin with the death of Joshua. That could mean about 1375 BC or perhaps 200 years later. Bible experts debate when Joshua led his armies in the conquest of Canaan. The stories end shortly before Saul becomes Israel's first king, in about 1050 BC.

LOCATION:

Most of the stories take place in what are now the countries of Israel and Jordan.

NOT QUITE conquerors

"You were not to make any covenants with the people living in this land; instead, you were to destroy their altars. But you disobeyed my command. Why did you do this? So now I declare that I will no longer drive out the people living in your land. They will be thorns in your sides, and their gods will be a constant temptation to you."

JUDGES 2:2–3

With many of the Canaanite armies defeated and most of the highland territory in Israel's control, phase one of the conquest is over. Israel's dozen tribes, previously united into one fighting force, disband their army. Each tribe withdraws to its assigned territory. Phase two begins. Each tribe is to mop up the resistance in its own territory.

They seem eager to finish the job. The tribe of Judah strikes first, capturing individual towns and decimating coalition armies. They even capture the hilltop city of Jerusalem, though they don't manage to hold it. Jerusalem is apparently on the tribal border between Judah and Benjamin. And a few verses later in the story, the writer reports that Benjamin "failed to drive out the Jebusites, who were living in Jerusalem. So to this day the Jebusites live in Jerusalem among the people of Benjamin" (Judges 1:21). Later, in about 1000 BC, David will capture Jerusalem again and make it his capital.

Neighboring tribes sometimes team up to fight a common enemy. That's how Judah and Simeon capture the town of Zephath.

But there's apparently a limit to cooperation. No one comes to Judah's aid when the tribe fails to defeat a coastal army equipped with iron chariots. This may have been the powerful Philistines, who live on the coast and who horde the secret technology of iron-making.

Eventually, tribe after tribe gives up its conquest—in breech of their contract with God. Canaanites continue living among them and worshipping idols—some idols that are particularly nasty, requiring human sacrifice and sex rituals.

God sends a messenger to deliver bad news to the Israelites: The people have lost the will to fight, so God will no longer give them the power to fight. As Moses and Joshua had warned the people years earlier, failure to finish the job is a punishable offense under Israel's agreement with God.

This failure "made the LORD burn with anger against Israel, so he handed them over to raiders who stole their possessions. He turned them over to their enemies all around, and they were no longer able to resist them" (Judges 2:14).

THE TWELVE

Each time the Israelites repented of their sins and asked God for deliverance from their attackers, God sent a leader called a "judge."

That word's a bit outdated now, since we associate judges with court cases. The Hebrew term had a much broader meaning, which included "ruler" or "leader." "Tribal ruler" is probably a better way of describing them.

These heroic leaders often rallied the Israelites and drove off the oppressors.

The stories are generally regional, not nationwide. Israel wasn't yet a united nation, but a loosely knit confederation of tribes. So there was likely some overlap between the dozen judges.

Judge	Years of activity	Claim to fame
Othniel	40	Defeated king of Aram, in what is now Syria
Ehud	80	Assassinated an oppressive king in what is now Jordan, then led a successful revolt
Shamgar	Unknown	Killed 600 Philistines with an ox herder's stick
Deborah	40	Led an army of foot soldiers that defeated an invading chariot corps
Gideon	40	With 300 men, drove off 135,000 invaders from Midian, a nation in what is now Jordan or Saudi Arabia
Tola	23	Considered a minor judge, he was a descendant of Dodo—whoever that was
Jair	22	Had 30 sons who owned 30 towns in the rich grazing land of Gilead, in what is now Jordan
Jephthah	6	Defeated Ammonites in what is now Jordan, then honored his rash vow to celebrate victory by sacrificing the first thing to greet him at home: his only child, a daughter
Ibzan	7	Had 30 sons and 30 daughters
Elon	10	Unknown
Abdon	8	Had 40 sons and 30 grandsons, all of whom rode donkeys—suggesting a time of prosperity and peace
Samson	40	A strongman who killed a lion with his bare hands and who waged a one-man war against the Philistines, killing 1,000 with a donkey's jawbone and then killing himself and thousands more when he pushed down the support pillars of a temple

Ground zero. Deborah gathers her foot soldiers on this rounded hill, Mount Tabor. It's the perfect battlefield for infantry about to take on an invading chariot corps. Iron-plated chariots can't maneuver well on a steep hillside.

THE GENERAL is a lady

"You will receive no honor in this venture, for the LORD's victory over Sisera will be at the hands of a woman."

JUDGES 4:9

Those are the words of a prophet named Deborah, talking to a general named Barak. Deborah has just passed along God's order to Barak: Assemble 10,000 fighters at Mount Tabor and you'll defeat the invading chariot corps led by a Canaanite named Sisera.

"I will go," Barak replies, "but only if you go with me" (Judges 4:8).

Deborah is no soldier. She's a wife and "a prophet who was judging Israel at that time. She would sit under the Palm of Deborah. . .and the Israelites would go to her for judgment" (Judges 4:4–5).

Yet Deborah agrees to go, vowing that a woman will earn the battlefield praise.

King Jabin of the Canaanite city of Hazor hears about Deborah gathering her militia. His seasoned army is only a hard day's march away from Mount Tabor, about 25 miles north. Jabin has been raiding Israel's northland for 20 years, and he apparently doesn't plan to stop anytime soon. So he orders his general, Sisera, to take the army and 900 iron war chariots down to crush the uprising.

As the chariots approach Mount Tabor along the banks of the tiny Kishon River—which normally looks more like a creek than a river—a rainstorm explodes above them. Dry riverbeds called wadis (WAH-dees) funnel their fill to the Kishon, which swells into a torrent. Flash flood.

Deborah orders Barak to attack, and 10,000 screaming Israelites charge down the hill.

Floodwater snatches and sweeps many of the enemy chariots downstream away from the battlefield, drowning the attack crews. Mud sucks in most of the other chariots, forcing crews to run for their lives.

The enemy general, Sisera, runs, too. And he keeps running until he comes to a lone herder's camp, probably miles away. Only the herder's wife, Jael, is there to greet him. She offers him milk, a fine sedative for a wasted warrior on the run. Then when Sisera falls asleep, she drives a tent peg into the side of his head.

And with that, Deborah's prophecy is fulfilled. One woman started the battle. And another woman finished it.

GIDEON'S ELITE strike force

"Go with the strength you have, and rescue Israel from the Midianites."

JUDGES 6:14

Spoken by an angel sent from God, this line sounds like a joke. The clue is the angel's timing. The angel is addressing an Israelite named Gideon—who's hiding in a hole in the ground.

Gideon is hiding there because raiders have stormed into Israel's prime farming area in the fertile northland. They charge in on camels from Midian, a country in what is now Jordan or Saudi Arabia. Each spring they come to steal the freshly harvested barley and wheat, along with all the livestock they can find. Many Israelites have taken to hiding in caves and rock dens in the raiding season.

Gideon is hiding at the bottom of a winepress—which may have been just a hollowed out rock that looks like a big bowl. He's working in there, knocking grain kernels from stalks he had cut earlier. By working there, he won't be seen by Midianite scouts riding in the distance.

Gideon argues with the angel, insisting he doesn't have any strength to fight Midian. "My family group is the weakest in Manasseh, and I am the least important member of my family" (Judges 6:15 NCV).

History's first camel cavalry

Gideon's story is the world's first known report of anyone riding camels in battle.

Camel-riding raiders stormed in from the Arabian Desert. "These enemy hordes...arrived on droves of camels too numerous to count. And they stayed until the land was stripped bare" (Judges 6:5).

Fighters on camelback had several advantages over Israelite foot soldiers. Camels could:

- sprint twice as fast as the best Olympic runners;
- cover five times the distance most people can walk in a day; and
- cruise at 25 miles per hour for an entire hour—more than double the speed of a marathon racer.

Gideon's strategy was to strike the Midianite camel cavalry while they were asleep.

Bumpy but fast. Rifle strapped to his back, this camel-riding herder in the early 1900s can cover 100 miles in a day searching for pasture for his flocks. Camels, which Midianites rode while raiding Israel, can sprint up to 40 miles per hour—offering quite the element of surprise.

"I will be with you," the angel answers, speaking for God.

Gideon wants proof—miracles, in fact. And the angel complies. A fleece of wool left out overnight is soaked with dew the next morning—but the ground around it is dry. The next day the opposite happens: dry fleece, wet ground. Gideon is convinced.

An army of 32,000 rallies to Gideon's call—though that doesn't seem nearly enough to engage Midian's coalition of 135,000. Still, God says it's too many. God wants to make it clear that ridding the Midianite infestation is *his* doing, not the work of Gideon's soldiers. So Gideon, acting on God's order, cuts his army down to an elite fighting force of 300.

His men surround the Midianite camp at about midnight, then light torches and blow rams' horns. Horrified and confused by the nighttime sound and light show, the Midianite soldiers assume the enemy is already in their camp. So they start killing each other. Gideon chases down the runaways, killing them and their kings.

After Gideon dies, the memory-challenged Israelites go back to worshipping idols of Baal, main god of the Canaanites. "They forgot the LORD their God, who had rescued them from all their enemies surrounding them" (Judges 8:34).

THE HERO who kills his daughter

"I will give to the LORD whatever comes out of my house to meet me when I return in triumph. I will sacrifice it as a burnt offering." . . .*When Jephthah returned home. . .his daughter came out to meet him, playing on a tambourine and dancing for joy.*

JUDGES 11:31, 34

God responds to Israel's sin by letting the Ammonite people, in what is now Jordan, oppress Israelites who live east of the Jordan River. In time, those Israelites again call on God to save them.

Salvation comes through the son of a prostitute. Jephthah's half brothers had run him off so they wouldn't have to share the family inheritance with him. Abandoned, Jephthah forms a band of not-so-merry men described as "worthless rebels." But they can fight.

In time, the Israelites ask him to organize and lead an army against Ammon. In return, they promise to let him rule the territory.

Acting much like a wise king, Jephthah tries out some diplomacy on the Ammonites. He reminds Ammon's king that the Ammonites lost their land to Israel after an unprovoked attack on Israelite refugees. Moses had asked for safe passage through the land, and Ammon responded with a doomed military assault. So it was God who gave Israel the land, Jephthah argues—and that was 300 years ago. So Jephthah asks why Ammon has waited so long to reclaim the land.

Ammon's king ignores this message. But he can't ignore Jephthah's army, which crushes the Ammonites and destroys about 20 of their cities.

Before the battle, Jephthah had made a rash vow to God. If he won, he promised to sacrifice whatever came out of his house to greet him when he returned. His only child, a daughter, is the first to welcome him. Jephthah ignorantly keeps the vow, though Jewish law clearly shows that God detests human sacrifice: "Never sacrifice your son or daughter as a burnt offering" (Deuteronomy 18:10).

Jephthah apparently hadn't read that. He "kept the vow he had made" and his young daughter "died a virgin" (Judges 11:39).

Samson's weakness. Delilah holds the braids of Samson's hair, which she clipped off while he was sleeping. Samson had to keep a vow to God—that he'd never cut his hair—in order to keep his extreme strength. But Delilah, pretending to be the love of his life, weaseled the secret out of him and collected a big reward.

SAMSON, Philistine-killer

He found the jawbone of a recently killed donkey. He picked it up and killed 1,000 Philistines with it.

JUDGES 15:15

Samson is an odd hero. He's not a leader like the other judges. He's a maverick—a one-man army. And he's not interested in spiritual things. He's driven by animal instincts—especially by his insatiable desire for women, and for revenge.

Yet his story begins with the promise of hope, and it ends with that hope fulfilled.

"You will become pregnant and give birth to a son," an angel tells the woman who will become Samson's mother. "He will be dedicated to God as a Nazirite from birth. He will begin to rescue Israel from the Philistines" (Judges 13:5).

As a lifelong Nazirite, Samson isn't supposed to cut his hair. And as long as he keeps this vow, God will bless him with incredible strength.

Samson is born at a turning point in Israel's history. Philistines and Israelites are learning to live together in peace. But it's with Israel as the lesser nation—a nation in danger of becoming assimilated into Philistine culture. Philistines have both the stronger army and a secret weapon: knowledge of how to forge iron weapons that can slice through Israel's soft, bronze weapons.

Samson's early years actually show how well the two nations are getting along. He marries a Philistine, over the objections of his parents. But it's at the weeklong marriage celebration that Samson starts to sour on the Philistines. Samson bets all 30 of his Philistine guests that they can't solve his riddle. On the line are 30 sets of clothing.

His guests cheat. They extort the answer from his bride by threatening to kill her. So Samson storms off to a neighboring Philistine town, where he kills 30 men and takes their clothes to pay his debt. Then he abandons his bride and goes back home to his parents. By the time Samson cools off and returns to his bride, her father has married her to the best man.

Revenge takes over the rest of Samson's story. "I cannot be blamed for everything I am going to do to you Philistines," Samson tells his ex-father-in-law (Judges 15:3).

Samson torches Philistine farms, vineyards, and olive groves. Philistines retaliate by torching his ex-wife and her father. Then they start terrorizing Israelites, who eventually convince Samson to surrender. But once in custody, Samson breaks his ropes and kills 1,000 Philistines. Their iron swords prove no match for Samson's improvised weapon: a donkey's jawbone.

Philistine iron can't stop him. But Philistine flesh manages quite nicely. Samson falls in love with Delilah, a Philistine who loves money more than him. Philistine leaders offer her a reward equal to several thousand dollars if she can find the source of Samson's strength. She nags it out of him, cuts his hair while he's napping, and turns him over to the Philistines.

The arresting soldiers gouge out Samson's eyes and put him to work grinding grain. Months later, they parade him as a war trophy in front of thousands crowded into a temple. In his only recorded prayer, Samson asks for revenge: "Let me pay back the Philistines for the loss of my two eyes" (Judges 16:28). Samson pushes on twin support pillars, which were probably towers of stone blocks stacked on top of one another. That was a common design in Samson's day. The temple collapses, killing Samson and more Philistines than he had killed during his lifetime.

Israel is no longer in danger of a polite assimilation into Philistine life. The two nations are now suspicious of each other and evolving into enemies. Years later, King David will finish the job Samson started. He will break the back of Philistine power. And it will be the Philistines, not the Jews, who become a lost nation—assimilated into Middle Eastern culture.

NOTHING but chaos

In those days Israel had no king; all the people did whatever seemed right in their own eyes.

JUDGES 21:25

After a dozen rotations of the cycle—Israel slipping into sin, God sending oppressors, Israel repenting, and God responding with a deliverer—anarchy takes over. It's illustrated in several stories at the end of Judges.

- A Levite hires himself out as a rich man's priest. This Levite practices a smorgasbord religion, worshipping God as well as Canaanite idols.
- Israelites in the tribe of Benjamin gang-rape a man's concubine (a woman who's a bit like a common-law wife).
- Tribal leaders of Benjamin refuse to turn over the rapists. So the other tribes start a civil war, and nearly wipe out the tribe of Benjamin.
- To fix the near annihilation, Israelite leaders allow the surviving men of Benjamin's tribe to kidnap Israelite women from other tribes to serve as their wives.

The book ends with what sounds like a not-so-subtle plea for a king who can unite Israel and restore the peace. Indeed, the book that follows is a bridge to stories about the kings of Israel. The book is Ruth, named after its starring character—the great-grandmother of Israel's most revered king, David.

RUTH

THE ARAB MOTHER OF ISRAEL'S KINGS

Escaping a drought in Bethlehem, a husband and wife take their two sons east into Moab, a territory in what is now Jordan. There, the sons marry Moabite women. But within 10 years, all three men are dead, leaving their widows destitute.

The elderly mother, Naomi, decides to walk back to Bethlehem, perhaps hoping a relative will take her in. She advises her daughters-in-law, Ruth and Orpah, to go home to their mothers. Orpah reluctantly agrees. But Ruth insists on staying with Naomi.

After the two women arrive in Bethlehem, a rich farmer named Boaz takes an interest in Ruth. He admires her loyalty to Naomi, perhaps partly because he's related to Naomi's dead husband.

His interest and admiration are good news for the women because it makes him a prime target for becoming Ruth's next husband. It's ancient Jewish custom for the closest relative of a deceased man to marry the widow, to make sure she's cared for. It's an ancient form of social security.

Naomi convinces Ruth to propose marriage to Boaz by asking him to fulfill his role as a "family redeemer." He gladly agrees. The couple has a son named Obed. He will grow up to become the grandfather of Israel's most famous king: David.

Not Jewish. Dressed in the clothes of an Arab Bedouin, this herder's daughter from the early 1900s is no more Jewish than Ruth who came from what is now Jordan. Yet Ruth, the great-grandmother of David, became the mother of Israel's most revered family of kings.

LOYAL daughter-in-law

"Don't ask me to leave you and turn back. Wherever you go, I will go; wherever you live, I will live. Your people will be my people, and your God will be my God."

RUTH 1:16

A long drought dries up the farmland and grazing fields in southern Israel. So a Bethlehem couple, Elimelech and his wife Naomi, gather up their two boys and move across the Jordan River. They settle in Moab, a fertile strip of land perched on a plateau above the Dead Sea. Perhaps it's in northern Moab, the area Moses gave to the Israelite tribe of Reuben. Whether it's north or south Moab, the walk from Bethlehem takes just a few days.

Elimelech dies in Moab. His sons, Mahlon and Kilion, marry Moabite women: Orpah and Ruth. But within about 10 years after moving to Moab, both sons are dead, as well. Suddenly, the three women are destitute. They have no source of income, since earning a living in ancient times is considered a man's job.

Typically, childless widows like Orpah and Ruth would go home to their parents and hope to marry again. And that's what Naomi

MAIN POINT:

A non-Jewish woman is the ancestor of Israel's greatest dynasty of kings—from David to the King of kings, Jesus.

WRITER:

One of the most beautifully written stories in the Bible, the book of Ruth never reveals the name of its writer.

DATE:

Ruth probably lived in about 1100 BC, since she was David's great-grandmother, and he ruled as king in about 1000 BC. Bible experts are left to wonder when the story was written. Guesses on the timing start about 950 BC, when David's son Solomon reigned. But some guess the book was written during Israel's exile in Babylon (modern-day Iraq) in the 500s BC.

LOCATION:

The story shifts from Bethlehem to Moab in what is now Jordan, and then back to Bethlehem.

WHAT'S SO BAD ABOUT A MOABITE?

If God had been looking for a way to impress people with the family tree of Israel's greatest dynasty of kings, he wouldn't have imported the tree from Moab.

What king would want to admit that his family got its start from a drunken old man who impregnated his daughter?

But that's where the Moabites came from—that's the family heritage that Ruth brought to her wedding with a Bethlehem Jew. When God seared Sodom off the planet, Lot and his two daughters ran to the nearby hills and hid in a cave. The girls thought Lot was the last man alive in the area, so they got him drunk and had sex with him. They wanted his family to live on.

"When the older daughter gave birth to a son, she named him Moab. He became the ancestor of the nation now known as the Moabites" (Genesis 19:37). The Moabites eventually settled on a narrow strip of fertile land east of the Dead Sea, in modern-day Jordan.

Since Lot was Abraham's nephew, and Abraham was the father of the Jews, the Jewish people considered the Moabites their distant relatives. But these relatives didn't always get along.

Naomi's Long Walk Home

Red Sea

Gulf of Aqaba

Ruth pleads to leave Moab with Naomi

MOAB

Dead Sea

Jericho

Bethlehem

Jerusalem

ISRAEL

Jordan River

Mediterranean Sea

recommends. She says she'll walk back to Bethlehem to spend her final years with whatever family she has left.

Both daughters-in-law begin walking with her. But Naomi eventually talks Orpah into leaving, and going home. Ruth, however, refuses to budge. She absolutely won't allow Naomi to make this trip alone. Why Ruth saddles herself with an elderly mother-in-law, the Bible doesn't say. Perhaps she loved Naomi that much. Or maybe the home she came from wasn't worth going back to.

PICKING UP leftovers

"Let me go out into the harvest fields to pick up the stalks of grain left behind by anyone who is kind enough to let me do it."

RUTH 2:2

Naomi and Ruth arrive in Bethlehem sometime in April or May, when farmers are cutting their first grain harvest: barley.

By law, Jewish harvesters can make only one pass through the fields. Anything left after that belongs to the poor. So Ruth goes out to gather grain for her and Naomi. In what appears to be an incredible stroke of luck, she finds herself in the field of a rich farmer named Boaz. He's a relative of Naomi's dead husband.

Boaz has heard about this young widow who refused to abandon Naomi. He admires Ruth for this, and he rewards her. He thanks her for her loyalty to Naomi, and he tells her to follow a group of women harvesters. Then he orders the harvesters to leave some extra grain for Ruth. Boaz also invites Ruth to drink from his well whenever she's thirsty and to share the lunchtime meal he prepares for his workers.

By day's end, Ruth goes back to Naomi with this story of incredible kindness—and half a bushel of grain.

"Good!" Naomi says. "Stay with his young women right through the whole harvest. You might be harassed in other fields, but you'll be safe with him" (Ruth 2:22).

God's social security program

Widows, along with orphans and immigrants, were among the most vulnerable people in Bible times.

It was a man's world. Women were minors in a court of law—like kids today. Women were also the property of men—fathers, husbands, or sons. So women generally weren't allowed to own property or conduct business. They weren't considered capable of that since their education was typically limited to household matters: cooking, sewing, and hauling water.

Widows with no one to look after them became destitute. Some begged on street corners. Others turned to prostitution.

God ordered his people to take care of each other with this remarkable goal in mind: "There should be no poor among you" (Deuteronomy 15:4).

And he set up laws to make sure the most vulnerable people got the support they needed.

- Widows could call on a close relative, such as their husband's brother, to marry them and take care of them (Deuteronomy 25:5–10). That's exactly what Ruth did.
- Farmers weren't supposed to harvest every bit of their crops. Instead, they were to skip the edges of grain fields, leave some grapes on the vine, and not pick up grapes that had fallen on the ground. "Leave them for the poor and the foreigners living among you" (Leviticus 19:10).

Home is a Bethlehem cave. A Bethlehem widow poses for a photo in front of her cave home. For the picture, she switched out her everyday scarf for this white one, the best she owned—frayed and patched, but clean. American charity workers had brought her a fuel-fed lamp to use for light and heat.

- Every third year, a tenth of the harvest was donated and stored for distribution. Some went to the Levites, a tribe of priests without a territory assigned to them. The rest went to "foreigners living among you, the orphans, and the widows in your towns, so they can eat and be satisfied" (Deuteronomy 14:29).
- Charity was law. "Give generously to the poor, not grudgingly, for the LORD your God will bless you in everything you do" (Deuteronomy 15:10).

HOW RUTH gets her man

"Take a bath and put on perfume and dress in your nicest clothes. Then go to the threshing floor, but don't let Boaz see you until he has finished eating and drinking. Be sure to notice where he lies down; then go and uncover his feet and lie down there. He will tell you what to do."

RUTH 3:3–4

"Put your cover over me." Following ancient tradition, a Jewish groom extends his prayer shawl to cover his bride. When Ruth asked Boaz to cover her, she was following a tradition throughout the region. The groom would put a cloth over his bride as a symbol of his protection.

Naomi decides that Boaz has husband potential for Ruth. For one thing, he's a relative of Naomi's husband and sons. That means he's eligible to fulfill the Jewish law requiring a relative of the dead man to marry the widow. Besides, Boaz has already shown interest in Ruth.

Naomi's strategy looks a bit like entrapment, at least to readers today. It looks like she's helping a young widow trap an older rich man into getting married.

Boaz and his workers are sleeping outside near the pile of cut grain stalks. It's to protect the harvest from thieves. Ruth secretly joins them, apparently after sunset—which comes about 7:30 p.m. in early May. Freshly bathed and sprinkled in the scent of romance, Ruth waits until Boaz falls asleep. Then she glides over to him and slips under the covers at his feet.

About midnight, Boaz wakes—pleasantly surprised.

What pleases him is Ruth's reply after he asks who she is.

"I am your servant Ruth. . . . Spread the corner of your covering over me, for you are my family redeemer" (Ruth 3:9).

WHY THIS STORY WAS WRITTEN

It's anyone's guess why Ruth's unnamed writer penned this story onto a leather scroll. Fortunately, Bible experts love to guess. Here are a few of their most popular theories.

• David is the surprising climax of the story—and the reason it was written. The book of Ruth is a great slice of history from the family of Israel's greatest king.

• It's a captivating story that wonderfully illustrates the value and reward of loyalty.

• It's the counterpoint to what some Jews considered an outdated and callous teaching that spanned many centuries and was championed by a priest named Ezra. After Jews returned home from exile in what is now Iraq (then Babylon), Ezra ordered all Jewish men to divorce their non-Jewish wives. Why? "The holy race has become polluted by these mixed marriages" (Ezra 9:2). But Ruth's story shows that Israel's greatest dynasty of kings came from a mixed marriage.

That reply has something special going for it.

It's a sly take-off on something Boaz told her earlier: "May the LORD, the God of Israel, under whose wings you have come to take refuge, reward you fully for what you have done" (Ruth 2:12). The Hebrew word for "wing" and "cover" are the same. Boaz had said he hoped God would protect Ruth under his wings. And now Ruth is asking Boaz to become God's protective "wing" by spreading his "cover" over her.

Boaz, described as an older man, apparently believes that Ruth could have her pick of any number of young men. But she opts for an older man like him, to honor Naomi's family tradition. Boaz is liking this lady more and more.

He says there is another family member who is a closer relative. So that fellow would have first dibs on marrying Ruth. Boaz promises to talk with the man in the morning.

Boaz lets Ruth spend the night, but he has her sneak off before daybreak—perhaps to preserve both of their reputations. Also, if the other relative finds out that Boaz is interested enough in Ruth to share the covers with her, Boaz could lose some negotiating leverage.

HAPPILY ever after

Boaz took Ruth into his home, and she became his wife. When he slept with her, the LORD enabled her to become pregnant, and she gave birth to a son. . . . And they named him Obed. He became the father of Jesse and the grandfather of David.

RUTH 4:13, 17

In front of 10 witnesses at the city gate, Boaz makes an offer to the man first in line to marry Ruth. And Boaz does it with the savvy of a warrior leading a surprise attack.

He says Naomi needs to find a man to take her husband's property. Some translations say she's selling it. But the word can also mean "give away." Jewish widows in Ruth's day don't seem to have legal rights to inherit and sell their husband's property. The land passes on to a son, daughter, brother, uncle, or the nearest male relative—in that order (Numbers 27:8–11). Widows aren't on the list.

"If you want the land," Boaz says, "it's yours. But if not, I'm next in line."

"All right, I'll take it," the man says.

Here comes the surprise.

"Of course, your purchase of the land from Naomi also requires that you marry Ruth, the Moabite widow," Boaz says. "That way she can have children who will carry on her husband's name and keep the land in the family" (Ruth 4:5).

Deal breaker.

Boaz gets the land, the lady, and presumably the mother-in-law.

The couple has a son whom they name Obed. He will become the father of Jesse and the grandfather of David—Israel's most celebrated king in a thousand years of kings.

Eventually, Ruth will become one of a select five women who show up in the published family tree of Jesus.

1 SAMUEL

From donkey herder to king. Israel's first king—Saul—grew up as the son of a donkey herder. When the prophet Samuel told him that God had chosen him to become the nation's first king, Saul wasn't happy. He preferred tending donkeys to tending people.

HERE COME THE KINGS

God is Israel's king. At least he is during the nation's early years, while the Israelites get settled in Canaan. When God needs human leaders to rally the people for something important, like a battle, he manages to round up some leaders just fine. Notable leaders like Deborah and Gideon. Samuel becomes the last of these unique leaders known as "judges."

Samuel is a miracle baby, born to a previously infertile woman. His mother, Hannah, is so grateful to God for her son that while Samuel is still young, she gives him back to God. She allows her boy to grow up in the sacred worship center—serving God by helping the priests.

Samuel becomes both a spiritual and political leader. He settles disputes as a circuit-walking judge. He represents the people before God, as a priest. And he delivers God's messages to the people, as a prophet.

Yet in Samuel's old age, the Israelites worry that his bribe-loving sons will take the reins. So they insist on Samuel picking a king for them. Samuel feels rejected. But God comforts him by explaining that the people aren't rejecting Samuel. They're rejecting God as their king.

Samuel anoints a donkey herder named Saul as Israel's first king. Saul proves himself a gifted military leader. But he disobeys God by performing rituals reserved for priests and by stealing possessions from a defeated enemy.

Saul loses God's support. Depression sets in and begins to take control of him. When David as a young shepherd kills a Philistine champion named Goliath in one-on-one mortal combat, the Israelites cheer him as a hero. Saul grows insanely jealous, decides to kill David, and spends much of his energy and resources trying to hunt down David instead of trying to build up his nation.

Saul's story ends on the battlefield, in suicide. Philistines overrun his forces, killing three of his sons. And rather than be taken alive, Saul falls on his own sword.

PRICE TAG FOR A KING

Samuel tried to talk the Israelites out of adopting a monarchy. He said kings come at a high price. Each king would demand from the citizens:

- sons to fight in his army and farm his fields;
- daughters to do his household chores such as making meals and perfume; the best fields, farmland, and orchards—confiscated for royal use; and
- one-tenth of all the crops and livestock, as taxes.

MAIN POINT:

Israel insists on having kings like other countries, even though God warns against it.

WRITER:

Unknown.
First and Second Samuel were originally one book. About a century before Jesus was born, scholars translating the Jewish scriptures into Greek split this book in half so it would fit on regular-sized scrolls. The combined books of Samuel feature stories that spin around three people: Samuel, Saul, and David. But the stories were apparently compiled by someone who lived at least half a century after David. That's because the book often refers to the Israelite people by country names used after the nation split into the competing kingdoms of Israel and Judah. This split happened after David's son, King Solomon, died in about 930 BC.

DATE:

1100–1000 BC. Spanning about a century, the stories start with the prophet Samuel's birth a few years before 1100 BC, and they end with King Saul's death a little before 1000 BC.

LOCATION:

Israel

A BABY BOY for an infertile lady

"O LORD of Heaven's Armies, if you will look upon my sorrow and answer my prayer and give me a son, then I will give him back to you. He will be yours for his entire lifetime."

1 SAMUEL 1:11

In Bible times, a woman isn't considered a success in her career as the household engineer unless she produces a son who will grow up to help her husband and inherit his estate. Hannah can't even have a daughter. Her husband's second wife taunts her, perhaps figuring that God is punishing Hannah, who's getting what she deserves.

Hannah knows better. She pleads with God to give her a son, promising to give the boy back to him for a lifetime of service. A priest, Eli, witnesses one of her prayers. Hannah is praying at Israel's worship center in Shiloh, a village in central Israel and just a few miles north of her hometown, Ramah. Eli sees her lips moving, but there's nothing coming out.

Eli jumps to the wrong conclusion: "Must you come here drunk?" (1 Samuel 1:14).

Hannah politely explains that she's talking to God about something deeply troubling. Eli, hopefully with some apology in his tone, tells her, "Go in peace! May the God of Israel grant the request you have asked of him" (I Samuel 1:17).

Hannah seems to take this as God's answer, and she leaves in great joy.

Samuel is born within a year. Hannah raises him until he's fully weaned from breast milk and eating only solid food. In this culture, he's probably several years old by that time (1 Samuel 1:26).

True to her vow, she walks little Samuel up to Shiloh and turns him over to Eli, who will raise him with his own sons at the worship center. Hannah and her husband will visit often, bringing gifts of clothing to their boy.

Messages from God are rare at this time in Israel's history. But one night while young Samuel is sleeping in the worship center, God calls out his name. Samuel thinks it's Eli, and he goes to him. This happens three times that night before Eli realizes God is calling the boy. So he tells Samuel, "If someone calls again, say, 'Speak, LORD, your servant is listening'" (1 Samuel 3:9).

And the Lord does speak. Unfortunately, it's bad news for Eli. His sons are horrible priests. They eat sacrificial meat reserved for God. And they sleep with the help—women who work at the worship center. Since Eli hasn't disciplined his evil sons, God says he will take care of it.

God says he'll carry out all the threats delivered earlier by another prophet: "The time is coming when I will put an end to your family, so it will no longer serve as my priests. All the members of your family will die before their time. None will reach old age" (1 Samuel 2:31).

MISPLACING God's "magic box"

"Let's bring the Ark of the Covenant of the LORD from Shiloh. If we carry it into battle with us, it will save us from our enemies."

1 SAMUEL 4:3

Actually, the Ark of the Covenant—a gold-plated chest that holds the 10 Commandments—isn't really God's "magic box." That's just how this particular generation of Israelites decides to treat their most sacred relic—as though power comes from the box instead of from God.

The Israelite army is losing a crucial battle with the Philistines. The battleground lies 20 miles west of the Shiloh worship center. That's just a day's march away. Perhaps the Israelites remember some of their history of the Exodus and the early conquest of Canaan, and they recall that priests carried the chest into battle. What they forget, however, is that the priests did this specifically because God told them to.

Israelite messengers rush to Shiloh and quickly convince their priests to bring the chest into battle. These are the same priests—Eli's sons—whom God has promised to kill for their spiritual contempt and hypocrisy.

When the priests arrive with the sacred chest, the soldiers cheer so loud that the vibration shakes the ground. The Philistines remember stories about the Ark of the Covenant. So when they hear that this chest has just arrived in Israel's camp, they figure they're as doomed as every other enemy of Israel that had fought and died beneath its dreadful shadow.

Terrified Philistine generals warn their soldiers, "This is a disaster! We have never had to face anything like this before! . . . Fight as never before, Philistines! If you don't, we will become the Hebrews' slaves" (1 Samuel 4:7, 9).

The sacred chest may have motivated the Israelites. But it motivates the Philistines even more. They win the battle.

Back at Shiloh, 98-year-old Eli sits anxiously beside the city gate waiting for news. He must be worried that this might be the day God had warned him about—the day of punishment for his sons.

A battlefront messenger arrives, his clothes torn and his body covered in dirt—customary expressions of grief. Eli doesn't see any of this, because he's blind. But he hears the rush of frantic voices, and he asks what the noise is all about.

"Israel has been defeated by the Philistines," the messenger replies. "The people have been slaughtered, and your two sons, Hophni and Phinehas, were also killed. And the Ark of God has been captured" (1 Samuel 4:17).

Shocked, Eli falls backward out of his seat. The fall breaks his neck, and he dies. In a single day, Israel has lost its top priests and its most sacred relic.

Philistine ark of the covenant. Captured as a war trophy, Israel's most sacred object—the gold-covered chest containing the 10 Commandments—sits on display in a Philistine temple. But by morning, a nearby statue of the Philistine god has mysteriously fallen, as though bowing before the holy chest.

Plague in a box

The Philistines thought they captured quite the prize—Israel's cherished Ark of the Covenant. But it brought them nothing but a brand of trouble that sounds like the bubonic plague.

The Ark of the Covenant was a four-foot-long wooden chest covered with gold inside and out and topped with gold statues of two angelic beings. Inside rested the 10 Commandments, Israel's most basic laws etched in stone and delivered to Moses by the Lord. The Israelites kept this chest in the most sacred room of their worship center. They considered it God's throne on earth.

When the Philistines captured the Ark in battle, they put it on display in their temple at Ashdod, a city near the seacoast. But overnight, the statue of their god Dagon somehow fell on its face beside the chest. They stood Dagon back up the following day. But the next night the statue not only fell over again, it broke into pieces, sending its head rolling.

A plague of tumors broke out among the Philistines. So they sent the chest to another Philistine town. More tumors. Another town. More tumors. This continued for seven months.

First Samuel's description of the disease and the cure suggests bubonic plague. This is a disease carried by rats and common in coastal towns where shipboard rats escape their floating prisons.

Plague victims developed lumps—swellings called "buboes" from which "bubonic" takes its name.

The Philistine cure: Send the chest back to Israel with gifts. "Make five gold tumors and five gold rats, just like those that have ravaged your land. Make these things to show honor to the God of Israel" (1 Samuel 6:4–5).

ISRAEL'S FIRST KING, a donkey herder

"Give us a king to judge us like all the other nations have."

1 SAMUEL 8:5

Samuel leads Israel as a judge, settling disputes. When he grows old, he appoints his two sons to take over. But they're greedy, and they sell justice to the highest briber. Israel's leaders take their complaint to Samuel by asking for a king.

Though the request leaves Samuel feeling rejected, God tells him not to take it personally and to do as the people ask.

"It is me they are rejecting," God says, "not you. They don't want me to be their king any longer" (1 Samuel 8:7).

God selects Saul, son of a donkey herder as well as "the most handsome man in Israel—head and shoulders taller than anyone else in the land" (1 Samuel 9:2). Samuel first meets him when Saul is out looking for some of his father's stray donkeys. And it's in that roadside meeting that Samuel announces, "I am here to tell you that you and your family are the focus of all Israel's hopes."

Saul doesn't want the pressure. And he doesn't want the job.

Samuel calls Israel's leaders to the village of Mizpah to introduce them to their first king. Saul reluctantly goes with him. But when it comes time for Samuel to present Saul, he's hiding among the baggage. Perhaps that's his comfort zone, among the baggage haulers of the day: donkeys.

Someone spots him, which shouldn't have been too difficult given his height. And the people proclaim him king.

Saul is not your typical king who quickly adjusts to privilege and wraps himself in luxury. In his very next scene, he's back home plowing a field with oxen. Not especially kingly. But what happens in that field proves regal. Messengers arrive with horrible news. A foreign king has surrounded an Israelite city. He says he'll sign a peace treaty with them, but only if he can gouge out the right eye of every citizen, "as a disgrace to all Israel" (1 Samuel 11:2).

Saul cuts his oxen to pieces, right there in the field he has been plowing. Then he sends out messengers as army recruiters, giving each of them a piece of dead meat. He orders them to show it to Israelite men throughout the region and to say this is what will happen to them if they don't join him immediately to fight off the invader. With his dead-meat militia of 300,000, Saul wins the battle and the hearts of his people.

Iron Age meets Stone Age and loses. Goliath's state-of-the-art iron weaponry is no match for one well-placed stone. Swirling a sling around his head to build momentum, David releases a stone like a miniature missile. Flying 100 yards a second, it drops Goliath like a rock.

DAVID the giant-killer

As Goliath moved closer to attack, David quickly ran out to meet him. Reaching into his shepherd's bag and taking out a stone, he hurled it with his sling and hit the Philistine in the forehead.

1 SAMUEL 17:48–49

For a donkey herder, Saul becomes one fine commander and chief. His army enjoys one battlefield success after another, engaging a variety of neighboring enemies. The toughest of the lot are the Philistines, who settled along the west coast about the same time Joshua and the Israelites arrived from the east.

One day the two armies prepare for battle, eyeballing each other from their camps on opposite hillsides, with a valley between them. Each day the Philistines send out their champion, a giant named Goliath, offering to settle the fight man-to-man. Goliath will battle Israel's best warrior in mortal combat, winner take all.

No takers.

The shepherd boy David arrives at the Israelite camp, on an errand for his father. He's bringing food to his big brothers, who had joined Saul's militia to push back this Philistine advance into Israel's territory.

David hears Goliath's challenge. And he accepts.

King Saul tries to talk him out of it. But David assures Saul that God has helped him kill lions and bears that threatened his father's sheep. And God will help him kill this Philistine, too.

David walks into the valley. He pauses at a stream just long enough to pick up five stones, worn aerodynamically smooth from the water's current. He needs only one. It strikes Goliath in the forehead, perhaps knocking him unconscious. David quickly takes the giant's own iron sword and ends the battle, cutting off Goliath's head.

The Philistine army runs, and Saul's men chase them clear back to their walled cities.

Back in Israel, out come the dancing women. They're singing: "Saul has killed his thousands, and David his ten thousands!" (1 Samuel 18:7).

This song, it seems, changes history. For it plants a seed of jealousy in Saul that grows into a consuming obsession: Get rid of David.

REASONS NOT TO FIGHT GOLIATH

- **He was a giant.** He stood nearly seven feet tall—or almost 10 feet according to some ancient copies of the story.
- **State-of-the-art weaponry.** Philistine weapons were made of iron, in a forging process they kept secret. Iron could slice through Israel's soft bronze weapons.
- **Massive spear.** His spear shaft was two inches thick or more—the thickness of a weaver's beam. His iron spearhead alone weighed 15 pounds, and soaring through the air would make quite an impression on a person's rib cage.
- **Armor.** An assistant walked ahead of him carrying a shield. Goliath himself wore a bronze helmet, leg armor, and a coat of mail. The mail alone probably outweighed young David: 125 pounds.

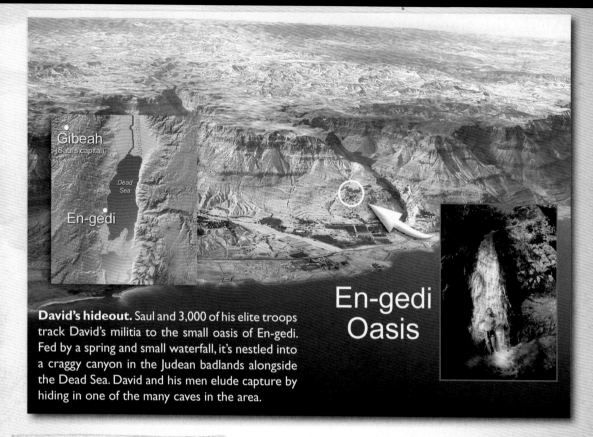

Gibeah
(Saul's capital)

Dead
Sea

En-gedi

En-gedi
Oasis

David's hideout. Saul and 3,000 of his elite troops track David's militia to the small oasis of En-gedi. Fed by a spring and small waterfall, it's nestled into a craggy canyon in the Judean badlands alongside the Dead Sea. David and his men elude capture by hiding in one of the many caves in the area.

DAVID runs for his life

Saul sent troops to watch David's house. They were told to kill David when he came out the next morning.

1 SAMUEL 19:11

King Saul slips into deep depression, with good reason. Because Saul had looted an enemy's possessions against God's order, "the Spirit of the LORD had left Saul, and the LORD sent a tormenting spirit that filled him with depression and fear" (1 Samuel 16:14).

Jealousy toward David only makes things worse. Saul tries several times to kill young David—twice while David is playing a harp to calm him. The king throws a spear and misses. Saul tries again, in a sneaky way, when David asks to marry Saul's daughter, Princess Michal. The king sets a high and dangerous price for the hand of his daughter in marriage. David has to bring him the foreskins of 100 Philistines—or die trying. Preferably the latter.

David brings back 200 foreskins. And suddenly he's King Saul's son-in-law, with his popularity still soaring.

Saul makes a desperate move. He orders troops to stake out the home of his own daughter and to kill her husband when he steps outside in the morning. Michal somehow finds out about it and helps David sneak away at night. Then she stalls the soldiers the next morning by telling them David is sick in bed.

Furious, Saul dissolves their marriage and forces Michal to marry another man. Then Saul spends the rest of his life in a search-and-destroy operation targeting David.

Now a fugitive, David flees into southern Israel where he grew up. There, an army gathers around him, drawn like steel to a magnet—"men who were in trouble or in debt or who were just discontented" (1 Samuel 22:2).

SAUL'S dynasty dies

The Philistines closed in on Saul and his sons, and they killed three of his sons— Jonathan, Abinadab, and Malkishua. . . and wounded him severely. . . . So Saul took his own sword and fell on it.

1 SAMUEL 31:2–4

Saul's army squares off again with the Philistines. But this time they stage the battle in Israel's northland. Perhaps they're fighting for control of the lucrative trade routes through the Jezreel Valley.

From his camp on the slopes of Mount Gilboa, Saul watches Philistines pour into the sprawling valley below. Their numbers look overwhelming. Frantic with fear, Saul wants direction from God. Middle Eastern kings going into battle often seek assurance of victory from their holy men. But the prophet Samuel has died, and God's Spirit has long since left Saul.

Dogs on the Philistine menu. Philistines loved their dogs, nicely cooked. And we're not talking hot dogs. Butchering marks were found on canine bones in the ruins of an ancient Philistine town: Ashkelon. Archaeologists conclude that Philistines enjoyed their dogs, dead or alive. None of their Canaanite neighbors appear to have had a taste for canine cuisine.

In desperation, Saul goes hunting for a psychic who can conjure up Samuel's spirit. He hears about one at Endor, a small village behind the enemy lines. So under the black of night Saul slips around the Philistine flank and visits the psychic, who agrees to call up Samuel.

Apparently planning to put on a show for her client, she screams in shock when Samuel's spirit actually appears.

"Tell me what to do," Saul asks.

"Why ask me, since the LORD has left you and has become your enemy?" Samuel replies. "The LORD will hand you and the army of Israel over to the Philistines tomorrow, and you and your sons will be here with me" (1 Samuel 28:16, 19).

Saul returns to his camp that night, inconsolable. In the battle that follows the next day, Philistines overrun the Israelite defenders. Saul's three oldest sons die in the fighting. Philistine archers hit Saul and are about to capture him. Fearing torture, he asks his battlefield assistant to kill him. But the assistant refuses. So Saul ends his own life, falling on his sword. His assistant does the same.

2 SAMUEL

GOOD KING DAVID, FLAWED FAMILY MAN

With King Saul and his sons dead, the Israelites rally around their favorite hero and giant-killer. They crown David king. At first, he's declared king only of his native southland tribe: Judah. But later, all of Israel embraces him as their ruler.

Saul had been a fine warrior king on the battlefield. But David manages to accomplish what Saul only dreamed of. David secures Israel's borders on all sides, even overpowering the Philistines. He captures Jerusalem and establishes it as Israel's political and spiritual capital.

On the family front, though, the king who masters the Middle East seems lost in his own home. He forces his ex-wife, Michal, Saul's daughter, to leave her beloved husband and return to his harem. She hates him for it. David has an affair with a soldier's wife, getting her pregnant and then murdering her husband in a cover-up. And David lets his oldest son get away with raping a half sister— ignoring the Jewish law about how to deal with such an offender. So the sister's full brother—who's also a son of David—takes the law into his own hands. He murders the prince and eventually leads a coup against his father.

Throughout most of David's reign, the country he's leading grows more secure while the family he's raising falls apart.

Warrior king. David earns his fame in war, defeating every enemy on Israel's perimeter. But the toughest battles of his life are the ones he loses in his very own home.

MAIN POINT:

God helps David establish Israel as a sovereign nation strong enough to secure its borders against enemies.

WRITER:

The writer isn't identified, but he probably lived sometime after David and Solomon. For more, see page 86.

DATE:

The story takes place from about 1010–970 BC, during David's 40-year reign.

LOCATION:

Israel, with some battles in what are now Jordan and Syria

Rock-solid proof of David. Highlighted in white, "House of David," meaning "Dynasty of David," is engraved on this stone from about 100 years after David's reign. Archaeologists found it in 1993. Before that—without any hard evidence that David existed—some Bible experts speculated he was nothing more than a bigger-than-life legend, like King Arthur.

FROM FUGITIVE to king

There at Hebron, King David made a covenant before the LORD with all the elders of Israel. And they anointed him king of Israel. David was thirty years old when he began to reign, and he reigned forty years in all.
2 SAMUEL 5:3–4

Still on the run from King Saul, David gets news that the Philistines have crushed Saul's army. A soldier who said he fought beside Saul delivers the report. Lying, he also says he put the mortally wounded king out of his misery.

"Why were you not afraid to kill the Lord's anointed one?" David asks. Then David gives an order to his own men: "Kill him!" (2 Samuel 1:14–15). David believes that no one has a right to kill the man God has chosen as Israel's king. That's why David didn't kill Saul earlier when he had opportunities.

Saul's commanding general proclaims a new king for Israel: Ishbosheth, the 40-year-old son of Saul. But David's tribe of Judah remains loyal to their legendary son, and they proclaim David king of their tribe.

Ishbosheth clashes with his general, Abner, accusing him of having sex with a woman in the royal harem. If Abner slept with a member of the king's harem—which he doesn't deny—it's like saying he is the rightful king. In fact, Abner is probably running the country at the time and feels he has a right to some of the fringe benefits.

The theory that Abner is the power behind the throne seems confirmed by what happens next. In his anger, he makes a deal with David to give Ishbosheth's kingdom to David. Unfortunately, David's general—Joab—kills Abner before the deal gets sealed. It's a revenge murder. Abner had killed Joab's brother in a battle.

With Abner gone, fear paralyzes Ishbosheth. He knows that Abner had been defending Ishbosheth's right to rule.

Two captains murder Ishbosheth. Then they hack off his head and take it to David, thinking he'll be pleased. But King David is developing a pattern of hostility toward anyone who kills a king in Israel. He orders the two executed.

Without a king, leaders of Israel's northern tribes travel south to Hebron, David's capital. There they proclaim him king of the reunited nation of Israel.

Euphrates River

Mediterranean Sea

PHOENICIA

Sea of Galilee

Jordan River

Jerusalem

PHILISTIA

Dead Sea

Solomon's add-on

Gihon Spring

CITY OF DAVID

David's Kingdom

EGYPT

Gulf of Aqaba

David's capital and kingdom. Israel in David's day stretched into what are now Lebanon in the north, Egypt in the south, along with Syria and Jordan east of the Jordan River. (Inset) Shaped a bit like Florida, David's Jerusalem covered just the bottom half of this ridge, below the white dots. His son Solomon later added the square section above, where he built the temple. Today, a 1,300-year-old, gold-domed Muslim shrine called the Dome of the Rock now sits on the temple hilltop.

DAVID takes Jerusalem

David then led his men to Jerusalem to fight against the Jebusites, the original inhabitants of the land who were living there. The Jebusites taunted David, saying, "You'll never get in here! Even the blind and lame could keep you out!"

2 SAMUEL 5:6

Perched on top of a steep ridge and surrounded by stone walls, Jerusalem looks invincible to David's army standing in the valley below. The soldiers must wonder what makes David think they can take it.

After all, Israelites have been in the country for at least 200 years—perhaps 400; scholars debate the timing of Joshua's conquest. And so far, the Israelites still haven't managed to capture and hold the city.

There is one report from shortly after Israel's conquest of the country that suggests otherwise: "The men of Judah attacked Jerusalem and captured it, killing all its people and setting the city on fire" (Judges 1:8). Perhaps many Jebusites fled the city before the battle, then came back afterward to build it even stronger.

David targets Jerusalem because he thinks it will make a perfect capital for Israel. Location is the reason. It sits in no-man's-land on the border between the tribes of Judah and Benjamin. That means if David conquers it and declares it the nation's capital city, he won't be showing favoritism to any of Israel's 12 tribes.

Besides that, this is a city that's easy to defend and hard to capture.

David gives his troops plenty of motivation for battle. "Whoever is first to attack the Jebusites will become the commander of my armies!" (1 Chronicles 11:6).

He also gives a word of advice: "Whoever attacks them should strike by going into the city through the water tunnel" (2 Samuel 5:8). He may have been talking about the 52-foot-high vertical shaft that functioned like a city well. Protected inside the city, people could drop a water bucket down this shaft. The bucket would land in Gihon Spring—a pool of water inside a small cave below Jerusalem, at the base of the ridge.

Joab, the son of David's sister, is the first one up the shaft. What happens next is a mystery. Perhaps he throws open the city gates, allowing his comrades to charge inside. However the battle unfolds, David's army wins.

David expands the city and turns it into Israel's political center. Then he begins the long process of transforming it into Israel's spiritual center, too. He does this by bringing to town Israel's most sacred relic: the Ark of the Covenant—a gold-covered chest that holds the 10 Commandments. David also builds an altar on a bedrock threshing floor near the city. And there he offers sacrifices to God.

Israel's main worship center, though, lies a few miles north at the sacred tent in the city of Gibeon. But within a few decades, at God's command, David's son Solomon will build a temple in Jerusalem. And from that time on, Jerusalem will remain for the Jewish people the most sacred city on earth.

BATHSHEBA the bathing beauty

Late one afternoon, after his midday rest, David got out of bed and was walking on the roof of the palace. As he looked out over the city, he noticed a woman of unusual beauty taking a bath. . . ."Bathsheba. . . the wife of Uriah the Hittite." Then David sent messengers to get her; and when she came to the palace, he slept with her.

2 SAMUEL 11:2–4

David already has at least seven wives and 16 sons, not counting daughters. He's managing a country as large as the Jewish people have ever controlled—before or since. And his army is fighting a battle no more than a three-day walk from his front door.

How David can find the time, energy, and libido for an affair is a tribute to the power of a deadly combo: testosterone and bad judgment.

David probably isn't looking for trouble, but he gets an eye full. He's probably out for a breath of fresh air, since people in Bible times used their flat roofs the way we use balconies, decks, and porches. Bathsheba is probably taking her bath in the walled courtyard of her home below. City homes are often built around a central courtyard.

It isn't just any bath she's taking. She's observing Jewish law by taking a purification bath one week after her menstrual flow stopped. This means that after her bath she's not only fresh and fragrant, she's fertile.

David invites her to the palace and the two have sex. The Bible doesn't say if it's consensual or if Bathsheba is fearfully obliging the Alpha Hebrew. In either case, she gets pregnant.

Her husband, Uriah, is off fighting for king and country. He's laying siege to a city about 60 miles away, near what is now Jordan's capital of Amman.

David has a bright idea. Bring Uriah home for a few days. Bathsheba will give him a warm welcome. And when the baby comes, Uriah might think it resembles him more than the king.

Uriah, however, refuses to sleep with his wife while his comrades are suffering through a battle. David tries a second time, getting Uriah drunk. But even wasted, Uriah displays more honor than the king.

David decides to have him killed. So David sends Uriah back to the battle with a message for the commander: Put Uriah on the front line, order a charge, and then pull back—leaving Uriah exposed. Uriah and several other soldiers die. David marries Bathsheba.

The prophet Nathan confronts David. "You have murdered Uriah the Hittite with the sword of the Ammonites and stolen his wife. . . . This is what the LORD says: Because of what you have done, I will cause your own household to rebel against you" (2 Samuel 12:9, 11).

David immediately confesses his sin and repents. In response, God immediately forgives him. Sadly, Bathsheba's son dies after seven days.

RAPING little sister

Absalom had a beautiful sister named Tamar. And Amnon, her half brother, fell desperately in love with her. . . .He grabbed her and demanded, "Come to bed with me, my darling sister". . .and since he was stronger than she was, he raped her.

2 SAMUEL 13:1, 11, 14

David's oldest son, Amnon, is first in line to become king after his father dies. Amnon sets a sex trap for one of his half sisters, Tamar. They both claim David as their father, but they have different mothers. Amnon pretends he's sick, and he convinces Tamar to fix a meal and feed him. But when she comes to his bedroom, he rapes her.

In the afterglow, "Amnon's love turned to hate, and he hated her even more than he had loved her" (2 Samuel 13:15). So he runs her off in disgrace—"damaged goods" is what other men would consider her.

Jewish law in that culture forbids "sexual relations with your sister or half sister" (Leviticus 18:9). It also requires a rapist to "marry the young woman because he violated her, and he may never divorce her as long as he lives" (Deuteronomy 22:29).

Yet King David—though angry—refuses to punish the crown prince or force him to marry Tamar. David doesn't even discuss the subject with his son.

Shamed, young Tamar moves out of the palace and into the home of her full brother, Absalom. There's no indication she ever gets married.

It takes two years for Absalom to find an opportunity to avenge his sister and himself—for he considers this rape of his sister as personally humiliating. It's as though Amnon is taunting him, calling him a weakling who can't defend his own sister.

Absalom invites his half brother to a feast during sheep-shearing season—the happy time when herders reap a payday for their sheep's wool. Amnon gets drunk at the party, and Absalom orders his men to kill the prince. Then Absalom flees to the home of his maternal grandfather, the king of Geshur, in what is now Syria.

A COUP against father

A messenger soon arrived in Jerusalem to tell David, "All Israel has joined Absalom in a conspiracy against you!"

2 SAMUEL 15:13

David eventually gets over the shock of Amnon's murder. But after three years, David is still missing Absalom. So he invites his son home. Oddly enough, David refuses to see him for another two years.

This infuriates Absalom, who is now the crown prince—David's oldest surviving son and next in line to become king.

Absalom starts plotting a coup. He hires 50 bodyguards, and each morning he goes to the city gate where court cases are tried. There, he ingratiates himself to the citizens who have come with complaints. He says they have a good case. "Too bad the king doesn't have anyone to hear it," he adds. "I wish I were the judge. Then everyone could bring their cases to me for judgment, and I would give them justice!" (2 Samuel 15:3–4).

When the grateful folks start to bow before him, he stops them, stands them up, and hugs them. Within several years, handsome prince Absalom is the toast of Israel. And he's just about ready to toast his father. With widespread support, he declares himself king. He does this in Hebron, the city where the people crowned David king years earlier.

Supporters rally to Absalom's cause, and an army emerges. David flees Jerusalem. But he leaves behind a mole—a palace advisor named Hushai whose mission is to give Absalom bad advice. Hushai advises the rookie king to take some time to build a vast army before chasing down David. But this also gives David time to build his army of seasoned soldiers.

In the forest battle that follows, Absalom's army can't stop the charge of David's angry warriors. Running for his life, Absalom gets jerked off his mule—headfirst. His long, thick hair snags an oak tree, and he's suddenly dangling from a branch like an acorn painted with a bull's-eye.

David has given orders to spare Absalom. But the soldiers spear him instead. Three daggers to the heart, compliments of the commander, Joab. Then come the blades and spearheads of 10 other soldiers.

When David gets the news, he bursts into tears: "O my son Absalom! My son, my son Absalom! If only I had died instead of you!" (2 Samuel 18:33).

WHERE PALESTINE GETS ITS NAME

Palestinians owe their name to the Philistines.

About the time Joshua and the Israelites arrived in Israel, the Philistines were getting there, too. They settled on the west coast, where many Palestinians live today in the area of the Gaza Strip. In fact, Gaza—a city in the Gaza Strip—was one of five key Philistine cities.

For centuries, Philistines dominated the Israelites. But David broke their power. In time, the Philistines were assimilated into other Middle Eastern groups.

Though their culture died, their name survives as "Palestine." It's from the word that Greeks used to refer to a Philistine: *Palaistine*.

Mothers in court. Pleading their case to King Solomon, two women roommates claim the same infant son—while neither claims the dead one. Pointing an angry finger at the living child, who's dangling before a soldier's sword, one of the women encourages King Solomon to carry out his threat—split the boy so each woman gets half. Solomon knows right then that she's not the mother. And Israelites know they've got a wise king.

FROM GLORY TO SHAME, KINGS LEAD THE WAY

King David grows old. On his deathbed he declares that Israel's next king will be the son he had with Bathsheba: Solomon.

Since David has already overpowered Israel's enemies, Solomon is free to develop the nation. For 40 years—Israel's most glorious generation—he reigns in prosperity and peace. During that time, he builds Israel's first permanent worship center, a temple in Jerusalem. Then he adds a palace, and he fortifies cities throughout Israel, making them easier to defend.

Solomon's biggest claim to fame, however, is his wisdom. Yet he marries 1,000 women—not particularly wise. In his old age, these women lure him into worshipping their idols.

For this sin, God declares that Solomon's dynasty will lead only a fraction of Israel—just the single tribe of Judah.

After Solomon dies, his son threatens to tax the people even more harshly than Solomon had done. So the northern tribes secede from the union and form their own country: Israel.

The southern nation takes the name of Judah, after the tribe.

Bible writers give the kings of Israel a poor evaluation, calling them men who do "evil in the Lord's sight." Two of the worst rulers are Ahab and Jezebel. Many of Judah's kings get bad marks, too. So God starts sending prophets like Elijah and Elisha. They warn the Jewish leaders that God will punish their nations unless the Israelites honor their agreement to obey him.

In most cases, sadly, the kings ignore God's prophets.

HOW SOLOMON'S MOM
crowned him king

[Bathsheba to dying David:]
"All Israel is waiting for you to announce who will become king after you. If you do not act, my son Solomon and I will be treated as criminals as soon as my lord the king has died."

I KINGS 1:20–21

Solomon is not the crown prince. He's not next in line to become king after David. Solomon is way down the line. David had at least 16 sons by the time he met Solomon's mother, Bathsheba.

Adonijah is the current crown prince. And he's already throwing a precoronation bash—while his father lies dying. The prince has already lined up the backing of most of his younger brothers, Israel's commanding general, and an influential priest.

But the prophet Nathan favors young Solomon—perhaps an insight he gets from God. The way the Bible reports it, Nathan

MAIN POINT:
Israel splits into two nations, north and south. It's God's punishment because King Solomon led the Israelites into worshipping idols.

WRITER:
Unknown. First and Second Kings were originally one book. About a century before Jesus was born, scholars translating the Jewish scriptures into Greek split this book in half so it would fit on regular-sized scrolls. The stories in this two-part book stretch about 400 years, from the time of David until invaders destroy Jerusalem in 586 BC. That means the writer or editors probably compiled the material from royal records and other sources sometime later—perhaps while the Jews were still exiled in what is now Iraq, then called Babylon.

DATE:
The stories in 1 Kings cover a little more than a century. They start during the final years of David's reign, which ended in about 970 BC. And they continue a few years past the death of King Ahab in about 850 BC.

LOCATION:
Israel

tricks old David. Nathan convinces Bathsheba to plant the idea in David's memory-fogged head that he vowed to make Solomon king. "And while you are still talking with him," Nathan tells Bathsheba, "I will come and confirm everything you have said" (1 Kings 1:14).

Nathan asks if David has changed his mind about Solomon, since Adonijah is already celebrating. David responds by crowning Solomon that day.

News travels quickly to Adonijah's party. And the guests stumble over each other in their rush to get out. Party over.

Apparently not ready to give up, Adonijah later asks his little brother Solomon if he can marry one of the women in the royal harem. Perhaps he thinks Solomon won't realize that this would give Adonijah added support for arguing that he's the rightful king. As David's oldest son, who would also be married to one of David's former wives, Adonijah would have a good case for the kingship. Kings often married the wives of the previous king for this very reason, to justify their right to the throne.

Solomon figures it out instantly, and orders his brother executed.

WISEST HUMAN EVER

"I will give you a wise and understanding heart such as no one else has had or ever will have!"
I KINGS 3:12

God appears to Solomon in a dream. The Bible says that's one of the most common ways God communicated to his prophets and others. "What do you want?" God says. "Ask, and I will give it to you."

"Give me an understanding heart so that I can govern your people well and know the difference between right and wrong," Solomon replies.

God grants that request—and then some. God promises that Solomon will become the wisest man in human history, as well as rich and famous. The queen of Sheba later pays Solomon a visit, perhaps intending to open trade negotiations. His wisdom and wealth leave her breathless.

"I heard in my country about your achievements and wisdom," she says. "I had not heard the half of it! Your wisdom and prosperity are far beyond what I was told" (1 Kings 10:6–7).

The Bible credits Solomon with writing "3,000 proverbs" (1 Kings 4:32) along with writing or at least inspiring many of the wise sayings and songs in Proverbs, Ecclesiastes, and the Song of Solomon.

Yet, proving that even wise people sometimes do stupid things, in his old age he gives into the temptation of worshipping idols.

SOLOMON'S prefab temple

"I am planning to build a Temple to honor the name of the LORD my God."
1 KINGS 5:5

Almost 500 years after leaving Egypt as slaves, the Israelites start to build their first permanent worship center. They've been worshipping in a tent that some older Bible translations call the tabernacle. David had wanted to build a temple, but God rejected the idea. David had too much blood on his hands. God wanted a man of peace to build it. So the job falls to Solomon.

It's a project that takes an army of about 200,000 drafted workers seven years to complete. Solomon recruits 30,000 loggers to cut cedar in Lebanon, 80,000 quarry workers and stone cutters, 70,000 general laborers to tote the timber and stone, and 3,600 foremen to manage the crews.

Surprisingly, it's a prefabricated building that masons piece together on site. "The stones used in the construction of the Temple were finished at the quarry, so there was no sound of hammer, ax, or any other iron tool at the building site" (1 Kings 6:7).

This may be out of respect for what the Israelites know will become their holiest spot on earth. Or perhaps the site is already sacred and used for sacrifices. Decades earlier, David bought a bedrock threshing floor on what some say became the temple hilltop. Then he "built an altar there to the LORD and sacrificed burnt offerings and peace offerings" (2 Samuel 24:25).

By today's standards, Solomon's temple is a small building: 30 yards long, 10 yards wide, and 15 yards high—about as high as a four-story building. Inside, where only priests are allowed, there are three rooms:

- **porch;**
- **sanctuary**, a cedar-paneled room where priests burn incense, light golden lampstands, and set out 12 sacred loaves of bread each Sabbath—the bread representing Israel's 12 tribes and their devotion to God; and
- **inner sanctuary**, a gold-paneled, 10-yard cube where Israel keeps its holiest object: the chest that holds the 10 Commandments.

Outside, in the courtyard, people bring their offerings. There, priests burn the offerings on top of a 15-foot-high altar.

TEMPLE TRIVIA

- Jews considered the temple God's home away from heaven—a holy palace among his people. As Solomon put it: "I have built a glorious Temple for you, a place where you can live forever" (1 Kings 8:13).
- Solomon spent nearly twice as long building his own palace: 13 years for his palace, seven years for God's temple.
- The temple survived 400 years. Babylonian invaders from what is now Iraq stripped it of gold and leveled it in 586 BC.

Israel's first temple. Solomon drafts nearly 200,000 men to work seven years building the Jerusalem temple. Once it's finished, only priests are allowed inside the sanctuary. All others stay out in the courtyard, where they sacrifice animal offerings and burn them on top of a huge altar. The massive basin in the foreground holds water for the washing rituals.

SOLOMON'S HAREM

Solomon loved many foreign women.... He had 700 wives of royal birth and 300 concubines... they turned his heart to worship other gods.

1 KINGS 11:1, 3–4

King Solomon's 1,000 wives might seem a few hundred too many, especially given God's warning: "The king must not take many wives for himself, because they will turn his heart away from the LORD" (Deuteronomy 17:17). But Middle Eastern custom allowed men to have as many wives as they could afford. Solomon's harem housed 700 wives by marriage and 300 other wives with less status.

Rulers sometimes grew large harems for several reasons:

- **Testosterone.** They enjoyed gorgeous women.
- **Peace treaties.** They sealed peace treaties with other rulers by exchanging royal daughters in marriage. The premise: What king would attack a nation if his daughter and grandchildren lived in the palace of that nation?
- **Bragging rights.** The bigger the harem, the bigger the man—or so the man thought.

Filled with kingly daughters, Solomon's harem was thick with political intrigue. Divas jockeyed for power. In time, some of Solomon's wives convinced him to build shrines so they could worship their gods. Solomon worshipped with them. And he paid the price—losing most of his kingdom.

A man and his harem. A wealthy Egyptian pauses for a portrait with his trio of wives in about 1880. Harems were common among wealthy people in the Middle East for thousands of years, and still exist in some Muslim societies.

ONE JEWISH NATION splits in two

When all Israel realized that the king had refused to listen to them, they responded, "Down with the dynasty of David!"... And to this day the northern tribes of Israel have refused to be ruled by a descendant of David.

1 KINGS 12:16, 19

Because Solomon worships idols during his senior years, God gives notice: "I will surely tear the kingdom away from you and give it to one of your servants. But for the sake of your father, David, I will not do this while you are still alive. I will take the kingdom away from your son" (1 Kings 11:11–12).

That son is Rehoboam, who decides to play hardball with the complaining citizens.

Solomon had worked and taxed the nation to the brink of revolt. He needed their muscle and money to build a glorious nation. Now, the masses want a break. And they're bold enough to ask for it.

Rehoboam meets with his advisors to discuss the request. Seasoned advisors encourage him to agree—to become a servant to the people so the people will become servants to him. But the younger men argue that he needs to present himself as a strong leader. So, on their advice, he tells the citizens, "Yes, my father laid heavy burdens on you, but I'm going to make them even heavier!" (1 Kings 12:11).

The people respond with a short history lesson, set to poetry. They know that their grandparents had rallied around David by chanting a chorus:

"We are yours, David!
We are on your side, son of Jesse."
1 CHRONICLES 12:18

But now the Israelites are singing a different tune:

"Down with the dynasty of David!
We have no interest in the son of Jesse."
1 KINGS 12:16

All the northern tribes go home, leaving Rehoboam to rule nothing more than his own tribe of Judah on Israel's southern border.

In the northland, the people select a new king: Jeroboam, a one-time foreman in Solomon's drafted workforce. Jeroboam builds up the city of Shechem and makes it capital of what becomes known as the nation of Israel. And to keep his people from going back to Jerusalem in Judah to worship, he sets up two worship centers: one golden calf idol in Bethel, 12 miles north of Jerusalem, and another calf idol in Dan.

"These are the gods who brought you out of Egypt!" he tells his people.

450 YEARS OF KINGS

	UNITED ISRAEL	
1000s BC	Saul, becomes king about 1050 BC* **David,** 1010 **Solomon,** 970	

	JUDAH (South Israelite Nation)	ISRAEL (North Israelite Nation)
900s BC	Rehoboam, 930 Abijam, 913 **Asa,** 910	Jeroboam I, 930 Nadab, 909 Baasha, 908
800s BC	**Jehoshaphat,** 872 Jehoram, 853 Ahaziah, 841 Athaliah (queen), 841 Joash, 835	Elah, 886 Zimri, 885 Omri, 885 Ahab, 874 Ahaziah, 853 Joram, 852 Jehu, 841 Jehoahaz, 814
700s BC	Amaziah, 796 Azariah (Uzziah), 792 Jotham, 750 Ahaz, 735 **Hezekiah,** 715	Jehoash, 798 Jeroboam II, 793 Zechariah, 753 Shallum, 752 Menahem, 752 Pekahiah, 742 Pekah, 740 Hoshea, 732 *Assyrians destroy Samaria, 722*
600s BC	Manasseh, 697 Amon, 642 **Josiah,** 640 Jehoahaz, 609	
500s BC	Jehoiakim, 609 Jehoiachin, 598 Zedekiah, 597 *Babylonians destroy Jerusalem, 586*	

* Most dates are approximate. Predominantly good kings are listed in bold type.

Israel's king on the record. Etching his thanks onto a stone slab 2,800 years ago, King Mesha of Moab (in what is now Jordan) gives credit to his god for a successful rebellion. Mesha says he won his nation's freedom from Israel's king Omri, father of the infamous Ahab.

PROPHETS on alert

Once when Jezebel had tried to kill all the LORD's prophets, Obadiah had hidden 100 of them in two caves.

1 KINGS 18:4

Idol worship had come to Israel on Solomon's watch. In his old age, he had let some of his foreign wives talk him into building shrines to some of the most bloodthirsty gods that humans ever invented—including Molech, who demanded child sacrifices.

That's when the Israelites—on a national scale—started treating pagan religion as an acceptable option or supplement to worshipping God. All Israelite kings in the northern Jewish nation of Israel are portrayed in the Bible as godless. And so are most kings in the southern nation of Judah.

God responds by sending prophets. Their job is to warn the people about the consequences of breaking their centuries-old contract with God. Line item one in the contract is: Don't worship any god but the Lord. Failure to comply will produce tragedies that will make the 10 plagues of Egypt look like a slight inconvenience.

Elijah is one of the first of these prophets. He lives in the northern Jewish nation during the reign of King Ahab, who is married to a foreign woman: Jezebel, formerly a Phoenician princess from what is now Lebanon. Jezebel wants to wipe out the Jewish religion and replace it with her own, which reveres Canaanite gods such as Baal. So she creates an 850-member congress of pagan prophets, which she helps fund. Then she begins exterminating Israelite prophets, forcing the lucky survivors into hiding.

Killer prophet. Sword-swinging Elijah towers over a doomed false prophet. This statue, resting on a hilltop in the Mount Carmel range, commemorates Elijah's victory over 850 of Jezebel's prophets. Elijah challenged them to call fire from the sky—seemingly an easy task for their rain god, Baal.

Some live in caves. Others, like Elijah, leave the country for a time.

But Elijah eventually returns with a vengeance—on a mission from God. He challenges all Jezebel's prophets to a spiritual duel. They meet on a hill in the Mount Carmel range—one prophet against 850. The challenge is to call down fire from the sky to burn up a sacrificed bull. That's right up the alley of Baal, the god who is sometimes pictured with thunderbolts in his hands. As the god of fertility in family, flocks, and field, he's considered the source of rain that keeps everything alive.

Jezebel's prophets pray all day. They dance, scream, and even cut themselves to get their god's attention.

"Perhaps he is daydreaming, or is relieving himself," Elijah taunts. "Or maybe he is away on a trip" (1 Kings 18:27).

Jezebel's prophets give up in the evening.

On Elijah's turn, he soaks the altar with water. Then he prays a short prayer: "O Lord, God of Abraham, Isaac, and Jacob, prove today that you are God in Israel and that I am your servant" (1 Kings 18:36). Fire flashes from heaven, burning up even the stone altar.

At Elijah's command, the crowd executes Jezebel's prophets as Jewish law requires: "False prophets or visionaries who try to lead you astray must be put to death, for they encourage rebellion against the Lord your God" (Deuteronomy 13:5).

The victory, however, is short-lived. King and queen continue worshipping false gods. And most of the nation follows their lead.

VEGETABLES to die for

One day Ahab said to Naboth, "Since your vineyard is so convenient to my palace, I would like to buy it to use as a vegetable garden."

1 Kings 21:2

Ahab and Jezebel have a getaway palace in Jezreel, on a hilltop overlooking the sprawling Jezreel Valley. Some Bible students call it the Valley of Armageddon. Ahab wants a vegetable garden nearby, so he asks a farmer named Naboth to sell him a vineyard that has been in Naboth's family for centuries. By law, the land needs to stay in Naboth's family.

So Naboth refuses. Ahab pouts. And Jezebel plots.

As a former princess from a country where the king could do just about anything he wanted, Jezebel must think Ahab is acting more like a peasant than a king.

Writing in Ahab's name, she orders the elders in Naboth's hometown to set him up for execution. They're to call a public meeting and arrange for two liars to accuse him of cursing God and the king—a capital offense. The meeting ends with citizens stoning Naboth to death.

Ahab confiscates Naboth's land. While he's there claiming it, Elijah arrives with a message from God.

"I am going to destroy your family," Elijah says, quoting God. "The members of Ahab's family who die in the city will be eaten by dogs, and those who die in the field will be eaten by vultures" (1 Kings 21:22, 24).

2 KINGS

Jerusalem falls. Invaders push the doomed Jewish defenders into the temple courtyard and slaughter them at the altar in front of the sanctuary.

THE JEWISH NATION DIES

Many Jews feel secure in their homeland—home free, home forever. After all, God told their forefather, Abraham: "I will give the entire land of Canaan, where you now live as a foreigner, to you and your descendants. It will be their possession forever, and I will be their God" (Genesis 17:8).

But what happens when they decide that God is no longer their god?

In the agreement that the Jewish people have with God, they receive protection and blessing as long as they honor their part of the contract. But God has warned the people that if they break the contract by trading him in for fake gods and by persistently breaking his other laws, he will drive them out. "The LORD will scatter you among all the nations from one end of the earth to the other" (Deuteronomy 28:64).

Apparently, the Jews forget this warning. They sin up a storm, from generation to generation.

God sends prophets to remind the people and their leaders of the consequences. For the most part, the prophets get about as much attention as people today carrying a sign, THE END IS NEAR.

But for the northern Jewish nation of Israel and the southern Jewish nation of Judah, the end truly is near.

God sends Assyrian invaders from what is now Iraq to conquer Israel, scatter the people, and resettle the land with foreigners. About 150 years after that, God performs an encore. He sends the Babylonians to destroy Judah and to exile the Jewish survivors.

As a nation, Israel is dead—erased from the world map.

ELIJAH'S CHARIOTS of fire

Suddenly a chariot of fire appeared, drawn by horses of fire. . .and Elijah was carried by a whirlwind into heaven. Elisha saw it and cried out, "My father! My father! I see the chariots and charioteers of Israel!"
2 KINGS 2:11–12

MAIN POINT:

God allows invaders to wipe both Jewish nations off the world map, leveling the cities and exiling the survivors. It's punishment for centuries of sin, especially for worshipping idols.

WRITER:

Unknown. First and Second Kings were originally one book. Since the stories end with the fall of Jerusalem in 586 BC, the material was probably compiled sometime after that—perhaps by Jewish scholars living as exiles.

DATE:

The stories cover about 300 years. They pick up where I Kings leaves off, starting well into the ministry of the prophet Elijah, in the 800s BC, and ending with the fall of Jerusalem in 586 BC.

LOCATION:

Israel, followed by exile in the empires of Assyria and Babylon in what is now Iraq

Elijah's ministry is ending. King Ahab has died in battle, but his son Joram has taken over and Ahab's widow, Jezebel, continues her reign of terror as queen mother.

At God's instruction, Elijah has selected a successor: Elisha. The two take one last walk together, through Jericho and toward the Jordan River. When they reach the river, Elijah rolls up his cloak and dips it in the water. Just as the water had stopped flowing for the Israelites so they could cross into Israel several centuries earlier, it stops again. The prophets cross the riverbed and walk into what is now the country of Jordan.

Both know that something's coming and Elijah's going. Other prophets in Israel know, too, for a group of 50 approaches Elisha during the walk and asks if he knows his master will be leaving today. Elisha knows.

In their final moments together, old Elijah asks if there's anything he can do for Elisha. What Elisha wants is to follow in the footsteps of his mentor—to become Elijah's successor, with miracle-working power from God.

"You have asked a difficult thing," Elijah says. "If you see me when I am taken from you, then you will get your request. But if not, then you won't" (2 Kings 2:10). This put the request in God's hands.

Fire and wind are both common symbols of God and his power throughout the Bible—from Moses and the burning bush to the strong wind that fills an upper room where Jesus' disciples gather at Pentecost. Both appear now. Chariots and horses of fire storm in from the heavens, riding a whirlwind that scoops up Elijah and carries him away.

Not only does Elisha witness it, he catches Elijah's cloak as it falls. If Elisha has any doubt that God has granted his request, that's cleared up at the Jordan. Elisha rolls up the cloak, dips it in the water, and watches as the river stops so he can cross.

Israel's king on his knees. Jehu, king of Israel, bows before the Assyrian King Shalmaneser III. Chiseled onto this black limestone monument, the illustrated Assyrian report from 825 BC says Jehu brought gifts of silver, gold, spears, and a staff for the king.

QUEEN JEZEBEL becomes dog meat

They threw her out the window, and her blood spattered against the wall and on the horses. . . . When they went out to bury her, they found only her skull, her feet, and her hands.

2 KINGS 9:33, 35

A chariot corps commander destined to end Ahab's dynasty gets a double anointing for the job. Years before he will lead the coup to overthrow Ahab's son, Jehu is anointed by Elijah as Israel's future king (1 Kings 19:16). And now, Elisha privately anoints him again.

Jehu reluctantly tells his men what Elisha has said. They immediately carpet Jehu's path with their cloaks, blow a ram's horn, and proclaim him king. Reluctance gone, Jehu climbs into his chariot, and with a unit of his soldiers he races the 40 miles to Jezreel. Ahab's son, Joram, is there recovering from a battle wound. Judah's king, Ahaziah, has come up to pay a royal visit—providing Jehu with two kings for the price of one coup.

Guards see Jehu racing frantically toward the city, and the king assumes there's urgent news from Jehu's post on the border. So both kings ride out to meet him. Both kings are met with arrows. Joram dies instantly. Ahaziah escapes but dies of his wounds.

Guards immediately tell Jezebel her son has fallen. Oddly, she fixes her makeup and then perches by the palace window. Perhaps she wants to maintain her queenly dignity to the very end. Jehu orders her servants to give her a big push in his direction, out the window. As she lies dead on the ground, he leads his chariot unit over her body, on a red carpet of blood. Then they go inside for a bite to eat.

While they're eating inside, the dogs are eating outside, enjoying a royal feast. Jehu later discovers that there's hardly anything left of the queen to bury. Apparently a student of religious history, he declares the prophecy of the late prophet Elijah fulfilled: "At the plot of land in

Jezreel, dogs will eat Jezebel's body. Her remains will be scattered like dung" (2 Kings 9:36–37).
Then Jehu turns her revered temple devoted to Baal into a public toilet.

THE KILLER GRANDMA QUEEN

When Athaliah, the mother of King Ahaziah of Judah, learned that her son was dead, she began to destroy the rest of the royal family.
2 KINGS 11:1

If there was any queen among the Jews meaner than Jezebel, it was Queen Athaliah. She killed her grandchildren to get rid of all the royal heirs—so she could run the country.

Actually, Athaliah may have been Jezebel's daughter. The Bible says she was King Ahab's daughter, though it stops short of naming her mother.

Surprisingly, Athaliah ended up ruling the rival Jewish nation. She grew up in the northern Jewish nation of Israel, but she ruled Judah in the south.

Ahab had given her away in marriage to Judah's prince, to seal a peace treaty. In time, her husband became king and then died. Then her son, Ahaziah, became king. He was assassinated while visiting Israel's king, Ahab's son, in the coup that ended Ahab's dynasty and Jezebel's life.

Instead of consoling her grandchildren over the death of their father, Athaliah killed them. Then she took the throne as queen of Judah.

Unfortunately for her, one infant grandson escaped: Joash. Priests hid him in the temple. Six years later, the high priest and military officers presented young Joash as the rightful ruler.

Grandma Athaliah got what she had given: an execution.

THE NORTHERN Jewish nation falls

Israel was exiled from their land to Assyria.

2 KINGS 17:23

God lets the northern Jewish nation of Israel survive about 200 years. That seems patient of him since the Jews worshipped idols throughout that time—and not one of their kings is described as good.

God's ancient contract with the Jewish people warned that he would punish them for breach of contract: "The Lord will bring a distant nation against you from the end of the earth" and "exile you and your king to a nation unknown to you" (Deuteronomy 28:49, 36).

During Israel's two centuries of disobedience, the Assyrian Empire had been expanding beyond its base in what is now Iraq. To feed its voracious appetite for power, it invaded neighboring countries and forced them to pay heavy annual taxes. The Jewish nations of Israel and Judah both complied.

But in a stab for freedom and sovereignty, Israel's king Hoshea stops the payments. The Assyrian king, Shalmaneser, invades. He surrounds Israel's capital city of Samaria and stays there for three years—until Israel's king surrenders in 722 BC.

Assyrians round up all the Jews they can find and then march them off into exile, to cities scattered throughout what is now Iraq. Then the Assyrians send their own pioneers into Israel to resettle the land. Some Jews escape the exile and remain in their homeland, but many end up intermarrying with the foreign pioneers. This mingling of cultures will, in time, produce a race of people called Samaritans. Many Jews in Jesus' day will hate them, calling them racial half-breeds and spiritual heretics who teach a distorted faith based on a condensed and edited version of the Jewish Bible. Samaritans revere only the first five books of the Bible.

Prophets had predicted Israel would fall. And afterward, other prophets begin pointing to the collapse of Israel as a wake-up call for Judah, warning that the same thing will happen to the southern Jews unless they honor their agreement to serve God.

It's a wake-up call that most southern Jews decide to sleep through.

How to treat a Jewish captive. Assyrian soldiers impale Jewish prisoners of war. Assyrians had captured them after conquering the city of Lachish, near Jerusalem, in 701 BC.

Vicious Assyrians

Ancient Middle Eastern terrorists, the Assyrians (based in what is now Iraq) considered scenes of terror suitable for framing on their palace walls. The stone carving at left is from their palace in Nineveh, the capital city.

Also etched in stone is an Assyrian king's brag after capturing a city in the 800s BC: "Their men, young and old, I took as prisoners. Of some I cut off the feet and hands. Of others I cut off the noses, ears, and lips. Of the young men's ears I made a mound. Of the old men's heads I built a minaret tower."

Rebels got no respect from Assyrians. Instead, they got themselves dead in creative ways. One style of execution that Assyrian soldiers enjoyed was to slice open a captive's abdomen, stuff a wild cat inside, quickly sew up the abdomen, and then back away—watching the animal claw itself out.

Terror, the Assyrians figured, was a great inhibitor. So they used it to keep enemies in their place—serving Assyria.

JERUSALEM survives Assyria's siege

That night the angel of the LORD went out to the Assyrian camp and killed 185,000 Assyrian soldiers. When the surviving Assyrians woke up the next morning, they found corpses everywhere. Then King Sennacherib of Assyria broke camp and returned to his own land.

2 KINGS 19:35–36

About 20 years after Assyria wiped the northern Jewish nation off the map, they get an invitation from the southern Jewish nation of Judah for an encore performance with a slight change of venue.

Assyria's King Sargon is dead. He died in a battle in 705 BC. His son, Sennacherib, takes a few years to get settled onto the throne and to consolidate his power base. During that time, several nations decide to rebel against Assyria by withholding their annual tax. These nations include Judah, Tyre, Philistia, and Egypt.

Sennacherib mobilizes his army in 701 BC and marches southwest. His own records, preserved on a clay prism, confirm the Bible's report of the invasion. "I approached Ekron [a Philistine city 25 miles west of Jerusalem] and killed the governors and nobles who had rebelled and hung their bodies on stakes around the city." In Judah, he says he took out 46 walled cities, saving Jerusalem for last.

While Sennacherib is finishing off Lachish, about 30 miles southwest of Jerusalem, Judah's king decides it's time to surrender. The king is Hezekiah, described in the Bible as the most godly king in Judah's nearly 350-year history. "There was no one like him among all the kings of Judah, either before or after his time" (2 Kings 18:5).

Hezekiah sends his apologies for the rebellion. And attempting to negotiate an end to the violence, Hezekiah offers to pay whatever Sennacherib demands in exchange for an Assyrian withdrawal.

Sennacherib's price: more than one ton of gold and 11 tons of silver. That's roughly $17,000,000 in gold and $3,000,000 in silver on today's market, when gold sells at $550 an ounce and silver sells for $10 an ounce. To cover that bill, Hezekiah empties the palace treasury and peels gold from the massive temple doors.

Sennacherib apparently accepts the payment but continues his vengeful crusade. He drives off an Egyptian army charging to Judah's rescue. Then he surrounds Jerusalem. Outside the city wall, an Assyrian spokesman yells up to the people.

"Don't listen to Hezekiah when he tries to mislead you by saying, 'The LORD will rescue us!'. . . . What god of any nation has ever been able to save its people from my power? So what makes you think that the LORD can rescue Jerusalem from me?" (2 Kings 18:32, 35).

Hezekiah's secret tunnel. Wading through knee-high water, a visitor explores the tunnel Hezekiah built to channel spring water into Jerusalem.

Water for Jerusalem

King Hezekiah knew he would have a water supply problem if invaders surrounded Jerusalem. And he certainly expected Assyrian soldiers to do just that because he intended to stop paying Assyria's annual taxes.

Jerusalem was built on a ridge. But the city's main source of water was Gihon Spring—outside the protective city walls—nestled in a cave at the base of the ridge. (See photo page 96.)

Hezekiah decided to bring that water into the city. So he "built a pool and dug a tunnel to bring water into the city" (2 Kings 20:20). Miners working from both ends cut a tunnel through nearly 600 yards of solid rock. Through this channel, spring water could flow into the lowest part of the city built at the ridge's low end.

In 1880 the tunnel was rediscovered, along with a stone plaque telling "the story of its cutting." Tourists have been wading through the tunnel ever since.

The prophet Isaiah, trapped inside the city with Hezekiah, has a word from God for the brash Assyrian king. "I will make you return by the same road on which you came" (2 Kings 19:28).

The next morning, Assyrian soldiers lucky enough to wake up find themselves among 185,000 dead comrades. Sennacherib gives the order to break camp and head for home— probably by the same road on which they came.

Jerusalem saved by the bubonic plague?

What killed 185,000 Assyrian soldiers who were laying siege to Jerusalem?

"The angel of the LORD," says the Bible (2 Kings 19:35).

"Rats," say some Bible experts. "The angel of the LORD" is a metaphor, they argue. It's a way of saying God was behind the attack that saved Jerusalem.

About 250 years after the disaster—several centuries before the Bible was compiled—a Greek historian named Herodotus wrote that Sennacherib's army was stopped one night by a rat infestation. Rats ate holes in the equipment and killed many soldiers. Perhaps this took place at Jerusalem.

Some Bible experts say the rats probably brought with them diseases such as the bubonic plague.

Caged king. "As for Hezekiah," reports the Assyrian king Sennacherib on this 2,700-year-old clay prism, "I made him a prisoner in Jerusalem...like a bird in a cage. I surrounded him." This battlefield brag stops short of claiming the Assyrians took Jerusalem—a restraint that substantiates the Bible's report that God drove off the Assyrians.

THE JEWISH country dies

King Nebuchadnezzar of Babylon led his entire army against Jerusalem. . . .
He burned down the Temple of the LORD, the royal palace, and all the
houses of Jerusalem. He destroyed all the important buildings in the city.
Then he supervised the entire Babylonian army as they tore down the
walls of Jerusalem on every side.

2 KINGS 25:1, 9–10

From the best king Judah would ever have—Hezekiah—Jewish history shifts to his son and successor, Manasseh, considered by many the worst Jewish king on record.

"Manasseh...sacrificed his own son in the fire. He practiced sorcery and divination, and he consulted with mediums and psychics. He did much that was evil in the LORD's sight, arousing his anger" (2 Kings 21:6). The Jewish Talmud, a collection of history and tradition, blames Manasseh for giving the order to saw the prophet Isaiah in half—using a wooden saw blade.

With just one exception—good king Josiah—the half-dozen kings that follow Manasseh are also spiritual losers. By this time, there's a new bully thumping nations on the international block. Babylon has overpowered Assyria, taking over the Middle Eastern turf. Babylon's empire has established its capital in the city of Babylon, in what is now the southern outskirts of Baghdad.

In a rerun of history, Judah's king of the moment—Zedekiah—decides to withhold the annual taxes that Babylon demands from weaker nations. The prophet Jeremiah warns him that God is on Babylon's side, and is taking a stand against Judah's persistent sin. Zedekiah revolts anyhow.

Babylon has already invaded Judah twice before. Once in 604 BC. And again in 597 BC, to put down a rebellion. This would be Babylon's third invasion in less than 20 years. So this time, they decide to strip the land like locusts and exile any of the troublemaking Jews who survive.

Babylon's siege of Jerusalem lasts two and a half years. That's long enough to starve Jewish mothers into eating their own children. This graphic story, reported by an eyewitness, is preserved in the saddest book in the Bible: Lamentations.

On July 18, 586 BC, Babylon finally breaks through Jerusalem's walls. They kill many of the citizens and dismantle the city stone by stone. Most survivors are taken captive to Babylon, exiled from their homeland.

For the first time since Joshua led the Israelites into the promised land, at least 600 years earlier, there is no longer a Jewish nation on the world map. And there won't be for another 50 years, until Persians overrun the Babylonians and free the Jews to go home.

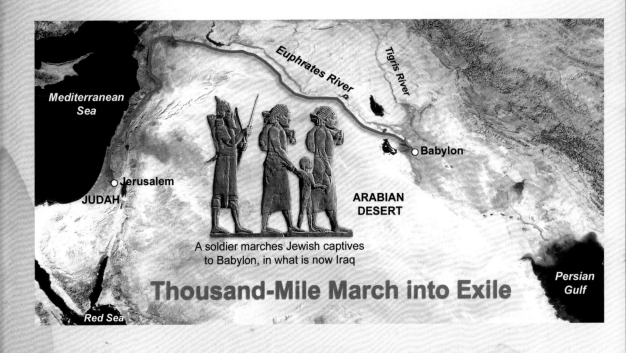

A soldier marches Jewish captives to Babylon, in what is now Iraq

Thousand-Mile March into Exile

1 CHRONICLES

Sacred touch up. A New York City rabbi carefully touches up the fading ink on an old scroll. When a scroll begins to wear out, Jewish scholars make a duplicate. Dead Sea Scrolls discovered in the 1940s—with copies of scripture a thousand years older than those used to translate the King James Version of the Bible—confirm that Jews were careful to accurately preserve their history.

THE HEAVILY EDITED HISTORY OF ISRAEL, PART 1

First and Second Chronicles, originally one book, read a bit like a political spin doctor's work on damage control—turning sad history into glad history.

Most of the stories in these two books also appear in 1 and 2 Samuel and 1 and 2 Kings. So Chronicles is a bit of a rerun, but with lots of unhappy scenes not included. Like stories of David's affair with Bathsheba, or Solomon worshipping idols in his senior adult years. Those don't make the cut in Chronicles.

Censorship, cover-up, and sugarcoating are not what's going on.

The Jews know their sad history all too well. They've just returned from a generation-long exile in what is now Iraq—God's punishment for their sad history of sinning. The two books of Chronicles, however, seem to be written to answer one burning question the returning Jews have: "Since we broke our covenant with God by sinning so badly that he took away our Promised Land, does that mean we're no longer his chosen people?"

With a carefully crafted history lesson, the writer of Chronicles assures the Jews that they are still God's chosen people. That's the point of the upbeat history. The writer is reminding the Jews about all that God has done for them. God has protected and blessed them throughout the ages. And now he has brought them home from exile, for a fresh start.

In God's ancient contract with Israel, he promised the nation a second chance: "Even though you are banished to the ends of the earth, the LORD your God will gather you from there and bring you back again. The LORD your God will return you to the land that belonged to your ancestors, and you will possess that land again. Then he will make you even more prosperous and numerous than your ancestors!" (Deuteronomy 30:4–5).

Now God begins delivering on his promise.

MAIN POINT:

God never gives up on people, in spite of their sinning. Even after punishing the Jews for centuries of sin by exiling them from Israel, he brings them home for a new beginning. "His faithful love endures forever" (1 Chronicles 16:34).

WRITER:

The book doesn't name the writer. Ancient Jewish tradition says it was written by Ezra, a priest who helped rebuild the Jewish faith and nation after the 50-year exile. His story appears in the books of Ezra and Nehemiah, two other books Jewish tradition says Ezra wrote.

DATE:

The books of 1 and 2 Chronicles cover about 500 years of Israel's history. This history starts with the first king, Saul, in the 1000s BC. And it ends with the Persian Empire releasing the Jewish exiles, allowing them to go home and rebuild their nation in the 500s BC.

LOCATION:

Israel, followed by exile in Babylon, an empire based in what is now Iraq

WHO'S WHO in the Hebrew family tree

The sons of Israel [Jacob] were Reuben, Simeon, Levi, Judah, Issachar, Zebulun, Dan, Joseph, Benjamin, Naphtali, Gad, and Asher.

1 CHRONICLES 2:1–2

Starting a book with a list of about 2,000 names might not seem like a great way to hook a reader's attention. It might seem like a waste of space—trivia that belongs in an appendix, if there. But to Jewish people who value tradition and their ages-old history with God, it's a perfect place to begin.

And the beginning is exactly where the book starts—with Adam and his most notable descendants spanning the first 10 generations of human history: "Seth, Enosh, Kenan, Mahalalel, Jared, Enoch, Methuselah, Lamech, and Noah" (1 Chronicles 1:1–4).

By no definition are these people Jews. The Jewish race starts with Abraham, who doesn't show up until nearly 100 names into the list. But the message those early names contain is an attention-getter: God's plan for Israel began at Creation.

The Jews were not God's afterthought.

COMING home

The first of the exiles to return to their property in their former towns were priests, Levites, Temple servants, and other Israelites.

1 CHRONICLES 9:2

The moment the writer finishes listing highlights of Israel's genealogy, from Adam to the exile in Babylon, he jumps to a list of Jews returning to Israel from exile. There's a connection that the writer expects the Jewish people to see: Jews not only have a history with God, they have a future. God began planning for the Jews at the beginning of time. And he isn't about to abandon them now.

That's the theological message. But there's practical value to the genealogy, as well.

For one, it traces the lineage of the current leaders. Their ruling governor, Zerubbabel, is a descendant of David. And that makes him a legitimate leader of the people.

Also, priests and other worship leaders are identified through their bloodline connection to Levi. He was the founding father of the tribe assigned the ministry of directing Israel's worship.

The writer's point: God has allowed the Jews not only to come home, but to come home with David's dynasty and the priesthood intact.

The writer hopes that people will see this as compelling evidence that God:
- still considers them his chosen people;
- still considers his covenant with them intact; and
- has given them a new beginning.

The writer also hopes that the Jews will learn from their past failures and serve God this second time around.

KING DAVID'S glory days

All Israel gathered before David at Hebron and. . .they anointed him king of Israel.

1 CHRONICLES 11:1, 3

Picking up the story of Israel when it became a nation, the writer wants to accent the positive. But that's hard when the story of Israel's first king, Saul, is such a sad one. Saul repeatedly disobeys God. And in the end, he and three of his sons die in a battle with the Philistines. Mortally wounded, rather than risk torture, "Saul took his own sword and fell on it" (1 Chronicles 10:4).

There's no bright side to that story, so the writer of Chronicles mercifully shortens it—a literary mercy killing. Saul's reign estimated at roughly 25 years gets a mere 23 verses—about a sentence or two for every year he reigned.

David, on the other hand, gets nearly as many chapters as Saul gets verses—19 chapters for David's story. That's because there's powerful evidence in David's life and throughout his 40-year reign that God was behind him. Even before David's reign started, when he was a young shepherd preanointed by Samuel as Israel's future king, "the Spirit of the LORD came powerfully upon David from that day on" (1 Samuel 16:13).

The stories that follow are upbeat variations on the same stories scattered in 1 and 2 Samuel and 1 Kings. What's missing are several notable downers—sad history about David that would detract from the writer's goal of encouraging the Jewish people. Why bother them with downers since they have just returned home from perhaps the biggest downer their race has ever experienced: the decimation of their country and the exile of their surviving citizens?

So, missing from 1 Chronicles are:

- David's affair with Bathsheba and the murder of her husband (2 Samuel 11);
- David's refusal to punish his son, the crown prince, for raping the prince's half sister (2 Samuel 13);
- the raped sister's full brother, Absalom, murdering the rapist (2 Samuel 13); and
- Absalom's doomed coup against David (2 Samuel 15).

David's upbeat history begins with the fractured coalition of Jewish tribes uniting to declare him king over all Israel.

With that mandate, David begins his lifetime of work defeating Israel's neighboring enemies, securing and expanding the nation's borders, and setting up Jerusalem as both a political and spiritual center for the Jewish people. He makes it his capital city. And by bringing into Jerusalem the nation's most sacred object—the Ark of the Covenant, a chest that holds the 10 Commandments—he makes it clear that this is where God will live among the Jews. This chest, after all, is considered God's throne on earth. It's at this chest that God promises, "I will meet with you there and talk to you from above the atonement cover between the gold cherubim that hover over the Ark of the Covenant" (Exodus 25:22).

David erects a tent for the chest, and people apparently start bringing sacrifices there—"burnt offerings and peace offerings to God" (1 Chronicles 16:1). This is perhaps a precursor to the temple Solomon will later build.

ISRAEL'S HOLY CHEST

Israel's most sacred object was a portable, gold-plated chest that held the original 10 Commandments etched onto stone slabs—Israel's bedrock laws on which all other laws were built.

But it was more than a box with sacred cargo. It was a spiritual throne for God (2 Samuel 6:2), sometimes described as his earthly "footstool" (1 Chronicles 28:2). It would rest in the most sacred room of the tent worship center, and later of the temple. There, only the high priest could approach it—and only once a year, at Yom Kippur, the annual Day of Atonement when the nation repented of its sin.

Built during the time of Moses, while the Hebrews traveled out of Egypt and toward Israel, the chest was about four feet long and two feet deep and wide. Made of acacia, a Sinai desert hardwood, it was covered inside and out with solid gold. Two gold-covered acacia poles, slipped into a pair of golden rings on each side of the chest, allowed priests to carry it when necessary. That's how they transported it: during the Exodus, into battle as a sign that God was with them, and when David brought it to Jerusalem.

Topping the chest was a single block of molded gold, decorated with two winged cherubim—a type of angel that served as guards or attendants. Sword-carrying cherubim made sure Adam and Eve didn't return to the Garden of Eden (Genesis 3:24). And cherubim guarded the heavenly temple in a prophet's vision (Ezekiel 10:3).

It's unclear what they looked like. In Ezekiel's vision, they each had four faces: human, ox, lion, and eagle.

No one seems to know where the chest is now. Some scholars guess that the Babylonians, led by King Nebuchadnezzar, took it when they sacked Jerusalem in 586 BC. And the scholars have some Bible support: "Nebuchadnezzar carried away all the treasures from the LORD's Temple and the royal palace. He stripped away all the gold objects that King Solomon of Israel had placed in the Temple" (2 Kings 24:13).

But a Jewish legend says the prophet Jeremiah, living at the time, hid it in a cave on the mountain where Moses died and then "sealed up the entrance" (2 Maccabees 2:5 NRSV).

Earlier, Jeremiah had predicted that the chest would be lost. But he said Israel would not miss it or need to rebuild it. "In that day Jerusalem will be known as 'The Throne of the LORD'" (Jeremiah 3:17).

TEMPLE plans

"You have shed so much blood in my sight, you will not be the one to build a Temple to honor my name. But you will have a son who will be a man of peace. . . . He is the one who will build a Temple to honor my name."

1 CHRONICLES 22:8–10

David has a palace in Jerusalem. And he wants to build a temple for God there, too. David has the spot picked out: land around a bedrock threshing floor he had bought from a farmer. David had already built an altar there.

God wants a temple in the city so people can worship him there. But he says he wants it built by a man of peace. David is a man of war. The man of peace who will build the temple is Solomon, David's son and successor.

Though David stops short of actually building the temple, he assembles much of the supplies, and he even organizes the temple ministries.

He puts stonecutters to work chiseling blocks from the white limestone native to the area. He imports rot-resistant cedar from the forests of Lebanon. He stockpiles bronze for some of the massive temple accessories, such as a water basin big enough to hold 18,000 gallons of water. And he provides a huge supply of nails shaped from the newest, strongest metal: iron.

Perhaps most impressive of all, he amasses a staggering inventory of precious metals to decorate and furnish the temple: about 4,000 tons of gold and 40,000 tons of silver. On today's market when gold sells for $550 an ounce and silver for $10 an ounce, that translates into more than $70 billion in gold and almost $13 billion in silver.

Beyond stockpiling temple resources, David calls together the Levites—Israel's tribe of worship leaders. After taking a census of all Levite men age 30 and above, he comes up with 38,000 eligible temple workers. Then he organizes them into what appears to be rotating ministry teams that will take turns serving in the temple. Only descendants of Aaron can serve as priests. The rest will work in other capacities, such as administrators, judges, musicians, guards, maintenance workers, and assistants who help priests perform the sacrificial rituals.

First Chronicles ends with elderly David, 40 years into his reign, naming Israel's new king: Solomon—the man destined to build God's temple.

What's wrong with a census?

Satan rose up against Israel and caused David to take a census of the people of Israel.... God was very displeased with the census, and he punished Israel for it.
1 CHRONICLES 21:1, 7

After securing Israel by defeating hostile nations on his borders, David ordered a census of men old enough to fight in battle. Seems harmless enough. Moses had taken a census twice, to count the Exodus refugees.

But David's census, also reported in 2 Samuel 24, angered God. And David's commanding general had warned that it would. Bible experts today, however, aren't sure what David did that was wrong enough to warrant God's punishment: 70,000 killed in a plague.

Theories:
- With wars ended, David didn't need to know what his available manpower was. He took the count to feed his pride, with numbers he could brag about.
- The census suggests Israel needed a huge fighting force more than they needed God—the same God who once helped Gideon and 300 men rout 135,000 Midianite invaders.
- David didn't collect the census tax, which was used in the worship center—a mere two-tenths of an ounce of silver per person. "Whenever you take a census of the people of Israel, each man who is counted must pay a ransom for himself to the LORD. Then no plague will strike the people as you count them" (Exodus 30:12).

2 CHRONICLES

An inside look. Solomon's temple, seen in this cutaway drawing, shows the large sanctuary inside where only priests are allowed to go. The back room (right) is even more holy. Only the high priest can go there, where the Jews keep their most sacred object: the Ark of the Covenant, a gold-covered chest that holds the 10 Commandments.

THE HEAVILY EDITED HISTORY OF ISRAEL, PART 2

Focusing mainly on Israel's best kings, the writer continues the story of the Jewish nation chosen by God. They're chosen not just for privilege, but for a mission: to become a light that draws people from all over the world to God.

Jerusalem's most famous prophet put their mission this way: "Let your light shine for all to see. For the glory of the LORD rises to shine on you. Darkness as black as night covers all the nations of the earth, but the glory of the LORD rises and appears over you. All nations will come to your light" (Isaiah 60:1–3).

And come, they do. Solomon builds the most glorious Jewish nation that has ever existed, reigning over a golden age. Kings and queens come calling to admire his wisdom and wealth.

In the 400 years that follow, God blesses other Jewish kings who devote themselves to him and who encourage their people to do the same. But in the end, idolatry, injustice, and other sins demand God's attention. He cleanses the land much like he once cleansed the world with a flood. Only this time, he sends a flood of invaders to drive out the sinful Jews.

A generation in exile changes the Jewish remnant. They determine never to repeat the horrendous mistakes of the past. And God brings them home, forgiven.

SOLOMON builds Israel's first temple

Solomon began to build the Temple of the LORD in Jerusalem.

2 CHRONICLES 3:1

Solomon's reign is a dream come true—literally. He travels to Israel's main worship center, the tent tabernacle in Gibeon about six miles north of Jerusalem. There, in a dream, God offers to give him anything he wants. Solomon asks for wisdom. And God promises to give it to him, along with wealth and fame "as no other king has had before you or will ever have in the future" (2 Chronicles 1:12).

Solomon apparently spends the first three years of his 40-year reign securing his power base, reinforcing his army, and setting up defensive military stations around the country. Then he begins a building project that will transform Jerusalem into a spiritual center and the most sacred Jewish city on earth. He builds the first permanent Jewish worship center, a temple.

Since the time of the Exodus out of Egypt—480 years earlier, according to 1 Kings 6:1—Jews had worshipped God in a tent. But now they worship at a white limestone temple that shimmers like a jewel set into the Jerusalem hilltop. (For a description and a painting of the temple, see page 104 in 1 Kings.)

Solomon's 15-day dedication ceremony is over the top. He sacrifices "22,000 cattle and 120,000 sheep and goats" (2 Chronicles 7:5). For the most part, the animals are probably eaten by worshippers who gather for this historic occasion. But some Bible experts say the numbers are probably an exaggeration to emphasize the importance of the event. Or perhaps it's a mistake that some scribe made years later, while copying the story onto another scroll. Otherwise, the priests are sacrificing 16 animals a minute, 10 hours a day, for 15 days. Other students of the Bible, however, say these numbers are realistic given the crowds coming to

MAIN POINT:

God blesses the Jewish people during the reigns of godly kings, and he punishes them for disobedience during the reigns of evil kings. But he never gives up on them.

WRITER:

Unknown. Ancient Jewish tradition says it was written by Ezra, a priest who helped rebuild the Jewish nation after the 50-year exile.

DATE:

The books of 1 and 2 Chronicles cover about 500 years of Israel's history, from the time of Israel's first king, Saul, in the 1000s BC to the time when the Persian Empire releases the Jewish exiles to go home and rebuild their nation in the 500s BC. Second Chronicles starts with the reign of Israel's third king, Solomon, in the mid-900s BC.

LOCATION:

Israel, followed by exile in Babylon, an empire based in what is now Iraq town for this monumental dedication of the first temple in Israel's history.

Afterward, God appears to Solomon, probably in a dream again. "I have heard your prayer and have chosen this Temple as the place for making sacrifices," God says. "At times I might shut up the heavens so that no rain falls, or command grasshoppers to devour your crops, or send plagues among you. Then if my people who are called by my name will humble themselves and pray and seek my face and turn from their wicked ways, I will hear from heaven and will forgive their sins and restore their land" (2 Chronicles 7:12–14).

For the next 400 years, this temple will serve as the one place on earth where Jews can expect to encounter God by presenting their requests and finding atonement for their sins.

QUEEN of Sheba

When the queen of Sheba heard of Solomon's fame, she came to Jerusalem to test him with hard questions.

2 CHRONICLES 9:1

If Bible experts are right, curiosity isn't the only reason the queen visited Solomon. She came to jump-start trade with one of the wealthiest kings in the Middle East.

The Bible story helps substantiate that theory. The queen comes with expensive gifts for Solomon: camels loaded with spices, jewels, and four and a half tons of gold. And she leaves with "whatever she asked for—gifts of greater value than the gifts she had given him" (2 Chronicles 9:12).

The two rulers make natural trade partners.

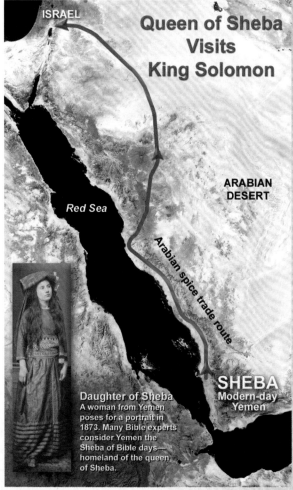

Queen of Sheba Visits King Solomon

ISRAEL

ARABIAN DESERT

Red Sea

Arabian spice trade route

SHEBA
Modern-day Yemen

Daughter of Sheba
A woman from Yemen poses for a portrait in 1873. Many Bible experts consider Yemen the Sheba of Bible days—homeland of the queen of Sheba.

Solomon controls the land bridge to nations farther north, for caravans that don't want to risk traveling through the Arabian Desert. He also owns a port with a fleet of ships at the north end of the Red Sea. And Sheba, many experts theorize, lies some 1,500 miles away at the other end of the Red Sea, on the southwest corner of Arabia in what is now Yemen. Solomon has access to goods from Israel and farther north: fruits, vegetables, wine from the fields of Israel, and cedar from the forests of Lebanon. Sheba, from across the 17-mile narrowing of the southern Red Sea, has access to African products: gold, jewels, rare wood, and exotic animals.

Ethiopian legend says the queen converts to Solomon's faith and gives birth to his son. That son, Menelik, is said to have founded Ethiopia's royal dynasty. Legend adds that he later brings Israel's sacred Ark of the Covenant to Ethiopia.

THE UNHOLY north

To this day the northern tribes of Israel have refused to be ruled by a descendant of David.

2 CHRONICLES 10:19

After Solomon dies, the northern tribes secede from the united tribes of Israel. They're tired of working on the king's pet building projects and paying for them with high taxes. So they ask Solomon's son and successor, Rehoboam, to relax the demands. Instead, he vows to ratchet up the royal demands. So the northerners form their own country, called Israel. Rehoboam is left to rule his native tribe of Judah, which becomes a separate country.

The writer of 1 and 2 Chronicles says very little about the northern tribes. The Jews there generally worship idols, and the rulers are evil. So their sad story doesn't contribute to the upbeat history in Chronicles, which is intended to highlight scenes of God's faithfulness toward the Jews.

God patiently endures the sinful northern nation for about 200 years, sending prophets to warn them of tragic consequences if they persist. In 722 BC, Assyrian invaders overrun the nation, exile the survivors, and repopulate the land with Assyrian pioneers.

WHY WOULD GOD CHANGE HIS MIND?

King Hezekiah fell deathly ill. It was punishment for sin: "he became proud" (2 Chronicles 32:25).

The prophet Isaiah delivered a message from God, advising the king to get his affairs in order since he wouldn't recover. Isaiah left. And Hezekiah, weeping, repented.

Before Isaiah had gotten out of the palace, God sent him back with a new message: "I have heard your prayer and seen your tears. . . . I will add fifteen years to your life" (2 Kings 20:5–6).

Why did God flip-flop, changing his mind like that?

The Bible doesn't say. Theologians insist that Hezekiah's repentance came as no surprise to the all-knowing God. Many suggest that it was Hezekiah who changed, not God. Because Hezekiah changed, God's plans for him changed, as well.

One thing is clear. Prayer made a difference—15 years' worth.

JUDAH'S few good kings

Asa became the next king. There was peace in the land for ten years. Asa did what was pleasing and good in the sight of the LORD his God.

2 CHRONICLES 14:1–2

Downplaying Judah's godless kings, the writer spotlights many of the nation's best kings. Asa, for example, merits only a few verses in 1 Kings. But the writer of Chronicles decides to stretch Asa's story into several chapters, portraying him as a tireless spiritual leader and a brilliant warrior like David, once driving back a million-man invasion force from Ethiopia. Other featured kings:

- **Jehoshaphat.** Asa's son, Jehoshaphat, follows his father's example, tearing down idol worship centers and fortifying the nation with defensive garrisons. "He did what was pleasing in the LORD's sight" (2 Chronicles 20:32).

- **Hezekiah.** Though he foolishly tries to free his tiny nation from Assyrian domination by withholding the required annual taxes, he's a godly king—and God protects him. Assyrian invaders devastate most of Judah's cities. But at Jerusalem an angel kills much of the invading army, forcing the Assyrian king to "return home in disgrace" (2 Chronicles 32:21). For a theory about how God may have used a plague as his angelic messenger, see 2 Kings, page 116, "Jerusalem saved by the bubonic plague?"

- **Josiah.** Judah's last good king, Josiah restores Jewish worship after a priest finds in the temple a long-lost scroll of Jewish laws. Josiah is upset because the nation hasn't been living by these laws. So he assembles the people, reads the scroll, and promises "to obey all the terms of the covenant that were written in the scroll" (2 Chronicles 34:31). And he requires everyone else to do the same.

Cyrus on the record. Persian warriors like this archer defeat the Babylonians and free the Jewish captives. (Inset) A nine-inch-long clay cylinder, dating from 536 BC, confirms the Bible's report that the Persian king Cyrus freed the Jews. The cylinder says he freed all captives to go home, rebuild their temples, and to say a prayer for him each day.

GOOD-BYE Jerusalem

The Babylonians killed Judah's young men. . . . The few who survived were taken as exiles to Babylon. . . .until the kingdom of Persia came to power.

2 Chronicles 36:17, 20

The southern Jewish nation of Judah outlasts Israel in the north by about 150 years. Then a trio of Judah's kings—one after another—reject the advice of God's prophets and try to break free of Babylon, an empire that overran and replaced Assyria. The kings withhold their required annual taxes from Babylon.

Three times the Babylonians are forced to invade: 604 BC, 597 BC, and 586 BC. As far as the Babylonians are concerned, the third time is one time too many. They destroy all the fortified cities—Jerusalem included. They take everything of value, slaughter many citizens, and then deport the survivors to Babylon, in what is now Iraq, where they can keep a close eye on them.

The Jewish nation no longer exists, at least not on Jewish soil. The land rests, "lying desolate until the seventy years were fulfilled, just as the prophet had said" (2 Chronicles 36:21). "The prophet" is Jeremiah, who witnesses the fall of Jerusalem. He has warned that the Jews would endure 70 years of captivity (Jeremiah 25:11).

About 70 years after Babylon's first invasion, when Babylonians took captives from among Judah's leaders, a new empire comes to power: Persia. That's about 50 years after the fall of Jerusalem. The Persian king Cyrus frees the Jews to go home and rebuild their nation.

EZRA

Caravanning home. Pushing on to sundown, a camel caravan passes near Jerusalem in the early 1900s. Ezra and other Jews followed a thousand-mile caravan route from what is now Iraq to Jerusalem—in a journey that took four months.

ISRAEL GETS A SECOND CHANCE

Persians from what is now Iran overrun the Babylonian capital near what is now Baghdad in Iraq. Suddenly, the Middle East changes hands. The Babylonian Empire gives way to the Persian Empire, stretching from India in the east to the North African countries of Egypt and Libya in the west.

The Persian king Cyrus issues a decree. He frees Babylon's political prisoners—refugees deported from their conquered homelands. This includes the Jews. Cyrus urges the Jews to rebuild their Jerusalem temple. He even gives them back the temple furnishings that the Babylonians had stolen.

And so 50 years after the deported Jews arrived in Babylon, they load up caravans and head back home. Once there, they rebuild the temple.

A priest named Ezra arrives in Jerusalem almost a century later, and he begins teaching the people the laws of Moses.

This sparks a dramatic revival, leading to widespread repentance. And in what must be a bitterly controversial decision, many Jewish men even divorce their non-Jewish wives. They do this because the law urges them not to marry outside the Jewish faith. Such marriages, the law explains, can lead people into idolatry. And idolatry is why the Jews spent the past generation exiled in a foreign country. They don't want to go through that misery again.

ISRAEL'S second Exodus

"Any of you who are his [God's] people may go to Jerusalem in Judah to rebuild this Temple of the LORD. . . . And may your God be with you!"

EZRA 1:3

For 50 years the Jewish people have been living a thousand-mile walk from their homeland. Babylonian invaders deported them out of Israel in 586 BC and forced them to move to what is now Iraq. But in 539 BC, Persians conquer the Babylonian Empire. The ruler of this new superpower, King Cyrus, issues a decree releasing the Jews to go home and rebuild their temple along with their nation.

A clay cylinder surviving from Cyrus's day confirms that this was his policy for all Babylon's former deportees (see photo on page 128.)

An entire generation of Jews has grown up in Babylon. They don't all decide to return home. But more than 42,000 do.

In some ways, the Exodus home is reminiscent of the Israelite Exodus out of Egypt nearly a thousand years earlier. But instead of having to buck a hostile ruler determined to hang onto the Jews as a cheap source of slave labor, this generation enjoys a Persian ruler who sends them off with his blessing.

Cyrus gives the Jews 5,400 articles of gold and silver previously confiscated from them by the Babylonians, including some sacred furnishings from the temple. Cyrus also orders their Babylonian neighbors to send them off with gifts of gold, silver, and livestock to help them on their way.

MAIN POINT:

God gives the Jewish people a fresh start—a chance to rebuild their nation on godly principles. And after spending half a century in exile because they didn't do this the first time, the Jews are highly motivated to get it right this time.

WRITER:

The writer isn't identified. Ancient Jewish tradition says it was written by Ezra, a priest who helped rebuild the Jewish nation after the 50-year exile. In the first copies of the Hebrew Bible, Ezra and Nehemiah appeared as a single book.

DATE:

The story covers about 100 years, from the time the first Jews return from exile in about 538 BC until Ezra's arrival and ministry in the mid-400s.

LOCATION:

The stories are set it two locations: Israel, and the Persian Empire based in what is now Iran.

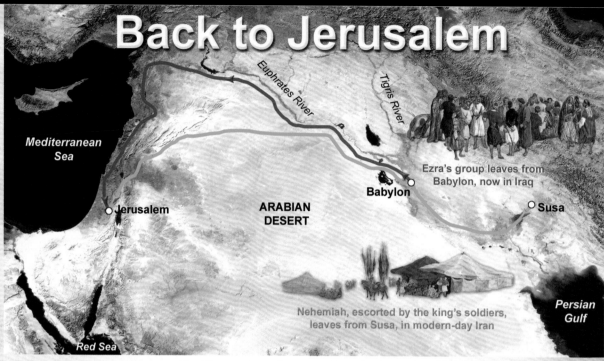

Back to Jerusalem

Mediterranean Sea

Euphrates River

Tigris River

Jerusalem

ARABIAN DESERT

Babylon

Ezra's group leaves from Babylon, now in Iraq

Susa

Nehemiah, escorted by the king's soldiers, leaves from Susa, in modern-day Iran

Persian Gulf

Red Sea

Exiles come home. Deported for 50 years into what is now Iraq, the first wave of Jews returns home. Ezra and Nehemiah follow about 70 years later—Ezra from Babylon and Nehemiah from Susa, in what is now Iran.

REBUILDING the temple

Construction of the Temple of God began in midspring, during the second year after they arrived in Jerusalem. The work force was made up of everyone who had returned from exile.

EZRA 3:8

The returning Jews take up an offering among themselves to buy supplies for rebuilding the temple. They come up with about half a ton of gold and three tons of silver.

That sounds like a lot, but it's a miniscule fraction of what David had stockpiled for his son, Solomon, to use in buying supplies for the first temple: 4,000 tons of gold and 40,000 tons of silver. It's easier to see the staggering difference in money raised when we convert the gold and silver to dollars. When gold sells for $550 an ounce and silver for $10 an ounce on today's market, the amount David raised was about $83 billion compared to about $9 million raised by the returning refugees.

The Jews take a couple of years to get settled into their homes and establish their gardens and flocks. They also build an altar so they can begin offering sacrifices to God. Then during their second spring back, perhaps in April or May of 536 BC, they lay the foundation for the temple.

Perhaps the foundation looks small or it lacks the high quality craftsmanship of Solomon's temple. For though the young people cheer for joy at what they see, the older people who remember the first temple begin crying. The writer doesn't say why they cry. But the implication is that they know they're getting what they paid for—an inferior temple.

Non-Jewish locals who have settled in the land hate to see the Jews returning and rebuilding their nation. They start lobbying the Persian government to make the Jews stop working on this first major building project. The locals eventually succeed. First they bribe Persian officials who somehow slow the Jewish efforts. Then they convince a new king, Artaxerxes, that the Jews have a long history of rebelling against the empires they are supposed to serve. So the king orders all work stopped.

The work resumes a couple of decades later, during the reign of King Darius. That's after the Jews convince him to search the royal records and find Cyrus's original decree urging the Jews to rebuild their temple. Darius finds the records. Then he not only orders the work to continue without interference; he also orders his governor to use tax money to pay for the construction.

On March 12, 515 BC, the temple is finished. The date is this precise because Ezra cross-references events that match surviving Persian records. Putting the two together provides the date.

Though this temple is just a shadow of Solomon's elegant worship center—and the humblest of the three temples that the Jews build during their history—it lasts longer than any other: 500 years. That compares to about 400 years for Solomon's temple and less than 100 years for Herod's temple in New Testament times.

A PRIEST condemns interracial marriage

"You have committed a terrible sin. By marrying pagan women, you have increased Israel's guilt. So now confess your sin to the LORD, the God of your ancestors, and do what he demands. Separate yourselves from the people of the land and from these pagan women."

EZRA 10:10–11

About 70 years after the first wave of Jews leave Babylon for Israel, a priest named Ezra joins a second wave headed home. There are perhaps a few thousand Jews in this group. Ezra refers to about 1,500 men, but he's apparently not counting women and children.

The priest leaves Babylon on April 8, 458 BC. Following one of several caravan routes up the Euphrates River and then turning south, he arrives in Jerusalem four months later, on August 4.

He's met by a group of Jewish leaders with a complaint. Many Jewish men have married non-Jewish women, "So the holy race has become polluted by these mixed marriages" (Ezra 9:2).

The Jewish elders are concerned about a particular law from the time of Moses. This law forbids Jews from marrying non-Jewish locals who "will lead your children away from me to worship other gods" (Deuteronomy 7:4). This is what led to the exile. Oddly, it all began with a king famous for his wisdom. Solomon brought idolatry to Israel on a national scale when he married non-Jewish women who eventually convinced him to build shrines to their gods.

The Jews don't want a repeat of their recent, tragic history—complete with another invasion and deportation.

Ezra goes to the temple where he lies on the ground, weeping and confessing the nation's fresh sin. There, a man makes a plea to Ezra. The man is Shecaniah, a son of Jehiel and a descendant of Elam. He urges Ezra to order all Jewish men to divorce their non-Jewish wives and to send them away, along with their children.

Ezra does as requested, though his demand seems both harsh and controversial. Some Jews of the day likely considered the ancient law out of date—pertinent only to the Israelites in Joshua's time. After all, it referred to Canaanites of the conquest era. Also, David's dynasty began specifically because a Jewish man married a non-Jew: Ruth. She was from Moab, in what is now Jordan. She became David's great-grandmother. And she loved God. In fact, it's possible that Ruth's story survived in the Bible partly because it's an effective counterpoint to Ezra's order.

Some Bible experts wonder if Shecaniah had an ulterior motive for his request. His father is listed among the 113 Jewish men married to non-Jews: "From the family of Elam: Mattaniah, Zechariah, Jehiel" (Ezra 10:26). Perhaps Jehiel had two or more wives. If Shecaniah was Jehiel's son by a Jew, Shecaniah might have had plenty to gain by eliminating his half brothers. At the least, he would have increased his inheritance because his disowned brothers would have gotten nothing. And if Jehiel's oldest son had been from a non-Jewish woman, Shecaniah might have taken that son's place as the new head of the clan once Jehiel died. In that case, Shecaniah would have received a double share of inheritance—twice as much as any of his younger brothers.

Whether or not God wanted the men to divorce their wives, Ezra and other leaders come to that conclusion. Jewish law, however, does not call for divorce after such a marriage. If it did, the Jews might have missed out on the greatest dynasty of kings in their history.

Ezra's numbers don't add up

The books of Ezra and Nehemiah, originally one book, each say there were 42,360 Jews who returned to Israel in the first wave (Ezra 2:64; Nehemiah 7:66). But when the two passages break down the list by families, the numbers don't add up.

Ezra's list adds up to only 29,818. Nehemiah's list adds up to 31,089.

Bible experts can only guess why the Bible ends up with three different totals.

- Scribes copying worn-out, faded scrolls onto new scrolls made mistakes, perhaps skipping some of the families listed on earlier manuscripts.
- The breakdown by family was just a partial listing even in the original.
- The total of 42,360 includes women, while the family listings include only men. But this wouldn't explain why the family totals in Ezra fall 1,271 short of those in Nehemiah. Perhaps a scribe got some numbers wrong. Ezra lists 1,222 men in the family of Azgad, for example. And Nehemiah lists 2,322 in that family. Several other family numbers are off as well.

Though there are occasional discrepancies like this in the Bible, the discrepancies are incredibly few—a tribute to the care that scribes took in creating fresh copies. The discrepancies don't affect the Bible's teaching.

The Great Scroll of Isaiah, for example, was found among the famous Dead Sea Scrolls and was 1,000 years older than the Isaiah scroll that scholars used to translate the King James Version of the Bible. Yet it's nearly identical to the copy a millennium younger. The discrepancies are only minor changes that seem like copying mistakes and that don't affect the message of the book.

NEHEMIAH

Repairing Jerusalem. Tourists stroll by as a craftsman works inside this huge model of ancient Jerusalem. Nehemiah organized a crew that—in just 52 days—rebuilt the city walls destroyed by attackers.

GOD JOINS A CONSTRUCTION CREW

Nearly 100 years after the first wave of Jews return from exile in what is now Iraq, they have a temple in Jerusalem. But they have no protection for it, or for the people living there. The city walls are a wreck—either from recent attacks or from the Babylonian invasion nearly 150 years earlier.

Nehemiah gets word of this. He's a Jew working in the Persian palace more than a thousand miles away. The news spins him into a depressed funk. He can't believe that his people are allowing the holy city to lie in ruins. He considers this neglect a national disgrace.

Nehemiah convinces the Persian king to grant him a leave of absence so he can go back to his Jewish homeland and oversee the rebuilding of Jerusalem's walls.

Non-Jews living in the area object to the building project. They're afraid that refortifying Jerusalem will become just the first step in rebuilding a Jewish nation that will eventually oppress them, and perhaps deport them.

In spite of this opposition, and perhaps inspired by it, Nehemiah orchestrates a team of construction crews that finish the job in 52 days. Jews and non-Jews alike see this astonishing feat as evidence that the construction miracle "had been done with the help of our God" (Nehemiah 6:16).

Ezra gathers the people and reads to them from the writings of Moses—perhaps laws in the book of Deuteronomy. Then he leads them in pledging allegiance to God and in promising to live according to ancient Jewish traditions.

More than the king's wine taster

Nehemiah describes himself as "the king's cup-bearer" (Nehemiah 1:11). That's a palace servant who brings the king his wine, after tasting it to make sure no one has spiked it with poison.

Sounds like a lowly position, staffed by an expendable human being.

But if that's true, why would the king give Nehemiah:
- an extended leave of absence;
- supplies to rebuild Jerusalem's walls;
- lumber to build himself a house in Jerusalem; and
- an armed escort of soldiers and charioteers for a round trip of more than 2,000 miles.

Official cupbearers for many kings carried a lot of influence at the palace. After all, cupbearers generally saw the king every day and had his ear. And they certainly had the king's confidence since he trusted them with his life.

The job's prestige shows up in a book in the Roman Catholic Bible: Tobit, part of a collection of ancient Jewish writings called the Apocrypha. Tobit describes a particular cupbearer as the number two man in the Assyrian Empire. King Esar-haddon, son of the infamous Sennacherib, appointed Ahikar "chief cupbearer, keeper of the royal seal, and chief of administration" (Tobit 1:22).

A drink fit for a king. A servant offers his master a drink. Cupbearers like Nehemiah made sure the king drank the best wine. (Inset) Nehemiah may have served the king in a golden goblet like this one. It's from Nehemiah's time and location, in what is now Iran.

MAIN POINT:

In what appears to be a miracle, the Jews rebuild Jerusalem's broken walls in just 52 days.

WRITER:

Written as a first-person story, this book represents "the memoirs of Nehemiah" (Nehemiah 1:1). Jewish tradition says a priest named Ezra—who knew Nehemiah—added these memoirs to his book. The books of Ezra and Nehemiah were originally a single volume, apparently written as a sequel to 1 and 2 Chronicles, which were also a single volume.

DATE:

The story takes place in about 445 BC and was probably written shortly after the events took place.

LOCATION:

Persia and Israel. Nehemiah leaves Susa, capital of the Persian Empire in what is now Iran. He travels to Jerusalem.

ASKING the king a big favor

"Send me to Judah to rebuild the city where my a[...]"

Nehemiah is a Jewish man working as a palace official in Susa, capital [...] Empire that stretches from Northern Africa to India. One of his brothers ha[...] from visiting Jerusalem, and he gives Nehemiah a distressing status report.

"Things are not going well," he says. "They are in great trouble and disgrace. The [...] Jerusalem has been torn down, and the gates have been destroyed by fire" (Nehemiah 1:[...]

Nehemiah doesn't say if this is a fresh development—the result of a recent attack. Perhaps the Jews who have been living in Jerusalem for two generations still haven't bothered to rebuild the walls that Babylonian invaders tore down in 586 BC. In either case, this news hammers Nehemiah. He sits and cries. Then he begins praying and fasting, skipping meals as he pleads with God.

Nehemiah gets this disturbing news in November or December of 446 BC. For some reason he has to wait four to six months to act on it, sometime in April or May of 445 BC. That's the first time King Artaxerxes notices Nehemiah is depressed and asks why. Perhaps the king was traveling during the cool winter season.

Whatever caused the delay, it has given Nehemiah plenty of time to consider what he'll say to the king. Nehemiah asks for a leave of absence to repair the most sacred Jewish city on earth. He also asks for letters granting him safe passage, and a letter granting him local timber for the construction.

The king gives him all this and more—an armed escort. Nehemiah apparently leaves right away since the journey of more than 1,000 miles takes several months and his memoirs say he's busy working on the wall by mid-August.

REBUILDING Jerusalem's walls in 52 days

Laborers carried on their work with one hand supporting their load and one hand holding a weapon.

NEHEMIAH 4:17

Three days after arriving in Jerusalem, Nehemiah climbs on his donkey and takes an evening ride around the city, inspecting the broken walls and gateway entrances. There's so much destruction in some areas, he says, "my donkey couldn't get through the rubble" (Nehemiah 2:14).

Nehemiah meets with city leaders and tells them about his mission and the king's support. There's no hesitation. They want in on this plan to rebuild the walls. So they mobilize the citizens.

Nehemiah organizes the workers into construction crews, assigning each crew to a section of the wall. This may have sped up the work by spurring some friendly competition among crews.

...of the vast Persian ...s just returned

...wall of ...)

Solomon ... (top). That's abou... walls enclosing 50 acres. ... right of the city lies the Kidron Valley and the Mount of Olives.

NEHEMIAH

Non-Jews in the area—Arabs, Samaritans, and Ammonites—condemn the project. And with good reason. If the Jewish nation manages to pull itself up out of the rubble, non-Jewish settlers in the area can expect to forfeit their land. This is the Jewish homeland.

A coalition of opponents to the project plots to stop the work. They accuse the Jews of rebellion against Persia. They criticize the work as sloppy. They threaten to attack the workers. And they offer to meet with Nehemiah in a negotiation, intending to kill him. At least that's what Nehemiah figured. So he didn't go.

After the threats of attack, half the workers take up guard duty. The other half arm themselves and keep on working. On October 2, after just 52 days, the Jewish workers finish closing all breaks in the wall. They've also plugged each of the city's gateway entrances with massive, wooden doors.

It's unclear how much repair was needed or if Nehemiah's job was just a temporary patchwork. Josephus, a Jewish historian writing several hundred years later, said it took two years and four months to finish the job—perhaps a more permanent repair. Archaeological evidence suggests that there was some extensive work, and that Nehemiah's construction crews rebuilt the eastern wall, facing the Mount of Olives. That's the area where Nehemiah reported that the damage was too extensive for his donkey to maneuver through.

Whether the work was temporary or permanent, what the workers manage to accomplish in under two months astounds even their critics, putting the fear of God in them.

PROMISE to God

They swore a curse on themselves if they failed to obey the Law of God as issued by his servant Moses.

Before the week is over, the Jews gather to thank God. The priest Ezra reads from the "Law of Moses." That's possibly sections of Deuteronomy that summarize the agreement God has with the Jewish people and the laws they're supposed to obey.

Unfortunately, the words are in Hebrew. And most of the Jews there have grown up in Babylon, where they spoke Aramaic—a language the Jews would continue speaking even in the time of Jesus. Temple workers scatter among the crowds and apparently translate the words into Aramaic.

The Jews gather several times over the next few weeks, to observe a Jewish holiday they had forgotten and to listen to more from the Law of Moses. Then they agree to commit themselves to the agreement God made with their ancestors. They promise to follow all the laws written on the sacred scroll, emphasizing several.

They won't:
- marry outside the Jewish faith;
- do business on the Sabbath; or
- neglect caring for the temple.

They will:
- let the land rest and cancel all debts every seventh year;
- pay the annual temple tax; and
- tithe a tenth of their harvest and bring it to the temple.

In doing this, the Jews become a people of the Book—they live by the teachings of Moses. When they step out of line, leaders confront them.

Nehemiah says that after he saw merchants bringing produce into Jerusalem to sell on the Sabbath, he ordered the city gates closed at the beginning of the Sabbath, on Friday evenings. And when he meets Jewish men with foreign wives, he says, "I made them swear in the name of God that they would not let their children intermarry with the pagan people of the land" (Nehemiah 13:25).

To do less, many Jews feared, would be inviting God to once again drive them out of their homeland. And this is an encore performance they want to skip at all costs.

ESTHER

Jewish queen of Persia. After an empirewide hunt for a queen, the Persian king Xerxes chooses a Jewish orphan. "The king loved Esther more than any of the other young women. He...set the royal crown on her head and declared her queen" (Esther 2:17).

STOPPING A HOLOCAUST

It sounds like the plot of a fairy tale: Jewish orphan girl wins beauty contest, marries king, and saves her people from genocide.

But it's a page out of Jewish history. The Jews fall into grave danger during the reign of the Persian king Xerxes. But his Jewish queen, Esther, becomes an advocate for them.

The danger erupts after another Jew, Mordecai, refuses to bow to a top palace official: Haman. In retaliation, Haman plots to wipe out the entire Jewish race—not realizing that Esther is Jewish or that Mordecai is her older cousin, the man who raised her.

Haman convinces the king to issue an irrevocable decree against "a group of troublemakers"—apparently without even bothering to tell the king who these trouble-makers are. Under the rules of engagement, soldiers and citizens will be free to kill the Jews on March 7, 473 BC, and confiscate their property.

All Jews are fair game, from one end of the empire to the other— from what is now India in the east to Libya some 6,000 miles away in northern Africa.

Mordecai convinces Esther to tell the king that this plot targets her and her people. Enraged at Haman's manipulation of him, the king orders him executed. Bible experts debate exactly how Haman dies. Some say he's impaled, which was a common form of execution in the region—popularized centuries earlier by the Assyrians. But most Bible translations say Haman dies by hanging.

Persian law prohibits the king from revoking his previous decree. But he issues a counterdecree allowing the Jews to defend themselves and the Persian troops to help them.

The Jews survive. And they add a new holiday to their calendar, celebrating the holocaust missed.

LOOKING for a beauty queen

"Let us search the empire to find beautiful young virgins for the king. . .the young woman who most pleases the king will be made queen."

ESTHER 2:2, 4

Wine is apparently the reason the Persian king Xerxes loses his first queen and suddenly finds himself in need of a replacement.

It all starts when the king, three years into his reign, throws a six-month party to show off his wealth. As a finale to the celebration,

MAIN POINT:

Esther, Jewish queen of the Persian Empire, saves the Jews from an empirewide holocaust.

WRITER:

Unknown. And that's unfortunate since this is one of the best-written short stories in all of Hebrew literature. Possible writers include Ezra or Nehemiah, since the writing style of the stories in Ezra and Nehemiah is similar to the style in Esther's story. Mordecai is another possibility since he's at least a key source of information.

DATE:

Esther's story takes place during the reign of King Xerxes, known in Hebrew as Ahasuerus. He reigned for 21 years, from 486–465 BC. Esther became queen in about 479 BC, more than 30 years before Ezra and Nehemiah left Persia for Jerusalem.

LOCATION:

Susa, capital of the Persian Empire and now the Iranian city of Shush

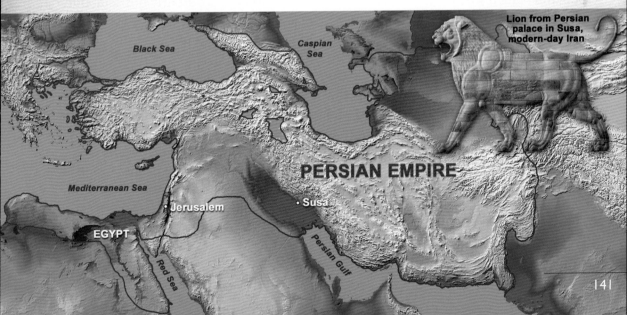

Lion from Persian palace in Susa, modern-day Iran

Black Sea

Caspian Sea

Mediterranean Sea

Jerusalem

Susa

PERSIAN EMPIRE

EGYPT

Red Sea

Persian Gulf

The king's ladies. Persian king Xerxes has a harem full of wives. But only Esther wears the crown as queen.

he hosts a weeklong feast. He entertains the nobles while his wife, Queen Vashti, entertains their wives. On the last day of the banquet, Xerxes is feeling his grapes—"in high spirits because of the wine" (Esther 1:10). He sends for Queen Vashti, and tells her to wear her crown. He's planning to put her on display as a trophy wife because she's enviably gorgeous.

Beyond good looks, Vashti also has a mind of her own. And the very idea of walking into a room full of men who have been drinking wine for a week is apparently not something she considers regal. She declines the invitation.

Publicly embarrassed, the king asks his advisors how to deal with the impudent queen. Male chauvinism is at risk, they warn. They advise him to put the queen in her place. Otherwise, women throughout the empire might follow her lead and start acting like they're equal to men.

Vashti gets her wish, and then some. She doesn't want to come to the king, so he grants her wish forever. She's banished from his presence. Xerxes then orders officials in all of his provinces to start bringing into his harem the empire's most beautiful young virgins. These women will remain in the king's harem, but only one will receive the title of queen.

A young Jewish orphan named Esther becomes one of the many candidates. She was adopted and raised by her cousin, Mordecai, who works somewhere in the palace.

Like other candidates for queen, Esther spends a year indulged in beauty treatments. She's massaged and marinated in oils, creams, and perfume until she's fragrant to the bone. When it's her turn to spend the night with the king, she carefully follows last-minute advice from the harem's chief eunuch—who seems quite the romantic. He obviously gives Esther great advice because she wins the heart of her king, who crowns her queen.

As a result, the queen of the world's only superpower is a Jew. But she keeps it a secret, as well as her family ties to Mordecai.

PLANNING a holocaust

When Haman saw that Mordecai would not bow down or show him respect, he was filled with rage. He had learned of Mordecai's nationality, so he decided it was not enough to lay hands on Mordecai alone. Instead, he looked for a way to destroy all the Jews throughout the entire empire of Xerxes.

ESTHER 3:5–6

King Xerxes promotes a man named Haman to become the empire's top official. Other palace workers bow when Haman walks by—everyone except Mordecai. When colleagues ask Mordecai why he doesn't bow, he cryptically answers only that he's a Jew.

That's no answer at all. Jews bow to rulers. Jewish law doesn't prohibit that.

We're left to guess why Mordecai refuses to bow. Some Jewish scholars in ancient times said Haman may have worn a picture of an idol on his clothing. Other experts guess that Mordecai was expressing his disapproval of Haman's family history, which was marked by hatred toward the Jews. Haman descended from King Agag of the Amalekites, a race that launched an unprovoked attack on Israelite refugees during the Exodus (Exodus 17).

Whistle-blowers report Mordecai to Haman, who apparently assumes that no Jew will show him the respect he deserves. So he works up a final solution: kill them all and confiscate their property.

With minimal detail, he presents his plan to the king. "There is a certain race of people scattered through all the provinces of your empire. . .and they refuse to obey the laws of the king. So it is not in the king's interest to let them live" (Esther 3:8). Haman asks the king to decree that patriotic citizens be allowed to kill the troublemakers and take their belongings. In return for this decree, Haman offers to contribute 375 tons of silver to the palace treasury. That's more than all the tax money Persia raises in a year. On today's market when silver sells for $10 an ounce, that's $240 million. Haman probably plans to raise this money from confiscated Jewish property.

A holocaust fee is essentially what Haman is proposing—with a gentleman's agreement to kill now and pay later. The slaughter date is set about a year ahead, for March 7, 473 BC. This gives Haman time to spread the word.

ESTHER'S mystery party

[Queen Esther to the king:] "Please come with Haman tomorrow to the banquet I will prepare for you. Then I will explain what this is all about."

ESTHER 5:8

Mordecai pleads with his cousin, Esther, to meet with the king and intercede for their fellow Jews. But Esther is reluctant, with good reason. "Anyone who appears before the king in his inner court without being invited is doomed to die unless the king holds out his gold scepter," Esther replies, citing a Persian law. "And the king has not called for me to come to him for thirty days" (Esther 4:11).

Mordecai quickly responds. "Don't think for a moment that because you're in the palace you will escape when all other Jews are killed" (Esther 4:13).

Esther agrees to go to the king, but only after Mordecai leads the Jews in three days of fasting. Surprisingly—for a book in the Bible—Esther's request stops short of asking for prayer. But many see prayer implied, since Esther and Mordecai are Jewish. Secular readers, however, may have taken the reference to skipping meals as an expression of grief or worry. Mourners and others in distress often fasted, covered themselves in ashes, and wore torn clothes.

When Esther shows up uninvited, the king is delighted to see her. He asks what he can do for her. Esther says nothing of the planned holocaust. Instead, she invites him and Haman to a banquet.

The king is smart enough to know she wouldn't risk her life to invite him to dinner. So during the meal he says, "Tell me what you really want." Instead, Esther invites him and Haman to another banquet the following day, promising to explain then what this is all about. The king can taste the suspense.

Haman, however, remains clueless to everything but the royal attention he's getting. After the first banquet, he calls in a group of friends to brag about his growing popularity.

Does Esther belong in the Bible?

Jews in New Testament times didn't consider Esther part of their Holy Bible—judging by the Dead Sea Scrolls. These scrolls are the oldest surviving library of sacred Jewish writings. Jews stuffed the scrolls in clay jars and stashed them in caves during a Roman attack in the late AD 60s. Esther is the only Old Testament book missing from the Dead Sea library.

There's something important missing from the book of Esther, too: God.

He's not mentioned. The only other Old Testament book that overlooks God is the Song of Solomon—another book that barely made it into the Jewish Bible.

Esther earned its way into the Bible because on closer inspection Jewish readers saw God at work behind the scenes, directing an incredible string of coincidences. They saw him, too, in the words of Mordecai who told the queen that if she didn't step up to protect the Jews, deliverance would come "from some other place" (Esther 4:14).

Here's the intriguing question: If Esther is a religious book, intended to show God at work protecting the Jews, why would the writer downplay the religious angle?

Some Bible experts say it may have been to entice secular readers—and to let them draw their own conclusion that the God of the Jewish people left his fingerprints all over this remarkable story.

HAMAN on a stick

They impaled Haman on the pole he had set up for Mordecai.

ESTHER 7:10

During Esther's second banquet the king repeats his earlier request. He wants to know what's on Esther's mind.

"My people and I have been sold to those who would kill, slaughter, and annihilate us," she says.

"Who would be so presumptuous as to touch you?" the king asks.

"This wicked Haman," she answers.

Enraged, the king storms out into the palace garden, perhaps to consider how to handle Haman's apparent attempt at a coup.

Meanwhile, back at the banquet, Haman rushes over to Esther to beg for his life. The queen is reclining on a couch. Haman, in terror, collapses on top of her—just as the king walks in. The king's eyes must have bugged. And he may well have jumped to some incorrect conclusions: Haman was leading a coup, and he was going to take the queen as his prize right away. New kings in those days did that sort of thing after ousting the previous king; it was a show of authority.

There's strict protocol on how to approach any of the king's wives, especially the queen. Jumping on top of her at a banquet is not considered proper etiquette. One of the palace eunuchs, perhaps a guard from the harem, knows that Haman has committed a fatal faux pas. So he offers the shocked king a suggestion.

"Haman has set up a sharpened pole that stands seventy-five feet tall in his own courtyard. He intended to use it to impale Mordecai, the man who saved the king from assassination" (Esther 7:9).

"Impale Haman on it," the king replies.

ESTHER, THE COMEDY

Many Jewish scholars say Esther's story is a comedy, and we should read it that way.

They say storytellers in ancient times would have expected big laughs in several places, including the following:

1) **Mordecai rides on the king's horse while Haman, acting on the king's order, leads it and shouts praises about his enemy Mordecai.**

   What makes it funny: The king asked Haman for advice about how to honor someone, and Haman assumed the king was talking about him. But the king wanted to reward Haman's enemy, Mordecai, for reporting an assassination plot. Haman came up with the idea for this honor. But he thought he'd be the one riding the horse instead of the one leading it like a servant (chapter 6).

2) **Haman falls on the queen as the king walks in.**

   What makes it funny: Haman is pleading for his life, but it looks to the king like he's getting a bit too familiar with the queen (chapter 7). Some Bible translations say the king thinks Haman is "assaulting" Esther. But the Jewish translation has Haman trying to "ravish" her (Tanakh Translation).

3) **The king orders Haman impaled.**

   What makes it funny: First, Haman gets impaled on a pole he built for Mordecai—poetic justice. Second, the narrator's line after the king passes sentence is a hoot by any standard: "Then the king was not so angry anymore" (Esther 7:10 NCV).

CELEBRATING a holocaust missed

Mordecai recorded these events and sent letters to the Jews near and far. . . calling on them to celebrate an annual festival.

ESTHER 9:20–21

The king gives Haman's job to Mordecai after Esther reveals that Mordecai raised her. As for the king's holocaust decree, Persian law says he can't revoke the order. So instead he issues a counterdecree, declaring his support for the Jews.

In this decree, he gives the Jews permission not only to defend themselves against attack, but to confiscate the property of their attackers. Persian governors, out of respect for the king, help defend the Jews.

Clashes erupt on March 7–8, 473 BC, as many Persians decide to go ahead with their yearlong plan for a land and wealth grab at the expense of the Jews. Some 800 Persians, including Haman's 10 sons, die in the fighting at the capital city of Susa. Throughout the empire, the Jews kill 75,000.

Mordecai decides that surviving this near-holocaust is worthy of celebration. So, with Esther's backing, he establishes the annual Jewish festival of Purim (POOR-um). That's the Hebrew word for "lots," which was a dicelike object that Haman used to select the slaughter date of March 7.

Observant Jews today still celebrate Purim each spring. It's their most fun-filled holiday— entered into with the spirit of a Mardi Gras. Kids dress up as characters in Esther's story. Friends and family exchange gifts. And worshippers gather in the synagogue to hear Esther's entertaining story read aloud from a scroll. But every time the reader comes to Haman's name, the listeners scream and use noisemakers to drown out his villainous name.

Persians in battle. Persian soldiers defend Jews from an uprising in which thousands of Persian citizens try to kill Jews and steal their property. The violence is sparked by a Persian official who tricks the king into writing a law that lets citizens conduct ethnic cleansing against the Jews.

JOB

WHY GOD LETS BAD THINGS HAPPEN TO GOOD PEOPLE

Job is a rich herder—at least until a string of disasters take just about everything important to him.

In a single day, raiders and a freak firestorm take all of his livestock—11,000 animals—and kill his shepherds. Worse, a windstorm destroys the house where Job's 10 children are eating together, killing every one of them. Later, sores erupt all over Job's body.

His friends tell him to repent, since they're convinced he's being punished by God. His wife tells him to curse God and die, apparently expecting God to put Job out of his misery. Job refuses. He says he hasn't done anything wrong, and he doesn't plan to start now.

But there's one thing Job does decide to do. In a spirit not particularly patient, he demands an explanation from God.

"You, God, are the reason I am insulted and spit on. . .so you must be the one to prove them wrong" (Job 17:6, 4 CEV).

God does, in fact, come to Job's defense—but without explaining himself. Instead, God asks Job to explain the wonders of creation.

Job gets the point: trust in the one whose insight is beyond human understanding. And Job decides to do that.

By story's end, Job has 10 more children and herds double the size of before. People who later listen to Job's story benefit, too. They learn an important lesson in theology: Don't assume people suffer because God is punishing them for sin. That's a common misunderstanding in Bible times—which Job's story tries to correct.

Why? That's the single most important question Job has for God. Job has suddenly, tragically lost his health, his children, and his herds. And he wants God to explain why.

MAIN POINT:
Bad things sometimes happen to good people who've done nothing to deserve them.

WRITER:
The book doesn't name the writer.

DATE:
It's unclear when Job lived or when his story was written down. Several clues suggest Job lived about 4,000 years ago, in the time of Abraham or earlier. Some clues: Job serves as the family priest apparently before an established priesthood, his wealth is measured by the size of his herds instead of his currency, and he is raided by Sabeans—a nation of tribes living in that era.

LOCATION:
Unknown. He lived in the land of Uz. But no one knows where Uz was.

A MEETING in the air

One day the members of the heavenly court came to present themselves before the LORD, and the Accuser, Satan, came with them.

JOB 1:6

Job's misery isn't just a string of bad luck. It all starts with a meeting in heaven. God meets with a representative described as the Accuser. Most English Bible translations call him by the Hebrew word for *Accuser*: Satan. In Hebrew, anyone described as an accuser or an enemy is a "satan." That word is sometimes applied even to God, when he becomes an enemy to Israel.

Bible experts debate whether or not this particular Accuser is the same Satan who will later tempt Jesus. But given what this Accuser does to Job, he seems like one devil of an angel.

JOB'S IRAQI CLONE

Job's story isn't the only ancient tale of a good man suffering.

There are several. One is from the same era—more than 4,000 years ago. It's called "A Man and His God," and it took place in the world's first known civilization: Sumer. That's a kingdom in what is now southern Iraq.

The Iraqi Job and the Bible Job each suffered unfairly and complained bitterly.
Bible Job: "Why wasn't I born dead? Why didn't I die as I came from the womb?" (Job 3:11).
Iraqi Job: "Let my mother who gave birth to me not stop weeping for me."

Both complain that God was ignoring them.
Bible Job: "But it is God who has wronged me,

capturing me in his net. I cry out, 'Help!' but no one answers me" (Job 19:6–7).
Iraqi Job: "For how long will you ignore me and not take care of me?"

In the end, both men put their trust in God.
Bible Job: "I take back everything I said, and I sit in dust and ashes to show my repentance" (Job 42:6).
Iraqi Job: "I have set my sights on you as on the rising sun."

One big difference is that the Iraqi Job's trust comes only after God helps him. The Bible Job's trust comes before God helps. The Iraqi Job shows gratitude. The Bible Job shows faith.

In this meeting God brags about Job, calling him the finest person on earth. The Accuser begs to differ, arguing that Job's righteousness grows out of the fertile fields of God's blessing. Plant Job on a barren mound of ashes and we can all watch him wither. "Take away everything he has," the Accuser tells God, "and he will surely curse you to your face!" (Job 1:11).

So God tells the Accuser to go ahead and put Job to the test.

DISASTER, day one

"Fire of God has fallen from heaven and burned up your sheep and all the shepherds. . . . Raiders have stolen your camels. . . . The house collapsed, and all your children are dead."

JOB 1:16–17, 19

Four disasters strike Job, one right after another. The writer describes them with a repetitive cadence as powerful as a burst of machine-gun fire that pummels Job to the ground.

- Sabean raiders steal his oxen and donkeys and kill the farmhands. One worker survives to deliver the news. While he's still talking, in comes the next messenger.
- Fire from the sky, perhaps a fire started by lightning, incinerates Job's sheep and shepherds. One worker survives to deliver the news. While he's still talking, in comes the next messenger.
- Chaldean raiders steal his camels and kill Job's herders. One worker survives to deliver the news. While he's still talking, in comes the last messenger.
- A windstorm blows down the home of Job's oldest son, where all of Job's 10 children are enjoying a meal. One servant survives to deliver the news.

Finally, Job gets some time to react. He rips his robe and shaves his head—common expressions of grief, a bit like our custom of wearing black clothes or a black armband.

Then he collapses to the ground and proves the Accuser wrong. "I came naked from my mother's womb, and I will be naked when I leave," Job says. "The LORD gave me what I had, and the LORD has taken it away. Praise the name of the LORD!" (Job 1:21).

That's not even close to cursing God to his face.

DISASTER, day two

Satan. . . struck Job with terrible boils from head to foot.

JOB 2:7

"Skin for skin," the Accuser argues in his second meeting with God.

That's a baffling phrase. Bible experts aren't sure what it means. But in context, it's as though the Accuser is saying Job is out to save his own skin—and that even if it costs the skin of his 10 children, Job will refuse to curse God because he doesn't want to die. It's a common belief in those days that anyone who curses God is inviting death.

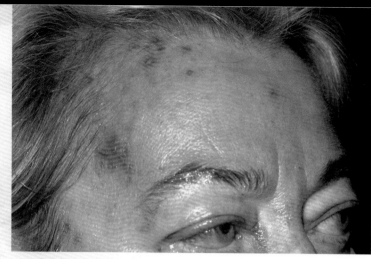

Job's disease: shingles? Open sores produced by shingles can cover a person from head to foot, like chicken pox. Most common among older people and sometimes brought on by stress, shingles is one contender for the disease that afflicted Job.

God gives the Accuser permission to do anything to Job that he wants, short of killing him. And with a brilliant stroke of poetic injustice, the Accuser goes after Job's skin.

It's unclear exactly what Job suffered. Various Bible translations call them painful sores, boils, or ulcers with dried-over scabs. Whatever the disease, it peppered Job from head to toe with painful, itching sores that came on quickly. There are many skin diseases that match the Bible's broad description, including eczema, psoriasis, and smallpox.

Another disease, most common in older people, is shingles. It's an incredibly painful chicken pox virus that lies dormant in the skin's nerve roots for many years before waking up. It's most likely to occur in people over age 50 who have had chicken pox and who suffer from immune systems weakened by stress, injury, or other problems.

Job would have had no way of knowing if this was a curable disease or a lethal one. Either way, as far as Job's wife is concerned this tragic string of coincidences is all the proof she needs to reach this conclusion: God has painted a bull's-eye on her husband, and Job is doomed. She advises euthanasia, an end to the suffering: "Curse God and die" (Job 2:9).

"You talk like a foolish woman," Job answers. "Should we accept only good things from the hand of God and never anything bad?" (Job 2:10).

Again Job proves his Accuser wrong. Job refuses to curse God even when his skin doesn't seem worth saving.

WITH FRIENDS like these. . .

When three of Job's friends heard of the tragedy he had suffered, they got together and traveled from their homes to comfort and console him.

JOB 2:11

It seems odd, but when Job's friends arrive they say nothing—for an entire week. The pleasure of their company is all the comfort Job gets.

Sadly, when they do start talking their words are harsh enough to qualify as a bonus torment—as though the Accuser got God's permission to send them.

These three men take Job's misery into a new dimension—from physical to spiritual.

Job has already lost just about everything this world has to offer: riches, family, health. That couldn't be much clearer, with Job sitting on a pile of ashes and scratching around his pus pockets. Now his friends arrive and call him a sinner. They say God is punishing him.

That's a common belief in ancient times: Blessed people are blessed because God is rewarding them for living a good life, and afflicted people suffer because God is punishing them for sin. Many Bible experts say that the whole point of Job's story is to refute this warped theology.

Jesus would later refute it, too. When his disciples see a man born blind, they ask Jesus whose sin is to blame—the man or his parents. Neither, Jesus answers. "This happened so the power of God could be seen in him" (John 9:3). Then Jesus heals the man.

It's from the warped school of theology that Job's three friends and an apparent late-comer, Elihu, make accusations like these:

Eliphaz: "My experience shows that those who plant trouble and cultivate evil will harvest the same" (Job 4:8).

Bildad: "Does the Almighty twist what is right? Your children must have sinned against him, so their punishment was well deserved" (Job 8:3–4).

Zophar: "Listen! God is doubtless punishing you far less than you deserve!" (Job 11:6).

Elihu: "Job, you deserve the maximum penalty" (Job 34:36).

These are his friends.

"Stop assuming my guilt," Job argues, "for I have done no wrong" (Job 6:29).

"Sinner!" Pointing the finger at him, Job's friends insist he must have sinned terribly to deserve the horrible things happening to him.

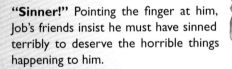

COMPLAINING JOB

"Patient as Job" is an old saying that doesn't capture the spirit of the man.

Job suffered terribly. And he wasn't shy about complaining.

He complained about:

His right to complain. "God's terrors are lined up against me. Don't I have a right to complain? Don't wild donkeys bray when they find no grass?" (Job 6:4–5).

The bedside manner of his friends. "What miserable comforters you are! Won't you ever stop blowing hot air?" (Job 16:2–3). "As physicians, you are worthless quacks. If only you could be silent! That's the wisest thing you could do" (Job 13:4–5).

The extent of his suffering. "I would rather be strangled—rather die than suffer like this. I hate my life" (Job 7:15–16).

God's unfairness. "For he attacks me with a storm and repeatedly wounds me without cause" (Job 9:17).

Yet in spite of all his complaining, Job vows never to turn from God. For as he explains it, "What hope do the godless have when God cuts them off?" (Job 27:8).

"Where were you when I created the earth?" Questions like this from God abruptly halt Job's complaining. Job realizes there are limits to his understanding. So he decides to trust in the God who understands everything.

GOD ENDS the theology debate

"Who is this that questions my wisdom with such ignorant words?"

JOB 38:2

Job has been blunt with God, charging him with cruelty and demanding that he explain himself: "Don't simply condemn me—tell me the charge you are bringing against me" (Job 10:2).

Now it's God's turn to get blunt.

God arrives on the scene in a whirlwind. There are other times in Bible stories when God shows up on the wings of the wind. He carries Elijah to heaven in a whirlwind. He uses wind to blow into Egypt a plague of locusts, and later to part the sea before the fleeing Israelite refugees. And with the sound of a windstorm, the Holy Spirit arrives in Jerusalem at Pentecost to empower the disciples of Jesus.

Job has been asking "why" questions.

God responds with "who" questions.

Essentially, God wants to know who Job thinks he is. And God makes his point with curt questions like these:

- "Where were you when I laid the foundations of the earth? Tell me, if you know so much" (Job 38:4).
- "Can you direct the movement of the stars—binding the cluster of the Pleiades or loosening the cords of Orion?" (Job 38:31).
- "Is it your wisdom that makes the hawk soar and spread its wings toward the south?" (Job 39:26).

Job gets the point. He answers God's "who" question. "I am nothing," Job says. "I will cover my mouth with my hand" (Job 40:4).

All Job does now is listen. And God gives him an earful—continuing a barrage of questions that only the Creator could answer.

Job now realizes that all his deep-sounding philosophical questions about suffering are the mutterings of a fool. He can't begin to understand why God lets good people suffer. And he doesn't have the creativity or the foresight to think of ways God could actually use suffering to help the sufferer, as well as to help others. Jesus had that insight, though, and he showed it by healing a blind man so others could see "the light of the world" (John 9:5).

"I take back everything I said," Job replies, "and I sit in dust and ashes to show my repentance" (Job 42:6).

God turns his attention to Job's guests, accusing them of spreading lies about the kind of God he is. He orders them to offer an animal sacrifice and to have Job—the man they accused of sinning—to pray for them. Then, in what sounds like punitive damages for emotional distress, God orders each of them to give Job a gold ring and some money.

God blesses the second half of Job's life, as he had blessed the first half. Job raises 10 more children, including three of the most beautiful daughters in the land. His herds and flocks double. And he lives 140 years, long enough to see four generations of children—including his great-great-grandchildren.

JOB'S RESURRECTION HOPE

Go ahead, try to find any reference in the Old Testament to life after death.

They're all over the New Testament. But it seems that most people in Old Testament times had no idea they could rise again and spend forever with God.

Most Old Testament characters talking about death had nothing to say about an afterlife, though a few mention a shadowy place of the dead where they expect to live with their ancestors.

The godly king Hezekiah had an even bleaker take on the afterlife. In a song of praise to God for healing him, he wrote: "For the dead cannot praise you. . . .Those who go down to the grave can no longer hope in your faithfulness. Only the living can praise you as I do today" (Isaiah 38:18–19).

Job is an exception.

Speaking from what must feel to him like the brink of death, he sounds like a man with New Testament savvy—living 2,000 years ahead of his time:

"But as for me, I know that my Redeemer lives, and he will stand upon the earth at last. And after my body has decayed, yet in my body I will see God! I will see him for myself. Yes, I will see him with my own eyes. I am overwhelmed at the thought!" (Job 19:25–27).

PSALMS

SINGING THE BLUES TO GOD

In Bible times, Psalms was the closest thing the Jews had to a hymnbook.

Written on leather scrolls, Psalms was a collection of 150 songs, prayers, and sacred readings that the Jews used in worship. The musical notes are missing, but the lyrics survive. And so do some instructions to the music director—for example: "to be accompanied by a stringed instrument."

Many people think of Psalms as a praise book. Jews, in fact, call the book *Tehilim*—Hebrew for "songs of praise." And readers will certainly find a lot of songs praising God in Psalms. But they'll also find many complaining to him.

Nearly half the psalms qualify as complaints—songs or prayers of grief, disappointment, or urgent pleas for help. They're songs sung blue. Yet even in complaining, most of the poets wrap up their complaints with expressions of trust in God.

Jews recited or sang some of these psalms at home and in worship services at the temple. The Jews also

Royal music. Lyre strapped to his chest, a musician playing the part of King David strolls the streets of Jerusalem. David wrote 3,600 songs, according to the Psalms scroll copied in the time of Jesus and discovered in 1956 among the ancient library of Dead Sea Scrolls.

sang selected psalms for special occasions, such as weddings, religious holiday festivals, and the coronation of a king.

Some of these psalms are the most cherished and most quoted verses in the entire Bible.

Perhaps none is more familiar than Psalm 23, often read at the bedside of the dying: "The LORD is my shepherd; I shall not want. He maketh me to lie down in green pastures: he leadeth me beside the still waters" (Psalm 23:1–2 KJV).

The survival of these psalms is a tribute to their inspired writers and to the God who inspired them. For God gave these poets the gift of expressing in words what most of us can only feel. So people of faith throughout the centuries have latched onto these psalms, singing and praying them as their own.

The apostle Paul wrote that the Holy Spirit prays for us, "making prayer out of our wordless sighs, our aching groans" (Romans 8:26 THE MESSAGE). Psalms does that, too.

THANKING God for life

When I look at the night sky and see the work of your fingers—the moon and the stars you set in place—what are people that you should think about them?

PSALM 8:3–4

In a song of praise attributed to David, the poet raises his sights to the brilliant canopy of the nighttime sky—just as David must have done on countless nights while guarding his sheep. In a moment of awe, the poet asks why a God who could create such a magnificent display would give a second thought to human beings.

But God does far more than think about

MAIN POINT:

God is open to whatever we want to say to him—the full range of life's sorrow and joy. We can thank him, or we can tell him we're mad at him. Whether we're happy, depressed, worried, or hopeful, God welcomes us.

WRITER:

Almost half the psalms—73 of 150—are attributed to David. But these bylines weren't in the earliest scrolls. And they're phrased vaguely. Calling a psalm "of David" can mean it's "by David," "about David," or even "inspired by David." Other psalms are attributed to Solomon and Moses, along with music ministry leaders Korah and Asaph. Some psalms aren't attributed to anyone.

DATE:

Most psalms are impossible to date because they express intimate feelings instead of historical facts. Some psalms, though, refer to life during the Jewish exile in Babylon—in the 500s BC. So the psalms could span about a thousand years, back to the time of Moses in the 1400s BC.

LOCATION:

Most psalms are about people in Israel. But some are set in Egypt. And others are set in Babylon, which is now Iraq.

God's canvas. For a moment at sunset, the desert sky transforms into a brilliant canvas. Looking to the night sky, the psalmist sees God's hand at work. And he declares God's glory "is higher than the heavens."

people, the poet says. He places them on a pedestal of prestige.

"You made them only a little lower than God and crowned them with glory and honor. You gave them charge of everything you made, putting all things under their authority" (Psalm 8:5–6).

Centuries later, the writer of Hebrews would quote these verses. He used them as a way of describing Jesus: given a position lower than the angels while he ministered on earth, but after his death and resurrection, he was "crowned with glory and honor" (Hebrews 2:9).

Yet to the psalmist, people don't have to wait for an afterlife to receive God's glory. God has already honored human beings simply by giving them life and entrusting to them the job of taking care of his creation—"putting all things under their authority" (Psalm 8:6).

The poet doesn't even try to explain why God would do such a thing. He simply responds in gratitude and praise: "Your majestic name fills the earth" (Psalm 8:9).

MUSIC WITHOUT RHYME

Like the lyrics of most songs today, the words in Psalms are poetry. But unlike most poems today, ancient Hebrew poetry doesn't rhyme.

Instead of repeating sounds, Hebrew poetry repeats ideas. So there's no rhyme, but plenty of reason.

The poet makes a one-line statement. Then in the next line, he might repeat his statement in a slightly different way. Or he might contrast it with an opposite idea. Sometimes he extends the idea, further explaining what he's talking about.

In the following psalm, the second line both extends and repeats the idea in the first:

"I know the LORD is always with me. I will not be shaken, for he is right beside me" (Psalm 16:8).

WHEN GOD forgets us

O LORD, how long will you forget me? Forever?

PSALM 13:1

Does this sound like a song that most folks would want to sing in church? Yet the introductory note to the song leader, describing this as a psalm of David, suggests that people did use it in worship services.

The trouble is that the words of this particular psalm don't seem to track with what many think our objective should be when we gather with a praise band and a choir: "Make a joyful noise unto God, all ye lands" (Psalm 66:1 KJV).

This psalm doesn't seem to qualify as a joyful noise. It's just a noise. Or so it seems.

But it's a noise repeated in several psalms, including these:

- "My God, my God, why have you abandoned me?" (Psalm 22:1).
- "O God my rock," I cry, "Why have you forgotten me?" (Psalm 42:9).
- "Why do you look the other way?" (Psalm 44:24).
- "All night long I prayed, with hands lifted toward heaven, but my soul was not comforted" (Psalm 77:2).

If David wrote this song, perhaps he wrote it during those long years as a refugee. That's when he was on the run from an insanely jealous King Saul, and sometimes hiding in caves. But no matter who wrote it, this is a song many people have lived. Desperate, they pray to God and get nothing but dead air:

- a Jew in a World War II concentration camp;
- a loyal employee laid off and unable to find work; or
- a son praying for his father who's dying of cancer.

It's not the complaint that distinguishes this psalm and others like it. The complaint is common to humanity. What distinguishes this is the faith of the psalmist at the end of the song.

In the hanging dead air, without any kind of response from God, the poet makes a seemingly irrational promise.

"I will sing to the LORD because he is good to me" (Psalm 13:6).

On the basis of God's track record, the writer gives God the benefit of the doubt and tells him, "I trust in your unfailing love."

THE LORD, our shepherd

The LORD is my shepherd; I have all that I need. . . . Even when I walk through the darkest valley, I will not be afraid, for you are close beside me.

PSALM 23:1, 4

In one of the most famous and most comforting chapters in the entire Bible, a poet compares God to a shepherd lovingly guarding his sheep.

Attributed to David, this sounds like a song he would write. Once a shepherd himself, there were times when he risked his life to protect his sheep—clubbing away at dangerous predators such as "lions and bears" (1 Samuel 17:36). Sheep had little to fear when protected by such a devoted shepherd.

The divine shepherd, says the poet, "lets me rest in green meadows; he leads me beside peaceful streams" (Psalm 23:2). Still waters run deep. So these quiet streams and green meadows—in their abundance—are heaven on earth for sheep.

Even in dark valleys where danger lays waiting to pounce from the shadows, there's nothing to fear. For one thing, the shepherd has a long staff. He uses it to gently tap a sheep at risk of nibbling itself into trouble, off the path, and into the shadows. For another, the shepherd is armed with the same kind of short club that David used to beat off wild animals.

The poet's point: It's a comfort to know we're protected by a shepherd who's loaded for bear.

There's a shift in the last two verses. It's as though we leave the combo-metaphor of God and David as shepherds. And we move to a metaphor of royalty. "You prepare a feast for me in the presence of my enemies. You honor me by anointing my head with oil" (Psalm 23:5).

As king of Israel, David could lavish his guests with more food than they could possibly eat, and with expensive perfumes that would transform a scentless stone room into a Himalayan flower garden. Jews imported some scented oils, like spikenard, from India's Himalayan Mountains.

If King David could do this, how much more could the King of kings offer his guests? It's the comfort of such unlimited hospitality that the poet enjoys.

This reassuring scene—the climax of the song—makes it a natural at the bedside of the dying and at the graveside of the dead. The poet's promise is that those people so loved by God can rest in peace, for they "will live in the house of the LORD forever" (Psalm 23:6).

SEARCHING for God

As the deer longs for streams of water, so I long for you, O God. . . .
My heart is breaking.

PSALM 42:1, 4

The byline associates this sad song with the descendants of Korah, a family of musicians who ministered at the Jerusalem temple. It's a sad song because the person portrayed in the song is essentially exiled from God. At least that's how he feels about being unable to worship at the Jerusalem temple, which Jews in his day consider God's home on earth.

This lonely, heartbroken exile wanders about on Israel's northern border, in the area of Mount Hermon—the snowmelt source of the Jordan River. That places him about 120 miles north of Jerusalem, as the turtledove flies.

He never says exactly what's keeping him from returning to Jerusalem. Perhaps he's too sick to make the trip. Or maybe he's exiled from the city. Or his route might be blocked by enemies. For whatever reason, he's stuck somewhere on the fringe of Israel. There, unidentified enemies harass him with taunts: "Where is this God of yours?" (Psalm 42:3).

"O God my rock," the exiled man cries. "Why have you forgotten me? Why must I wander around in grief, oppressed by my enemies?" (Psalm 42:9).

There shouldn't be a Psalm 43.

When Archbishop Stephen Langton divided the Old Testament into chapters in the 1200s, he made the mistake of breaking in two the single song that spans both chapters—psalms 42 and 43. Both of these chapters share the same chorus: "Why am I discouraged? Why is my heart so sad? I will put my hope in God! I will praise him again—my Savior and my God!" (Psalm 42:5–6/Psalm 43:5).

Though Jerusalem's temple is now long gone, leveled by the Romans in AD 70, this song is timeless and enduring. Most people understand the feeling of separation from God—of not sensing his presence when they desperately need him.

And it's not just the complaint that people throughout the ages have responded to. They also respond to the persistent trust they see in this exiled man. He's determined to hang onto God even when it doesn't feel like there's anything to hang on to. For his faith and apparently his experience convince him that it's the smart thing to do.

Still heartbroken, the poet declares: "I will put my hope in God" (Psalm 42:5).

FIVE BOOKS IN ONE

Psalms is divided into five books, each ending with a short doxology—a hymn of praise to God. Each one of these doxologies starts with the words "Praise the Lord," which helps clearly mark the beginning and end of each section.

Jewish scholars say it's no coincidence that there are five books.

These five sections parallel the five books of Moses—the most revered material in the Jewish Bible. The books of Moses contain the heart of Jewish law and tradition.

One rabbi in ancient times described the connection this way: "Moses gave the five books of the Law to Israel and David gave the five books of Psalms to Israel."

Book 1: Chapters 1–41, containing most of David's songs.

Book 2: Chapters 42–72, including some songs of the musicians Korah and Asaph.

Book 3: Chapters 73–89, almost exclusively songs of Korah and Asaph.

Book 4: Chapters 90–106, mostly psalms with no bylines.

Book 5: Chapters 107–150, mostly songs for special occasions such as festivals and pilgrimages to Jerusalem.

FORGIVE me

Purify me from my sins, and I will be clean; wash me, and I will be whiter than snow.

PSALM 51:7

A short introduction sets the scene. It says this is a psalm about David asking for God's forgiveness. The sin David committed is that he had an affair with Bathsheba, got her pregnant, and then arranged for her husband to die in battle so David could marry Bathsheba. This tragic story appears in 2 Samuel, chapters 11 and 12.

The psalm's introduction, like the byline, wasn't part of the original song. It was added later, perhaps when Jewish worship leaders compiled the collection. So it's possible this isn't the prayer David prayed after the prophet Nathan confronted him with his sin.

One clue that it's not David's prayer: "Against you, and you alone, have I sinned" (Psalm 51:4). The fact is, David certainly sinned against Bathsheba's husband. But this quote does track with David's admission in the original story: "I have sinned against the LORD" (2 Samuel 12:13).

Perhaps it's not that David—or whoever else wrote the psalm—is overlooking the others he hurt. Instead, perhaps he's focusing on the one above all who is offended: the holy God.

If this isn't the prayer David prayed, it could have been.

What makes the prayer timeless is that it's a wonderful prayer of repentance for anyone who has sinned. It guides us through the journey of seeking forgiveness.

"Have mercy on me, O God."

"I have done what is evil in your sight."

"Create in me a clean heart, O God. Renew a loyal spirit within me."

"Restore to me the joy of your salvation."

"You will not reject a broken and repentant heart, O God."

Whatever David said to God, it was enough. For the moment David repented, Nathan announced, "The LORD has forgiven you" (2 Samuel 12:13).

THE LONGEST SONG

With a whopping 176 verses—every one of them praising the hundreds of Jewish laws delivered by Moses—Psalm 119 is the longest chapter in the Bible.

It's long on purpose.

The purpose: to make a statement—and to do it the hard way.

The poet's statement: I love God's law, from A to Z.

Why it's the hard way: The song is an acrostic. It has 22 sections, one section for each letter of the ancient Hebrew alphabet. Every section begins with a different letter of the alphabet, starting with *aleph*, the first Hebrew letter, and working all the way through *tav*, the last letter.

That's love of the law, from A to Z.

A SONG for the road

I look up to the mountains—does my help come from there? My help comes from the LORD.

PSALM 121:1–2

This psalm is called a song of ascent—something to sing when walking uphill. It's one of 15 songs of ascent clustered together in chapters 120–134.

The hills the travelers are climbing are those around Jerusalem. In the Bible, when travelers talk about going to Jerusalem they say they're going "up" to Jerusalem—even if they're coming down from the northland in Galilee, heading south. Jerusalem is still up. That's because the city is perched on a ridge of hills, surrounded by hills. No matter what direction travelers come from—north, south, east, or west—they're going to have to climb to get to Jerusalem.

Since the Jerusalem temple is the only place Jews are allowed to offer sacrifices to God throughout much of Bible-time history, Jews often take trips there. The city is especially

Road to Jerusalem. Travelers approach Jerusalem from the south, in this painting from 1839. From any direction, the only way to Jerusalem is up—because the city rests like a crown on a hill in the Judean highlands.

crowded during each of the three important festival celebrations observed in the spring, summer, and fall.

"Each year every man in Israel must celebrate these three festivals: the Festival of Unleavened Bread [also called Passover], the Festival of Harvest, and the Festival of Shelters. On each of these occasions, all men must appear before the LORD your God at the place he chooses" (Deuteronomy 16:16). And that "place he chooses" becomes the temple that Solomon builds in Jerusalem.

Why does the poet look to the mountains and ask if his help comes from there? Bible experts don't know.

Maybe the poet is saying yes, his help comes from the hills since that's where he's headed—to God's temple on the Jerusalem hilltop.

Or maybe he's saying no, that his help doesn't come from pagan shrines commonly built on hilltops. Or no, his help doesn't come from the cavalry or some other army appearing in the nick of time on the crest of a hill at the moment he needs rescuing. Instead, his help comes from God.

Whatever the poet is trying to say, the hilly area around Jerusalem is a great setting to sing about hills. And with robbers hiding in the crevices along the path, it's also a great place to sing of God's protection: "The LORD keeps watch over you as you come and go, both now and forever" (Psalm 121:8).

Jerusalem

Qumran

Jordan River

Dead Sea

Bible stash. Copies of the Bible 1,000 years older than those used to translate the King James Version of the Bible were found in caves like this, at Qumran near the Dead Sea. Among the stash of Dead Sea Scrolls was a partial copy of Psalms—with extra psalms.

LONG-LOST PSALM

The oldest surviving copy of Psalms, written on a leather scroll in the time of Jesus, includes some previously unknown psalms that don't appear in Bibles today.

Many of today's Bibles are based on scrolls copied about 1,000 years after this older scroll, discovered in 1956.

Called the Psalms Scroll, it was copied about AD 30–50—probably from an older scroll. And it was redis-covered among an ancient library known as the Dead Sea Scrolls. Jews living beside the Dead Sea stashed their sacred scrolls in nearby caves when a Roman army attacked, annihilating their community.

Here is the author's paraphrase of an excerpt from one of the long-lost psalms:

A maggot can't praise you;
    Insects can't sing of your grace.
But the living can praise you;
    Even those who have fallen sick can sing your praises.
You teach them kindness and holiness through your example
    Because their souls are in your loving hands.
    And you care for each one, providing their every breath.
Take care of us, O Lord.
    Treat us with your typical goodness, mercy, and compassion.
You hear the voices of those who love you.
    You don't hold back your love from them.
Thanks be to God who does good things,
    showering his people with kindness and mercy.
From my very soul I cry out to praise your name—
    to give you glory for all you do,
    to declare your faithful devotion.
    When it comes to praising you, there is no such thing as an end.

PROVERBS

Sages at work. Jewish men compare thoughts about scripture. Proverbs is a collection of practical advice about godly living—and it comes from elderly men.

ADVICE FROM WISE OLD MEN

No plot. No stories. No characters. Proverbs has none of it.

Yet it's one of the most quoted books in the Bible. Here's an example of why: "It's better to stay outside on the roof of your house than to live inside with a nagging wife" (Proverbs 21:9 CEV).

That's why it's quoted so much. It's quotable.

Proverbs, for the most part, is a book of snappy one-liners—advice written by old men, for young men. The genre is called wisdom literature. And by the time of Solomon, who is said to have written most of Proverbs, wisdom lit had been popular throughout the Middle East for about 1,000 years.

Topics in Proverbs cover just about everything old men think young men should know about life in the real world. That includes money, sex, marriage, raising kids—even the danger of cosigning loans and the proper etiquette for dinner meetings:

"When you are invited to eat with a king, use your best manners. Don't go and stuff yourself! That would be the same as cutting your throat" (Proverbs 23:1–2 CEV).

Some of this grandfatherly advice is just that, advice by someone's granddad. And it shouldn't be taken as promises from God. Often, the God-loving grandfathers of Proverbs are simply making note of trends and principles they've observed in their years on the planet. For example, "Lazy people are soon poor; hard workers get rich" (Proverbs 10:4).

Tell it to a coal miner.

Or tell it to a factory worker punching a clock 12/6 to make ends meet. There are exceptions to the rule.

Wise readers read Proverbs wisely.

STREET smarts

Don't be tempted by sinners or listen when they say, "Come on! Let's gang up and kill somebody, just for the fun of it."

PROVERBS 1:10–11 CEV

Like most wisdom literature, Proverbs is loaded with practical advice for everyday life. There are some short essays on matters of philosophy, such as the nature of wisdom

MAIN POINT:

These wise sayings are intended "to teach people to live disciplined and successful lives, to help them do what is right, just, and fair" (Proverbs 1:3).

WRITER:

Most are introduced as "the proverbs of Solomon, David's son, king of Israel" (Proverbs 1:1). Solomon reportedly wrote 3,000 proverbs (1 Kings 4:32). Other proverbs are by a group of unidentified men simply called "the wise" (Proverbs 24:23). And one proverb each is attributed to the otherwise unknown Agur along with a king named Lemuel.

DATE:

Solomon reigned from about 970–930 BC. Some proverbs, however, were probably added several centuries later. King Hezekiah's advisors were working on the collection during his reign, nearly 300 years after Solomon (Proverbs 25:1).

LOCATION:

Israel

and how it's different from foolishness. But for the most part, if Proverbs were part of a shoe it would be the sole—where the rubber hits the road. Avoiding bad company is one of the first pieces of advice the elderly sages give their young students. "My child, don't go along with them!" the teachers say. "They are trying to get themselves killed" (Proverbs 1:15, 18).

A sampling of other practical advice:

- **Settling disagreements.** "Drawing straws is one way to settle a difficult case" (Proverbs 18:18 CEV).
- **Cosigning loans.** "If you have put up security for a friend's debt. . .follow my advice and save yourself. . .swallow your pride; go and beg to have your name erased" (Proverbs 6:1, 3).
- **Calming someone down.** "A gentle answer deflects anger, but harsh words make tempers flare" (Proverbs 15:1).

Solomon of Egypt. Mummy mask of an Egyptian author named Amenemope—from whom Solomon may have borrowed some proverbs. The mask along with a copy of the Egyptian's book—a collection of wise sayings called "Instruction of Amenemope"—each date to about 1000 BC. That's just a few decades before King Solomon is said to have written much of Proverbs.

Borrowing some Bible from Egypt?

Jewish editors who compiled the wise sayings in Proverbs may have drawn on some writings from Egypt. That's a country famed for its wisdom literature as early as a thousand years before Solomon could have penned his first wise nugget.

One section of Proverbs in particular—30 sayings by a group of sages identified only as "the wise" (Proverbs 22:17–24:22)—bears striking resemblance to an Egyptian book of 30 sayings.

"Instruction of Amenemope" is named after its Egyptian writer, who seems to have lived about a century before Solomon, in the 1000s BC or perhaps earlier. The collection has 30 short chapters, with most chapters just a few lines long and each chapter covering a different topic.

Compare the following excerpts from Proverbs and Amenemope. These are just a few of the many similarities.

Proverbs	Instruction of Amenemope
"Listen to the words of the wise; apply your heart to my instruction" (Proverbs 22:17).	"Give your ears to hear the sayings, give your heart to understand them."
"Don't rob the poor just because you can" (Proverbs 22:22).	"Don't steal from the poor or attack a cripple."
"Don't befriend angry people or associate with hot-tempered people" (Proverbs 22:24).	"Don't start a quarrel with a hot-mouthed man."

SEX ADVICE from old men

The man who commits adultery is an utter fool. . . . His shame will never be erased.

PROVERBS 6:32–33

Sex is a hot topic in Proverbs—in a couple of ways. It's a common topic, showing up in many chapters. And it's a steamy topic at times, perhaps a bit too descriptive for reading in a public worship service.

The best sex advice these elderly mentors have for their young, male students can be summed up in a single sentence: Don't have sex with anyone but your wife.

A sampling of pertinent one-liners:

- "A prostitute will bring you to poverty, but sleeping with another man's wife will cost you your life" (Proverbs 6:26).
- "Why spill the water of your springs in the streets, having sex with just anyone? . . . Rejoice in the wife of your youth. . . . Let her breasts satisfy you always" (Proverbs 5:16, 18, 19).
- "Don't even think about that kind of woman [another man's unfaithful wife]. . . . Her house is a one-way street leading straight down to the world of the dead" (Proverbs 7:25, 27 CEV).
- "Stay away from her! Don't go near the door of her house!" (Proverbs 5:8).

Lady of the house. Young men should take pleasure in their wives, the sages of Proverbs advise. It's dangerous, they warn, for men to have affairs with prostitutes or other men's wives.

A WORD ABOUT WIVES

When old men in Bible times talked about wives, any woman within earshot really needed to brace herself.

It was a chauvinistic day. Men ruled, for better or worse. Sometimes for worse. The old men of Proverbs were no exception. Not everything they say about women is fair and balanced, or stated with sensitivity.

- **The wife as a bone cancer.** "A worthy wife is a crown for her husband, but a disgraceful woman is like cancer in his bones" (Proverbs 12:4).
- **The drip.** "A quarrelsome wife is as annoying as constant dripping" (Proverbs 19:13).
- **A desert upgrade.** "It is better to live alone in the desert than with a quarreling and complaining wife" (Proverbs 21:19 NCV).

That said, one of the Bible's most beautiful tributes to wives is preserved as a chapter in Proverbs. It was written by an otherwise unknown king: Lemuel. Sadly for men, the tribute isn't his own. He credits his mother.

Lemuel's wise mother produced a long list of chores that hardworking wives did for their families. Then she gave this advice to husbands everywhere, encouraging them to reward their wives: "Show her respect—praise her in public for what she has done" (Proverbs 31:31 CEV).

So ends the book of Proverbs, with a lady getting the last word.

WATCH your mouth

Keep your mouth shut, and you will stay out of trouble.

PROVERBS 21:23

There's a New Testament book like Proverbs: James, a book of practical Christian advice. James is famous for its chapter about the power wielded in a tiny tongue—power enough to flail up the perfect storm.

"People can tame all kinds of animals, birds, reptiles, and fish, but no one can tame the tongue" (James 3:7–8).

Yet a key message in James as well as Proverbs is that trying to tame the tongue is well worth the effort—even if we're only partly successful.

In hopes of at least beginning to control the tongue, the elders of Proverbs offer some how-to advice.

- "Don't respond to the stupidity of a fool; you'll only look foolish yourself" (Proverbs 26:4 THE MESSAGE).
- "Gossip separates the best of friends" (Proverbs 16:28).
- "Some people make cutting remarks, but the words of the wise bring healing" (Proverbs 12:18).

RAISING kids

Direct your children onto the right path, and when they are older, they will not leave it.

PROVERBS 22:6

More than a dozen proverbs deal with raising kids. Most of the advice zeroes in on discipline—urging young fathers to consider disciplining their children as an expression of love.

"A father corrects a child in whom he delights," reads one proverb (3:12).

Another proverb adds a sense of urgency: "Discipline your children while there is hope. Otherwise you will ruin their lives" (Proverbs 19:18).

Yet another adds motivation: "Discipline your children, and they will give you peace of mind" (Proverbs 29:17).

But does Proverbs encourage spanking?

Some Bible translations leave parents feeling as though they have a biblical mandate to hit their disobedient kids—and if they don't they're negligent.

Examples from two passages that sound pro-spanking:

- "Don't be afraid to correct your young ones; a spanking won't kill them. A good spanking, in fact, might save them from something worse than death" (Proverbs 23:13–14 THE MESSAGE).
- "Those who spare the rod of discipline hate their children. Those who love their children care enough to discipline them" (Proverbs 13:24).

This makes it sound like parents who don't spank their kids don't love them.

Yet many Bible translations take out the spanking verbiage, to focus attention on the need for discipline rather than the manner of the discipline. Also, some shepherds remind us that a shepherd's rod isn't for walloping sheep. It's for gently nudging them back on the path and away from danger.

Many Bible experts, on the other hand, argue that spanking unruly children was a common method of discipline throughout the ancient world, including among Jewish families. So some scholars say that the elderly sages of Proverbs were presuming that some spanking would be necessary.

The question that godly parents face today is whether or not this ancient practice is still necessary for their particular children, given the other options available. Some children are sensitive enough to melt into tears of regret at the mere tone of disappointment in a parent's voice. Others may need their cell phone taken away for a week. Still, some Christian people insist that on occasion their particular kid needs the sharp sting of a wallop.

LAZY is crazy

As a door swings back and forth on its hinges, so the lazy person turns over in bed.

PROVERBS 26:14

Hard work is a headliner in Proverbs. In dozens of proverbs scattered throughout this collection, elderly sages praise hard work—sometimes as though it's a matter of life or death.

Bullish on plowing. With a team of bulls and a wooden plow like those used in Bible times, a farmer in the early 1900s turns the rocky soil of what is now Israel. Elders of Proverbs would have praised him for his hard work.

"Take a lesson from the ants, you lazybones," says one sage. "They labor hard all summer, gathering food for the winter. But you, lazybones, how long will you sleep? . . . A little extra sleep. . .a little folding of the hands to rest—then poverty will pounce on you like a bandit" (Proverbs 6:6, 8–11).

This reads a bit like one of the many animal fables in ancient Middle Eastern writings. There was a widespread feeling back then that people could learn important lessons about life by studying animal behavior. Animal fables show up in many collections of wisdom literature. Here in Proverbs, the moral behind the fable of the ant is that snoozers are losers—and they'll discover it soon enough.

When it comes to getting a job done right, these mentors aren't fans of shortcuts, quick fixes, or get-rich-now schemes.

- "Good planning and hard work lead to prosperity, but hasty shortcuts lead to poverty" (Proverbs 21:5).
- "Wealth from get-rich-quick schemes quickly disappears; wealth from hard work grows over time" (Proverbs 13:11).
- "Work hard and become a leader; be lazy and become a slave" (Proverbs 12:24).

For some reason elderly sages—not just of Proverbs but of wisdom writings throughout the ancient Middle East—figure they have to keep jack-hammering away at this topic if they have any hope of getting their message through the thick skulls of young men.

WISDOM IS A LADY

Wisdom is a "she" in Proverbs.

"Wisdom shouts in the streets. She cries out in the public square. . . . 'How long, you simpletons, will you insist on being simpleminded?' " (Proverbs 1:20, 22).

The good lady Wisdom shows up in chapters 1 and 8, both times as a female.

That's odd, since it was a man's world back then.

There's at least one good guess why the sages of Proverbs personified wisdom as a woman instead of, say, an old man. It's because a woman fits the context better.

The good lady Wisdom isn't the only one shouting in the streets. There's another woman out there. And she's no lady.

Not even close to Wisdom, this other woman "is often in the streets and markets, soliciting at every corner. . . . with a brazen look she said, . . .'Come, let's drink our fill of love until morning. Let's enjoy each other's caresses, for my husband is not home' " (Proverbs 7:12–13, 18–19).

The good lady Wisdom, offering safety (Proverbs 1:33), is a fine alternative to the woman light on morals: "She runs a halfway house to hell, fits you out with a shroud and a coffin" (Proverbs 7:27 THE MESSAGE).

ECCLESIASTES

WHEN LIFE SEEMS SENSELESS

The wisest man who ever lived takes on the hardest question of all.

Who wouldn't want to know what happens?

The wise guy is Solomon—at least that's who the writer strongly hints that he is. Solomon was the Israelite king who was "wiser than anyone who has ever lived or ever will live" (1 Kings 3:12 CEV).

The tough question he tackles is this: "What's the point of life—why are we humans here?"

Ecclesiastes sounds a bit like a lab experiment in logic, with all the tests taking place in the writer's mind. In one experiment after another, he searches for the meaning of life.

He looks in all the logical places, where people measure their worth: by the work they do, the wealth they accumulate, the education they gain, the pleasures they seek, and the relationships they cherish.

But when the writer closes the lab door after his final experiment and he stands ready to report his findings, the word is grim. "Everything is meaningless."

That's the conclusion of the wisest human being who would ever swim in humanity's gene pool. If there's an answer to the tough question he grappled with, it's beyond him.

He finds no lasting value in humanity. We humans make no enduring difference in the world. We're born. We live. We die. And life goes on without us, as though we never existed.

That said, he reaches a surprising conclusion.

Instead of urging us to eat, drink, and party like there's no tomorrow, he suggests that we live in a way that would express gratitude to the one who gave us life. Honor God, he says, and "do what he tells you" (Ecclesiastes 12:13 THE MESSAGE).

A philosophical approach. Tight-lipped, the unidentified philosopher portrayed in this statue seems at a loss for words. So is the sage of Ecclesiastes. He can't explain the purpose of life. Yet he advises people to live in a way that honors God, the giver of life.

WHAT'S the point of living?

God has dealt a tragic existence to the human race. I observed everything going on under the sun, and really, it is all meaningless—like chasing the wind.

ECCLESIASTES 1:13–14

The Teacher identifies himself as a longtime student of wisdom—a sage. In fact, his book fits the genre called wisdom literature, like the books of Job and Proverbs. Books like these can offer fast-food brain nuggets of practical insight, condensed to no longer than the sentence we find inside a fortune cookie. Or they can serve up a banquet of profound insight, in the form of stories or poetic essays.

Ecclesiastes does all of this, in an attempt to find meaning in life.

But as wise as the Teacher is, he finds no meaning. People just don't make a difference in the long scope of history. "Generations come and generations go, but the earth never changes" (Ecclesiastes 1:4).

Dying young. An Egyptian couple mourns their child. The Teacher says he has witnessed "the death of good young people and the long life of wicked people" (Ecclesiastes 7:15). And he says this injustice makes no sense to him.

MAIN

"I have thought deeply ab[ou]t [what is going] on here under the sun. . . . Her[e is my] final conclusion: Fear God and obey his commands" (Ecclesiastes 8:9; 12:13).

WRITER:

"These are the words of the Teacher, King David's son, who ruled in Jerusalem" (Ecclesiastes 1:1). That suggests Solomon. So do other clues: The writer is wise, has lots of wives, and talks about receiving treasures from foreign leaders. But many Bible experts say his choice of certain Hebrew words sounds like they're coming from 400 to 600 years after Solomon's time. The disconnect would be a bit like Romeo catching sight of Juliet in the distant moonlight and declaring, "Did my heart love till now? Forswear it, sight! She's a bad mama jama." Perhaps an editor revised Solomon's original work, some Bible experts speculate, the way Bible translators have updated the 400-year-old Shakespearean English of the King James Version. Or maybe someone else wrote the book, giving Solomon the credit. The reverse of plagiarism, this was a common way of honoring someone in ancient times. Many students of the Bible, however, prefer the traditional position: that Solomon wrote this book. They argue that translating ancient words is a tricky business, especially since the Jews used shorthand, skipping the vowels. Even with vowels, many given Hebrew words could have a variety of meanings.

DATE:

If Solomon wrote it, he did so in the 900s BC.

LOCATION:

Israel

f the writer were alive today, he might change this a bit. Given the environmental tastrophes that humanity seems to be spawning these days, the Teacher might complain that our only enduring quality is to make things worse—to exploit God's creation instead of taking care of it.

For some bewildering reason, the Teacher says, we're born. We live our moment in the sun. Then we're gone, leaving behind not so much as a shadow. The sun doesn't even notice we're missing. It just goes on rising and setting each day, while the wind keeps blowing and the rivers rush on to the ocean.

People may remember us for a time, but before long even that is lost. "We don't remember what happened in the past, and in future generations, no one will remember what we are doing now" (Ecclesiastes 1:11).

Where Ecclesiastes gets its name

If we gave this book an English title, it might be "The Teaching."

But we don't. We hang onto the Greek title: *ekklesiastes*. That's odd because the book wasn't written in Greek. It was written in Hebrew.

The Hebrew word is *koheleth*. That's what the writer calls himself: *Koheleth*. Unfortunately, no one is certain what *koheleth* means. The root word, *khl*, means "to assemble." So scholars often guess that *koheleth* means "the assembler," as in someone who assembles knowledge or who assembles a class of students. That's why most modern Bible versions translate *Koheleth* as "the Teacher."

About 200 years before Christ, Greek-speaking Jews translated their sacred Hebrew writings into Greek—the main language of the day. *Koheleth* became *ekklesiastes*, the Greek word for "the one of the assembly."

When Christian scholars started translating the Bible into other languages—such as the Roman Empire's preferred language of Latin—they decided to keep the Greek word as the title.

Even the Teacher's own mission in life—to learn as much as he can about everything—is as foolish as chasing the wind. The faster he runs, the faster the wind blows. The more questions he answers, the more questions those answers raise. And in frustration he laments, "The greater my wisdom, the greater my grief" (Ecclesiastes 1:18).

WORK is a waste

What do you get from a life of hard labor? . . . You hand over what you worked for to someone who never lifted a finger for it.

ECCLESIASTES 2:22, 21 THE MESSAGE

Of the many experiments the Teacher conducts, three focus on trying to find meaning in work, wealth, and pleasure. They're all a bust.

- **Work.** "I came to hate all my hard work here on earth, for I must leave to others everything I have earned" (Ecclesiastes 2:18).
- **Wealth.** "How meaningless to think that wealth brings true happiness! The more you have, the more people come to help you spend it. So what good is wealth—except perhaps to watch it slip through your fingers!" (Ecclesiastes 5:10–11).
- **Pleasure.** "I denied myself no pleasure," the Teacher says. He built huge homes, with gardens and parks. He married many beautiful women. He bought slaves to take care

of his family and his vast herds. He hired musicians to entertain him. He says, "I had everything a man could desire!" (Ecclesiastes 2:8). Yet he sees no lasting value to it. "What good does it do to seek pleasure?" (Ecclesiastes 2:2).

The Teacher makes a judgment call. Even though work, wealth, and pleasure are meaningless, as far as he can tell, that doesn't mean we should cut them out of our lives. He advises just the opposite: "The best thing we can do is to enjoy eating, drinking, and working. I believe these are God's gifts to us" (Ecclesiastes 2:24 CEV).

He trusts God more than he trusts his understanding. He sounds like the sage who offered this advice: "Trust in the LORD with all your heart; do not depend on your own understanding" (Proverbs 3:5).

If he's not the wise Solomon, he's at the very least an incredibly insightful and godly sage.

SEASONS of life

For everything there is a season, a time for every activity under heaven. A time to be born and a time to die.

ECCLESIASTES 3:1–2

In one of the most famous poems of the Bible, the Teacher describes some of life's most notable experiences. And he does it in a way that points to God, showing that God is in control of our destiny. God sets the timeline of our lives.

Count the verses describing the "seasons." It's no coincidence there are seven. In the Bible, seven is the perfect number. It symbolizes completion. This symbolism goes back to Creation. On day seven, God's work was finished and he rested. And on the seventh day of the week, the Sabbath, God's people rest. Everything we need to do—work and rest—takes place in seven days of the week.

All of life's experiences are summed up in these seven verses, with each verse covering one extreme to the other. The first line of each verse describes the experience, and the second line repeats the idea—either by saying it another way or contrasting it with

Eat, drink, and be merry. Raising a cup of wine in her courtyard, this young lady is fortunate enough to taste opulence. But wealth doesn't bring true happiness, warns the Teacher. Still, he encourages people to enjoy the blessings God gives them—and to share with others. "Someday you will be rewarded" (Ecclesiastes 11:1 CEV).

the flip side of the coin. That's a trait of Hebrew poetry. Lines don't rhyme. Instead of repeating sounds, they repeat ideas. No rhyme, just plenty of reason.

In life's seven basic seasons, there are times:

- to be born and to die;
- to kill and to heal;
- to cry and to laugh;
- to hug and to push away;
- to find something and to lose something;
- to tear and to mend; and
- to love and to hate.

We might be in control of how we respond to life's situations. But the timing of the events is beyond our control. Another poet put it this way, in a prayer to God: "My times are in your hands" (Psalm 31:15 NIV).

It's striking to read it this way. What makes it so jarring is this: Though our time is in God's hands, eternity is in our hearts. God "has planted eternity in the human heart" (Ecclesiastes 3:11). Bible experts debate what that means. But one idea is that we have a sense of eternity. We know it's there. We want it. And we want to know how our life fits into the eternal scheme of things.

But the sage says we can't see that far: "People cannot see the whole scope of God's work."

Yet one more time, the Teacher has a suggestion. He repeats something he said earlier, in 2:24. "I concluded there is nothing better than to be happy and enjoy ourselves as long as we can. And people should eat and drink and enjoy the fruits of their labor, for these are gifts from God" (Ecclesiastes 3:11–13).

We can't begin to understand the seasons of life, and why things happen when they do. But we can enjoy the good times when they come.

A BARMAID'S ADVICE IN THE BIBLE?

Chunk of a legend. One of many surviving copies of an ancient adventure story—the Epic of Gilgamesh—this fragment was found in Israel. It was copied into clay about 400 years before Solomon. The writer of Ecclesiastes, possibly Solomon, seems to borrow some advice from this story.

One snippet of advice from the wise Teacher of Ecclesiastes—who is traditionally considered to be Solomon—seems incredibly similar to some advice an ancient Iraqi hero got from a barmaid.

The hero was Gilgamesh. He's a king thought to have lived more than 2,000 years before Solomon, in what is now Iraq. His story is called the Epic of Gilgamesh. And most of this story was found on a dozen clay tablets in the ruins of an Assyrian king's library in Nineveh. That's near modern-day Mosul in northern Iraq. As the story goes, Gilgamesh was on a quest for the secret of immortality.

The barmaid was Siduri. Here's part of her advice, alongside similar advice in the Bible.

Ecclesiastes 9:7–9 CEV	Epic of Gilgamesh, tablet 10, author's paraphrase
Be happy and enjoy eating and drinking! (verse 7).	Fill your belly. Enjoy yourself day and night—eating, dancing, and playing.
Dress up, comb your hair, and look your best (verse 8).	Take a bath, wash your hair, and wear sparkling fresh clothes.
You love your wife, so enjoy being with her (verse 9).	Let your wife enjoy being with you.
This is what you are supposed to do as you struggle through life on this earth (verse 9).	This is what people are supposed to do.

SONG OF SONGS

LOVE TALK

What is a song about sex—with no mention of God—doing in the Bible?

That's a question that people of faith, Jews and Christians alike, have been asking for more than 2,000 years. Most believers in ancient times couldn't handle what many scholars today insist is the truth about this book. And the truth is that it's an erotic celebration of love between a man and a woman who graphically praise the physical features of each other and trade fantasies about making love. Though their words aren't obscene, they are unapologetically sensual.

Too sensual, it seems, for most believers until the 1800s.

Until then, most read the book as an allegory. They thought the symbolic meaning was more important than the literal meaning.

For many Jews the Song was

Black and beautiful. In an erotic poem, two lovers confess their most intimate desires for each other—exchanging compliments and occasionally bragging about themselves. "I am black and beautiful," the woman says. "Ah, you are beautiful," her lover agrees (Song of Songs 1:5, 15 NRSV).

a symbol of God's love for Israel. The man in the story is God. The woman is Israel. The bedroom is the land now called Israel. The kissing is God giving Israel the laws they're to follow. And the woman's confession of having black skin is Israel's confession of sin—worshipping idols.

Christians did much the same thing, with the man usually representing Jesus. Even John Wesley, a preacher in the late 1700s who became the father of the Methodist Church, insisted that the Song "could not with decency" refer to a literal man and woman. "This book is to be understood allegorically concerning that spiritual love and marriage, which is between

MAIN POINT:

Love between a husband and a wife is something to celebrate and enjoy, both in words and in sexual intimacy.

WRITER:

"This is Solomon's song of songs, more wonderful than any other" (Song of Songs 1:1). But most Bible experts say they doubt Solomon wrote the book—for several reasons.

• The first verse seems to act like a title added later by an editor compiling the songs—as editors did with many psalms.

• In Hebrew, the byline is phrased vaguely: "of Solomon." That could mean it's by him. Or it's for him, perhaps for one of his weddings. Or it's about him, though there's little mention of him afterward.

• Some of the phrasing seems to come from hundreds of years after Solomon.

Many Bible experts say this book is probably a collection of poetry and love songs used in wedding celebrations. Others say a single writer wrote it, perhaps a woman. That's because the starring female character in the Song speaks 61 of the 116 verses—more than the starring male or the minor characters.

Many students of the Bible take the traditional approach, arguing that Solomon wrote the song. Among the supporting evidence: names of cities in the song fit the time of Solomon, before the nation split in two. The writer talks about many exotic spices, plants, and jewels—which fits this era when Solomon was trading with countries throughout the Middle East and Africa. Also, this genre of writing is similar to songs that Egyptians were writing at and before the time of Solomon.

DATE:

Unknown. Solomon ruled from about 970–930 BC.

LOCATION:

Israel. The lovers mention many locations in Israel, such as Jerusalem, the coastal plains of Sharon, and Mount Hermon.

Saint Bernard of Clairvaux

Christ and his church."

Only in the 1800s did Bible experts start tiptoeing away from the allegorical interpretation. The bedroom is real, they began arguing. So is the kissing and so are the breasts. Most Bible experts today seem to agree.

What remains confusing is the storyline. Many don't see one. They see just a collection of love songs, a bit like the "Best of Johnny Mathis." But in this case, the "Best of King Solomon."

Yet other experts see plot possibilities.

- Solomon picks a country girl as a bride. But she rejects him for her country boy.
- Solomon is the country boy, so he gets the girl after all.
- Country girl falls in love with country boy, and she sees her man as kingly—every bit as regal as Solomon.

LOOKING good

You are so handsome, my love, pleasing beyond words.

SONG OF SONGS 1:16

A lovesick man and woman pummel each other with compliments. Their dialogue reads like a how-to manual for couples who don't know how to put their love into words.

Compliments from the gentleman:

"You are beautiful, my darling, beautiful beyond words. Your eyes are like doves behind your veil. . . . Your lips are like scarlet ribbon; your mouth is inviting. . . . Your breasts are like two fawns, twin fawns of a gazelle grazing among the lilies" (Song of Songs 4:1, 3, 5).

Compliments from the lady:

CELIBATES IN LOVE WITH THE SONG

Some monks and other early Christian leaders who took the vow of chastity seemed uncommonly preoccupied with the Song of Songs—the most explicitly sexual book in the Bible.

Some might wonder if they read it for the same reason many today read *National Geographic* magazine: to explore the sights they'll never get to visit in person.

But if their writings are any clue, they wanted to convince others that the Song isn't about sex. Instead, they saw the poems as a metaphor about the spiritual love between God and humanity.

Bernard of Clairvaux. Living in the 1100s, this French monk wrote 86 sermons about the Song of Songs. And that covered only the first two chapters and one verse from chapter 3. That's more than two sermons a verse—from a celibate monk.

He argued that the Song's literal meaning was only the "outer husk," hiding the real, symbolic meaning.

Here's his take on the real meaning of: "How lovely are your cheeks; your earrings set them afire!" (Song of Songs 1:10).

"Heavenly goldsmiths...will fashion glorious tokens of truth and insert them in the soul's inward ears."

Origen. An Egyptian Christian in the AD 200s, this theologian wrote 10 books about the Song of Songs—and many sermons.

Oddly, he shooed people away from the Song and the commentaries he wrote about it.

He said, "I advise everyone who is not yet rid of the distractions of the flesh and has not stopped feeling the passion of physical desires to stay completely away from reading this little book and the comments that will be said about it."

Then he went on to argue that the Song had nothing to do with "bodily functions" but, instead, with the "divine senses of the inner man."

"His body is like bright ivory, glowing with lapis lazuli. His legs are like marble pillars set in sockets of finest gold. His posture is stately, like the noble cedars of Lebanon. His mouth is sweetness itself; he is desirable in every way" (Song of Songs 5:14–16).

HERE comes the groom

Look, it is Solomon's carriage.

SONG OF SONGS 3:7

The woman has what some Bible experts say is a dream—a nightmare ending in a delightful fantasy.

The lady in love waits in bed for her lover, but he never comes. So she ventures out into the darkness to look for him, asking village guards if they've seen him. She eventually finds him and takes him home to the same bed where her mother conceived her. The implication is that she's going to follow her mother's example—if not by conceiving, at least by having sex.

What follows in the same chapter is a description of Solomon's wedding party storming into the village with a huge entourage, including 60 bodyguards. It's a song completely unrelated to the previous "dream" section, some scholars say. Yet it fits nicely into at least one possible

JOHN WESLEY'S CODE KEY TO THE SONG

Like most church leaders during Christianity's first 1,800 years, Methodist founder John Wesley taught that the Song of Songs was not about a couple in love.

Writing commentaries in the 1700s, Wesley said the Song symbolizes spiritual love between Jesus and the church.

Here's part of the code key Wesley used to explain what he said the book was really talking about. It's from his commentary, *John Wesley's Notes on the Song of Solomon.*

Bible description	Symbolic meaning
Young woman (1:1)	Church
Young man (1:8)	Jesus
Kisses (1:2)	Any unusual tokens of God's love
Black skin (1:6)	A person contemptible and deformed
The man lying between the woman's breasts (1:13)	A description of the church's intimate union and hearty affection to Christ
Bed (1:16)	Wherever believers enjoy sweet fellowship with Christ
Solomon's 60-man bodyguard (3:7)	Angels and others God use to protect his church
Solomon's chariot (3:7)	The word of Christ, preached by ministers
The woman's lovely neck (4:4)	Faith. It unites the church with Jesus. Rationale: The Bible sometimes calls the church the body of Christ, and Jesus the head of the church. The neck connects the body and head.
Lips as sweet as nectar (4:11)	Prayer and praise
A little sister too young to have breasts (8:8)	Big sister is the early church dominated by Jews. Little sister is the later church, dominated by non-Jews called Gentiles.

timeline: The bride-to-be dreams of making love and here comes her groom ready to wed.

The king drives an import—a chariot crafted of wood from Lebanon. It's likely the best available builder's wood: cedar. This chariot is loaded, trimmed in gold and silver, and padded in cushions colored with the most expensive dye: purple. The king has no air-conditioning and wears no deodorant, because neither is available in this ancient desert nation. But he smells great, lathered in the sweet scents of imported perfume: frankincense and myrrh.

Many Bible experts say the groom isn't really Solomon. Instead, the ladies telling this part of the story are complimenting the country boy groom. He may be riding a rat-eared donkey instead of an imported chariot. His entourage may include only his family and a few goat-herder friends. And he may smell like sheep dip. But to his waiting bride, he's regal. And she couldn't love him any more if he were the king himself.

PASSION fire

[Young Man:] "You are slender like a palm tree, and your breasts are like its clusters of fruit. . . . I will climb the palm tree and take hold of its fruit."

SONG OF SONGS 7:7–8

If in fact the Song of Songs is an allegory, as most Christian scholars taught for the first 1,800 years, imagine God saying something like this to the nation of Israel—or Jesus saying something like this to the church. In the allegorical interpretation, that's what would be going on. This would be a dialogue between God and his beloved people about the spiritual love they share for one another.

But most of today's scholars say that's the wrong way to interpret this passage.

They admit there are allegories in the Bible. Paul creates one when he tells the Galatians that Abraham's two wives symbolized God's two covenants. Hagar, the slave wife, represented Israel's binding obligation to the Jewish laws—the old covenant. But Sarah, the freeborn wife, represented freedom from Jewish laws—the new covenant (Galatians 4:21–26).

Aphrodisiac. With roots that look like a human torso, the flowering mandrake was considered an aphrodisiac and fertility enhancer. The young woman in Song of Songs said she wanted to lie with her lover in a field of mandrakes. Childless Rachel—one of Jacob's two wives—once bought mandrake roots from the other wife, Leah. In trade, Rachel gave up her night with Jacob. The roots worked, but on the wrong woman. Leah got pregnant that night.

179

Yet the Song of Songs, most experts today agree, is simply a celebration of love. And this celebration is expressed no more sensually than in the final two chapters of the book. It sounds as though the couple is on their honeymoon, or anticipating it with every hormonally charged fiber in their bodies.

After the young man compares his lady to a fruit tree and declares his intention of picking some fruit—making love—the lady responds with eager willingness. "I am my lover's, and he claims me as his own" (Song of Songs 7:10).

Not only does she say yes, she offers an idea for enhancing the pleasure.

"Let us get up early and go to the vineyards to see if the grapevines have budded. . . . There I will give you my love" (Song of Songs 7:12).

She wants to make love outside, surrounded by the fragrance of budding flowers and where "wildflowers. . .pomegranates. . .and mandrakes [considered aphrodisiacs] give off their fragrance."

MAKING a commitment

"Always keep me in your heart and wear this bracelet to remember me by."
SONG OF SONGS 8:6 CEV

This isn't just a collection of songs about a young couple who wants to make passionate love in bed, in the vineyard, under an apple tree (Song of Songs 8:5), and wherever else they can find a little privacy. It certainly is that. But it's more.

It's about the enduring nature of love, and the power love has to sustain people—even after a mate has died.

In what many Bible experts say is the greatest song in this Song of Songs, the young woman assures her man that the love she has for him will never die. And she asks him to make the same commitment to her.

"Always keep me in your heart," she says. "The passion of love bursting into flame is more powerful than death, stronger than the grave. Love cannot be drowned by oceans or floods; it cannot be bought, no matter what is offered" (Song of Songs 8:6–7 CEV).

Cupid armed and dangerous. Helping romance along, Cupid does what comes natural for a mythological son of Venus, the goddess of love. When some Presbyterians in the 1600s started suggesting that the Song of Songs might be about physical love instead of spiritual love, British church leaders condemned them. Known as the Westminster Assembly, these British leaders insisted it was blasphemous to treat the sacred Song as "a hot carnal pamphlet formed by some loose Apollo or Cupid."

God is nowhere mentioned in this book.

But many see him in the joy that love brings to this couple, and in the woman's declaration that love isn't something we can control or buy. It's a gift. And people of faith see God as the giver, for it was God who created people and told them, "Be fruitful and multiply" (Genesis 1:28).

This is the one and only law of God that human beings have consistently obeyed, with pleasure.

EGYPTIAN LOVE SONG

Israel wasn't the only place in Bible times where lovers quoted erotic poetry and sang intimate love songs to each other.

Ancient love songs have been discovered throughout the ancient Middle East.

Many of them sound like they would fit quite nicely into the Song of Songs.

The following Egyptian song would work well in the Bible's Song, if it weren't for references to a goddess. The song was written in the 1100–1200s BC, at least a century before Solomon. The writer calls his lover "sister" just as the man in the Bible's Song does.

Sister without rival,
        most beautiful of all.
She looks like the star-goddess,
        rising at the start of the good New Year.
Perfect and bright, shining skin,
        seductive in her eyes
        when she glances,
        sweet in her lips
        when she speaks,
        and never a word too many
Slender neck, shining body,
        her hair is true lapis,
        her arm gathers gold,
        her fingers are like lotus flowers.
Ample behind, tight waist,
        her thighs extend her beauty,
        shapely in stride
        when she steps on the earth.
She has stolen my heart
        with her embrace.
She has made the neck of every man
        turn around at the sight of her.
Whoever embraces her is happy,
        he is like the king of lovers.

Source: Papyrus Chester Beatty I, Song One. Chester Beatty Library and Gallery, Dublin.

ISAIAH

FIRST THE BAD NEWS

In a vision, a Jerusalem prophet named Isaiah steps into heaven. There, he sees God surrounded by angels.

"Whom should I send as a messenger to the people?" God asks.

"Here am I," Isaiah replies. "Send me."

Isaiah gets the sad job of delivering the worst news the Jewish people have ever heard in their more than a thousand years of history. Invaders will overrun their two nations, Israel in the north and Judah in the south. Most Jews lucky enough to survive the carnage will be led off as captives.

Israel will no longer exist on the world map. That's the bad news.

God is carrying out the punishment written into his ancient contract with the Jewish people. He said he would bless them for obedience, but he would punish them for persistent sin: "The LORD will scatter you among all the nations from one end of the earth to the other" (Deuteronomy 28:64).

Fortunately, Isaiah's message doesn't end on this bitter note. God will bring the Jewish survivors home for a fresh start. And he will send a messiah from King David's family to set up a kingdom more wonderful than the Jews could ever imagine.

Purifying a prophet. An angel touches a hot coal to the lips of Isaiah, purifying him to speak God's holy message to the Jews.

MAIN POINT:

God is patient, but he eventually punishes individuals and nations for their persistent sin. Yet his punishment is not vindictive. It's intended as a remedy, to turn people away from sins that hurt themselves and others.

WRITER:

Bible experts debate who wrote this book. They say there may have been one writer, two, or three.

The traditional view says Isaiah wrote it. The book begins by announcing, "These are the visions that Isaiah son of Amoz saw" (Isaiah 1:1).

But only the first 39 chapters are set in Isaiah's time, the 700s BC. Chapters 40–66 describe conditions about 150 years later. That's when the Jews are exiled into Babylon, modern-day Iraq. The book even names the Persian king who will defeat Babylon and free the Jews: Cyrus, who reigned from 559–530 BC (Isaiah 45, 48).

Many scholars say at least two writers worked on this book, perhaps three:

- Writer 1, probably Isaiah, chapters 1–39, set in Isaiah's time.
- Writer 2, chapters 40–55, during the exile in the 500s BC.
- Writer 3, chapters 56–66, after the Jews return home from exile in the 400s–500s BC.

Many scholars argue that chapters 40–66 could be predictions. Even the specific reference to Cyrus, though uncommon, wasn't unheard of in prophecies. One prophet looked 250 years into the future and predicted that Israel would have a good king named Josiah (1 Kings 13:2).

One other clue that points to the traditional view is the oldest copy of Isaiah. It was found among the famous Dead Sea Scrolls and copied about 100 years before Jesus. The scribe who copied it apparently believed the original document was written by only one writer, for there is no break after chapter 39.

DATE:

Isaiah ministered from about 740–700 BC.

LOCATION:

Isaiah lived in Jerusalem, and most of his prophecies focus on the Jewish people. But many prophecies involve other nations throughout the Middle East.

Oldest Isaiah scroll. Hidden for nearly 2,000 years in a cave beside the Dead Sea is a nearly complete copy of Isaiah. Written on leather about 100 years before Jesus' time, it's the oldest copy of Isaiah yet discovered—1,000 years older than the copy used to translate the King James Version of the Bible. (For photo of the cave in which it was found, see page 162.)

BAD NEWS for Jerusalem

[God:] "I am sick of your burnt offerings of rams and the fat of fattened cattle."

ISAIAH 1:11

Even before reporting his vision, Isaiah unleashes a bombardment of prophecies on sinful nations of the Middle East. And he starts with his own homeland: Judah and its Jerusalem capital.

Israel had split into two countries 200 years earlier, with the 10 northern tribes seceding from the union in a bloodless tax revolt. Their nation became known as Israel, while southern Jews took the name of the dominant tribe there, Judah.

Isaiah tells his homeland Jews that God is sick and tired of their hypocrisy. Written to sound like a lawsuit, the prophecy presents God's case against the Jews. The charge: sin—a capital offense.

God says the Jews go through the motions of religion, offering sacrifices and praying when others are watching. But it's just an act.

As for their offerings, God says, "I cannot stand them." And as for their prayers: "I will not listen" (Isaiah 1:14, 15).

God isn't concerned about the mere motions and words of worship rituals. He's concerned about what the rituals are intended to invoke in people: "Do good. Seek justice. Help the oppressed. Defend the cause of orphans. Fight for the rights of widows" (Isaiah 1:17).

But it's too late. The Jews have already decided to do as they please. And in a stinging rebuke God reveals their fate by referring to them as two cities he seared off the planet some 1,300 years earlier. "Listen to the LORD, you leaders of 'Sodom.' Listen to the law of our God, people of 'Gomorrah' " (Isaiah 1:10).

Scattered through the book are repeated warnings to the southern Jewish nation and to the capital city.

- "The LORD of Heaven's Armies, will take away from Jerusalem and Judah everything they depend on: every bit of bread and every drop of water. . . . In those days a man

Prophets in a row. Ten of Israel's prophets surround Moses holding the 10 Commandments. From the left, they are Amos, Nahum, Ezekiel, Daniel, Elijah, Moses, Joshua, Jeremiah, Jonah, Isaiah, and Habakkuk.

will say to his brother, 'Since you have a coat, you be our leader! Take charge of this heap of ruins!' " (Isaiah 3:1, 6).

- "I will be your enemy, surrounding Jerusalem and attacking its walls. I will build siege towers and destroy it" (Isaiah 29:3).
- "Without consulting me, you have gone down to Egypt for help. You have put your trust in Pharaoh's protection. . . . But by trusting Pharaoh, you will be humiliated" (Isaiah 30:2–3).

Isaiah had warned the Jews not to make a military alliance with Egypt. But the Jews did it anyway. This was an attempt to join forces and break free of the oppressive Assyrians, the world superpower of the moment. Assyrians led by King Sennacherib respond in 701 BC by invading Judah, destroying most of the cities, and fighting off Egyptian soldiers who come charging to the rescue of their allies.

Jerusalem survives that invasion, which Isaiah witnesses. But the city and the nation will eventually fall to the world's next superpower: Babylon. That will happen more than a century later, in 586 BC.

A VISIT to heaven

I saw the Lord. He was sitting on a lofty throne. . . . Attending him were mighty seraphim, each having six wings. . . . They were calling out to each other, "Holy, holy, holy is the LORD of Heaven's Armies! The whole earth is filled with his glory!"

ISAIAH 6:1–3

In a terrifying vision, Isaiah finds himself standing in heaven's throne room in the presence of God. The time is 740 BC, the year King Uzziah dies.

"It's all over!" Isaiah says. "I am doomed, for I am a sinful man" (Isaiah 6:5). He knows God is holy and that sin can't survive in God's presence.

But instead of destroying Isaiah, God purifies him in a ritual somewhat similar to a ritual the Jewish high priest performs on Yom Kippur (Day of Atonement), the nation's annual day of repentance. The priest brings into the Jerusalem temple's most holy room an incense burner with burning coals taken from the temple altar. There, he sprinkles fragrant incense onto the coals, filling the room with a scented cloud.

In Isaiah's vision, God's throne room looks like a temple, too—a more wonderful version of the Jerusalem temple. In this heavenly temple, a mysterious angelic being called a seraphim uses tongs to pick up a piece of coal from the altar. Then he touches it to Isaiah's lips in an apparently painless act, representing a cleansing by fire. Isaiah can now speak the holy words God has for the Jewish people.

Isaiah's first message seems to describe the spiritual condition of the Jewish people. He's to say to them: "Listen carefully, but do not understand. Watch closely, but learn nothing" (Isaiah 6:9). In more than two centuries as a nation, they still don't understand what it means to be God's people.

When Isaiah asks how long he has to keep delivering God's message to the Jews, he gets a grim reply: "Until their towns are empty, their houses are deserted, and the whole country is a wasteland; until the LORD has sent everyone away, and the entire land of Israel lies deserted" (Isaiah 6:11–12).

BABYLON
Daniel, 600s–500s BC
Ezekiel, 593–571 BC

ASSYRIA
Jonah, 700s BC
Nahum, 600s BC

Sea of Galilee

Mediterranean Sea

ISRAEL
Hosea, 700s BC
Amos, 760 BC

Jordan River

JUDAH
Micah, 742–687 BC
Isaiah, 740–700 BC
Zephaniah, 640 BC
Habakkuk, 600s BC
Jeremiah, 627–586 BC
Haggai, 520 BC
Zechariah, 520–518 BC
Malachi, 400s BC

Dead Sea

LOCATION UNKNOWN
Joel, date unknown

EDOM
Obadiah, after 586 BC

When and Where Prophets Ministered

THE FIFTH Gospel

"The virgin will conceive a child! She will give birth to a son and will call him Immanuel. . .'God is with us.' "

ISAIAH 7:14

Writing more than 700 years before Jesus is born, Isaiah sounds like a time traveler who witnessed the birth, ministry, and execution of Jesus. New Testament writers recognize the prophecies about Jesus, and quote Isaiah some 50 times—more than any other book in the Old Testament.

This is why some scholars call Isaiah "The Fifth Gospel." Matthew, Mark, Luke, John, and Isaiah.

Like many prophecies, most of Isaiah's apparent predictions about Jesus seem to fit two eras in history: Isaiah's day as well as a time in the distant future.

Isaiah's prophecy about a virgin giving birth to a child refers first to Isaiah's day. The northern Jewish nation of Israel has teamed up with Syria to rebel against the Assyrian Empire. When Judah refuses to join the coalition, Israel and Syria plan to attack Judah. Isaiah tries to reassure his king, Ahaz, that the invasion will never happen.

Isaiah points out a particular "virgin"—the Hebrew word can also be translated "young woman." This woman might be Isaiah's wife, or perhaps the king's wife. Whoever the woman is, by the time her son is old enough to know right from wrong, "the lands of the two kings you fear so much will both be deserted" (Isaiah 7:16).

Matthew's Gospel picks up this passage, uses a word that can mean only "virgin," and then declares that it's one of many prophecies from Isaiah that point to Jesus. A few others:

- "For a child is born to us, a son is given to us. The government will rest on his shoulders. And he will be called: Wonderful Counselor, Mighty God, Everlasting Father, Prince of Peace. His government and its peace will never end" (Isaiah 9:6–7).
- "There will be a time in the future when Galilee. . .will be filled with glory. The people who walk in darkness will see a great light" (Isaiah 9:1–2). Galilee, in northern Israel, was Jesus' hometown region and main area of ministry.
- "Say to those with fearful hearts, 'Be strong, and do not fear, for your God is coming.' . . .And when he comes, he will open the eyes of the blind and unplug the ears of the deaf. The lame will leap like a deer, and those who cannot speak will sing for joy" (Isaiah 35:4–6).
- "The LORD has anointed me to bring good news to the poor. He has sent me to comfort the brokenhearted and to proclaim that captives will be released and prisoners will be freed" (Isaiah 61:1). Jesus read this passage to His hometown crowd in Nazareth and declared, "The Scripture you've just heard has been fulfilled this very day!" (Luke 4:21).

DEAD SAVIOR

One of the biggest surprises in the Bible is the kind of Messiah God sent to save Israel.

Jews expected a warrior. Someone like King David, only better. A leader who would free them from oppressors, restore Israel's lost glory, and even create heaven on earth:

"In that day the wolf and the lamb will live together... a little child will put its hand in a nest of deadly snakes without harm. . . . The earth will be filled with people who know the LORD" (Isaiah 11:6, 8–9).

Jesus won't be that kind of Messiah—at least not in his first coming. Many scholars say the Bible's scenes of a glorious Messiah have to wait for Jesus' second coming.

In the first coming, Jews won't get a victorious king on a golden throne. They'll get an executed rabbi on a stone slab. New Testament writers point to Isaiah 53 and say that this should have come as no surprise.

Isaiah describes the suffering and death of Jesus with such theological and historical accuracy that the words read more like history than prophecy. Yet a surviving copy of Isaiah's book, found among the Dead Sea Scrolls, dates to 100 years before Jesus. There's no way it could be history passed off as prophecy.

In what many Christians have come to call the Suffering Servant passage, Isaiah describes Jesus as a servant-minded Savior who gives his life for others:

- "Despised and rejected—a man of sorrows, acquainted with deepest grief."
- "Pierced for our rebellion, crushed for our sins. . . . He was whipped so we could be healed."
- "The LORD laid on him the sins of us all."
- "Led like a lamb to the slaughter...he did not open his mouth."
- "He had done no wrong."
- "He was buried like a criminal; he was put in a rich man's grave" (Isaiah 53:3, 5–7, 9).

BAD NEWS for Israel

In a single day the LORD will destroy both the head and the tail. . . . The leaders of Israel are the head, and the lying prophets are the tail.

ISAIAH 9:14–15

By the time Isaiah begins his ministry, in 740 BC, the breakaway northern Jewish nation has had nothing but godless kings—for its entire 200-year existence.

Even their system of worship is set up to encourage idolatry. Their first king, Jeroboam, erected golden calves at worship centers in two cities. He did this to encourage northern Jews to worship in their own country instead of at the Jerusalem temple in the southern Jewish nation of Judah. If he could keep his people home, he figured, they wouldn't be tempted to reunite with the southern Jews under a king from David's dynasty.

Compliant prophets, eager to please their kings and enjoy the rewards it brought them, mislead the people—speaking out against true prophets and justifying nationwide injustice and exploitation of the helpless. During the reign of King Ahab and Queen Jezebel, the queen executes as many true prophets as she can round up. Her plan is to turn Israel into a nation that worships Baal, the Canaanite god of fertility in field, flock, and family. The prophet Elijah sidetracks that plan in a battle of the gods on Mount Carmel. He's able to call down fire from the sky—something Jezebel's 850 prophets can't do. Afterward, Jewish onlookers rally to Elijah's command to execute the pagan prophets, as God's law instructs: "Anyone who sacrifices to any god other than the LORD must be destroyed" (Exodus 22:20).

Yet in spite of this dramatic miracle and the people's support for God, the godless leaders win out in the long run.

Isaiah lives to see the northern kingdom fall.

The collapse begins when Israel decides to unite with some neighboring nations to break free from the Assyrian Empire and its high taxes. Israel and Syria, led by their kings Pekah and Rezin, try to strong-arm Judah into joining the coalition. Judah refuses. Israel and Syria fear this means they might have to fight battles on two fronts: Assyria in the north and Judah in the south. So they plot a preemptive strike against Judah, intending to install a king who will join their coalition.

Judah's king Ahaz—acting against Isaiah's advice—calls on Assyria for help. The Assyrians arrive in 732 BC and crush the coalition army. But they also decimate much of Judah, as well, reducing both Jewish nations to near starvation.

Ten years later, in 722 BC, Israel's king Hoshea tries again to break free of Assyria. This time the Assyrians, their patience exhausted, wipe out Israel's cities—including the capital, Samaria. Most Jews lucky enough to survive are led off into captivity, never to return. Assyria repopulates the land with their own pioneers, many of whom marry the few Jews left behind.

This mixed race will become Samaritans, hated by Jews in Jesus' time as half-breeds and heretics said to practice a distorted form of Judaism. Samaritans revere only an edited version of the first five books in the Bible. And they worship on Mount Gerizim instead of Jerusalem. Gerizim is the "hill of blessing" where Moses told the Jews to read God's promises of blessing after they entered the promised land of Canaan (Deuteronomy 11:29).

DOOMSDAY

Look! The LORD is about to destroy the earth and make it a vast wasteland.

ISAIAH 24:1

Nicknamed the "Apocalypse of Isaiah," chapters 24–27 paint the horrifying picture of a dead planet. Something terrible happens—something so devastating that it changes the contours of the earth's surface.

Any number of natural disasters could do this: global droughts or global flooding,

Planet killer. Thundering thousands of miles an hour, a meteor the size of a nation crashes to earth in an artist's rendering. Some wonder if this is what Isaiah meant when he warned that God would demolish the world: "He devastates the surface of the earth. . .only a few are left alive" (Isaiah 24:1, 6).

earthquakes, volcanoes, massive meteors. Any one of these could decimate life on a planetary scale. So could another world war that draws from the arsenals of nuclear, biological, and chemical weapons.

But any search for clues to identifying the specific disaster will end in frustration. The clues lead in too many directions:

"They are destroyed by fire" (verse 6). Could this refer to volcanoes or war?

"Grapevines waste away" (verse 7). Drought?

"Destruction falls like rain from the heavens" (verse 18). Meteors?

"The earth has broken up. It has utterly collapsed; it is violently shaken. The earth staggers like a drunk. It trembles like a tent in a storm" (verses 19–20). Earthquakes?

Actually, Isaiah may not have any of these disasters in mind. His prophecy, like most in the Bible, is written in poetic verse and is full of symbolism.

Whatever disaster takes place, one thing is clear: God is behind it. "The earth suffers for the sins of its people, for they have twisted God's instructions, violated his laws, and broken his everlasting covenant. Therefore, a curse consumes the earth. Its people must pay the price for their sin" (Isaiah 24:5–6).

After the disaster, chaos follows. "Every home is locked to keep out intruders. Mobs gather in the streets, crying out for wine. . . . The city is left in ruins. . . ." Throughout the earth the story is the same—only a remnant is left (Isaiah 24:10–13).

Even if this disaster leads to the end of human life on earth, it's not the end as far as God is concerned.

In supernatural scenes that look like they are rerun in the closing chapters of Revelation,

Isaiah describes a great banquet for God's people. "He will swallow up death forever! The Sovereign LORD will wipe away all tears. . . . In that day the people will proclaim, 'This is our God! We trusted in him, and he saved us!' " (Isaiah 25: 8–9; see Revelation 21:3–4).

BAD NEWS for the Middle East

The LORD *is enraged against the nations. His fury is against all their armies. He will completely destroy them, dooming them to slaughter.*

ISAIAH 34:2

God will see to it that invaders overrun Israel and Judah. It's going to happen because, generation after generation, the two Jewish nations break their agreement to obey God's laws. Instead of obeying and reaping the promised rewards of blessing, they choose disobedience and the punishment that comes with it—punishment written into the ancient contract in Moses' time.

But punishment for sin isn't reserved just for God's chosen people.

The prophet Habakkuk once asked God why he would punish the Jews by sending invaders from Babylon. As sinful as the Jews are, Habakkuk complains, they are still "more righteous" than "the wicked" Babylonians (Habakkuk 1:13).

God's answer to Habakkuk, and his promise to Isaiah, is that the other nations will get what they deserve, too. The punishment for sin is death. It has been that way since the beginning of human history, when God warned Adam and Eve that eating forbidden fruit would be a fatal mistake. Those first nibbles, many Bible experts speculate, not only brought sin into the world—they brought death, as well. Until then, there is no mention of death in the creation story.

One nation at a time, Isaiah reveals what God has in store for them. It's nothing to look forward to. These are some of the key nations, and the fate that Isaiah says awaits them.

- **Assyria.** Based in what is now Iraq, this empire stretches from modern-day Iran to Egypt. Famed for its vicious terror tactics, such as impaling captives, this empire erases Israel from the political map in 722 BC.

  God's word for them: "After the Lord has used the king of Assyria to accomplish his purposes. . .he will turn against the king of Assyria. . . . When you are done destroying, you will be destroyed" (Isaiah 10:12; 33:1).

- **Babylon.** Also based in Iraq, Babylonians overpower Assyria in 612 BC and become the world's new superpower. They erase Judah from the map in 586 BC. But a coalition force of Persians and Medes from what is now Iran crushes Babylon in 539 BC.

  God's word for them: "I will stir up the Medes against Babylon. . . . I will make an end to all the groaning Babylon caused" (Isaiah 13:17; 21:2).

- **Philistia.** A seafaring Mediterranean race perhaps from Crete, the Philistines immigrate to the coast of what is now Israel about the same time Joshua arrives with the Israelites. The two neighbors fight off and on for centuries, until the Philistines are gradually assimilated into other Middle Eastern cultures.

God's word for them: "Melt with fear, you Philistines! A powerful army comes like smoke from the north" (Isaiah 14:31).

- **Moab.** Located in modern-day Jordan, the Moabites fight many battles with Jews over the centuries. An ancient record etched in stone and called the Moabite Stone (photo on page 107) reports one of Moab's victories over the Jews.

  God's word for them: "The bravest warriors of Moab will cry out in utter terror. . . . The people of Moab will worship at their pagan shrines, but it will do them no good. . . no one will be able to save them" (Isaiah 15:4; 16:12).

- **Damascus.** Oasis town and capital of Syria, Israel's neighbor to the northeast was often Israel's enemy and sometimes an ally.

  God's word for them: "The city of Damascus will disappear! It will become a heap of ruins" (Isaiah 17:1).

- **Ethiopia.** In Bible times, this nation was in what is now southern Egypt and its neighbor to the south, Sudan.

  God's word for them: "Listen, Ethiopia—land of fluttering sails that lies at the headwaters of the Nile. . . . Your mighty army will be left dead in the fields" (Isaiah 18:1, 6).

- **Egypt.** Like Damascus, Egypt was sometimes Israel's best ally and sometimes its worst oppressor.

Bad News
for two empires and nine nations

God's word for them: "I will hand Egypt over to a hard, cruel master. . . . The king of Assyria will take away the Egyptians and Ethiopians as prisoners. He will make them walk naked and barefoot, both young and old, their buttocks bared, to the shame of Egypt" (Isaiah 19:4; 20:4).

- **Edom.** South of the Dead Sea, in what is now Jordan, the Edomites refused to let Moses and the Israelites of the Exodus cross through their land on the way to Canaan.

  God's word for them: "Night will soon return. . . . Edom will be paid back for all it did to Israel. The streams of Edom will be filled with burning pitch, and the ground will be covered with fire" (Isaiah 21:12; 34:8–9).

- **Tyre.** A busy seaport city in what is now Lebanon, these people were once business partners with David and Solomon, providing cedar lumber for the Jerusalem palaces and temple. Queen Jezebel came from this land, bringing to Israel the worship of Baal and other pagan gods.

  God's word for them: "Weep, O ships of Tarshish, for the harbor and houses of Tyre are gone!" (Isaiah 23:1).

Within about a century after Isaiah, all of these nations and empires fall to invaders—if not the Assyrians or the Babylonians, or both, to the Persians who come next.

NOW SOME good news

How can you say the LORD does not see your troubles. . . . Those who trust in the LORD will find new strength. They will soar high on wings like eagles. They will run and not grow weary. They will walk and not faint.

ISAIAH 40:27, 31

Sometimes called Second Isaiah—because the setting jumps about a century and a half after Isaiah's time—chapters 40 through the rest of the book describe a new and upbeat era in Jewish history. God has heard the prayers of his people, who are exiled in Babylon for their sins. Their punishment is ending. The people are coming home to rebuild their country.

In 586 BC Babylonian invaders had overrun Judah, the last surviving Jewish nation. They took their Jewish captives back to Babylon, where they could keep an eye on them. But about 50 years later, Persia crushed Babylon and took control of the Middle East, becoming the world's new superpower. The Persian emperor Cyrus, named half a dozen times in Isaiah's prophecy (chapters 44, 45, 48), released the Jews to go home and rebuild their nation. One of Cyrus's documents, a clay cylinder etched in wedge-shaped cuneiform writing, confirms that he freed all Babylon's political prisoners. (See picture on page 128.)

God tells the Jews what's behind all this: "Though I have destroyed you in my anger, I will now have mercy on you through my grace" (Isaiah 60:10).

Israel's rebuilt Jerusalem will become a shining city. In some of Isaiah's poetic descriptions, it sounds like he's describing more than the capital and nation rebuilt in the 500s–400s BC. It sounds like he's extending the description to some era in a distant idealistic future—one that sounds remarkably like the New Jerusalem of Revelation.

Many Bible experts, in fact, say that though much of Isaiah deals with ancient history that has already been played out, some of the closing chapters don't. They deal with events still ahead.

Isaiah 60	Revelation 21
No longer will you need the sun to shine by day, nor the moon to give its light by night, for the LORD your God will be your everlasting light (v. 19).	The city has no need of sun or moon, for the glory of God illuminates the city, and the Lamb is its light (v. 23).
All nations will come to your light (v. 3).	The nations will walk in its light (v. 24).
Your gates will stay open around the clock (11).	Its gates will never be closed at the end of day because there is no night there (25).

Still ahead is the day of judgment: "See, the LORD is coming with fire, and his swift chariots roar like a whirlwind. He will bring punishment with the fury of his anger and the flaming fire of his hot rebuke" (Isaiah 66:15).

But there's life after judgment, as well. With excitement, Isaiah points to "new heavens and earth" and the fulfillment of God's plan of salvation when the Lord says, "All humanity will come to worship me" (Isaiah 66:22–23).

WHAT HAPPENED TO ISAIAH?

A Jewish legend says there were two Isaiahs, literally.

Scholars today argue about the possibility of two Isaiahs—two writers of the book. But an ancient Jewish book called the Martyrdom and Ascension of Isaiah says there really were two Isaiahs—two halves of the one man. The evil king Manasseh, this book reports, ordered Isaiah cut in two with a wooden saw. It was punishment for predicting the fall of Judah.

Some Bible experts say one of the New Testament writers probably had this story in mind when he spoke about Old Testament saints getting "sawed in half" (Hebrews 11:37).

JEREMIAH

WATCHING THE LIGHTS GO OUT IN JERUSALEM

Jeremiah not only predicts what is perhaps the worst disaster in Jewish history, on a scale with the Holocaust, he lives to see it—and to curse the day he was born.

He's just a young boy when God chooses him to deliver messages to the only Jewish nation that's left: Judah, in what is now southern Israel. The northern Jewish nation of Israel is already nothing but a tragic page in history. Assyrian invaders decimated the country a century before Jeremiah, exiling the survivors and resettling the land with foreign pioneers.

Judah is doomed to the same destiny. Invasion. Decimation. Exile. That's Jeremiah's message. That's what he lives to see.

But like most prophets in the Bible, he also delivers good news: God will restore the nation. The Jews will get a second chance.

With creativity and persistence Jeremiah delivers God's message. Sometimes he acts out the prophecies. And when the king in anger burns Jeremiah's scroll of prophecy, Jeremiah writes the expanded edition we have today.

Babylonian invaders from what is now Iraq destroy the Jewish cities, saving the capital stronghold of Jerusalem for last. Jeremiah survives the attack. And because he had urged the Jewish king to surrender—advice the king ignored—the Babylonians free Jeremiah.

He wants to stay in his homeland. But some Jewish survivors force him to flee with them to Egypt. They do so even after Jeremiah warns that if they go, "You can be sure that you will die from war, famine, and disease" (Jeremiah 42:22).

They go anyhow, and take Jeremiah with them. He is never heard from again.

Getting it in writing. Sitting comfortably on display in the Louvre Museum of Paris is this statue of an ancient Middle Eastern scribe—a professional writer who hired out his skills in literacy. Jeremiah dictated his prophecies to just such a writer, a man named Baruch.

MAIN POINT:

God will punish the Jewish people for their long history of sinning. He will allow invaders to overrun the country and exile the Jews from their homeland. But in 70 years he will bring the Jews home and give them a fresh start.

WRITER:

"As Jeremiah dictated all the prophecies that the LORD had given him, Baruch wrote them on a scroll" (Jeremiah 36:4). Baruch was Jeremiah's assistant. Stories accompanying the prophecies may have been added by Baruch or another writer.

DATE:

Jeremiah's ministry spans about 40 years, from 627–586 BC. That's from "the thirteenth year of the reign of Josiah... until the eleventh year of the reign of King Zedekiah. ... In August of that eleventh year the people of Jerusalem were taken away as captives" (Jeremiah 1:2–3).

LOCATION:

Jeremiah delivers his prophecies in Jerusalem, capital of the southern Jewish nation of Judah.

THE BOY prophet

"O Sovereign LORD," I said, "I can't speak for you! I'm too young!"

JEREMIAH 1:6

Jeremiah starts his book by reporting that he tried to talk God out of turning him into a prophet.

Jeremiah has good reason for trying to get out of this divine appointment. Prophecy at this moment in history is a thankless job. Prophets deliver mostly bad news. News like this: "The bodies of my people will be food for the vultures. . . . I will put an end to the happy singing and laughter in the streets of Jerusalem. . . . The land will lie in complete desolation" (Jeremiah 7:33–34).

People hate prophets for talking like that. And people running the country hate it even more because it sends the signal that they're doing a lousy job.

Jeremiah isn't the only Bible prophet who has tried to get out of the job. Moses tried, too. He said he wasn't a good speaker. Jonah tried, as well. But instead of arguing with God, he simply ran away. He boarded a ship sailing in the opposite direction he was supposed to go. But a fish caught him and tossed him back.

Jeremiah's excuse is that he's too young. He never says how young. But the Hebrew word that describes him is often translated as "boy" or "child." He may have been just a teenager, perhaps as young as 13. That's the age at which Jewish tradition says boys can start accepting religious responsibilities.

Whatever his age, he loses the debate. He is, after all, arguing with God. Appearing in a vision, God says he created Jeremiah for this job. "Before you were born I set you apart and appointed you as my prophet to the nations" (Jeremiah 1:5).

"Don't say, 'I'm too young,' " God tells the boy. "Go wherever I send you and say whatever I tell you. And don't be afraid of the people, for I will be with you and will protect you. I, the LORD, have spoken" (Jeremiah 1:7–8).

GOD AS a trade-in

"My people have exchanged their glorious God for worthless idols! The heavens are shocked at such a thing."

JEREMIAH 2:11–12

Just as Isaiah did earlier, Jeremiah lays out God's case against the Jews. Parts of the message actually sound a bit like a trial lawyer's opening statement.

"My people have done two evil things," God says. "They have abandoned me—the fountain of living water. And they have dug for themselves cracked cisterns that can hold no water at all" (Jeremiah 2:13).

This is a word picture—a graphic way of saying the people have abandoned God and put their trust in something as useless as a cracked pot. A cistern is an underground storage pit, often chiseled out of the native limestone bedrock and waterproofed with plaster. People dug cisterns close to a home or a village and stored water in them. The water may come from runoff during occasional showers in this dry region. And sometimes people haul water from distant streams and wells.

Pouring water into a cracked cistern is good for only a cardiovascular workout. So doing that is actually smarter than what the Jews are doing. Instead of worshipping God, they're worshipping idols—which is good for nothing but trouble.

Different prophets in the Bible focus on different offenses the Jewish people have committed. Amos, for example, zeroes in mainly on rich folks exploiting everyone else. But Jeremiah's complaint is about the underlying problem: The people have rejected God. They've traded him in on idols. And they act like it—lawless. Every man for himself.

How bad have the Jews become? "Even faithless Israel is less guilty than treacherous Judah!" (Jeremiah 3:11).

That should have given the Jews a clue about where they were headed. As punishment for persistent idolatry—and as predicted by various prophets—God erased the northern Jewish nation of Israel from the world map. He did it in 722 BC, about a century before Jeremiah started his ministry. Assyrians from what is now Iraq leveled the Israelite cities and exiled most of the Jewish survivors.

"How can I pardon you?" God asks the Jewish people in another graphic word picture. "I fed my people until they were full. But they thanked me by committing adultery and lining up at the brothels" (Jeremiah 5:7).

God won't pardon those who refuse to admit their guilt. So he tells his prophet, "Pray no more for these people. . .for I will not listen to you" (Jeremiah 7:16).

Time is up for the last surviving Jewish nation. The end is near.

CRYING time

"If only my head were a pool of water and my eyes a fountain of tears, I would weep day and night for all my people who have been slaughtered."

JEREMIAH 9:1

Jeremiah's nickname is "the Weeping Prophet." It's not only because he cries—and with good reason. It's also because he's credited with writing the saddest book in the Bible: Lamentations. This is a horrifying eyewitness account of the siege and sack of Jerusalem—with starving Jewish mothers cooking their own children for food.

Knowing what lies ahead for his people, Jeremiah cries out to God. There's no point in praying for deliverance. God has already told him not to bother—the nation has chosen its fate. So Jeremiah pours out his pain: "Oh, how I hurt! How I hurt! I am bent over in pain. Oh, the torture in my heart! My heart is pounding inside me" (Jeremiah 4:19 NCV).

When God called young Jeremiah as a prophet, God said Jeremiah was born for this mission. That's why it's so shocking to hear Jeremiah say, "I curse the day I was born! . . . I curse the messenger who told my father, 'Good news—you have a son!'. . . Oh, that I had died in my mother's womb, that her body had been my grave" (Jeremiah 20:14–15, 17).

Yet that's how hopeless he feels. A holocaust is coming. And there is nothing he can do to stop it.

ACTING OUT PROPHECIES

Like Isaiah and Ezekiel, Jeremiah acted out some of his prophecies. It made a bigger impression, and it helped people remember what he said.

Jeremiah's act	God's message
Jeremiah hid a linen belt in a hole until the cloth rotted.	"This shows how I will rot away the pride of Judah and Jerusalem" (Jeremiah 13:9).
He didn't marry.	Families in Jerusalem will die and "no one will mourn for them or bury them" (Jeremiah 16:4).
He didn't go to parties.	"In your own lifetime…I will put an end to the happy singing and laughter in this land" (Jeremiah 16:9).
He bought a clay jar and shattered it in front of city leaders.	"As this jar lies shattered, so I will shatter the people of Judah and Jerusalem beyond all hope of repair" (Jeremiah 19:11).
With Babylonian invaders surrounding Jerusalem, he bought a nearby plot of land.	"Someday people will again own property here in this land and will buy and sell houses and vineyards and fields" (Jeremiah 32:15).

END OF JEWISH nation is near

Hear the terrifying roar of great armies as they roll down from the north. The towns of Judah will be destroyed.

JEREMIAH 10:22

For two centuries before Jeremiah's prophecy, the world's superpower hailed from north of the Jewish homeland. First the Assyrians. Then the Babylonians. Both empires made their capital in what is now Iraq. Assyrians had wiped out the northern Jewish nation of Israel in 722 BC. Then the Babylonians overpowered the Assyrians about 15 years into Jeremiah's ministry, in 612 BC. Babylon remains in control during the rest of Jeremiah's lifetime. So depending on when people hear Jeremiah's gloomy prediction, those who believe it probably figure the "great armies" are either Assyrian or Babylonian.

Both fit Jeremiah's description: "A great nation is rising against you from far-off lands" (Jeremiah 6:22). Assyria was headquartered in Nineveh, near what is now Mosul in northern Iraq. Babylon made its capital in the city of Babylon, about 50 miles south of Baghdad. Either army would have to march between 700–900 miles to get to Jerusalem, depending on the riverside trade route they follow.

Jeremiah eventually identifies the invader: "I will hand the people of Judah over to the king of Babylon" (Jeremiah 20:4).

But who's coming and how far they'll have to travel is the least of the Jewish peoples' concerns. The big worry—at least for Jeremiah—is what's going to happen after the invaders get there.

He breaks the news with eloquence, drama, and vivid images.

- "I hear a cry, like that of a woman in labor, the groans of a woman giving birth to her first child. It is beautiful Jerusalem gasping for breath and crying out, 'Help! I'm being murdered' " (Jeremiah 4:31).
- "I will raise my fist to destroy you. I am tired of always giving you another chance. I will winnow you like grain at the gates of your cities and take away the children you hold dear" (Jeremiah 15:6–7).
- "I will hand this city over to the Babylonians and to Nebuchadnezzar, king of Babylon. . . . The Babylonians outside the walls will come in and set fire to the city. They will burn down all these houses where the people provoked my anger by burning incense to Baal. . . . Israel and Judah have done nothing but wrong since their earliest days" (Jeremiah 32:28–30).

GOD, the potter

"As the clay is in the potter's hand, so are you in my hand."

JEREMIAH 18:6

This single line from a message God sends to the Jewish people could sound reassuring. A reminder that God is in control. But the message comes from an unsettling scene in a potter's shop: The potter working at his wheel doesn't like how the pot is shaping up. So he smashes it into a ball and starts over.

"O Israel," God says, "can I not do to you as this potter has done to his clay?" (Jeremiah 18:6).

God has started over before. The Flood was a do-over. Humanity had become so sinful that God decided to start again with the family of one righteous man: Noah. God offered to start over with Moses, after the Israelites worshipped a golden calf at Mount Sinai. "Leave me alone so my fierce anger can blaze against them," God tells Moses, "and I will destroy them. Then I will make you, Moses, into a great nation" (Exodus 32:10). But Moses convinced God to give the Israelites another chance.

Even now it's not too late for the nation to repent. It's never too late. "If I announce that a certain nation or kingdom is to be uprooted, torn down, and destroyed," God says, "but then that nation renounces its evil ways, I will not destroy it as I had planned" (Jeremiah 18:7–8).

Yet most of Jeremiah's prophecies sound as though the smashing of Judah is a done deal. Does that mean the reference to God's possibly changing his mind is an escape clause Jeremiah inserted, in case the Babylonians don't come? Hardly. When we keep reading we see that the day of smashing is near. And we see why. The Jewish people hear God's offer to forgive them, but they reply, "Don't waste your breath. We will continue to live as we want to, stubbornly following our own evil desires" (Jeremiah 18:12).

It's not too late for Judah to repent, but God knows it's not going to happen. And he knows that the nation needs a big event to serve as a lesson for future generations. Erasing Judah from the world map qualifies.

Pottery lesson. A Middle Eastern potter spins soft clay on a turntable, making a water jug. God told Jeremiah to go to a potter's shop. The potter didn't like how the bowl looked. So he smashed the clay into a ball and started over. God said he was going to do the same thing with the Jewish nation. He would destroy it and start over.

Written in stone. The name of Jeremiah's assistant, Baruch, appears on this dried plug of clay (below)—an impression of his professional seal. It reads "Belonging to Baruch, son of Neriah, the scribe," just as the Bible identifies him. Scribes often sealed a private letter with a glob of wax or clay marked with an imprint of their name. (Picture at left) In notes scribbled on pieces of broken pottery, a Jewish outpost commander reports to Lachish, the last Jewish city Babylon faced on its march to Jerusalem. In this note called "Lachish Letter 1," written shortly before Babylon reached the city, the officer says he hopes God will "cause my Lord [the Lachish commander] to hear words of peace." Tragically, Babylon destroyed Lachish. Archaeologists found the officer's notes among charred ruins by the main gate.

ISRAEL'S promised rebirth

"The time is coming when I will restore the fortunes of my people of Israel and Judah. I will bring them home to this land that I gave to their ancestors, and they will possess it again."

JEREMIAH 30:3

Exiled a thousand miles away in what is now Iraq, Jews lament the loss of their nation. They also fear they have become God's "unchosen people." But Jeremiah says they still have reason to hope.

Each Bible prophet who predicted doom for the Jewish nation—Jeremiah included—assured the people that God would give them a second chance. God would save a remnant and bring them home to rebuild Israel.

"After the seventy years of captivity are over," God promises the Jews, "I will punish the king of Babylon and his people for their sins" (Jeremiah 25:12).

Actually, the captivity lasts only 50 years after the fall of Jerusalem. Persians overrun Babylon in 538 BC and free the Jews and other political prisoners. But the full captivity does last almost 70 years. That's measuring from 605 BC, when Babylon first invades Judah and takes captives—the prophet Daniel among them. Also, the temple is lost for exactly 70 years, from the time of its destruction in 586 BC until its rebuilding and dedication in 516 BC.

THE FIRST Bible burning

After the king had burned the scroll on which Baruch had written Jeremiah's words, the LORD gave Jeremiah another message. He said, "Get another scroll, and write everything again."

JEREMIAH 36:27–28

Baruch is a scribe, a secretary with clout. He's one of relatively few people in the Jewish nation who can read and write. And he makes his living from it. Folks hired scribes when they needed to put something in writing, such as a contract or a bill of sale. Baruch recorded Jeremiah's prophecy on a long strip of leather rolled up into a scroll.

In 605 BC, after about 22 years of ministry, Jeremiah dictates his prophecies to Baruch. This is during the fourth year of Jehoiakim's reign. That's the year Babylon will make its first of three invasions into Judah and will force Jehoiakim to start paying annual taxes to the empire.

It apparently takes about a year to finish the scroll. With the writing done, Jeremiah tells Baruch to read the scroll to worshippers who gather at the Jerusalem temple for the next day of fasting, held sometime in November or December of 604 BC. Afterward, palace officials invite Baruch for a private reading.

Shocked by what they hear, the officials report to King Jehoiakim. One of the officials reads it to the king, who is keeping warm beside a fire in the palace. Each time the official finished reading about three or four columns, "the king took a knife and cut off that section of the scroll. He then threw it into the fire, section by section, until the whole scroll was burned up" (Jeremiah 36:23).

At God's instruction, Jeremiah dictates a new scroll—adding more material, including an ominous message for the king: "He will have no heirs to sit on the throne of David" (Jeremiah 36:30).

King Jehoiakim dies six years later, in 598 BC—shortly after deciding to withhold taxes from Babylon. By the time the Babylonian army arrives, the king's son, Jehoiachin, has ruled for only three months. He surrenders and is promptly replaced with a king of Babylon's choosing. Then Jehoiachin is taken to Babylon as a political prisoner. But he is treated well there, allowed "to dine in the king's presence for the rest of his life" (2 Kings 25:29).

JERUSALEM falls

The Babylonians burned Jerusalem, including the palace, and tore down the walls of the city.

JEREMIAH 39:8

Jeremiah is the only known prophet on record to witness the final destruction of Jerusalem—the last act of erasing the Jewish nation off the world map. Jeremiah describes it briefly

in chapter 39 and again in chapter 52. But the Bible's detailed description waits for the book of Lamentations, an anonymous book that ancient Jewish tradition says Jeremiah wrote.

After Babylon's King Nebuchadnezzar dethrones 18-year-old King Jehoiachin, he replaces him with 21-year-old Zedekiah, a Jew who promises to pay taxes to Babylon. That's in 597 BC. But less than a decade later, a rebellion breaks out in Babylon. Zedekiah figures that Babylon has its hands full with this distraction, so he declares Judah's independence—and stops sending tax money to Babylon.

Nebuchadnezzar arrives at Jerusalem on January 15, 588 BC. (Several date references in Jeremiah can be cross-checked with dates on Babylonian documents, allowing scholars to convert the dates to the modern calendar.) The Babylonian army surrounds the city so no one can come or go. Then they begin the tedious work of breaking through Jerusalem's thick stone walls. One common technique is to tunnel under the wall and then collapse the tunnel. With the ground suddenly falling away, sometimes the stone wall above will drop into the hole—creating a break in the wall.

The siege lasts two and a half years. Lamentations describes Jerusalem's suffering in heartbreaking detail. On July 18, 586 BC, part of the wall collapses. King Zedekiah waits for the cover

Weeping for the exiles. Women grieve over Jews deported from Babylon's apparent staging ground for captives: Ramah, a city north of Jerusalem. Jeremiah prophesied, "A cry is heard in Ramah—deep anguish and bitter weeping. Rachel weeps for her children, refusing to be comforted— for her children are gone" (Jeremiah 31:15). Rachel was the wife of Israel's founding father, Jacob. His dozen sons produced descendants who became the 12 tribes of Israel. Rachel's crown of thorns points to what a New Testament writer considered another fulfillment of this prophecy in the distant future: grief over Bethlehem babies slaughtered by King Herod in his attempt to kill Jesus.

of night, then he abandons his people. Instead of surrendering, as Jeremiah had advised, or fighting as he must have promised his citizens he would do, he runs for his life. And he takes with him what's left of his army.

His army scatters, but Zedekiah heads for food and water in the oasis town of Jericho, 20 miles north. That's where the Babylonians catch up with him. Nebuchadnezzar has a special punishment for this handpicked king of his. Zedekiah gets his eyes gouged out. But only after watching his sons and palace advisors slaughtered. Zedekiah will spend the rest of his cursed life in a Babylonian prison.

In August, Babylonians begin the job of burning and then dismantling Jerusalem, stone by stone: temple, palace, houses, walls. Most Jerusalem survivors, 832 of them, are taken captive to Babylon. Some of the poorest are left to tend the vineyards and fields. Jeremiah is freed because he had advised Zedekiah to surrender. He decides to stay in his homeland. But he doesn't stay long.

Nebuchadnezzar appoints a governor to rule the area, but within a few years—no more than four—Jewish guerrillas assassinate him. Then they flee to Egypt, fearing retaliation. In fact, that retaliation comes in 582 BC. Babylon takes 745 more Jewish captives then.

Jews who flee to Egypt force Jeremiah and Baruch to go with them. It's in Egypt that Jeremiah delivers his last known prophecy. He warns his fellow Jews that Nebuchadnezzar will follow them and "destroy the land of Egypt" (Jeremiah 43:11). The invasion takes place in about 568 BC.

LAMENTATIONS

SADDEST BOOK IN THE BIBLE

As tragic as the Holocaust was in the 1940s, with six million Jews exterminated in a wave of genocide that swept over Europe, there's an event in Jewish history every bit as horrifying. The body count is much less. But the pain and the sense of hopelessness for the survivors are almost unbearable.

The Jews lose more than their holy city, Jerusalem, which invaders burn and methodically disassemble stone by stone. The Jews also lose more than their nation, politically dismantled by the execution or exile of its leaders and most of the citizens. Worst of all, the Jewish people lose their God. Or so they think.

That fear is reflected in the writer's final word—the last note sounded in this short collection of bitterly blue songs called laments:

> Restore us, O LORD, and bring us back
>   to you again!
> Give us back the joys we once had!
> Or have you utterly rejected us?
> Are you angry with us still?
>
> LAMENTATIONS 5:21–22

The writer seems to have been an eyewitness to Babylon's invasion of the southern Jewish nation of Judah in 586 BC. Now, writing from exile in Babylon, he describes the starvation and cannibalism he saw inside Jerusalem during Babylon's two-and-a-half-year siege. The poet

Babylonian blues. Asked to sing about their lost city of Jerusalem, Jewish captives in Babylon refuse. "Beside the rivers of Babylon, we sat and wept as we thought of Jerusalem. We put away our harps, hanging them on the branches of poplar trees" (Psalm 137:1–2). Babylonian soldiers had leveled Jerusalem, stone by stone.

talks, too, about the heartbreak of having to live so far from home.

Then, expressing his sorrow at the nation's sin that caused all this in the first place, he sings his last song. He pleads with God for one more great exodus. He wants to go home.

TEARS for Jerusalem

I have cried until the tears no longer come; my heart is broken.

LAMENTATIONS 2:11

Exiled a thousand miles from Jerusalem, a homesick Jew writes about the city and nation to which he can never return. They don't exist anymore.

The last authentic political king the Jews would ever have—the final branch from David's family tree—Zedekiah made a fatal decision. He stopped sending the taxes Babylon required of all nations in their Middle Eastern empire. Since this was a repeat offense, Babylon's King Nebuchadnezzar decided to waste no more time with the Jewish nation. Instead, he laid it waste. He plundered everything of value, leveled the walled cities, and exiled many of the citizens to Babylon, where he could keep a close watch on them.

The heartbroken songwriter, a survivor of the decimation, writes a collection of songs that sounds like a bizarre cross between a eulogy, a prayer, and an eyewitness police report. In painful, pitiful detail he describes how the Jerusalem citizens suffered through two and a half years of siege and how the invaders demolished the holy city.

A scene sampler of the siege, from chapter 4:

Children of Jerusalem. "Parched tongues... stick to the roofs of their mouths in thirst" (verse 4).

MAIN POINT:

Grief consumes the Jews who survive the decimation of their country and are exiled in what is now Iraq. Deeply repentant for bringing this on themselves because of their sins, they wonder if God will ever forgive them. And they fear he won't.

WRITER:

The book doesn't name its writer. Ancient Jewish tradition credits the prophet Jeremiah. For one reason, the writer seems to have been an eyewitness to the fall of Jerusalem—as was Jeremiah. Also, Jeremiah wrote at least one other book of laments: "funeral songs for [King] Josiah. ...These songs of sorrow have become a tradition and are recorded in *The Book of Laments*" (2 Chronicles 35:25). That's probably a different book, but it shows that Jeremiah knew how to write laments.

DATE:

There's a 50-year window of opportunity for writing Lamentations. The author describes events beginning with Babylon's two-and-a-half-year siege and sack of Jerusalem (588–586 BC). But he writes before the Jews start returning from exile in 538 BC.

LOCATION:

The book is written from exile in Babylon, an empire headquartered in what is now Iraq.

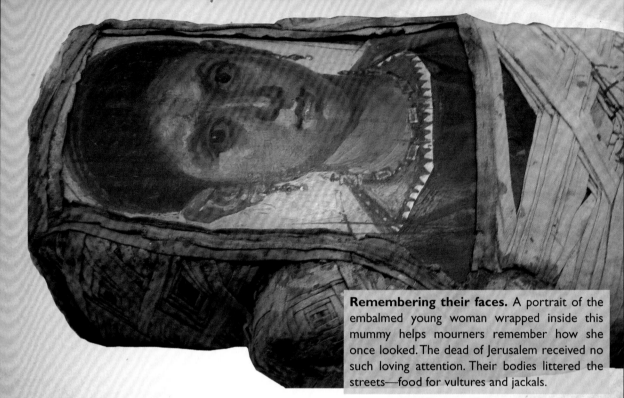

Remembering their faces. A portrait of the embalmed young woman wrapped inside this mummy helps mourners remember how she once looked. The dead of Jerusalem received no such loving attention. Their bodies littered the streets—food for vultures and jackals.

Princes. "Their faces are blacker than soot. No one recognizes them in the streets. Their skin sticks to their bones" (verse 8).

Mothers. "Tenderhearted women have cooked their own children. They have eaten them to survive the siege" (verse 10).

After this grueling siege comes a vicious attack, transforming the glorious city into a rock city—piles of stone blocks from destroyed homes, palaces, temple, and walls. "Jerusalem, once so full of people, is now deserted" (Lamentations 1:1). The roads to Jerusalem, once crowded during festival seasons with happy pilgrims on their way to the temple, are empty.

"For all these things I weep," the poet writes. "My children have no future, for the enemy has conquered us" (Lamentations 1:16).

MENU DURING A SIEGE

Children eventually make it onto the menu, not only in Jerusalem but in other cities besieged in ancient battles.

In Samaria, besieged capital of the northern Jewish nation of Israel, one mother went to the king and complained about another woman. "This woman said to me: 'Come on, let's eat your son today, then we will eat my son tomorrow.' So we cooked my son and ate him. Then the next day I said to her, 'Kill your son so we can eat him,' but she has hidden her son" (2 Kings 6:28–29).

The king ripped his robe in despair.

Invaders knew that one of the best ways to capture a walled city was simply to surround it and wait for the people to die of thirst, starvation, and disease.

A book to take to the wall. A Jewish man prays at Jerusalem's Western Wall, also known as the Wailing Wall because of the crying that occasionally takes place here. Some Jews read Lamentations here each week. It's fitting. The book laments the fall of Jerusalem and the temple. The Western Wall—the holiest place in Judaism—is all that's left of the temple. This stone wall is actually just part of a retaining wall that holds up the hillside where the temple once stood. (For a photo of the Western Wall and the temple hilltop, see page 282.)

ANCIENT SONGS SUNG BLUE

Lamentations' poet didn't break new ground when he wrote a blues song about Jerusalem.

Also on the top ten list of ancient Middle Eastern laments over destroyed cities:

- **Ur**, Abraham's hometown in what is now Iraq. Invaders destroyed it a few decades after Abraham left for Canaan.
- **Sumer**, the world's first known civilized empire, in what is now Iraq.
- **Nippur**, an Iraqi city between the Tigris and Euphrates rivers.

Like Lamentations and similar ancient songs, each of these laments paints graphic images of the dead.

Lament for Jerusalem	Lament for Ur	Lament for Sumer	Lament for Nippur
"See them lying in the streets—young and old, boys and girls, killed by the swords of the enemy....The enemy has killed all the children whom I carried and raised" (Lamentations 2:21–22).	"The streets were piled with dead. In those wide streets, where feasting crowds once gathered, bodies lie jumbled....In open fields once filled with dancers, the corpses lay in heaps. The country's blood pours into ditches, like metal in a mold. Bodies dissolve, like butter in the sun."	"They piled up in heaps, they spread out like stalks of grain cut and scattered.There were corpses floating in the Euphrates River."	"They have piled up the young women, young men and their little children like stacks of grain....They have splashed their blood on the ground like a rainstorm."

THE CULPRIT: sin

Why should we, mere humans, complain when we are punished for our sins?

LAMENTATIONS 3:39

Though it doesn't make the pain any easier to bear, the poet knows the reason for the Jewish tragedy. "Jerusalem has sinned greatly, so she has been tossed away like a filthy rag" (Lamentations 1:8).

It's God doing the tossing. "The Lord in his anger has cast a dark shadow over beautiful Jerusalem. . . . In his day of great anger, the Lord has shown no mercy even to his Temple" (Lamentations 2:1).

For many Jews, the temple was their secret weapon—the source of their invincibility. It was God's home on earth. They couldn't imagine God allowing invaders to violate it, let alone destroy it.

At the temple's dedication God himself told the builder-king, Solomon, "I have set this Temple apart to be holy—this place you have built where my name will be honored forever. I will always watch over it, for it is dear to my heart" (1 Kings 9:3).

Yet the nation's sin is so pervasive and enduring that God withdraws his protection.

FAITH in God anyhow

Great is his faithfulness; his mercies begin afresh each morning. I say to myself, "The LORD is my inheritance; therefore, I will hope in him!"

LAMENTATIONS 3:23–24

The poet understands that his nation is being punished for sin. And he encourages his Jewish readers to repent. Yet he really seems to think that God went over the top in the punishment department.

So he asks God a few questions:

- "Should mothers eat their own children, those they once bounced on their knees?"
- "Should priests and prophets be killed within the Lord's Temple?"
- "See them lying in the streets—young and old, boys and girls, killed by the swords of the enemy. You have killed them in your anger, slaughtering them without mercy. . . . O LORD, think about this! Should you treat your own people this way?" (Lamentations 2:21, 20).

God sometimes answers spiritual leaders such as prophets, usually in a dream or a vision. But there's no indication he ever answers this poet. If Jeremiah is the writer, then he already knows the end of the story. Within a few decades God will take the exiles home and allow them to rebuild their nation. But this writer seems to waffle on that belief.

It's as though he desperately wants to believe it, but he's not sure it will happen. On the one hand, he says, "The anger of the LORD is satisfied" (Lamentations 4:11), and "No one is abandoned by the Lord forever. Though he brings grief, he also shows compassion because of the greatness of his unfailing love" (Lamentations 3:31–32). But his last lines in this sad song raise doubts. "Why do you continue to forget us? Why have you abandoned us for so long? Restore us, O LORD, and bring us back to you again! Give us back the joys we once had! Or have you utterly rejected us? Are you angry with us still?" (Lamentations 5:20–22).

With memories of corpses littering an annihilated Jerusalem, with doubts about his future, and with a sense that he has reached the end of his rope—that he has done all he can do, and it still isn't enough—the poet makes an amazing declaration.

He finds reason to hope.

His reason is God. The writer knows what kind of being God is. God is kind and compassionate. And the evidence is that he spared some of the Jews. If God had not been merciful, the poet argues, all the Jews would have died.

Trusting in God's mercy, the poet exiled from a dead nation declares, "Deep in my heart I say, 'The LORD is all I need; I can depend on him!' " (Lamentations 3:24 CEV).

This poet has walked into a dead end, expecting to find God waiting there to save him.

Suffering from A to Z

There are 22 verses in every Lamentations chapter but one. Chapter 3 has three sets of 22 verses, for a total of 66.

There's a reason for building each chapter around 22 verses. The ancient Hebrew alphabet has 22 letters. Each verse in Lamentations starts with a letter of the alphabet, working from first to last. Verse 1 begins with the letter *aleph*. Verse 2, *beth*. Verse 3, *gimel*. The Hebrew "A, B, C."

A songwriter in Psalms did the same thing with Psalm 119, writing about his love of Jewish laws and tradition (see page 160).

Neither writer explains why he goes to so much trouble. But in the case of Lamentations, some Bible experts wonder if the poet is saying the Jews have suffered everything from A to Z, many times over.

EZEKIEL

MISERY IS GOING TO GET COMPANY

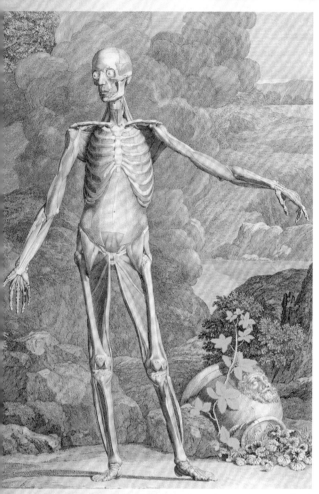

Alive again. The human anatomy, drawn by a medical artist in 1749. Ezekiel's most famous vision takes place in a valley full of human skeletons. Suddenly the bones snap together. Tissues erupt and engulf them. Then, with heaving lungs resuscitated by the wind, the bodies stand—alive. God says what he did for these bones, he'll do for Israel. The nation will live again.

Ezekiel is writing from a bad situation to more than 10,000 fellow Jews in the same situation. They're all exiled a thousand-mile walk from home and living in the heart of the Babylonian Empire, in what is now Iraq.

Babylon had already invaded the Jewish nation twice. First in 605 BC. That was to introduce themselves as the new world super-power replacing Assyria, which they had just crushed. They also took the occasion to demand that the Jews send them tax money each year. The Babylonians came again eight years later, in 597 BC. They did this to collect their taxes after the Jewish king decided to stop sending money.

It was during this second invasion that Babylon took thousands of Jews with them, Ezekiel included. Political prisoners, of sorts, many were free to live as they pleased in Babylon—as long as they didn't try to go home.

Ezekiel is a priest, which means he now has nothing to do. The work of a priest takes place in the Jerusalem temple, which for Ezekiel is a long and forbidden commute. But God gives him a new job. Ezekiel becomes a prophet to the Jewish exiles.

Boiled down to the basics, Ezekiel's message has two points:

- God is going to allow the Babylonians to destroy what remains of the Jewish nation and to exile most Jews who survive the onslaught.
- God will eventually send the Jews back home to rebuild their nation to levels of glory never seen before.

Ezekiel's message, though hard to hear, at least offers hope. It assures the Jews that even though they're in breach of contract for breaking their ancient promise to serve God, they are still the chosen people. God will punish them for their centuries of sin. But punishment isn't God's final word. Ezekiel and the other Bible prophets don't end their messages with doom and gloom. Their messages end with God's punishment achieving its effect: repentance, forgiveness, and restoration.

For Jews in exile, Ezekiel says they can count on going home.

MAIN POINT:

God is going to allow invaders to shut down the Jewish nation, destroying the cities and exiling the citizens. But in time, God will restore the Jewish nation.

WRITER:

Ezekiel, a priest and a prophet. Most of the book is written in the first person of Ezekiel himself. But there are occasional insertions that seem added later, such as "The LORD gave this message to Ezekiel son of Buzi, a priest, beside the Kebar River in the land of the Babylonians" (Ezekiel 1:3).

DATE:

At age 25, in 597 BC, the priest Ezekiel is taken captive to Babylon. Five years later he begins 22 years of ministry as a prophet, from 593–571 BC.

LOCATION:

Babylon, an empire headquartered in what is now Iraq. The empire's capital is also called Babylon, located about 50 miles south of Baghdad. But Ezekiel's first vision takes place beside an irrigation canal called Kebar. That's near the ancient city of Nippur, about 100 miles south of Baghdad.

Mark and his lion. The four Gospel writers are each symbolized by a creature. The lion represents Mark. These connections come from Ezekiel, who sees a vision of four creatures pulling the chariot of God. Early Christian scholars said these creatures symbolize the four evangelists whose Gospels carried God's message to the world.

EZEKIEL'S bizarre calling

"Son of man, go to the people of Israel and give them my messages."

ROMANS ... EZEKIEL 3:4

There's nothing especially unusual about the words God speaks to Ezekiel, calling him to become a prophet. But the pomp and circumstance surrounding those words are so wildly bizarre that some modern readers speculate that Ezekiel sees a UFO. Whatever he sees, it flies. It can turn instantly in any direction. And it's accompanied by creatures that look part human, part animal, and part angel.

Bible books rated PG-30

Some scenes in Ezekiel are horrifying—with symbolic writing at times beyond comprehension. For these reasons, some early rabbis banned the book for anyone under the age of 30. The Song of Solomon was banned by some, as well, because of its erotic dialogue.

Some Jewish interpreters say Ezekiel's description brings to mind the Ark of the Covenant, the gold-plated chest that held the 10 Commandments. That's partly because the flying object contains God, as though it's a celestial chariot carrying his throne. The ark is described as the Lord's "chariot," complete with "gold cherubim whose wings were stretched out over the Ark" (1 Chronicles 28:18).

Everything Ezekiel sees is part of a vision, perhaps during a trancelike state. God generally spoke to prophets through dreams and visions.

Five years into Ezekiel's exile, in the year 593 BC, 30-year-old Ezekiel has this vision in which he sees God approaching him. At first, it looks like a storm coming—led by a massive cloud consumed in light, some flashing.

Out of the cloud emerge four humanoid creatures, each with four wings and four faces: human, lion, ox, and eagle. They're pulling what appears to be God's throne loaded onto a chariot. "On this throne high above was a figure whose appearance resembled a man" (Ezekiel 1:26).

Some early Christian writers, such as Irenaeus in the AD 100s, said these four creatures symbolize the evangelists believed to have written the four Gospels. Those symbols stuck, and paintings of the evangelists often show them alongside the symbol that represents them: Matthew, with the man; Mark, the lion; Luke, the ox; and John, the eagle. In the minds of some early Christian scholars, these evangelists did what the four creatures of Ezekiel's vision did—they delivered the glory of God.

Ezekiel sees God himself, glowing and surrounded by a halo of light.

Ezekiel falls facedown. But God orders him to stand up and then commissions him as a prophet.

When God, in a vision, called Isaiah into ministry about 150 years earlier, an angel prepared Isaiah to deliver sacred messages by purifying his lips with a piece of coal taken from heaven's altar. Ezekiel,

EZEKIEL'S TEL AVIV

Israel's most cosmopolitan city took its name in 1909 from the first Jewish community to hear Ezekiel's message. The prophet went to "Tel-abib" (Ezekiel 3:15). It means "hill of the spring." It was located beside an irrigation channel near Nippur, between the Tigris and Euphrates rivers. Changing the Arabic spelling to Hebrew, the Jews named their coastal city Tel Aviv to symbolize the rebirth of Israel, which Ezekiel predicted.

however, is given a scroll—to eat. He notices that the scroll is filled with writing on both sides: "funeral songs, words of sorrow, and pronouncements of doom" (Ezekiel 2:10). Even so, Ezekiel says the scroll tastes as sweet as honey. Although no other prophet had a scroll-eating experience like this, Jeremiah at least uses a similar metaphor. "When I discovered your words," Jeremiah said, referring to the full extent of God's message, which included the restoration of Israel, "I devoured them. They are my joy and my heart's delight" (Jeremiah 15:16).

The scene of Ezekiel feasting on the celestial scroll is a graphic way of letting everyone know that the words he will speak are not his own, but God's.

BAD NEWS for Jews

"I am about to bring war upon you. . . . I will kill your people in front of your idols. . . . The place will be littered with corpses, and you will know that I alone am the LORD."

EZEKIEL 6:3–4, 7

Perhaps more than any other Bible prophet, Ezekiel delivers bad news with a flair for drama. Words aren't enough. He draws pictures—sometimes with his actions and sometimes with actual drawings. His first prophecy, in fact, begins with a picture drawn on a clay brick.

"Draw a map of the city of Jerusalem," God tells him. "Surround the city with siege ramps and battering rams" (Ezekiel 4:1–2). This is to show the Jewish exiles what is going to happen back in their homeland.

Next, God tells Ezekiel to show the people why it's going to happen—and why it had already happened to the northern Jewish nation of Israel more than a century earlier. Ezekiel shows them. He lies on his left side for 390 days, described as one day for each year of Israel's

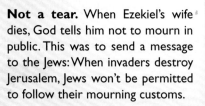

Not a tear. When Ezekiel's wife dies, God tells him not to mourn in public. This was to send a message to the Jews: When invaders destroy Jerusalem, Jews won't be permitted to follow their mourning customs.

Not quite messiah. Immersed in mystical Jewish teachings called *Kabbalah*, Sabbatai Zevi (1626–76) declared himself the promised messiah. Confirming his claim was a young kabbalist rabbi, who considered himself the messiah's forerunner. The young rabbi said he got this insight from a trance. And he predicted that the year of salvation would come in 1666. And so it did, for Zevi. Arrested by Turks that year, Zevi was given a choice: convert to Islam or die. Zevi converted.

JEWISH MYSTICS WITH SECRETS

Ezekiel's strange vision of a flying heavenly throne, in chapter 1, helped launch a new brand of Jewish faith during the time of Jesus: *Kabbalah*. It means "tradition." Believers taught that through fasting, prayer, and secret incantations, a select few could experience Ezekiel-like visions—and more. They could actually encounter God in a personal, mystical way.

God supposedly passed secret knowledge about this on to Moses at Mount Sinai—unwritten law to be hidden from most people. These secrets, passed on by word of mouth, were said to supplement the hundreds of written laws now preserved in the Bible. But only certain people could be entrusted with this special knowledge.

Followers grew to believe that some of their leaders, who served as personal spiritual guides, had achieved this heightened state of insight. These leaders taught about the divine world and its hidden connections to life on this planet, as well as hidden meanings to scripture.

In today's world, rational thinking is generally more popular than a mystical approach. Yet some Jews—especially Hasidic Jews—still practice one of many forms of Kabbalah.

sin. Then he lies on his right side for 40 days, representing 40 years of Judah's sin.

These numbers baffle Bible experts. The northern nation of Israel survived on its own for only about 200 years. And Judah's sinning off and on, depending on the king of the moment, extended more than 300 years. If Ezekiel's numbers are to be taken literally, perhaps the 390 years represent when Israel started sinning during the time of the judges. And perhaps the 40 years represent the especially evil periods of Judah's existence. Scholars offer a variety of other theories, as well.

Numbers aside, the point is that God will punish the Jews for a long history of sinning. In other prophecies that Ezekiel acts out, he:

- *Eats bread cooked over a fire fueled by manure* (Ezekiel 4:15). This shows that the Jews will have to eat unclean (nonkosher) food to survive.
- *Shaves his head and beard, then divides the hair into "three equal parts"* (Ezekiel 5:1). He puts a third in the center of his picture map of Jerusalem and burns it, representing

Jews who will die when the city is burned. He scatters another third on the map and chops it with a sword, representing those killed in the vicinity. And he scatters the final third to the wind, representing those who survive, though many end up exiled.

- *Trembles while eating* (Ezekiel 12:18). This shows that the Jews in Jerusalem and throughout the nation will tremble with fear for their lives as they eat.

What does God have against the Jews?

God had set them apart as a holy nation, as an example of how he wants everyone to live—devoted to him. But not only do the Jews fail to live up to those higher standards, God says, "You have not even lived up to the standards of the nations around you. . . . Because of your detestable idols, I will punish you like I have never punished anyone before or ever will again" (Ezekiel 5:7, 9).

Bare Tyre. Ezekiel predicts the fate of Tyre: The city will be leveled to bedrock. Alexander the Great fulfilled the prophecy some 250 years later. Tyre citizens retreated to a fortress just offshore, on a small island. But Alexander dismantled their city and used the stones, wood, and dirt to build an attack road to the island. Ezekiel's prophecies about Judah's neighbors appear in chapters 25–32.

GOD leaves town

The glory of the LORD moved out from the door of the Temple.

EZEKIEL 10:18

Living in exile, Ezekiel and the other Jews have no place to worship. Many historians speculate that the synagogue got its start here, during the exile. Jews would meet in one another's homes to worship as best they could by reading their sacred writings. One tiny shred of evidence comes from Ezekiel 8. The prophet is at his home, meeting with former leaders of Judah. It's a little more than a year into his ministry—September 17, 592 BC. This precise date is possible because Ezekiel refers to several events in his prophecy that can be cross-checked with dates in Babylonian records.

During this meeting he has another vision. He's transported a thousand miles to Jerusalem. There he sees God's first and most important commandment being broken—in the temple precincts. The commandment: "You must not have any other god but me" (Exodus 20:3). The offense: A statue of an idol, the god of some other nation, stands near the temple altar.

"Do you see the detestable sins the people of Israel are committing to drive me from my Temple?" God asks the prophet (Ezekiel 8:6).

As the vision continues, Ezekiel sees a "cloud of glory" hovering inside the courtyard where the altar is kept. That's the courtyard closest to the sanctuary, where only priests and Jewish men are allowed.

The "cloud of glory" has a long history with the Jews. It starts with the glowing pillar of cloud that led them out of Egypt and into the Promised Land that became Israel.

It continues when they build their first worship center, a tent tabernacle that they carried with them during their 40 years in the badlands. When the tent was completed, "the cloud covered the Tabernacle, and the glory of the LORD filled the Tabernacle" (Exodus 40:34). Whenever the cloud left the tent, this was the cue for Moses and the Israelites to follow along on the next leg of their journey.

When Solomon built and dedicated this very temple that Ezekiel is seeing in his vision, God responded with the honor of his presence: "At that moment a thick cloud filled the Temple of the LORD. The priests could not continue their service because of the cloud, for the glorious presence of the LORD filled the Temple of God" (2 Chronicles 5:13–14). Seeing this, Solomon declared, "O LORD, you have said that you would live in a thick cloud of darkness. Now I have built a glorious Temple for you, a place where you can live forever!" (2 Chronicles 6:1–2).

Forever ends on September 17, 592 BC.

God has left the building. And the city. And the nation.

The Jews will have no one but themselves to stop the next wave of Babylonian invaders. And it won't be enough.

The invaders arrive at Jerusalem four and a half years later, on January 15, 588 BC—after destroying the other walled cities of Judah. The Babylonians surround Jerusalem, sealing it up and starving the citizens for two and a half years. Babylon's soldiers break through the walls on July 18, 586 BC. Then they start killing the citizens and setting fire to the buildings. August is spent dismantling the stone buildings and walls, one stone at a time, until the capital of the Jewish nation looks like a junkyard for cut rock.

Many Jewish survivors are taken captive to Babylon, where they join Ezekiel and the community of Jews exiled years earlier. Some Jews are left behind to tend the fields.

VISIONS of God returning

The glory of the LORD came into the Temple through the east gateway. . . . The LORD said to me, "Son of man, this is the place of my throne and the place where I will rest my feet. I will live here forever among the people of Israel."

EZEKIEL 43:4, 7

WHY "SON OF MAN"?

God addressed Ezekiel with an unusual title—which will later become Jesus' favorite way of referring to himself. The title is "son of man." In the original Hebrew language, it's literally *ben Adam* or "son of Adam" since Adam means "human."

"Mortal" is how some Bible versions translate it.

It seems easy to understand why God would address Ezekiel this way. It's to remind the prophet who is the mighty God revealed in the visions, and who is not.

But why would the divine Son of God pick up where Ezekiel leaves off and adopt the title for himself?

Some Bible experts say it's one way Jesus emphasized his humanity. He came to suffer and die. And he put his glory on hold until he accomplished that.

On the other hand, Jesus may also have had a certain Bible passage in mind. It's one that he figured his followers would notice after he was dead, risen from the grave, and preparing a second coming:

"I saw someone like a son of man coming with the clouds of heaven. . . . He was given authority, honor, and sovereignty over all the nations of the world, so that people of every race and nation and language would obey him. His rule is eternal—it will never end. His kingdom will never be destroyed" (Daniel 7:13–14).

Once the hammer falls on Jerusalem, Ezekiel's message takes a turn for the better. The Jews have lost just about everything. And the good news at the bottom of a pit is that the only way to go is up. That's the message Ezekiel starts preaching. Things are going to get better.

First he targets Judah's neighbor nations. He warns that they'll get what they deserve for treating God's people so horribly for so many years.

Then he gives the Jews a peek into their destiny, with the help of his best-known vision. God whisks him away in spirit to a valley covered in a scattering of human bones. It must have looked like a massacre took place there, with the bodies abandoned. That's exactly what happened to many of the Jews in Jerusalem.

Suddenly, bones all over the valley begin to rattle—snapping back into their joints. Then out of nowhere, tendons, muscles, and skin begin erupting onto the bones, lacing them with humanity. A wind sweeps into the valley, blowing life into the mouths and nostrils of the newly formed bodies. Then those bodies come to life. Much the same thing happened when God blew the breath of life into the first human at creation, and when the Holy Spirit rushed like a windstorm into the upper room at Pentecost, bringing Jesus' disciples back to spiritual life.

"These bones represent the people of Israel," God tells Ezekiel. "Prophesy to them and say, 'This is what the Sovereign LORD says: O my people, I will open your graves of exile and cause you to rise again. Then I will bring you back to the land of Israel'" (Ezekiel 37:11–12).

God is coming back with them. Ezekiel sees this in a vision of a wonderful temple, rebuilt. He sees God returning in that familiar cloud of glory.

Bible experts don't agree on what temple Ezekiel is talking about. Is it the temple that the returning Jews built and dedicated in 516 BC? Some Jewish scholars wonder if it's the temple the Messiah will build when he comes. Or perhaps it's a symbol of some wonderful day ahead—maybe at the end of time—when people worship God as they should in a place forever called by a new name: "The LORD Is There" (Ezekiel 48:35).

Celestial tour guide. A divine being "whose face shone like bronze" (Ezekiel 40:3)—perhaps an angel or God himself—leads Ezekiel through a series of visions. The prophet sees a rebuilt temple and God returning to Jerusalem.

DANIEL

Iraqi Daniel. Escorted out of Jerusalem to Babylon, Daniel spends the rest of his life advising foreign kings of two empires. First in Babylon, 50 miles south of modern-day Baghdad. Later in Susa—modern Shush, Iran—where he advises Persians who over-powered Babylon.

Black Sea

Caspian Sea

Mediterranean Sea

● **Jerusalem**

Babylon ●

Susa ●

Jewish captives bound for Babylon

Persian Gulf

Babylonian Empire

Red Sea

FROM KING'S PALACE TO LIONS' DEN

A prince in Israel, Daniel is just a young man—perhaps in his twenties or even younger—when he's marched into exile a thousand miles from home. He's taken with other Jews to Babylon, in what is now Iraq.

This forced exile is a Babylonian policy of intimidation, intended to show weaker countries who's boss and to arm-twist rulers into sending annual tax money to the empire—or risk losing more top-tier citizens.

Once in Babylon, Daniel impresses the leaders with his intellect and good sense. The king eventually appoints him as one of his advisors. But he's not just another voice in the royal think tank. He earns a reputation for two specialties: dream interpretation and prophecy.

Both of these gifts endear him to one king after another, in both the Babylonian Empire and the Persian Empire that follows. But all the gratitude and special consideration he gets from the king only stirs up jealousy among his fellow advisors. So they conjure up a scheme that lands Daniel in a lions' den. But the plot backfires. Daniel survives. And the king feeds the other advisors to the lions.

After six chapters of storytelling, the book shifts to reporting Daniel's bizarre visions—some so strange that the angel Gabriel has to explain them. Even then, many Bible experts say the explanations could use explanations.

GROOMED for palace duty

"Select only strong, healthy, and good-looking young men. . . . Make sure they are well versed in every branch of learning, are gifted with knowledge and good judgment, and are suited to serve in the royal palace."

DANIEL 1:4

King Nebuchadnezzar is looking for advisors among his political prisoners. So he describes for his chief of staff the qualities that he's looking for among "the young men of Judah's royal family and other noble families, who had been brought to Babylon as captives" (Daniel 1:3).

Those who qualify will enter a three-year course of study at the palace. They'll learn the language and literature of Babylon and everything possible to prepare them for advising the king.

Four Jews impress the staff and are admitted to the program: Daniel and three others, best known by their Babylonian names: Shadrach, Meshach, and Abednego.

As royal students in the king's palace, they are to eat what the king provides. But the Jews want to stay kosher. They don't want to defile themselves spiritually by eating food

MAIN POINT:
Despite appearances, God controls history. In time, he'll prove it.

WRITER:
Bible experts debate who wrote this book. The first seven chapters are stories in the third person, describing events in the life of Daniel and others. The last five chapters are prophecies in Daniel's voice. These prophecies so accurately describe events up until the mid-100s BC that many wonder if this final part of the book was added later—by someone else. Daniel is also written in two languages. About half is in the Jewish language of Hebrew: the introduction and most of the prophecies. But the stories are in Aramaic, the international language spread by Babylonians and Persians. Pieces of a Daniel scroll dating to the 100s BC were found among the famous Dead Sea Scrolls. Some scholars argue that if the book of Daniel had been such a relatively new release, it probably wouldn't have found space in this sacred Jewish library.

DATE:
Daniel's story begins around 600 BC. He serves about 60 years as an advisor to Babylonian and Persian kings.

LOCATION:
Daniel lives in Jerusalem until taken as a political prisoner to Babylon. He serves two empires: Babylon (in what is now Iraq) and Persia (modern Iran).

forbidden in Leviticus 11. This includes pork, animal fat, or any meat not completely drained of blood. "No matter where you live, you must never consume the blood of any bird or animal" (Leviticus 7:26).

Daniel asks if he and his colleagues can observe their kosher diet.

But the chief of staff says, "If you become pale and thin compared to the other youths your age, I am afraid the king will have me beheaded" (Daniel 1:10).

Daniel convinces the man to conduct a 10-day test. Daniel and his colleagues eat only

DREAM INTERPRETER'S HANDBOOK

A dream is sometimes a hint of what lies ahead. That's what many people in ancient times believed: Jews, Egyptians, Assyrians, Babylonians, Persians, Greeks, and Romans.

Dream specialists wrote handbooks about how to interpret dreams. Here's a sampling—for curiosity's sake, not for recommendations:

THE DREAM	THE MEANING
A dog rips your clothing.	Get ready for a financial loss.
You see a "little person" adult.	Your life will be cut in half.
You see stars.	Great fortune awaits you.
You are submerged in water.	You are spiritually clean.
You see yourself sitting naked.	You will lose your possessions.
A white horse appears.	An angel is coming.
Dogs bark.	Crooks are going to steal from you.
You're falling.	You're going to suffer something unpleasant.
You're flying.	You're going to experience some success.
Your hair is cut off.	Get ready for a business failure.
You're running.	Your life is in good shape and secure.
You see yourself dead.	Expect a long life.

vegetables. After 10 days, they look healthier than any others in the program. So the chief of staff allows them to live as vegetarians—which is the only way they can be certain the food prepared for them is kosher. They have no way of knowing if the Babylonian butcher drained the meat of all its blood.

God gives these four Jewish men "an unusual aptitude for understanding every aspect of literature and wisdom" and Daniel "the special ability to interpret the meanings of visions and dreams" (Daniel 1:17).

At the end of their training period, the king chooses all four as his advisors. Daniel will serve Babylonian kings until there is no more Babylonian Empire. About 60 years later, Persians will crush Babylon. But the Persian king will see Daniel's gifts and will keep him on as a valued advisor.

SWEET and sour dreams

"If you don't tell me what my dream was and what it means, you will be torn limb from limb."

King Nebuchadnezzar has two dreams. The first is so troubling that he is fully prepared to kill every palace advisor if one of them can't interpret the dream for him. And to make sure the dream specialist isn't just pretending to interpret the dream, he insists that the interpreter prove himself by telling the king what he dreamed.

The dream specialists draw a blank. So the king orders all of his advisors executed, including Daniel. The first that Daniel hears of this is when guards come to arrest him. Not yet considered a dream specialist, he manages to convince the desperate king to give him time to consider the matter. Daniel and his friends pray. And God reveals the dream to Daniel, who immediately reports it to the king.

In his dream, the king saw a huge and terrifying statue of a man. Topped with a head of gold, the statue's material diminishes in value as it moves downward: silver chest and arms; bronze belly and thighs; iron legs; clay-iron mixture for the feet. A single rock cut from a mountain shatters the statue.

Daniel says the statue's golden head represents the king and his great Babylonian Empire. The other three metals represent inferior kingdoms that will come later. Some scholars point to Medes, Persians, and Greeks.

Daniel says the mountain rock comes from God, who will eventually destroy all other kingdoms and "set up a kingdom that will never be destroyed or conquered" (Daniel 2:44).

In dream number two the king sees a huge tree that provides fruit and shade for the entire world. But then a messenger from heaven chops it down. In what reads like a mixed metaphor, the messenger declares that the tree will go temporarily insane, having "the mind of a wild animal instead of the mind of a human" (Daniel 4:16).

Dreams about a "world tree" show up in other ancient writings and often represent an empire. But in this case, Daniel says the tree represents the king. He will lose his mind, and for a time he'll behave like an animal—eating grass and living outdoors.

This happens a year later while the king is standing on the flat roof of his palace, surveying his kingdom and bragging about how great he is. It's unclear how long the insanity lasts. Daniel simply calls it "seven periods of time," perhaps months, seasons, years, or as long as God considers necessary. "Seven" symbolizes completion in the Bible. God rested on day seven after creation.

However long the insanity lasts, it's long enough for the king's hair to grow as long as "eagles' feathers" and for his nails to look like "birds' claws" (Daniel 4:33). Fingernails, on average, grow about one and a half inches a year. A one-inch nail starts looking clawish.

There's no report of Nebuchadnezzar being sick for a long time. But the Greek historian Megasthenes, who lived about 200 years later, reports that Nebuchadnezzar climbed to his palace roof one day and was inspired by a god. This might be a reference to the insanity, since the ancients sometimes looked on insanity as the opposite of demon possession: divine possession. Or it might refer to what happened next in the king's life.

When his insanity subsides, he turns from bragging about himself to bragging about the most high God, whose "rule is everlasting, and his kingdom is eternal" (Daniel 4:34).

FIREPROOF Jews

"Look!" Nebuchadnezzar shouted. "I see four men, unbound, walking around in the fire unharmed! And the fourth looks like a god!"

DANIEL 3:25

Daniel's three Jewish friends—Shadrach, Meshach, and Abednego—had gotten tossed into a huge furnace for refusing to worship the king's new statue. The statue may have been of the king or of a god; the Bible doesn't say.

The furnace is probably a kiln for melting and refining metal. One ancient furnace discovered in Nippur, about 50 miles south of Babylon, was shaped like a railroad tunnel with a wall sealing one end. Heated by charcoal, ancient kilns could top 1800°F. That's at the high end of a typical cremation chamber today: 1400°F–1800°F.

The heat actually kills the soldiers who push the Jews inside. But when the king looks into the flames, he sees four men walking around. The fourth is described as an angel sent to protect them.

Coded message. Babylon's last king, Belshazzar, is having a party when a hand appears out of nowhere. It writes a cryptic message on the wall: "numbered, numbered, weighed, divided." Daniel interprets the meaning. The days of the king and his kingdom are numbered. Belshazzar's value as a ruler has been weighed and found lacking. So his kingdom will be divided among others. Persian invaders arrive and kill him that very night.

"Come here!" the king calls to them. The three Jews step out, and the king forbids anyone from speaking out against their God.

DANIEL in the lions' den

"Daniel, servant of the living God! Was your God, whom you serve so faithfully, able to rescue you from the lions?"

DANIEL 6:20

That's the sound of a frantic Persian king yelling into a sealed lion's den.

When Babylon falls to Persian invaders in 539 BC, the new ruler springboards elderly Daniel to the top of the political heap. Daniel becomes one of three leading administrators in charge of the new empire's 120 provinces.

The king, according to this story, is Darius the Mede. But this name hasn't turned up among king lists for the Medes, who lived in what is now northern Iran. Nor has the name shown up on king lists among the Persians, in southern Iran. Cyrus was the first king of the Persian Empire. So some Bible experts wonder if Darius was just a governor whom Cyrus put in charge of the region. After all, Daniel never calls Darius king of Persia—only the new king of Babylon.

Whoever Darius is, the favor he shows Daniel feeds the jealousy of other administrators. They plot Daniel's downfall. It's ironic that they decide God is his Achilles' heel—God, as the weak link.

Knowing that Daniel prays three times a day, they convince Darius to sign an irrevocable law about prayer. The law requires all citizens to pledge their allegiance to Darius by praying only to him for the next 30 days.

Daniel's political enemies catch him praying and turn him in.

Panic attack. That might describe the

Daniel and his cats. Cutthroat palace intrigue lands Daniel in a lion pit overnight. His political enemies had played on the king's vanity, convincing him to sign a law ordering everyone to pray only to him for 30 days—or face lions. They turn in Daniel for praying to God. Daniel survives. And the king, angry about being manipulated, sends the connivers to the carnivores.

king's reaction. He spends all day looking for a loophole in the law. Queen Esther's Persian husband faced a similar dilemma after unwittingly ordering a holocaust of the Jews. He wrote a counterlaw, allowing the Jews to protect themselves and encouraging Persian officials to offer their help. But Darius could hardly order the lions not to chew.

God could.

Darius orders the sentence carried out. But he doesn't sleep that night. Early the next morning he rushes to the pit, delighted to find Daniel alive.

Furious at the officials who had put Daniel and him through this ordeal, the king decides to give those men a taste of their own medicine—and the lions a taste of nobility. The officials and their families are fed to the lions. In ancient times, the entire family often paid the price for the father's stupidity. This prevented a son from growing up and trying to get even.

VISIONS of end times

I, Daniel, saw a great storm churning the surface of a great sea, with strong winds blowing from every direction.

DANIEL 7:2

Daniel's book closes with a series of visions so bewildering that the angel Gabriel has to come and explain them. Even then, Gabriel's explanations don't begin to answer all the questions.

In chapter 2, Daniel spoke of four kingdoms. Visions now bring him back to that theme. He sees four animals that represent four world powers. In one vision the beasts are a winged lion, a bear, a winged leopard, and a horrifying creature with iron teeth. And in a second vision he sees a shaggy goat breaking off both horns of a strong ram.

Without naming nations, Gabriel explains that the four creatures of Daniel's first vision represent four world superpowers. In explaining the second vision, however, Gabriel does name nations.

The two-horned ram represents the kings of Media and Persia. The shaggy male goat represents the king of Greece (Daniel 8:20–21). The fourth kingdom may be Babylon—suggested by an earlier reference to a winged lion. Archaeologists have recovered from Babylon's ruins many pictures of winged lions.

As powerful as these four empires are—with Alexander the Great commanding the most territory, from India to Libya—they're just the hint of a speck in the universe compared to what's coming.

"As my vision continued that night, I saw someone like a son of man coming with the clouds of heaven. He approached the Ancient One and was led into his presence. He was given authority, honor, and sovereignty over all the nations of the world, so that people of every race and nation and language would obey him. His rule is eternal—it will never end. His kingdom will never be destroyed" (Daniel 7:13–14).

In his final visions, Daniel sees suffering ahead, along with cosmic battles between angels and demons. But we also read a clear reference to resurrection and eternal life—a rarity in the Old Testament. (For a similar reference in Job, see page 153.) "Many of those whose

Attack of the shaggy goat. Alexander the Great spears a Persian warrior as the king flees for his life in a chariot. Alexander and his Greeks win the battle of Issus in 333 BC, despite 20 to 1 odds against them. Daniel's vision portrays the Greek king as a shaggy goat breaking the two horns of a powerful ram: the Medes and the Persians.

bodies lie dead and buried will rise up, some to everlasting life and some to shame and everlasting disgrace" (Daniel 12:2).

Daniel's most famous vision, however, has Gabriel talking about a perplexing "period of seventy sets of seven" (Daniel 9:24). That, Gabriel says, will mark the end of rebellion and the coming of an "anointed one."

Many scholars interpret the "seventy sets" as 70 years. So "70 years of seven" becomes "70 years times seven"—490 years. Yet others consider the numbers symbolic, meaning that all of these events are completed in God's perfect timing.

Bible experts and those not so expert have interpreted this vision every imaginable way. Some see Daniel's closing visions as a source of clues about the second coming. William Miller, a Bible teacher in the early 1800s, used Daniel's numbers to predict that Jesus would return on October 22, 1843. Miller started by presuming that "2,300 evenings and mornings" (Daniel 8:14) refers to years and that the "anointed one" in chapter 7 points to Jesus.

But many scholars today say Daniel's visions do an excellent job of describing the reign of a Greek tyrant named Antiochus IV Epiphanes (175–164 BC). He executed the Jewish high priests, who, like Israel's kings, were sometimes called God's "anointed ones." He also banned the Jewish religion and desecrated the Jerusalem temple in some way, perhaps by setting up pagan symbols or by sacrificing a forbidden animal such as a pig.

Many Bible experts say Daniel is referring to these events when he says this: "He will put an end to the sacrifices and offerings. And as a climax to all his terrible deeds, he will set up a sacrilegious object that causes desecration, until the fate decreed for this defiler is finally poured out on him" (Daniel 9:27).

Jews rebelled against Antiochus and won their independence.

Daniel's visions have one main point: Suffering lies ahead for God's people, but the suffering will eventually end.

These prophecies point to Daniel's future, in our past. Yet at times it seems that they point to our future, as well: the end times, when God sets up a perfect kingdom. Bible prophecies sometimes get their job done in two time zones. Some of Isaiah's prophecies, for example, spoke of events in his time that later applied to Jesus, as well.

Daniel presses for details. "How will all this finally end?" he asks Gabriel.

Gabriel's answer sounds like good advice for all believers craving more details about future events: "What I have said is kept secret and sealed until the time of the end," Gabriel says. "Go your way until the end. . . . At the end of the days, you will rise again to receive the inheritance set aside for you" (Daniel 12:9, 13).

Killing a snake god with a hair ball. Some Bibles—like those used by many Catholics—tell an extra story about Daniel. Babylonians worship a massive snake as a god. But Daniel feeds it a hair ball lathered with tar. Gradually the tar soaks into the hair, making the hair ball puff up bigger than the snake's stomach. The snake pops and dies.

HOSEA

THE PROPHET AND THE HOOKER

Mrs. Hosea. In perhaps the most bizarre request God makes of any prophet in the Bible, he tells Hosea to marry a prostitute. It's to show how Israel has acted like a prostitute, committing spiritual adultery by worshipping other gods.

This is the story of a match made in heaven.

Far from an ideal marriage, it's a disaster—but that's the point. God wants to give the Jews a living, breathing, physical example of what they are doing to him on a spiritual level.

What they are doing is committing adultery.

They are worshipping foreign gods, especially the chief Canaanite god: Baal. This is a fertility cult. Many Jews consider Baal the source of fertility in field, flock, and family. Though it's disgusting to think about, many of Baal's faithful followers teach that the arid region's life-giving rain is his semen. So they try to stimulate him to shower the earth. They do this by having ritual sex with shrine and temple prostitutes. Some scholars speculate that this reenacts the consummation of Baal's celestial marriage to the goddess Asherah.

So Israel's adultery isn't just spiritual. For many worshippers, it's physical, as well.

God takes dramatic action. He tells one of his prophets, Hosea, to actually marry a prostitute. This is so weird that many ancient rabbis and early Christian leaders didn't believe it. They argued that it's just a story with a moral—about a nation with no morals. A kind of parable, or perhaps a vision the prophet has.

The majority opinion today agrees that it's a type of parable—but a living one. Hosea is a real man who marries a prostitute, Gomer. She has three children, perhaps none of them by Hosea. She runs away. But on God's command, Hosea hunts her down and buys her back from the man who considers her his newly acquired property.

The point of this acted-out parable is not only to show the Jews what they are doing to God. It's to show them what God wants to do to them. He wants to forgive them. He wants reconciliation. But the choice is theirs.

MAIN POINT:

Israel has committed what amounts to spiritual adultery. By embracing foreign gods, the people have been unfaithful to the Lord. Yet God loves them so much that he seeks reconciliation by asking them to give up their false gods and come back to him.

WRITER:

Hosea is typically considered either the writer or the main source behind the book that bears his name.

DATE:

Hosea ministered from roughly 750 to 722 BC, the year Assyrian invaders overran Israel. That means he witnessed the destruction he warned his people about. Rulers at the time were Jeroboam II, in the northern Jewish nation of Israel, and Uzziah, Jotham, Ahaz, and Hezekiah in the southern nation of Judah.

LOCATION:

Hosea lived and prophesied in the northern Jewish nation of Israel.

Fertility god. On display in the Louvre Museum of Paris, Baal, chief god of the Canaanites, carries a club and a budding spear that might represent lightning or fertile crops. Canaanites and many Jews prayed to him for rain and for fertility in fields, flocks, and family.

HOSEA'S arranged marriage

"Marry a prostitute, so that some of her children will be conceived in prostitution. This will illustrate how Israel has acted like a prostitute by turning against the LORD and worshiping other gods."

HOSEA 1:2

Hosea son of Beeri is Israel's prophet of last chance. He's living in this northern Jewish nation during its final two decades. Assyrian invaders will storm in during 722 BC, destroy the cities, exile many of the survivors, and then repopulate the land with foreign pioneers.

God is behind all this. He's punishing Israel for two centuries of sin rooted in idolatry.

But it doesn't have to be this way. There doesn't have to be an invasion. That's the message Hosea delivers more dramatically than any other prophet. God has had other prophets act out some of his messages. Isaiah, Jeremiah, and Ezekiel performed skitlike performances to illustrate a point. Ezekiel throws hair into the wind to show that God will scatter the sinful Jews to the four winds. Hosea, on the other hand, must embrace an entirely new life—and a wife. He doesn't just act out a short scene to make God's point. His life becomes the point.

For Hosea, it's a tough life. But for Israel, it's a tough point. They are committing spiritual adultery by worshipping idols. In fairness, many Jews in Hosea's day don't think of it that way. They believe in God, they perform the right worship rituals, and they give their offerings. But they think of God as just one deity in a gallery of gods—perhaps the strongest god. And they certainly consider him the God of war, since he gave their ancestors victory over the Egyptians and the Canaanites.

But for abundant crops, herds, and lots of children, many Jews turn to Baal and related deities worshipped throughout the ancient Middle East.

Yet rule number one for the Jews is this: "You must not have any other god but me" (Exodus 20:3). It's the first and most important of the 10 Commandments. Spiritual polygamy is nothing but adultery. Hosea's marriage to Gomer illustrates this truth.

It's unclear what kind of prostitute Gomer is. She might be a temple prostitute who works at a pagan temple or shrine. She might scout for customers on the streets and at the busy gateways into the city. Or she might simply be a woman with an earned reputation for promiscuity. Whatever the case, she's not the kind of woman to take home to Mother.

PATTER of little feet

Gomer. . .became pregnant and gave Hosea a son.

HOSEA 1:3

In time, Gomer gives Hosea two sons and one daughter. But the phrasing leaves readers wondering what part Hosea played in the blessed events—if any.

The writer never even hints that Hosea is the biological father of any one of the children. And it's certainly on the minds of readers because God has already told Hosea that his wife would have children "conceived in prostitution" (Hosea 1:2).

Like other prophets, Hosea gives his children symbolic names. They have to live out a message from God just as their father has been doing.

Child 1: a son, Jezreel. "I am about to punish King Jehu's dynasty to avenge the murders he committed at Jezreel. In fact, I will bring an end to Israel's independence. I will break its military power in the Jezreel Valley" (Hosea 1:4–5).

PROPHETS IN THE MINORS

Hosea is the first of a dozen prophets called "Minor Prophets."

It's not that he and his colleagues are minor leaguers compared to the four heavy hitters who appear earlier in the Bible lineup: Isaiah, Jeremiah, Ezekiel, and Daniel—known as the "Major Prophets."

Hosea and the others are "minor" mainly because their books are shorter. Tally the chapters of all 12 books together. The total is 67 chapters. That's just one more than we'll find in the single book of Isaiah.

Jews called the dozen by a different name: The Twelve. And they grouped the dozen together because, as one rabbi taught, "they are small; they might get lost."

Hosea comes first not just because at 14 chapters it's one of the longest. It's also because the story is set at the start of the 300 years covered in these dozen prophecies. Hosea and Amos both prophesied in the mid-700s. Malachi, possibly written in the mid-400s BC, closes the book on the Minor Prophets as well as the Old Testament.

(For stats on the Minors—when and where they ministered—see the map on page 186.)

There seem to be two messages here, one direct and one less obvious. This more direct message targets the Jewish king Jeroboam. He's a great-grandson of Jehu, the chariot corps commander who led the coup a century earlier that overthrew the dynasty of Ahab and Jezebel. Ahab was already dead, but Jehu murdered Ahab's reigning son and the queen mother, Jezebel.

The king and his mother were staying at their getaway palace in Jezreel, overlooking the sprawling valley where armies have fought scores of battles throughout history. The king of the southern Jewish nation of Judah had the bad luck of visiting Jezreel at the time. So Jehu killed him, as well. Then Jehu killed all of Ahab's family, friends, and officials in Jezreel. On top of that, he demanded the heads of Ahab's 70 sons. These sons were living in Israel's capital, Samaria. Jehu had their heads brought to Jezreel and piled them "in two heaps at the entrance of the city gate" (2 Kings 10:8).

The less direct message is wrapped up in the meaning of the word *Jezreel*. The name means "sowing." Back then, farmers sowed most seeds by scattering them on plowed ground. That's how God is going to punish the Jews for their sins. Moses had said as much centuries earlier, warning his fellow Israelites bound for the Promised Land that sin would generate this response: "The Lord will scatter you among all the nations from one end of the earth to the other" (Deuteronomy 28:64).

The chosen ones will become the scattered ones.

Hosea's homeland. Hosea lived in the northern Jewish nation of Israel (see map page 233). He named his first child Jezreel, after the murders that took place there. God promises to crush Israel's military power in the Jezreel Valley (below). It's the site of many ancient battles and a place Napoleon called the perfect battlefield. Some speculate this is the Valley of Armageddon where Revelation says the forces of good and evil will fight one last battle in the end times.

Child 2: a daughter, Lo-ruhamah. Her name means "not loved." This name represents God's message for the Jews if they don't break off their affair with idols: "I will no longer show love to the people of Israel or forgive them" (Hosea 1:6).

Child 3: a son, Lo-ammi. His name means "not my people." God explains the boy's name this way: "Israel is not my people, and I am not their God" (Hosea 1:9).

Israel became God's people at least 500 years earlier, when Moses and the Israelites entered into a binding agreement with God. As long as the Israelites obeyed the laws God gave through Moses, God would protect and bless the nation. But God warned that disobedience was a deal-breaker. Deuteronomy 28 sums up the consequences for any breach of contract. One consequence on the long list: "The LORD will cause you to be defeated by your enemies" (Deuteronomy 28:25).

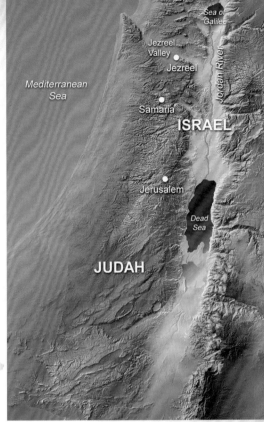

GOD FILES charges against Israel

"Bring charges against Israel. . .for she is no longer my wife, and I am no longer her husband."

HOSEA 2:2

As God does through other Bible prophets, he lays out his charges against Israel. And he does it much as a lawyer would in an opening statement in court.

He starts with a generalization: "There is no faithfulness, no kindness, no knowledge of God in your land" (Hosea 4:1).

Then he gets specific, rattling off a list of offenses:
- lying;
- stealing;
- adultery;
- violence;
- murder;
- idolatry;
- prostitution; and
- sex with temple prostitutes.

These sins break some of the most basic Jewish laws—those from the 10 Commandments, the foundation of all other Jewish laws preserved in the first five books of the Bible.

When a person breaks these laws, there's no point in going through the motions of observing other Jewish laws and traditions. There's no reason to eat only kosher food, practice circumcision, or bring sacrifices and offerings to the priests.

God says he's going to punish the nation for its serial sinfulness. He makes that point in one of the Bible's most famous lines: "They have sown the wind, and they shall reap the whirlwind" (Hosea 8:7 KJV).

Their behavior is as foolish as trying to plant a wisp of air. And for this, they will harvest a fool's crop: a national disaster. "I will send down fire on their cities" (Hosea 8:14). Jews hearing this can't help but think of Sodom and Gomorrah, twin cities seared off the map for their sins.

This isn't God taking out his anger on the Jews, beating them up and walking away. It's punishment with a purpose.

REUNITED

"Go and love your wife again, even though she commits adultery with another lover. This will illustrate that the LORD still loves Israel, even though the people have turned to other gods and love to worship them."

HOSEA 3:1

It looks as though Gomer abandons Hosea and returns to prostitution. Or perhaps she runs off with some other man. Wherever she lands, she's treated as someone else's legal property. If Hosea wants Gomer back, he has to buy her—a bit like a groom paying his father-in-law for the right to marry the man's daughter. The bridal fee is considered compensation for the loss of a household servant.

"Holy" prostitution. A young priestess at a pagan worship center. God accuses Israel's men of visiting shrines of fertility cults to have sex with temple priestesses. In some cults, priestesses perform sex as part of the worship ritual. The sex act supposedly stimulates the gods into blessing the worshipper with whatever is requested: rain for the crops, more sheep in the flocks, or more children.

Hosea buys back his ex-wife. The price: some wine, five bushels of barley, and six ounces of silver—about $60 on today's market when silver sells for $10 an ounce.

Hosea's willingness to take back such a sinful woman has to make an impression on many people, especially Gomer. The message it sends is that Hosea loves Gomer no matter what. It's almost like the irrational love that many parents have for their kids. Our children can do terrible things—even commit robbery or murder. But they're still our kids. We have a history with them that binds us together in love. And it's a love that is stronger than any evil.

God loves Israel that way. He often expresses his love with metaphors we can relate to: as a father who loves his children, or as a husband who loves his wife. There is discipline—punishment to fit the crime. But God never severs the relationship.

The punishment God levies on the Jewish people is to allow the Assyrians to overrun Israel in 722 BC and the Babylonians to overrun Judah in 586 BC. This punishment will turn the Jews around. Sitting in exile, they will recognize their sins and repent.

Anticipating this, God promises, "I will heal you of your faithlessness; my love will know no bounds, for my anger will be gone forever. . . . My people will again live under my shade. They will flourish like grain and blossom like grapevines" (Hosea 14:4, 7).

The scattered people will come home.

JOEL

Locusts do lunch. Fleeing the beach, vacationers on the Canary Islands off the coast of North Africa fight their way through a swarm of locusts. Numbering in the millions, these migratory grasshoppers devastate one-third of the crops in the North African nations they infest during November 2004. Joel uses an infestation like this to warn the Jews that something more destructive is coming: invaders.

DAY OF THE LOCUST

Despite the best efforts at pest control throughout the Middle East, locusts still manage to swell into horrifying swarms.

Born in the African and Arabian deserts, where predators are few, Middle Eastern locusts can rise up in soaring towers 5,000 feet high before dropping onto a momentarily green field. One massive swarm in 1889 crossed the Red Sea in a sun-blackening shroud stretched out an estimated 2,000 square miles.

Agricultural societies fear these critters. Joel uses this fear to deliver a warning. Instead of acting out his message, which many other prophets do, Joel lets Mother Nature and her locusts do the acting. Perhaps Joel's homeland has recently suffered a locust outbreak. Or maybe he's expecting the people to draw on a more distant memory. In either case, he figures they know the damage that locusts can do.

Something worse is coming, Joel warns. A desert locust is usually only an inch long, if that. But the prophet tells the people to imagine locusts the size of warhorses. In fact, they are warhorses. And war chariots. And uncountable, sword-rattling soldiers scurrying over city walls to satisfy their hunger for Jewish blood.

Joel says the Jews have only one hope of stopping this deadly invasion: Repent.

MAIN POINT:

God is sending invaders to punish the Jewish people if they don't repent.

WRITER:

"Joel son of Pethuel" (Joel 1:1). Beyond that, the Bible says nothing more about him—including when or where he ministered.

DATE:

Guesses about when Joel lived span 500 years. They start around 800 BC, which would make him the earliest of the 16 prophets with Bible books named after them. And the guesses end around 300 BC, which would make him the last of the prophets.

Clues favoring an early date, such as the 700s BC:

• **Joel comes after Hosea in the Bible.** This suggests that those who compiled the Bible thought he ministered around the time of Hosea, in the mid-700s BC.

• **Jerusalem has walls (Joel 2:7).** Babylonians tore them down in 586 BC, though the Jews rebuilt them in 445 BC.

Clues favoring a late date, such as the 300s BC:

• **Joel mentions the sale of Jews to the Greeks (Joel 3:6).** This suggests Joel lived after Alexander the Great conquered what is now Israel in 332 BC. But Greeks were buying foreign slaves even in the 700s BC.

• **There's no mention of kings.** This points to sometime after 586 BC, when Babylon dethroned the last Jewish king.

• **Priests and elders weep in the temple (Joel 2:16–17).** This, in combination with the absence of a king, points to sometime after Babylon destroyed Jerusalem and exiled the Jews in 586 BC. Freed Jews rebuild the temple in 515 BC and have no king.

LOCATION:

Joel seems to direct his prophecy toward the southern Jewish nation of Judah. But this isn't completely certain. He does refer to Judah and its capital, Jerusalem. Yet he also briefly mentions Israel, possibly the northern Jewish nation (Joel 2:27; 3:16). This, however, could be a generic reference to the Jewish people instead of the northern nation that the Assyrians overran in 722 BC.

LOCUST-KILLER'S GUIDE
circa early 1900s

Break up their torpedo-shaped egg pods with a plow. Each pod packs a wallop: 80 to 150 eggs.

Torch them while they're eating or when they're crawling and too young to fly.

Poison them with bait scattered around plants they'll want to eat.

Surround their hatching ground with a sheet metal wall. Shoo the young, wingless hoppers into a pit.

Stomp the pit like you're dancing on their grave.

KNOW YOUR LOCUST

Even with today's locust-busting technology, complete with chemical cocktails sprayed from planes and truck-mounted mist blowers, it's nearly impossible to stop a swarm of locusts.

The best defense is a good offense. But the best offense works only when the locusts have no defense. That's when they're hatching underground.

Plow their egg pods to bits. That's what farmers in Bible times did after each swarm.

When locusts invade, they not only eat the plants, they plant their own new crop: Generation Next.

Desert locusts bury their eggs four to six inches underground, packing 80 or more eggs into each egg pod. Up to 1,000 egg pods have been found under a square yard of soil. That's potentially 80,000 locusts hatching sometime within 10 days to two months, depending on soil conditions. Females will usually lay eggs at least three times.

Once hatched, desert locusts usually live three to five months, growing from wingless hoppers to flying adults. Swarms can span several hundred square miles, with 60 to 120 million locusts in each square mile. These swarms can travel many miles, depending on the wind. They regularly cross the Red Sea, nearly 200 miles wide. And in 1988, a West African swarm caught a 10-day wind that carried them 3,000 miles to England.

Locusts don't attack people or animals. Nor do they carry any known diseases that harm humans.

People, on the other hand, kill locusts any way they can. In addition to the techniques shown in the photos, people today
- spray insecticide on swarms and breeding grounds;
- dig trenches to catch young hoppers;
- drive wheeled boxes or screens into swarms, trapping locusts in a trough of water and kerosene or sticky tar; and
- eat the locusts stir-fried, roasted, grilled, boiled, dried, or still kicking.

Desert locust. Photographed during a 1915 locust plague in what is now Israel, this short-legged cousin of a grasshopper eats its weight in food each day. A small one-ton swarm can out-eat 10 elephants. The bigger the swarm, the more agitated and aggressive the locusts become.

SWARM

A vast army of locusts has invaded my land.

JOEL 1:6

Joel describes an invasion of what sounds like four waves of locusts, with each wave featuring a distinctly different kind of locust.

- "Cutting locusts" attack first, eating everything they touch.
- "Swarming locusts" arrive and eat what is left.
- "Hopping locusts" come next.
- "Stripping locusts" end the feeding frenzy.

Bible experts aren't sure what locusts Joel is describing. Entomologists say the desert locust grows through six stages of development as it matures to an adult in two to four months. Perhaps Joel is thinking of some of these stages. But Joel's description also seems to fit the two main stages. By mentioning four waves of locusts, perhaps Joel is tracing the damage of two generations, with Generation Next coming a few weeks after the first infestation.

So the "cutting locusts" and the "hopping locusts" might both refer to the young, wingless locusts that cut plants off at ground level. And the "swarming locusts" and "stripping locusts" might refer to the flying adults that devour plants from top to bottom.

On the other hand, Joel may have nothing like this in mind. He might be simply exercising some poetic license to describe the extreme damage caused by a locust infestation. "Our food disappears before our very eyes" (Joel 1:16).

Some scholars suggest that Joel's four types of locusts refer to four future empires that will rule God's people: Babylon, Persia, Greece, and Rome. Or perhaps they refer to the four empires that rule them during Old Testament times: Assyria, Babylon, Persia, and Greece.

When Joel describes the locusts as "a vast army," he's actually saying they are as vast as "a nation." That's a more literal translation of Joel's description in the original Hebrew language. In fact, the real threat Joel wants to warn the Jews about is a military invasion from another country.

BARBARIANS at the gate

Sound the alarm in Jerusalem! . . . A great and mighty army appears.

JOEL 2:1–2

This time it's not an army of locusts attacking plants. It's an army of warriors that will attack and decimate the Jewish people. Walled cities like Jerusalem generally have several guard towers rising above the walls. From there, soldiers scan the horizon and hilltops. At the first sign of an invasion force, they alert the city by blowing a ram's horn. It sounds a bit like a squeaky bugle playing beside a lemonade stand.

The massive invasion force—well equipped with infantry, cavalry, and charioteers—moves in choreographed unison: "They never jostle each other; each moves in exactly the right position" (Joel 2:8).

"Look at them as they leap along the mountaintops," Joel says. "The earth quakes as they advance" (Joel 2:5, 10).

The invasion of Jerusalem that Joel describes could fit several during the 500-year period when Bible experts say Joel might have lived, including:

- Assyrian armies led by Sennacherib in 701 BC; or
- Babylonians led by Nebuchadnezzar in 597 BC and 586 BC.

But if Joel's references to Jerusalem are just a way of identifying the Jewish homeland, he could be pointing to other invasions, as well. One possibility: Assyria erasing the northern Jewish nation of Israel from the world map in 722 BC. Another: Alexander the Great overrunning regional defenders after battling them for a couple of months at the coastal city of Gaza in 332 BC. This city, about 45 miles southeast of Jerusalem and now in Palestinian control in the Gaza Strip, was managed at the time by a Persian governor. The Persian Empire, headquartered in what is now Iran, was the superpower of the day, controlling the Middle East. But that was only until Alexander and his Greek army brushed them aside to become the world's newest superpower.

Two-legged locust. Like a locust wearing its protective skeleton on the outside, this Greek infantryman of the 300s BC is cloaked in a hide of body armor. Joel warns the Jews that invaders are coming. But it's unclear which ones—Assyrians, Babylonians, Persians, or Greeks.

> *The day of the LORD is near, the day when destruction comes from the Almighty. How terrible that day will be!*
> JOEL 1:15

THE FLIP-FLOPPING DAY OF THE LORD

Once upon a time the "day of the Lord" was a good thing.

It was something to look forward to—God stepping into history to fight for Israel.

Many Bible experts trace the idea back to the beginning of Israel's story, when God stormed onto the pages of human history by freeing the Israelite slaves in Egypt. The miracles he performed in the process are among the most famous in the Bible. Ten plagues pressured Egypt's king into freeing the slaves. After that, the sea split in two, giving the Israelites a backdoor escape route when Egypt's army came to take them back.

"Day of the Lord" shows up in some Bible translations as a word or a phrase such as "on that day," "then," or "day of visitation."

By the 700s BC, Israel's prophets had started flipping the phrase upside down, turning it into bad news for Jews.

Joel—who uses the phrase five times in his short book—flip-flops it as well as any. When describing the invasion force coming to destroy Jerusalem, Joel says, "The LORD is at the head of the column....This is his mighty army, and they follow his orders. The day of the LORD is an awesome, terrible thing" (Joel 2:11).

On this particular day of the Lord, God isn't coming to help the Jews. He's coming to defeat them.

But Joel foresees another day of the Lord in the more distant future. It's judgment day, a good day for God's people. It's a day when "everyone who calls on the name of the LORD will be saved" (Joel 2:32).

REPENT, the end is near

The LORD *says, "Turn to me now, while there is time. Give me your hearts. Come with fasting, weeping, and mourning."*

JOEL 2:12

Unlike other prophets in the Bible, Joel tells the Jews to repent—but without telling them what they did wrong.

He doesn't say anything about them breaking their ancient agreement to serve God in return for protection and blessing. He says nothing about them worshipping idols, exploiting the poor, or selling justice in court to the highest bidder.

Still, by warning them to turn back to God, the implication is that they've turned away. And in this era of history, there's only one way to turn from God. It's by breaking his laws.

Even if the Jews repent, Joel doesn't seem certain how God will respond. "Who knows?" Joel says. "Perhaps he will give you a reprieve, sending you a blessing instead of this curse" (Joel 2:14).

But it's possible that Joel's implied uncertainty is a subtle lesson in theology: God is the one in charge. He doesn't take marching orders from us—even if we repent. "Forgive me" isn't a magic phrase that forces God to do what we want him to do.

That said, Joel expresses what seems to be genuine hope that the Jews can avoid the coming disaster. And it's a hope based on God's nature: "He is merciful and compassionate, slow to get angry and filled with unfailing love. He is eager to relent and not punish" (Joel 2:13).

For that reason, Joel calls for heartfelt repentance. Even an uncaring professional mourner could pretend to be sorry by wailing, rubbing dirt on her face, and ripping her clothes—all of which are customary expressions of grief in Bible times. "Don't tear your clothing in your grief," Joel says, quoting God, "but tear your hearts instead" (Joel 2:13).

JEWISH revival

"I will pardon my people's crimes, which I have not yet pardoned; and I, the LORD, *will make my home in Jerusalem with my people."*

JOEL 3:21

Whatever happens to the Jews, whether or not they have to suffer the punishing invasion Joel has described, destruction isn't the last word. At some point, the Jews will come to their senses. They will repent. God will forgive them. And the relationship between them and God will be revived.

God promises:

- "I will drive away these armies from the north" (Joel 2:20).
- "I will give you back what you lost" (Joel 2:25).
- "I will gather the armies of the world. . . . I will judge them for harming my people" (Joel 3:2).

God names the armies he's talking about. They're Israel's two west coast, seafaring neighbor nations: Philistia, along with Tyre and Sidon—two major cities of Phoenicia, in what is now Lebanon. With their seaports and sailing savvy, Philistia and Phoenicia harvested crops of Jewish people, then sailed them to slave markets in distant lands such as Greece.

It's to these nations that God delivers one of the most famous messages in the book of Joel: "Get ready for war! . . . Hammer your plowshares into swords and your pruning hooks into spears" (Joel 3:9–10).

Philistia and Phoenicia both suffered during invasions by Assyrians in the 700s BC, Babylonians in 500s BC, Persians in the 500s–300s BC, and Greeks led by Alexander the Great in 332 BC. In addition, an earthquake dropped much of Sidon into the Mediterranean Sea in 146 BC. Philistines gradually lost their national identity and were assimilated into neighboring cultures.

God's most famous promise in the book of Joel is this one, later picked up by the apostle Peter in his sermon that launched the Christian church: "I will pour out my Spirit upon all people. Your sons and daughters will prophesy. Your old men will dream dreams, and your young men will see visions" (Joel 2:28).

To this point in Jewish history, God has poured out his Spirit only in special situations and for select people, such as prophets, priests, and kings. But when the Holy Spirit fills Jesus' followers who are gathered in a Jerusalem house during a Pentecost festival, they consider it a turning point in history. They run outside with this message for Jewish pilgrims who had come from distant lands for the holiday: Joel's prophecy has come true (Acts 2). The Holy Spirit is now available to everyone.

More than 3,000 Jews believe what they hear, convinced by miracles accompanying the message. And the Christian church is born.

AMOS

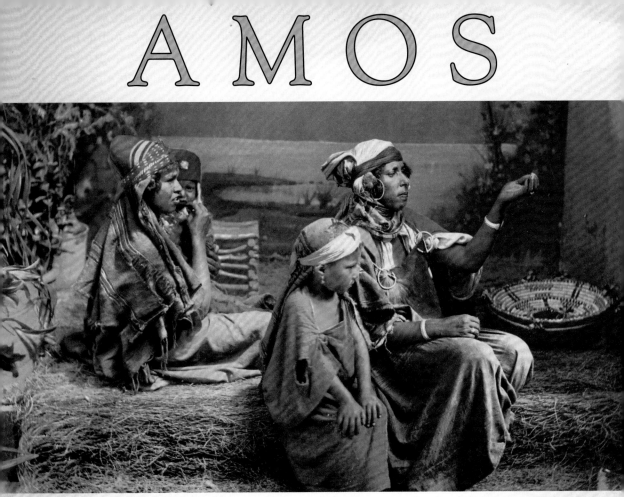

Reduced to begging. With her children watching, a Middle Eastern mother begs for money in 1899. Amos complains that Israel's rich upper class feeds off the poor: charging unjust taxes, cheating them in business, and driving them deeper into poverty.

THE POOR MAN'S PROPHET

Maybe it takes one to know one. Perhaps that's why God skips over the professional prophets and calls a lowly farmer to deliver what becomes a message so forceful and majestic that civil rights advocates today still quote this man.

His name is Amos. He farms and shepherds in a remote village more than half a day's walk south of Jerusalem. Usually, prophets minister in their own countries. But God orders Amos across the border, into the northern Jewish nation of Israel. There, in the capital city of Samaria, he delivers a string of prophecies that teaches an unbelievable lesson in theology.

Jewish movers and shakers, fat cats, and aristocrats have plenty of reason to believe God is smiling on them. After all, they're enjoying peace and prosperity. Many ancients, including the Jews, consider blessings like these as gifts from above. God himself promised that if the Jews lived in a way that pleased him, "they and their descendants would prosper" (Deuteronomy 5:29).

This particular prosperity, however, has nothing to do with God's blessing. Instead, Amos says, it has everything to do with rich people exploiting the poor, cheating their customers, and buying off judges.

Amos says this corruption is going to stop, one way or another.

If the people don't stop it, Amos warns, God will. The Lord will level the playing field.

Invaders can do that quite effectively. A few decades later, when Assyrian soldiers line up captive Jews and march them 1,000 miles into exile, the has-been princes with hooks in their noses look very much like commoners.

MAIN POINT:

God is going to punish the northern Jewish nation of Israel for a long list of sins—especially for exploiting the poor and selling justice to the highest-bidding briber.

WRITER:

Amos delivered these prophecies. He describes his job: "I do not make my living as a prophet, nor am I a member of a group of prophets. I make my living as a shepherd, and I take care of sycamore trees" (Amos 7:14 NCV). His grove produces sweet figs.

Amos's eloquent writing style suggests he's well educated. Or perhaps he has some help from a professional scribe—as did Jeremiah, who dictated his prophecies. Some Bible experts say the book's upbeat ending—the last five verses—reads like a disjointed add-on that came later. But

without those verses of hope, Amos would be the only prophet in the Bible who preached nothing but doom for the Jews. All the others included a promise that God would restore the Jewish nation.

DATE:

Amos ministered in the middle to high-numbered 700s BC. He comes first among all the writing prophets whose dates are known. He offers several clues about when he ministered.

- Uzziah is king of Judah (reigning about 783–742 BC).
- Jeroboam II is king of Israel (about 786–746 BC). The time of peace and prosperity (for the rich) that's reflected in Amos suggests the final decade or so of Jeroboam's reign, perhaps in the 760s BC.
- "Two years before the earthquake" (Amos 1:1). Archaeologists have recently found evidence in city ruins of a massive earthquake in the region during the mid-700s BC.
- "I will make the sun go down at noon" (Amos 8:9), perhaps a reference to the solar eclipse of 763 BC.

LOCATION:

Amos lived in the southern Jewish nation of Judah, in the village of Tekoa. That's about a dozen miles south of Judah's capital, Jerusalem. He took his prophecy on the road to the northern Jewish nation of Israel, with its capital in Samaria.

Bad News for Israel's Neighbors

Persian Gulf

Nineveh • Babylon
ASSYRIA

"You will be taken captive"

"Your capital will burn" ARAM
PHOENICIA • Damascus "Your leaders will be taken captive"
Tyre • AMMON
ISRAEL
Jerusalem • MOAB "You will die in a great noise"
JUDAH
"The last of the PHILISTIA EDOM "Your cities will be destroyed"
Philistines will die" "Jerusalem will
be destroyed"

Mediterranean Sea

Red Sea

SEVEN sinners

"The people of Damascus have sinned again and again, and I will not let them go unpunished!"

Amos 1:3

Farmer Amos leaves his sycamore grove and his flock—presumably in someone else's care. And he starts walking north. He walks past Jerusalem and right out of his country, the southern Jewish nation of Judah. Three days and 50 miles from home, he arrives in Samaria, capital of the northern Jewish nation of Israel.

There he begins telling the people about messages he received from God in a vision. At first, the messages must sound reassuring. That's because Amos starts by announcing that God is going to lower the doom-boom on seven of Israel's nearest neighbors. Every oracle against these nations—sometimes represented by their leading city—begins with the same ominous warning: "For the many crimes of [nation's name inserted], I will punish them."

- **Damascus,** capital of Aram in what is now Syria. The Arameans committed war crimes. "They dragged logs with spikes over the people" (Amos 1:3 cev).
- **Gaza,** a leading city of the Philistines in what is now the Palestinians' Gaza Strip.

They deported entire Jewish villages and sold many Jews into slavery.

- **Tyre,** main seaport city of Phoenicia in what is now Lebanon. Ditto the Philistine charge. And add a broken peace treaty.
- **Edom,** in what is now southern Jordan. Descended from Jacob's brother, Esau, and therefore related to the Jews, Edomites fought the Jews and showed them no mercy.
- **Ammon,** in what is now northern Jordan. Ammonites committed genocide against the Jews, even cutting open pregnant women in merciless attacks.
- **Moab,** in what is now central Jordan. The Moabites desecrated a corpse, burning the bones of Edom's king. Some ancients taught that cremation deprived the person's spirit of the rest he or she could enjoy from a burial.
- **Judah,** the southern Jewish nation. They disobeyed God's law.

Each of these nations is eventually devastated by war—either by Assyrians, Babylonians, or regional armies. By the time Alexander the Great and his Greeks arrive in the 300s BC, all seven of these nations are gone. Even the Jews, controlled by Persians, remain a kingless community.

ONE BIG sinner

"The people of Israel have sinned again and again, and I will not let them go unpunished!"

AMOS 2:6

Seven—the number of nations Amos addresses—is often the perfect number in the Bible. It's the number symbolizing a job completely finished. God rested on the seventh day of creation. And he told his people to finish each week by resting, as well. But Amos doesn't stop with the seven sinful nations. In fact, he's just getting started.

Amos has devoted a total of 18 verses to those seven nations. But up next, Israel all by itself gets that much—and 100 verses more.

The prophet's biggest complaint is social injustice. Amos complains about oppression of the poor (2:6–7); sexual immorality (2:7); corruption (3:10; 8:5); injustice in the courts (5:7, 12); selfishness (6:1–6); and the worship of idols (7:9).

Throughout the Bible—Old Testament and New—there's one thing God repeatedly says his people should do: help the helpless. In that ancient society without organized welfare programs, orphans, widows, and immigrants are especially vulnerable. That's why Bible writers describe God like this: "He is the great God, the mighty and awesome God, who shows no partiality and cannot be bribed. He ensures that orphans and widows receive justice. He shows love to the foreigners living among you and gives them food and clothing" (Deuteronomy 10:17–18).

That's the model Israel is to follow. Instead,

- "They sell honorable people for silver and poor people for a pair of sandals" (Amos 2:6). Perhaps an exaggeration, but the point is that rich people are collecting the tiniest of debts by going so far as to sell the debtors themselves. Owe a few bucks and can't pay? Take a stand on the slave block—proceeds of the sale go to the person you owe.

- "They trample helpless people in the dust and shove the oppressed out of the way" (Amos 2:7).
- "At their religious festivals, they lounge in clothing their debtors put up as security. In the house of their god, they drink wine bought with unjust fines" (Amos 2:8). These people have the gall to think they're religious, even though they're stealing from the poor.
- "How you hate honest judges! . . . You oppress good people by taking bribes and deprive the poor of justice in the courts" (Amos 5:10, 12).
- "You trample the poor, stealing their grain through taxes and unfair rent" (Amos 5:11). These are folks who would tax widows selling a few loaves of bread and then use the money to buy a cruise ticket to Greece.

Amos has a message for hardcore crooks like these: "Prepare to meet your God in judgment" (Amos 4:12).

ISRAEL'S judgment day

"The people of Israel will certainly become captives in exile, far from their homeland."

AMOS 7:17

To show just how crooked Israel is, God makes his point with a plumb line—a tool that builders use to make sure walls go up straight. "I will test my people with this plumb line," God says. He obviously finds the nation crooked, because he quickly adds, "I will no longer ignore all their sins" (Amos 7:8).

God doesn't call the rich elite of Israel "fat cats." This late into their sinning, God isn't that polite. Instead, he says, "Listen to me, you fat cows living in Samaria, you women who oppress the poor and crush the needy, and who are always calling to your husbands, 'Bring us another drink!' " (Amos 4:1).

In the original language, Amos is talking about the top breed of cattle—pampered in the fertile pastures of Bashan, in what is now Jordan.

"The time will come," God adds, "when you will be led away with hooks in your noses.

Crooked as a lopsided wall. Egyptian builders used this plumb line about 3,000 years ago. With a longer string, they would drop the stone bob beside a wall they were building. If the string remained the same distance from the wall all the way down, the wall was straight. In a vision, Amos sees God building a wall and using a plumb line. God determines that Israel is crooked. So he decides to do with Israel what a builder does with a crooked wall: tear it down and start over.

Every last one of you will be dragged away like a fish on a hook! You will be led out through the ruins of the wall" (Amos 4:2–3).

That time is 722 BC. Israel boldly decides to stop paying its required annual taxes to the Assyrian Empire. So Assyria's king, Shalmaneser, brings an invasion force to collect the taxes—and everything else of value.

After surrounding the capital city of Samaria—and for three years cutting off their supplies—the Assyrian soldiers force the starving citizens to surrender. Shalmaneser doesn't want to deal with this rebellious nation again. So he deports all the leading citizens. Israel, and the 10 Jewish tribes that once made up this nation, are scattered abroad.

RESURRECTED nation

"I will bring my exiled people of Israel back from distant lands, and they will rebuild their ruined cities and live in them again."

Amos 9:14

This upbeat promise ends the book. But it might seem perplexing to those who know history. That's because of the "Lost Tribes of Israel." They're still lost. The 10 northern Jewish tribes never return home, as far as the Bible tells.

Assyrians repopulate the northern Jewish homeland with foreign pioneers who intermarry with the sparse Jewish population left behind. They produce a race that the southern Jews grow to despise: Samaritans. Many Jews come to think of Samaritans as racial and spiritual half-breeds, with mixed blood and a mixed-up religion that recognizes only the first five books in the Bible—and an edited version at that.

God's promise is to "restore the fallen house of David" (Amos 9:11). That doesn't necessarily include the northern Jewish nation. The northern nation seceded from the Jewish union and from David's dynasty about 200 years earlier.

Judah in the southland is the tribe that kept crowning David's descendants as king. That ended in 586 BC, when Babylon did to them what Assyria had done to Israel in 722 BC. The difference is that the exiled southern Jews were released about 50 years later. Many returned home to rebuild their country.

Some Jewish scholars say Amos's promise about the restoration of David's dynasty refers to more than just the repatriation of Jews after the Persians overrun Babylon and free the political prisoners. They say it points to an ideal time in the future, when the Messiah reigns over Israel.

Many Christian scholars, too, say it refers to the Messiah—and to his second coming. They describe the church as the new Israel. And they say that "all the nations" refers to the Messiah's kingdom: "Israel will possess what is left of Edom, and all the nations I have called to be mine. . . . They will never again be uprooted" (Amos 9:12, 15).

Some Bible prophecies work on two timelines at once—in the prophet's era and in the distant future. It could be that God wants readers to see both in this promise: Israel's restoration in ancient times and the world's restoration still to come.

OBADIAH

Red Rock City. An easily defended, narrow passage through towering cliffs leads to Petra—ancient capital of Edom, a city carved into red rock cliffs. *Edom* means "red," and *Petra* means "rock." The prophet Obadiah warns that Edom's rock fortresses high in the mountains won't protect them from the punishment God is sending their way. Today Petra is a ghost town, visited by tourists.

A TASTE OF THEIR OWN MEDICINE

The shortest book in the Old Testament, Obadiah takes only 21 verses to deliver its message of doom. Far less than a book, it's just a 291-word essay in its original Hebrew language.

And for a change, the Jews aren't the ones getting doomed. They've already met their doom.

Invaders swept through the Jewish homeland, sacking the capital city of Jerusalem. The prophet Obadiah never bothers to identify who the invaders are—or which Jewish nation he's talking about: Israel in the north or Judah in the south. Most Bible experts, however, guess that Obadiah is talking about the Babylonian invasion of Judah in 586 BC.

If this guess is right, the attackers came from the north in what is now Iraq. But whatever invasion it was, Jewish war refugees fled to their nearest neighbor in the south: Edom.

It's a brother nation. Israel descended from Jacob's family. Edom descended from the family of Jacob's older brother, Esau. Like brothers, sometimes these two nations worked together as allies. But more often, they fought. Edom wouldn't give Moses and the Israelites of the Exodus permission to pass through their land on the way to what is now Israel. Rather than fight their brothers, the Israelites took a long detour southward around Edom, eventually entering

Israel from east of the Jordan River.

Israel's first king, Saul, fought Edom. David conquered the nation, and the Jews collected taxes from them for generations. But Edom eventually broke free.

When Jewish war refugees poured across the border into Edom's territory, the Edomites didn't quite lay out the red carpet of welcome. Instead, they killed some of the Jews. And they arrested others and delivered them to the invaders. Then they plundered the decimated cities and gloated over Israel's hard luck.

Obadiah warns that before God is done with Edom, there won't be anyone left there to gloat.

Petra painting. Petra's temple, carved from solid rock and captured on canvas in 1839.

ROCK WALLS won't stop God

The LORD says to Edom, "I will cut you down to size."

OBADIAH 2

South of the Dead Sea, rugged mountains towering some 5,000 feet high provide a natural barrier for the people of Edom. Some of their strongest fortresses are built in these mountains because the area is easy to defend and hard to attack.

MAIN POINT:
God is going to pay back the country of Edom for arresting and killing Jewish refugees who were running for their lives from invaders.

WRITER:
Obadiah is the prophet who delivered this short message. Because his name means "servant of God," some Bible experts speculate that Obadiah wasn't the writer's name, but a description of the writer. Supporting this theory is the fact that Obadiah's father isn't mentioned. Typically, important Bible characters are identified by their name and their father's name. Obadiah, however, was a common name in Bible times. Another Obadiah is mentioned in 1 Kings 18:3.

DATE:
Obadiah probably delivered this message sometime during a 30-year stretch: after Babylon overran the southern Jewish nation of Judah in 586 BC, but before Edom fell to Babylon in 553 BC. This isn't certain, however, because Obadiah doesn't identify the invaders he mentions. Many Bible experts say their best guess is this is the Babylonian invasion—a pivotal event for the Jews because it erases their sovereign nation from the world map.

LOCATION:
Obadiah targets the nation of Edom, south of the Dead Sea in what is now Jordan.

This gives them a false sense of security.

"You live in a rock fortress and make your home high in the mountains," Obadiah tells them. " 'Who can ever reach us way up here?' you ask boastfully" (Obadiah 3).

The prophet answers that question for them by quoting God: "Even if you soar as high as eagles and build your nest among the stars, I will bring you crashing down" (Obadiah 4).

Edom's crime: inhospitality on a par with the Holocaust. An invasion force—probably the Babylonian army in 586 BC—storms through Judah, scattering the Jews who run for their lives. Some run to Edom, about a four-day trip south of Jerusalem.

One of the most important customs in ancient times is to show hospitality to strangers in the land. With God, it's law: "You must not oppress foreigners," God told the Jews. "You know what it's like to be a foreigner, for you yourselves were once foreigners in the land of Egypt" (Exodus 23:9).

It's common knowledge in Bible times, long before national welfare programs, that the people most at risk are orphans, widows, and foreigners—outsiders who might be travelers or immigrants. So God orders his people to help these helpless people.

But instead of helping the Jewish refugees, Edom

- rejoices at Israel's misfortune;
- arrests some of the refugees and turns them over to the invaders;
- kills some of the refugees; and
- picks through the ruins of destroyed Jewish cities, taking whatever it wants.

"As you have done to Israel," God vows, "so it will be done to you" (Obadiah 15). This is the flip side of the Golden Rule: "Do to others whatever you would like them to do to you" Jesus said. "This is the essence of all that is taught in the law and the prophets" (Matthew 7:12).

REMAKING the Middle East

"Just as you swallowed up my people on my holy mountain, so you and the surrounding nations will swallow the punishment I pour out on you. . . and disappear from history."

OBADIAH 6

Like other Bible prophets, Obadiah ends with good news for the Jews. Their enemies will fall. And the people of Israel will return from exile to rebuild their nation.

In what reads like sweet retribution, the invaders who most likely were the ones to decimate the Jewish homeland do the same to Edom. It happens about 33 years after Jerusalem falls. A Babylonian king named Nabonidus, in 553 BC, crushes Edom. Adding to the irony, Edom's refugees flee to the Jewish homeland. They set up a base in Hebron, 20 miles south of Jerusalem. By this time, they're called Idumeans. Sweeter still, a Jewish ruler named John Hyrcanus in 120 BC defeats the Idumeans and forces them to convert to Judaism or die.

Herod the Great, born about 50 years later, comes from just such a family of converted Idumeans. Courting the Roman conquerors who arrive, he gets himself appointed king of the Jews. Not quite sovereign, he answers to Rome. He's also a few genes short of a Jew.

The Edomite nation evaporates from history sometime after Rome crushes a Jewish uprising in AD 70—destroying cities throughout the region, including Jerusalem. One by one, Israel's neighbors all evaporate, as well. These include both of those named by Obadiah: Phoenicia in what is now Lebanon, along with Philistia, on what is now the west coast of Israel and the Palestinian Gaza Strip.

Obadiah ends with what sounds like a utopian world where "the LORD himself will be king!" (Obadiah 21). Many Jewish scholars say this refers to life after the Messiah comes. And many Christians point to the kingdom of eternal life after the second coming of Jesus.

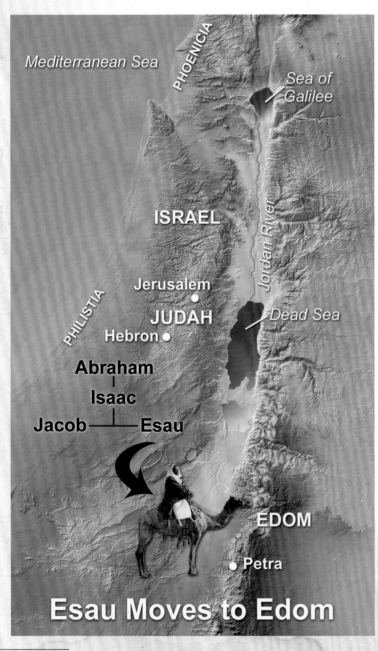

Esau Moves to Edom

Brother nations. The Jewish nations of Israel and Judah descended from Abraham, Isaac, and Jacob. Esau—Jacob's older brother—moved to Edom, in what is now Jordan. Generations later, Edom and the Jewish nations became bitter enemies. God vowed to erase Edom from the world map, along with other neighboring enemies of the Jews.

JONAH

Fish bait. Thrown overboard to appease an angry God, Jonah gets himself swallowed by a big fish. But he survives inside the fish for three days. Judging this a whopper of a tale, some Bible scholars say Jonah's story might be make-believe. They suggest it's more like Jesus' story of the Good Samaritan—a parable with an important message. Others insist it's a fish tale that's true.

THE PROPHECY THAT DOESN'T COME TRUE

There's only one sentence of prophecy in this book. And it turns out wrong: "Forty days from now Nineveh will be destroyed!" (Jonah 3:4).

Never happened.

This isn't the only thing strange about the book of Jonah. Of all the 16 Bible prophets with books named after them, Jonah is the only one who rebels against God. And he does it twice.

- **Rebellion 1.** Ordered to deliver the doom message to Nineveh, Jonah sails off in the opposite direction. But getting thrown overboard in a storm and swallowed by a big fish convinces him to do as God told him.
- **Rebellion 2.** After Nineveh repents and God spares the city, Jonah pouts. He's embarrassed that his prophecy didn't come true. And he's mad that God didn't go ahead and kill Nineveh's 120,000 citizens anyhow.

All of this makes Jonah look like a lowlife—lower than a whale's belly. Jonah really doesn't need his biographer to accentuate the negative. But the writer does.

In four short chapters, nearly everyone and everything obeys God. The only exception is Jonah, God's holy prophet.

The wind and sea obey, churning up a storm to rock Jonah's boat. The sailors obey, agreeing to throw Jonah overboard. The big fish obeys, swallowing Jonah and spitting him out as a loogie. The pagan king of one of the world's cruelest empires obeys, ordering his people to repent. And the citizens of Nineveh obey, asking God's forgiveness for their sins.

Everyone's on board with God except Jonah, God's prophet.

MAIN POINT:

God forgives the worst of sinnerswhen they genuinely repent—even the Assyrians, famed for their vicious terror tactics.

WRITER:

The story is about Jonah, son of Amittai. But it's not written in the first person. So it's possible that someone else told Jonah's story for him. "Jonah, son of Amittai" is mentioned elsewhere in the Bible. He's a prophet from the small Galilean village of Gath-hepher (2 Kings 14:25), which is near Nazareth in northern Israel.

DATE:

Jonah ministered during the reign of Jeroboam II in Israel (about 793–753 BC). He correctly predicted that Jeroboam would regain lost territory east of the Jordan River in what is now Jordan. Jeroboam's reign ended about 30 years before Assyrian invaders wiped Israel off the political map and exiled the Jewish survivors.

LOCATION:

Jonah's story begins in the northern Jewish nation of Israel. It continues on the Mediterranean Sea with a short, stormy cruise. And it ends after a thousand-mile walk to Nineveh, capital of the Assyrian Empire. Nineveh's ruins are near what is now the northern Iraqi town of Mosul.

Atlantic
Ocean

ITALY
Sardinia

SPAIN
Tartessus

GREECE

Black Sea

TURKEY

Nineveh

Carthage

Mediterranean Sea

Jonah's destination:
unknown site called Tarshish.
Possibly Tartessus,
Sardinia, or Carthage.

ISRAEL
Joppa

EGYPT

Jonah's Scenic Route to Nineveh

LOOKING FOR TARSHISH

Instead of going to Nineveh, as God asked, Jonah boarded a ship bound for Tarshish. Trouble is, no one today seems to know where Tarshish was.

The name is associated with:

Mining and refining of metal. "They bring beaten sheets of silver from Tarshish" (Jeremiah 10:9). "Tarshish sent merchants to buy your wares in exchange for silver, iron, tin, and lead" (Ezekiel 27:12).

Seafaring traders from a distant land. "The western kings of Tarshish and other distant lands will bring him tribute" (Psalm 72:10).

Bible experts suggest four contenders for Tarshish—each of which match these two descriptions.

•Tartessus. The top candidate, this city in southwestern Spain was famous for its metal and trade. Phoenicians from what is now Lebanon—probably the sailors who transported Paul—maintained a port here. Also, if Jonah wanted to get away from Nineveh, this is about as far as he could get

in his day. A Greek history writer in the 400s BC, Herodotus, pointed to this city as Tarshish.

•Carthage. This port town in the North African country of Tunisia seemed the top contender when Jewish scholars translated their sacred Hebrew scriptures into Greek. The Greek Bible, called the Septuagint, used "Carthage" instead of "Tarshish" when translating Ezekiel 27:12,.

•Sardinia. A Phoenician inscription from the 800s BC suggests Tarshish is on this island. Some Bible experts narrow it further to Nora, now a ruins near a southern port.

•Mediterranean Sea. Many Bible experts say the Hebrew word for Tarshish has a broader meaning: open sea. In this case, Jonah simply caught a ship headed out to sea. A ship going just about anywhere on the Mediterranean would have taken him away from Nineveh.

JONAH GETS a sense of direction

"Get up and go to the great city of Nineveh." . . . Jonah got up and went in the opposite direction.

JONAH 1:2–3

Every Bible prophet except Jonah works with the Jewish community. Even Obadiah's one-chapter message of doom for the country of Edom has a Jewish angle: God is punishing them for mistreating the Jews. Jonah is the exception. He is the one and only prophet God picks to go on a mission that has nothing to do with the Jews.

God orders Jonah to Nineveh, capital of Assyria.

There's good reason Jonah doesn't want to go. It's called survival instinct.

The Assyrians are perhaps the most vicious empire this world has ever seen. Their idea of art, suitable for framing and hanging on their palace walls, includes stone-chiseled images of dead Jews impaled on poles as thick as fence posts (see photo on page 114). Ordering a Jew to go to Nineveh and deliver a death threat would have made as much sense as sending a rabbi to Berlin in the early 1940s to tell Hitler he's in big trouble.

Jonah apparently considered this a suicide mission.

He must have figured he had nothing to lose by visiting the opposite side of the planet. So he goes to the port city of Joppa, now engulfed by the twin cities of Tel Aviv and Jaffa. There he catches a ship bound for Tarshish. It's uncertain exactly where Tarshish was, but one of the most persistent and plausible theories places it at Tartessus in southwestern Spain. That's nearly the end of the world in Bible times—next stop due west: a swamp now reclaimed as Washington, DC.

Phoenician sailors from what is now Lebanon do a brisk business with Spanish merchants. But on this trip, a storm catches them somewhere along the way. Centuries later, gale-force winds would snatch the apostle Paul's ship about 600 miles offshore. The storm would push Paul's ship another 600 miles before running it aground near Italy.

Sailors on Jonah's ship throw cargo overboard. Discarding the weight allows the ship to ride higher in the sea. They also try rowing and steering the ship to shore, without success. They figure the gods are behind the fierce storm, so they cast lots to find out who on board has offended a god. Lots were probably a bit like flipping a coin to get a yes or no answer. The last flip indicts Jonah. He admits his guilt and says the storm will stop if they toss him overboard. Eventually, as a last resort, they do just that.

CAUGHT by a fish

The LORD *had arranged for a great fish to swallow Jonah. And Jonah was inside the fish for three days and three nights.*

JONAH 1:17

This part of the story is one reason some Bible experts say the book of Jonah is fiction—a short parable with a moral, like some of the stories Jesus told.

There are urban legends about whalers cutting up their catch and finding a live person inside. But these are just tall tales. And that includes the 1896 story appearing in Joseph Pulitzer's prestigious *New York World* newspaper. The story, illustrated with a drawing of a man sitting inside an open-mouthed whale, claims that a British whaler named James Bartley spent a day and a half inside a sperm whale before his crew caught the beast and cut Bartley free. Though Bartley said he sailed on *Star of the East*, his name wasn't on the crew list. And the captain's wife later said Mr. Bartley never sailed with her husband.

The Bible never says a whale swallowed Jonah.

The Bible describes the creature only as a big fish. Jews in Jonah's day aren't seafarers. They're sea-fearers—shepherds who prefer grass under their feet. So Jonah may not have recognized a whale if he saw one. Especially during what sounds like a near-typhoon.

Even if the prophet saw something during his flush down the critter's throat, it may have been nothing more than tongue and tonsils. Some Bible experts, doubting that Jonah could have survived three days of stomach acid, suggest he remained in the oral cavity like a wad of gristle that eventually gets spit out.

Oddly, while still inside the fish, Jonah thanks God for saving him: "I sank beneath the waves, and the waters closed over me. . . . But you, O LORD my God, snatched me from the jaws of death!" (Jonah 2:5–6).

Poetry like that isn't what we'd expect from someone sitting inside any part of a sea creature. We'd expect something more like the scream of a banshee. This is another reason some scholars say this story is a few facts shy of reality. Yet other scholars argue that Jonah, resting in the whale's mouth, might have seen that the storm had died and that he had not—and that the creature was keeping him on the surface.

After Jonah's prayer, at God's command the fish spits its catch onto the beach. The fish that had caught a man throws him back.

A book that says "I'm sorry"

Each autumn, Jewish people read the book of Jonah during the afternoon service on their annual day of repentance: Yom Kippur (Day of Atonement).

The point isn't to identify with the starring character, a Jewish prophet. Instead, the people are encouraged to emulate the ancestors of Iraq—the people of Nineveh—by expressing sorrow for their sins.

TOURING Nineveh

The people of Nineveh believed God's message, and from the greatest to the least, they declared a fast and put on burlap to show their sorrow.

JONAH 3:5

Unlike most other prophets in the Bible, Jonah's message gets through. The Assyrians do what the Jews rarely do—believe the message and repent.

Some historians say they had good reason to believe the end was near. If this Jonah is the same prophet mentioned in 2 Kings, then he probably arrived at Nineveh in the mid-700s. That was a tough time for Assyria. They were facing revolts. They had lost some battles. And they were experiencing persistent drought. In the middle of all this, the solar eclipse of 763 BC probably stirred up the worry pot.

Seeing Nineveh's repentance, God spares the city. This shows that God is flexible enough to change his plan to accommodate a changed people.

Jonah, on the other hand, isn't flexible enough to get over his preconceived notion that prophecies should always come true. Moses had said as much: "If the prophet speaks in the LORD's name but his prediction does not happen or come true, you will know that the LORD did not give that message" (Deuteronomy 18:22).

That might have been true during the Exodus, but it doesn't fit Jonah's story. And perhaps

Moses wasn't intending to squeeze God into this particular mold for all time.

In the history of Israel's prophets, Jonah scores the rare success. He turns people to God and saves 120,000 lives. Yet this unlikely, rare success of a prophet actually considers himself a failure. If God won't kill Nineveh's 120,000 people, Jonah says he wants God to kill him.

The book closes with God insisting that

Delayed doom. Nestled along the banks of the Tigris River, Nineveh is protected by nearly eight miles of walls. The Assyrian capital is "so large that it took three days to see it all" (Jonah 3:3). After Jonah warns the people of approaching doom, they repent and escape destruction. But a generation later, in 612 BC, Babylonians sack the city.

he has every right to spare this massive city. And 120,000 is a lot of humanity. Line them up shoulder to shoulder and they'd string out a line some 45 miles long.

Bible experts debate the point of Jonah's story. Possibilities:

- God's love isn't limited to Jews.
- God is eager to forgive and slow to punish. His justice is balanced by his merciful grace.
- Everyone and everything yields to God: wind and waves, pagans and prophets.

FACT OR FICTION?

Some Bible scholars say they don't believe Jonah's fish story.

They say it's more likely a parable—a make-believe story with a spiritual message—than a snippet of real history from someone's life.

Here are a few of their key arguments, along with counterpoints from Bible experts who disagree with them.

- **It reads like a parable.** It's immediately captivating, short, and with an abrupt thunderbolt of an ending that leaves the reader thinking. **Counterpoint:** Jonah was a real person in history, mentioned in 2 Kings 14:25.
- **It doesn't read like a prophecy.** It's a single short story, with a one-sentence prophecy that doesn't come true. **Counterpoint:** There are plenty of short stories in the Bible's other books of prophecy—especially in Daniel and Jeremiah.

- **How could anyone possibly survive inside a fish for three days? Counterpoint:** Couldn't a God who created the universe arrange for a comparatively minor event like this? Besides, Jesus seemed to believe Jonah's story: "For as Jonah was in the belly of the great fish for three days and three nights, so will the Son of Man be in the heart of the earth for three days and three nights" (Matthew 12:40).
- **Extensive records that have survived from Nineveh don't mention anything about Jonah's visit or a spiritual awakening. Counterpoint:** Keep looking. Many scholars said Bible writers made up the Hittites—until Hittite records started showing up in the late 1800s and their royal archive surfaced in 1906.

MICAH

DOOM FIRST, SALVATION LATER

Small-town prophets seem to have a special connection to the poor—and stern words for rich people who exploit the poor.

Like Amos who ministered a few years before him, Micah comes from a small village. And just like Amos, he targets people who abuse power and privilege:

- the rich who get richer through extortion and violence;
- merchants with scales weighted in their favor, like loaded dice;
- judges who sell judgment for a bribe;
- prophets and priests who say whatever the people will pay to hear; and
- rulers who do whatever it takes to live in luxury and preserve their power.

But Micah doesn't stop with society's elite. He goes after their victims, as well. These less privileged Jews could have taken their pleas to God, asking him for help. Instead, they go to

Turning swords into plow tips. Cloth padding on his shoulder, a Middle Eastern farmer carries his heavy wooden plow. It's tipped with a metal insert—called a plowshare—for slicing through soil. Micah promised the Jews peace—a day when soldiers would "hammer their swords into plowshares" (Micah 4:3).

idols. Many seem to feel they can satisfy God by treating him as one of the many gods they worship—offering his required sacrifices but living as they please.

Micah sets them straight. "The LORD has told you what is good," Micah says, "and this is what he requires of you: to do what is right, to love mercy, and to walk humbly with your God" (Micah 6:8).

Yet most of the people and their leaders do none of this. So Micah warns them of the consequences. Invaders will dismantle the two Jewish nations and exile the citizens.

But after the doom, salvation comes. God will bring the Jews home to rebuild their nation.

Micah doesn't want the Jews to lose sight of the hope ahead. Perhaps that's why he weaves salvation into his message, matching all three rounds of bad news with rounds of good news:

Round one: doom (1:1–2:11), salvation (2:12–13).

Round two: doom (chapter 3), salvation (4:1–5:15).

Round three: doom (6:1–7:7), salvation (7:8–20).

Doomsday is coming for the Jews of Micah's day. They will pay for their sins. But the generation to follow can expect God's grace: a clean slate, a fresh start, and a hopeful future.

MAIN POINT:

For sins of injustice and idolatry, God is going to let invaders demolish both Jewish nations: Israel in the north and Judah in the south. Survivors will be exiled. But in time, God will bring the Jews home to rebuild their nation.

WRITER:

Micah, a small-town prophet, is the source of these messages. Either Micah wrote them himself, or someone recorded them for him. Many scholars say another writer added material more than a century later. One reason they say this is because Micah lived in the 700s BC, yet he predicts that the people of Jerusalem "will soon be sent in exile to distant Babylon" (Micah 4:10). It's unusual to mention Babylon at all—but especially so since Babylon won't snatch the "world superpower" title from Assyria for another century. The exile Micah mentions took place in 586 BC.

DATE:

Micah said his ministry spanned the reigns of three kings of Judah: Jotham, Ahaz, and Hezekiah. That covers 55 years, from about 742 to 687 BC.

LOCATION:

Micah lived in Moresheth. That's a small village about a day's walk, 20 miles, southwest of Jerusalem.

PROPHETS FOR A TOUGH CENTURY: 700S BC

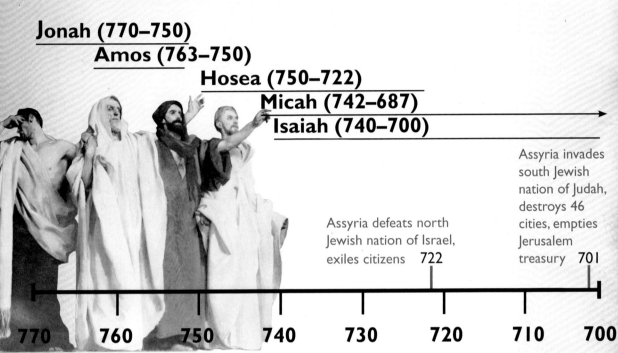

Jonah (770–750)
Amos (763–750)
Hosea (750–722)
Micah (742–687)
Isaiah (740–700)

Assyria defeats north Jewish nation of Israel, exiles citizens 722

Assyria invades south Jewish nation of Judah, destroys 46 cities, empties Jerusalem treasury 701

770   760   750   740   730   720   710   700

BAD NEWS for Jews

Shave your heads in sorrow, for the children you love will be snatched away.

MICAH 1:16

Micah has a message of doom, and he spreads it around. Though he lives in the southern Jewish nation of Judah, there's more than enough doom for Israel in the northland as well.

God's complaint against the people of both nations is that they're breaking the first and most important of the 10 Commandments—the 10 laws on which all other Jewish laws rest. They're worshipping idols.

Idolatry headquarters is none other than the capitals of both Jewish nations: Samaria in the north and Jerusalem in the south. Ironically, Jerusalem is supposed to be the holy city—the city of God. In one of the songs that Jews sing, they praise Jerusalem as "the city of our God, the sacred home of the Most High. God dwells in that city; it cannot be destroyed" (Psalm 46:4–5).

As it turns out, this isn't quite true—at least not as many Jews understand the promise.

Some of the Jews in Micah's day are counting on Jerusalem's invincibility to protect them from their sins. They figure they can do as they please and count on God to protect his turf no matter what.

It will come as quite a surprise to many that God cares more about his people than he does about his real estate. God will give up his home on earth, as many Jews consider Jerusalem to be, if this is what it takes to win back his people.

Not only is it possible for Jerusalem to be destroyed, Micah warns. It *will* be destroyed. That's Micah's warning for both Jewish capitals—Jerusalem and Samaria.

Oddly, the destruction will come in just the way the Jews expected protection: "God will protect it," they sang of Jerusalem, in one of many Bible songs praising the city. "The nations are in chaos, and their kingdoms crumble! God's voice thunders, and the earth melts!" (Psalm 46:5–6).

But not this time.

For Jerusalem and Samaria, "The LORD is coming! . . . The mountains melt beneath his feet" (Micah 1:3–4). But it's not the foreign nations in chaos. It's the Jewish nations.

Micah's World

Sea of Galilee

ISRAEL

Samaria

Mediterranean Sea

Jordan River

Jerusalem

Moresheth

Dead Sea

JUDAH

Small-town prophet with big news. From the tiny village of Moresheth, Micah delivers tragic news to leaders of both Jewish nations: Their kingdoms will fall.

God promises to turn both cities—and the countries they represent—into a plowed heap of ruins. In Jerusalem, "a thicket will grow on the heights where the Temple now stands" (Micah 3:12). God's heaven on earth will become a weed patch.

BAD NEWS for the high and mighty

What sorrow awaits you who lie awake at night, thinking up evil plans. You rise at dawn and hurry to carry them out, simply because you have the power to do so.

MICAH 2:1

Like Amos, Micah seems especially concerned about injustice. With stern warnings of judgment ahead, Micah unloads God's complaints on several elite groups in Jewish society.

- **The greedy rich.** "When you want a piece of land, you find a way to seize it. When you want someone's house, you take it by fraud and violence. You cheat a man of his property, stealing his family's inheritance" (Micah 2:2).
- **Exploitive political leaders.** "You skin my people alive. . . . You chop them up like meat for the cooking pot" (Micah 3:2–3).
- **Prophets prophesying from the gut.** "You promise peace for those who give you food, but you declare war on those who refuse to feed you" (Micah 3:5).
- **Priests looking for a profit.** "You priests teach God's laws only for a price" (Micah 3:11).

These people are supposed to be community leaders who look out for the good of the people they serve. Instead, they serve themselves the good of the people—taking whatever they want.

They're no different than raiders. They covet. They plot. They attack. And they do whatever it takes to get what they think they deserve. Micah warns that God is about to give them what they deserve: a taste of their own medicine.

The little kingdoms they have built for themselves are about to be confiscated. And instead of singing their own praises, they'll be singing a new song: "We are finished, completely ruined!" (Micah 2:4).

Micah lives to see both countries invaded.

The Assyrians decimate Samaria in 722 BC, exiling many Jewish survivors—who apparently never return.

Then in 701 BC the Assyrians invade the southern Jewish nation of Judah. Led by King Sennacherib, the invaders fail to capture Jerusalem. But they devastate the countryside, destroying 46 Judean cities before surrounding Jerusalem. The Jewish king Hezekiah responds by emptying the palace treasury and peeling the gold paneling off the temple doors—delivering it all to Sennacherib. The Assyrians eventually leave, but only after God sends an angel that kills 185,000 soldiers in their camp. A Greek history writer, Herodotus, reported that Sennacherib's army was stopped by a rat infestation—perhaps carrying diseases such as the bubonic plague—that killed many soldiers.

Judah survives for another century. But in 586 BC Babylonian invaders finish what the Assyrians started. Babylon's soldiers tear down Jerusalem stone by stone. Then they exile most of the Jews who survive the two-and-a-half-year siege and the vicious attack that comes after Babylon breaks through the city walls.

THE MESSIAH from Bethlehem

You, O Bethlehem Ephrathah, are only a small village among all the people of Judah. Yet a ruler of Israel will come from you, one whose origins are from the distant past. . . . He will be the source of peace.

MICAH 5:2, 5

Like every other Bible prophet pronouncing doom on the Jews, Micah ends on a positive note. God won't leave the survivors exiled in foreign lands scattered all over the Middle East, from Iran to Egypt.

God promises to bring the remnant of Israel home to rebuild their nation. "Those who were exiles will become a strong nation" (Micah 4:7).

He also promises to send a mysterious ruler. This ruler won't come from a king living in the capital. Instead, he'll be born in the same little village of Israel's most beloved king, David. The village is Bethlehem, six miles south of Jerusalem.

The connection between Ephrathah and Bethlehem is uncertain. Perhaps Ephrathah was an earlier name for the village. Or it might have been the name of the dominant family there, or the first Jewish family to settle there.

Many Jewish scholars in ancient times said these verses point to the Messiah whom God promised to send—a deliverer from David's family who would restore Israel's glory. One ancient Jewish commentary on Micah, the Targum Jonathan, interpreted Micah's prediction this way: "And you, O Bethlehem Ephrath, you who were too small to be numbered among the thousands of the house of Judah, from you shall come forth before Me the Messiah, to exercise dominion over Israel, he whose name was mentioned from before, from the days of creation."

Early Christian scholars would later add that these Jewish scholars were right. The Messiah, Jesus, was born in Bethlehem.

When star-following wise men come to King Herod on a mission to honor what they think is the newborn King of the Jews, Herod presumes they are talking about the Messiah. Many Jews at the time are weary of Rome's century-long occupation. So they're pleading with God for deliverance and expecting it at any moment. The Messiah is very much on their minds.

When Herod asks his scholars where the Messiah will be born, they answer, "In Bethlehem in Judea" (Matthew 2:5). Then they cite their source: Micah 5:2.

O little town. Bethlehem rests quietly on a hilltop while a woman in the early 1900s draws water from a well. Micah predicts that this tiny village, former hometown of King David, will one day produce another great ruler. Seven hundred years later, Jesus is born here.

NAHUM

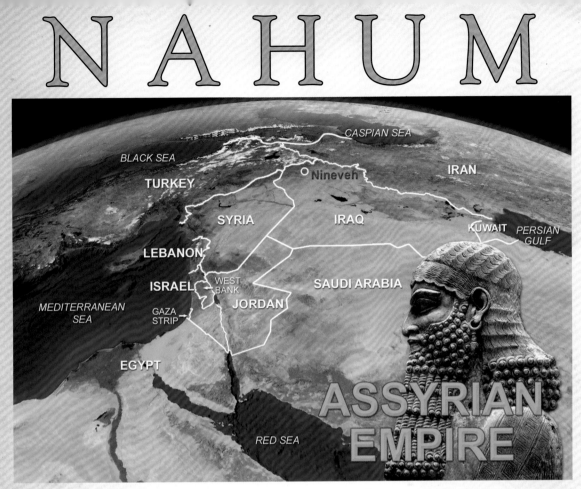

CASPIAN SEA
BLACK SEA
TURKEY
IRAN
○ Nineveh
SYRIA
IRAQ
KUWAIT
PERSIAN GULF
LEBANON
ISRAEL
WEST BANK
SAUDI ARABIA
MEDITERRANEAN SEA
GAZA STRIP
JORDAN
EGYPT
RED SEA

ASSYRIAN EMPIRE

Green and mean. Most of the livable areas between Iran and Egypt were controlled by the Assyrian Empire, marked in green. From their capital in Nineveh, in what is now northern Iraq, they dominated most Middle Eastern nations, forcing them to pay taxes.

JONAH FINALLY GETS HIS WISH

It's about a hundred years too late for Jonah to see it, but his wish comes true. Nineveh—capital of the brutal Assyrian Empire—gets what's coming to it.

God had sent Jonah there to warn the citizens that God was about to destroy the city. But the people repented. So God changed his plans for the changed people.

Instead of feeling like a success for turning the people to God, Jonah felt like a failure because his prediction didn't come true.

"If you won't kill them, kill *me*!" Jonah pouted. "I'm better off dead!" (Jonah 4:3 THE MESSAGE).

That's how the book ends—with Jonah whining and God reminding him that he's God, so he's allowed to forgive people who repent.

But a century later, times have changed. God calls on Nahum to deliver Jonah's message all over again: Nineveh is about to fall. There's no indication that God told Nahum to deliver the message in person, though one legend says Nahum lived near the city. But the context of the book makes it seem more likely that Nahum is living in the southern Jewish nation of Judah, since these folks appear to be his audience. Nahum is writing to assure them that the Assyrians are going to get the punishment to fit their crimes: death.

The Assyrians have already scratched Jonah's northern Jewish nation of Israel off the world map, exiling many of the citizens and resettling the territory with foreign pioneers. And they've bullied Judah big-time, destroying 46 walled cities and forcing the king to pay heavy taxes each year.

Nahum probably lives long enough to see his prediction come true. Within 50 years of his prophecy, perhaps much less, Nineveh is a ghost town and a free source of used bricks—all you can carry.

Getting it in writing. Babylonian records like this—one of several tablets from the Babylonian Chronicle—confirm that many of Nahum's predictions about the fall of Assyria come true. Written in wedge-shaped cuneiform characters, the chronicle tells of the Babylonian attack on Assyria's capital, flooding that collapses the city walls, along with the looting and burning of the city—all predicted by Nahum.

MAIN POINT:

A superpower like the Assyrian Empire is no match for God. He'll punish the Assyrians for a long list of sins, including war crimes and idolatry.

WRITER:

"Nahum, who lived in Elkosh" (Nahum 1:1). No one seems to know where this village was. Various stories place it in northern Israel's region of Galilee, in southern Israel, and even on the outskirts of Nineveh. Some Jewish scholars writing in the Targum, an ancient collection of Bible commentary and interpretations, say Elkosh wasn't a real place. The word means "God is harsh." So the scholars speculate that it's a symbol for what God was about to do to Assyria.

DATE:

Clues in the book suggest Nahum delivered his prophecy sometime during a 50-year span: between 663 and 612 BC. He reports the fall of Egypt's capital, Thebes, which took place in 663 BC (Nahum 3:8). And he predicts the fall of Assyria's capital, Nineveh, which happens in 612 BC.

LOCATION:

Nahum targets Nineveh, capital of the Assyrian Empire. The city was located near Mosul, in northern Iraq. Nahum's message, however, seems directed at the only surviving Jewish nation: Judah, in what is now southern Israel.

Assyrian sport. Backed up by bodyguards, an Assyrian king takes the game of shooting fish in a barrel to the arena—which is stocked like a lions' den. Assyrians, famed for their violence, terrorized neighboring nations into paying taxes to the empire.

ASSYRIA is a goner

This is what the LORD says concerning the Assyrians in Nineveh: "You will have no more children to carry on your name. . . . I am preparing a grave for you because you are despicable!"

NAHUM 1:14

The Assyrians weren't always the meanest Middle Easterners you'd never want to meet. But they certainly were by Nahum's day.

It took them nearly 15 centuries to get that nasty. But by the 900s BC—a couple of hundred years before Nahum—they were well on their way to controlling much of the known civilized world, from what is now Iran to Egypt.

In fairness to Assyria, the Bible paints a portrait of this empire that some historians say is too lopsided. From a secular point of view, the Assyrians have a lot going for them. They create the first international empire, kicking open the door to trade, to artistic ideas, and even to an exchange of religious ideas.

But from a spiritual point of view, Bible writers portray them as bottom dwellers. Nahum sums up God's complaint about them with a single sentence: "Where can anyone be found who has not suffered from your continual cruelty?" (Nahum 3:19).

With nations and city-size kingdoms throughout the Middle East paying the bills, Assyria builds an elegant capital. (For a painting of Nineveh, see page 258.) The palace alone covers three large city blocks. And the desert city—nearly three square miles of lakes, gardens, parks, homes, and businesses—is surrounded by a river and moats and further protected by some eight miles of walls.

Yet these natural and man-made barriers won't be enough to protect it, Nahum warns. Nineveh's elegance, built from bones and blood, will turn to dust.

Many of Nahum's predictions are confirmed by history.

- "Your enemy is coming to crush you, Nineveh" (Nahum 2:1). A coalition force marches on Assyria in 612 BC. This includes the long-oppressed Babylonians in Iraq's southland along with Medes from Iran and Scythians from farther north, near the Black Sea.
- "The river gates have been torn open! The palace is about to collapse! . . . Nineveh is like a leaking water reservoir!" (Nahum 2:6, 8). The Babylonian Chronicle, Babylon's ancient report of the battle, says a flood washed away part of the wall—throwing out a welcome mat for the invaders.
- "Loot the silver! Plunder the gold! There's no end to Nineveh's treasures—its vast, uncounted wealth" (Nahum 2:9). The Babylonian Chronicle confirms the massive wealth looted from the city.
- "Fire will devour you" (Nahum 3:15). Charred ruins show that invaders torched the city.
- "Never again will you plunder conquered nations" (Nahum 2:13). Invaders demolish Nineveh so thoroughly that it has never been rebuilt. Sandstorms covered it within a few centuries. Today it's a grassy mound—a bump on the flat plains. People call it Tell Kuyunjik, "mound of many sheep."

Not quite how Assyrian warriors would want to be remembered.

BAD-MOUTHING the bad boys

"I will lift your skirts and show all the earth your nakedness."

NAHUM 3:5

Nahum calls the Assyrian warriors a bunch of girlie men.

And he does it during patriarchal times. *Patriarch* is from a Greek word that means "father." As in, "not mother." It was a man's world. And most women stayed in the house, where the men said they belonged.

It was quite an insult to call a man a woman. And it was worse to call a man a woman who sells her body, which is exactly what Nahum was saying. "You were nothing more than a prostitute using your magical charms and witchcraft to attract and trap nations" (Nahum 3:4 CEV).

Common punishment for prostitution and adultery was public humiliation, such as stripping the offender naked.

Nahum was promising Assyria similar treatment in front of a gawking international public.

Head count. Assyrian soldiers pile up the severed heads of their victims. Similar scenes show scribes counting heads for the royal record.

TERRORISTS BC

Terror was a tool for Assyria, perhaps the most vicious empire in ancient times. The more their enemies and allies feared them, the less trouble they'd cause. That's what Assyrian leaders figured.

Assyrians took pride in their terror tactics. They actually turned this grisly art form into art suitable for framing—which they proudly mounted on their palace walls. These included scenes of warfare, torture, and the impaling of captives on poles as big as fence posts.

Terror tactics

- Swing babies by their ankles and pop their heads against a stone wall.
- Dismember the soldiers. King Ashurnasirpal bragged, "I captured many troops alive: I cut off of some their arms and hands; I cut off of others their noses, ears, extremities. I gouged out the eyes of many troops."
- Behead the defeated. King Shalmaneser III bragged about building a pyramid of chopped-off heads at the city he demolished. King Ashurnasirpal hung the heads on trees around the conquered town.
- Stack the corpses. Commanders often made a show of the enemy body count, stacking corpses like firewood at the city gate.
- Mutilate the bodies. King Sennacherib, who destroyed 46 Jewish cities, said after filling a plain with enemy corpses, "I cut off their testicles, and tore out their privates like seeds of a cucumber."
- Feed them to the dogs. King Ashurbanipal said he had the bodies of his enemies hacked up so he could feed them to dogs and pigs.
- Humiliate and torture the leaders. Ashurbanipal also said he put a dog chain on one leader and imprisoned him in "a kennel at the eastern gate of Nineveh." There, travelers coming and going could pay their respects to the leader of the pack.

Skinned alive. Palace art from Nineveh shows Assyrian soldiers peeling skin off captives. King Ashurnasirpal bragged, "I skinned all the nobles who rebelled against me and hung their skins on the walls."

HABAKKUK

ARGUING THAT GOD'S NOT FAIR

The prophet Habakkuk wants God to straighten out the Jews—not wipe them off the map.

Habakkuk is a prophet living in the southern Jewish nation of Judah, apparently during its last two or three decades. He's troubled by all the sin he sees:

- violence;
- destruction;
- injustice in the courts; and
- wicked people outnumbering the righteous.

The first Protestant. Martin Luther—father of the Protestant movement—nails to the door of a church his list of 95 criticisms of the Roman Catholic Church. Catholics taught that people are saved through obedience to the church. But Luther argued that salvation comes through faith in God. He got this idea from the apostle Paul (Romans 1:17), who got the idea from the prophet Habakkuk, who got the idea from God: "Only those who live by faith are acceptable to me" (Habakkuk 2:4 CEV).

So he prays about it. And he gets frustrated when God doesn't do anything to fix the problem. So he complains, "How long, O Lord, must I call for help? But you do not listen!" (Habakkuk 1:2).

Not much longer. That's God's answer.

He says he's sending the cruel Babylonians to punish the Jews.

Habakkuk can't believe God would do something so unfair. Babylonians are worse than the Jews, Habakkuk argues.

God assures his prophet that the Babylonians will eventually face their own judgment day. But in the meantime, God will use them to punish the Jews.

Like Job—who questioned God's justice many centuries earlier for dumping so much suffering on him—Habakkuk finally comes around. Neither Job nor Habakkuk figures out why God does what he does. But both decide to trust him nonetheless.

In the entire Bible, there's no statement of faith in God that's more moving, more powerful, and yet more tender than Habakkuk's last words—his closing prayer that he sets to music and sings to God.

MAIN POINT:

Trust God in the hardest times, even when it looks like God is unfairly or callously doing nothing while good people suffer.

WRITER:

"This is the message that the prophet Habakkuk received in a vision" (Habakkuk 1:1). As with most Bible prophets, scholars know almost nothing about him.

DATE:

Bible experts say Habakkuk probably debated God sometime during the quarter century between 612 and 586 BC. The Babylonians became the world's superpower in 612 BC by defeating the Assyrian Empire. Then they destroyed Jerusalem about 26 years later, in 586 BC.

LOCATION:

The southern Jewish nation of Judah. This is where Habakkuk lives and ministers. It's the bull's-eye for the invasion force God is sending.

DISAGREEMENT with God

You can't be serious! . . . Evil men swallow up the righteous and you stand around and watch!

HABAKKUK 1:13 THE MESSAGE

Some Bible experts wonder what the book of Habakkuk is doing in the "prophets" section of God's sacred library. Habakkuk is certainly a prophet—a holy man who delivers God's message to people. That's how he's introduced. But in this book, he delivers no message to the Jews. His words are just a conversation with God—a prayer.

What makes it unique, and prophetlike, is that God answers.

What makes it even more unique is that Habakkuk doesn't like God's answer. And he says so—in much the same style of confrontation that Job used after suddenly losing his children to a windstorm, his herd to raiders, and his health to a skin disease: "He attacks me with a storm and repeatedly wounds me without cause" (Job 9:17).

Habakkuk has asked God to step into Jewish history and stop the sinning that's going on. God replies by saying he's raising up the Babylonian Empire to do just that.

Shocked, Habakkuk doesn't understand how God could do such a thing. The Babylonians are no better than the evil Assyrian Empire they defeated.

God knows. And he lists some of their sins.
- "In their greed they have gathered up many nations" (Habakkuk 2:5).
- They got "rich by extortion" (Habakkuk 2:6).
- They "committed murder throughout the countryside" (Habakkuk 2:17).

In return, God vows, survivors among the people the Babylonians hurt will rise up against them. Babylon will fall.

TALKING to a stone wall

"To speechless stone images you say, 'Rise up and teach us!' Can an idol tell you what to do?"

HABAKKUK 2:19

Worshipping lifeless idols is another complaint God has about the Babylonians. In books by other prophets of Habakkuk's time, it's also one of the most serious complaints God has against the Jews.

"How foolish to trust in your own creation," God says, "a god that can't even talk! What sorrow awaits you who say to wooden idols, 'Wake up and save us!' " (Habakkuk 2:18–19).

Both kingdoms fall. The Jewish nation is erased from the political map in 586 BC when Babylon invades from what is now Iraq. And the Babylonian Empire is erased from the map some 50 years later, in 539 BC, when the Persians invade from what is now Iran.

Babylonian idol. A priest (left) worships Ishtar, queen of heaven and top goddess in Babylon's gallery of gods. (Small photos) Clay and metal idols of the goddess were mass-produced from molds.

THE SINGING prophet

Though the flocks die in the fields, and the cattle barns are empty, yet I will rejoice in the LORD! I will be joyful in the God of my salvation!

HABAKKUK 3:17–18

As hard as it is for Habakkuk to understand why God would send the evil Babylonians to punish the Jews, it's even harder for some people to understand Habakkuk's response.

God is sending vicious invaders into Habakkuk's homeland. They will destroy cities, kill many of the people, exile others, and take whatever they want. Habakkuk himself might be killed or exiled. Certainly some of his family and friends will die.

In a moving prayer, he imagines all of this. He surrounds himself by the devastation of war, with nearly everything of value lost. He has nothing to his name. Yet in this moment he decides he's not going to make the same mistake the Babylonians do: trusting that "wealth will buy security" (Habakkuk 2:9).

HABAKKUK IN THE LIONS' DEN

Daniel wasn't the only prophet in the lions' den. Habakkuk joined him.

That's according to one book in some Christian Bibles: Bel and the Dragon—a 42-verse addition to the book of Daniel. It's printed in many Catholic and Eastern Orthodox Bibles.

"The prophet Habakkuk was in Judea; he had made a stew and had broken bread into a bowl" (Bel and the Dragon 1:33 NRSV). He was about to take this food to field workers. But an angel transported him more than a thousand miles to the lions' den in Babylon, a city about 50 miles south of modern-day Baghdad.

Habakkuk fed Daniel and was returned home.

Habakkuk is going to put his trust in God, no matter what happens.

Everything Habakkuk once owned might be gone—taken from him. But his faith has never been in what he owned—possessions like barns full of cattle. His faith is in the God who owns "the cattle on a thousand hills" (Psalm 50:10).

That's why he goes out singing. Chapter 3 isn't just a prayer; it's a prayer song "sung by the prophet" (Habakkuk 3:1). Most Bible prophecy is written as poetry—and would work as the lyrics to a song, whether or not anyone ever put musical notes to it. But Habakkuk's prayer was almost certainly sung in worship services. Like the psalms, it includes several instructions for the music leader.

From its beginning, this prayer has been a song that people of faith believe is worth singing.

Habakkuk's oldest commentary. This four-and-a-half-foot-long commentary on Habakkuk was discovered among the Dead Sea Scrolls—a sacred library from Jesus' time. The commentator, writing sometime in the first century before Jesus was born, says Habakkuk isn't just a book about Jewish history; it's about the present, as well. The Babylonians, he writes, are just an earlier version of the Romans who can expect the same fate as Babylon. Rome fell in AD 410 to invaders called Goths, from what is now Germany.

ZEPHANIAH

LAST CHANCE TO REPENT

It's no wonder Zephaniah is the most overlooked book in the Bible—one that many Christians have never even heard of.

Besides being one of the shortest books in the Bible—three chapters tallying 53 verses—it delivers a message that's hard to warm up to, and tough to preach. So we shouldn't expect to hear many sermons from Zephaniah.

Here's the prophet's message in a sentence: "I, the LORD, now promise to destroy everything on this earth—people and animals, birds and fish. . . . And I will wipe out the entire human race" (Zephaniah 1:2–3 CEV).

Who wants to hear that?

The prophet does offer an escape clause. But it's weak.

He says if the people repent, "perhaps even yet the LORD will protect you—protect you from his anger on that day of destruction" (Zephaniah 2:3). But repentance or not, the day of destruction is already marked on the calendar.

Each of the Bible prophets who predicts Jewish doom wraps up his message with hope—the restoration of Israel. Oddly—after what appears to be a planet-killing catastrophe—Zephaniah does the same.

He quotes God as saying, "I will give glory and fame to my former exiles, wherever they have been mocked and shamed. On that day I will gather you together and bring you home again. I will give you a good name, a name of distinction, among all the nations of the earth" (Zephaniah 3:19–20).

Do or die. Zephaniah warns the people of the last surviving Jewish nation that the end is near. If they don't do something to stop the sin in their country, God will make the entire nation pay the price. In the eyes of a holy God, sin is a capital offense. The punishment is death.

This puts a perplexing twist on everything Zephaniah has said.

Some scholars insist that Zephaniah is exaggerating—using poetic license to describe the end of the Jewish world, not the end of planet Earth. Others wonder if he's doing double duty and talking about both—the end of the Jewish nation in the near future, and the end of the planet in the distant future. This is another reason people overlook this book. It's a tough book to figure out.

MAIN POINT:

God is giving the Jews one last chance to repent. If they don't take it, God will destroy their nation. But after the punishment, God promises to raise up a new generation of Jews devoted to him.

WRITER:

"The LORD gave this message to Zephaniah ...the son of Cushi, son of Gedaliah, son of Amariah, son of Hezekiah" (Zephaniah 1:1). This is the only time a prophet's family tree gets traced back four generations. And many scholars say it's probably to connect him to one of the most beloved Jewish kings: Hezekiah. If they're right, Zephaniah is a distant relative of the current king, Josiah. Other scholars disagree because:
- The writer doesn't actually say Zephaniah's great-great-grandfather is Hezekiah.
- Hezekiah was a common name.
- There were only three generations between King Hezekiah and his great-grandson Josiah, the king of Zephaniah's day. Not four.
- Amariah isn't listed in the Bible as one of King Hezekiah's sons.

Other prophets living in Zephaniah's time include Nahum, who began ministering before Josiah's reform, along with Jeremiah and Habakkuk, who ministered after Josiah's short-lived reform.

DATE:

"When Josiah son of Amon was king of Judah" (Zephaniah 1:1). Josiah reigned from 640 to 609 BC, taking the throne at age eight after his father was murdered. Many scholars say Zephaniah's description of the Jewish nation tracks well with conditions between 640–621 BC. After that, the grown-up Josiah led the nation in a spiritual reform movement—perhaps in response to Zephaniah's message.

LOCATION:

The southern Jewish nation of Judah. The Assyrians had defeated and dispersed Jews in the northern Jewish nation of Israel about a century earlier.

CREATION in reverse

"I will sweep away people and animals alike. I will sweep away the birds of the sky and the fish in the sea."

ZEPHANIAH 1:3

Bible experts have taken a close look at the order of the targets on this divine hit list:

- people
- animals
- birds
- fish

What's jarring about this order is that it's the exact opposite of the order in which God created life.

- "Let the waters swarm with fish" (Genesis 1:20).
- "Let the skies be filled with birds" (Genesis 1:20).
- "Let the earth produce every sort of animal" (Genesis 1:24).
- "God created human beings" (Genesis 1:27).

As complete as creation is now—on a planet teeming with life—that's how complete the destruction will be after God's judgment. No life at all.

Optimist in trouble. Surrounded by floodwater from the rising Mississippi River, this homeowner sends his message to the sky. Zephaniah warns of a coming disaster as destructive as the flood in Noah's day—wiping out all life on earth.

GOOD-BYE, world, good-bye

"I will wipe humanity from the face of the earth."

Extreme to the max, Zephaniah dooms not only the Jewish nation. He dooms all life on the planet. Even the animals of land, sea, and air—as though they did something wrong.

Oddly, Zephaniah delivers this message during the reign of one of Judah's few godly kings.

Josiah inherits the throne at age eight when his father, King Amon, angers palace officials so much that they murder him. By age 16, Josiah starts exploring the religion of his ancestor David. That's a radically new direction for his family, since his father, as well as his grandfather Manasseh, worshipped idols. By age 20, Josiah is launching a religious reform, destroying pagan shrines. And by age 26, he's renovating Solomon's neglected, 300-year-old temple in Jerusalem.

Some Bible experts speculate that Zephaniah delivered his message during Josiah's early years, before the Jewish revival started. The sins Zephaniah describes certainly fit Judah during those years:

- Its leaders are like roaring lions hunting for their victims.
- Its judges are like ravenous wolves at evening time who by dawn have left no trace of their prey.
- Its prophets are arrogant liars seeking their own gain.
- Its priests defile the temple by disobeying God's instructions (Zephaniah 3:3–4).

What's clear in Zephaniah is that the Jews have sinned, judgment day is coming, and the prophet is pleading with his people to repent. "Gather around, before it's too late. . . . If you do right and are humble, perhaps you will be safe on that day when the LORD turns loose his anger" (Zephaniah 2:1–3 CEV).

What's not clear is the extent of this doomsday judgment. Zephaniah, like most other prophets in the Bible, uses poetry to deliver his message. So it's sometimes hard to know how literally to take his words. Some scholars say that a rose by any other name is still a rose, and worldwide doom is still worldwide doom.

Others argue that Zephaniah is using a technique that Jesus would later employ—exaggeration for emphasis. Zephaniah uses this to describe the horrific fall of Judah that will take place within a generation, in 586 BC. If Zephaniah's prophecy helps spark Josiah's reform in 621 BC, as many scholars suggest it did, then Babylon would crush Judah only 35 years later.

Still other scholars say there could be elements of both the near future and the distant future in Zephaniah's message.

Isaiah did this kind of thing, most scholars agree, when he predicted the birth of a son in a futile attempt to stop King Ahaz from joining forces with Assyria. "The virgin [young woman] will conceive a child! She will give birth to a son and will call him Immanuel" (Isaiah 7:14). That newborn child was a sign in Isaiah's day. But New Testament writers said Isaiah's prophecy also worked on a second level, pointing to Christ.

Jesus also did this when he talked about when "the end will come" (Matthew 24:14). Much of what he said was fulfilled when Rome sacked Jerusalem 40 years later. But part of his prophecy seems to await a future fulfillment.

WHO DIES—JEWISH NATION OR EVERYONE?

Is Zephaniah exaggerating when he talks about the end of the world?

Some Bible experts say he means exactly what he says. Others argue that he's poetically describing the upcoming fall of Judah. Here are a few of the key points from both arguments, followed by counterpoints from those who disagree.

Everyone dies

- Zephaniah plainly and repeatedly says God is going to wipe out all life on the planet. *Counterpoint:* This is poetry and should be read that way. Besides, if everyone dies, how can God say to the Jews, "I will gather you together and bring you home again" (Zephaniah 3:20)? Who's left to bring home?
- Zephaniah names countries north, south, east, and west of Judah—all four points of the world compass. *Counterpoint:* The few nations mentioned are those of special concern to Judah during Josiah's reign.
  1. **Philistia.** Assyria had exiled some Jews there, and Josiah wanted them back.
  2. **Moab and Ammon.** In what is now Jordan, these countries took land from the Israelite tribes of Gad, Manasseh, and Reuben.
  3. **Ethiopia.** Egypt's defeat of this country signaled the possible end of Assyrian domination in the Middle Eastern southland.
  4. **Assyria.** This empire controlled Judah.

Only the Jewish nation dies

- "That terrible day of the LORD is near" (Zephaniah 1:14). Judah fell a few decades later. But the world is still here—2,600 years later. *Counterpoint:* "A day is like a thousand years to the Lord, and a thousand years is like a day. The Lord isn't really being slow about his promise, as some people think. No, he is being patient for your sake. He does not want anyone to be destroyed, but wants everyone to repent" (2 Peter 3:8–9).
- Zephaniah predicts that after the destruction, God will bring home "my former exiles" (Zephaniah 3:19). So he's obviously talking about the upcoming exile into Babylon. *Counterpoint:* Perhaps he's referring to more than one judgment day in his book—one for the Jews in the immediate future and one for everyone at the end of human history.

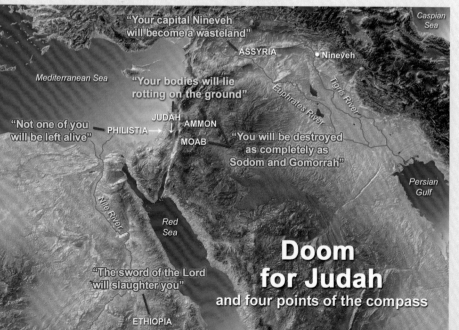

"Your capital Nineveh will become a wasteland"

ASSYRIA • Nineveh

Caspian Sea

Mediterranean Sea

"Your bodies will lie rotting on the ground"

Euphrates River

Tigris River

JUDAH AMMON

"Not one of you will be left alive"

PHILISTIA → ↓

MOAB

"You will be destroyed as completely as Sodom and Gomorrah"

Persian Gulf

Nile River

Red Sea

"The sword of the Lord will slaughter you"

Doom for Judah
and four points of the compass

ETHIOPIA

Doom in four directions. After warning that God will destroy Judah, Zephaniah turns his doom to Judah's neighbors in all four directions: north, south, east, and west. This symbolizes worldwide disaster, according to some Bible experts. Others disagree, saying the localized predictions came true. Nineveh is still a rock pile. The nations of Philistia, Ammon, and Moab are gone. And Judah and Ethiopia were both conquered within a few decades.

THE DAY after judgment

At last your troubles will be over, and you will never again fear disaster.

After judgment day comes restoration day. Zephaniah ends his short prophecy with what sounds a bit like double-talk—a description of two scenarios at once.

Scene one. Clearly he's talking about God bringing the Jewish exiles home to rebuild their nation: " 'The accumulated sorrows of your exile will dissipate. . . . I'll bring you back home—a great family gathering! You'll be famous and honored all over the world. You'll see it with your own eyes—all those painful partings turned into reunions!' God's Promise" (Zephaniah 3:18–20 THE MESSAGE).

Scene two. But there's more than a return from exile going on here. Perhaps looking to a distant future, Zephaniah envisions a perfect world ruled by a loving God.

The description sounds much like this utopian vision of a New Jerusalem at the end of human history and at the beginning of a new life with God: "Look, God's home is now among his people! He will live with them, and they will be his people. . . . He will wipe every tear from their eyes, and there will be no more death or sorrow or crying or pain. All these things are gone forever" (Revelation 21:3–4).

Zephaniah's similar version of utopia: "The remnant of Israel will do no wrong; they will never tell lies or deceive one another. They will eat and sleep in safety, and no one will make them afraid. . . . The LORD himself, the King of Israel, will live among you! At last your troubles will be over, and you will never again fear disaster" (Zephaniah 3:13, 15).

HAGGAI

God vs. farmer. In a backbreaking job, a woman in Israel tills the soil with a mattock. Haggai delivers a warning to farmers of his day: They can expect nothing but one pitiful harvest after another until the Jerusalem temple is rebuilt.

PUTTING GOD ON HOLD—FOR 18 YEARS

Israel's holiest site on earth, the Jerusalem temple, is a rock pile.

Invaders from Babylon, in what is now Iraq, tore down most of the city in 586 BC and then deported the Jews to Babylon.

That exile lasted about 50 years, until 539 BC when Persians from what is now Iran defeated Babylon and freed the political prisoners. The Persian emperor Cyrus respected religion. And he gave the freed prisoners his blessing to rebuild their temples. He said so in a clay document that has survived from his reign: the Cyrus Cylinder (see photo on page 128). In this document he asked the freed prisoners to do him a favor: Say a prayer for me.

About 50,000 Jews returned in the first wave back to Israel. They quickly built a foundation for a new temple. But the work stopped when a new emperor came to the throne. Non-Jewish settlers in the Jewish homeland complained to this emperor about the rebuilding project. They said the Jews had a long history of rebelling against empires, first the Assyrians, then the Babylonians, and perhaps the Persians next.

The emperor halted the work. And for the next 18 years the Jews went about their business, living without their temple. They didn't seem to appeal the emperor's decision—not even after a new emperor arrived in year 17.

In the fall of year 18, after what appears to have been a terrible year for the crops, Haggai calls on the Jews to finish rebuilding the temple. Only then will God bless the land again, Haggai warns.

By this time, the Jews have been without a temple for 66 years. An entire generation of Jews has learned to live without it. Haggai must feel that if the temple isn't rebuilt soon, there will be no one left with memories of the old temple or with the desire to build a new one.

MAIN POINT:

If the Jewish people pick up where they left off nearly two decades earlier, and finish rebuilding the Jerusalem temple that Babylon demolished, God will end the drought and bless the nation.

WRITER:

The prophet Haggai is the writer. He's possibly an old man since he seems to remember how majestic Solomon's temple looked before the Babylonians tore it down 66 years earlier. If he was an elderly man at the time, that could help explain why his ministry was so short.

DATE:

Haggai delivers his prophecies during a span of just four months: August 29 to December 18, 520 BC. The dates are unusually precise because Haggai identifies the day, month, and year, along with historical landmarks preserved in dated Persian records. Haggai begins his work about 18 years after the first wave of Jews return from exile in Babylon.

LOCATION:

Jerusalem

GOD: Build me a house

The LORD sent this message through the prophet Haggai: "Why are you living in luxurious houses while my house lies in ruins?"

HAGGAI 1:3–4

The prophet Haggai takes his message to the top Jewish official: Zerubbabel, governor of what used to be the southern nation of Judah. Now it's the Persian province of Judah. Though Zerubbabel is just a governor, he's a descendant of King David and the lead candidate for king if Judah ever regains its independence.

Mount of Olives ridge

Temple hillto

Western Wall

Holy hill. The Jewish temple once sat on this Jerusalem hilltop, where Islam's Dome of the Rock took up residence 1,300 years ago. This gold-domed shrine—Islam's third holiest site in the world—commemorates Muhammad's ascent into heaven. The Western Wall below it is the holiest Jewish site on earth—and a place where many Jews come to pray. It's just a retaining wall that holds up the hillside. But it's all that remains of the ancient Jewish temple.

It's late in August, when most crops have been harvested. Apparently, it has been a tough year for farmers and herders—the two main jobs of Jews at the time. Quoting God, Haggai says, "I have called for a drought on your fields and hills—a drought to wither the grain and grapes and olive trees and all your other crops, a drought to starve you and your livestock and to ruin everything you have worked so hard to get" (Haggai 1:11).

This is just one of Haggai's several warnings, which are based on curses and blessings from the nearly 1,000-year-old laws of Moses:
- bad harvest (Deuteronomy 28:38);
- food shortages (Deuteronomy 8:10); and
- lack of clothing (Deuteronomy 10:18).

Haggai's point is that these curses will remain Judah's fate until the temple is rebuilt. He drives home this message with a piece of logic that even the most uneducated could understand: The Jews have been living in homes for 18 years, so isn't it about time to build a home for God?

Many people throughout Haggai's world think of temples as the earthly dwelling place of the gods. So do the Jews, though they understand that God isn't limited to the temple.

Solomon expressed this eloquently when he started planning the first temple. "This must be a magnificent Temple because our God is greater than all other gods. But who can really build him a worthy home? Not even the highest heavens can contain him!" (2 Chronicles 2:5–6).

By law, this temple becomes the one and only place where God accepts sacrifices.

- "Be careful not to sacrifice your burnt offerings just anywhere you like. You may do so only at the place the LORD will choose within one of your tribal territories. There you must offer your burnt offerings" (Deuteronomy 12:13–14).
- "I have heard your prayer," God tells Solomon, "and have chosen this Temple as the place for making sacrifices" (2 Chronicles 7:12).

WORK begins

They began to work on the house of their God. . . .on September 21 of the second year of King Darius's reign.

HAGGAI 1:14–15

Zerubbabel believes Haggai's message and enthusiastically jumps into the building project. It takes him only about three weeks to get organized. Then the work begins.

Temple Timeline
1,000 years of history

AD

691 Muslims build Dome of the Rock on temple mount

70 Romans destroy temple
AD 64 Herod's renovation complete
20 Herod starts expanding temple

March 12, 515 Second temple completed
August 29, 520 Haggai tells Jews to finish the building
September 21, 520 Work resumes

536 Jews lay foundation for second temple

622 Josiah repairs aging temple
586 Babylonians destroy Temple

960 Temple completed
967 BC Solomon starts first temple

BC

283

Darius the Great has been on the throne for more than a year, the first of his 35 years as emperor of Persia. Ezra's book fills in the gaps about what happens after the building starts, even mentioning Haggai by name.

Non-Jewish settlers don't want to see the Jewish nation rebuilt. So they file a complaint with Darius. They remind him that a previous emperor, Artaxerxes, ordered the work stopped because of the Jews' tendency for rebellion. Darius asks his archivist to check this in the royal records. The archivist does confirm Artaxerxes' order, but he also finds the original ruling by Cyrus. This ruling not only gives the Jews permission to rebuild the temple, it orders their neighbors to pay for it.

"I hereby decree," Darius writes, "that you are to help these elders of the Jews as they rebuild this Temple of God. You must pay the full construction costs, without delay, from my taxes collected in the province west of the Euphrates River so that the work will not be interrupted" (Ezra 6:8).

A month into the rebuilding, Haggai admits that the temple isn't shaping up to look like much—at least not compared to Solomon's temple. (For a painting of Solomon's temple, see page 104.) But Haggai promises, "The future glory of this Temple will be greater than its past glory" (Haggai 2:9).

This is a promise that has to wait for 500 years. Ezra reports that Zerubbabel's temple is finished on March 12, 515 BC, some four and a half years after the work started. Not until 20 BC does King Herod the Great launch such an expansion and upgrade to Jerusalem's second temple that many Bible historians refer to it as the third temple—and by far the largest and most majestic.

Herod even expands the hilltop and shores it up with retaining walls, one of which survives: the Western Wall, sometimes called the Wailing Wall. Work continues for more than 80 years, finally ending in AD 64.

Shekel for shekel, Zerubbabel's temple—the most modest of the three—is the best buy. It lasts longer than Herod's temple and Solomon's temple combined. In fact, the more elegant the temple, the shorter its life span. Herod's temple, the most magnificent of all, survived only six years. The Romans tore it down in AD 70 while crushing a Jewish revolt. Solomon's temple lasted 400 years before Babylonians pulled it down. But Zerubbabel's temple survived 500 years before Herod began the makeover—and almost a century beyond that.

ZECHARIAH

FINALLY, A PROPHET WITH GOOD NEWS

It's not that other Bible prophets were pessimists, delivering only bad news. They just seem that way compared to Zechariah.

Heaven-sent. Angels appear in visions to Zechariah, acting out symbolic scenes and then explaining the messages behind them. Artists often paint angels with wings, though the Bible rarely describes them that way. Wings may have started appearing in paintings because the ancients couldn't image how messengers would travel from the heavens, unless they flew like birds.

Most other Bible prophets lived before God punished the Jews by exiling them to Assyria and Babylon, in what is now Iraq. So those earlier prophets warned the Jews where they were headed if they didn't stop sinning. But even those prophets offered hope, promising that God would bring the Jews home one day.

Zechariah lives after the exile. Jews are back in their homeland, rebuilding their nation.

But 18 years after their return, it's still a struggle for them.

- They live under the shadow of another superpower: Persia. The Persians treat Judah as a province of the empire, not as an independent nation.
- Farming and herding are tough work, especially given the drought that Zechariah's prophet colleague, Haggai, describes.
- There's no temple in which to seek God's help, though Haggai has just recently convinced the Jews to start rebuilding it.

These are people who need good news. So with visions and prophecies, Zechariah delivers just that.

He promises the Jews that God is in control and that he'll help them finish the temple.

Beyond that, Zechariah promises that God will send Jesus—at least that's how some New Testament writers interpret his prophecies. In just 14 chapters, Zechariah delivers more prophecies about Jesus than any other book in the Old Testament, with the single exception of Isaiah's megabook of 66 chapters.

Zechariah sees even beyond the first coming of Jesus. The prophet sees what appears to be an end-time, utopian world when "the LORD will be king over all the earth. On that day there will be one LORD—his name alone will be worshiped" (Zechariah 14:9).

MAIN POINT:

"My Temple will be rebuilt, says the LORD of Heaven's Armies. . . . The towns of Israel will again overflow with prosperity" (Zechariah 1:16–17).

WRITER:

Most Bible experts agree that the first eight chapters of this book were written by "the prophet Zechariah son of Berekiah and grandson of Iddo" (Zechariah 1:1).

But many aren't so sure about the final six chapters: 9–14. There are several reasons:

- The tone and writing style are different.
- The message seems to deal more with Israel's distant future than with Zechariah's time, reflected in chapters 1–8.
- Zechariah speaks of a threat coming from the Greeks (Zechariah 9:13), though Persia was the superpower of the day. Greece didn't defeat the Persians until 332 BC—about 200 years after Zechariah.

Bible experts who say Zechariah wrote the whole book argue that a writer's style can change with time and that prophets are in the business of talking about the future—immediate and distant.

Also, they argue that the Greeks were a rising threat to Persia as early as 490 BC. That's when their much smaller army stopped Persia's 25,000-man invasion force at the famous battle of Marathon. There, a Greek soldier started the tradition of 26-mile marathon races by running to Athens with the news of their victory.

DATE:

Zechariah's ministry spans at least two years, beginning in October or November of 520. That's the autumn when the Jews, at Haggai's prodding, start rebuilding the temple. The last date mentioned is December 7, 518 BC, when Zechariah receives a message from God urging the people to show mercy to each other, and especially to the poor.

LOCATION:

Jerusalem

ONE NIGHT of visions

In a vision during the night, I saw a man sitting on a red horse. . . .
Behind him were riders on red, brown, and white horses. I asked the
angel who was talking with me, "My lord, what do these horses mean?"

ZECHARIAH 1:8–9

February 15, 519 BC, turns out to be a memorable night for Zechariah. Angels on horseback appear to him in a vision—the first of eight visions he'll have that night. This date and several other dates in Zechariah are this precise because the writer identifies the day by landmark events in surviving Persian records.

Zechariah may be terrified by the army of angels appearing suddenly before him, but the point of the vision is just the opposite. It's intended to calm and reassure him and all Jews.

Zechariah learns that these angels have been patrolling the earth and are perhaps the

ZECHARIAH'S EIGHT VISIONS

Zechariah has eight bizarre visions in a single night. These visions seem intent on assuring the Jews that God is watching out for them and that better days are ahead for Jerusalem and the entire Jewish nation.

What Zechariah sees	What it means
An army of angels mounted on horseback (Zechariah 1:7–17).	Apparently a peacekeeping force, they've been patrolling the earth.
Four animal horns and four blacksmiths (Zechariah 1:18–21).	The horns represent nations that hurt Judah. The blacksmiths, perhaps angels, have come to destroy those nations.
A man with a tape measure, on his way to measure Jerusalem (Zechariah 2:1–5).	Jerusalem will become so prosperous that there won't be enough room for all the people who want to live there.
An angel gives clean clothes to a high priest dressed in filthy clothes and then forgives him of his sins and puts him in charge of the temple (Zechariah 3:1–10).	God has purified Israel's priests for service in the temple. Many also see this as a symbol of the coming Messiah and the forgiveness of sins that will follow.
A golden lampstand, seven smaller lamps fueled by olive oil, and two olive trees (Zechariah 4:1–14).	God is in charge. The seven lamps symbolize God's all-seeing eyes. Many scholars guess that the golden lamp represents God himself and that the trees represent God's chosen Jewish leaders: Governor Zerubbabel and the high priest.
A huge, flying scroll (Zechariah 5:1–4).	The scroll has curses for anyone in the land below who sins.
A woman sitting inside a grain basket that is carried off to Babylon to be worshipped (Zechariah 5:5–11).	The woman symbolizes wickedness.
Four chariots (Zechariah 6:1–8).	The charioteers are spirit beings sent from God to patrol the earth in all four directions and to do his work.

ones responsible for the relative peace that the Jews experienced during and after their exile. Then he listens as the commanding angel says a prayer. God has been angry at Jerusalem for 70 years, the angel reminds him. So the angel asks how much longer God will withhold his mercy from the Jews.

Seventy is a round number. It has actually been 69 years since Babylonian soldiers lay siege to Jerusalem, and 67 years since they destroyed it.

God answers the angel, saying the days of mercy have come.

"I have returned to show mercy to Jerusalem. My Temple will be rebuilt. . .and measurements will be taken for the reconstruction of Jerusalem" (Zechariah 1:16).

Actually, the rebuilding of the temple had started almost five months earlier, on September 21. But the Jews had started that project once before and stopped. This time God urges them to finish what they started.

"Among the other nations, Judah and Israel became symbols of a cursed nation," God says. "But no longer! Now I will rescue you and make you both a symbol and a source of blessing. So don't be afraid. Be strong, and get on with rebuilding the Temple!" (Zechariah 8:13).

In a fourth vision, Zechariah sees the high priest purified for ministry in the temple by changing his old, dirty clothes for new ones.

The angel handling the purification says that this purified priest and the others serving with him are symbols of a ser-

VISION-INDUCING MUSIC

At least one prophet in the Bible used soothing harp music to induce a trance that would allow him to hear from God. That prophet was Elisha.

It happened when three kings on a march into battle ran out of water holes. They asked Elisha if God would help them. That's when Elisha called for a harp.

The gentle strums worked, since God delivered his message "while the harp was being played" (2 Kings 3:15). Elisha told the kings that God would produce pools of water in the valley where the army was camped. The next morning, pools mysteriously appeared.

One of the main ways God communicated to prophets was through visions experienced during a trancelike state. God also used dreams to deliver messages.

Music from many ancient cultures, especially Asian countries, is known for its sedating, hypnotic, trance-inducing effects. This music usually has a level tone and a steady rhythm. Spiritual leaders, such as shamans of India, used music like this to create a trance that they said blurred the distractions of this world and helped them communicate with the spirit world.

vant whom God will send—a "Branch" (Zechariah 3:8). Years earlier, Isaiah and Jeremiah each spoke of a future leader who would be a branch from King David's family tree. Jews came to think of this branch as the Messiah, a great ruler for a new and wonderful day. Early Christians saw Jesus as this Messiah.

BETTER DAYS are coming

On that day the LORD their God will rescue his people, just as a shepherd rescues his sheep. They will sparkle in his land like jewels in a crown.

ZECHARIAH 9:16

Much of the second half of Zechariah, beginning with chapter 9, has an end-time apocalyptic feel. It reads a bit like Revelation and similar end-time passages scattered throughout the New Testament.

Zechariah says that nations will gang up on Jerusalem and try to move it like a person would pick up a rock and toss it away. "On that day," God says, "I will make Jerusalem an immovable rock" (Zechariah 12:3). Other nations will try to move it, but they'll only hurt themselves trying.

After crushing Israel's enemies and restoring the glory of his people, God will throw open the doors to a wonderful age of righteousness and peace. Zechariah makes it sound like heaven on earth—or maybe just heaven.

• "On that day a fountain will be opened. . .a fountain to cleanse them from all their sins" (Zechariah 13:1).

Compare: "The water I give. . .becomes a fresh, bubbling spring within them, giving them eternal life" (John 4:14).

• "On that day the sources of light will no longer shine, yet there will be continuous day! Only the LORD knows how this could happen. There will be no normal day and night, for at evening time it will still be light" (Zechariah 14:6–7).

Compare: That sounds very much like a Bible passage talking about the New Jerusalem, where people will live forever with God: "The city has no need of sun or moon, for the glory of God illuminates the city, and the Lamb is its light" (Revelation 21:23).

• "Two-thirds of the people in the land will be cut off and die. . . . But one-third will be left in the land. I will bring that group through the fire and make them pure. I will refine them like silver and purify them like gold" (Zechariah 13:8–9).

Compare: "There is wonderful joy ahead, even though you have to endure many trials for a little while. These trials will show that your faith is genuine. It is being tested as fire tests and purifies gold—though your faith is far more precious than mere gold. So when your faith remains strong through many trials, it will bring you much praise and glory and honor on the day when Jesus Christ is revealed to the whole world" (1 Peter 1:6–7).

In the end, Zechariah sees a wonderful existence: God reigns and everyone is grateful—and worshipping him for it.

PREDICTING JESUS

Writing 500 years before Jesus, Zechariah makes astonishingly accurate predictions about Jesus' life and ministry. New Testament writers took notice and declared that Jesus fulfilled those prophecies. Here are three of the more obvious prophecies about Jesus.

Zechariah's prediction	Jesus' fulfillment
Donkey rider "Shout in triumph, O people of Jerusalem! Look, your king is coming to you. He is righteous and victorious, yet he is humble, riding on a donkey's colt" (Zechariah 9:9).	With Jesus riding a donkey into Jerusalem on what becomes known as Palm Sunday, cheering crowds welcome him as the Messiah, shouting, "Praise God for the Son of David!" (Matthew 21:9).
Sold for 30 pieces of silver A good shepherd is paid what he's worth: 30 pieces of silver. But God tells him, "Throw it to the potter" (Zechariah 11:13).	Judas betrays Jesus for what priests think Jesus is worth: "thirty pieces of silver" (Matthew 26:15). Judas later returns the money and hangs himself. Priests use the money "to buy the potter's field, and they made it into a cemetery for foreigners" (Matthew 27:7).
Scattering the sheep "Strike down the shepherd, and the sheep will be scattered" (Zechariah 13:7).	The night of his arrest, Jesus tells his disciples: "Tonight all of you will desert me. For the Scriptures say, 'God will strike the Shepherd, and the sheep of the flock will be scattered' " (Matthew 26:31).

MALACHI

Bad bull. Sheep, goats, and bulls were the most common animals Jews sacrificed to God in Bible times. These sacrifices paid the penalty for sin. By God-given law, the Jews were to sacrifice only animals in perfect health. But Malachi accused the Jews of sacrificing sick and crippled animals. That means the Jews were sinning at the very moment they were asking God for forgiveness.

FRAUDS AT WORSHIP

Malachi gets the last word in the Old Testament.

As far as many Jews are concerned, Malachi and his contemporaries—Haggai and Zechariah—are the last prophets to walk the planet. Prophecy ends with them, at least according to conventional Jewish wisdom in the centuries that follow.

That makes Malachi's message all the more important.

Apparently ministering about a century after the Jews return to their homeland and rebuild Jerusalem, Malachi warns that God is upset with the Jews. Again.

To their credit, the Jews aren't worshiping idols—which was the main sin that got them divinely deported to Babylon in modern-day Iraq. But other sins are creeping into their culture:

- Many Jews are bringing defective animals to the temple as sacrifices for God.
- Priests are letting them get away with it.
- Some men are marrying non-Jewish women who worship idols.
- Many Jews have stopped tithing a tenth of their income for the upkeep of the temple and its ministries.
- Some Jews are cheating their employees, oppressing the poor, and depriving the helpless of justice.

Judgment day is coming, Malachi warns. When that happens, the wicked will be "burned up like straw," while those who serve God "will go free, leaping with joy like calves let out to pasture" (Malachi 4:1–2).

GIVING GOD the leftovers

"When you give blind animals as sacrifices, isn't that wrong? And isn't it wrong to offer animals that are crippled and diseased? Try giving gifts like that to your governor, and see how pleased he is!"

MALACHI 1:8

When it comes time to offer sacrifices to God, many Jews are bringing good-for-nothing livestock—including "animals that are stolen and crippled and sick" (Malachi 1:13).

That's not only insulting to God, it's against God's law: "Do not present an animal with defects, because the LORD will not accept it on your behalf. . . . You must not offer an animal that is blind, crippled, or injured, or that has a wart, a skin sore, or scabs" (Leviticus 22:20, 22).

MAIN POINT:

Don't expect to please God by going through the motions of worship. He expects sincerity and obedience.

WRITER:

Malachi is the prophet behind this book, but the Bible says nothing about him. Many scholars doubt this was the writer's real name. *Malachi* means "my messenger." So the book could have been written by an anonymous prophet. In fact, the first Bible translation—from Hebrew to Greek in the 100s BC—translates the word that way: "my messenger."

DATE:

No date is given. But there are several clues that suggest the book was written in the 400s BC: First, Jews were sacrificing in the temple, which was rebuilt in 515 BC. Second, A Jewish governor led them, which is the system Persians set up when they dominated the Middle East. Third, Jews were marrying non-Jews, a problem Ezra addressed in the mid-400s BC.

LOCATION:

Israel, probably when the region was known as the Persian province of Judah

Some of these sacrifices that the Jews are offering are intended to atone for sin—a capital offense in the eyes of a holy God. Sin demands the death penalty. But God created the sacrificial system as a way for sinners to find forgiveness by substituting the death of an animal: "The LORD will accept its death in your place to purify you, making you right with him" (Leviticus 1:4).

Such an important offering for such a great being—the Lord of creation—demands the best a person can afford. Whether it's a bird offered by a poor person or a bull brought by someone wealthy, it has to be fit for the ritual and free of defects.

Yet many Jews are bringing the bane of the barn and the flake of the flock.

"How I wish one of you would shut the Temple doors so that these worthless sacrifices could not be offered!" God says. "I am not pleased with you. . .and I will not accept your offerings" (Malachi 1:10).

Perhaps only a generation or two after their exile in Babylon—where God sent them for disobedience—the Jews already need a refresher course in the Jewish faith. They haven't quite learned their lesson.

A TENTH for the temple

"You have cheated me of the tithes. . . . Bring all the tithes into the storehouse so there will be enough food in my Temple. If you do. . . I will pour out a blessing so great you won't have enough room to take it in! Try it! Put me to the test!"

MALACHI 3:8, 10

As far as many Jews are concerned, they're good religious people.

They believe in God and they obey the ancient laws that God gave them through Moses. They're bringing sacrifices to the temple, though some of the animals can barely walk. Many are probably bringing gifts to the temple: crops and livestock, which serve as salary for the priests and as merchandise that priests can trade for supplies and labor to maintain the temple and its ministries.

But the Jews seem to have gaps in their memory. They act as though it's okay to bring only a token offering.

Yet the law is specific: "One tenth of the produce of the land, whether grain from the fields or fruit from the trees, belongs to the LORD. . . . Count off every tenth animal from your herds and flocks and set them apart for the LORD" (Leviticus 27:30, 32).

Priests collect the crops and livestock much like governments today collect taxes. One of the ministries at the temple is to distribute part of these supplies to poor people in the community, such as widows and orphans.

But many Jews are shortchanging God, the community, and themselves, as well. All the faithful Jews benefit from the ministries of the temple and the priests. There the people find forgiveness for their sins, spiritual renewal, religious education, and a compassionate hand when they're facing a personal crisis. God set up the tithing system to sustain these ministries.

Rather than beating the offending Jews with a verbal club, Malachi offers a carrot. He says God promises that if the people bring the full 10 percent, God will bless them for their obedience. "Your crops will be abundant, for I will guard them from insects and disease. Your grapes will not fall from the vine before they are ripe" (Malachi 3:11).

Why early Christians didn't tithe

Cheerful giver? Digging deep for his wallet, this worshipper seems anything but happy. The picture, from *Harper's Weekly* magazine, was published in 1872—when tithing was still a new idea among Christians.

Christians didn't start tithing 10 percent of their income to the church until the 1800s.

That was the surprising discovery of Paul Merritt Bassett, emeritus professor of the history of Christianity at Nazarene Theological Seminary.

When he began looking into the history of tithing, he already knew that the early Christians didn't tithe. They rejected the practice as one of many Jewish laws rendered obsolete under God's new covenant through Jesus—like the laws about animal sacrifice, kosher food, and circumcision.

Christians said they gave offerings—not tithes. There's no mention of Christians tithing in the New Testament. Instead, they donated what they could. "Whatever you give," Paul said, "is acceptable if you give it eagerly" (2 Corinthians 8:12).

In later centuries, the church in some areas collected a tax from all the citizens. But this wasn't a tithe.

When Bassett started searching for the first Christian sermon on tithing, it didn't show up until the 1800s, just before the Civil War. That's when many Protestant churches got aggressive with religious education, missions, and charitable work. And they needed extra money to pay those bills.

Some pastors found a solution. They started to preach that tithing was a timeless moral law—like the laws about helping the poor. So it was a law that was still in effect—not obsolete as the early Christians had taught.

The idea caught on.

Bassett insists that tithing is still a good idea, since it takes money to maintain church ministries. "But let's free ourselves from the burden of trying to prove the theologically unprovable," he says, "and from the attempt to transform a wonderfully pragmatic device into a holy commandment. God loves a cheerful giver."

SECOND COMING of Elijah

"I am sending you the prophet Elijah before the great and dreadful day of the LORD arrives. His preaching will turn the hearts of fathers to their children, and the hearts of children to their fathers."

MALACHI 4:5–6

Elijah never died. Celestial chariots of fire and a whirlwind carried him away.

Since his body wasn't destroyed, some Jews consider it reasonable that he can return.

Malachi's promise leads many Jews to believe that Elijah will become the advance man for the Messiah—or as Isaiah put it, "the voice of someone shouting, 'Clear the way through the wilderness for the LORD! . . . Then the glory of the LORD will be revealed, and all people will see it together'" (Isaiah 40:3, 5).

At each springtime Passover meal, Jews set out a cup for Elijah in case he should come. And at circumcision ceremonies, they reserve a chair for him.

But Christians teach that Elijah has already come—symbolically and literally.

Symbolically. Jesus said John the Baptist fulfilled Malachi's prophecy. "He is Elijah, the one the prophets said would come" (Matthew 11:14). John qualified as Jesus' advance man by preaching about repentance and by introducing him as "the Lamb of God who takes away the sin of the world!" (John 1:29).

Literally. Later, before Jesus' crucifixion, Elijah and Moses both met with Jesus on a hilltop known as the Mount of Transfiguration. That's where Jesus' body temporarily transfigured into a glowing celestial form. "His clothes became dazzling white, far whiter than any earthly bleach could ever make them" (Mark 9:3).

Malachi ends with the world waiting for the Messiah.

Matthew, the next book in the Christian Bible, begins with the Messiah's arrival as a newborn baby boy: Jesus.

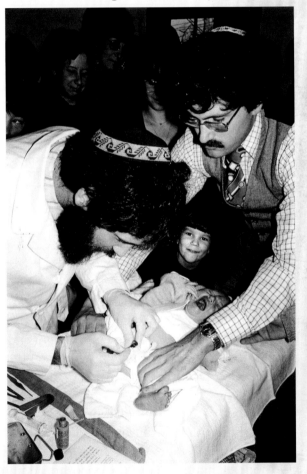

Inviting Elijah. Family and friends gather for the circumcision of an eight-day-old boy, marking his entrance into the Jewish faith. Some Jews reserve a chair for Elijah—in case he comes to announce that this little boy will grow up to become the Messiah God has sent to fix the broken world.

THE APOCRYPHA

Extra books in Christian Bibles

	Protestant	Catholic	Orthodox	Other Christians
39 Books of Old Testament				
Tobit				
Judith				
Esther additions				
Wisdom of Solomon				
Sirach				
Baruch				
Letter of Jeremiah				
Prayer of Azariah & Song of Three Jews				
Susanna				
Bel and the Dragon				
1 Maccabees				
2 Maccabees				
1 Esdras				
Prayer of Manasseh				
Psalm 151				
3 Maccabees				
2 Esdras				
4 Maccabees				

Library of Alexandria. The Apocrypha first appears in a Greek translation of the revered Jewish writings. An Egyptian king comissioned it for his famous library.

BOOKS THAT DIDN'T MAKE THE OLD TESTAMENT CUT

A stack of more than a dozen sacred scrolls never made it into the Jewish Bible.

This stack has a name: Apocrypha (ah-POC-ruh-fuh). It's Greek for "hidden." And that's what many early Christians thought should be done with these scrolls. Written mainly between 300 BC and 70 AD, they weren't considered reliable enough for the Jewish Bible.

Like the Old Testament, the Apocrypha spans many genres: history, romance, prayers, poems, songs, and wise sayings like the proverbs.

Roman Catholics include in their Bible seven books of the Apocrypha, calling them "Deuterocanonical." It means "added later."

When Protestants broke from the Catholics, they dropped the add-ons. The Eastern Orthodox Church did just the opposite, adding several. Some smaller Christian groups, such as the Slavonic Church, added still others. There's no general agreement about which books belong in the Apocrypha.

The library, condensed

Tobit. This is the story of a Jewish man deported to Nineveh, in what is now Iraq. Against Assyrian law, he bravely gives executed Jews a proper burial.

Judith. A Jewish widow, Judith saves her city from attacking Assyrians by going to Assyria's camp, seducing the enemy general, and then cutting off his head.

Esther additions. With 107 extra verses, this Greek version of Esther's story adds more than 50 references to God. The Hebrew version doesn't mention him at all.

Wisdom of Solomon. Sounding a lot like Proverbs, this collection of wise sayings and essays points people to righteous living.

Sirach. Also known as Ecclesiasticus ("Church Book"), this 51-chapter book reads like a combo of Psalms and Proverbs. It features songs and wise advice.

Baruch. Claiming to be the prophet Jeremiah's assistant, Baruch writes a letter to Jews in Jerusalem. Writing from exile in Babylon, modern-day Iraq, he confesses the Jewish nation's sins and prays for deliverance.

Letter of Jeremiah. Jeremiah writes a letter to the exiles in Babylon, warning them not to worship idols.

The Prayer of Azariah and the Song of the Three Jews. This add-on to the book of Daniel is said to be the prayer and the song that Daniel's three friends prayed and sang when Nebuchadnezzar put them in a furnace.

Susanna. A beautiful young woman, Susanna is wrongly accused of having an affair with a mystery man who runs away. Jewish elders—in this case dirty old men—accuse her after she refuses to have sex with them. Daniel proves the elders are lying.

Bel and the Dragon. Daniel uncovers hoaxes about two fake gods. He proves that priests are sneaking into the temple at night to eat food left for Bel—which they claimed the god had been eating. And he feeds a tar-covered hair ball to a "divine" dragon—probably a snake. The ball swells, exploding the snake and proving it's no god.

1 Maccabees. A Jewish priest leads a revolt against Syrian occupiers, winning Israel's independence.

2 Maccabees. More on the war of independence and how God helped the Jews.

1 Esdras. Repackaging much of the material in Ezra, this book tells about the fall of Jerusalem, the exile of Jews into Babylon, and their return home to rebuild Jerusalem and the temple.

Prayer of Manasseh. King Manasseh, perhaps the most evil Jewish king who ever lived, confesses his sins in a 15-verse prayer. This is the king who sacrificed his son to an idol.

Psalm 151. David's song after killing Goliath.

3 Maccabees. Contrary to what the title suggests, this isn't the Jewish war of independence, part 3. Instead, it's about God protecting Jews in Egypt from a king who tries to trample them with a herd of elephants.

2 Esdras. The prophet Ezra's visions of the end times.

4 Maccabees. This is set in the days just before the revolt against Syria, described in 1 Maccabees. The writer urges Jews to keep observing Jewish laws even though the Syrians are executing Jews who don't abandon their faith.

**CHURCH LEADERS SETTLE
ON NEW TESTAMENT BOOKS.**

	Marcion, AD 140	Irenaeus, 180	Tertullian, 200	Origen, 250	Codex Sinaiticus Bible, 325	Athanasius, 367	Council of Carthage, 397
Matthew		■	■	■	■	■	■
Mark		■	■	■	■	■	■
Luke	■	■	■	■	■	■	■
John		■	■	■	■	■	■
Acts		■	■	■	■	■	■
Romans	■	■	■	■	■	■	■
1 Corinthians	■	■	■	■	■	■	■
2 Corinthians	■	■	■	■	■	■	■
Galatians	■	■	■	■	■	■	■
Ephesians	■	■	■	■	■	■	■
Philippians	■	■	■	■	■	■	■
Colossians	■	■	■	■	■	■	■
1 Thessalonians	■	■	■	■	■	■	■
2 Thessalonians	■	■	■	■	■	■	■
1 Timothy		■	■	■	■	■	■
2 Timothy		■	■	■	■	■	■
Titus		■	■	■	■	■	■
Philemon	■		■	■	■	■	■
Hebrews			■	■	■	■	■
James				■	■	■	■
1 Peter		■	■	■	■	■	■
2 Peter				■	■	■	■
1 John		■	■	■	■	■	■
2 John		■	■		■	■	■
3 John					■	■	■
Jude		■	■	■	■	■	■
Revelation		■	■	■	■	■	■
Shepherd of Hermas*		■		■	■		
Epistle of Barnabas*		■		■	■		

For more about this book, see page 401.

**LOCKING IN
THE NEW TESTAMENT.**

It took 300 years for church leaders to agree on which books to put in the New Testament. A short list started the ball rolling: A scholar named Marcion approved one Gospel—Luke—and most of Paul's letters. But as Christian writings continued to circulate among churches, the list grew. Bishop Athanasius, writing an Easter letter to church leaders in AD 367, became the first on record to approve the 27 books of the New Testament. Thirty years later, church leaders meeting in the North African city of Carthage adopted this same list, though some disagreement lingered.

NEW TESTAMENT

By the time Jesus was born, sometime around 6–4 BC, Jews had been waiting for at least six centuries for God to do something new. He said he would.

Through the prophets, God had promised to send a Messiah—a King above all kings who would bring peace to Israel and to the world.

God even promised to radically change the Jewish religion. "The day is coming," God said, "when I will make a new covenant with the people of Israel and Judah" (Jeremiah 31:31). The old covenant—which is a testament or binding agreement—was summed up in the laws of Moses. But the new agreement—the New Testament—between God and his people would come with the Messiah and be summed up in his teachings.

Jesus began his ministry of perhaps three years in about AD 27. It took miracles to convince the Jews he was this promised Messiah. And though his ultimate miracle—the Resurrection—finally convinced his skeptical disciples, even that megamiracle failed to nudge most Jewish scholars away from their entrenched traditions.

But some Jews believed. And through the work of Jesus' disciples, the church was born and began to grow.

At first, stories about Jesus were passed along by word of mouth from eyewitnesses. But as the Jesus generation began to die, writers started putting the stories on paper, making copies of them, and then passing those copies along for local churches to read in their worship meetings. Traveling ministers such as Paul and Peter wrote letters to churches, offering encouragement, teaching, and attempting to solve local problems. These letters, too, were copied and circulated.

In AD 397, church leaders gathered at a council meeting to agree on which writings were authentic:

- those written by apostles or their close associates;
- those widely recognized in local churches as messages from God; and
- those in line with traditional Christian teachings.

They agreed on the 27 books that now make up the library called the New Testament.

MATTHEW

Messiah quest. Sages lead a caravan from what may have been modern-day Iraq or Iran. They're headed to Jerusalem in hopes of honoring a newborn Jewish boy they believe is destined to become a great king—perhaps even the promised Messiah.

FINALLY, THE MESSIAH HAS COME

What makes Matthew so special? Why did early church leaders bump it to the front of the line in the New Testament, ahead of three other books about Jesus?

It probably wasn't the first Gospel written. Most Bible experts guess that Mark holds that distinction.

It certainly isn't the most cerebral. John is the thinking man's Gospel (a word that means "good news").

And it isn't the most compassionate take on Jesus and his ministry. Luke, said to have been written by a medical doctor, holds that title.

But Matthew—better than any other Gospel about Jesus—picks up where the Jewish Bible leaves off. Malachi closes the Old Testament with a promise: God will send a Messiah to fix Israel's problems and bring peace and joy to the people. Matthew opens the New Testament by declaring that this promise from centuries past is now fulfilled: The Messiah has come at last.

And Matthew does it convincingly, quoting one ancient Jewish prophecy after another and explaining how Jesus fulfills each promise—57 in all. Mark comes in a distant second, quoting 30 prophecies.

Matthew and the other Gospels go to great lengths to convince readers that Jesus is the Messiah—for good reason. Jesus is not what anyone expected. The Jews were looking for a warrior, but they got a pacifist. They anticipated a new kingdom of Israel, but they got the spiritual kingdom of God.

Jews—then and now—point to a long list of failed expectations. Promises Jesus didn't meet. But Matthew and the other Gospels point to fulfilled prophecies, divinely insightful teachings, and miracles to convince Jews and others of faith that their expectations were off the mark—that Jesus is the Messiah who has come to fix the world. He's the one whom Israel's last prophet said "will rise with healing in his wings" (Malachi 4:2).

MAIN POINT:

The promised Messiah arrives as a newborn baby boy: Jesus. But most Jews don't recognize him. They're expecting a warrior king like David—someone to restore the independence and glory of Israel. The salvation Jesus brings isn't political. It's spiritual. It's for everyone. And it's forever.

WRITER:

The book doesn't identify the writer. But church leaders beginning in at least the AD 100s said Matthew wrote it. He was a tax collector in Capernaum when Jesus recruited him as a disciple.

DATE:

Matthew's story covers more than 30 years—from sometime before 4 BC to about AD 30. King Herod the Great died in 4 BC. Since the Bible says Herod tried to kill the newborn Jesus in Bethlehem by slaughtering all boys ages two and under, Jesus could have been born in 6 BC. Maybe earlier, if Herod ordered the murders a year or more before he died. Jesus' death in about AD 30 means he lived into his mid to late 30s. Most Bible experts say Matthew was probably written after AD 70—the year Romans destroyed the temple—since the writer emphasizes Jesus' predictions about that destruction.

LOCATION:

Israel. Most of Jesus' ministry takes place in the rolling hills of Galilee, a region in what is now northern Israel.

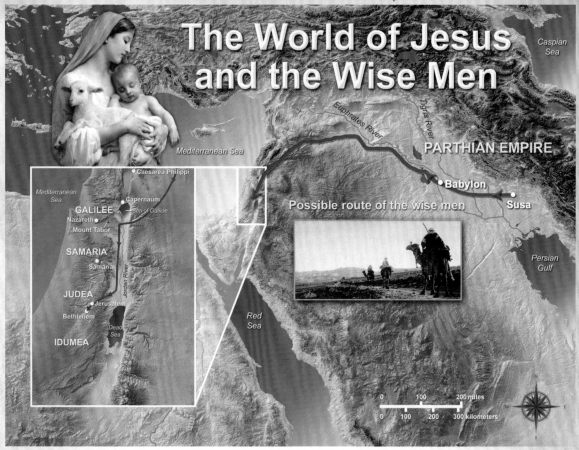

The World of Jesus and the Wise Men

Caspian Sea

Euphrates River

Tigris River

Mediterranean Sea

PARTHIAN EMPIRE

•Babylon

Possible route of the wise men

Susa

Persian Gulf

Caesarea Philippi

Mediterranean Sea

GALILEE
Capernaum
Sea of Galilee
Nazareth•
Mount Tabor

SAMARIA
Samaria•

Jordan River

JUDEA
•Jerusalem
Bethlehem

Dead Sea

Red Sea

IDUMEA

0   100   200 miles
0   100   200   300 kilometers

Wise Easterners. Wise men come from the East looking for a newborn Jewish king. But where in the East? The Bible doesn't say. Many experts guess what is now Iraq or Iran, where large cities such as Babylon and Susa were famous for their astrologers. Jews lived there, too, and may have told these sages the prophecies about a coming Messiah.

SHAKING JESUS' family tree

This is a record of the ancestors of Jesus the Messiah, a descendant of David and of Abraham.

MATTHEW 1:1

A genealogy? What a boring way to start a book.

That's what many readers today think of Matthew's opening chapter.

Jews from Matthew's day would have disagreed. Tradition-minded Jews kept a record of their ancestors partly because certain rights and responsibilities were inherited. Priests descended from Aaron, the brother of Moses. Kings—and the coming Messiah—would descend from David, Israel's most revered king.

Matthew's genealogy is a legal document. By comparing it to other genealogies, Jews of the day could confirm that Jesus met the ancestral requirements for the Messiah. He was

THE JEWISH GOSPEL

Matthew seems to target Jewish readers more than any other Gospel does. The writer
- traces Jesus' family tree to Abraham, father of the Jews;
- points out 57 prophecies that Jesus fulfills;
- uses common Jewish phrases such as "kingdom of heaven"; and
- compares Jesus to Israel. Like the Jews of the Exodus, Jesus
   —returned from Egypt (where his family fled when King Herod killed the Bethlehem boys);
   —suffered in the desert badlands (where he was tempted);
   —passed through the waters of the Jordan River (where he was baptized); and
   —presented laws on a mountain (his Sermon on the Mount).

a Jew, descended from Abraham. And he was a contender for Israel's throne, since he was related to King David.

This family tree is a bit odd, though. In a couple of ways.

For one thing, it only randomly matches Luke's genealogy—just a few of the same names show up in both. But each list is condensed, skipping generations. And one genealogy might reflect Jesus' legal ancestry, through Joseph, while the other reflects his biological ancestry through Mary.

Another oddity: Matthew's genealogy includes women. Most genealogies of the time didn't. Even more odd, Matthew's women aren't the notable ones, like Sarah and Rachel—ancestral mothers of the Jews. He spotlights what some would consider the rotten apples:
- Tamar, who had twins by her father-in-law (Genesis 38);
- Rahab, the Jericho prostitute who helped the Israelite spies (Joshua 2);
- Ruth, an Arab who became King David's great-grandmother (Ruth 4); and
- Bathsheba, wife of Uriah, who had an affair with David (2 Samuel 11).

Scholars debate why Matthew included these women. One guess is that it shows God is capable of working through the most unusual people. And that includes a young virgin named Mary.

A PREGNANT VIRGIN?

Some Christians join skeptics on this point. They doubt Matthew's claim about Mary: "While she was still a virgin, she became pregnant through the power of the Holy Spirit" (Matthew 1:18).

Matthew says this fulfills prophecy: "The virgin will conceive a child!" (Isaiah 7:14). But *virgin* in Hebrew—Isaiah's language—can mean "young woman" or "virgin." In either case, Isaiah wasn't talking about a pregnant virgin.

He was talking about a specific woman in his time, perhaps someone the king was about to marry. This young woman would soon get pregnant—the normal way—and have a son. And by the time this boy was old enough to eat solid food, two nations threatening the Jewish kingdom would be destroyed. So the son was a sign.

Matthew sees the prophecy as a sign for his time, too, 700 years after Isaiah. The Greek word that Matthew uses for "virgin" means just that—a woman who hasn't had sex. Perhaps Matthew gets this insight from Jesus. But he doesn't say.

Early Christians came to accept the teaching literally. They saw it as a miraculous expression of an unsolvable mystery—evidence supporting the Christian teaching that Jesus is fully human and fully God.

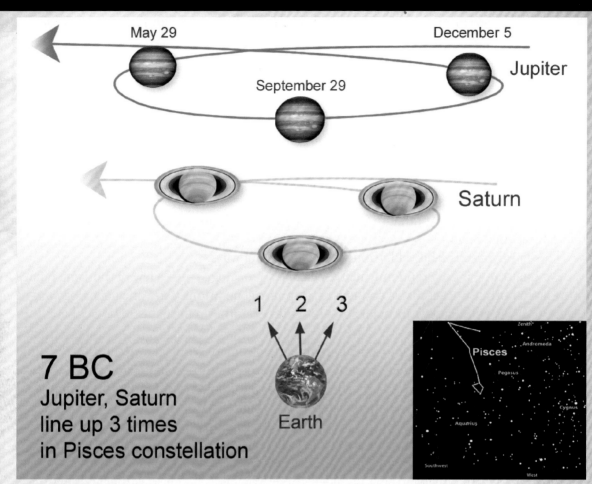

7 BC
Jupiter, Saturn
line up 3 times
in Pisces constellation

Star of Bethlehem? About once a millennium, Jupiter and Saturn line up with earth three times in a single year. In 7 BC, some astronomers calculate, they lined up inside the Pisces constellation. On the ancient Middle Eastern horoscope, Jupiter represented kings, Saturn the Jews, and Pisces ("fish") the Jewish homeland. This rare triple conjunction may have led the star-savvy sages to Israel looking for a newborn king.

WISE MEN with shocking news

Wise men from eastern lands arrived in Jerusalem, asking, "Where is the newborn king of the Jews? We saw his star as it rose, and we have come to worship him."

MATTHEW 2:1–2

Picture a small group of Iraqis riding their camels more than a thousand miles to Jerusalem. They want to pay their respects to the Jewish king and his newborn son, who they believe is destined to become a great leader.

That may be exactly what happened. "Eastern lands" may have been the empire of Parthia, stretching across what is now Iraq and Iran. This is a land where sages study the stars in search of clues about the future.

Scholars make lots of guesses about the star that led these men to Jerusalem:

- a supernova the Chinese observed for more than two months in 5 BC;
- a glowing spirit being, perhaps like the pillar of light that led the Israelites through the Exodus badlands; or
- an unusual conjunction of Jupiter and Saturn in the Pisces constellation in 7 BC.

The conjunction theory seems most sensible to many, since on the ancient horoscope Jupiter represented kings, Saturn represented Jews, and Pisces represented the land of Israel. So the wise men concluded that a new king of the Jews would be born in Israel.

That means the wise men didn't follow a star; they just followed where the heavenly lights led: to Jerusalem, capital of the Jewish homeland.

Perhaps the journey began after sages asked Jews living among them if there were any prophecies about a great Jewish leader. And then hearing about the Messiah, the sages headed out on a caravan trip that could have taken several months—perhaps after many months of planning. That means they could have arrived in Bethlehem a year or two after they first saw the astrological surprise.

Were there three wise men? That's just a guess. It grows out of the number of gifts

that Matthew says they brought: gold, frankincense (dried sap burned as fragrant incense), and myrrh (scented oil used in perfume and incense).

The sages may have been shocked to discover that Herod, king of the Jews, didn't have a newborn son. Given Herod's habit of killing off his competition—including two of his own sons and his wife—they should have been terrified, as well, since they came to honor a competing king.

Fortunately for them, Herod decides not to kill the messengers. Instead, he uses them like detectives to find his next target. Herod's Bible scholars say Micah predicted the Messiah would come from Bethlehem, six miles south. So Herod sends the sages there,

Bethlehem massacre. On orders from King Herod, Jewish authorities slaughter Bethlehem boys age two and under. Herod is targeting young Jesus. Foreign sages and hometown scholars convince Herod that the Messiah—Israel's long-awaited king—has been born in this tiny village.

asking them to report back. They don't. God warns them in a dream to go home another way.

Herod responds with a vicious order: Kill all the Bethlehem boys age two and under. Joseph, warned of this in a dream, flees with his family to Egypt, where they stay until Herod dies. If Herod died soon afterward, then the story of the wise men may have taken place the year he died: 4 BC. And if Jesus was two years old at that time, as Herod's execution order might suggest, Jesus could have been born in 6 or 7 BC.

Herod's horrible death

The king who tried to kill the baby Jesus died at about age 70 with these symptoms:
- intense itching,
- painful intestinal problems,
- difficulty breathing,
- convulsions, and
- gangrene of the genitals.

That's how Josephus, a Jewish historian writing a few decades after Herod, described the king's death.

Doctors today say Herod may have suffered from chronic kidney disease and a sexually transmitted disease such as gonorrhea.

JESUS goes public

Jesus went from Galilee to the Jordan River to be baptized by John.

MATTHEW 3:13

Skipping the next 30 years in Jesus' life, Matthew jumps to the start of his ministry, marked by two events: baptism and temptation.

Perhaps the biggest question is why Jesus bothers with baptism. A prophet named John the Baptist is baptizing people who confess their sins. A dip in the water symbolizes the spiritual cleansing of God's forgiveness. But the Bible portrays Jesus as the Son of God who "came to take away our sins, and there is no sin in him" (1 John 3:5). Even John the Baptist says so, and tries to talk Jesus out of the baptism.

Jesus is cryptic in his response: "We must carry out all that God requires" (Matthew 3:15). Some Bible experts speculate that Jesus was referring to God's plan of salvation, which involves Jesus' taking responsibility for humanity's sin and then taking the punishment, which is death. By stepping into the water, Jesus confesses the sins of the human race as though they are his sins. Or perhaps Jesus is showing everyone the path he wants them to follow.

Jesus goes a step further in identifying with the people he came to save. He walks into the nearby rocky Judean badlands, where Satan tempts him. Jesus spends 40 days, perhaps a rounded number intended to help connect his testing to the 40 years of testing that the Israelites faced during the Exodus.

Satan, in an effort to get Jesus to worship him, uses some of the same general enticements that every human faces—the desire for comfort, prestige, and power:
- bread to satisfy Jesus' appetite during a spiritual fast;
- rescue by God's angels, to remind him of who he is; and
- worship by the entire world.

Jesus refuses it all and remains focused on his mission.

JESUS CONDENSED

Headlines from the Sermon on the Mount

Golden Rule. "Do to others whatever you would like them to do to you. This is the essence of all that is taught in the law" (Matthew 7:12).

Anger. "Settle your differences quickly" (Matthew 5:25).

Revenge. "Do not resist an evil person" (Matthew 5:39).

Judging others. "The standard you use in judging is the standard by which you will be judged" (Matthew 7:2).

Enemies. "Love your enemies! Pray for those who persecute you" (Matthew 5:44).

Charity. "Don't do your good deeds publicly, to be admired by others" (Matthew 6:1).

Money. "You cannot serve both God and money" (Matthew 6:24).

Assets. "Don't store up treasures here on earth.... Store your treasures in heaven" (Matthew 6:19–20).

Worry. "I tell you not to worry about everyday life—whether you have enough food and drink, or enough clothes to wear" (Matthew 6:25; see also Matthew 6:32).

Prayer. "Don't babble on and on...your Father knows exactly what you need" (Matthew 6:7–8). For an example, see the Lord's Prayer (Matthew 6:9–13).

Sermon on the Mount. Nestled among hilltop trees, the Chapel of the Beatitudes commemorates the place where tradition says Jesus preached the Sermon on the Mount. Luke calls it the Sermon on the Plain. But the rolling hills along the Sea of Galilee can fit either description, as the plain at the left shows.

JESUS' MOST famous sermon

Jesus went up on the mountainside and sat down. His disciples gathered around him, and he began to teach them.

MATTHEW 5:1–2

Jesus moves from his hometown of Nazareth to the fishing village of Capernaum, a day's walk north. The village rests on the northern banks of a huge freshwater lake called the Sea of Galilee. Five of Jesus' dozen disciples live in the area: fishermen brothers Peter and Andrew, fishermen brothers James and John, and tax man Matthew.

On one of the gently sloping hills nearby, Jesus preaches what is perhaps the most famous sermon in history: the Sermon on the Mount. The Gospel of Luke lowers the elevation and shortens the sermon, calling it the Sermon on the Plain and condensing Matthew's three chapters to just half a chapter. But the gently rolling hills in the area could be described either way—hills or plain. And the sermon, many Bible experts say, sounds more like a series of talks: The Best of Jesus, a condensed version of all his most important teachings.

Jesus begins with a famous section called the Beatitudes—his prescription for spiritual happiness. What follows is anything but a promise of comfort or success in the world. Instead, it's an assurance in the middle of discomfort and failure. And it's an urging to press on anyway, humbly serving God and others—even when it hurts.

In a way, Jesus is flipping conventional wisdom upside down.

Rich folks can afford the most expensive objects on earth, but "God blesses those who are poor and realize their need for him, for the Kingdom of Heaven is theirs" (Matthew 5:3).

Aggressive go-getters might corner a tiny clump of success, but "God blesses those who are humble, for they will inherit the whole earth" (Matthew 5:5). The strength of a gentle soul catches the attention of heaven and earth—and is honored in both.

FEEDING 5,000-plus

Jesus took the five loaves and two fish, looked up toward heaven, and blessed them. . . . About 5,000 men were fed that day, in addition to all the women and children!

MATTHEW 14:19, 21

Jesus develops an incredible following because he's an incredible attraction.

His teachings don't sound like those of other rabbis. Yet they ring true to the best of Jewish tradition and to the sense of everything good and right and just. What he teaches may not be the way most Jews live their lives. But it's the way they want to live—and the way they know God wants them to live. Crowds are drawn to Jesus because of his words.

Miracles don't hurt the draw, either. And Jesus heals people everywhere he goes: lepers, the blind, the crippled, the demon-possessed. He even heals a Roman officer's paralyzed servant—from long distance. Jesus tells the officer, "Go back home. Because you believed, it has happened" (Matthew 8:13).

As Jesus walks from place to place, crowds follow him—even when he needs a break. Once, he slips away in a boat. But the people follow along the shoreline in a massive crowd of 5,000 men—not counting the women and children. Jesus could have had the equivalent of several villages tagging behind.

They catch up with Jesus in a remote area. Weary as Jesus is, compassion drives him to heal their sick. But evening approaches. So the disciples advise Jesus to send the crowds away so they can buy food somewhere.

Instead, Jesus suggests a potluck. It's an idea the disciples have already considered—and rejected. Fives loaves of bread and two fish are all they can turn up, which is barely enough to silence the rumble of two growling stomachs.

In a miracle as quiet as a fish sandwich, Jesus shows his power over creation. He blesses the food. The disciples distribute it. The crowd of at least 5,000—perhaps double that—eats its fill. And the disciples collect a dozen baskets of leftovers—one for each disciple.

1,600-year-old fish. Mosaic tile of two fish and a basket of bread survives on the floor of a church built in the AD 400s—a few decades after Romans legalized Christianity. This Church of the Multiplication of Loaves and Fishes marks the lakeside slope where tradition says Jesus fed 5,000 hungry people. The site today is called Tabgha, located about two miles from Capernaum, Jesus' ministry headquarters.

PETER'S VIEW of Jesus

"You are the Messiah, the Son of the living God."

MATTHEW 16:16

Perhaps to get away from the crowds, Jesus takes his disciples a day's walk north of the Sea of Galilee. They go to a predominantly non-Jewish area called Caesarea Philippi. There, Jesus asks his disciples who the people say he is.

They answer that some say he's John the Baptist back from the dead. That's what the Galilean ruler Herod Antipas said. Guilt-ridden after beheading John, Herod seems certain that Jesus is John: "This must be John the Baptist raised from the dead! That is why he can do such miracles" (Matthew 14:2).

Others say Jesus is a prophet or perhaps Elijah, returning from the heavens as predicted to prepare the way for the promised Messiah.

"Who do you say I am?" Jesus asks. Peter answers that Jesus is the Messiah and more—the Son of the living God. This was apparent in the virgin birth as well as in later evidences of God's involvement in Jesus' life. At Jesus' baptism, a voice from the sky declared, "This is my dearly loved Son, who brings me great joy" (Matthew 3:17).

Jesus blesses Peter, as rabbis often did when a student gave a correct answer to an important question. Simon was Peter's name until Jesus invited him to become a disciple and then renamed him Peter—a word that means "rock."

"You are Rock," Jesus says, "and on this rock I will build my church." Bible scholars debate what is happening here, with Jesus giving Peter "the keys of the kingdom of heaven." Many Catholics say that Jesus put Peter in charge of the church and that Peter became the first in a long line of popes entrusted with God's authority on earth.

Others say Jesus was simply declaring what would soon happen. Peter was already leader of the disciples. He would also be a key leader of the Christian movement. After Jesus' death, resurrection, and ascension, Peter would preach the first sermon. More than 3,000 Jews assembled for the Passover festival in Jerusalem would convert.

Blessing Peter. Jesus blesses Peter, calling him the rock upon which Jesus will build the church. In fact, Peter later preaches a sermon in Jerusalem that converts more than 3,000 Jews—jump-starting the church. This statue outside the Church of Peter's Primacy, near the Sea of Galilee, commemorates the blessing and Peter's leadership.

JESUS GLOWS on a mountaintop

Jesus' appearance was transformed so that his face shone like the sun, and his clothes became as white as light.

MATTHEW 17:2

Jesus' ministry lasts about three years. That's an estimate based on the number of times he seems to have gone to Jerusalem for festivals. As the end approaches, he starts telling his disciples about what's coming: he'll be killed in Jerusalem, but he'll rise from the dead after three days.

A week after Peter declares Jesus the Son of God, he sees evidence of it that's probably more remarkable than anything he has seen so far. Jesus takes his closest friends—Peter, James, and John—to an unidentified mountain. Some scholars guess the mountain was Mount Hermon, near Caesarea Philippi. It's the highest in the region and the snowmelt source of water for the Jordan River. But early church leaders said it was Mount Tabor, about a two-day walk south, near his hometown of Nazareth.

As the disciples watch, Jesus seems to transform into a celestial being. He glows. Bible writers sometimes describe angels and God that way, shimmering with light. Suddenly Moses and Elijah appear. They start talking with Jesus as though they all know each other.

Church of the Transfiguration. A church crowns the snow-covered top of Mount Tabor, where early Christians said Jesus transformed into a glowing being. Jesus denied Peter's request to build a memorial, but Christians built a church there by the early AD 400s, shortly after Rome legalized Christianity.

SAVIOR in the saddle

"Look, your King is coming to you. . .riding on a donkey's colt."

MATTHEW 21:5

On the last Sunday morning before his death, Jesus climbs onto a donkey that's saddled with cloth garments. The donkey is a loaner, borrowed from a village on the Mount of Olives—probably Bethany, about a mile from Jerusalem.

Jesus knows the prophecy about Israel's Messiah arriving on a donkey (Zechariah 9:9). So he arranges to fulfill it.

Leading a procession of followers, Jesus crests the Mount of Olives and begins descending into the Kidron Valley. Then he climbs the facing hillside, entering Jerusalem.

Crowds are gathered for the biggest festival of the year: Passover, a springtime holiday commemorating God's deliverance of the Jews from slavery in Egypt. It's an exciting time, but even more so this year because of Jesus. The Jews have been praying for a deliverer—a Messiah from King David's family. They expected the Messiah to deliver them from slavery once again, this time from Roman occupiers.

Jesus is that deliverer, many believe. So they greet him like a king, spreading cloaks and palm leaves on the path before him. They cheer him, too, as the answer to their prayers: "the Son of David. . .the one who comes in the name of the LORD!" (Matthew 21:9).

JESUS PREDICTS the future

As Jesus was leaving the Temple grounds, his disciples pointed out to him the various Temple buildings. But he responded. . ."I tell you the truth, they will be completely demolished."

MATTHEW 24:1–2

Kingdom of heaven on earth

Jesus had a pet topic. Bible writers usually call it by one of two names: kingdom of heaven or kingdom of God.

It's not a substitute word for "heaven." It's the kingdom that God rules in heaven and on earth. Jesus spent much of his time teaching people about this kingdom—what it's like and how to live as kingdom citizens.

Jesus often used word pictures to describe it.

When asked who the greatest person in this kingdom is, Jesus called over a child. Then he said, "Anyone who becomes as humble as this little child is the greatest in the Kingdom of Heaven" (Matthew 18:4).

He used parables, too. A shepherd leaves his flock of 99 sheep to find one missing sheep. When he finds it, he rejoices. Jesus said God rejoices, too, when a lost person returns to the heavenly kingdom where he belongs.

Finding lost sheep is the ministry of Jesus. And it's the ministry he passes on to his disciples.

During the five days before his arrest, Jesus teaches in Jerusalem. Often it's at the temple, still being remodeled into the largest and most beautiful Jewish temple in history. On their way out of the temple one day, the disciples start talking about the wonderful architecture. Jesus tells them that someday every stone will be torn down.

Of course, they want to know when this will happen—and when the earth will end, since they're on the general subject of endings.

Jesus answers with a speech that sounds like it belongs in Revelation. It's really quite hard to follow because it seems Jesus is doing on purpose what some of the prophets in Old Testament times did without knowing it: prophesying on different timelines, with some statements intended for the immediate future and others intended for the distant future.

He talks about wars and famines, along with the desecration and destruction of the temple. And he says of these and other signs, "This generation will not pass from the scene until all these things take place" (Matthew 24:34). He will die in about AD 30. Forty years later, Romans will destroy the temple in the process of crushing a Jewish revolt for independence.

In fact, early Christian writers say some people in Jerusalem escaped Rome's final assault on Jerusalem because they remembered Jesus' speech and took his advice: "Those in Judea must flee to the hills" (Matthew 24:16).

Other predictions seem to refer to a time still in the future, when everyone sees "the Son of Man coming on the clouds of heaven with power and great glory" (Matthew 24:30). The timing of this future event, Jesus says, remains a mystery even to him. "Only the Father knows" (Matthew 24:36).

But when the time comes, so does judgment.

Jesus uses analogies and parables to describe what will happen. He says God will separate the good people from the evil ones as easily as a shepherd separates sheep and goats.

Judgment criteria, at least in this analogy, involve good deeds. Jesus says good people will feed him when he's hungry, give him something to drink when he's thirsty, give him clothing when he needs it, and visit him when he's in jail.

But here's the clincher. When asked how anyone could possibly do this for him, he says, "I tell you the truth, when you did it to one of the least of these my brothers and sisters, you were doing it to me!" (Matthew 25:40).

Citizens of God's kingdom help people who need it.

THE LAST supper

Jesus took some bread and blessed it. Then he broke it in pieces and gave it to the disciples, saying, "Take this and eat it, for this is my body."

MATTHEW 26:26

Every springtime around Easter since the time of Moses, observant Jews have eaten a Passover meal. It's to celebrate the first event in the Jewish nation's history: God's deliverance of the Israelites from Egyptian slavery. In Jesus' time, Jewish pilgrims flock to Jerusalem to celebrate the holy day there.

The weeklong celebration begins on Nissan 15 (Jewish calendar), which falls in March or April. Jews gather in a home to eat the Passover supper, called the *seder*. They eat after sunset on Friday night, which is when the Jewish Sabbath begins.

Jesus would be dead by then. So he seems to celebrate the Passover a day early, on Thursday night—a few hours before his arrest. God had instituted the Passover meal as a way of helping Jews throughout the generations remember how much he loved them. Jesus does much the same, creating a new ritual that Christians have been observing for 2,000 years. It's called by various names: Holy Communion, the Lord's Supper, and the Eucharist (from the Greek word for "thankful").

Jesus breaks some bread into pieces, gives it to the disciples, and tells them to eat it. Then he takes a cup of wine and passes it among them, telling them to drink it. He says the broken bread is his body and the wine is his blood "poured out as a sacrifice to forgive the sins of many" (Matthew 26:28).

Early Christians established this as their first sacrament, or sacred ritual, because Jesus told his disciples, "Do this to remember me" (Luke 22:19). Christian groups treat the ritual differently. Most Protestant groups celebrate Communion just a few times a year and consider the bread and wine (or grape juice) as symbols of Christ's body and blood. Catholics and Orthodox churches teach that the bread and wine actually become the body and blood of Jesus.

Judas leaves the meal early to arrange for the ritual to become reality.

SPEEDY TRIAL, slow execution

Pilate responded, "Then what should I do with Jesus who is called the Messiah?" They shouted back, "Crucify him!"

MATTHEW 27:22

Most Jewish leaders detest Jesus. They disagree with him theologically on many points, especially with this casual observance of the Sabbath. That's a day Jesus feels free to heal people, take long walks, and pick a snack of grain kernels while walking through a wheat field. They envy his popularity, too.

But what troubles them most is that he might capitalize on his popularity and launch a revolt against Rome—a revolt they fear the Romans would crush. And he might do it during Passover, while he's surrounded by enthusiastic supporters who believe he's the Messiah sent by God to free them.

The trick is how to get rid of him without sparking a riot.

Judas comes to the rescue. He offers to lead arresting officers to Jesus at night. No one is sure why Judas does this. Greed is a possible motive, since he accepts a reward: 30 pieces of silver, an amount predicted 500 years earlier (Zechariah 11:12). But Judas later returns the money and hangs himself in shame. Another guess is that he hoped to prod Jesus to defend himself and to start the Jewish Revolution.

Judas leads a group of temple guards to Jesus, who's praying in an olive grove across the valley on the slopes of the Mount of Olives.

HOW TO SPOT A PHARISEE

Not all Jews in Jesus' day believed the same things.

There were distinct groups, just as Christians today have different denominations: Baptist, Methodist, Catholic, Greek Orthodox. There are distinct Jewish groups today, as well: Orthodox (the most traditional), Conservative, and Reform (the most liberated from ancient traditions).

Two leading groups in Jesus' day were the Pharisees and the Sadducees. And Jesus didn't care much for the distinct teachings of either.

PHARISEES

Beyond staunchly conservative, the Pharisees were oppressively legalistic.

They not only insisted that Jews observe all the laws that God gave through Moses, they added extra laws. And they taught that those extra laws were just as important. A modern variation would be to argue that a denomination's church manual of policy and expected behavior is as important as the Bible.

Pharisees added their laws to protect the Law. It was a bit like building a fence around the 10 Commandments to make sure no one accidentally wandered into forbidden territory.

For example, God's law tells people not to work on the Sabbath. So the Pharisees defined "work." The Talmud, a collection of ancient Jewish laws and commentary, preserves 234 Sabbath-day prohibitions. Among them:

- Cooking. Food was prepared the day before Sabbath.
- Treating an injured person or helping an animal out of a ditch, unless life was at risk.
- Walking farther than about half a mile.

SADDUCEES

Mainly priests and the social elite, these Jewish leaders controlled temple worship and were well represented on the governing Jewish council called the Sanhedrin, which tried Jesus.

More liberal-minded than the Pharisees, the Sadducees felt bound only to the laws in the books of Moses—not to the hundreds of extra laws that the Pharisees added.

Sadducees argued that there was no such thing as immortality of the soul or resurrection. "That is why they are 'sad you see.' " Some Bible professors use this line to help their students remember the Sadducees' distinctive teachings.

The way of the cross. Jesus carries his cross, outside the walled city of Jerusalem, to his execution. He's followed by a crowd, including the several women and the "beloved" disciple who stayed with him while he died. Italian artist Biagio d'Antonio painted this picture in the 1400s. The cloth portrait of Jesus, lower right, is reminiscent of the famous Italian Shroud of Turin—carbon-dated to the 1300s and said to contain an impression of Jesus' face and body.

Peter, bold for the moment, draws a sword and cuts off the ear of the high priest's slave. But Jesus warns Peter that those who live by the sword will die by the sword. Jesus heals the man's ear.

Arresting officers take Jesus to the home of Caiaphas, the high priest. Jewish leaders are waiting for him. They are members of the Jewish ruling body, a 70-member council that enforces Jewish law. They scramble to find witnesses so they can try him on the spot. But the witnesses can't seem to agree, or they don't offer testimony that would lead to the death penalty.

In frustration, Caiaphas demands to know if Jesus is the Son of God.

Jesus replies, "In the future you will see the Son of Man seated in the place of power at God's right hand and coming on the clouds of heaven" (Mathew 26:64).

As far as Caiaphas is concerned, this is arrogant blasphemy that disrespects God. He condemns Jesus to death. But the Roman occupiers reserve the right to execute prisoners. So after sunrise the Jews take Jesus to the regional governor, Pilate. The governor doesn't want to execute a man over religion. So he gives the Jews a choice. Pilate will free either Jesus or a death-row prisoner named Barabbas. The Jews choose Barabbas.

By 9 a.m. Jesus is beaten and nailed to a cross. After six hours of hanging there, he dies. And before sunset, when the Sabbath begins and work ends for a full day, the corpse of Jesus lies in a stone tomb guarded by Roman soldiers.

HE'S back

"I know you are looking for Jesus, who was crucified. He isn't here! He is risen from the dead, just as he said would happen."

MATTHEW 28:5–6

An angel appears at the garden tomb, glowing like Jesus did during his transfiguration earlier on the mountain. The angel announces what Jesus himself had predicted: the Resurrection. It is Sunday, the first Easter.

Several women come to the tomb at daybreak. It's their first opportunity to wash Jesus' body and wrap it in scented spices for a proper burial. Matthew says the women are Mary Magdalene and another Mary. Mark's Gospel says the second Mary is the mother of James. And Mark adds that Salome came along, too.

The timing of everything that happens this famous morning isn't clear. Each Gospel presents snippets of information, but it's impossible to piece them all together into a well-defined flow of events. Perhaps it's because all the witnesses are overdosed on emotion and dazed by their senses. And in the jumbled mix of fear, confusion, shock, and joy, some of the details get blurred.

There's an earthquake. An angel pushes aside the massive, Frisbee-shaped stone that blocks the entrance to the tomb. The guards faint and then wake up and run off to report what happened. The women arrive at the empty tomb guarded by an angel—with a face shining like "lightning" and clothes "white as snow."

In time, Jesus appears. The women fall at his feet and worship him. And he sends them on their way, with good news for his disciples.

MARK

THE ACTION-PACKED STORY OF JESUS

Fishers of men. Nets ready to cast, fishermen on the Sea of Galilee in the early 1900s prepare for a day's work. Jesus' first disciples are two teams of brothers, all fishermen at work: Peter and Andrew, James and John.

This is the Gospel for readers with a short attention span. For two reasons.

- It's the shortest of the four Gospels.
- It's light on talk, heavy on action.

Forget Jesus' family tree. And don't bother with his birth. At least Mark doesn't. Instead, he jumps feet first into the Jordan River, where John the Baptist is baptizing people, and adds this disclaimer: "Someone is coming soon who is greater than I am—so much greater that I'm not even worthy to stoop down like a slave and untie the straps of his sandals. I baptize you with water, but he will baptize you with the Holy Spirit!" (Mark 1:7–8).

One verse later, Jesus is in the water, too. Getting baptized.

A few dozen words after that, Satan is tempting him in the Judean badlands—a scene that lasts only two verses—with no dialogue. Then Jesus is off to work, rounding up disciples, healing hundreds, feeding thousands, freeing the tongues of the speechless, tying the tongues of snooty scholars, calming storms, walking on water, dying, and coming back to life.

It's a frantic pace.

But it's an action-lover's book.

MAIN POINT:

Jesus, the Son of God, came to earth to take the punishment for humanity's sin by suffering and dying.

WRITER:

The book doesn't identify the writer. But since at least AD 130, church leaders have credited one of Peter's associates: John Mark. John was his Hebrew name. Mark was the Latin name he used among Romans and other non-Jews. John Mark's source was supposedly Peter, since there's no indication that he ever met Jesus.

DATE:

The story covers about three years, the length of Jesus' ministry ending in about AD 30. The story was probably written in the AD 60s. At least that's the most common guess among Bible experts. Many prefer this decade partly because Romans started executing Christians then, in AD 64. That's the year Emperor Nero blamed them for burning down most of Rome. Mark's Gospel emphasizes the suffering of Jesus, perhaps to remind suffering Christians of the 60s that even Jesus suffered and died.

LOCATION:

Israel

THE MESSIAH'S dream team

"Come, follow me, and I will show you how to fish for people!"

MARK 1:17

Jesus begins his ministry in a strange way. He calls a group of 12 men to become his disciples—to travel with him and learn from him. That's not normal. Students pick rabbis they want to learn from. Rabbis don't pick students.

There's no degree program Jesus had to follow to become a rabbi. People simply recognize him as a rabbi because he sounds like one. He knows the Jewish scriptures like an expert, and he teaches them with authority.

Mark, by skipping a lot of Jesus' story, makes it sound as though Jesus starts picking his disciples even before he begins teaching and healing people. Not true. And it sounds like the disciples are just waiting for a chance to quit their jobs. Andrew and his brother Simon, whom Jesus later names Peter, are fishing along the shore in the lake called the Sea of Galilee when Jesus makes them an offer they can't seem to refuse. If they follow him, he will make them fishers of men. "And they left their nets at once and followed him" (Mark 1:18). A little farther down the shore, Jesus makes the same offer to brothers James and John—with the same results.

Offering to make these fishermen "fishers of men" could have meant anything: ancient Amway, slave trading, or tax collecting. Though Mark skips a lot, other Gospels fill in the gaps. The four fishermen know plenty about Jesus by this time. Andrew had heard John the Baptist call Jesus "the Lamb of God who takes away the sin of the world." So Andrew tagged along with Jesus for a bit and then rushed to his brother, declaring, "We have found the Messiah" (John 1:41).

Jesus continues his ministry, headquartered in Capernaum. Peter has a home there, just a few feet from the synagogue. There, Jesus picks up another disciple: Matthew, a tax collector working at a tollbooth. Most Jews of the day hate tax collectors. Some Jewish leaders even consider them ritually unclean, which means a Jew who comes in contact with them must go through purification rituals before worshipping at the temple.

Tax collectors are Jews who collaborate with the Roman occupying force. They bid for the right to collect taxes. Then they pay Rome its share and keep the rest as a salary. To up their salary, many overcharge and grow rich.

Jesus' choice of disciples—and the rest of the company he keeps—mystifies the Jewish leaders. They can't understand why he hangs out with "scum," as they put it. So he tells them, "Healthy people don't need a doctor—sick people do. I have come to call not those who think they are righteous, but those who know they are sinners" (Mark 2:17).

By chapter 3, Jesus has assembled his full team of disciples: "Simon (whom he named Peter), James and John (the sons of Zebedee, but Jesus nicknamed them 'Sons of Thunder'), Andrew, Philip, Bartholomew, Matthew, Thomas, James (son of Alphaeus), Thaddaeus, Simon (the zealot) [perhaps referring to the organized group seeking Jewish independence], Judas Iscariot (who later betrayed him)" (Mark 3:16–19).

Not a scholar or an aristocrat among them. Just average men.

The suffering Gospel

A third of this short book zeroes in on the last week of Jesus' life—6 of 16 chapters.

Passion Week, it's called. That's from the old days when "passion" meant "suffering."

We don't have to wait until chapter 11 to see Jesus under attack. That happens right away, and many times.

- First he has to deal with representatives of hell: hostile demons.
- Then it's folks who are supposed to represent heaven: Jewish leaders. As it turns out, they don't recognize God when they look him in the eye. It's Jesus' theology that throws them. It just doesn't seem kosher. So they try to publicly humiliate him. When that backfires, they hatch a plot to kill him.
- Then it's his hometown folks. They, too, are "deeply offended" by his teachings (Mark 6:3).
- Even his own family comes to a painful conclusion: "He's out of his mind" (Mark 3:21).

Mark is working a theme. And it's hard to miss.

JESUS BREAKING Sabbath rules

"Why are they breaking the law by harvesting grain on the Sabbath?"

MARK 2:24

That's the question Jewish scholars have for Jesus.

They saw Jesus and his disciples walking through a grain field, with the disciples plucking grain snacks as they walked. The disciples would snap off the kernel-loaded grain heads at the top of the tall stalks. Then they'd rub the grain heads in their hands to break off the chaff and release the tiny grain kernels, which they'd then pop into their mouths.

Jesus' critics are scholars from a rule-minded group in the Jewish religion: Pharisees. As far as the Pharisees are concerned, Jesus' disciples are breaking the Sabbath by harvesting.

These Pharisees get even more upset when, on perhaps the very same Sabbath, Jesus heals a man with a deformed hand. They teach that it's a sin to treat the sick on the Sabbath, unless the patient is in danger of dying. A deformed hand doesn't qualify.

The Bible doesn't forbid picking snacks of grain or healing people on the Sabbath day of rest. But commandment number four of ten does say, "Remember to observe the Sabbath day by keeping it holy. You have six days each week for your ordinary work, but the seventh day is a Sabbath day of rest dedicated to the LORD your God. On that day no one in your household may do any work" (Exodus 20:8–10).

The Pharisees had taken it upon themselves to apply this law to everyday life—so Jews would know exactly what they could and could not do on the Sabbath. (See "How to Spot a Pharisee," page 314.) One famous rabbi of the time, Shammai, not only opposed helping sick people unless their lives were at risk. He opposed visiting them or even praying for them. He argued that the Sabbath was a day for joy.

Jesus might have told him to tell it to the hand—a moment before Jesus healed it.

What he does say to Shammai's kindred spirits is this:

- "The Sabbath was made to meet the needs of people, and not people to meet the requirements of the Sabbath" (Mark 2:27).
- "Does the law permit good deeds on the Sabbath, or is it a day for doing evil?" (Mark 3:4).

Jesus' words make common sense to thoughtful people, which is one reason why crowds start following him. But most Jewish leaders are so saturated with the traditions they've learned that they can't process fresh insight—even if it's more kosher than their tradition.

Looking for the Messiah

For nearly 600 years, Jews had been waiting for God to make good on his promise.

That's how long it had been since a Jewish king ruled Israel—a legit king from David's family, not a Rome-appointed king like Herod the Great. God promised David, "Your kingdom will continue before me for all time, and your throne will be secure forever" (2 Samuel 7:16).

Forever ended in the summer of 586 BC.

Babylonian invaders from what is now Iraq destroyed Jerusalem and dismantled David's dynasty of kings.

But prophets insisted that God would send an "anointed one" ("Messiah" in Hebrew; "Christ" in Greek). That's a term used throughout the Old Testament to describe some of God's special leaders, including selected kings, priests, and prophets.

The future Messiah would be the most special of all. Prophets painted pictures of a victorious warrior king who would restore the peace and glory of Israel. But they also painted pictures of a suffering servant who would die to save others.

Most Jews latched onto the warrior theme and ran with it. By the time Jesus began his ministry, the Jews had endured a century of oppressive Roman occupation. Messiah expectations were soaring. And the miracle-working Jesus looked like the right man at the right time.

But he didn't even try to free Israel. He declared at his trial, "My Kingdom is not of this world" (John 18:36). What a disappointment to his followers, with their preconceived notions of the Messiah.

But the Resurrection turned that frown upside down. Suddenly it dawned on his disciples what God meant when he promised that David's throne would be secure forever. They started spreading the "good news" ("Gospel" in Old English). The Messiah from David's family had come as a suffering servant. And one day he's coming back as a victorious king who will rule a glorious and timeless kingdom.

Jesus tries to pound some intellectual sense into them. He reminds them that David and his men ate sacred temple bread reserved for priests. And he reminds them that a holy day is for doing holy things, like helping people in need.

But all the Pharisees seem capable of processing is the punishment for desecrating the Sabbath: "Anyone who desecrates it must be put to death" (Exodus 31:14). So they plot to kill him.

BETTER than a sermon

He taught them by telling many stories in the form of parables.

MARK 4:2

Long-winded, pharmaceutically sedative sermons are not in Jesus' repertoire.

Or if they were, Mark doesn't seem to remember them any more than we remember last week's sermon if the preacher numbed us with abstract theological clichés.

A masterful teacher, Jesus prefers to play off of his immediate surroundings, using colorful stories to help people understand what he's trying to teach. And sometimes he uses these stories as coded messages to enlighten his followers, while mystifying his enemies.

But on occasion he mystifies both groups.

It happens once while he's teaching from a floating stage—a fishing boat anchored near the shore. Water from the lake amplifies his voice, lifting it to the crowds scattered on the sloping hillside. Perhaps in the distance a farmer is sowing seeds, or maybe the crops are already growing tall and swaying in the lakeside breeze.

Jesus begins, "A farmer went out to plant some seed" (Mark 4:3).

Then he tells a short tale about four seed groups. Some seeds

- are gobbled up by birds;
- develop shallow roots blocked by underground rocks, so they produce plants that wither and die in the sun;
- fall among weeds and thorns that choke them to death; and
- fall on fertile soil, producing a wonderful harvest.

"Anyone with ears to hear," Jesus says, "should listen and understand." But even his disciples, early in their education, don't get it. So Jesus breaks down the code.

The seed is God's message of salvation.

Seed group one represents people who hear the message, but Satan distracts them and takes them in a different direction.

Group two embraces the message but abandons it when critics ridicule them for their faith or when other problems develop.

Group three are people who eventually lose their faith, which gets crowded out by worries and a desire for money.

Group four represents believers who thrive.

By implication, Jesus—and later his disciples and other followers—sows the seed of God's message. Many people will reject it or give it up. But some won't. And they'll produce even more seeds like themselves: "thirty, sixty, or even a hundred times as much as had been

BIBLE AG-ED 101

Imported scents. Perfumed oils, posed beside flowers and herbs that produce the aroma. The Gospels of Matthew, Mark, and John tell of a woman pouring spikenard perfume on Jesus. Worth a year's salary, it was probably imported from India's Himalayan Mountains.

Middle Eastern scents

Mustard by the millimeter. At a millimeter in diameter, the mustard seed is one of the smallest seeds among garden plants. It takes 25 seeds lined up in a skinny row to stretch an inch. Jesus said the kingdom of God starts like this—tiny, but it grows tall. And like mustard plants, considered weeds by many farmers, God's kingdom spreads fast and far.

Forbidden snack. Jesus' disciples walking through a grain field snap off some grain heads and knock out the kernels for a snack. This offends some Jewish leaders who say the disciples are working—that they're conducting a miniharvest on the Sabbath day of rest.

Mustard seeds

Wheat stalks and grain

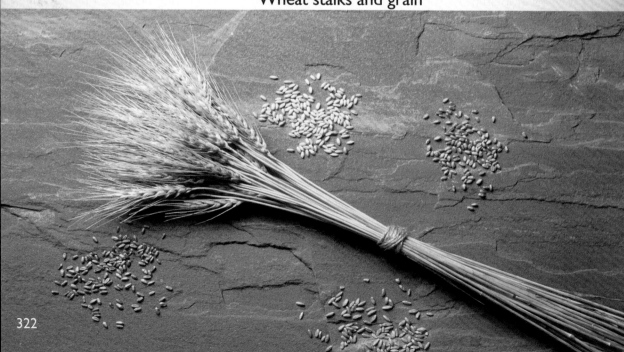

planted!" (Mark 4:20).

So Jesus is telling the disciples they shouldn't be discouraged when they're rejected.

HOW GOD'S garden grows

"How can I describe the Kingdom of God? What story should I use to illustrate it? It is like a mustard seed planted in the ground."

MARK 4:30–31

Not much bigger than a dot at the end of a sentence, the mustard seed in Jesus' time is a common symbol for smallness. "If you had faith even as small as a mustard seed," Jesus once said, you could move a mountain (Matthew 17:20) or uproot a huge tree (Luke 17:6).

The Mishnah, a collection of ancient Jewish commentary, uses a similar phrase to describe the smallest possible amount: "even as little as a grain of mustard." Actually, mustard seeds a millimeter thick aren't the smallest garden seeds around. Orchid seeds, at a fourth of a millimeter, are the smallest on record so far. It would take 100 of those tiny orchid dots lined up to reach an inch.

Jesus' point is that from a miniscule beginning, the mustard seed grows huge—becoming "the largest of all garden plants" (Mark 4:32). It's not actually the largest garden plant, either. There's a flower in Indonesia, the *Rafflesia arnoldii*, that can grow 7 to 12 feet tall, span 3 feet across, and weigh in at 170 pounds. The mustard plant in Israel seldom grows higher than 5 feet tall. But that's certainly one of the tallest garden plants in Israel. And Jesus' listeners wouldn't have quibbled over his botanical exaggerations. They'd understand the picture he's painting: small beginning, big ending.

What's confusing, though, is his reference to birds making "nests in its shade" (Mark 4:32). It would be one wobbly nest when the wind blew. But not quite so wobbly in a thick field of mustard, where the plants often flourish.

Some Bible experts wonder if Jesus is using the birds or the shade as symbolism. "Birds of the air" was one way Jews referred to non-Jews. And "shade" was a common symbol for shelter, refuge, and protection.

So perhaps Jesus is saying more than that God's kingdom starts small (with him and a dozen disciples) and grows large (into a Christian movement spanning the world). Perhaps he's also saying that it becomes a haven for everyone, Gentiles included.

JOHN the beheaded

"I want the head of John the Baptist, right now, on a tray!"

MARK 6:25

After reporting several of Jesus' parables, Mark jumps to some of the miracles: calming the storm and then healing people. Jesus is well into the beginning of his ministry when his predecessor, John the Baptist, is beheaded.

TOP 10 MIRACLES AND PARABLES

Miracle	Matthew	Mark	Luke	John
Raising Lazarus				11:1–44
Walking on water	14:22–32	6:47–52		6:16–21
Feeding 5,000	14:13–21	6:30–44	9:10–17	6:1–14
Turning water to wine				2:1–11
Calming a storm	8:23–27	4:37–41	8:22–25	
Healing a Roman officer's servant	8:5–13		7:1–10	
Healing a bleeding woman	9:20–22	5:25–34	8:43–48	
Healing a man born blind				9:1–41
Healing a paralyzed man	9:2–7	2:3–12	5:18–26	
Withering a fig tree	21:18–22	11:12–14, 20–25		
Parable				
Good Samaritan			10:30–37	
Prodigal (lost) son			15:11–32	
Lost sheep	18:12–14		15:4–7	
Farmer planting seeds	13:3–8, 18–23	4:3–8, 14–20	8:5–8, 11–15	
Mustard seed	13:31–32	4:30–32	13:18–19	
Ten virgins at a wedding	25:1–13			
Lost coin			15:8–10	
Three servants with investment money	25:14–30		19:12–27	
Worst seat at the party			14:7–14	
Rich man and Lazarus			16:19–31	

John is a distant relative of Jesus. Their mothers, Elizabeth and Mary, are related, though the Bible doesn't say how (Luke 1:36).

Jesus said John fulfilled the Old Testament prophecies about Elijah returning to announce the coming of the Lord: "Elijah is indeed coming first to get everything ready [for the Messiah]. But I tell you, Elijah has already come, but he wasn't recognized, and they chose to abuse him. . . . Then the disciples realized he was talking about John the Baptist" (Matthew 17:11–13).

John is a traveling prophet, baptizing people who repent of their sins and telling about someone greater than him who is coming soon: "I'm not even worthy to stoop down like a slave and untie the straps of his sandals" (Mark 1:7). When Jesus arrives, John points him out as the one he was talking about—the one who would baptize people with the Holy Spirit.

Some of John's disciples leave him and start following Jesus. John is arrested during those waning days of his ministry. He had publicly condemned the incestuous marriage of Galilee's ruler, Herod Antipas. Herod, a son of Herod the Great, married his own brother's ex-wife, Herodias. She had divorced her first husband. But Jewish law said it was wrong for a man to marry his brother's wife if the brother was still alive. "If a man marries his brother's wife, it is an act of impurity. He has violated his brother" (Leviticus 20:21).

Herodias doesn't appreciate being called a sexual pervert. So when she sees a chance to get even, she takes it. Her daughter, called Salome according to a first-century Jewish historian named Josephus, dances for her stepfather on his birthday. It must be quite the dance, since he promises to reward her with anything she wants.

Salome consults her mom. Then she comes back asking for John's head on a platter.

Herod respects John as a holy man who is loved by the people. He doesn't want to kill him. But Herod's pride is on the line. He made a promise in public. So he keeps his promise and John loses his head.

JESUS LOVES the little children

"Let the children come to me. Don't stop them! For the Kingdom of God belongs to those who are like these children."

MARK 10:14

Jesus spends a lot of time talking about the kingdom of God, which Matthew calls the kingdom of heaven. This is Jesus' favorite topic. He's not talking about heaven alone in some distant future. He's also talking about here and now. The kingdom of God is anywhere God rules. And it's anywhere that souls have pledged their allegiance to him. (See "Kingdom of Heaven on Earth," page 312.)

One day, Jesus uses children to make an important point about the kingdom. Parents are bringing their kids to him so he can touch them and bless them.

Jews of the day believe there's power in both. Merely touching a holy man can heal a person or turn an unlucky life toward happier days. Receiving a spoken blessing can do much the same.

Jesus' disciples aren't pleased. They think Jesus has more important things to do. Children live at the bottom of society's barrel in much of the ancient Middle East. People today debate abortion, but in Bible times most parents had the legal right to do what comedian Bill Cosby jokingly threatened, as father to son: "I brought you into the world. I can take you out."

An Egyptian letter from Jesus' time says as much. In 1 BC, a man named Hilarion writes from Alexandria to his pregnant wife, Alis. He says, "If you have the good luck to deliver another child, if it's a boy keep it. But if it's a girl, set it outside and let it die."

As Jesus has done before, he turns social values upside down. He not only treats children with the same respect he gives their parents, he flips the barrel. Suddenly the bottom of the barrel is the top. And grown-ups are left looking up to their kids as models of what it takes to become a citizen in God's kingdom.

What it takes to become a citizen of heaven is something that children in this ancient culture have: humility and a sense of total dependence on others. The kingdom of God isn't populated with crowds of the self-reliant and self-assured. It's full of people who depend on their Father.

JESUS gets violent

Jesus entered the Temple and began to drive out the people buying and selling animals for sacrifices.

MARK 11:15

In the last week before his crucifixion, Jesus rides a donkey into Jerusalem. Crowds of Jewish pilgrims have come to their holy city to celebrate Passover. Many cheer Jesus' arrival, greeting him as a Messiah King and carpeting his path with cloaks and palm branches. The day is Sunday—history's first Palm Sunday.

Jesus visits the temple and takes notice of how religious business is being conducted. There are four main worship areas:

- **Huge, outer courtyard.** Anyone can go into this area. But it's as close as non-Jewish believers are allowed to the sanctuary.
- **Inside courtyard for Jewish women.** All Jews are allowed here. But non-Jews caught this close to the sanctuary risk execution. And they can read the warning engraved in stone, painted blood red, and set into the walls.
- **Altar courtyard for Jewish men.** Located just outside the front doors of the sanctuary, this courtyard contains the altar where sacrifices are burned. No women allowed.
- **Sanctuary.** Only priests can enter the building.

Jesus sees that the temple leaders have allowed merchants to set up a market in the outer courtyard—the sanctuary for non-Jewish believers. Perhaps the merchants have to rent the space from the priests.

It must have seemed a win-win-win situation. The temple gets rental money. Merchants make a shekel. And worshippers get animals to sacrifice along with currency exchange services, which allow them to trade their pagan coins with pictures of Roman rulers and gods for the temple-approved currency needed to pay their annual temple taxes. Of course, the worshippers probably paid convenience-store premium prices.

In this scene, Mark mentions just one type of sacrificial animal: doves—which poor people could offer as sacrifices. But there were probably other sacrificial animals, too: sheep, goats, and bulls.

The merchants probably weren't scattered all over the Gentile courtyard. Archaeological evidence suggests the temple market was mainly under a tile-roofed, colonnade hallway called the Royal Stoa. Almost 200 yards long, it opened without a wall into the courtyard.

There are two main theories about why Jesus flipped over the merchant tables and drove off the entrepreneurs and their customers.

Theory One. He is protecting the holiness of this international worship center and allowing non-Jews to worship in peace. "The Scriptures declare, 'My Temple will be called a house of prayer for all nations,' " Jesus says, "but you have turned it into a den of thieves" (Mark 11:17).

Theory Two. Jesus is symbolically acting out God's judgment on the system of temple worship and reinforcing his prediction that the temple will be destroyed (Mark 13:2). Romans dismantle it 40 years later, in AD 70. Jesus' sacrificial death for the sins of everyone would make the temple's sacrificial system obsolete.

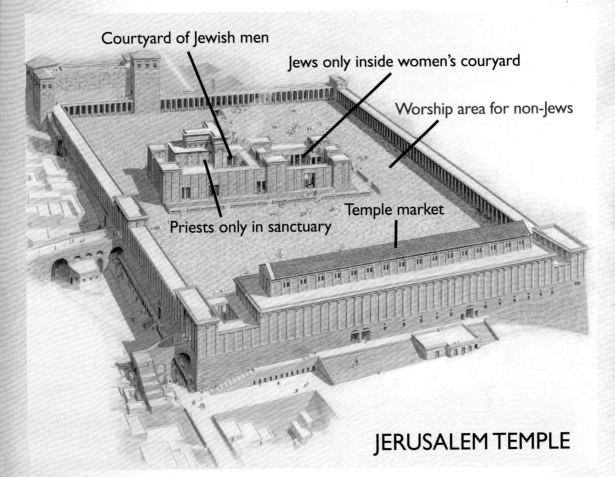

Courtyard of Jewish men

Jews only inside women's couryard

Worship area for non-Jews

Priests only in sanctuary

Temple market

JERUSALEM TEMPLE

Keeping non-Jews with the livestock. The sprawling courtyard surrounding the sanctuary complex is as close as non-Jews are allowed to the sanctuary. It's their worship center. Jesus becomes furious when he sees merchants selling sacrificial animals there. So he runs off merchants and customers alike.

COLOGNE for Jesus

Jesus was in Bethany. . . . While he was eating, a woman came in with a beautiful alabaster jar of expensive perfume. . . . She broke open the jar and poured the perfume over his head.

MARK 14:3

The timing of this incident is up for debate. The Bible places it "two days before Passover and the Festival of Unleavened Bread" (Mark 14:1). That could mean Wednesday, two days before the Friday Passover and Jesus' execution. Or it might mean the previous Saturday, which is two days before the beginning of the weeklong Passover celebration. If that's the case, Mark is backtracking, since he has already described events on Sunday, when Jesus entered Jerusalem on a donkey.

John's Gospel tells a story so similar that many Bible experts say it's just another witness's recollection of the same event. John sets it on Saturday. But he places the meal at the home of Lazarus, whom Jesus raised from the dead—not at the home of Simon the onetime leper, where Mark places it. Both live in Bethany, a small village on the outskirts of Jerusalem. Both Simon and Lazarus may have attended the meal.

A woman whom Mark doesn't identify pours a flask of expensive perfume over Jesus' head. This scented oil is imported spikenard, worth the salary that an average man makes in a year. John says the woman honoring Jesus is Mary, the sister of Lazarus and Martha. The perfumed oil is the same type and value as Mark mentions, but in John's version, Mary pours it on Jesus' feet, not on his head. Yet with 12 ounces, she would have had plenty for both head and feet.

Mark says the disciples complain about the extravagant waste, saying the perfume should have been sold and the money given to the poor. John's Gospel says Judas is the complainer—adding that he's also the group treasurer who skims money for himself.

Jesus defends the woman. "Leave her alone," he says. "She has done what she could and has anointed my body for burial ahead of time" (Mark 14:6, 8).

It's customary in Jesus' day to wash the corpse before burial. Then, in this hot region at the edge of the Arabian Desert, the body is covered with perfumed oil and wrapped in layers of scented cloth. It's to help mask the odor of decaying flesh while mourners grieve over the corpse.

This is all part of a proper burial, which Jesus won't get. He will be taken off the cross too late in the day on Friday for burial preparations. The workless Sabbath begins at sunset. So his body will go straight into a tomb, where it will wait for tending on Sunday morning.

KISS of betrayal

"You will know which one to arrest when I greet him with a kiss."

MARK 14:44

On Thursday evening Jesus eats one last meal with his disciples. They sing a hymn and then walk down into the narrow Kidron Valley on Jerusalem's east side. Then they climb the gentle slopes of a ridge called the Mount of Olives, where Jesus wants to pray. It's a favorite spot for him, perhaps in an olive grove called Gethsemane—from a word that means "olive press." Some speculate it was a cave. That's because there's a cave in the area where an ancient olive press was kept. The press wouldn't have been in use, since this is springtime, and olives aren't harvested until late in the summer.

Jesus is deeply upset and grieving. He's bravely committed to his mission, but he is certainly willing for a last-minute change of plans. Maybe God would send the same angel who had stopped Abraham from sacrificing his son Isaac. "Everything is possible for you," Jesus prays. "Please take this cup of suffering away from me. Yet I want your will to be done, not mine" (Mark 14:36).

Judas had left the group earlier. But now he returns with an armed escort. Jewish leaders want to arrest Jesus privately, without starting a riot. And Judas agrees to help them for what Matthew's Gospel says is 30 silver coins, probably shekels—the coins Jews used to pay their temple taxes. That's about 12 ounces total, or $120 on today's market when silver sells at $10 an ounce.

Bible writers don't say why Judas sold out Jesus. Perhaps they didn't know why. Some Bible experts guess it was for the money. Others guess it was to force Jesus into starting an uprising by taking a stand against Jewish leaders and the Roman authorities who supported them.

Judas's signal to the arresting officers is a kiss on Jesus' cheek. Kisses like this are a common way of greeting in Jesus' day, just as they are in many parts of the world today. They're like handshakes in some areas. When the officers arrest Jesus, the disciples run away to avoid getting arrested themselves.

Jesus wept here. "O Jerusalem, Jerusalem, the city that kills the prophets," Jesus once lamented. The Church of the Lord Wept—or Dominus Flevit, the Latin name it goes by—commemorates this moment of grief in Jesus' life. The window design with a chalice and thorns serves as a grim reminder that Jerusalem eventually killed him, too.

Why did Jesus have to die?

You'd think the almighty God could have figured out a better plan of salvation.

Something less bloody.

Something that didn't involve his Son on a slab.

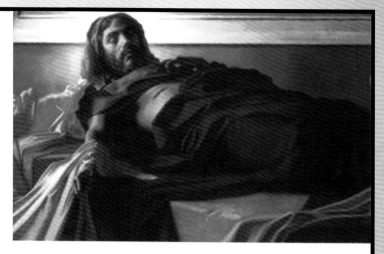

To be quite frank, God isn't famous for explaining himself. Suffering Job would testify to that. God essentially told Job there are some things that physics-bound humans can't understand about the spiritual dimension. In those cases, God expects people to trust him.

Perhaps that's the case with Jesus' death. Yet the Bible does offer a few clues about possible reasons.

Sin is a capital offense.

It has been from the beginning. God told Adam that if he broke the one and only law—eating forbidden fruit—"you are sure to die" (Genesis 2:17). The apostle Paul added, "The wages of sin is death" (Romans 6:23).

It's as though God can't tolerate sin any more than matter can tolerate anti-matter. We're not going to find them in the same vicinity.

Life is in the blood.

God said as much when he set up the system of animal sacrifices. "The life of the body is in its blood. I have given you the blood on the altar to purify you, making you right with the LORD. It is the blood, given in exchange for a life, that makes purification possible" (Leviticus 17:11).

Jesus' death fulfilled the death penalty requirement for everyone.

"Our High Priest offered himself to God as a single sacrifice for sins, good for all time. . . . When sins have been forgiven, there is no need to offer any more sacrifices" (Hebrews 10:12, 18).

Jesus' death set the stage for the Resurrection.

It was the Resurrection that finally convinced Jesus' disciples that he was God's Son. They were convinced enough that most of them died as martyrs. After seeing Jesus risen from the dead, and hearing him promise the same future for them, they died expecting that "everyone who believes in him will not perish but have eternal life" (John 3:16).

THE VERDICT: death

They took Jesus to the high priest's home where the leading priests, the elders, and the teachers of religious law had gathered.

MARK 14:53

Temple security officers take Jesus to the home of the Rome-approved high priest, Caiaphas. Other Jewish leaders have gathered there, as well. Peter follows from a safe distance. Once Jesus is inside, Peter joins the group of guards and servants waiting outside.

Inside, Jesus faces a barrage of lying witnesses who manage to contradict one another. Frustrated with them, Caiaphas asks Jesus if he is God's Son. When Jesus confirms that he will one day sit at God's right hand, no more lying witnesses are necessary. The truth is enough to condemn Jesus.

Jews don't have a formal creed—a concise statement of their key beliefs. But this one sentence comes close enough that some Jews wear it on tiny scrolls stashed inside boxes (phylacteries) tied to their foreheads and forearms: "Listen, O Israel! The LORD is our God, the LORD alone" (Deuteronomy 6:4).

Not the Lord and his Son.

Running the universe isn't a family business—not as far as the Jews are concerned. And to insist otherwise is considered blasphemy, even for a miracle-working prophet who raises the dead.

"What is your verdict?" Caiaphas asks the hastily assembled Jewish council. The Jewish council has 70 members. "Guilty!" they all cried. "He deserves to die!" (Mark 14:64).

Outside, several people accuse Peter of being a follower of Jesus since he has the northern accent of a Galilean. Peter denies the charge three times, until a rooster crows at the approaching dawn. Suddenly, Peter remembers that Jesus had predicted this denial and the crowing rooster. Peter breaks down sobbing. Matthew's Gospel adds that he runs off.

At daybreak the Jews take their condemned prisoner to Pilate, the Roman governor. Only he can order the death sentence. He does so reluctantly, at the insistence of the early-morning crowd of Jewish leaders. Roman historians of the time, such as Seneca (about 4 BC–AD 65), confirm that Roman trials could begin at sunrise or earlier.

At 9 a.m. Jesus is nailed to the cross and hoisted up. Six hours later, at about 3 p.m., he cries out a mystifying statement: "My God, my God, why have you abandoned me?" (Mark 15:34).

Some think he's calling for Elijah, since in the original language "My God" is *Eloi*. The word sounds a bit like the name of the prophet who Jews thought would come back to announce their Messiah's arrival: Elijah. So "Elijah, Elijah, why have you abandoned me?" must have sounded like the pitiful cry of a crazy person who really thought he was the Messiah.

Bible experts disagree over why Jesus said what he did. Some speculate that in this last moment of life, Jesus took on the sins of the world—and that God had no choice but to back away from him.

Others say Jesus was sending a message, quoting the first line of Psalm 22—a prophecy about the misery he has experienced.

- "My tongue sticks to the roof of my mouth" (verse 15).
- "They have pierced my hands and feet" (verse 16).
- "They divide my garments among themselves and throw dice for my clothing" (verse 18).

Jesus dies.

Surprisingly, a member of the council that condemned him—Joseph of Arimathea—asks Pilate for the body. Sabbath is quickly approaching, arriving at sunset. So Jesus is hurriedly wrapped in cloth and placed in Joseph's own tomb, recently cut from the rock wall of a nearby garden.

BACK from the dead

"He isn't here! He is risen from the dead!"

MARK 16:6

Sabbath ends at sunset on Saturday. That's the first chance anyone has to prepare Jesus' body for a proper burial. Mary Magdalene and another woman go to the market and buy fragrant burial spices to put on the body.

By sunrise the next day, the women are already on their way to the tomb—wondering how they're going to move the massive, disk-shaped stone that's parked in front of the tomb entrance.

Needless worry.

The stone is already rolled aside, and an angel is waiting for them. The angel says Jesus is gone, risen from the dead, and that he'll meet the disciples up in Galilee.

The oldest copies of Mark end here, after verse 8. Some early Christian writings seem to confirm this cutoff. Early Christian writers who quoted Mark but who either questioned the authenticity of verses 9-20 or who skipped any reference to those verses include: Origen (died about AD 254), Eusebius (died about AD 340), Jerome (died about AD 420).

At some point, perhaps, an editor copying the book decided that this ending was too abrupt—especially considering the endings available in the other Gospels. Scholars guess that this editor created an add-on ending by adapting material from all three other Gospels: Matthew, Luke, and John.

- verses 9–11 (John 20:11–18);
- verses 12–13 (Luke 24:13–24);
- verse 14 (John 10:24–31);
- verses 15–18 (Matthew 28:16–20); and
- verses 19–20 (Luke 24:50–53).

What's remarkable and ironic about this is that most scholars consider Mark the first Gospel written, and a main source that the others drew from.

Still, of all the stories in the Bible, Christians consider the Resurrection the most reliable—and the most critical to the faith. Paul put it this way: "If Christ has not been raised, then all our preaching is useless, and your faith is useless" (1 Corinthians 15:14).

JESUS IN APPEALS COURT

Had there been an appeals court in Jesus' day, his case would have qualified for a retrial.

The Jewish council that tried him seems to have broken several laws in the process. That's according to rules of procedure preserved in the Mishnah, a collection of Jewish laws passed along by word of mouth and finally written down by about AD 220.

- Trials weren't allowed on the day before Sabbath or the day before a festival such as Passover.
- The trial was supposed to be held on temple grounds—not in the house of one of the judges.
- Death-penalty cases had to be tried in daylight.
- Conviction required confirmation at least one day later, after a night's sleep.

LUKE

Shepherds visit the Lamb of God. A portrait in contrasts, this painting of Jesus' humble beginning hangs in one of the world's most prestigious museums, the Louvre in Paris. From a makeshift crib—a feeding trough—the baby Jesus gazes up at his first visitors: shepherds. They represent a humble class of people. Placing them at the Nativity is one reason Luke's story earned its nickname: Gospel of the Outcasts.

GOOD NEWS ISN'T JUST FOR JEWS

Somewhere lost in history is a fellow named Theophilus. So far, archaeologists poking around in the dirt have turned up nothing about him. But many Christians would really love to know who he was—since he's the reason nearly a third of the New Testament was written.

The two huge books of Luke (the story of Jesus) and Acts (the story of how the church got started) are actually letters to this mystery man. It seems as though the writer—identified by early Christian leaders as a non-Jewish doctor named Luke—is trying to teach Theophilus about the widely misunderstood Christian religion.

One theory is that Theophilus was a Roman official in charge of Paul's trial in Rome, and that Luke wrote these letters in Paul's defense. This would help explain why Acts ends with Paul awaiting trial in Rome, with no word about the outcome.

Yet perhaps Theophilus was a Christian who hired Luke to research the birth of Christianity and to get it in writing before all the eyewitnesses had died.

Whoever Theophilus was, we owe him. Without Luke's letter to this man, we'd be missing:

- a Christmastime favorite—the story of the baby Jesus lying in a manger;
- the parable of the good Samaritan;
- the widow who donated her last mite, a pennylike coin of measly value;
- the parable of the prodigal son, a young man who loses nearly everything but eventually finds his way home to his loving father.

But perhaps what we'd miss most of all is a single word: *Savior*. Matthew and Mark skip the word. John uses it just once. But Luke's entire Gospel spins around this word and the idea behind it.

Luke's story isn't just good news for Jews. It's great news for everyone. An angel puts it this way: "I bring you good news that will bring great joy to all people. The Savior— yes, the Messiah, the Lord—has been born today in Bethlehem" (Luke 2:10–11).

SHEPHERDS at the baby crib

There were shepherds staying in the fields nearby, guarding their flocks of sheep.

LUKE 2:8

Around the time of Jesus' birth, the angel Gabriel makes at least two visits to earth, perhaps three.

First he goes into the Jerusalem temple to tell an old priest, Zechariah, that his wife, Elizabeth, will have a son. "He will be a man with the spirit and power of Elijah," Gabriel says. "He will prepare the people for the coming of the Lord" (Luke 1:17). Gabriel is talking about John the Baptist.

Later that year, when Elizabeth is beginning her sixth month of pregnancy,

MAIN POINT:

Jesus has come to save everyone, not just the Jews.

WRITER:

The book doesn't name the writer. At least as early as the AD 100s, church leaders said a non-Jewish physician wrote this Gospel and its sequel, the Acts of the Apostles. The doc was Luke, a traveling companion and colleague of the apostle Paul. If this is correct, Luke is probably the only non-Jewish author whose work appears in the New Testament.

DATE:

Luke's story stretches more than 30 years—the lifetime of Jesus on earth— from about 6 BC to about AD 30. It's uncertain when Luke wrote the story. Some guess in the AD 50s or 60s. That would place it before Paul's execution— which would explain why Acts ends without telling the results of Paul's trial in Rome. Others guess in the AD 70s or 80s, after the gospel had spread throughout the Roman Empire as Jesus predicted: "to the ends of the earth" (Acts 1:8).

LOCATION:

Israel. Most of Jesus' ministry takes place in Galilee, in what is now northern Israel.

Gabriel pays a startling visit to Mary in the village of Nazareth. Mary is a young virgin engaged to marry Joseph. She's also related to Elizabeth, though the Bible doesn't say how.

Gabriel tells Mary, "You will conceive and give birth to a son, and you will name him Jesus. He will be very great and will be called the Son of the Most High. The Lord God will give him the throne of his ancestor David. And he will reign over Israel forever; his Kingdom will never end!" (Luke 1:31–33).

Gabriel's third visit may have been the most famous of all. He isn't named this time, but he may well have been the angel who told a group of Bethlehem shepherds to go into town to see "the Savior—yes, the Messiah, the Lord. . . . You will recognize him by this sign: You will find a baby wrapped snugly in strips of cloth, lying in a manger" (Luke 2:11–12).

Late in Mary's pregnancy, she and Joseph make the three-day, 60-mile trek from Nazareth to Bethlehem. The Roman emperor Augustus ordered an empire-wide census, perhaps to get an idea about what taxes he could expect from each region. Everyone had to register for this census in their family's ancestral hometown. Joseph was an ancestor of King David, who grew up in Bethlehem. Apparently there are so many people coming to tiny Bethlehem that the village inn fills up.

So the Son of God ends up getting born in a barn—probably a cave that sheltered livestock. This story is odd on many levels, provoking questions:

- Why would God allow his Son to be born in such humble surroundings?
- And of all people in the area—Jerusalem was only six miles north—why would the angel tell social bottom dwellers like shepherds to go and see the baby Jesus? That's like inviting a crew of street cleaners into the White House to see the First Lady's new baby. It wouldn't make sense—unless the president really was a man of the people.

Jesus is exactly that. And in the years to come he will make this promise to the common people: "Those who humble themselves will be exalted" (Luke 14:11).

BOY prodigy

When Jesus was twelve years old, they attended the festival as usual. . . . Jesus stayed behind in Jerusalem. . .sitting among the religious teachers, listening to them and asking questions. All who heard him were amazed at his understanding and his answers.

LUKE 2:42–43, 46–47

When did Jesus realize he was something more than human—the Son of God? The Bible doesn't say. Perhaps while Jesus was still a little boy, Mary and Joseph told him the remarkable story of his birth.

The Bible does suggest that Jesus knew he was unique by the time he was 12. That's one year before a Jewish boy's coming-of-age ritual: *bar-mitzvah*, an idea that developed several centuries later.

Jesus and his family had come to Jerusalem for the springtime Passover festival, probably traveling with a group of family and friends from Nazareth. That would explain why Mary and Joseph didn't miss him until the end of the first travel day, when the large group that's headed home camps for the night.

Rushing back to Jerusalem, his parents spend at least one day pushing through the crowds in what must have been a frantic, terrifying search for their lost son. Luke says they spent three days, but that may include the one-day walk away from the city and another day to walk back again.

They find Jesus in one of the temple courtyards, wowing the Jewish teachers with his insights about the Jewish religion. Perhaps in a scolding voice, Mary asks young Jesus why he did this to his parents, frightening them so. It's a complaint, not a polite query.

"Didn't you know that I must be in my Father's house?" he answers (Luke 2:49).

Luke says his parents don't understand. And Bible experts today aren't so sure about it, either. Some guess that Jesus was saying he was headed into a ministry of teaching people about God. So it would be natural for him to spend as much time as he could studying. And the place to study the Jewish faith is among Jewish scholars at the temple.

But by referring to God as "my Father," Jesus seems to be doing more than calling himself a faithful Jew who serves his heavenly Father. Given the context, separated from Mary and Joseph for at least a day, he already seems to understand that he has a unique relationship to his spiritual Father—and a mission to fulfill.

VIOLENT home folks

When he came to the village of Nazareth, his boyhood home, he went as usual to the synagogue on the Sabbath and stood up to read the Scriptures.

LUKE 4:16

Jesus' relative John the Baptist baptizes him. And Jesus begins his ministry as a traveling rabbi who visits synagogues throughout his home region of Galilee, in what is now northern Israel. He quickly earns a name for himself as a miracle worker and an insightful but controversial teacher.

Jesus returns to his hometown of Nazareth, a day's walk from his ministry headquarters in the lakeside village of Capernaum. As a visiting rabbi, he is invited to take part in the Sabbath worship services. Jewish worship has a particular order, which probably includes reading from different parts of the Jewish scriptures, a sermon, and perhaps singing some psalms. The oldest written accounts of Jewish services confirm this, but no one can be sure that this reflects worship in Jesus' time. So it's uncertain if Jesus chooses to read from Isaiah 61 or if that passage is simply the next one on the weekly schedule.

It's a passage that many Jews believe talks about the Messiah and the end times. It speaks of a God-anointed messenger—a Messiah—sent "to bring Good News to the poor. . .to proclaim that captives will be released, that the blind will see, that the oppressed will be set free, and that the time of the LORD's favor has come" (Luke 4:18–19).

Boldly, Jesus says he is that messenger.

He anticipates that his hometown people will tell him to prove it by performing the kind of miracles they've heard he has done in other villages. Mark's Gospel says he has already done some in Nazareth, but very few: "Because of their unbelief, he couldn't do any mighty miracles among them except to place his hands on a few sick people and heal them" (Mark 6:5).

By the time of this Sabbath service, Jesus apparently knows about the people's lack of faith. So he refuses to do any more miracles—and he refuses with a warning that sounds like an insult. He says there were plenty of needy Jews in the days of Elijah and Elisha, yet Elijah helped a starving widow in what is now Lebanon. And Elisha healed a Syrian leper.

In other words, Jesus is implying that Gentiles are more worthy of God's help than the Jews are.

Furious, the worshippers decide to stone him to death. But instead of throwing stones at him, they're going to throw him at the stones. They'll pitch him off one of the cliffs in the area. But Jesus slips out of the rioting crowd and returns to Capernaum.

Nazareth cliff-diving. Steeper and higher than it looks—especially from the precarious perch on top—this cliff lies on the outskirts of the hilltop city of Nazareth. Hometown folks dragged Jesus to the edge of a hill, intending to shove him off.

A ROMAN with more faith than a Jew

"I am not even worthy to come and meet you. Just say the word from where you are, and my servant will be healed."

Luke 7:7

Luke continues to build a case for the value of non-Jews. Jesus has left his Jewish hometown, where "he was amazed at their unbelief" (Mark 6:6). Now, back in Capernaum, he comes across a Roman soldier whose faith leaves him "amazed."

The soldier has a servant who is dying. Jesus has probably performed many healing miracles in and around Capernaum, so the soldier hopes Jesus will help.

There's a problem. The soldier is a Gentile. And he knows that some rabbis avoid contact with non-Jews. Some, in fact, consider Gentiles ritually unclean. That means as far as the rabbis are concerned, if a Jew touches a Gentile, or even steps inside a Gentile home, the Jew has to go through cleansing rituals before worshipping God at the temple.

Rather than risk offending Jesus, the soldier sends messengers: Jewish leaders in the city. "If anyone deserves your help, he does," they tell Jesus, "for he loves the Jewish people and even built a synagogue for us" (Luke 7:4–5). That's probably the same synagogue that archaeologists found just a few feet from what seems to have been Peter's house. Christians later built a church over the ruins of Peter's home, right next door to the synagogue.

Jesus agrees to help. But once the soldier learns of it, he sends another delegation. These messengers tell Jesus the soldier doesn't feel worthy of hosting Jesus in his home. So he asks Jesus to simply give the healing order from where he is, just as a commander gives orders to his subordinates. "My servant will be healed," the soldier says. "I know this."

Astonished, Jesus turns to the crowd and says, "I tell you, I haven't seen faith like this in all Israel!" (Luke 7:9).

Coming from a rabbi, that's quite the compliment for a Gentile. And quite a put-down for the Jews.

DOING SOMETHING about the weather

When Jesus woke up, he rebuked the wind and the raging waves.
Suddenly the storm stopped and all was calm.

LUKE 8:24

Matthew, Mark, and Luke all tell this story. Healing people is one thing. In Jesus' day, like today, it's not unheard of for sick people to suddenly get well. But who ever heard of a miraculous weatherman who could actually do something about the weather? Certainly not the disciples. That's why this miracle catches their attention.

Jesus decides to leave Capernaum, a village located on the Sea of Galilee's north shore. He plans to sail to the Gerasene region across the lake. Bible experts aren't sure where this is.

Nearly half the disciples are experienced fishermen. So the question is how they could have gotten themselves into this fix—caught in a life-threatening storm on a lake they had been fishing all their lives.

This is an unusual lake, seemingly tailor-made for sudden storms. It sits like a bowl on the edge of a desert, buried deep in the dirt—700 feet below sea level. As the sun bears down on it, evaporating the surface water, muggy, moist heat rises. But cool breezes lie just 30 miles east. Depending on the way the wind blows, this cool air can pour in from the Mediterranean Sea, rolling down the Galilean valleys and crashing into the hot air that's lifting from the lake. That's a prescription for an instant storm, which can churn waves six feet high.

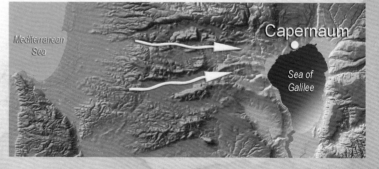

Storm Rx. Cool ocean breezes plummet 700 feet below sea level, crashing into hot air rising from the desert lake. The result: a sudden storm.

Beyond the storm chaser. When a sudden storm on the Sea of Galilee threatens to sink their small boat, frantic disciples wake Jesus. He immediately orders the wind and waves to quiet down.

Jesus must be exhausted. He keeps on sleeping—right up until he hears the alarm: "Master, Master, we're going to drown!" (Luke 8:24).

Jesus wakes and shows the disciples that he's more than the Master of men.

"Silence! Be still!" he says, addressing the storm (Mark 4:39).

Then he addresses his disciples. "Where is your faith?" (Luke 8:25).

This band of brothers, Jews each one, still can't muster faith the size of a mustard seed. That's Luke's implication. Even witnessing Jesus stopping a storm won't produce the miracle of faith within them. It will take the mother of all miracles to do that: the Resurrection.

A MIRACLE for women only

A woman in the crowd had suffered for twelve years with constant bleeding, and she could find no cure.

LUKE 8:43

A menstrual period that drags on and on. That's the most common guess about what this woman has endured for a dozen years. If Dr. Luke were alive today, he might diagnose her problem as menorrhagia. It's a disease that produces excessive or prolonged menstrual bleeding—or both.

Normally, a menstrual period lasts four to five days every 28 days, generating anywhere from four tablespoons to one cup of blood. But a woman suffering from menorrhagia can experience menstrual periods that stretch out to a week or more, producing enough blood to soak a pad or a tampon every hour for several consecutive hours. This condition can cause chronic pain in the lower abdomen, extreme weariness, and even shortness of breath.

There's an extra side effect in Jesus' day: ritual uncleanness. If this is what the woman in Luke's story has, many rabbis would condemn her for going out in public. She is ritually unclean—which means she's not fit to worship God until her period stops and she undergoes purification rituals: waiting a week, sacrificing two birds, and taking a bath. Also, anyone she touches during her period becomes as unclean as she is. That's Jewish law (Leviticus 15:19).

Still, she works her way through the crowd and manages to touch the fringe of Jesus' robe. Some believe that touching a holy man can work miracles.

Right away the bleeding stops. Jesus feels healing energy flow, and he asks who touched him.

Terrified and trembling, the woman is probably afraid to admit what she did. But she seems even more afraid of telling a lie to this holy man. So she confesses, explaining her problem in front of the entire crowd. That means we can probably add humiliation to what she's feeling.

Perhaps that's why Jesus responds the way he does: "Daughter." What single word could have put her more at ease, and more quickly?

"Your faith has made you well," he says. "Go in peace" (Mark 5:34).

Jesus is shaping up to be anything but a typical Jewish rabbi.

THE GOOD Samaritan

"A despised Samaritan came along, and when he saw the man, he felt compassion for him. Going over to him, the Samaritan soothed his wounds with olive oil and wine and bandaged them."

LUKE 10:33–34

Jesus tells the parable of the good Samaritan in response to one of the most important questions of all. "Teacher, what should I do to inherit eternal life?" (Luke 10:25).

The question—a popular one of the day, showing up in ancient Jewish writings—is a test from a Jewish scholar. He wants to know if Jesus agrees with other rabbis.

Jesus answers with a kosher response, quoting what many Jews believe are the two most important commandments:

- Love God with all your heart.
- Love your neighbor as yourself.

The scholar presses Jesus, asking who qualifies as a neighbor. This is where Jesus gets nonkosher, expressing his unconventional idea in a story. Conventional Jewish wisdom says the "neighbors" God expects Jews to love are other Jews—not sinners and foreigners.

Writing about 200 years before Jesus, a Jewish scholar put it this way: "Give to the godly person, but don't help a sinner. Do good to humble people, but don't give to the ungodly. Don't even give them food" (*Wisdom of Jesus Ben Sirach* 12:4–5).

In Jesus' parable, robbers mug a man traveling on the desolate road from Jerusalem to Jericho. It's an isolated stretch of nearly 20 miles, through rocky Judean badlands.

Two Jewish leaders walk right past him. First a priest. Then a priest's assistant. Perhaps they were afraid of becoming ritually contaminated. Touching a corpse would do that, leaving them unfit to conduct services at the temple until after going through a week of cleansing rituals (Numbers 19:11). Or maybe they didn't want to get involved.

But a "despised Samaritan"—a non-Jew—does get involved. He treats the man's wounds, takes him to an inn, and pays the innkeeper to take care of him.

Many Jews despise Samaritans, considering them racial and spiritual half-breeds. Samaritans are a race of Jews who intermarried with Assyrian pioneers from what is now Iraq. The Assyrian Empire overran what is now northern Israel, then sent in pioneers to repopulate the land with settlers friendly to the empire.

The half-Jews developed what traditional Jews considered a warped, quasi-Jewish religion. Samaritans don't revere Jerusalem as a worship center. Instead, they worship at Mount Gerizim near modern-day Nablus. That's where Joshua and the Israelites renewed their agreement with God after entering the Promised Land. Samaritans also have their own Bible, which Jews consider an edited version of the first five books in the Bible.

"Which of these three would you say was a neighbor to the man who was attacked by bandits?" Jesus asks the scholar.

"The one who showed him mercy."

"Yes, now go and do the same," Jesus replies (Luke 10:36–37).

THE REBELLIOUS prodigal

"The younger son told his father, 'I want my share of your estate now before you die.' So his father agreed. . . . A few days later this younger son packed all his belongings and moved to a distant land, and there he wasted all his money in wild living."

LUKE 15:12–13

Jewish leaders can't understand why Jesus hangs out with sinners. Rabbis are respected people who keep respectable company. That's the general rule. But it's not Jesus' practice.

He explains himself with a trio of parables about lost things and how important it is to recover them: lost sheep, lost coin, lost son.

In the last parable—a famous one told only in Luke—a son asks for his share of the family inheritance. As the younger of two sons, he would get a third of his father's estate. Two-thirds usually goes to the oldest son, who eventually becomes leader of the extended family.

It's a callous request, just as it would be today. But the father gives the boy what he wants—perhaps the cash value of the livestock and land, essentially buying him out. The boy leaves and quickly spends the money on "wild living." That's probably a kind way of saying "drunken orgies."

Money gone, the young man winds up tending hogs—nonkosher animals the Jews are supposed to avoid. The Talmud, an ancient collection of Jewish teachings and Bible commentary, says, "Cursed is the man who raises pigs."

The young man gets so hungry that he eats pig food: pods that many Bible experts say are the carob pods eaten by animals and the poorest of poor people.

In time, the fellow decides survival is more important than pride. So he heads home to ask his father if he can work there as a servant.

Jesus' description of the reunion is a heart-melt. The father isn't pouting. He's grieving—missing his son and watching for him every day. When he spots him, as a small dot on the distant path, he takes off running toward him.

Many parents—then and now—know the feeling. Children might grow up to make stupid choices, hurting themselves and others. But they're still our children. And we love them. No matter what. We might hate what they've done. But our love for them overpowers all else.

The father in this story represents God. The lost son represents those who have been spiritually lost but who want forgiveness. And the older brother, unhappy about the glad reunion, may represent the Jewish leaders who don't like seeing Jesus in the company of sinners.

But Jesus wants the Jewish leaders to see sinners as children whom God is eager to welcome home.

TAX MAN up a tree

Zacchaeus. . . .was the chief tax collector in the region, and he had become very rich.

LUKE 19:2

On his way to Jerusalem, Jesus comes to the oasis town of Jericho, a thriving city known for its year-round fruits and vegetables. He has about another 20 miles to go, a full day's walk.

Zacchaeus lives in this crossroads town near what is now Israel's eastern border, a few miles from the Jordan River. He's in charge of collecting taxes throughout the region, including tolls for produce and other goods shuttled in or out of the city. He apparently won the bid to collect taxes from his fellow Jews, agreeing to give Rome the tax it required.

Jews hate tax collectors for collaborating with the Roman occupiers and for gouging them with excessive taxes. Gouging is how tax collectors get rich. They keep any tax money above the amount they promise Rome.

Zacchaeus wants to catch a look at the notable visitor, but he can't see over the crowds. So he climbs a tree, where Jesus spots him. Calling the well-known official by name, Jesus says, "Come down! I must be a guest in your home today" (Luke 19:5).

Instead of avoiding outcasts, Jesus seeks them out—like a rabbi looking for trouble. That's how most Jews see it. But not Jesus. He says, "The Son of Man came to seek and save those who are lost" (Luke 19:10).

Many Bible experts say this one sentence sums up the "Gospel of the Outcasts," as Luke's Gospel is sometimes called. Jesus, on his way to Jerusalem to give up his life, takes an evening in Jericho to save a life.

After his encounter with Jesus, Zacchaeus becomes a new person. He vows to give half his money to the poor. And he offers a quadruple payback to anyone he has cheated. The Jewish penalty of restitution for stealing a basic commodity like sheep is "four sheep for each sheep stolen" (Exodus 22:1).

CRUCIFIED

When they came to a place called The Skull, they nailed him to the cross.
LUKE 23:33

Jesus arrives in Jerusalem on Sunday. Crowds welcome him like he's a king. In fact, they hope he is. Many believe he's the Messiah they've been praying for God to send to free them from their Roman occupiers.

But on Thursday night one of Jesus' disciples, Judas Iscariot possessed by Satan, helps Jewish leaders arrest him. Then, in an all-night trial, the 70-member Jewish council convicts him of insulting God by claiming to be God's Son. They sentence him to death.

By daybreak, the council marches him across town to Pilate, the Roman governor. According to Roman law, only officials of Rome can order criminals executed. Pilate doesn't agree with the sentence, and, like a savvy politician, he tries to pass the buck.

Jesus is from Galilee. And Galilee's ruler, Herod Antipas, is in town for the Passover festival. A son of Herod the Great, Herod Antipas is the ruler who executed John the Baptist. Pilate sends Jesus to Herod. When Herod asks Jesus to do a miracle, Jesus refuses, standing silent.

To mock Jesus, who's charged with claiming to be king of the Jews, Herod dresses him in a royal robe and sends him back to Pilate—who enjoys the joke. The two rulers become friends over this.

Still, Pilate objects to the death sentence. But the angry Jewish council prevails.

Pilate orders Jesus crucified between two criminals. All three are executed outside the city walls at a place called Calvary—Rome's native Latin word for "skull." "Golgotha" means the same thing in Hebrew. Perhaps people call the place "skull" because it's the city's execution site, or because it's near some tombs.

Nails pierce Jesus at about 9 a.m. At noon, darkness covers the land for three hours—perhaps heavy cloud cover, maybe a miracle sun-stopper. At 3 p.m. Jesus shouts his last breath: "Father, I entrust my spirit into your hands!" (Luke 23:46).

A DOCTOR'S GUIDE TO JESUS' CRUCIFIXION
Illustrated by the Mayo Clinic

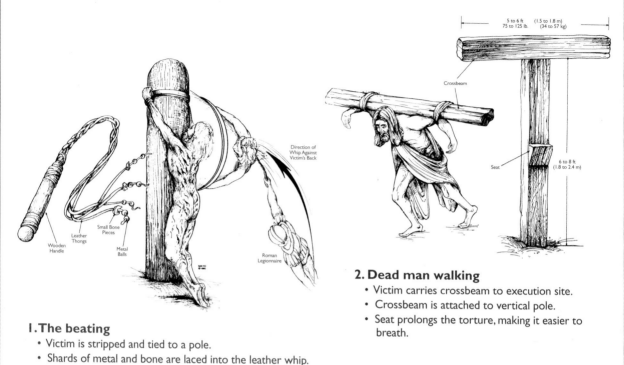

5 to 6 ft   (1.5 to 1.8 m)
75 to 125 lb.   (34 to 57 kg)

Crossbeam

Direction of
Whip Against
Victim's Back

6 to 8 ft
(1.8 to 2.4 m)

Seat

Small Bone
Pieces

Leather
Thongs

Wooden
Handle

Metal
Balls

Roman
Legionnaire

2. Dead man walking
- Victim carries crossbeam to execution site.
- Crossbeam is attached to vertical pole.
- Seat prolongs the torture, making it easier to breath.

1. The beating
- Victim is stripped and tied to a pole.
- Shards of metal and bone are laced into the leather whip.
- Romans aren't limited to 40 strokes, as are the Jews.
- Pain and blood loss set stage for shock.

Source: "On the Physical Death of Jesus Christ," *Journal of the American Medical Association.* Details about crucifixion are taken from the Bible and from other ancient sources.

BACK-FROM-THE-DEAD man walking

Two of Jesus' followers were walking to the village of Emmaus. . . . As they talked. . .Jesus himself suddenly came and began walking with them.
LUKE 24:13, 15

As the other Gospels report, Jesus is buried before sunset on Friday. That marks the beginning of the Jewish Sabbath—24 hours of rest and worship. Jesus rises from the dead on Sunday morning. That's when several women discover the empty tomb and report it to the 11 disciples—minus Judas, who has hanged himself.

That same day, in a story only Luke reports, two of Jesus' followers who live in the neighboring village of Emmaus start walking home. Jesus meets them on the path. But for some reason they don't recognize him.

Jesus asks what they're talking about. They can't believe his question. He's obviously

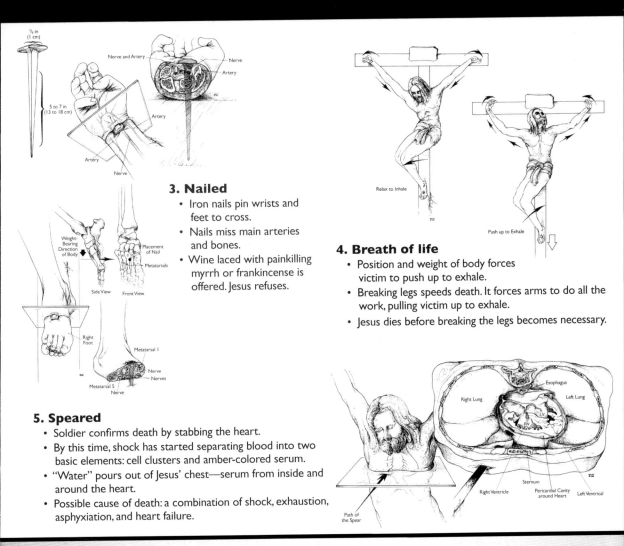

3. Nailed

- Iron nails pin wrists and feet to cross.
- Nails miss main arteries and bones.
- Wine laced with painkilling myrrh or frankincense is offered. Jesus refuses.

4. Breath of life

- Position and weight of body forces victim to push up to exhale.
- Breaking legs speeds death. It forces arms to do all the work, pulling victim up to exhale.
- Jesus dies before breaking the legs becomes necessary.

5. Speared

- Soldier confirms death by stabbing the heart.
- By this time, shock has started separating blood into two basic elements: cell clusters and amber-colored serum.
- "Water" pours out of Jesus' chest—serum from inside and around the heart.
- Possible cause of death: a combination of shock, exhaustion, asphyxiation, and heart failure.

coming from Jerusalem. Yet he doesn't seem to know what happened to the prophet who so many people thought was the Messiah. So they tell him.

Jesus responds with a history lesson from all three major sections of the Jewish Bible: Law, Prophets, and Writings. He quotes predictions about how the Messiah would suffer—predictions fulfilled by this crucifixion.

Perhaps he quotes some of these, which the disciples would later use in their sermons:

- "He was pierced for our rebellion, crushed for our sins. . . . He was whipped so we could be healed" (Isaiah 53:5).
- "He was buried like a criminal; he was put in a rich man's grave" (Isaiah 53:9).
- "You will not leave my soul among the dead or allow your holy one to rot in the grave" (Psalm 16:10).
- "My righteous servant will make it possible for many to be counted righteous, for he will bear all their sins" (Isaiah 53:11).
- "The stone that the builders rejected has now become the cornerstone" (Psalm 118:22).

Messiah roadblock. Seen from the Garden of Gethsemane, Jerusalem's Eastern Gate is now sealed. A Muslim ruler plugged it with stone after hearing prophecies that the Jewish Messiah would come to save Israel and enter through the Eastern Gate.

When the three reach Emmaus, the two locals invite Jesus to spend the night. He agrees and joins them for a meal. Only at mealtime do the hosts suddenly recognize him, after he breaks a loaf of bread and blesses it. In that instant, he disappears.

With night approaching, the two rush back to Jerusalem to tell the disciples about their mysterious encounter. But as the two are still talking, Jesus suddenly appears—to the horror of the disciples. They think he's a ghost.

Jesus assures them it's him, in the glorified flesh. He proves it by inviting them to touch him and by eating a piece of fish.

Forty days later, according to Luke's sequel, the Acts of the Apostles, Jesus leads the disciples to Bethany on the Mount of Olives. There, he rises into the sky, disappearing from sight.

This is the amazing story the disciples feel compelled to tell—or die trying.

JESUS IN THE ROMAN HISTORY BOOKS

The Bible isn't the only ancient book that talks about Jesus.

- "There was a wise man who was called Jesus, and his conduct was good. . . . Pilate condemned him to be crucified. . . . His disciples didn't abandon their loyalty to him. They reported that he appeared to them three days after his crucifixion, and that he was alive."

  Antiquities of the Jews, by Josephus (about AD 37–101)

- "Christ suffered the ultimate penalty at the hands of procurator Pontius Pilate when Tiberius was emperor of Rome."

  Annals of Imperial Rome, by Tacitus (about AD 55–120)

- "Chrestus" caused the riots in Rome in AD 49. This is probably a reference to Christ and to the hostility that erupted when traditional Jews clashed with Jews who believed Jesus was the promised Messiah. Acts 18:2 supports this theory, reporting that Claudius Caesar expelled all Jews from Rome at the time.

  The Lives of the Caesars, by Suetonius (about AD 70–130)

JOHN

Raising Lazarus. To prove Jesus is God's Son, John reports seven signs—miracles that Jesus performs. Raising Lazarus from the dead is the last and most dramatic, for it shows that even death is no match for the Son of God.

THE CASE FOR JESUS AS GOD'S SON

If all four Gospels could pose for a family picture, John would stand out like a seven-foot-tall Watusi adopted into a family of redheaded pygmy triplets. John is that different from Matthew, Mark, and Luke.

Bible experts call the triplets the Synoptic Gospels, from a Greek word that means "viewing together." They're so much alike that it's easy to compare them side by side.

But John is its own Gospel—in a category by itself.

Skip Jesus' parables. John does.

And forget most of Jesus' miracles. John reports only seven, which he calls "signs"—evidence that Jesus is God's divine Son.

John writes with only one purpose: to prove the deity of Jesus. Every miracle and story John reports nudges readers in that direction. He starts his Gospel at the Creation, placing Jesus there. And John includes long discussions Jesus has with people, explaining who he is and why he came to earth.

By the time John writes this Gospel, he may have already read the other three. He knows he's skipping a lot, and he says so: "Jesus also did many other things. If they were all written down, I suppose the whole world could not contain the books that would be written" (John 21:25).

But what John adds are some of the most famous stories and teachings in all of the Bible—not the least of which is John 3:16, "For God loved the world so much that he gave his one and only Son, so that everyone who believes in him will not perish but have eternal life."

That one sentence sums up the message in all four Gospels, according to Martin Luther. He's the Catholic priest who, in the 1500s, launched the Protestant movement by arguing that we're saved by faith, not by obedience to church leaders.

MAIN POINT:

John says he wrote this Gospel "so that you may continue to believe that Jesus is the Messiah, the Son of God, and that by believing in him you will have life by the power of his name" (John 20:31).

WRITER:

"This is the same disciple who was eyewitness to all these things and wrote them down. And we all know that his eyewitness account is reliable and accurate" (John 21:24 THE MESSAGE). As with all three other Gospels, this writer isn't identified by name. Church leaders at least as early as the AD 100s said it was the apostle John, one of Jesus' closest disciples. In fact, John is the only disciple not mentioned by name in the book—perhaps an act of humility.

DATE:

This Gospel was written late in the first century, perhaps in the AD 90s, according to most Bible experts. Clues include the well-developed Christian teachings. The writer seems to have had many decades to draw conclusions about what he witnessed during Jesus' ministry.

LOCATION:

Israel, known in Roman times as Palestine. The Roman word comes from "Philistine," a warrior race that settled in the land the same time Joshua and the Israelites arrived.

JESUS at Creation

In the beginning the Word already existed. The Word was with God, and the Word was God.

JOHN 1:1

This is a great way to start a book if you don't want anyone to read it. That's how it seems to many readers today. But John's first sentences, which seem puzzling to us, would have captivated Greek and Jewish readers in his day.

With a single idea John gets his point across to two different cultures. Greeks and Jews read the same words and react with radically different thought patterns, but they reach the same conclusion: John is introducing Jesus as a divine being.

John does this by calling Jesus the Word, *Logos* in Greek.

Greek philosophers of the day teach that *Logos* is the mysterious principle behind the universe—the eternal force that drives everything.

Jewish scholars, on the other hand, teach, "In the beginning God created the heavens and the earth" (Genesis 1:1). And God did this by simply speaking the word. "God said, 'Let there be light,' and there was light" (Genesis 1:3). The word of God created the universe.

John is telling Greeks and Jews alike that Jesus is the divine force behind the universe.

It's a startling statement. So John spends the rest of his Gospel proving it.

THE THINKER'S GOSPEL

John's Gospel probably wowed the religion scholars of his day. Quite a feat for a has-been fisherman.

Two wow factors:

- **Describing Jesus as the Word.**

Greek philosophers used "Word" (*Logos*) as a name for the cosmic reason behind the universe. The Ephesian philosopher Heraclitus said the Word is a mysterious power that "always exists" and that makes "all things happen."

- **Using layered meanings.**

We think it's clever when a comedian comes up with a double entrendre that we can take in two radically different directions. John makes many statements that can go in a bunch of directions—each direction correct.

For example, he calls Jesus the "bread of life," a symbolic description that works on a lot of levels:

Mealtime bread, the food that people relied on most to sustain their lives. Jesus is the source of our spiritual nourishment.

Passover bread, eaten at an annual festival as a reminder that God delivered the Jews from Egyptian slavery. Jesus delivered people from slavery to sin.

Manna, bread that fell from heaven to feed the starving Jews during the Exodus. Jesus came from heaven to feed a spiritually hungry world.

Communion bread, a reminder that Jesus sacrificed his body, paying the death penalty for humanity's sins.

JESUS the reluctant winemaker

The wine supply ran out during the festivities, so Jesus' mother told him, "They have no more wine."

"Dear woman, that's not our problem," Jesus replied.

JOHN 2:3–4

Jesus begins his ministry by allowing his relative John the Baptist to baptize him in the Jordan River. Then he assembles a dozen disciples. They will travel with him, learn from him,

No wine before it's time. Farmers stomp grapes into grape juice, then run it through a sieve to filter out the skin. It takes about six weeks for wine to ferment. In his first reported miracle, Jesus turns water into wine.

WAS IT GRAPE JUICE OR WINE?

Jesus drank full-bodied wine that would make him slur the Sermon on the Mount if he drank enough of it. That's the kind of wine he served up in Cana, according to most Bible experts.

It's a matter of timing and location. Grapes are harvested in the heat of summer—mostly August to September, depending on the variety. And this is in a hot country that borders the Arabian Desert. In this summer heat, grape juice starts to ferment right away.

Jesus enjoyed good food and fine wine enough that his critics called him "a glutton and a drunkard" (Matthew 11:19).

Yet it seems unlikely that he ever overindulged in wine. The Bible repeatedly warns people to drink in moderation, without getting drunk: "What sorrow for those who get up early in the morning looking for a drink of alcohol and spend long evenings drinking wine to make themselves flaming drunk" (Isaiah 5:11).

and help him spread his teachings.

Jesus and his entourage are invited to a wedding at Cana, a village near his hometown of Nazareth. Cana's exact location is unknown, but many guess it's now a vacant ruin called Khirbet Qana, eight miles north of Nazareth.

Weddings are even bigger events in Jesus' time than they are now. The celebrations last a week. And the guests—some who have traveled a day or more—expect plenty of good food and wine.

Unfortunately for the groom, who's responsible for supplying the food, the guests drink the wine jugs dry. Mary, the mother of Jesus, seems to be one of the first to realize this. Perhaps she's helping with the wedding of her neighbor. That would explain why she later gives orders to the wedding servants.

Mary reports the problem to Jesus, who seems inclined to do nothing about it. Then he adds an odd and cryptic remark: "My time has not yet come" (John 2:4). Elsewhere in John, this statement refers to the Crucifixion: "The leaders tried to arrest him; but no one laid a hand on him, because his time had not yet come" (John 7:30). So it seems that Jesus is saying if he miraculously produces wine, he'll set in motion a chain of events leading to his execution.

Mary apparently doesn't understand, so she insists. She orders servants to follow whatever instructions Jesus gives them. Jesus notices six empty stone jars, and he tells the servants to fill them with water. These stone jars typically hold about 20 gallons each—120 gallons for all six.

Jesus instantly turns the water into wine so fine that the wedding reception coordinator compliments the groom for saving the best for last.

This story is one of only seven miracles that John reports. And John's the only Gospel to report it. But it's an excellent choice to follow the introduction, which places Jesus at Creation in the beginning of time. For it shows that Jesus is still the master of his creation.

YOU MUST be born again

"I tell you the truth, unless you are born again, you cannot see the Kingdom of God."

JOHN 3:3

In Jerusalem, Jesus gets a nighttime visit from one of the most influential Jewish leaders in the country. His name is Nicodemus. He's a biblical scholar and one of about 70 Jews on the ruling Jewish council known as the Sanhedrin. Members of this council create and enforce Jewish laws. That makes this council a bit like a Congress/Supreme Court combo—or Parliament/House of Lords in England.

Nicodemus seems to represent the minority view on the council, for he tells Jesus, "Your miraculous signs are evidence that God is with you" (John 3:2).

Jesus replies with several perplexing statements that still stir up debate among Bible experts. First, he says that anyone who wants to become a part of God's kingdom—on earth as well as in heaven—must be "born again." That's a phrase that can be translated several

Seven miracles of Jesus	
We could go to any other Gospel and find nearly three times as many miracles as we'll discover in John's Gospel.	John reports only seven. But five of these appear nowhere else in the Bible. And all seven are called "signs" proving that Jesus is divine.
The Miracle	**The Message**
1. Turns water into wine (John 2:1–12)*	Jesus is still the master of creation.
2. Heals an official's son without even going to see the boy (John 4:46–54)*	Jesus isn't limited by geography.
3. Heals a crippled man on the Sabbath (John 5:1–17)*	Jesus isn't limited by time. Some Jewish scholars say it's wrong to treat the sick on the Sabbath unless the patient is on the brink of dying.
4. Feeds 5,000 people with five loaves of bread and two fish (John 6:1–14)	Jesus, who declares himself "the bread of life," is the source of nourishment, both physical and spiritual.
5. Walks on water (John 6:16–21)	Jesus isn't limited by physics.
6. Heals a man born blind (John 9:1–41)*	Jesus brings light into the world, both physical and spiritual.
7. Raises Lazarus from the dead (John 11:17–44)*	Even death is no match for the Son of God.

Miracle reported only in John's Gospel

ways, including "born from above," implying a spiritual awakening.

Then Jesus explains himself. He says that a person must be "born of water and the Spirit" (John 3:5). Some scholars say this refers to one event. Some say two. Theories of the Bible experts:

- Jesus is talking about (1) physical birth, when the water breaks, followed by (2) spiritual birth. But writings of the day don't show anyone else using "born of water" to refer to physical birth.

- Jesus is talking about (1) water baptism followed by (2) a life changed by the Spirit's daily guidance.

- Jesus is talking about the one spiritual experience he mentioned earlier: being born again. The prophets occasionally mentioned water and spirit together when predicting a great day ahead for Israel, when the Messiah would come:

    "Then I will sprinkle clean water on you, and you will be clean. . . . And I will put my Spirit in you so that you will follow my decrees and be careful to obey my regulations" (Ezekiel 36:25, 27).

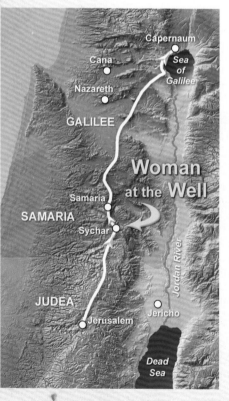

The road less traveled. Jesus leaves Jerusalem and walks home through the heart of Samaria, a region many Jews avoid. Not fond of Samaritans, Jewish travelers in Jesus' day prefer one of the Samaritan bypasses: routes along the coast or beside the Jordan River. At a well near Sychar, Jesus meets a Samaritan woman and tells her about living water that quenches spiritual thirst forever.

THE RABBI and the divorcée

A Samaritan woman came to draw water, and Jesus said to her, "Please give me a drink."

JOHN 4:7

Jesus leaves Jerusalem and travels home to Galilee, a region in what is now northern Israel. Most Jews refuse to take the shortest route because it goes through the center of Israel, where Samaritans live. And Jews hate Samaritans (see "The Good Samaritan," page 340). Even today, Israelis often drive around the same area because many Palestinians live there.

Jesus, however, doesn't take the Samaritan bypass along the coast or beside the Jordan River. He walks right into the heart of the region of Samaria.

At noon he arrives at Jacob's Well outside Sychar, a village about 30 miles north of Jerusalem. That puts him about a day and a half into his trip, and nearly halfway home.

He sends his disciples into town to buy food, while he sits by the well and waits. The well is more than 100 feet deep today, but it measured 240 feet deep in AD 670. So it may have been even deeper in Jesus' day. Jesus doesn't get anything to drink, since the custom of the day is to BYOB—bring your own bucket. And he didn't.

Women usually come to the well in groups during the cool of the morning or evening. Gathering water is both a chore and a social event.

But suddenly, in the heat of the day, a solitary woman shows up, bucket in hand. Jesus asks her for a drink. It's a shocking request for several reasons.

- Jews typically don't talk to Samaritans.
- Jews teach that Samaritans and everything they touch are ritually unclean. So drinking water from a Samaritan would make a Jew unclean, forcing that person to undergo purification rituals.
- Rabbis don't usually talk to women in public. It's considered inappropriate behavior.

The woman recognizes Jesus as a Jew, perhaps from his northern accent. So she says she can't believe he's asking her for a drink.

"If you only knew the gift God has for you and who you are speaking to," Jesus replies, "you would ask me, and I would give you living water" (John 4:10).

"Living water" means running water. It's from a stream, or a river, or a spring, or a well that's fed by the underground water table. It's not water from a pond or an underground cistern that stores water in a plaster-coated rock pit.

But Jesus isn't talking about water at all.

The woman doesn't realize this. She thinks he's talking about some magic water—an eternal thirst-quencher. But Jesus is talking about everlasting life—the eternal death-quencher.

This woman eventually realizes that Jesus is a holy man. She figures this out after Jesus tells her she has been married five times and is currently living with a man who is not her husband. Jewish law limits women to three divorces. So the Jews would have considered her a serial sexpot—all the more reason for a respectable rabbi to avoid her. But Jesus has a different perspective: "I have come to call not those who think they are righteous, but those who know they are sinners and need to repent" (Luke 5:32).

THE COMPLETE GUIDE TO THE BIBLE

The woman rushes back to her village to tell the people about Jesus. The villagers invite Jesus to stay, and he does, for two days. During that time he convinces many that "he is indeed the Savior of the world" (John 4:42).

SEEING GOD through a blind man's eyes

"Rabbi," his disciples asked him, "why was this man born blind? Was it because of his own sins or his parents' sins?"

JOHN 9:2

Jesus and his disciples return to Jerusalem to celebrate the harvesttime Feast of Tabernacles. While walking along, the disciples notice a man born blind. They ask Jesus who's to blame for this man's suffering, since many rabbis of the day teach that suffering is God's punishment for sin. That's a theological blunder that Job's story sets straight, according to many Bible experts. Job suffered though he did nothing to deserve it.

In the case of a child born blind, some rabbis blame the parents. For biblical support they point to Exodus 34:7, "I lay the sins of the parents upon their children and grandchildren; the entire family is affected—even children in the third and fourth generations."

But this verse more likely means that a parent's sin can affect the children, as it would if a parent gambled away the family savings. God holds people accountable only for their own actions. As one prophet put it: "All people will die for their own sins—those who eat the

---

JESUS, THE GREAT "I AM"

Jesus tells people who he is, using seven dramatic one-liners—each pointing to God.

Every statement begins with "I am." That's God's name.

When Moses asked who he should tell the enslaved Hebrews in Egypt had sent him, God replied, "I AM WHO I AM. Say this to the people of Israel: I AM has sent me to you" (Exodus 3:14).

I am...
- "The bread of life" (John 6:35).
  The source of every believer's spiritual life.
- "The light of the world" (John 8:12).
  The source of spiritual insight and direction.
- "The gate for the sheep" (John 10:7).
  The doorway into the kingdom of God.
- "The good shepherd" (John 10:14).
  The one who knows his sheep and lays down his life to save them.
- "The resurrection and the life" (John 11:25).
  The one who not only gives people life after death, but is the source of eternal life.
- "The way, the truth, and the life" (John 14:6).
  The one who not only shows people the way to God and salvation, but is the way. No one can reach the Father except through Jesus, the bridge between heaven and earth.
- "The true grapevine" (John 15:1).
  The source of spiritual nourishment for everyone connected to him in faith, just as a grapevine feeds water and nutrients to the branches.

sour grapes will be the ones whose mouths will pucker" (Jeremiah 31:30).

A child can be born blind for many reasons. For example: lack of nutrition during pregnancy, problems with the delivery, or inherited diseases. One disease is LCA, or Leber Congenital Amaurosis. Recessive genes, which have to come from both parents, cause light sensors in the eye to malfunction. There's still no treatment for this.

"It was not because of his sins or his parents' sins," Jesus answers the disciples. "This happened so the power of God could be seen in him" (John 9:3).

Prophets had said that when the Messiah comes, "he will open the eyes of the blind" (Isaiah 35:5). And that's what Jesus does. He spits on the ground and mixes up a tiny mud plaster that he applies to the man's eyes. Then he tells the man to wash it off in the Pool of Siloam, fed by the "living water" of a spring. Perhaps Jesus used these two techniques to help build the man's faith. Many people in ancient times taught that spit had healing properties, though many rabbis taught that spit was ritually unclean. The running water of a spring, however, washes away ritual uncleanness.

Jewish leaders interrogate the healed man because Jesus healed him on the Sabbath—a day when many rabbis insist that doctors should rest from treating the sick, unless the patient is in danger of dying. Some leaders condemn Jesus for breaking this rule that they've established, even though the rule isn't in the laws of Moses. Other leaders agree with the healed man: "Ever since the world began, no one has been able to open the eyes of someone born blind. If this man were not from God, he couldn't have done it" (John 9:32–33).

LAZARUS, alive again

Jesus shouted, "Lazarus, come out!" And the dead man came out.
JOHN 11:43–44

Jesus remains in Jerusalem for Hanukkah, a December festival in which Jews celebrate an important event that took place about 200 years earlier: rededication of the temple after the Jews won their war of independence against Syria.

While teaching in the temple courtyard, Jesus gets into a bitter debate with some Jewish leaders. They try to arrest him, but he escapes. He goes to a village or perhaps a region called Bethany on what is now Jordan's side of the Jordan River. It's the place "where John was first baptizing" (John 10:40). Bible experts aren't certain exactly where this is. One possibility is just a few hundred yards east of the river. Archeologists recently found the remains of baptismal pools there, along with a church they say is perhaps the one mentioned by early pilgrims—a church marking the place where tradition says John baptized Jesus.

Jesus is there when he hears that one of his friends has become deathly ill. Lazarus is that friend. He's the brother of Mary and Martha. All three live in the village of a different Bethany—on the outskirts of Jerusalem.

The sisters send word for Jesus to come right away. But he delays leaving for two days. He starts the trip only after Lazarus dies. By the time Jesus arrives, Lazarus has been dead four days. That's one day longer than any hope of resuscitation, according to ancient Jewish sources. As one rabbi put it in the AD 200s, "For three days the soul hovers over the body, hoping to re-enter." After that, the body's appearance begins to change and the soul moves on.

When Jesus sees Mary and others crying about Lazarus, he responds the way many people do in the face of death. He gets angry. And then he cries. Some scholars say that "bursts into tears" is a phrase that best communicates the sharp tense of the original Greek word.

Jesus—still angry—orders the stone pushed away from the entrance blocking the cave tomb. And he does so despite Martha's protest that Lazarus's decaying corpse must smell terrible by now.

Then, in the last and most remarkable of John's seven "signs," Jesus calls Lazarus back from the dead. Lazarus comes out, "his hands and feet bound in graveclothes, his face wrapped in a headcloth" (John 11:44).

Word spreads throughout the village and into Jerusalem. There, Jewish leaders apparently doubt the story because they decide that the man who has just overpowered death needs to die. They're afraid his popularity is cresting and that the people are ready to embrace him as the promised Messiah. This, they fear, could provoke a Jewish war of independence that Rome would crush.

"It's better," says Caiaphas, the high priest, "that one man should die for the people than for the whole nation to be destroyed" (John 11:50). There's a speck of unintentional prophecy in Caiaphas's words. Jesus, in fact, will die to save all people. "Christ died once for all time as a sacrifice to take away the sins of many people" (Hebrews 9:28).

JESUS WASHES the disciples' feet

"Since I, your Lord and Teacher, have washed your feet, you ought to wash each other's feet. I have given you an example to follow. Do as I have done to you."

JOHN 13:14–15

At what will become his last Passover celebration on earth, Jesus arranges to eat the Passover meal in Jerusalem with his disciples. Christians today call this meal the Last Supper. After eating, Jesus washes the feet of his disciples. It's a dramatic object lesson.

It's customary for a host to arrange for guests to wash their feet. Feet are almost always dirty because people travel by walking in sandals along dusty trails. A single step on Israel's dry land can create a tiny explosion of dust that envelops the foot.

Usually, people wash their own feet. If a servant does it for them, it's generally the servant who always gets the worst jobs. Some rabbis in ancient times said footwashing was too menial for Jewish slaves—and that non-Jewish slaves should do the dirty work.

In our culture today, the status of this servant might compare roughly to that of a poor immigrant or to a migrant farmworker—folks who work hard but who often get little reward and no respect.

Jesus takes on that humble role. He strips down to his underclothing and wraps himself in a towel. Then, one by one, he washes the feet of each disciple. Peter objects, probably for the same reason John the Baptist hesitated to baptize Jesus: "I'm not even worthy to be his slave and untie the straps of his sandal" (John 1:27).

Jesus insists.

Washing done, Jesus makes his point. "Slaves are not greater than their master," he says. This probably jogs the memory of the disciples, reminding them of a popular saying of the day: "Students are not greater than their teacher, and slaves are not greater than their master. Students are to be like their teacher, and slaves are to be like their master" (Matthew 10:24–25).

Jesus wants his followers to become servants, just as he has done.

Many churches today have a footwashing ritual at Easter time. And though this ritual may be a helpful reminder of the humility Jesus expects of his followers, it's not the "ritual" that Jesus wants to preserve. The humble lifestyle is what he wants to see his disciples practice.

PETER CHICKENS out as the rooster crows

"You're not one of that man's disciples, are you?" . . . Peter denied it. And immediately a rooster crowed.

JOHN 18:17, 27

Later that evening, Peter swings from gutsy to gutless in a matter of minutes—a duo of extremes, both of which are inappropriate at the time.

After the meal, Jesus leads the disciples to a nearby olive grove where he prays and waits to be arrested. Judas, the treasurer for the disciples, has sold Jesus out to the Jewish leaders. For a reward, he leads temple police to Jesus so they can arrest him when there are no crowds around to protest and start a riot.

Peter pulls out a sword and hacks off the ear of the high priest's slave. The Gospel that many Bible experts say was written by a doctor is the only one to add that Jesus "touched the man's ear and healed him" (Luke 22:51).

As arresting officers lead Jesus away, Peter follows from a safe distance—accompanied by an unidentified disciple, perhaps John himself or a Jerusalem-area follower. Either way, it's someone who's "acquainted with the high priest" (John 18:15) and allowed into his private, walled courtyard. He sneaks Peter in, too, convincing the woman watching the gate to let him in.

Earlier that evening, at the Last Supper, Jesus had predicted that before morning Peter would deny he even knew Jesus—three times. Peter's first denial comes after the woman who let him in asks if he's a disciple of the arrested rabbi.

"No, I am not," Peter lies.

Later, standing by the fire with guards and servants, Peter gets the question again. "No, I am not."

One of the servants in the arresting party—a man related to the slave Peter had cut—pressed the matter. "Didn't I see you out there in the olive grove with Jesus?" (John 18:26).

Again Peter denies it. "A curse on me if I'm lying—I don't know the man!" (Matthew 26:74).

In this very moment a rooster crows, probably announcing the dawning of what will become a tragic day. For Peter, it may be the worst moment in the worst day of his life.

WHERE WAS JESUS BURIED?

Tradition #1
Church of the Holy Sepulchre

Trying to wipe out the memory of Christian holy sites, Hadrian built Roman shrines over them. He built a temple to Jupiter and Venus over the spot where Christians said Jesus was buried.

Two centuries later—in the AD 300s—the emperor Constantine legalized Christianity, demolished Hadrian's temple, and built an early version of the Church of the Holy Sepulchre.

This painting from the 1800s (left) shows a small chapel inside the church's domed rotunda. What remains of Jesus' cave tomb is supposedly inside.

Though the church is protected inside the walls of Jerusalem today, the site was outside the walls in Jesus' time. Jewish law required that cemeteries be kept outside the city.

Source of the tradition:
Roman Emperor Hadrian (AD 76–138)

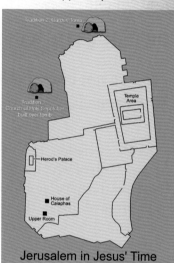

Jerusalem in Jesus' Time

Tradition #2

Garden Tomb

Surrounded by trees and flowers, the Garden Tomb (below left) seems to fit the Bible's description of Jesus' tomb, "near a garden" (John 19:41) yet outside the city in compliance with Jewish law. But it misses the "new tomb" description.

Located several hundred yards from the Church of the Holy Sepulchre, this tomb was part of a cemetery of stone tombs carved from rock several centuries before Jesus.

General Charles Gordon picked this as Jesus' possible burial site not only for the tomb but because of a hill a minute's walk away. The hill's cliff is eroded into a shape resembling a skull (below right). Romans executed Jesus on a hill called Golgotha, Hebrew for "Place of the Skull."

But this name may have come from bones of the victims or from the nearby cemetery. Also, the erosion on the cliff may not have resembled a skull 2,000 years ago.

Source of the tradition:
British General Charles Gordon
(1833–1885)

EXECUTING the Son of God

They nailed him to the cross.

JOHN 19:18

After an all-night trial, the Jews take Jesus to Pilate, Roman governor of the Judean territory. Only he has the authority to execute.

Pilate refuses to give the order until the Jews accuse Jesus of declaring himself king. "If you release this man, you are no 'friend of Caesar,' " they tell Pilate. It's a veiled threat—a hint that they'll appeal the case to Rome and criticize Pilate for not punishing a rebel leader.

Pilate orders Jesus crucified right away. Getting nailed to a cross is more than just a torturous way to die. Many Jews consider it spiritually humiliating—proof that God condemns the sinful victim. Quoting Deuteronomy 21:23 years later, Paul writes to Christians in the city of Galatia: "When he was hung on the cross, he took upon himself the curse for our wrongdoing. For it is written in the Scriptures, 'Cursed is everyone who is hung on a tree' " (Galatians 3:13).

For many Jews of the day, the manner of Jesus' execution proves that he's not even close to being God's Son. Instead, he's cursed of God.

Before Jesus dies, after six hours on the cross, he entrusts the care of his mother to "the disciple he loved" (John 19:26). Early church leaders identify this disciple as John, who they say is also the author of this Gospel. They add that John and Mary later move to Ephesus, a city on what is now Turkey's west coast.

DOUBTING Thomas

"I won't believe it unless I see the nail wounds in his hands, put my fingers into them, and place my hand into the wound in his side."

JOHN 20:25

Jesus rises from the dead on Sunday morning and appears to the disciples that evening. Thomas is the only one not with the group at the time. When Thomas returns and hears that Jesus has come back from the dead, he can't believe it.

He must have thought that it's one thing to raise others from the dead—Lazarus, Jairus's daughter (Mark 5:21–43), and a widow's son (Luke 7:11–17). But it's quite another to resurrect one's dead self.

Thomas has to wait eight days to see Jesus for himself. But then Jesus suddenly appears inside the locked house where the disciples are all staying. Jesus invites Thomas to touch the wounds in his hands and side.

No need. Thomas trusts his eyes and ears. "My Lord and my God!" he declares (John 20:28).

And with gentle words of rebuke for Thomas, Jesus offers a blessing on generations of believers yet to come: "You believe because you have seen me. Blessed are those who believe without seeing me" (John 20:29).

ACTS

HOW THE CHURCH IS BORN

In this sequel to the Gospel of Luke, Acts tells the story of what happens after Jesus leaves the planet.

Jailbreak. An angel frees imprisoned Peter. Like the other disciples, Peter is no longer afraid of prison or death now that he has seen the resurrected Jesus. In this selfless abandon, the church is born.

The writer, whom most Bible experts agree was probably Luke, starts by closing the book on the Jesus story. The disciples gather on the slopes of the Mount of Olives and watch Jesus ascend into the sky.

As he leaves, Jesus gives one final instruction to the disciples: Wait in Jerusalem for the Holy Spirit. This divine Spirit fills them with the courage to spread the teachings of Jesus everywhere—even in Jerusalem, where Jewish leaders had orchestrated the execution of Jesus only a few weeks earlier.

Thousands of Jews who've come to Jerusalem for a religious festival convert in a single day, embracing the teachings of the disciples. Jewish leaders retaliate. They bring pressure to bear on leaders and members of what they consider an emerging heretical Jewish cult:

- ordering them to stop the blasphemous teaching that Jesus is God's Son and that he rose from the dead;
- arresting and trying many of those who refuse; and
- executing some.

This violence eventually drives many believers out of town. But wherever they go, they take their new faith with them. And soon the teachings of Jesus are spreading all over the Roman Empire.

UP NEXT, the Holy Spirit

"Do not leave Jerusalem until the Father sends you the gift he promised . . . . In just a few days you will be baptized with the Holy Spirit."

ACTS 1:4–5

Even before Jesus was crucified, he told his disciples he would soon have to leave.

"I am going away to the One who sent me," Jesus tells them. "If I don't, the Advocate won't come" (John 16:5, 7). *Advocate* can also mean Comforter or Encourager. Jesus makes it clear that he's talking about the Holy Spirit who "will guide you into all truth" (John 16:13).

Now is the time for Jesus to leave, in an event Luke uses to begin Acts of the Apostles, his sequel to the Gospel of Luke. Forty days earlier Jesus rose from the dead and started appearing to his disciples from time to time, teaching them. Now he leads this small band of disciples to just outside Jerusalem. They walk to Bethany on the eastern slope of the Mount of Olives. There, Jesus tells them to go back to Jerusalem and wait for the Spirit.

"You will receive power when the Holy Spirit comes upon you. And you will be my witnesses, telling people about me everywhere—in Jerusalem, throughout Judea, in Samaria, and to the ends of the earth" (Acts 1:8).

Jesus ascends into the sky, and the disciples walk back to Jerusalem to wait. They select Matthias to replace Judas Iscariot, who had killed himself after helping Jewish leaders arrest Jesus. So they're back to a dozen. Word spreads that the Spirit is coming. So about 120 believers wait and pray together. Included in the group are Jesus' brothers and mother.

MAIN POINT:

Jesus' followers are to spread the good news about him and his teachings "everywhere—in Jerusalem, throughout Judea, in Samaria, and to the ends of the earth" (Acts 1:8).

WRITER:

The writer isn't identified, though the book is written to a mysterious person named Theophilus. (For more about Theophilus, see Luke's Gospel, page 333). Church leaders at least as early as the AD 100s said the Gospel of Luke and Acts of the Apostles were both written by Luke, a non-Jewish physician who traveled with Paul.

DATE:

The story of Acts covers more than 30 years, from the ascension of Jesus in about AD 30 to the trial of Paul in the 60s. Luke may have written this book while waiting for Romans to try Paul in the AD 60s. Or he may have written it in the 70s or 80s, long after the Romans executed Paul.

LOCATION:

The Roman Empire, sprawled throughout the Mediterranean world. Scenes play out in what are now the countries of Israel, Egypt, Syria, Lebanon, Turkey, Greece, Italy, Cyprus, and Crete.

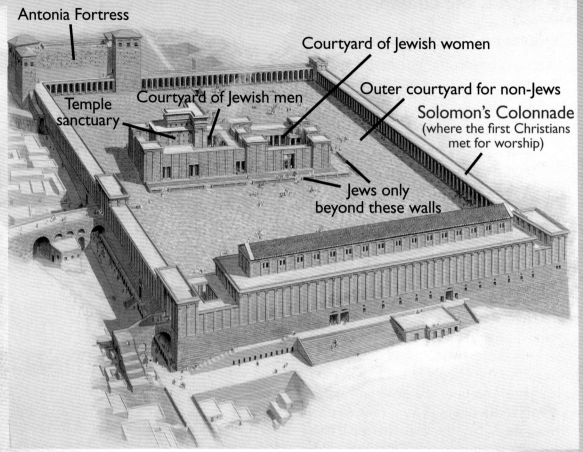

Antonia Fortress

Courtyard of Jewish women

Temple sanctuary

Courtyard of Jewish men

Outer courtyard for non-Jews

Solomon's Colonnade
(where the first Christians
met for worship)

Jews only
beyond these walls

First church of the temple. The first Christians gathered for worship at a spot under Solomon's Colonnade at the Jewish temple. Covered with a cedar roof, the colonnade stretched 300 yards long. Most believers were Jews, but some were Gentile converts to the Jewish faith. Solomon's Colonnade was in the outer courtyard, where non-Jews were allowed.

The wait lasts about 10 days, with the Spirit arriving on the day of Pentecost. This is an annual harvest festival that usually falls in late May or early June. It took place 50 days after Jesus' execution on Passover eve.

"Suddenly, there was a sound from heaven like the roaring of a mighty windstorm, and it filled the house where they were sitting. Then, what looked like flames or tongues of fire appeared and settled on each of them. And everyone present was filled with the Holy Spirit and began speaking in other languages, as the Holy Spirit gave them this ability" (Acts 2:2–4).

In the Bible, wind and fire often accompany divine appearances.

- **Burning bush.** "The angel of the LORD appeared to him [Moses] in a blazing fire from the middle of a bush" (Exodus 3:2).
- **Ten Commandments.** "All of Mount Sinai was covered with smoke because the LORD had descended on it in the form of fire" (Exodus 19:18).
- **Valley of dry bones.** "This is what the Sovereign LORD says: Come, O breath, from the four winds! Breathe into these dead bodies so they may live again" (Ezekiel 37:9).

Jewish pilgrims have crowded Jerusalem for the Pentecost festival. They have come from regions throughout the Roman Empire and beyond. These include what are now Israel, Iran, Iraq, Turkey, Egypt, Libya, Italy, Crete, and Jordan.

Many people hear the loud noise. So they come running to check it out. What they discover astonishes them. "We all hear these people speaking in our own languages about the wonderful things God has done!" (Acts 2:11).

With a crowd assembled, Peter launches into a dramatic sermon. Quoting the Old Testament, he points out prophecies about the resurrection of Jesus and the coming of God's Spirit. Then he announces that all of this has just happened.

Convinced in part by miracles, about 3,000 people believe what Peter says. They are "baptized and added to the church that day" (Acts 2:41).

The Christian movement has started. And most believers, if not all, are Jewish.

A CEASE and desist order

They [the Jewish governing council known as the Sanhedrin] called the apostles back in and commanded them never again to speak or teach in the name of Jesus.

ACTS 4:18

The church of Jesus Christ is born right in front of the same Jewish leaders who had schemed Jesus' execution several weeks earlier.

Surprisingly, the men behind the church movement are the same disciples of Jesus who scattered when temple police arrested Jesus, and who hid while Roman soldiers crucified him. But the courage they show by preaching in the very town that killed Jesus is often cited as proof that they saw Jesus raised from the dead. For in less than two months, they no longer fear death.

Their preaching, backed up by the kind of healing miracles Jesus did, keeps the church growing: now at 5,000 men, not counting their family members. This growth catches the attention of the 70-member Jewish governing council that had tried Jesus and sentenced him to death.

Before long, Peter and John find themselves standing before this very council, after spending a night in jail. They were arrested the day before, after healing a crippled man in the temple area and then preaching about Jesus to the crowd that gathered.

The council faces much the same problem it did with Jesus. Disciples have a wide base of support because of the wonderful miracles they're doing. Executing Peter and John could cause a riot. So the Jewish leaders simply order them to stop teaching about Jesus.

"Do you think God wants us to obey you rather than him?" the disciples reply. "We cannot stop telling about everything we have seen and heard" (Acts 4:19–20).

The council threatens the men further and then releases them.

Peter and John meet with the believers and tell them what happened. Then they all pray for courage to keep on spreading the word about Jesus.

DO-GOODERS drop dead

"Ananias, why have you let Satan fill your heart? You lied to the Holy Spirit, and you kept some of the money for yourself."

ACTS 5:3

Jews rich and poor join the movement. Many of the richer members sell some of their land and give the money to the disciples, who distribute it among the poor believers.

Apparently, this generosity draws praise, which one couple—Ananias and Sapphira—decides to cash in on. They think they can kill two birds with one stone:
- help the poor and
- buy themselves some glory in the process.

But Ananias and Sapphira end up as the two dead birds. And their claim to fame is shame.

They sell a hunk of their property. Then Ananias brings part of the money to the disciples, claiming he's donating all of it. Somehow, Peter knows better. Perhaps the buyer told him. Or maybe it was an even more reliable Source. Peter scolds Ananias. "The property was yours to sell or not sell, as you wished. And after selling it, the money was also yours to give away. How could you do a thing like this? You weren't lying to us but to God!" (Acts 5:4).

Ananias drops dead, with the speed of a massive heart attack or a bolt of lightning from the sky. The same thing happens to his wife three hours later. She hasn't heard that her husband is dead, so she repeats the lie. She drops dead the moment Peter shocks her with bad news wrapped around a horrifying prophecy: "How could the two of you even think of conspiring to test the Spirit of the Lord like this? The young men who buried your husband are just outside the door, and they will carry you out, too" (Acts 5:9).

The story reads like literal overkill. Why would God kill two people for exaggerating?

Bible experts say the original language suggests that it isn't shock that kills this couple. It's God who pulls the trigger. If so, it's gruesomely ironic—the name *Ananias* means "God is merciful." But apparently not today.

The Bible is full of stories about God killing sinful people. God even burned up two sons of Aaron, priests who got a worship ritual wrong. They "disobeyed the LORD by burning before him the wrong kind of fire" (Leviticus 10:1).

In many of these instances, including the death of Ananias and Sapphira, the punishment causes a snap-to effect. "Great fear gripped the entire church" (Acts 5:11). Suddenly everyone knows not to trifle with God or his ministers.

CHRISTIANITY'S first martyr

As they stoned him, Stephen prayed. . . . "Lord, don't charge them with this sin!" And with that, he died.

ACTS 7:59–60

There's a growth spurt in the church's compassionate ministry program—a ministry that includes providing food every day to needy people such as widows. The twelve disciples have been handling this personally. But now they delegate the responsibility so they can devote more time to teaching.

They select "seven men who are well respected and are full of the Spirit and wisdom" (Acts 6:3). All seven appear to be Jews from Greek-speaking regions. What's surprising about this is that the disciples decide to delegate the food program only after charges of discrimination. Greek-speaking Jews complain that their widows aren't getting as much food as the Hebrew-speaking Jewish widows. Many of the Greek-speaking Jews have moved to Jerusalem from other parts of the Roman Empire, where Greek is the preferred language. But the Hebrew-speaking widows are generally hometown ladies—the local favorites.

A man named Stephen is among the select seven. He eventually gets in deep trouble. But it's not because of his food pantry ministry, which apparently starts running smoothly. The problem starts in a local synagogue where he debates tradition-loving Jews who insist that Jesus is not God's Son.

This particular synagogue, one of many in Jerusalem, is called the Synagogue of Freed Slaves. Perhaps the synagogue started when some freed Jewish slaves moved to Jerusalem. The synagogue attracts Jews like Stephen who prefer worshipping in their native Greek language. One particular group from what is now Turkey engages Stephen in the debate and then convinces Jewish leaders to arrest him for blasphemy.

Appearing before the same council that had arranged Jesus' execution and ordered Peter and John to stop teaching about Jesus, Stephen gets politically incorrect.

He gives the Jewish history scholars a history lesson, which is offensive enough. It's like lecturing the Supreme Court justices about the law. Worse, Stephen emphasizes how Jewish leaders throughout the ages have repeatedly opposed God. Then Stephen makes it personal: "You stubborn people! You are heathen at heart and deaf to the truth. Must you forever resist the Holy Spirit? That's what your ancestors did, and so do you! Name one prophet your ancestors didn't persecute! They even killed the ones who predicted the coming of the Righteous One—the Messiah whom you betrayed and murdered. You deliberately disobeyed God's law" (Acts 7:51–53).

What happens next disobeys Roman law.

Jews aren't legally empowered to execute people. That's up to Roman officials, which is why the Jewish council took their case against Jesus to Pilate. But this time mob hatred sweeps Stephen off his feet and outside the city. There, his fellow Jews stone him to death. Watching the cloaks of the killers is a young man named Saul.

CHRISTIANITY'S most famous convert

Saul was uttering threats with every breath and was eager to kill the Lord's followers.

ACTS 9:1

Saul is his Hebrew name. But he's better known by his Greek name: Paul—the man who will become a Christian and write almost half the books of the New Testament.

In Roman times, most people speak their native language along with the universal trade language of Greek. Because of this, many Jews have two names. One is common among

Hebrew-speaking Jews. And the other is easier for Greek-speaking folks. In a modern variation, *Stephen* (STEVE-un) in English becomes *Stephane* (stef-FAWN) in French.

Call him Saul or call him Paul. Either way, he's a fanatic—an intolerant Jewish traditionalist. He believes that if any of his fellow Jews teach heresy—anything that he and other members of the Pharisee branch of Judaism consider as lies that dishonor God—those Jews need to be arrested, tried, and punished. Perhaps even executed.

Followers of Jesus qualify because the most basic Jewish belief is that there's only one God. Yet members of this new branch of Judaism say Jesus is divine, too—God's Son—and that Jesus is the only way to the Father: "I am the way, the truth, and the life. No one can come to the Father except through me" (John 14:6). Perhaps this is where they get the name of their religious movement: "the Way" (Acts 9:2).

After the Jewish mob kills Stephen, many believers move away. Saul knows they are taking their heresies with them. So he gets the high priest's permission to hunt them down in synagogues abroad. One of the largest cities in the region is Damascus, capital of what is now Syria. It's about 150 miles north of Jerusalem—about a week's walk.

As Saul and his traveling partners near the city, a mysterious light blinds him and drops him to the ground. Then a voice from out of nowhere asks, "Saul! Saul! Why are you persecuting me?" (Acts 9:4).

"Who are you?" Saul asks.

"I am Jesus, the one you are persecuting! Now get up and go into the city, and you will be told what you must do" (Acts 9:5–6).

In Damascus, a man named Ananias has a vision instructing him to heal Saul. A follower of the Way—as the early Christian movement is called—Ananias resists because he knows Saul has authority to arrest him.

"Go," the Lord insists, "for Saul is my chosen instrument to take my message to the Gentiles and to kings, as well as to the people of Israel" (Acts 9:15).

This is the closest the Bible comes to explaining why Jesus takes such drastic measures to convert Saul. Perhaps Jesus knows that the best way to battle intolerant Jewish traditionalists is with someone who used to be an intolerant Jewish traditionalist.

Ananias heals Saul, who converts. Instead of arresting believers in Damascus, Saul joins them and adds his amazing story to the good news about Jesus.

KOSHER FOOD, kosher people

"It is against our laws for a Jewish man to enter a Gentile home. . . . But God has shown me that I should no longer think of anyone as impure or unclean."

ACTS 10:28

Christianity starts as a Jewish sect—just another group of Jews with some distinct beliefs. Not unlike the Sadducees, a group of Jews who say there's no life after death. Or the Pharisees, who insist that the rules of rabbis passed along by word of mouth over the generations are as important as the laws of Moses. Followers of the Way are Jews who say the Messiah has come, and his name is Jesus.

In time, this new Jewish movement will part company with Judaism. By then, non-Jewish believers will start to outnumber the Jewish believers.

The time starts now with a noonday vision by Peter, Jewish leader of the movement that still holds on to many Jewish traditions.

While the midday meal is being prepared, Peter prays and falls into a trance. He sees a huge sheet coming down from the sky. The sheet holds all kinds of animals, including some that God, in Leviticus 11, told the Jews not to eat. Nonkosher food that Gentiles commonly eat around the world today includes pigs, rabbits, catfish, shrimp, and lobster.

A voice from heaven tells Peter to kill and eat the animals. Peter refuses, saying he eats only kosher food.

The voice replies, "Do not call something unclean if God has made it clean" (Acts 10:15).

When Peter comes out of the trance, he tries to figure out what the vision means. The answer is approaching his front door. And the Holy Spirit tells him so—that three messengers are coming and that he should go with them.

A Roman officer named Cornelius sent the messengers to invite Peter to come and tell him about Jesus. Cornelius commands an Italian regiment of about 100 soldiers, currently stationed at the seaside city of Caesarea. That's a day's walk north of where Peter is visiting in Joppa, part of the modern-day twin cities of Tel Aviv/Jaffa.

Cornelius isn't Jewish by race, but he is by faith. Described as a devout and God-fearing man who is well respected by the Jews, he apparently observes at least some Jewish laws and worships with the Jews. Still, he's a Gentile—probably not circumcised.

Peter has figured out the meaning of his earlier vision, thanks in part to the "coincidental" timing of the messengers' arrival.

"You know it is against our laws for a Jewish man to enter a Gentile home like this or to associate with you," Peter tells Cornelius. "But God has shown me that I should no longer think of anyone as impure or unclean" (Acts 10:28).

Peter tells Cornelius about his vision and about Jesus. Suddenly, the Holy Spirit fills Cornelius and the non-Jews with him. They begin speaking in other languages, as the disciples did at Pentecost. It's unclear what kind of languages they speak. At Pentecost, the disciples spoke in recognizable languages. But most Bible experts say in this case the writer is probably talking about unintelligible words spoken in moments of spiritual ecstasy—what Paul later describes as "unknown languages" (1 Corinthians 12:28).

Whatever the language, it shocks the Jews with Peter, for they recognize it as clear evidence that the Holy Spirit has filled these Gentiles. Peter knows a historic moment when he sees one. God has declared the unclean clean and the unchosen chosen.

The era of the new covenant has arrived. "I will make a new covenant," God vowed some 600 years earlier. Instead of having people follow a list of rules, such as the kosher food laws, God says, "I will put my instructions deep within them, and I will write them on their hearts" (Jeremiah 31:31, 33).

Peter baptizes Cornelius and his entire household. The church now includes one family of Gentiles.

HOW DID the disciples die?

King Herod Agrippa began to persecute some believers in the church. He had the apostle James (John's brother) killed with a sword.

ACTS 12:1–2

Though the Bible records the fate of only Judas Iscariot and James, early church leaders said most of the others died as martyrs—killed for preaching about Jesus.

Simon Peter. "Crucified at Rome with his head downward," wrote Origen, a church leader in the AD 200s. This seems to fulfill what Jesus told Peter would happen: " 'When you are old, you will stretch out your hands. . . .' Jesus said this to let him know by what kind of death he would glorify God" (John 21:18–19).

Andrew, Peter's brother. Crucified on an X-shaped cross, according to the Acts of Andrew, a book written in the AD 200s.

James, son of Zebedee. The first disciple to die as a martyr, he was executed by King Herod Agrippa—probably beheaded "with a sword" (Acts 12:2).

What is "speaking in tongues"?

There are two kinds of speaking in tongues.

- **Miraculously talking in a language the speaker hasn't learned.** This happened at the Pentecost festival in Jerusalem. Jesus' disciples preached to Jewish pilgrims—in the pilgrims' own languages (Acts 2).

- **In moments of spiritual ecstasy, using words that don't make sense without God's help.** These are usually words praising God or delivering a message from God. Christians in the early church considered speaking in tongues as a gift from God—and a sign that the Holy Spirit has filled a person.

Yet the apostle Paul called it one of the lesser Christian gifts. And he warned that it was a gift easily abused. People would interrupt church services by pretending to speak in tongues. And in this way, they called attention to themselves instead of to Christ.

That's why many churches prohibit this practice in their worship services today. And that's why Paul insisted that no one be allowed to speak in tongues during services unless God has provided an interpreter.

"I speak in tongues more than any of you," Paul once wrote. "But in a church meeting I would rather speak five understandable words to help others than ten thousand words in an unknown language" (1 Corinthians 14:18–19).

John, brother of James. Died a natural death in about AD 100 at what is now Ephesus, Turkey.

Philip. Crucified in Turkey, according to tradition.

Bartholomew. Skinned alive and beheaded after preaching in India, according to one tradition. But the *Martyrdom of Bartholomew* says he was stuffed in a sack and dumped in the sea.

Thomas. Speared to death in what is now India after starting several churches there. India's Syro-Malabar Catholic Church, with three million members, claims Thomas as its founding pastor.

Matthew. Martyred with an ax or a sword in Ethiopia, according to the most popular of many traditions. Other stories have him being burned to death or dying of natural causes.

James, son of Alphaeus. Crucified in Egypt, according to one tradition—in Iran, according to another.

Thaddaeus (Judas, son of James). Crucified or hacked to death with Simon the Zealot in what is now Iran, according to one story.

Simon the Zealot. Martyred with Thaddaeus in Iran, according to one tradition. Another story says he was cut in two with a saw.

Judas Iscariot. After helping Jews arrest Jesus, he "went out and hanged himself" (Matthew 27:5).

Matthias. Chosen to replace Judas Iscariot, he was stoned and beheaded, according to one story.

Skinned alive. This was the apostle Bartholomew's fate according to one legend that circulated among the early churches. The Bible reports the deaths of only two disciples: Judas, who committed suicide by hanging, and James, who was executed by sword.

THE FIRST MISSIONARIES

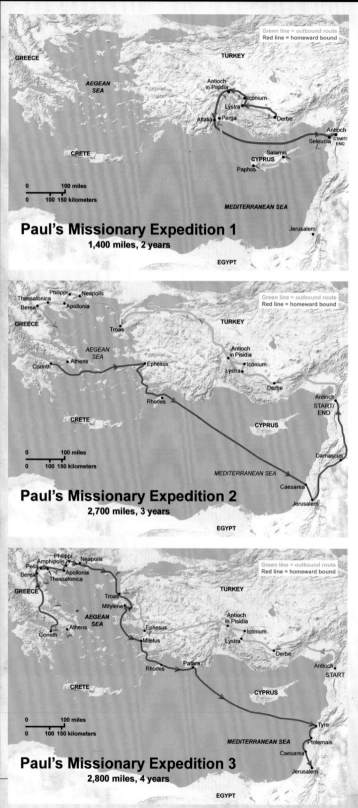

Paul's Missionary Expedition 1
1,400 miles, 2 years

Paul's Missionary Expedition 2
2,700 miles, 3 years

Paul's Missionary Expedition 3
2,800 miles, 4 years

Barnabas and Saul were sent out by the Holy Spirit. They went down to the seaport of Seleucia and then sailed for the island of Cyprus.
ACTS 13:4

After Saul's dramatic conversion to the Way in about AD 35, he disappears from history for about a dozen years. For part of that time he probably studies his Jewish Bible, or the Old Testament, looking for prophecies about Jesus and the new covenant God said he would make to replace the earlier set of rules he had given the Jews. In time, Saul probably teaches believers what he has discovered. He eventually returns to his hometown of Tarsus, in what is now Turkey. That's when he bursts back onto the pages of church history.

Barnabas pastors a church of mostly non-Jews in Antioch, Syria—about 150 miles southeast of Saul's hometown. The church must be growing, because Barnabas goes up to Tarsus and convinces Saul to join the ministry team as an associate pastor.

"It was at Antioch that the believers were first called Christians" (Acts 11:26). This nickname may have been an insult—much like the demeaning term for cult members of Sun Myung Moon's Unification Church: Moonies. But if so, believers eventually warm up to this new name and retire their former name, "the Way."

One day in a worship service at Antioch, the Holy Spirit impresses on the group to share Barnabas and Saul with others—to send the pastors out on a missionary expedition.

That one expedition turns into three, stretching roughly 7,000 miles over the next 20 years. By the end of these expeditions, new congregations made up mostly of non-Jews have sprung up throughout the Roman Empire—in what are now Cyprus, Turkey, and Greece. This includes churches in two of the empire's busiest cities—the seaport towns of Corinth in Greece, and Ephesus in Turkey.

THE FIRST church split

While Paul and Barnabas were at Antioch of Syria, some men from Judea arrived and began to teach the believers: "Unless you are circumcised as required by the law of Moses, you cannot be saved." Paul and Barnabas disagreed with them, arguing vehemently.

ACTS 15:1–2

Jews welcomed Gentile converts, as long as the Gentiles followed all the Jewish traditions—including the most intrusive: circumcision and kosher food restrictions. So when Gentiles began converting to the Way, many Jewish believers expected them to embrace not only the teachings of Jesus, but the laws of Moses, as well.

Paul and Barnabas, however, weren't requiring that of the Gentiles in Antioch. So when Jewish Christians visited there from Jerusalem, a fiery debate erupted.

Church leaders led by James, the brother of Jesus, met in Jerusalem to settle the argument.

- Peter defended Paul and Barnabas by telling about his nonkosher food vision and his experience with Cornelius.
- Paul and Barnabas added that the Holy Spirit was clearly working through the uncircumcised Gentiles of Antioch.
- James quoted the Jewish Bible, or the Old Testament, confirming that God spoke of a time when "the rest of humanity might seek the LORD, including the Gentiles" (Acts 15:17).

The council decided to ask Gentile believers to observe only three Jewish rules: "You must abstain from eating food offered to idols, from consuming blood or the meat of strangled animals, and from sexual immorality" (Acts 15:29).

Neither side was happy with this compromise.

Jewish believers kept pressing their case throughout the expanding church. And, in time, Paul started teaching that Jewish food laws are irrelevant in this day of the new covenant.

"One person believes it's all right to eat anything," Paul said. "But another believer with a sensitive conscience will eat only vegetables. Those who feel free to eat anything must not look down on those who don't. And those who don't eat certain foods must not condemn those who do, for God has accepted them" (Romans 14:2–3).

RIOT

"Paul has persuaded many people that handmade gods aren't really gods at all. And he's done this not only here in Ephesus but throughout the entire province!". . . At this their anger boiled, and they began shouting, "Great is Artemis of the Ephesians!"

ACTS 19:26, 28

Paul is too successful in Ephesus—at least as far as the idol-making lobbyists are concerned.

There are Seven Wonders of the World. But the most beautiful, according to one writer who said he saw all seven, is a temple in Ephesus dedicated to the Greek goddess Artemis. Romans call her Diana.

"I have seen the walls and hanging gardens of ancient Babylon, the statue of Olympian Zeus, the Colossus of Rhodes, the mighty work of the high pyramids, and the tomb of Mausolus," wrote the Greek scientist Philon in the 200s BC. "But when I saw the temple at Ephesus rising to the clouds, all these other wonders were put in the shade."

A lot of Ephesus citizens make their living off of Artemis. Artisans create statues and figurines of the goddess. Merchants sell them. And temple workers are happy for all the attention their goddess gets. Paul's preaching has thrown the idol industry into a recession.

Demetrius, a silversmith czar who runs an idol-manufacturing business, calls a meeting of everyone connected with the industry. He says he's worried about money and the diminishing respect for his industry. Then, implying that he's more concerned about spiritual matters than cash, he says he doesn't want to see Paul further erode the respect of "this magnificent goddess."

Archaeologists found the name of Demetrius on a list of men honored as protectors of the Ephesus temple, though it could have been another man by the same name. Also discovered is evidence of a guild of silversmiths, with an inscription reading, "May the guild of the silversmiths prosper!"

Double-barreled motivation—money and religion—quickly blasts the meeting into a mob. Onlookers, lured into the drama of the moment, join the hunt for Paul.

Mother of a riot. Devotees of Artemis, the great mother goddess of Ephesus, spark a riot that forces Paul out of town. Paul's ministry is so effective in Ephesus that it hurts the Artemis idol-making industry. This statue of Artemis, loaded with what some say are breasts for feeding the world, was crafted in the AD 100s and discovered at Ephesus.

What they find instead are a couple of Paul's associates, whom they drag to the city amphitheater. Paul hears about this and wants to go and meet the mob. Officials talk him out of it.

The mayor of the city goes to the theater and restores calm. He tells Demetrius and the trade workers to file a formal complaint instead of risking Roman intervention and punishment for causing a riot.

Paul decides it's time to move on. He travels west into Greece, briefly visiting congregations he started earlier and collecting an offering for believers suffering in Jerusalem.

RIOT encore

Jews from the province of Asia [western Turkey, where Ephesus is located] saw Paul in the Temple and roused a mob against him.
ACTS 21:27

Back in Jerusalem, Paul goes to the temple and begins a week of purification rituals. It's apparently a custom for Jews returning from Gentile lands. Gentiles are considered ritually unclean.

Jews from the Roman province where the Ephesus riot took place spot Paul in the temple. They're livid, apparently considering him unfit to worship there.

They incite a riot by making two charges, both unfair:

- They say he tells people to disobey the Jewish laws. Actually, he tells only the Gentile believers that they aren't bound by those traditions.
- Then they accuse him of bringing a Gentile into an inner temple courtyard reserved for Jews only—a crime punishable by death. They base this incorrect assumption on the fact that they saw him earlier in the day with a Gentile from Ephesus.

Jews swarm on Paul like killer bees on a hive burner. Roman soldiers stationed at the fortress overlooking the temple see the commotion. They rush in and stop the riot, arresting Paul.

20 churches to his credit

From Syria on the Roman Empire's eastern border to Italy in the west, Paul helped start at least 20 churches. He made believers in frontier towns, highland villages, and farming communities. But he gave most of his time to preaching in the empire's great coastal cities: Rome, Ephesus, Corinth, Philippi, and Thessalonica. For that's where the crowds were.

The commander plans to take Paul to the Jewish council for a hearing the next day. But he gets word that a group of 40 Jews plans to ambush the soldiers escorting Paul and then assassinate him. So the commander assembles a company of 70 cavalry and 200 foot soldiers to whisk Paul out of town that night.

They take him to Caesarea, Rome's headquarters in the Jewish homeland. Located on the Mediterranean seacoast about 60 miles northwest of Jerusalem, it's a thoroughly Roman city. Herod the Great built it in honor of Caesar, decorating the landscape with a theater, palaces, and temples to Roman gods.

The Roman governor, Felix, agrees to hear Paul's case. Five days later the Jewish high priest arrives with his entourage of scholars. The spokesman for the group, acting much like a lawyer would today, levels three charges against Paul:

- "We have found this man to be a troublemaker who is constantly stirring up riots among the Jews all over the world."
- "He is a ringleader of the cult known as the Nazarenes."
- "He was trying to desecrate the Temple when we arrested him" (Acts 24:5–6).

Paul then tells his side of the story, admitting that he's a member of the Way. But he denies that he tries to stir up riots or that he desecrated the temple.

Felix postpones his decision, saying he'll wait until the Jerusalem commander arrives to testify. Two years later, Paul is still in jail. Felix was hoping "that Paul would bribe him, so he sent for him quite often and talked with him" (Acts 24:26).

Paul finally gets a new hearing, but only after Festus replaces Felix as governor. When Festus suggests trying Paul in Jerusalem, where Jews had plotted to assassinate him, Paul exercises his right as a Roman citizen. He petitions to have his case tried in the empire's highest court—the court ruled by Caesar.

"Very well!" Festus says. "You have appealed to Caesar, and to Caesar you will go!" (Acts 25:12).

ROUGH sailing

A wind of typhoon strength (called a "northeaster") burst across the island and blew us out to sea.

Acts 27:14

Escorted by Roman soldiers, Paul probably sets sail in late summer or early fall, near the end of the safe season for voyages. Prevailing winds this late in the year—Etesian winds—blow from the northwest. That's the very direction Paul needs to go to get to Rome. So the 2,000-mile voyage into the wind will take well over a month. That means the ship will probably have to make port somewhere for the winter, or risk sailing in perilous seas.

After a one-day sailing leg north to Sidon, the soldier in charge arranges for passage on an Egyptian grain ship from Alexandria, bound for Rome. Passenger manifest: 276 passengers and crew.

By the time Paul's ship reaches Myra, on the southern coast of what is now Turkey, it's already after the Day of Atonement. That means it's after October 5, if Paul's trip takes place in AD 59 as many Bible experts speculate. This is well into the risky season for sailing. Still, the ship presses on toward the island of Crete.

With the zigzag route required to tack into the wind, the ship eventually makes it to Crete—about the halfway point in Paul's voyage. A well-sailed missionary, Paul advises the soldier guarding him to winter at Fair Havens. But the ship's captain prefers the better-protected harbor of Phoenix on the west side of the island. So he presses on, keeping the coastline in sight.

CHEAP-SEAT SAILING

Paul sailed during each of his four major trips. Sea voyages were relatively cheap.

A family's fare for passage from Athens to Alexandria, Egypt—a distance of about 600 miles—was only about two days' wages.

But since the main purpose of the ships was to carry cargo, the fare did not include food or cabins, though it did include water.

But a fierce storm called a northeaster engulfs the ship and drives it southwest—toward the Syrtis Major, treacherous shallows near North Africa, off the coast of Libya. Trying to slow this drive, the crew drops anchor. The winds apparently shift, turning the battered ship

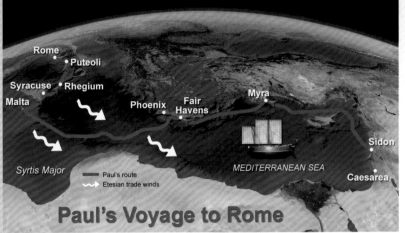

Rome
• Puteoli

Syracuse • Rhegium
Malta
Phoenix • Fair Havens
Myra

Sidon

Syrtis Major
— Paul's route
〜〜 Etesian trade winds
MEDITERRANEAN SEA
Caesarea

Paul's Voyage to Rome

WHEN TO SAIL, OR NOT

SAFE:
  May 27–September 14
RISKY:
  March 10–May 26 and
  September 15–November 11
DANGEROUS:
  November 12–March 9

Typhoon ahead. Summer is the safest time to sail the Mediterranean. But under Roman guard, Paul sails for Rome in a risky season—and with trade winds blowing in the wrong direction. They leave Caesarea in late summer and Myra in early October. This almost guarantees they'll need to find a winter harbor. They try for Phoenix. But a massive storm snatches them at Fair Havens and pummels the ship for two weeks before running it aground at Malta. Reconstruction proposal of a cargo ship from Paul's time, provided by Forum Navis Romana.

northwest toward its destination. Two weeks after the storm began, Paul's ship runs aground along the coast of the small island of Malta, south of Italy and Sicily. There, powerful waves quickly splinter the ship. Astonishingly, not one life is lost.

Three months later, in the spring of AD 60, Paul and his guards set sail on another Alexandrian ship. After two stops along the way, this ship delivers them to Puteoli (now Pozzuoli), a port city south of Rome. From there, Paul and his guards walk to Rome on two famous roads: the Via Campana and the Via Appia.

Paul is kept under house arrest for two years but is allowed to preach. The book of Acts abruptly ends here, without telling what happened to Paul. Perhaps the writer didn't know the end because he wrote Acts before the trial. Or maybe the writer believed his intended readers knew the tragic finale all too well.

Some scholars speculate that Paul was tried in AD 62 and executed. Others, leaning on snippets of writing from early Christian leaders, say he was released and made yet another journey: "I will come to see you on my way to Spain," he once wrote to believers in Rome (Romans 15:28).

The Roman bishop Clement, writing in about AD 96, confirmed that Paul "went to the limit of the West," implying Spain, on the empire's western perimeter. If this is what happened, Paul was probably arrested a second time, taken to Rome again, and executed perhaps during the persecutions that started after Nero blamed Christians for burning Rome in AD 64.

ROMAN ROADS

Rome had a network of more than 50,000 miles of paved roads and 200,000 miles of secondary roads. The paved roads were especially for soldiers and merchants, to help preserve peace and prosperity. But the roads also helped Paul and other Christians spread news about Jesus.

Roman roads, some of which survive, were generally 10 to 12 feet wide. Construction began by digging a straight trench about three feet deep. Workers filled this with a layer of tightly packed stones, followed by another layer of smaller stones bound with cement. The center rose higher than the sides, which allowed for good drainage. The road top was paved with large flat stones pieced together like a puzzle, with pebbles filling in any gaps. Brush was cleared from the roadside to make it harder for robbers to surprise travelers.

Paul's final leg to Rome. On his way to trial in Caesar's high court, Paul walked on this ancient Roman road—the Way of Appia, or Via Appia in Latin, the Roman language.

ROMANS

ROMAN EMPIRE

ICELAND · ENGLAND · GERMANY · FRANCE · ATLANTIC OCEAN · ITALY · Rome · SPAIN · SARDINIA · SICILY · GREECE · Ephesus · Corinth · BLACK SEA · TURKEY · ALGERIA · MOROCCO · MEDITERRANEAN SEA · CRETE · CYPRUS · ISRAEL · SYRIA · LIBYA · EGYPT · AFRICAN SAHARA DESERT · RED SEA · SAUDI ARABIA

Pastor to an empire. In Paul's day, Romans control all the land touching the Mediterranean Sea—an estimated 45 million souls. After starting churches on the empire's east side in what is now Syria, Turkey, and Greece, Paul writes to Christians in Rome. He says he hopes to stop by on his way to Spain.

EXPLAINING CHRISTIANITY TO STRANGERS

About 20 years into his missionary work, Paul writes this letter to Christians in Rome. He has startling news.

He says he has finished the work of planting house-church congregations in the eastern half of the Roman Empire. Now he wants to head over to the western tip: Spain.

Paul says he hopes to stop in Rome along the way to meet the Christians there, enjoy their fellowship, and invite them to "provide for my journey" (Romans 15:24).

Yep, he's asking for money.

It's a missionary offering for himself—fund-raising with savvy. Consider the next words out of his mouth in this dictated letter: "But before I come, I must go to Jerusalem to take a gift to the believers there. For you see, the believers in Macedonia and Achaia [modern-day Greece] have eagerly taken up an offering for the poor among the believers in Jerusalem" (Romans 15:25–26).

Paul is making a point. He's not just a taker. He's a giver. He does good things with the money he raises. The Greeks "eagerly" gave to Paul's cause. And he expects the Christians in Rome to do the same.

Paul has never been to Rome. But he knows that his reputation precedes him. His closing notes show that he has a lot of friends there—more than two dozen, including former ministry associates, people converted under his ministry, some who spent jail time with him, and one couple who risked their lives for him. Still, he feels the need to introduce himself and tell the Christians in Rome exactly what he believes and why.

In the process, Paul produces Christianity's first theology textbook—one that many Bible experts say is history's most concise, eloquent statement of the Christian faith. Even today, many Bible experts say that the best introduction to Christianity is to read someone else's mail: Paul's letter to Rome.

GOOD NEWS for sinners

Don't you see how wonderfully kind, tolerant, and patient God is with you? Does this mean nothing to you? Can't you see that his kindness is intended to turn you from your sin?

ROMANS 2:4

After a polite introduction, humbly calling himself a "slave of Christ," Paul jumps right into a subject that's tough enough for a pastor who knows the congregation, let alone a preacher who has never laid eyes on the folks. The topic is sin. Paul uses a typical Greek style of persuasion, often writing as though he's addressing one person.

MAIN POINT:

Paul introduces himself and his religious beliefs to Christians in Rome because he hopes to visit them soon. The most basic belief he wants to explain is that everyone has sinned and is worthy of the death penalty, but that God will forgive and pardon those who put their trust in Jesus.

WRITER:

Paul wrote this letter to Christians in Rome, apparently dictating it to an associate named Tertius (Romans 16:22). There are some New Testament letters that claim to be from Paul that some scholars doubt he actually wrote. Romans isn't one of them. In fact, Romans is the model—in writing style and teachings—that many Bible experts use to help determine the authenticity of his other letters.

DATE:

Paul wrote this letter in about AD 57, near the end of his third missionary trip.

LOCATION:

Paul is somewhere on his way back to Jerusalem after visiting churches in what is now Greece and Turkey. He's writing to Christians in Rome. If he wrote from Corinth, as many experts say is likely, he probably had Phoebe deliver the letter. She was from Cenchrea, a city neighboring Corinth, and she was headed to Rome. Paul asks the Romans to "welcome her" (Romans 16:2), implying that she has the letter.

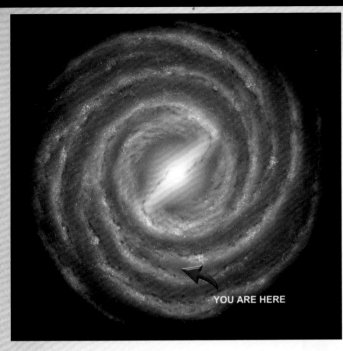

YOU ARE HERE

Milky Way theology. An artist's rendering of the Milky Way Galaxy helps illustrate the point a Hebrew poet once made. "The heavens proclaim the glory of God. The skies display his craftsmanship" (Psalm 19:1). Paul says this is the very reason people have no excuse for not believing God. Even those who believe the universe began with a Big Bang have to admit that someone pulled the trigger.

Good news first. The message Paul is about to deliver "tells us how God makes us right in his sight. This is accomplished from start to finish by faith" (Romans 1:17).

Now the bad news. Without faith, sinners have no excuse. And God will give them the punishment they deserve.

Paul says they have no excuses because the evidence is all around them: "For ever since the world was created, people have seen the earth and sky. Through everything God made, they can clearly see his invisible qualities—his eternal power and divine nature. . . . They know the truth about God because he has made it obvious to them" (Romans 1:20, 19).

Even if creation began with a Big Bang, Paul might argue today, someone had to load the universe and pull the trigger. In a physical universe, it's impossible for something to come from nothing. So there's more than a physical dimension at work in creating and sustaining the universe.

Paul says sinners ignore this fact. They write God off or create wacky theories about him. Then they do as they please. "Their lives became full of every kind of wickedness, sin, greed, hate, envy, murder, quarreling, deception, malicious behavior, and gossip" (Romans 1:29).

It's tempting to condemn them, Paul says. But it's hypocritical. We've all sinned. Judgment is God's business. And judgment day is coming.

Paul says that even Gentiles who were never taught religious laws such as the 10 Commandments "show that they know his law when they instinctively obey it, even without having heard it. They demonstrate that God's law is written in their hearts, for their own conscience and thoughts either accuse them or tell them they are doing right" (Romans 2:14–15).

For Jews and non-Jews alike, Paul's opening message is this: "The day is coming when God, through Christ Jesus, will judge everyone's secret life" (Romans 2:16).

PAUL'S TOUGH TAKE ON HOMOSEXUALITY

Shameful and *unnatural* are two words that sum up what Paul has to say about homosexuality.

Some Bible translators punch up his criticism with even stronger words: *indecent* and *perversion.* "Men committed indecent acts with other men, and received in themselves the due penalty for their perversion" (Romans 1:27 NIV).

For many Christians, that's uncomfortably close to name-calling: Perverts.

Some Bible students—in what most scholars describe as creative Bible interpretation—argue that Paul isn't saying what it sounds like he's saying. Their theories:

- He's condemning naturally heterosexual people who try to go against their nature and experiment with homosexuality.
- He's condemning homosexuals who don't lovingly commit themselves to their gay relationship. Instead, they're always on the hunt for sex.

But most Bible experts argue that Paul is writing from a Jewish background that condemns this practice as "a detestable act. They must both be put to death, for they are guilty of a capital offense" (Leviticus 20:13).

Jews get their message across outside the Bible, too. In an ancient collection of writings called the Sybilline Oracles, the writer says that Jewish men "honor their marriage vows and don't engage in evil intercourse with boys, as do Phoenicians, Egyptians, and Romans."

As the Oracles imply, Paul is also writing to a city that knows about homosexuality all too well. Nero—the emperor when Paul wrote this letter—married a young man named Sporus, who dressed like a woman. Some historians say that all but one of the first 15 Roman emperors had homosexual affairs, with Claudius as the sole exception.

Bible scholars say that with this background in mind, if Paul intended to attack some tiny slice of homosexuality instead of the entire practice, he would have made that clear.

WHY Jesus died

Everyone has sinned; we all fall short of God's glorious standard. Yet God, with undeserved kindness, declares that we are righteous.

ROMANS 3:23–24

A Jew would understand what Paul is saying here better than the typical Gentile would.

That's because Jews have a long history of offering blood sacrifices to pay for their sins. Since the time of Moses, some 1,400 years before Paul, Jews have known that God considers any sin a capital offense. Yet he graciously set up the sacrificial system, accepting the death of animals as a substitute for the sinful human beings.

That was the system in ancient times. It was part of God's old covenant, or agreement, with the Jews. But Jesus brought a new covenant, dying as the one and only sacrifice for everyone.

Old agreement: "The life of the body [of the sacrificial animal] is in its blood. I have given you the blood on the altar to purify you, making you right with the LORD" (Leviticus 17:11).

New agreement: "People are made right with God when they believe that Jesus sacrificed his life, shedding his blood" (Romans 3:25).

Paul says a normal person wouldn't even die to save a good soul. "But God showed his great love for us by sending Christ to die for us while we were still sinners. And since we have been made right in God's sight by the blood of Christ, he will certainly save us from God's condemnation" (Romans 5:8–9).

THE FIRST STEP is faith, not obedience

People are counted as righteous, not because of their work, but because of their faith in God who forgives sinners.

Paul appeals to an unlikely character when he makes this Jew-shocker of a point that faith is more important than obeying Jewish laws. He appeals to the father of the Jewish religion.

"Abraham believed God, and God counted him as righteous because of his faith," Paul writes, quoting Genesis 15:6.

God didn't consider Abraham righteous because Abraham kept the Jewish rules about circumcision, food restrictions, and resting on the Sabbath. There were no rules. Moses wouldn't bring them down the Sinai mountain for another 600 years or more.

Paul says there's something more basic to righteousness than obeying laws. And it's this foundation to righteousness that nudges us to obey. The foundation is faith. God wants us to obey him because we have faith in him.

Faith comes first, and obedience follows. Paul says it's faith that determines our eternal destiny.

"Because of our faith, Christ has brought us into this place of undeserved privilege where we now stand, and we confidently and joyfully look forward to sharing God's glory" (Romans 5:2).

Later in the New Testament, another writer will argue what appears to be the counterpoint: "I will show you my faith by my good deeds" (James 2:18).

Paul probably wouldn't argue. But he might add, "And I will show you my good deeds by my faith."

If faith is a chicken and a good deed is an egg, the chicken comes first. And it crosses the road to get to heaven.

BREAKING sin's grip

Don't you realize that you become the slave of whatever you choose to obey? You can be a slave to sin, which leads to death, or you can choose to obey God, which leads to righteous living.

Quicker than one, two, three, Paul draws on a trio of metaphors to help Christians understand why they shouldn't keep on sinning.

Baptism. He compares Christian baptism to the death of Jesus. When we're dipped under the water, we are symbolically dying with Jesus. And just as Jesus rose to life again, we rise from the baptismal water vowing to live new lives.

Crucifixion. Paul says our old, sinful selves were crucified with Jesus. He died "to break the power of sin" (Romans 6:10). And we died with him. We rose again with him, too, free of sin's power over us. Jesus took a journey to the grave and back again, overpowering both sin and death. And he took us with him.

Slavery. "Do not let sin control the way you live; do not give in to sinful desires" (Romans 6:12). Though sin is powerless because of what Christ did for us, that doesn't mean we can't raise up holy hands and invite sin to clamp the chains back on us. Christians can and sometimes do return to the slavery of sin.

Because we're human, we have natural desires. We want food, intimacy, financial security. But we can go overboard on just about any natural desire. Our stomach can lead us into sin. So can our eyes. Even our fingers, when we're counting a wad of cash.

"Do not let any part of your body become an instrument of evil to serve sin," Paul warns. "Instead, give yourselves completely to God, for you were dead, but now you have new life. So use your whole body as an instrument to do what is right for the glory of God" (Romans 6:13).

Paul admits there are times when it seems Christians can't control their behavior. They let their natural desires get the better of them, and they act as though they're slaves to sin.

"When I want to do what is right, I inevitably do what is wrong," Paul says, speaking for those believers struggling with sin. "I love God's law with all my heart. But there is another power within me that is at war with my mind. This power makes me a slave to the sin that is still within me. Oh, what a miserable person I am! Who will free me from this life that is dominated by sin and death?" (Romans 7:21–24).

Jesus.

He frees us, Paul says.

"Because you belong to him, the power of the life-giving Spirit has freed you from the power of sin that leads to death" (Romans 8:2).

At least to some extent, Paul says, it's mind over matter—holy mind over sinful matter. "Those who are dominated by the sinful nature think about sinful things, but those who are

SINFUL NATURE: THE SHORT COURSE

Paul spent a fair amount of time warning Roman Christians not to give in to the "sinful nature." Some Bible experts wish he had spent a little time explaining what in the world he was talking about.

"Sinful nature" is just a single word in the original Greek language: *sarx*. It means "flesh," as in, "The spirit is willing, but the flesh is weak."

Most Bible experts say Paul was talking about human weakness and our natural tendency to sin. Nobody has to teach us how.

In fact, it often seems we're more inclined to sin than to not sin. It's a bit like we're walking along the side of a hill and sin is the downward pull, while righteousness is the upward path. It's easier to go down than up.

Some call this downward tug the "indwelling sin."

And they say it's always there, as long as our flesh pumps blood. It's just part of this fallen world—and has been ever since Adam and Eve introduced sin into the world. (See "The Original Sin" page 14.)

A few Christian groups say the sinful nature can be destroyed by a spiritual experience sometimes called "entire sanctification." This is said to take place generally after a person matures as a Christian. It happens in an act of commitment to God, when we invite God to take control of every aspect of our lives. In this moment of spiritual crisis, the Holy Spirit cleanses the believer from the tendency to disobey God. Afterward, the Christian leans toward righteousness instead of toward sin. In a walk along a mountainside, it's gravity pulling us up.

controlled by the Holy Spirit think about things that please the Spirit" (Romans 8:5).

Paul says the choice is ours—and it's a matter of eternal life or death. "You have no obligation to do what your sinful nature urges you to do. For if you live by its dictates, you will die. But if through the power of the Spirit you put to death the deeds of your sinful nature, you will live" (Romans 8:12–13).

COPYCATS aren't us

Don't copy the behavior and customs of this world, but let God transform you into a new person by changing the way you think.

ROMANS 12:2

Dead sacrifices. That's what God wanted the Jews to give him during the era of the old covenant. These were animals slaughtered as substitutes for worshippers who deserved the death penalty for their sins.

But a new day has dawned. And with the rising Son comes a new covenant. Lifted up on the cross, Jesus has become the last dead sacrifice. His death paid the penalty for all sin. What God wants now, Paul says, are living sacrifices.

"Dear brothers and sisters, I plead with you to give your bodies to God because of all he has done for you. Let them be a living and holy sacrifice—the kind he will find acceptable. This is truly the way to worship him" (Romans 12:1).

Paul spends the last major section of his letter, chapters 12–15, painting a word picture. He wants the Romans to know what a living sacrifice looks like.

For those with God-given gifts:
- If your gift is serving others, serve them well.
- If you are a teacher, teach well.
- If your gift is to encourage others, be encouraging.
- If it is giving, give generously.
- If God has given you leadership ability, take the responsibility seriously.
- If you have a gift for showing kindness to others, do it gladly.

The to-do list:
- Love each other with genuine affection, and take delight in honoring each other.
- When God's people are in need, be ready to help them.
- Bless those who persecute you.
- Do all that you can to live in peace with everyone.
- Submit to governing authorities. For all authority comes from God, and those in positions of authority have been placed there by God.
- Pay your taxes.
- Accept other believers who are weak in faith, and don't argue with them about what they think is right or wrong.

The don't-do list:
- Never be lazy, but work hard and serve the Lord enthusiastically.
- Never pay back evil with more evil.
- Don't be too proud to enjoy the company of ordinary people.

Paul closes his letter with greetings to his many friends in Rome. And he says he hopes to visit all the believers there during a stop on his way to preach in Spain.

He does reach Rome—about three years later. But it's as a prisoner on his way to trial in the emperor's court.

After writing this letter, Paul returns to Jerusalem. Some Jews familiar with his rather un-Jewish ideas spot him in the temple. They don't like him being there, and they spark a riot with their accusations. Roman soldiers quickly arrest Paul. He languishes in jail for two years before appealing to Caesar's court and sailing to Rome, probably arriving in AD 60.

The book of Acts ends with a cliff-hanger: "For the next two years, Paul lived in Rome at his own expense. He welcomed all who visited him, boldly proclaiming the Kingdom of God and teaching about the Lord Jesus Christ. And no one tried to stop him" (Acts 28:30–31).

Some Bible experts say the trial probably ended in Paul's execution in AD 62. But many others say he was released and probably lived for another two years or more. Clement, a bishop in Rome, wrote in AD 96 that Paul "went to the limit of the West," implying Spain. If so, Paul's beheading in Rome probably came after Emperor Nero, in AD 64, blamed Christians for setting fire to the city.

LETTERS BY PAUL
A Time Line

DATE	BOOK	PAUL'S SITUATION
AD 51	1, 2 Thessalonians	Ministering in Corinth, some 200 miles south of Thessalonica
53	Galatians	Ministering in Ephesus; another theory says he wrote it in about AD 48, after his first missionary trip
55	1, 2 Corinthians	Ministering in Ephesus
57	Romans	At the end of his third missionary trip, perhaps in Corinth, on his way back to Jerusalem
60–62	Colossians, Philemon, Ephesians, Philippians	Under house arrest in Rome, awaiting trial
63	1 Timothy, Titus	After release from prison in Rome
67	2 Timothy	In prison at Rome again, awaiting execution

Dates approximate; debated among scholars

Image: Excerpt from Letter to Romans written about AD 200

ROMANS CHANGED MY LIFE

THE BOOK OF ROMANS IS THE REASON SOME OF THE MOST FAMOUS PEOPLE IN CHRISTIAN HISTORY BECAME FAMOUS.

AUGUSTINE

Outside of the apostles, he was the most respected theologian in the first 400 years of the Christian church.

The scene. At age 32, he was a party animal and sex addict who struggled with his addiction. After trying to read the Bible one day, he ran outside to the garden and wept.

His testimony. "Suddenly I heard a voice from the nearby house chanting. . . . 'Pick up and read.'. . . I rushed back to the place where. . .I had put down the book of the apostle when I got up. I grabbed it, opened it and in silence read the first passage on which my eye landed. 'Don't participate in the darkness of wild parties and drunkenness, or in sexual promiscuity and immoral living, or in quarreling and jealousy. Instead, clothe yourself with the presence of the Lord Jesus Christ. And don't let yourself think about ways to indulge your evil desires' (Romans 13:13–14). . . . With the last words of this sentence, it was as if a light of relief from all anxiety flooded into my heart."

MARTIN LUTHER

He was a Catholic priest whose teachings started the Protestant movement. He argued that we're not saved by obeying church leaders. We're saved by faith in Jesus.

The scene. He tried everything he could to earn his place in heaven, even fasting so much that it permanently damaged his digestive system. "If ever a monk could get into heaven by his monkery," he wrote, "it was me." But still he felt no assurance.

A scholar, he studied the book of Romans. But he hated an expression in the book: "the righteousness of God." He thought of it as something no one else could measure up to—and as the reason God had to punish people.

His testimony. "Night and day I pondered until...I finally realized that the righteousness of God is that righteousness which—through grace and sheer mercy—he justifies us by faith. . . . This passage of Paul became my gateway into heaven."

JOHN WESLEY

He was a circuit-riding preacher and theological father of many denominations, including the Methodists.

The scene. Disillusioned after a failed missionary trip to Georgia, in what later became the United States, Wesley returned to London. One evening he went unwillingly to a worship service. Someone began reading Martin Luther's preface to Romans.

His testimony. "While he was describing the change which God works in the heart through faith in Christ, I felt my heart strangely warmed. I felt I did trust in Christ, Christ alone for salvation; and an assurance was given me that he had taken away my sins."

1 CORINTHIANS

FOR CHRISTIANS BEHAVING BADLY

Paul is long gone from the church he started in the busy port city of Corinth.

He left them a couple of years earlier, during his second missionary trip. He needed to move on because he had work to do elsewhere. And he had already spent a year and a half getting the Corinthian church up and running—far more time than the few days or weeks he spent in most other towns.

Well into his third missionary trip, Paul gets a letter from the church. They have questions about serious problems they're facing—including some that they're apparently afraid to put in writing. So the messengers tell Paul about them.

- They have a potential church split in the works because they can't agree on who their leader is.
- They have a church member sleeping with his stepmother—appalling even by secular Roman standards.
- And they're suing the sandals off each other.

Paul on the defense. Founding pastor of the church at Corinth, Paul is an ocean away when he gets the bad news. The Corinthian church is on the verge of a split. And some members question his authority to do anything about it.

This is just the tip of the iceberg that the messengers tow over to the church's founding minister. Paul is about 250 nautical miles away, across the Aegean Sea. He's starting another church there, in the megacity of Ephesus. He can't drop everything he's doing. But he recognizes that the Corinthians need his help.

So he writes a letter—the first of several—addressing every one of the church's concerns.

UNHOLY power struggle

Let there be no divisions in the church. Rather, be of one mind, united in thought and purpose.

1 CORINTHIANS 1:10

Paul tackles the toughest problem first. The church is splitting into four groups. "Some of you are saying, 'I am a follower of Paul.' Others are saying, 'I follow Apollos,' or 'I follow Peter,' or 'I follow only Christ'" (1 Corinthians 1:12).

These aren't four people competing for the pastor's job. Jesus is off planet. Paul is off continent. And there's no report Peter ever visited Corinth. Apollos may be the only one of the four in town, if he's not back on the road. Alexandria, Egypt, is his home.

Bible experts aren't sure what kind of split is taking place. One of many guesses is that some Christians at Corinth are lining up behind a church leadership icon whose worship style or theological slant they prefer.

- Paul, perhaps for his Gentile-welcoming philosophy that people are saved through faith, not through following the Jewish laws.
- Apollos, maybe for his gift as a charismatic, "eloquent speaker" (Acts 18:24).

MAIN POINT:
"Live in harmony with each other" (1 Corinthians 1:10).

WRITER:
"This letter is from Paul...and from our brother Sosthenes" (1 Corinthians 1:1). But it's mainly from Paul—possibly dictated to some extent to Sosthenes, just as Paul later dictated Romans to Tertius. Throughout the letter, Paul writes from his own perspective: "I appeal to you..." (1 Corinthians 1:10). And at the end, he adds a personal note that begins: "HERE IS MY GREETING IN MY OWN HANDWRITING—PAUL" (1 Corinthians 16:21).

DATE:
About AD 55, during Paul's third missionary trip

LOCATION:
Paul is writing from Ephesus, a huge city on what is now Turkey's west coast. He's writing to Christians in Corinth, a busy trade center with ports in two oceans.

- Peter, possibly for his middle-ground approach to the Jewish-Gentile debate—calling on Jews to observe their laws and on Gentiles to follow only the minimal Jewish requirements imposed on them at the Jerusalem Council meeting a few years earlier (Acts 15:20).
- Christ, perhaps representing a more hard-line Jewish group that insists Gentile converts observe all Jewish laws—including circumcision and kosher diet.

These are just guesses. But it's clear that there's some kind of split going on. Paul says that job one for this particular church is unity.

"Has Christ been divided into factions? Was I, Paul, crucified for you? . . . Who is Apollos? Who is Paul? We are only God's servants. . . . I planted the seed in your hearts, and Apollos watered it, but it was God who made it grow. . . . The one who plants and the one who waters work together with the same purpose. . . . We are both God's workers. And you are God's field" (1 Corinthians 1:13; 3:5–6, 8–9).

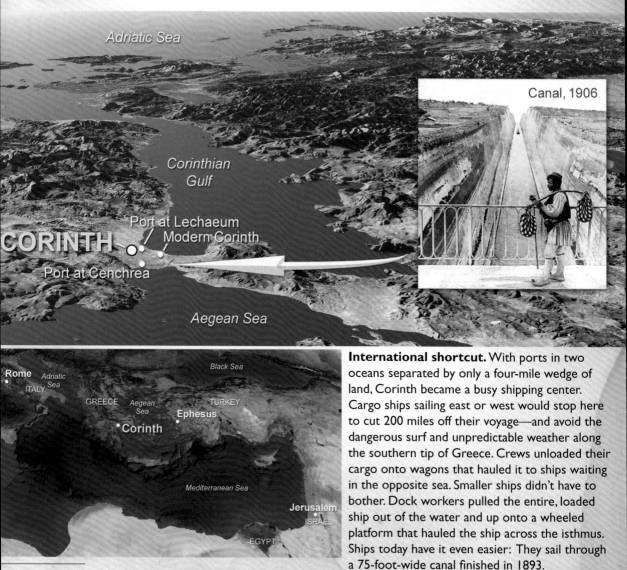

Adriatic Sea

Canal, 1906

Corinthian Gulf

Port at Lechaeum
Modern Corinth

CORINTH

Port at Cenchrea

Aegean Sea

Rome Adriatic
ITALY Sea

Black Sea

GREECE Aegean
        Sea
        Ephesus

TURKEY

Corinth

Mediterranean Sea

Jerusalem
ISRAEL

EGYPT

International shortcut. With ports in two oceans separated by only a four-mile wedge of land, Corinth became a busy shipping center. Cargo ships sailing east or west would stop here to cut 200 miles off their voyage—and avoid the dangerous surf and unpredictable weather along the southern tip of Greece. Crews unloaded their cargo onto wagons that hauled it to ships waiting in the opposite sea. Smaller ships didn't have to bother. Dock workers pulled the entire, loaded ship out of the water and up onto a wheeled platform that hauled the ship across the isthmus. Ships today have it even easier: They sail through a 75-foot-wide canal finished in 1893.

PAUL'S Q&A LETTER

Paul's letter to Christians in Corinth is a Q&A feast—all you can eat and then some.

The church wrote him a letter loaded with questions about problems in their church. Messengers who delivered the letter added a few more.

First Corinthians is Paul's reply, starting with the messengers' concerns. Paul didn't get around to the church's questions until chapter 7: "Now regarding the questions you asked in your letter..." (1 Corinthians 7:1).

Here are highlights.

Who's the spiritual leader of our church: Paul, Apollos, Peter, or Jesus?

"I planted the seed in your hearts, and Apollos watered it, but it was God who made it grow. It's not important who does the planting, or who does the watering. What's important is that God makes the seed grow" (3:6–7).

What should we do with a church member living in sin with his stepmother?

"Call a meeting of the church....Then you must throw this man out" (5:4–5). Paul hopes this will bring the man to his spiritual senses.

Is it okay for church members to sue each other?

"How dare you file a lawsuit and ask a secular court to decide the matter instead of taking it to other believers!" (6:1).

Can we do anything we want since Jesus already paid the price for our sins?

"Not everything is good for you....Don't you realize that your bodies are actually parts of Christ? Should a man take his body, which is part of Christ, and join it to a prostitute? Never!" (6:12, 15).

Should we get married or live celibate lives?

"I wish everyone were single, just as I am. But God gives to some the gift of marriage, and to others the gift of singleness" (7:7).

Is it okay to eat meat sacrificed to idols?

"We can't win God's approval by what we eat.... But you must be careful so that your freedom does not cause others with a weaker conscience to stumble" (8:8–9).

Is it okay to turn the Lord's Supper into a lively church potluck?

"You are not really interested in the Lord's Supper. For some of you hurry to eat your own meal without sharing with others. As a result, some go hungry while others get drunk. What? Don't you have your own homes for eating and drinking? Or do you really want to disgrace God's church and shame the poor?" (11:20–22).

Is speaking in a heavenly language the greatest of the special abilities the Spirit gives us?

"If I could speak all the languages of earth and of angels, but didn't love others, I would only be a noisy gong or a clanging cymbal" (13:1).

Will Christians really be raised from the dead?

"If there is no resurrection of the dead, then Christ has not been raised either. And if Christ has not been raised, then all our preaching is useless, and your faith is useless" (15:13–14).

What kind of resurrection bodies will we have?

"Just as we are now like the earthly man [Adam], we will someday be like the heavenly man [Jesus].... Our dying bodies must be transformed into bodies that will never die" (15:49, 53).

SEX SIN in the church

I can hardly believe the report about the sexual immorality going on among you—something that even pagans don't do. I am told that a man in your church is living in sin with his stepmother.

1 CORINTHIANS 5:1

Incest is what one church member is involved in. He's having an illicit sexual relationship with his stepmother. "Father's wife" is actually how Paul describes the woman. But most Bible experts say Paul phrases it this way because of a well-known Jewish law: "Do not have sexual relations with any of your father's wives" (Leviticus 18:8).

This incest is also illegal by Roman standards if the father is still alive. Emperor Augustus, fed up with gutter morality during his reign, made adultery illegal in 18 BC. Anyone found guilty could be exiled to an island. And that's what happened to his own daughter, Julia.

Even if the Corinthian man's father is dead, the scene is still disgusting to Romans, though not illegal. Leading Romans of this era say they are sickened by the idea of a marriage between a woman and her stepson. A lawyer and politician in the first century BC, Cicero, wrote about women who married their stepsons: "Oh, to think of the woman's sin, unbelievable, unheard of."

No wonder Paul is shocked when he learns that a church member is getting away with incest.

Paul advises the church to call a meeting and excommunicate the man: "You must throw this man out and hand him over to Satan so that his sinful nature will be destroyed and he himself will be saved on the day the

CELIBACY BEATS MARRIAGE

That's the personal opinion of Paul—a hard-working, hard-traveling single guy who wouldn't have gotten nearly as much accomplished if he had a family to tie him down.

"I say to those who aren't married and to widows—it's better to stay unmarried, just as I am. But if they can't control themselves, they should go ahead and marry. It's better to marry than to burn with lust" (1 Corinthians 7:8–9).

Why prefer the single life?

"I want you to be free from the concerns of this life. An unmarried man can spend his time doing the Lord's work and thinking how to please him. But a married man has to think about his earthly responsibilities and how to please his wife" (1 Corinthians 7:32–33).

For single and married folks alike, Paul knows the power of sexual desire. He has advice about that, too.

"Run from sexual sin. . . . Don't you realize that your body is the temple of the Holy Spirit, who lives in you?" (1 Corinthians 6:18–19).

Lord returns" (1 Corinthians 5:5).

Bible experts debate what Paul means by this. But many say his intent is to jolt the man into recognizing his sin and repenting.

The church probably takes this advice, since Paul doesn't address the matter again in his follow-up letter, 2 Corinthians. Some Bible students say this tactic may have worked, since Paul later writes about an ostracized church member, saying, "It is time to forgive and comfort him. Otherwise he may be overcome by discouragement" (2 Corinthians 2:7). But the context leads most Bible experts to conclude that this is a different man—one who insulted Paul.

CHAOS in the worship service

It sounds as if more harm than good is done when you meet together.

1 CORINTHIANS 11:17

Worship services have gotten out of hand. People at Corinth are apparently arguing about the following:

Worship fashions. Paul tells men to take off their hats. But he tells women to wear their head coverings. He's apparently working within the cultural rules of the day. For example, women who took off their head scarves in public were often considered immodest. Apparently some women in church are doing this when they pray and prophesy—perhaps to get more comfortable.

Communion versus potluck. The Lord's Supper at Corinth resembles a church potluck more than Communion. But this potluck doesn't involve much sharing—it's BYOF, bring your own food. So the rich bring a lot and sometimes get drunk. And the poor bring what little they have. Paul calls this disgraceful. For now, he tells them to eat their meals at home. He says he'll give them instructions about how to properly celebrate Communion next time he comes to town.

Speaking in tongues. Paul doesn't want this practice to take over a service. He limits each service to two or three people speaking in tongues, talking one at a time. And he doesn't want anyone to talk in heavenly languages unless there's someone to interpret. Otherwise, "they must be silent in your church meeting and speak in tongues to God privately" (1 Corinthians 14:28).

Women speaking in church. "Women should be silent during the church meetings. It is not proper for them to speak" (1 Corinthians 14:34). This statement is perplexing. Paul earlier said a woman should wear a head covering "if she prays or prophesies" (1 Corinthians 11:5).

Short of sign language, a body can't prophesy in church without speaking.

To figure out what Paul is saying about women, Bible experts advise readers to look at the rest of the passage. Paul is also talking about prophecy and the role of men as the head of the house in Roman and Jewish culture. Given this context, many scholars say Paul is telling women not to publicly question the prophecies of their husbands. "If they have any questions, they should ask their husbands at home" (1 Corinthians 14:35).

WHO DIED AND MADE YOU AN APOSTLE?

"Jesus."

That's the answer Paul gives to critics who say he isn't in the same league as Jesus' disciples—a dozen men who share the highest office in the early church.

The closest the Bible comes to defining *apostle* is when the word first shows up—when Jesus' 11 disciples search for someone to replace Judas.

Candidates must come "from among the men who were with us the entire time we were traveling with the Lord Jesus—from the time he was baptized by John until the day he was taken from us" (Acts 1:21–22).

There's no hint that Paul ever met Jesus during that time. Paul didn't even convert until about five years after Jesus died.

Yet Paul insists he's 100 percent apostle. He's clearly working with a different definition. The Greek word means "send."

Jesus sent his disciples on a mission: "You will be my witnesses, telling people about me everywhere—in Jerusalem, throughout Judea, in Samaria, and to the ends of the earth" (Acts 1:8).

After appearing to Paul on the road to Damascus, Jesus did much the same to him, declaring Paul "my chosen instrument to take my message to the Gentiles" (Acts 9:15).

Paul insists he was sent by Jesus—and he could prove it:

- "Even if others think I am not an apostle, I certainly am to you. You yourselves are proof that I am the Lord's apostle" (1 Corinthians 9:2).
- "When I was with you, I certainly gave you proof that I am an apostle. For I patiently did many signs and wonders and miracles among you" (2 Corinthians 12:12).

WHICH SPIRITUAL gift is tops?

There are different kinds of spiritual gifts, but the same Spirit is the source of them all.

1 CORINTHIANS 12:4

Folks at the church of Corinth seem to rank their spiritual gifts.

Perhaps it's a bit like the perception some churchgoers have today that a preacher or a soloist has the more important spiritual gift, beating out the lowly nursery worker.

Tell it to the kid with the messy diaper.

That's the point Paul makes. "The human body has many parts, but the many parts make up one whole body. So it is with the body of Christ" (1 Corinthians 12:12).

In other words, we're all essential to keeping the body up and running.

Well then, why are the next words out of Paul's mouth a ranking of spiritual gifts—with his title on top?

"First are apostles, second are prophets, third are teachers, then those who do miracles, those who have the gift of healing, those who can help others, those who have the gift of leadership, those who speak in unknown languages" (1 Corinthians 12:28).

Some Bible experts say Paul's list is a reaction to the Corinthian notion that speaking in unknown languages is the top gift; Paul lists that gift last. And some say the list is more about chronology. Christianity began with the apostles, and their work produced prophets, teachers, and other gifted leaders.

This much is clear. Paul says if we don't have love, it doesn't matter what gift we have.

"If I had the gift of prophecy, and if I understood all of God's secret plans and possessed all knowledge, and if I had such faith that I could move mountains, but didn't love others, I would be nothing" (1 Corinthians 13:2).

Spiritual gifts are only temporary, Paul adds. They're intended to help draw people to Christ. But character traits, three in particular, "will last forever—faith, hope, and love—and the greatest of these is love" (1 Corinthians 13:13).

DOUBTING the resurrection

Why are some of you saying there will be no resurrection of the dead?

1 CORINTHIANS 15:12

Immortality of a disembodied soul—Greeks can handle that idea. But they have big trouble with the idea of a physical body getting reanimated and living forever.

Paul learns that lesson 50 miles east of Corinth, when philosophers in Athens laugh him out of town.

He had them at "Hello." And he held them while he talked about the God who created and sustains everything in the world. After all, Greek philosophers such as Heraclitus teach that there's a mysterious force behind the universe that makes "all things happen" and that "always exists." But when Paul starts talking about the resurrection of the dead, the Athenian scholars "laughed in contempt" (Acts 17:32). That's why Paul moves on to Corinth, where he spends a year and a half starting a church among a more receptive crowd.

But with Paul gone for a couple of years, common sense sets in, reinforced by the prevailing Greek philosophy.

Paul reminds the Corinthians about all the witnesses who saw Jesus—500 plus of them.

Then Paul appeals to logic. For some skeptics, this would have been the stronger argument. Witnesses—and even apostles—could lie. But logic makes perfect sense. Paul's logic is this: Resurrection is the good news of Christianity. If you don't believe in the resurrection, what's the point of calling yourself a Christian?

"If Christ has not been raised," Paul says, "then your faith is useless and you are still guilty of your sins. In that case, all who have died believing in Christ are lost! And if our hope in Christ is only for this life, we are more to be pitied than anyone in the world" (1 Corinthians 15:17–19).

Point made, it seems. This is one topic Paul doesn't have to revisit in his follow-up letter.

Baptizing the dead. This portrait of a woman from Roman times decorates the outside of the casket that holds her mummified body. Paul makes a passing reference to "people being baptized for those who are dead" (1 Corinthians 15:29). This is one of the most debated statements in Paul's letter. One theory: Some people in Corinth are converting and getting baptized partly to honor the dying wish of a loved one—such as a mother's deathbed plea to her son.

2 CORINTHIANS

FIGHTING OFF A HOSTILE TAKEOVER

After writing 1 Corinthians, Paul revisits the congregation he started in the busy seaport town of Corinth. It's not a happy reunion.

The young congregation has been quarreling over a bunch of issues, including who the spiritual leader should be—and Paul is just one of several candidates. During this tense visit, one of the members verbally and viciously attacks him.

After Paul leaves town, life in the Corinthian church goes from bad to worse. Intruders come. Self-proclaimed apostles, they call Paul anything but an apostle.

Judging by the defense Paul puts up in 2 Corinthians—which is a letter he writes partly to respond to these intruders—they accuse him of

- being a fake apostle;
- promoting himself;
- lying to the Corinthians;
- keeping money he raised in offerings; and
- writing stern letters but not backing up his words with action.

Corinthian girl. Like "Valley Girl," this moniker was no compliment. In ancient Greek slang, it meant *hooker*. That's the reputation Corinth developed—but probably didn't deserve.

Paul answers each charge, reminding the Corinthians of what they saw for themselves when he was with them. What they saw was a genuine, miracle-working apostle of Christ who refused to accept offerings for himself and who cared deeply for the Corinthian believers. Though Paul did take offerings for himself from supporters in Philippi, and would later ask for financial help from Christians in Rome, he didn't collect offerings for himself in Corinth.

GOD'S NEW agreement with humanity

The old way, with laws etched in stone, led to death, though it began with such glory. . . . Shouldn't we expect far greater glory under the new way, now that the Holy Spirit is giving life?

2 CORINTHIANS 3:7–8

Paul begins his letter on an upbeat note. He offers a greeting that's typical for letters of the day, followed by a blessing that asks God to grant the people of Corinth grace and peace. Then, after dealing with a couple of quick concerns—a change in his itinerary and a plea to forgive the man who insulted him on his previous trip—Paul moves into his signature teaching. It's about God's new covenant that lays out the welcome mat for non-Jews.

Earning his reputation as "Apostle to the Gentiles," Paul says Jesus sent him on this mission to spread the good news everywhere, "like a sweet perfume" (2 Corinthians 2:14). He's comparing the new Christian religion with the old, rule-oriented Jewish faith that required worshippers to seek forgiveness by offering sacrifices as "a pleasing aroma to the

MAIN POINT:

Defending his ministry against intruders who pummel him with criticism, Paul pleads with believers at the church he founded in Corinth. "Please open your hearts to us. We have not done wrong to anyone, nor led anyone astray, nor taken advantage of anyone" (2 Corinthians 7:2).

WRITER:

"This letter is from Paul. . .and from our brother Timothy" (2 Corinthians 1:1). But it's written in the first person, as though Paul may be dictating to Timothy.

DATE:

Paul writes this follow-up to 1 Corinthians in about AD 55, a few months after writing the first letter.

LOCATION:

Paul is still traveling on his third missionary journey. Clues in the letter suggest he has already left Ephesus, where he stayed about three years. And now, in northern Greece, he writes this letter to the believers in and around Corinth.

CORINTH
FIRST · CENTURY

KEY
1. Lechaion Road
2. Propylaia (Entry Gate)
3. Peirene Fountain
4. Peribolos of Apollo
5. Julian Basilica
6. Bema (Judicial Seat)
7. Central Shops
8. South Stoa (market)
9. Bouleuterion (Senate House)
10. Statue of Poseidon and Fountain
11. Northwest shops
12. Archaic Temple (of Apollo)
13. North Market
14. Sanctuary of Athena Chalinitis
15. West Shops
16. Odeion
17. Theater

City in ruins. Seven columns from the Temple of Apollo guard the fallen ruins of one the busiest seaport cities in the Roman Empire.

THE FACTS AND MORE

Statistics about Corinth in Bible times come from ancient historical records and city ruins.

Corinth's sour reputation seems to come mainly from writers in the competing town of Athens. Most historians say there's more rivalry than accuracy in those comments. A sailor's town and home to the goddess of love, Corinth probably hosted its share of drunken bashes—but no more than other big cities.

Stats

- Population: 100,000 or more
- Size: 2.5 square miles
- Distance from Athens: 45 miles
- Distance from modern Corinth: 4 miles
- Destroyed by Romans: 146 BC
- Rebuilt by Romans: 46 BC
- Repopulated by freed slaves, poor Romans, Jews, foreign settlers. *Supporting quote from Paul: "Few of you were wise in the world's eyes or powerful or wealthy"* (1 Corinthians 1:26).
- Declared capital of Rome's Achaia province (southern Greece): 27 BC
- Declared free city of Roman citizens: after AD 54, by Nero
- Main attractions: nearby ports in two seas; Olympic-style Isthmian Games every two years

- Religion: Aphrodite, Apollo, Poseidon, Emperor, and other gods
- Destroyed by earthquake: 1886

Word on the street

- Aristophanes, a playwright of Greek comedies, coined the verb *corinthianize*. In English, it would be a four-letter word—a crass way of saying "fornicate."
- The city name shows up again in the title of an ancient Greek play. English translation: "Whore Lover."
- Two millennia before anyone thought up the demeaning tag of "Valley Girl," to insult ladies of San Fernando Valley, Greek philosopher Plato invented the "Corinthian Girl" (*korinthia kore*). It means "hooker." No reference to the nearby fishing industry.

Lord" (Leviticus 1:13).

Paul says the sweet perfume of Christianity is a stinker as far as some people are concerned: "To those who are perishing, we are a dreadful smell of death and doom. But to those who are being saved, we are a life-giving perfume" (2 Corinthians 2:16).

God's first covenant agreement with the Jews was glorious. After Moses had received the laws from God, his face glowed so much that people couldn't look at him. He had to wear a veil. Paul says God's new covenant—with all of humanity—is even more glorious.

The reason? Paul says the old covenant led to death.

That would shock an observant Jew. The Jews of Paul's day describe the covenant laws of Moses as "the law of life." You keep these laws to live. Breaking any one of the laws is a sin. And the punishment for sin is death—even if only the death of a sacrificial animal.

Under God's new covenant, Jesus has already provided the sacrifice. For those who put their faith in him, there is forgiveness and eternal life.

PAUL'S CORINTHIAN CONNECTIONS

Bible experts don't agree on how many times Paul visited and wrote the congregation at Corinth. Here's one possible flow of events—three visits and four letters.

- Visit #1, AD 50–52. Starts the church on his second missionary trip.
- Letter #1, AD 52. This letter, now lost, came before First Corinthians: "When I wrote to you before, I told you not to associate with people who indulge in sexual sin" (1 Corinthians 5:9).
- Letter #2, AD 55. First Corinthians, written probably in Ephesus during his third missionary trip.
- Visit #2, AD 55. This is a "painful visit" (2 Corinthians 2:1). It's apparently from Ephesus, directly to Corinth and back again—not reflected on most maps tracking Paul's third missionary trip.
- Letter #3, AD 55. This letter, also lost, was a stern one written "in great anguish, with a troubled heart and many tears" (2 Corinthians 2:4). Some say 2 Corinthians 10–13 was part of that high-voltage letter; others disagree.
- Letter #4, AD 55. Second Corinthians.
- Visit #3, AD 56. Stays in Corinth for three months and collects offering for Jerusalem poor.

PREACHING to a hostile crowd

We live in the face of death, but this has resulted in eternal life for you.

2 CORINTHIANS 4:12

Paul starts defending himself against his critics by reminding the Corinthians that he's putting his life on the line for this ministry. He's the genuine article, an authentic apostle with a ministry to die for.

Scattered throughout this letter is the evidence:

- "You ought to know, dear brothers and sisters, about the trouble we went through in the province of Asia [western Turkey]. We were crushed and overwhelmed beyond our ability to endure, and we thought we would never live through it" (2 Corinthians 1:8). *Paul is probably talking about the riot at Ephesus (Acts 19).*
- "We are pressed on every side by troubles, but we are not crushed. We are perplexed, but not driven to despair. We are hunted down, but never abandoned by God. We get knocked down, but we are not destroyed" (2 Corinthians 4:8–9). *Jews sometimes followed Paul from town to town trying to stop him. Once, Jews followed him to a neighboring town, stoned him, and left him for dead (Acts 14:19).*
- "Five different times the Jewish leaders gave me thirty-nine lashes. Three times I was beaten with rods. Once I was stoned. Three times I was shipwrecked. Once I spent a whole night and a day adrift at sea" (2 Corinthians 11:24–25).

Paul's point is that a fake apostle would never suffer through all of this. A fraud would have given up long ago.

Treasure in clay jars. A stash of silver ingots found in Israel. The ancient version of a hidden safe, clay jars were sometimes entrusted with great treasure: money, jewels, the Dead Sea Scrolls. Many thieves didn't think to look for valuables in such a common, plain container. Paul compares himself to a fragile jar containing the treasure of eternal life (2 Corinthians 4:7).

MACEDONIA   THRACE   Black Sea

MODERN-DAY
GREECE

Aegean
Sea

Adriatic Sea

MODERN-DAY
TURKEY

ASIA

Corinth   • Athens   • Ephesus

GREECE

Roman
Provinces
in Color

CRETE   Mediterranean Sea

PASSING the offering plate

Since you excel in so many ways. . .I want you to excel also in this gracious act of giving. I am not commanding you to do this. But I am testing how genuine your love is by comparing it with the eagerness of the other churches.

2 CORINTHIANS 8:7–8

Why would Paul—under attack for supposedly pocketing church offerings from Corinth—include in his letter of self-defense a fund-raising appeal?

It seems like bad timing. Worse, this appeal isn't just a polite invitation to give. It's high pressure. Hard sell.

Paul tells the Corinthians:

- "Finish what you started" (2 Corinthians 8:11). *They have apparently been donating to this particular cause for some time.*
- "I am testing how genuine your love is" (2 Corinthians 8:8).

- "I have been boasting to the churches in Macedonia [modern-day northern Greece] that you in Greece [now southern Greece] were ready to send an offering a year ago. . . . I don't want to be wrong in my boasting about you. We would be embarrassed—not to mention your own embarrassment" (2 Corinthians 9:2–4).
- "Churches in Macedonia. . .are very poor. But they are also filled with abundant joy, which has overflowed in rich generosity. For I can testify that they gave not only what they could afford, but far more" (2 Corinthians 8:1–3). *Paul's not-so-subtle message: If poor Macedonians can give generously, Corinthians in a thriving business center should make the Macedonian offering look like a tip for the waitress.*

There are two reasons Paul remains committed to this offering for poor Jewish Christians in Jerusalem.

First, Jerusalem church leaders asked Paul to "keep on helping the poor" (Galatians 2:10).

Second, he hoped that a generous gift from this non-Jewish sector of the church would help Jewish Christians accept these Gentiles—uniting the church.

Good idea. But it doesn't work.

When he takes the money to Jerusalem later, his presence at the temple sparks a riot. He spends the next four years under arrest, ending up in a trial for his life at the emperor's court in Rome. Some Bible experts say he's executed there. Others say he is released, only to get himself arrested a few years later and beheaded in Rome.

THORN in Paul's side

To keep me from becoming proud, I was given a thorn in my flesh.

2 CORINTHIANS 12:7

It's the Corinthian church. That's the thorn in Paul's side and the pain in his neck, according to some Bible experts.

Or it might be the Jews who dogged his trail to stir up the locals against him.

Evidence: The Greek word for *thorn* appears nowhere else in the New Testament. But when the Hebrew version of this word shows up in the Old Testament—Paul's Bible—it describes what the Canaanites would become to the Jews: "If you fail to drive out the people who live in the land, those who remain will be like splinters in your eyes and thorns in your sides" (Numbers 33:55).

Other thorn theories have Paul suffering from

- a physical problem such as malaria, epilepsy, poor eyesight, or a speech impediment;
- an emotional problem such as bipolar disorder, depression, or anger control; or
- a spiritual problem such as temptation.

INVASION OF THE
BODY OF CHRIST SNATCHERS

Bible experts aren't sure who intrudes on Paul's founding church at Corinth and then bad-mouths him.

One persistent guess is that it's a group of Jewish Christians who don't agree with his teaching that non-Jews can get saved without observing the Jewish laws. So they try to undermine his authority by criticizing him.

But some Bible experts say the intruders might be self-appointed apostles on a mission to harvest something other than souls in this trade hub teeming with money. Paul sarcastically calls them "super apostles" who preach "a different kind of gospel" (2 Corinthians 11:5, 4).

Paul doesn't give us a list of their charges against him. But many are implied in the defense he puts up.

"They call us impostors" (2 Corinthians 6:8).

Paul's reply: "In everything we do, we show that we are true ministers of God. We patiently endure troubles and hardships and calamities of every kind" (2 Corinthians 6:4).

Paul is no apostle.

"When I was with you, I certainly gave you proof that I am an apostle. For I patiently did many signs and wonders and miracles among you" (2 Corinthians 12:12).

He's a showoff who promotes himself.

"We don't go around preaching about ourselves. We preach that Jesus Christ is Lord" (2 Corinthians 4:5).

All he really wants is your money.

"The only thing I failed to do, which I do in the other churches, was to become a financial burden to you. . . . We are not like the many hucksters who preach for personal profit. We preach the word of God with sincerity and with Christ's authority, knowing that God is watching us" (2 Corinthians 12:13; 2:17). Paul served as a bivocational pastor when he started the church at Corinth. He paid his own way, working as a tentmaker (Acts 18:3).

He's unreliable. He said he was coming to visit you, then he changed his plans.

"The reason I didn't return to Corinth was to spare you from a severe rebuke" (2 Corinthians 1:23). Paul wrote a letter instead.

He's bold and stern when he writes, but timid in person.

"Those people should realize that our actions when we arrive in person will be as forceful as what we say in our letters from far away" (2 Corinthians 10:11).

Contenders for the New Testament

Not all books that belong in the New Testament are there, according to some early church leaders. Two were especially popular and widely read in churches.

Shepherd of Hermas. In this book written in the AD mid-100s, a shepherd from heaven—presumably an angel—gives spiritual advice to a former slave named Hermas. The book covers a lot of moral topics: sex, anger, and good deeds. But in a deviation from other New Testament books, the celestial shepherd says that people shouldn't sin after they're baptized. If

they do, the shepherd says, God will forgive them only once, and for a limited time.

Epistle of Barnabas. This letter reads like an essay about how non-Jewish Christians fit into God's covenant with the Jews. The writer says the Jews broke their agreement with God by worshipping idols and that Christians have become heirs to the new covenant that Old Testament prophets said God would make with his people. The letter was probably written sometime after the fall of Jerusalem in AD 70 but before Emperor Hadrian rebuilt it in AD 135.

GALATIANS

CLASH OF THE CHURCH TITANS

This is it. The fight of the century. Paul, chief apostle to the Gentiles, takes on Peter, lead disciple of Jesus.

It's not a fistfight, but the verbal blows pack quite a punch.

Paul wins. Not just because he's writing the history and he doesn't bother to tell us Peter's side of the heated argument. Even if Peter outdebates him in this titanic clash, Paul is the victor in the long run. His theological argument eventually wins over the emerging church.

This argument takes place in a predominantly non-Jewish church that Paul is helping pastor. Peter comes to town for a visit, eating and mingling with the Gentiles just fine until some Jewish Christians from Jerusalem come up, too. They refuse to eat with Gentiles, as Jewish custom dictates. Jews become ritually unclean when they associate with Gentiles. So Peter joins the visitors, giving the non-Jewish Christians the cold shoulder and extra elbow room. That's when Paul publicly confronts him, telling him off big-time.

This story—which takes place hundreds of miles from where the Galatian Christians live—is Paul's most dramatic case in point.

His point is this: Messianic Jews are dead wrong. Some of these Jewish Christians have come to Galatia teaching that Jesus is the Messiah—which is kosher Christian theology. But these Jewish Christians add that even Gentiles have to obey Jewish laws if they want God to save them from their sins.

Paul writes this letter to refute that idea. He gives one example after another to make his point—even drawing into the fray Abraham, father of the Jews. But no argument shows the passion of Paul's commitment better than his clash with a church titan.

Peter the hypocrite. Jesus may have promised Peter the keys to the kingdom, calling him a leader. But Paul called him a hypocrite. That was after Peter refused to associate with non-Jewish Christians. Peter had no trouble mingling with those Gentile believers until representatives from the Jerusalem church came for a visit. But Peter knew the Jerusalem guests disapproved of what he was doing, so he stopped.

TELLING Peter off

When Peter came to Antioch, I had to oppose him to his face, for what he did was very wrong.

GALATIANS 2:11

Paul goes to battle when he hears that Jewish Christians are intruding on some of the churches he founded in what is now Turkey. For these Jews by race are converting Gentile Christians to the Jewish brand of Christianity.

The back story is that there's a sharp split in the Christian church—one that a leadership conference in Jerusalem tried unsuccessfully to fix (Acts 15).

Pro-freedom. Some leaders, including Peter, Paul, and Barnabas, are convinced that faith in Jesus is enough to save people and that non-Jews don't have to adopt Jewish customs. God has set people free from the Jewish laws and has given them the Holy Spirit to guide them.

Pro-law. The church began as a Jewish movement. The first Christians were observant Jews—they followed Jewish laws about sacrifices, circumcision, and kosher food. Many of these Jewish Christians say anyone joining their movement should do the same. To become a Christian, a person also has to become an observant Jew.

"I am shocked that you are turning away so soon from God, who called you to himself through the loving mercy of Christ," Paul tells the Galatians in a letter. "You are following a different way that pretends to be the Good News" (Galatians 1:6).

Paul starts defending his freedom-from-Jewish-law message by giving the Galatians a short history lesson. He tells how Jesus himself gave him the job of taking the good

MAIN POINT:

Faith in Jesus is what saves us. We don't need to observe Jewish laws, such as circumcision or kosher food restrictions.

WRITER:

Paul writes this book, perhaps dictating it as he did others. He signs his John Hancock large: "NOTICE WHAT LARGE LETTERS I USE AS I WRITE THESE CLOSING WORDS IN MY OWN HANDWRITING" (Galatians 6:11). This note is one reason some Bible experts guess that Paul's thorn in the flesh was poor eyesight. (See "Thorn in Paul's Side," page 400.)

DATE:

There's confusion over the date. Some say Paul wrote Galatians in the AD mid-50s. Some say in the early 50s. And others say this is his first letter, written about AD 48. The key to the mystery is his intended audience.

LOCATION:

When it comes to this question, Bible experts generally pitch their tent in one of two camps. Paul addresses his letter to "the churches of Galatia" (Galatians 1:2). That's the name of a Roman province in what is now central Turkey. Some Bible experts say Paul had the southern churches in mind—those he and Barnabas founded on the first missionary trip. If so, he may have written this letter as early as AD 48, after he and Barnabas returned to the church they pastored in Antioch, Syria. Other Bible experts say Paul targeted churches he founded later in the original, ethnic Galatia farther north. He may have passed through northern Galatia during his second missionary journey, on his way to Greece.

WHO WERE THE GALATIANS?

Today we'd call them Irish, English, and French.

That's where this group of tribes came from when they invaded what is now Turkey in 278 BC.

Writers in ancient times called them Celts. One Roman writer in Paul's century—Livy—said the warriors had "tall bodies, long reddish hair, huge shields, very long swords" and they charged into battle with "songs, yells, and leaping."

They settled in north-central Turkey, in a hub around three main cities: Pessinus, Tavium, and Ancrya (modern Ankara, capital of Turkey).

The Romans later conquered the area and created the province of Galatia, expanding it south to include the four cities Paul visited on his first missionary trip. But ethnic Galatians—the long-legged redheads—lived up north.

That's the confusion.

When Paul addressed his book to Galatians, did he mean the cities he is known to have visited in the southland? Or was he talking about the ethnic Galatians who lived in cities up north?

The Bible doesn't mention any of these northern cities. But it's possible Paul passed through this area during his second missionary trip, when the Bible says he traveled "through the area of Phrygia and Galatia" (Acts 16:6).

Where in Galatia? Bible experts aren't sure if Paul wrote Galatians to churches he visited in south Galatia during his first missionary trip. Ethnic Galatians—called Celts—were mainly in the north, a territory Paul may have visited on his second trip. Solving this mystery could settle the debate about whether or not Galatians is Paul's earliest surviving letter.

news to non-Jews. And he reminds them that church leaders in Jerusalem bought into this idea and the theology behind it.

"In fact," Paul adds, "James, Peter, and John, who were known as pillars of the church, recognized the gift God had given me, and they accepted Barnabas and me as their co-workers. They encouraged us to keep preaching to the Gentiles, while they continued their work with the Jews" (Galatians 2:9).

History lesson over, Paul tells how he once had to jar Peter back to his theological senses—like he's trying to do with the Galatians.

Peter, of all the original disciples of Jesus, should have known better than to turn his back on the Gentiles. After all, it was his noontime vision that led him to convert and baptize the first known Gentile believer—a Roman soldier named Cornelius (Acts 10).

Yet turning his back on them is exactly what Peter did. He went up to the Syrian church in Antioch, perhaps to see for himself if the reports were true—that the Holy Spirit was working among a congregation of Gentiles. Reports apparently confirmed, Peter went so far as to eat with them—treating them as equals, and not as ritually unclean. But that all changed when some Jewish Christians arrived from Jerusalem—friends of the Jerusalem church's top leader, James the brother of Jesus. Peter quickly reverted to his old Jewish ways. He followed the lead of James's friends, refusing to eat with the Gentiles. "He was afraid of criticism from these people who insisted on the necessity of circumcision" (Galatians 2:12).

Paul actually calls Peter a hypocrite.

And he says that even Barnabas, the Antioch church's senior pastor, followed Peter's lead.

A public sin deserves public attention, Paul apparently concludes. He confronts Peter, if not in public, at least for public consumption. Paul puts it on the record.

Unfortunately for the curious, he never says how Peter responds. Had he convinced Peter to change his ways, most folks would have expected Paul to say so. His silence is ominous.

Dancing to ecstasy. Worshipping Bacchus, the Roman god of wine and revelry, dancers check their morals at the temple door. Lewd acts disgrace the rituals of this religion, which is popular in Galatia and throughout the Roman Empire during Paul's day. Many of these acts appear on Paul's not-to-do list: sexual immorality, impurity, lustful pleasures, idolatry, drunkenness, and wild parties (Galatians 5:19–21).

PAUL UNLEASHES all his defenses

Those who depend on the law to make them right with God are under his curse.
GALATIANS 3:10

Angry emotion, logic, common sense, mystical revelation—Paul uses all of these to combat the warped teachings of Jewish Christians. He even tries some experimental theology that seems a bit off the wall. Clearly, he's going all out to stop a consuming threat to his life's work.

Anger

This is Paul's angriest letter. Consider a few choice words:

- "I do not teach that a man must be circumcised. . . . I wish the people who are bothering you would castrate themselves!" (Galatians 5:11–12 NCV).
- "Let God's curse fall on anyone. . .who preaches a different kind of Good News than the one we preached to you. I say again. . .If anyone preaches any other Good News than the one you welcomed, let that person be cursed" (Galatians 1:8–9).

Common sense

"Let me ask you this one question: Did you receive the Holy Spirit by obeying the law of Moses? Of course not! You received the Spirit because you believed the message you heard about Christ. How foolish can you be? After starting your Christian lives in the Spirit, why are you now trying to become perfect by your own human effort?" (Galatians 3:2–3).

Logic

At least 600 years before God gave Moses the Jewish laws, Abraham founded the Jewish nation. " 'Abraham believed God, and God counted him as righteous because of his faith.' The real children of Abraham, then, are those who put their faith in God" (Galatians 3:6–7).

Metaphor

"The law was our guardian until Christ came; it protected us until we could be made right with God through faith. And now that the way of faith has come, we no longer need the law as our guardian" (Galatians 3:24–25).

Experimental theology

Case study 1. "God gave the promises to Abraham and his child. And notice that the Scripture doesn't say 'to his children,' as if it meant many descendants. Rather, it says 'to his child'—and that, of course, means Christ. . . . The law was designed to last only until the coming of the child who was promised" (Galatians 3:16, 19).

Who would have guessed that Abraham's "child" meant Jesus instead of Isaac?

Paul, and only Paul.

He's referring to the Old Testament promises about God blessing Abraham's "seed," a word that's singular in Hebrew.

Case study 2. "The Scriptures say that Abraham had two sons, one from his slave wife and one from his freeborn wife. . . . These two women serve as an illustration of God's two covenants. The first woman, Hagar, represents Mount Sinai where people received the law that enslaved them. . . . But the other woman, Sarah, represents the heavenly Jerusalem. She is the free woman, and she is our mother" (Galatians 4:22, 24, 26).

So how does Paul know these things?

Does the Holy Spirit clue him in—much like "prophets were moved by the Holy Spirit, and they spoke from God" (2 Peter 1:21)? Or is this the scenic and circuitous route that his logic takes—and, some might wonder, did he spot a unicorn along the way?

Paul's approach seems over the edge. How could he possibly get anything but an F if he tried writing something like this for a seminary exam in Old Testament exegesis, the interpretation of Scripture?

It's as though Paul has a point to make, and he's going to make it any way he can—even if he has to take ancient Bible passages out of context.

Yet rabbis of his day follow this same approach. They teach that the Bible has hidden meanings that only the most insightful readers can discern. So Paul adds this approach to his defensive arsenal.

Bloody ritual retired. Circumcision tools rest on display in a museum: cutting guides that hold foreskin in place, knives that cut along those guides, and a vial of ointment to soothe the wound. Eight-day-old Jewish boys experience this ritual, which welcomes them into God's covenant as God's chosen people. Paul argued that the covenant is obsolete because all people who have faith in Jesus are "the new people of God" (Galatians 6:16).

LEGALISM, be gone

Christ has truly set us free. Now make sure that you stay free, and don't get tied up again in slavery to the law.

GALATIANS 5:1

Now Paul goes on the offensive.

His approach is basically a question: Why would anyone freed from slavery want to go back? Those weren't the good old days.

Yet Jewish people—even today—say the law is what frees them. It offers security because it establishes right from wrong, black from white. And it provides guidance by setting up warning markers beside the moral boundaries.

But God's Spirit does it better. That's Paul's point. "Let the Holy Spirit guide your lives" (Galatians 5:16).

Many of the old Jewish laws are out of date, Paul says. This includes circumcision—the pivotal Jewish rite that welcomes baby boys into God's covenant. That covenant is obsolete. A new day has dawned.

In a graphic turn of phrase, Paul says that people who continue to trust in the flesh-hacking ritual of circumcision will themselves be "cut off from Christ" (Galatians 5:4).

But those who trust in Christ will be guided by the Spirit, producing godly character traits: love, joy, peace, patience, kindness, goodness, faithfulness, gentleness, and self-control.

"There is no law against these things!" Paul adds—one last cut at the enemy.

EPHESIANS

HOW TO LIVE THE CHRISTIAN LIFE

After three fiery letters in a row—two searing Corinth and one torching Galatia—Ephesians is a welcome relief.

Paul's not telling anybody off, complaining, or defending himself against critics.

Ephesians is an upbeat letter, Paul's most positive of all. And that's a bit odd since he's writing "in chains," probably waiting for trial in Rome.

That's assuming Paul actually wrote the letter—a leap of faith that many scholars aren't willing to take because of changes in writing style. Yet others insist it's a leap of faith *not* to believe, especially since the writer identifies himself as Paul and the book was added to the New Testament because early church leaders believed he wrote it.

Unlike in his other letters, Paul isn't telling stories or reacting to bad news. Instead, he's praising his readers for their solid Christian reputation. And he's reminding them that Jesus is the source of their salvation and the heart of Christianity's good news. Also, he's giving them practical advice for keeping up the good work of the good news:

• "Make every effort to keep yourselves united in the Spirit, binding yourselves together with peace" (Ephesians 4:3).

• "Don't let the sun go down while you are still angry, for anger gives a foothold to

Non-Jews welcome. A Palestinian living in East Jerusalem manages a smile, though Israelis and Palestinians argue over who should be living where. Paul reminds Jews and non-Jews that Christ "united Jews and Gentiles into one people. . .he broke down the wall of hostility that separated us" (Ephesians 2:14). Sadly—then and now—not everyone practices what Paul preaches.

the devil" (Ephesians 4:26–27).

- "Imitate God. . .in everything you do, because you are his dear children" (Ephesians 5:1).

MAIN POINT:

"Live a life filled with love, following the example of Christ" (Ephesians 5:2).

WRITER:

"This letter is from Paul" (Ephesians 1:1). Church leaders as early as the AD 100s quoted this letter, saying Paul wrote it. And no one seemed to doubt it until the late 1700s, when scholars started comparing it to his other letters. Now, many Bible experts—perhaps most—doubt Paul wrote Ephesians. Among their reasons:

- The words are more flowery than usual.
- Some words have a different meaning than they do in Paul's other letters.
- And some teachings are far more developed and seem to fit decades after Paul.

Many experts guess that someone such as Timothy may have written the letter in Paul's name. This was a common practice in ancient times. The writer humbly gives credit to his teacher—the opposite of plagiarism. Other scholars hold to the traditional view that Paul wrote Ephesians. They say Paul's writing style and insights may have changed over the years.

DATE:

If Paul is the author, he wrote while "in chains" (Ephesians 6:20), probably under house arrest in Rome sometime between AD 60 and 62. If one of Paul's students is the author, Ephesians may have been written 10 or 20 years later.

LOCATION:

"I am writing to God's holy people in Ephesus" (Ephesians 1:1). Yet several of the oldest and most reliable copies of this letter drop the phrase "in Ephesus." Also, the writer sounds as though he never met his readers: "Ever since I first heard of your strong faith. . .I have not stopped thanking God for you" (Ephesians 1:15–16). Yet Paul spent about three years starting the church in Ephesus. Many Bible experts say Ephesians may have been a general letter passed along from church to church. And it may have been sent from Ephesus, the third largest city in the Roman Empire, after Rome and Alexandria, Egypt.

HIGHWAY TO NOWHERE

Once the third largest city in the Roman Empire, Ephesus died after silt plugged up the riverside port that led to the sea.

From the amphitheater above—where Ephesians once rioted in protest of Paul (Acts 19)—a wide road led to the river port. But today, all the action in this ghost town comes from tourists, like those visiting what's left of the city library (left)—a mere façade.

It's unclear if Ephesians was written to the church in Ephesus, or perhaps to churches in neighboring cities. Most Bible versions include the address: "God's holy people in Ephesus." But several of the oldest and most reliable copies of the letter are addressed simply to "God's holy people."

Black Sea

TURKEY

Pergamum
Thyatira

Smyrna
Philadelphia

Laodicea

Ephesus

Mediterranean Sea

EGYPT

GOD'S NEW chosen people

Christ himself has brought peace to us. He united Jews and Gentiles into one people. . .he broke down the wall of hostility that separated us.

EPHESIANS 2:14

It takes God more than 2,000 years to get around to welcoming Gentiles into his plan of salvation. It's not that God is slow. Some things just take time.

God starts with one man of faith: Abraham. From Abraham, God builds a nation of faith: the Jews. And he promises those Jewish people that "all nations will come to your light" (Isaiah 60:3). Non-Jews are welcome into the Jewish faith at any time, through conversion. The Jews, however, tend not to let their little light shine as much as God would like. They treat other races as spiritually inferior. After all, it's the Jews who are God's chosen people.

Yet God vows that one day he will send a servant to point all people to himself, Jews and non-Jews. "You will do more than restore the people of Israel to me," God says of that servant. "I will make you a light to the Gentiles, and you will bring my salvation to the ends of the earth" (Isaiah 49:6).

Jesus was this servant.

When his parents took him to the temple for infant dedication, the priest said as much: "He is a light to reveal God to the nations, and he is the glory of your people Israel!" (Luke 2:32).

Paul reminds his Gentile readers that they were once outsiders. "You were called 'uncircumcised heathens' by the Jews, who were proud of their circumcision, even though it affected only their bodies and not their hearts" (Ephesians 2:11).

But Jesus changed all that by dying on the cross. His sacrifice put an end not only to the Jewish sacrificial system, but to the entire "system of law with its commandments and regulations" (Ephesians 2:15). It's obsolete.

From one man—Abraham—to one nation—the Jews—God has taken the next major step in his plan of salvation. Out of the Jewish nation comes one man—Jesus—the Savior of an entire world.

This is God's new plan: "Both Gentiles and Jews who believe the Good News share equally in the riches inherited by God's children" (Ephesians 3:6).

LIVE IN PEACE with each other

Be patient with each other, making allowance for each other's faults because of your love.

EPHESIANS 4:2

Paul calls for unity in the churches, but not unity at all costs. In his last words to church leaders at Ephesus—when he tells them they'll never see him again—he warns that "some men from your own group will rise up and distort the truth in order to draw a following" (Acts 20:30).

He expects church leaders to confront these kinds of people.

But Paul doesn't want confrontation and tension to be the norm among believers.

"Make every effort to keep yourselves united in the Spirit, binding yourselves together with peace. For there is one body and one Spirit. . . . There is one Lord, one faith, one baptism, and one God and Father, who is over all and in all and living through all" (Ephesians 4:3–6).

TO-DO LIST for the mature

Be mature in the Lord, measuring up to the full and complete standard of Christ.

EPHESIANS 4:13

We can measure our height and weight. But how can we measure our spirit? How can we gauge the maturity of our faith?

Paul doesn't give us a scale to let us know when we've arrived at the "full and complete standard of Christ." Perhaps that's because most of us never get there in this lifetime. Paul himself confesses in another letter, "I don't mean to say that I have already. . .reached perfection. But I press on to possess that perfection for which Christ Jesus first possessed me" (Philippians 3:12).

What Paul does give us is a list of spiritual characteristics.

It's actually a bit like a description of the scenery we can expect on the highway of holiness. If we see certain good characteristics along the way, we can know we're headed in the right direction. But if we see the bad characteristics he describes, we're headed into trouble.

Paul's list for keeping us on track:
- Stop telling lies.
- Don't let anger control you.
- Give generously to others.
- Don't use foul or abusive language.
- Be kind to each other, tenderhearted, and forgiving.
- Stay away from sexual immorality and obscene jokes.
- Don't get drunk.
- Instead, fill yourself with God's Spirit, and sing his praises.

Putting women in their place

Paul's plea for husbands and wives to "submit to one another" was a big step up from what other men were saying about wives in Roman times.

"A woman is inferior to her husband in everything. For that reason, she should obey him. . . . God has put the husband in charge."

Josephus
Jewish historian, first century AD

A Roman leader was asked why he was divorcing his wife, Papiria, who was beautiful, loyal, and who gave him two wonderful sons. Before adopting away their two sons and marrying another woman, he replied by comparing Papiria to a shoe. Holding it up he said, "This is attractive, isn't it? And it's new, isn't it? But you can't see where it pinches my foot."

Lucius Aemilius Paullus Macedonicus
Roman general, 100s BC

Women's work. Women carry water for household cleaning and cooking. In Paul's day, most women had a specific role to play, and it usually involved doing what their husbands told them to do.

LIFE in a Christian home

Submit to one another out of reverence for Christ.

EPHESIANS 5:21

Paul offers tips for healthy family relationships as he brings his letter to a close. He talks about husbands and wives, parents and kids, slaves and masters—calling for mutual respect in every relationship.

Husbands and wives. Countercultural in this male-run society, Paul asks husbands to submit to their wives—and wives to submit to their husbands.

It's not just blind obedience he's asking for. He wants husband and wife each to lovingly put the other first. Oddly, he's not asking them to do it out of respect for the person. It's out of respect for the Person.

It's a metaphor. Paul says that when husbands and wives do this, they're imitating Jesus. When the wife follows the lead of her husband in areas of his responsibility, she's doing what the church does: submitting to Christ. And when the husband treats his wife with loving devotion, he's imitating Christ, who "loved the church" and "gave up his life for her."

Healthy families don't spin around arguments over who's the boss. They spin around obedience to the new commandment Jesus gives: "Love each other" (John 13:34).

Parents and kids. In advising the kids, Paul could have used a stick. Maybe an ancient Bible quote such as, "Anyone who dishonors father or mother must be put to death" (Exodus 21:17). Instead, he uses a carrot. Two, in fact.

- "This is the right thing to do" (Ephesians 6:1).
- "If you honor your father and mother, 'things will go well for you, and you will have a long life on the earth' " (Ephesians 6:3, citing Exodus 20:12).

Even in Roman times, fathers have the power of life and death over their young children. Yet, staying true to his theme of mutual respect, Paul urges fathers not to exploit their authority by antagonizing the children.

Masters and slaves. How could Paul advise anything but "Masters, free your slaves just as Christ has freed you from slavery to sin"? That's what we want to hear Paul say.

Instead, he tells slaves to obey their masters— "with deep respect." You'd think he was a slave master, if not for the advice that follows: "Masters, treat your slaves in the same way. Don't threaten them; remember, you both have the same Master in heaven, and he has no favorites" (Ephesians 6:9).

He's one smart apostle.

Battlefield metaphor. The Centre Pompidou museum of modern art in Paris showcases an ancient Roman helmet— super-sized and impossible to miss. Paul uses battlefield armor to symbolize the spiritual resources Christians need for fighting off evil spirits in a world that's impossible to see.

When most of us try to change things, we generally jump right to the end of the process, telling people how to behave. But Paul tells them how to think. He nudges their attitude toward godliness, knowing that the appropriate behavior will follow.

Slavery was usually much different in Roman times than it was in the United States. Most slaves were freed by age 30. Many actually sold themselves into slavery to advance economically, rather than struggle on in poverty. Supported by a richer person, many were able to learn a trade, save money, raise a family, and even buy property.

That's not to excuse the exploitation. And it's certainly not to embrace the philosopher Aristotle's take on slavery: "A slave is a man's property. . .a living tool." But perhaps it helps us understand why Paul didn't go further in trying to change the social structure.

His advice to slaves makes even more sense when we consider what turned up in the garbage dump of a disappeared city in Egypt. The city was Oxyrhynchus. What turned up was a collection of writings called the Oxyrhynchus Papyrus, which includes a lot of information about the rise of Christianity during Roman times.

One document reports that a large group of slaves was set free because of the faithful devotion they showed to their master.

As Oxford lecturer Dirk Obbink describes this ancient report, Christianity "starts out as a small social phenomenon, then just takes over everything. . . . It's all reflected in the papyrus."

SUIT UP for spiritual battle

Put on all of God's armor so that you will be able to stand firm against all strategies of the devil.

EPHESIANS 6:11

In the most famous section of this letter, Paul tells Christians to suit up for battle.

Not against the Romans, but against forces that are more powerful: "We are not fighting against flesh-and-blood enemies, but against evil rulers and authorities of the unseen world, against mighty powers in this dark world, and against evil spirits in the heavenly places" (Ephesians 6:12).

Some Bible experts speculate that Paul closes his letter with this grim warning because he knows that most of his readers don't come from a Jewish background. Their spiritual background includes sorcery, astrology, and religious cults that prod their worshippers into ecstatic rituals that sound a lot like voodoo rites and demon possession in some African and Caribbean cultures.

To help his readers understand that this spiritual warfare is real, Paul seems to draw on word pictures from the Roman battlefront. But some Bible experts say it isn't so—that he creates his metaphor from Old Testament passages. Perhaps he has both in mind, knowing that Gentiles would connect with the battlefield images and that the Jews would pick up on the connections to their Bible.

PUT ON GOD'S ARMOR

Physical armor*	Spiritual equal	Jewish Bible background
Belt	Truth	"He will wear a belt of what is right and good and faithful" (Isaiah 11:5 NLV).
Body armor	God's righteousness	"He put on righteousness as his body armor" (Isaiah 59:17).
Shoes	Peace from the good news	"How beautiful on the mountains are the feet of the messenger who brings good news, the good news of peace" (Isaiah 52:7).
Shield	Faith	"My God is my rock, in whom I find protection. He is my shield, the power that saves me" (2 Samuel 22:3).
Helmet	Salvation	"He ... placed the helmet of salvation on his head" (Isaiah 59:17).
Sword	Word of God	"The LORD .... made my words of judgment as sharp as a sword" (Isaiah 49:1–2).

*Source: Ephesians 6:13–17

PHILIPPIANS

Philippi ruins 1861

MACEDONIA

Philippi

Thessalonica

Neapolis

MODERN-DAY GREECE

Troas

Aegean Sea

MODERN-DAY TURKEY

Adriatic Sea

GREECE

Olympia

Corinth

Athens

Ephesus

Olympic Games

Isthmian Games

CRETE

Mediterranean Sea

Voyage to Philippi. Prompted by a vision of a man pleading for help from Macedonia (Acts 16), Paul sails out of Troas, continuing his second missionary trip. Ten miles inland at the city of Philippi, named after Alexander the Great's father, King Philip, Paul starts the first church in Europe. This fledgling congregation proves intensely loyal, supporting their founding minister in good times and bad.

PAUL'S THANK-YOU LETTER

Funny thing about jail. It brings out the best in Paul.

He writes his most cantankerous letters when he's breathing free air. But in jail—as he is when he writes Philippians—he's usually gentle-spirited, reflective, and downright fatherly.

Philippians is a thank-you letter to a church that has a unique relationship with Paul. As far as the Bible tells us, it's the only church Paul lets support him with donations.

"You Philippians were the only ones who gave me financial help when I first brought you the Good News and then traveled on from Macedonia," he writes. "No other church did this. Even when I was in Thessalonica you sent help more than once" (Philippians 4:15–16).

In Corinth, where Paul spends nearly two years, he takes no money from Christians there. He earns his keep as a tentmaker.

In what is now Philippi, Greece, Paul starts the European church. The congregation meets at the home of Lydia, a businesswoman who sells "expensive purple cloth" (Acts 16:14). After Paul moves on, the church hears that Paul is in jail. So they put together a care package, perhaps money, warm clothes, and food. "I am generously supplied with the gifts you sent me with Epaphroditus," Paul writes (Philippians 4:18).

So he sends this letter of thanks back with Epaphroditus, who had gotten so sick on the trip to Paul that he nearly died. That certainly makes Paul all the more grateful for the church's help.

In this fatherly letter, Paul encourages the Philippians to
- "take an interest in others" (2:4);
- "live clean, innocent lives as children of God" (2:15); and
- "watch out for. . .people who. . .say you must be circumcised to be saved" (3:2).

MAIN POINT:

"Above all, you must live as citizens of heaven, conducting yourselves in a manner worthy of the Good News about Christ" (Philippians 1:27).

WRITER:

"This letter is from Paul and Timothy, slaves of Christ Jesus" (Philippians 1:1).

DATE:

Bible experts are divided over when Paul wrote this letter. Many say he wrote it sometime between AD 60 and 62, while he waited in Rome for his trial. The key to the date is figuring out where Paul was when he wrote the letter.

LOCATION:

Paul is "in chains because of Christ" (Philippians 1:13). But where? Many say Rome, since he refers to "the whole palace guard" (Philippians 1:13) and he sends greetings from believers in "Caesar's household" (Philippians 4:22). But the Romans have palace guards in key cities throughout the Roman Empire. And from time to time, members of Caesar's family visit those important cities. Other prime candidates for Paul's imprisonment include Corinth (about AD 50), Ephesus (between AD 54 and 56), and Caesarea (between AD 57 and 59). Wherever he's writing from, he's writing to the Roman city of Philippi in what is now Greece.

THE UPBEAT side of suffering

You have been given not only the privilege of trusting in Christ but also the privilege of suffering for him. We are in this struggle together.

PHILIPPIANS 1:29–30

Happier than any prisoner has a right to be, Paul starts his short letter by giving thanks.

He's grateful for the Christians at Philippi who have become his partners in ministry through their prayers, their financial support, and their continuing church work in their hometown.

Surprisingly, Paul says he's even grateful for his imprisonment and the suffering that goes with it. For two reasons:

- "Everyone here, including the whole palace guard, knows that I am in chains because of Christ" (Philippians 1:13).
- "Because of my imprisonment, most of the believers here have gained confidence and boldly speak God's message without fear" (Philippians 1:14).

Paul says he knows that the trial might end with his execution. But he says he's okay with that. In fact, he says that in eternity's long haul, that would be the best outcome for him personally: "For to me, living means living for Christ, and dying is even better" (Philippians 1:21).

But he says he expects that God will do as the Philippians have been asking and will free Paul to continue his ministry.

Paul warns that he won't be the last Christian who has to put his life on the line for the faith. Philippians will suffer, too.

If Paul writes this letter shortly before what many scholars say was his trial in about AD 62, the Philippians don't have long to wait for the suffering—if they have to wait at all.

Christians in Philippi already stand out as an odd group that refuses to worship the Roman emperor. And that's in one of only five cities in the Macedonian province that's designated as a Roman colony—privileged and exempt from many Roman taxes. Even worse,

---

Philippi, city of Alexander's dad

With gold and silver in the nearby hills and springs of water feeding the plain, the plot of land about 10 miles inland had excellent potential. So Greek settlers built a colony there in about 360 BC, naming it Krenides.

Alexander the Great's father, King Philip II of Macedon, saw the potential, as well. Two years after the colonists arrived, he overpowered them, took control of the settlement, built it up, and named it after himself: Philippi.

Romans took it next, capturing it in the 100s BC and creating the province of Macedonia in what is now northern Greece. Then they took steps to escalate the city's status:

- Building the Via Egnatia, the main land route connecting Italy with countries in the Middle East.
- Populating the city with retired army veterans, giving them plots of land.
- Giving Philippi the highest honor any provincial city could attain—"law of Italy" status. Roman law ruled and protected the people, who were considered Roman citizens, free to buy and sell property and exempt from many taxes.

Paul knew a well-placed ministry center when he saw one. Perhaps that's why he didn't bother stopping long at the seaport town of Neapolis. Instead, he walked half a day inland to Philippi. There he met a small group of Jews, told them about Jesus, and ended up planting the first congregation on the European continent.

Rome mysteriously catches fire in AD 64, and it's the Christians who take the heat. Emperor Nero blames them for starting the fire.

The persecution begins. Christians start dying on crosses, in prisons, and in the arenas.

"Don't be intimidated in any way by your enemies," Paul says. "They are going to be destroyed, but. . .you are going to be saved, even by God himself " (Philippians 1:28).

Not necessarily saved for longer life on earth, but saved for never-ending life with the Lord.

X-RATED ENTERTAINMENT

A few years after Paul writes to Christians at Philippi, warning them to prepare for suffering, the Roman Empire starts targeting the outlawed group.

Many Christians die entertaining packed arenas in cities throughout the Empire—fresh meat for wild animals and target practice for gladiators. The slaughter continues off and on for three centuries. Emperor Trajan (AD 98–117) hosts four solid months of games at Rome's Coliseum. Eleven thousand people die.

BE HUMBLE, like Jesus

Don't try to impress others. Be humble. . . . You must have the same attitude that Christ Jesus had.

PHILIPPIANS 2:3, 5

Whether Paul is writing to a church on the rocks or a church in the rose garden, he has one request that keeps showing up in his letters: unity in the congregation.

"Make me truly happy by agreeing wholeheartedly with each other, loving one another, and working together with one mind and purpose" (Philippians 2:2).

Easier said than done.

So Paul tells them how. And he does it with poetic flair. In fact, many Bible experts say Paul quotes one of the early Christian songs. Philippians 2:6–11 reads like the lyrics of a song that breaks into two stanzas. The first stanza (verses 6–8) describes Jesus' humility. The second stanza (verses 9–11) describes his reward.

Jesus was God, Paul reminds his readers. Yet Jesus took on the role of a humble servant, becoming human and dying on a cross—an execution method reserved for the lowest of lowlifes.

Yet for his willingness to go through all of this, God the Father elevated him to heaven's highest honor. And in time, Paul says, everyone will bow to this humble servant.

The implication is hard to miss.

Jesus is our model. He wants us to become God's servants, too—a plea Jesus made on the night before he died, when he washed the feet of his disciples. If stooping that low is not too low for Jesus, Paul would contend, then it shouldn't be too low for Jesus' followers. Or as Jesus put it, "I have given you an example to follow. Do as I have done to you. I tell you the truth, slaves are not greater than their master" (John 13:15–16).

Just as God rewarded Jesus, Paul further implies, God will reward those who follow Jesus' example.

Humility lasts a lifetime. But glory lives forever.

THE RACE of our lives

Forgetting the past and looking forward to what lies ahead, I press on to reach the end of the race and receive the heavenly prize for which God, through Christ Jesus, is calling us.

PHILIPPIANS 3:13–14

After Paul spends almost two years in Corinth, planting a church there, he starts doing something a little different. In past letters, he has often made a spiritual point by using an example from life—something familiar to the people. But after living in Corinth, he adds a new kind of illustration: metaphors from athletic competitions.

There's an excellent reason for this. On the outskirts of Corinth, the Greeks hold an Olympic-style competition every two years: the Isthmian Games. And about 75 miles west of Corinth, in the city of Olympia, they host a bigger event every four years: the Olympic Games.

Paul uses the illustration of a runner to make an important point in this letter.

The point he wants to emphasize is that he's on a spiritual journey. He hasn't arrived.

Some Greek philosophers teach that a person can reach intellectual enlightenment—a "complete mind." That kind of thinking worms its way into churches at Corinth and Ephesus. Some Christians start insisting that because of their religious training and insight, they've spiritually arrived. They're as perfect as perfect gets. Paul refutes that thinking in letters he sends to those churches. He advises his friend Timothy, pastor of the church in Ephesus, to avoid getting into debates with people full of "their so-called knowledge" (1 Timothy 6:20).

Greek runners in the homestretch of a race will lock their eyes on the post at the end of the track. It's the finish line. The prize that waits for them is a wreath—but not of gold, silver, or bronze. It's made from withered, pliable celery.

Like a seasoned Greek racer, Paul doesn't dwell on anything that happened earlier in the race—perhaps referring to his sufferings. Instead, his eyes are locked on the goal ahead: heaven. As he puts it in another letter, he's not running for a crown of celery that lasts only a short time. "We do it for an eternal prize" (1 Corinthians 9:25).

Stretching for the finish line. Greek athletes race for the prize: bragging rights and a wreath made of wilted celery. Paul says he races for a greater prize: eternal life. The Greeks hosted two major athletic competitions—the Olympics every four years and the Isthmian Games every two.

COLOSSIANS

DON'T GET CONNED INTO A FAKE RELIGION

Here's one more letter to a church in trouble.

That puts Colossians in Paul's "fix-it" file—a short stack of letters directed at churches in the Greek cities of Corinth and Thessalonica, and at churches in the Roman province of Galatia, in modern-day Turkey.

Bible experts are having a tough time trying to figure out exactly what Colosse's problem is. This letter is a bit like listening to one side of a phone conversation and trying to interpret what's happening on the other end.

Based on what Paul says, it looks like a minister named Epaphras started the church. And it's a reasonable guess that he did it during Paul's three-year stay at Ephesus, when Paul planted the church there during the AD mid-50s.

Now, perhaps almost a decade later, Epaphras tells Paul about a warped teaching that the Colossians are starting to warm up to. It's heresy. But which heresy?

Some guesses:

• **Mind-over-matter religion**—theological seeds that grow into a movement called Gnosticism a century later. Advocates teach that secret knowledge is the key to salvation.

• **Jewish Christianity**—arguing that even non-Jewish believers have to obey

Jesus' competition. "Lord of all being, father of the gods, and creator of men." That's one ancient description of the Egyptian god Amon, whose image is on display at the Louvre in Paris. Romans worship a crowded gallery of gods and spirits from all over the Roman Empire. An assortment of religions seems to converge in Colosse and rub off on Christians there.

Jewish laws to get saved.

- **Mix-and-match religion**—a blending of many teachings: Jewish, Gnostic, and local beliefs about evil spirits and astrology. That would give this accessorized heresy just enough truth to make it inviting—and more than enough fraud to make it dangerous.

Paul urges Christians in Colosse to trust the good news they were originally taught.

MAIN POINT:

"Just as you accepted Christ Jesus as your Lord, you must continue to follow him. Let your roots grow down into him, and let your lives be built on him.... Don't let anyone capture you with empty philosophies and high-sounding nonsense" (Colossians 2:6–8).

WRITER:

"This letter is from Paul...and from our brother Timothy" (Colossians 1:1). But many Bible experts doubt it. They doubt it for the same reasons they doubt Paul wrote Ephesians. In fact, there are some ideas that seem condensed from Ephesians, such as tips for a happy Christian family and characteristics of a Christian. Also, as with Ephesians, the author writes in long sentences with a lot of elegant prose. There are also some teachings not in letters that most scholars agree Paul wrote. Those who argue that Paul wrote this letter say it probably came late in his ministry, when his ideas were more developed. Writing style can change, too, they add. Especially when getting input from others, as Paul often did—Timothy in this case.

DATE:

Paul is writing from "prison" (Colossians 4:10). Similarities between Colossians and Ephesians suggest he wrote both letters about the same time—perhaps under house arrest in Rome (about AD 60–62).

LOCATION:

Paul wrote to Christians in Colosse, a small town about 120 miles east of Ephesus in what is now Turkey. That's roughly a week's walk from Ephesus, where Paul lived for about three years. But there's no indication Paul ever visited Colosse.

COLOSSE, OFF THE BEATEN TRAIL

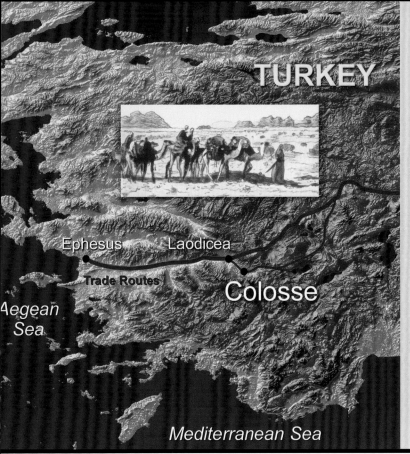

TURKEY

Ephesus   Laodicea

Trade Routes

Colosse

Aegean
Sea

Mediterranean Sea

A river town about 120 miles east of Ephesus, Colosse was once a busy city in the Lycus River Valley. But not in Paul's day.

A road is what made it busy in centuries past. Trade goods transported by land passed through Colosse on their way to Italy and Greece in the west, or to Turkey, Syria, Israel, and Egypt in the east.

But Romans later built a shortcut farther north, through Laodicea.

Colosse suffered. So did its main industry: textiles. The city was famous for producing dyed purple wool called *colossinus*.

It was perhaps only a few months after Paul wrote to Colosse that an earthquake nearly demolished the city—sometime between AD 60 and 64. Citizens rebuilt the town but later moved on—perhaps because of continuing earthquakes or repeated raids.

Today, all that's left of Colosse is a mound that archaeologists haven't started excavating.

FOR THOSE tempted to demote Jesus

Christ is the visible image of the invisible God. He existed before anything was created and is supreme over all creation.

COLOSSIANS 1:15

If Paul ever got around to visiting the Colossian church—located a week's walk from where he lived for about three years in Ephesus—it wasn't before he wrote this letter. He "agonized" over never visiting Colosse or the neighbor church at Laodicea, about 10 miles north (Colossians 2:1).

And now, in prison, he can't.

So he writes a letter, beginning with a greeting that's typical of Greek letters. Then he moves into a prayer—one that seems to set up what he intends to say about the problem the Colossians are facing. He prays that they'll thank God for the gift of their salvation. He's going to talk later about folks who say it's no gift at all—and that salvation is something they have to earn and protect.

One clue about the mysterious problem in Colosse shows up in what Paul writes next.

The words read like lyrics to an early Christian song about Jesus—and many Bible experts say that's exactly what Colossians 1:15–20 is. Paul also seems to quote a song about Jesus in another letter thought to have been written about the same time: Philippians 2:6–11. Perhaps songs about Jesus were on his mind in jail. He did seem fond of "singing hymns" in jail (Acts 16:25).

The song doesn't have a title. But it has a point: There's nothing superior to Jesus—who is God in the flesh. Jesus created everything, including the spirits in the "unseen world" (Colossians 1:16).

Bible experts say Jesus has competition in the church at Colosse. Some believers seem to be accessorizing their faith, mixing and matching Christianity with other religions, folk theology, and gods scattered around the empire. A sampling:

- **Jupiter.** Called Zeus among the Greeks, he's the top Roman god and chief of all the Roman gods.
- **Mithra.** Worshipped as a good spirit and ruler of the world, Mithra is popular among Roman soldiers and freed slaves—and widespread throughout Turkey. This faith has a lot in common with Christianity: honoring truth and courage and adopting Sunday as a holy day and December 25 as Mithra's birthday. It also teaches that there's a resurrection, judgment, and eternal life. On the other hand, it promotes astrology—the idea that the movement of planets and stars affects human destiny.
- **Local spirits.** Like some African tribes, many Romans believe that spirits live in trees, rivers, fields, and mountains. Romans give offerings to keep these spirits happy and wear amulets to protect themselves when spirits get upset.

THROWING OUT the rule book

Why do you keep on following the rules of the world, such as, "Don't handle! Don't taste! Don't touch!"? . . . These rules may seem wise because they require strong devotion. . . . But they provide no help in conquering a person's evil desires.

COLOSSIANS 2:20–21, 23

Chapter 2 of Colossians offers several more clues about what kind of warped teachings were making headway into the Colossian church.

- **"Empty philosophies and high-sounding nonsense that come from human thinking and from the spiritual powers of this world, rather than from Christ" (2:8).**

Mercury · Venus · Earth · Mars · Jupiter · Saturn · Uranus · Neptune

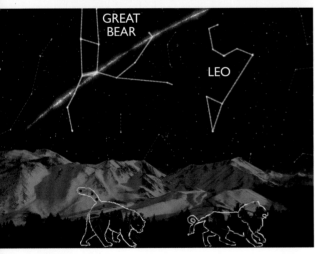

GREAT BEAR

LEO

Spirits in the sky. Like an arrow shot from a divine bow, a spray of stars courses through the northern sky. It soars above the constellation Leo, piercing the Great Bear. Many Romans in Paul's day believe that celestial spirits, planetary gods, and the movement of the constellations affect their day-to-day life. But Paul reminds Christians that Jesus created everything and "he disarmed the spiritual rulers and authorities.... He has set you free from the spiritual powers of this world" (Colossians 2:15, 20).

WICKED STARS

Astrology and hambone folk theology may have been part of the problem at the church in Colosse, some scholars say.

A church leader from Paul's century—Elchasai—may have given us a taste of this celestial hambone. His main teachings are preserved in a history written in the AD 200s by the church leader Hippolytus of Rome.

Here are three excerpts—bite-sized morsels that Paul would have found tough to swallow:

- "There are some wicked stars up there.... Don't do anything important when they're at their most powerful—especially on the days when the moon passes through them. That includes baptizing people."

- "Honor the Sabbath. That's one of the days when the wicked stars are strongest."

- "Don't start a big project the third day before the Sabbath. That's because three years into Emperor Trajan's reign, starting from the time he conquered the Parthians [modern-day Iran and Afghanistan, where astrology was revered], war will rage between the evil angels of the northern constellations. Because of this, all the wicked kingdoms of the world are in a state of confusion."

427

Philosophies is a word that, in ancient times, can refer to Greek ideas—such as those that teach eternal life but in a disembodied, impersonal state. The word can also refer to the occult: demons and sorcery.

Spiritual powers refers to demons. The Greek word behind this phrase shows up in Persian books about magic and astrology. The Persian Empire was the international center for the study of the stars and astrology. Based in what is now Iran, Persia once dominated all of Turkey.

Paul reminds the Colossians that Jesus is the head over every spirit being.

• **Insisting on circumcision, food restrictions, and observance of holy days (2:11–19).**

These clues seem to point to Jewish Christians who, throughout Paul's ministry, trail him like a clean-up crew devoted to mopping up his theological messes. Paul preaches that we're saved through faith in Jesus. Period. But many Jewish Christians insist that Christians also have to follow ancient Jewish laws, becoming Jews first and Christians second.

"When you came to Christ, you were 'circumcised,' but not by a physical procedure," Paul explains. "Christ performed a spiritual circumcision—the cutting away of your sinful nature" (Colossians 2:11). Paul adds that the Jewish rules were only shadows of the reality coming—and that reality is Jesus. This is a metaphor from Greek philosophy. Greeks teach that life on earth is just a shadow of the eternal life ahead. In time, what is real will replace what is shadow.

• **"Insisting on pious self-denial or the worship of angels" (2:18).**

Some Christians and Jews in the first century call on angels to help them, much like some Christians today pray to saints for help. Archaeologists have found many ancient protective amulets and other inscriptions from the region.

One inscription names the angels Gabriel, Michael, and Raphael. Then it offers this prayer: "Oh powerful angels, bless and prosper John and Georgia and this family while they live."

Angel magic. Etched into a jasper amulet is a plea for protection. A rooster-headed, snake-legged spirit raises a shield and cracks a whip to chase away evil. The amulet, worn as protective jewelry, invokes the power of four angels. Their names appear above the shield: Michael, Raphael, Gabriel, Ouriel.

Self-denial probably refers to the restrictive Jewish rules mentioned earlier. But it could involve some practices that later become widespread among Christians. These include fasting to the point of damaging the digestive system (as happened to the Protestant Reformer Martin Luther), carrying out self-beatings, and sleeping in the cold without a blanket. Christians did all of this in an attempt to express their devotion to God.

Paul admits that self-discipline can seem wise, but it really doesn't get at the heart of evil desires. It suppresses the evil desire instead of replacing it with a holy desire.

SPIRITUALLY NEW and improved

Put to death the sinful, earthly things lurking within you.

COLOSSIANS 3:5

As he does in his letters to the Ephesians and Philippians—which were also written from prison—Paul tells the Colossians how their new lives as Christians should look.

Colossian families should work hard at pleasing one another, Paul says.

And all Christians should consider their old, sinful lives as dead and gone.

"Since you have been raised to new life with Christ, set your sights on the realities of heaven," Paul says. "Think about the things of heaven, not the things of earth" (Colossians 3:1–2).

It's another way of saying, "Put God first." Jesus phrased it this way: "Seek the Kingdom of God above all else, and live righteously" (Matthew 6:33).

A list-maker, Paul offers a pair of lists to show the Colossians what exactly to avoid and what to pursue.

Avoid: lust, sexual immorality, greed, anger, malicious behavior, slander, dirty language, and lies.

Pursue: tenderhearted mercy, kindness, humility, gentleness, patience, forgiveness toward anyone who offends you, love, and unity in the church.

Paul closes this short letter by asking believers to keep on spreading the good news about Jesus, praising the Lord in songs, and living lives that attract nonbelievers to the faith. "Live wisely among those who are not believers, and make the most of every opportunity. Let your conversation be gracious and attractive" (Colossians 4:5–6).

1 THESSALONIANS

Church of the Archangels. Scattered throughout modern-day Thessaloniki, more than 300 churches stand in tribute to the staying power of Paul's ministry. This church, partly renovated, is dedicated to the archangels Michael and Gabriel—two among the "mighty angels" Paul said would return with Jesus (2 Thessalonians 1:7). Paintings on the original walls inside date the building to at least the 1300s. Several other churches in town are even older, one built in the 300s—the century Rome legalized Christianity.

LIVE HOLY LIVES UNTIL JESUS COMES

A nighttime vision convinces Paul to go to Greece. But given what happens to him in every Greek city where he preaches, some might say his vision was a nightmare.

Paul is traveling on his second missionary trip, planting house churches throughout what is now western Turkey. He intends to stay on the continent. But he has a vision: "A man from Macedonia in northern Greece was standing there, pleading with him, 'Come over to Macedonia and help us!'" (Acts 16:9). So Paul goes to Turkey's western port at Troas and catches a ship sailing north. He plants the first European church at Philippi. And he heals a demon-possessed slave girl, which strips away her power to tell the future anymore.

Her master is not impressed. He's livid. So he stirs up a mob, which ends up getting Paul beaten and tossed in jail with his associate, Silas. City officials later convince Paul to leave town.

He walks 90 miles along the Egnatian Way, a Roman road that brings him to the busy port town of Thessalonica. Paul preaches there for three weeks, converting some Jews and many non-Jews. But when tradition-minded Jews realize his teachings aren't what they'd consider kosher, they start a riot. Believers sneak Paul and Silas out of town that night.

Much the same happens at the next town, Berea. So Paul leaves for Athens, perhaps by ship. Athenian scholars laugh him out of town there, though some believe what he says.

That's when Paul moves on to Corinth, starting a church that will earn its reputation as the most trouble-plagued congregation in the New Testament.

It's in Corinth that Paul gets a status report on the church at Thessalonica. Some problems have cropped up. But Paul can't go back, so he comes up with an idea for dealing with troubles in the new churches he has left behind: correspondence school. He writes what most Bible experts say is his first surviving letter.

Based on what he says, the church seems to have three main questions:

- What should they do about the persecution they're facing?
- How should Christians behave?
- When is Jesus coming, and what happens to Christians who die before then?

MAIN POINT:

"Live your lives in a way that God would consider worthy" (1 Thessalonians 2:12).

WRITER:

"This letter is from Paul, Silas, and Timothy" (1 Thessalonians 1:1). But it's written in the voice of one person. So it probably represents the thinking of Paul more than that of his colleagues.

DATE:

Paul writes this letter in about AD 51, midway through his second missionary trip.

LOCATION:

Paul is writing from the southern Greek city of Corinth to new believers in Thessalonica. That's a Greek port town about a 300-mile walk to the north.

THESSALONICA: ANCIENT GREEK CAPITAL

This is probably a town Paul would have stayed at much longer, if angry Jews hadn't run him off.

It had everything he looked for in a major ministry center—like Ephesus and Corinth, where he had already set up churches.

A bustling port city of perhaps 100,000 souls, Thessalonica saw people coming and going by land and sea. Like Philippi, it sat on Greece's main east-west road: the Via Egnatia (Way of Egnatia). Merchants, soldiers, and others traveled on this road to cross Greece, heading toward Italy in the west or Middle Eastern countries in the east.

Thessalonica was also a "free city." That means Rome granted it special privileges such as the right to govern itself, freedom from military occupation, and exemption from some taxes.

Cassander, a former general of Alexander the Great, founded the city in 315 BC and named it after his wife, a half sister of Alexander. Romans captured it in 167 BC and later made it capital of the province of Macedonia, covering what is now northern Greece.

Ruins of the ancient city are scattered through the modern town of Thessaloniki. With a population of about 385,000, Thessaloniki is Greece's second largest city, after Athens.

Best port in Greece. A sprawling metropolis even in Paul's day, Thessaloniki has nearly four times more people now. The view southward, over the city, shows the best-protected natural harbor in Greece. Paul sails to Greece from Troas and then walks from Philippi to Thessalonica along the Egnatian Way—the main Roman road across the country.

JESUS SUFFERED, too

You received the message with joy from the Holy Spirit in spite of the severe suffering it brought you.

1 THESSALONIANS 1:6

New believers in Thessalonica are probably getting a taste of the nasty treatment that their founding pastor has been getting since he first set foot on the European continent: accusations, riots, beatings, and jail time.

Paul's ministry tips over two groups of people in Greek cities: business entrepreneurs and Jews who prefer their old-time religion. But mostly Jews.

Business entrepreneurs. Healing a demon-possessed slave girl is what gets Paul off on the wrong foot in Philippi. Suddenly, she can't tell the future anymore—which is a money-making venture for the girl's master. So he starts a riot that ends up getting Paul arrested, beaten, imprisoned, and asked to leave town.

Much the same thing happens later, in Ephesus. Paul's preaching about the one true God starts undercutting profits in the idol-making industry.

Jews. Paul is a Jew. And he believes that the good news he's delivering about Jesus is the next step for the Jewish faith. It's where God wants to take them—away from the laws of his old covenant agreement them and into the era of a new covenant. In this new arrangement, the Holy Spirit guides people toward holiness.

So as Paul moves from town to town, he introduces his message to worshippers in the synagogues. It's a natural place to start—Jews typically invite visiting Bible scholars to address the group. But it doesn't take long for the Jews to label Paul a heretic.

He tries taking them back into their Bible—a Christian's Old Testament—to show them how prophets predicted the life and ministry of Jesus. He convinces some. But most Jews can't handle the idea of God having a Son. And they're not keen about retiring the system of laws that God gave them through Moses. Old traditions die hard. So the Jews try to kill Paul instead.

After Paul sneaks out of Thessalonica for Berea, a group of angry Jews tracks him down. "When some Jews in Thessalonica learned that Paul was preaching the word of God in Berea, they went there and stirred up trouble" (Acts 17:13). Berean believers quickly escort him out of town for his own safety.

But the locals can't leave as easily as Paul does. For the Thessalonians, this city is their home. Jews and perhaps some local merchants start making life miserable for them.

Paul says he knows they are suffering "persecution from your own countrymen" (1 Thessalonians 2:14). But he commends the believers for remaining "strong in your faith" (1 Thessalonians 3:7). He also reminds them that they're not alone.

In suffering, Paul says, "you imitated the believers in God's churches in Judea who, because of their belief in Christ Jesus, suffered from their own people, the Jews. For some of the Jews killed the prophets, and some even killed the Lord Jesus. Now they have persecuted us, too" (1 Thessalonians 2:14–15).

HOW HOLY is holy enough?

God's will is for you to be holy.

1 THESSALONIANS 4:3

Some church groups say it's possible to live sin-free lives—to consistently fight off the temptation to do something that we know is wrong.

For biblical support, they often turn to Paul's first letter to the Thessalonians: "Now may the God of peace make you holy in every way, and may your whole spirit and soul and body be kept blameless until our Lord Jesus Christ comes again. God will make this happen, for he who calls you is faithful" (1 Thessalonians 5:23–24).

This sounds a bit like an echo from Jesus' Sermon on the Mount: "You are to be perfect, even as your Father in heaven is perfect" (Matthew 5:48).

Yet other Christians say it's unrealistic to expect sinless perfection in this lifetime—and that they've never witnessed it in anyone.

So what exactly is holiness?

Bible experts offer several ideas:

- Holiness is reaching a point of spiritual maturity that enables us to consistently refuse to do things we know are wrong. We'll make mistakes in judgment. But we won't choose sin over what we know God wants us to do.
- Holiness is a goal. We should follow the example of Jesus as best we can—growing from spiritual infants to strong, spiritual adults. On those occasions when we slip up and sin, God offers grace and forgiveness to those who repent.
- Holiness is a description of our one-of-a-kind God, who is superior to everything in creation. The Bible also uses this word to describe everything and everyone devoted to Him. Furnishings and utensils for the Jewish worship center were consecrated to "make them holy" (Exodus 40:9). We, too, become holy when we devote ourselves to God: "You. . .have been set apart as holy to the LORD" (Ezra 8:28). We become a one-of-a-kind people serving a one-of-a-kind God.

THE CHRISTIAN lifestyle

Live in a way that pleases God, as we have taught you.

1 THESSALONIANS 4:1

In most of his letters, Paul spells out the kind of behavior he expects to see from Christians. This is especially important in Thessalonica, where he stays for only about three weeks.

Holy seclusion. Many monks, like Baldassare Vallombrosano shown in this somber portrait from the 1500s, seek holiness by separating themselves from the sinful world. Some live alone. Others live in small monastic communities.

Jews have one set of expectations, much of which involves obeying Jewish rules and carefully following worship rituals. Romans have another. Many of the religions that the Romans practice don't require any particular moral behavior. If the worshippers offer the right sacrifices and follow the right rituals to keep their gods happy, all is well.

Not so for Christians. Paul reminds the Thessalonians that Christians

- stay away from sexual sin such as adultery;
- treat each other with loving respect;
- live quiet lives, minding their own business and working with their hands so that people who are not Christians will respect the way they live;
- "warn those who are lazy" (1 Thessalonians 5:14);
- encourage the timid;
- take care of the weak;
- are patient with everyone; and
- never stop praying.

SECOND Coming 101

We want you to know what will happen to the believers who have died.

1 THESSALONIANS 4:13

In the three weeks that Paul spends in Thessalonica, he couldn't teach much more than the basics of the Christian faith. But new converts have a lot of questions. And the Thessalonians are no exception. Christians there want to know what happens to believers who die before Jesus comes.

Apparently Paul—preaching about 20 years after the Resurrection—has told the Thessalonians that he expects Jesus to come back soon. That might explain why he later tells Christians in Corinth not to bother getting married unless their sexual desires are too strong to control—and that celibacy gives them more time to serve God (1 Corinthians 7:32). "The time that remains is very short," he says (1 Corinthians 7:29).

It seems as though Paul mistakenly thinks he'll live to see the second coming: "We who are still alive and remain on the earth will be caught up in the clouds to meet the Lord in the air" (1 Thessalonians 4:17). Later in his ministry, though, he seems to realize that the second coming isn't as imminent as he once thought.

In one of the clearest and most dramatic descriptions of the second coming, Paul writes as though he has seen a copy of the divine itinerary.

- Jesus comes with the sound of angel voices and the blast of a trumpet.
- Christians who are dead and buried rise from their graves.
- Christians still alive rise in the air, joining the celestial gathering.
- "Then we will be with the Lord forever," Paul says. "So encourage each other with these words" (1 Thessalonians 4:17–18).
- No one knows when this will happen. "The Lord's return will come unexpectedly, like a thief in the night" (1 Thessalonians 5:2).

2 THESSALONIANS

OBSESSION: THE SECOND COMING

Some new Christians can be a bit like little kids—you have to tell them more than once.

That's what Paul does in this second letter to a Greek church he started a few months earlier.

Paul spends a mere three weeks or so in Thessalonica, converting a group of people to Christianity. But then he gets run out of town by angry Jews. Moving on to Corinth, about a 300-mile walk south, he gets word about problems in the fledgling church at Thessalonica. So he writes them a pastoral letter of advice.

Apparently, Paul isn't happy with the response. He promptly turns around and writes another similar letter to them. But this time he comes across a bit more forcefully.

Persecution. In both letters Paul urges them to keep on serving God in spite of the persecution they're facing. But this time he adds, "God will provide rest for you who are being persecuted and also for us when the Lord Jesus appears from heaven" (2 Thessalonians 1:7).

Second coming. Paul also assures the Thessalonians that the second coming will take place in God's good timing. But in this letter he adds, "I ask you, my friends, not to be easily upset or disturbed by people who claim that the Lord has already come" (2 Thessalonians 2:1–2 CEV).

Work. In both letters he tells them to keep on working—perhaps a reference to some who have quit work because they think Jesus is coming back at any moment. This time Paul adds, "Those unwilling to work will not get to eat" (2 Thessalonians 3:10).

Robed and ready. Eager for Jesus' return, Christians have donned white robes and perched themselves on hilltops several times throughout history—at the bad advice of end-time specialists. But first on record to catch end-time fever is a small congregation of Greeks in the city of Thessalonica.

Clearly, Paul wants these believers to stop obsessing about when Jesus is coming back and to get down to the business of ministry.

That comes across in his prayer for the church. "We keep on praying for you, asking our God to enable you to live a life worthy of his call. May he give you the power to accomplish all the good things your faith prompts you to do. Then the name of our Lord Jesus will be honored because of the way you live" (2 Thessalonians 1:11–12).

JESUS' RETURN isn't next on the agenda

Let us clarify some things about the coming of our Lord Jesus Christ and how we will be gathered to meet him.

2 THESSALONIANS 2:1

Paul starts the letter with his typical greeting, introducing himself and his colleagues and asking God to bless his readers with grace and peace. Then he quickly mentions the persecution he knows is still going on in Thessalonica. It's probably coming mostly from tradition-loving Jews. They attack Christians as heretics, saying these people are intent on destroying the Jewish way of life and defaming God by insisting that he has a Son.

Paul then explains his main reason for writing. He wants to squelch rumors that Jesus has already come back.

It seems Paul isn't sure how the rumor got started—whether by a letter forged with his name or by a person claiming a vision. Either way, Paul says, "Don't believe them."

Certain things have to happen first, Paul says. Only then will Jesus come. Unfortunately,

MAIN POINT:

"Don't let anyone shake you up or get you excited over some breathless report or rumored letter from me that the day of the Master's arrival has come and gone. Don't fall for any line like that" (2 Thessalonians 2:2–3 THE MESSAGE).

WRITER:

"This letter is from Paul, Silas, and Timothy" (2 Thessalonians 1:1). But Paul speaks for the group. Some scholars say they doubt Paul wrote this short letter, for two reasons. The writing style is different from that of 1 Thessalonians. So is the teaching about Jesus' return; the first says Jesus will come unexpectedly, while the second says certain events will signal the return. Other Bible experts disagree. They say the letter is too short to analyze the writing—about 800 words in the Greek original. Also, the second letter simply expands on Paul's earlier teaching about Jesus' return; there's no clash.

DATE:

Those who say Paul wrote this second letter to the Thessalonians say he did so in about AD 51, perhaps after getting a reply to the first letter he wrote a few weeks or months earlier.

LOCATION:

Paul is writing from Corinth, a city in what is now southern Greece. He's writing to Christians in the northern Greek town of Thessalonica.

Paul isn't clear about what will happen first. He says a "man of lawlessness" will come, doing counterfeit miracles through Satan's power. "He will even sit in the temple of God, claiming that he himself is God" (2 Thessalonians 2:4).

Bible experts have tried guessing who this "man of lawlessness" is. One frequent guess is Emperor Caligula, who tried—unsuccessfully—to erect a statue of himself in the Jewish temple as a tribute to his divinity. But that was in AD 40, more than a decade before this letter. So that would support the idea that Jesus has already come or is next on the cosmic agenda.

So perhaps it's a reference to the Roman general Titus, who in AD 70 demolished the Jewish temple—which has never been rebuilt. Some scholars consider this a possibility. That's because of what Jesus said would happen before his return: "You will see what Daniel the prophet spoke about—the sacrilegious object that causes desecration standing in the Holy Place" (Matthew 24:15). Jesus added that the temple would be leveled and that God's people would be persecuted and killed—a prophecy that Titus fulfilled.

But Jesus also said that "the Good News about the Kingdom will be preached throughout the whole world, so that all nations will hear it; and then the end will come" (Matthew 24:14).

So Jesus' description is perplexing, too. Some scenes match the Roman army's destruction of Jerusalem. But other scenes don't.

Paul may have been parroting what Jesus said in an attempt to calm the Thessalonians' end-time hysteria. Perhaps Paul wasn't clearer because he didn't know how to be.

Many Christians speculate that the "man of lawlessness" is the future Antichrist. But that, too, is a guess.

DON'T BE a lazy bones

We hear that some of you are living idle lives, refusing to work.

2 THESSALONIANS 3:11

What most Bible experts really want to know is why these people aren't working.

In his first letter, Paul mildly encourages them to "make it your goal to live a quiet life, minding your own business and working with your hands, just as we instructed you before. Then people who are not Christians will respect the way you live, and you will not need to depend on others" (1 Thessalonians 4:11–12).

Later in that same letter he adds, "We urge you to warn those who are lazy" (1 Thessalonians 5:14).

But in this letter, Paul gets blunt. This is actually the third time he has dealt with the problem. The first was in person: "Even while we were with you, we gave you this command: 'Those unwilling to work will not get to eat' " (2 Thessalonians 3:10).

Paul gave them a good example to follow. As an apostle and a full-time minister, he could have taken up an offering or at least asked for free food. But while he was with them, he paid his own way—probably with help he got from the church he had just left, in Philippi. But he also worked with his hands, presumably at his family trade. He was a tentmaker. With an estimated 100,000 people in the port city of Thessalonica, there was certainly a market for tents and tent repair.

In this second letter, Paul advises Christians in Thessalonica to warn the lazy people among them—and to shun them if necessary.

Bible experts offer two main theories about why some of the people have stopped working.

Theory 1: Jesus is coming soon. Perhaps they didn't see the point of working. Why work for money when the end is near? You can't take it with you.

Some Christians who stopped working may have actually considered themselves spiritually superior to others. They, after all, had the faith to believe that Jesus was coming soon and that in the meantime God would take care of them.

Theory 2: Living off welfare. The Romans had at least a couple of welfare-like systems. First, they occasionally gave away free or cheap food to keep the masses happy. Also, some rich people in the empire would take on freebie-loving clients—a bit like celebrities today who attract entourages. Gratitude, emotional support, and an occasional chore were all the payback required.

In addition to this, early Christians created their own welfare system by looking out for each other—even selling off some of their property to provide food for the poor among them.

It remains a mystery why some Christians in Thessalonica stopped working, or who took care of them. But it's clear that Paul hates it. He thinks it sends the wrong signal about Christianity—that Christians are a parasitic people who feed off the hard work of others.

Paul wants nonbelievers to think highly of Christians.

"You don't work, you don't eat." Romans gather for a meal at a first-century restaurant. Paul writes to Christians in Thessalonica, warning them against laziness. He says if thinking about the second coming leaves them too busy to work, then they're too busy to eat.

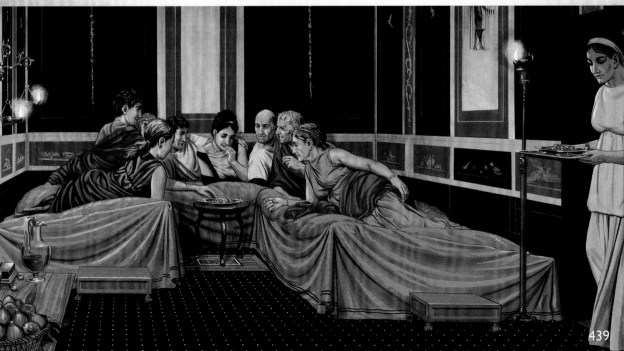

1 TIMOTHY

HOW TO BE A GREAT PASTOR

At some point in his travels with Timothy, Paul leaves the young man behind.

"When I left for Macedonia [northern Greece], I urged you to stay there in Ephesus," Paul writes (1 Timothy 1:3). The apostle Paul had spent nearly three years getting the Ephesus church up and running—far more time than he spent with any other church.

Ephesus is a megacity—one of the Roman Empire's main crossroads for traders and travelers. So Paul feels it's worth the extra effort.

Paul eventually leaves the church to continue his travels. When he and Timothy return later, he discovers a few problems cropping up. Some teachers are spreading ideas that clash with Paul's teachings. And there seems to be some trouble with the church leadership, along with distractions during worship services.

Paul apparently can't stay. But he leaves Timothy, his most trusted colleague, to straighten things out.

Afterward, Paul writes this letter to encourage Timothy and to give him some practical advice about how to

- deal with church people who are spreading warped ideas about Christianity;
- conduct worship services; and
- choose church leaders.

Like a son. Portrait of a young man painted in Roman times. Timothy, too, is young when he joins Paul's ministry team. Paul sends him on several long-distance assignments to settle problems in churches. Later, Paul assigns him to pastor the church in Ephesus. Their deep bond shows when Paul realizes he's about to die. He pens his last known letter: 2 Timothy. "Timothy, my dear son," he writes, "please come as soon as you can."

FRAUDS in church

Stop those whose teaching is contrary to the truth.

1 TIMOTHY 1:3

That's a mission statement—job one on Timothy's to-do list. Paul gives him that big chore.

Unfortunately, Bible experts can only guess what kind of contrarians Timothy is up against. But Paul gives us a few clues in scattered phrases.

"Myths and spiritual pedigrees. . . . they want to be known as teachers of the law of Moses" (1:4, 7). These could be Jewish Christians bragging about the heroes of the Jewish faith and telling legends about them. If so, they're also bragging about their bloodline connection to these heroes—something non-Jewish Christians can't do. These false teachers also teach that even non-Jewish Christians have to follow the laws of Moses. Throughout his ministry that's something Paul says is absolutely wrong.

"They will say it is wrong to be married and wrong to eat certain foods" (4:3). These people seem to be an early version of monks and other Christians who try to show their devotion to God by depriving themselves of what Paul calls "good gifts" God has given us.

"Unhealthy desire to quibble over the meaning of words" (6:4). Paul doesn't waste his time offering tips about how to debate philosophizing word people. In fact, he tells Timothy to "avoid godless, foolish discussions" (6:20). Instead, Paul points to the lifestyle of these spiritual frauds. Actions speak louder than words. And the actions of these frauds show that the one thing they want most of all is wealth.

MAIN POINT:

Paul wants to make sure that Timothy, pastor of the church at Ephesus, knows "how people must conduct themselves in the household of God. This is the church of the living God" (1 Timothy 3:15).

WRITER:

"This letter is from Paul. . .to Timothy, my true son in the faith" (1 Timothy 1:1–2). But some scholars aren't convinced. See "Who Wrote the Letters to Timothy and Titus?" page 445.

DATE:

It's uncertain when Paul writes this letter. Most Bible experts say it's after the events in Acts. They say Paul probably won his court case in Rome in about AD 62, went back to his travels, and wrote this letter around AD 63—or maybe a couple of years later.

LOCATION:

Paul is writing to Timothy, pastor of the church in the huge city of Ephesus—estimated population: several hundred thousand. It's the third largest city in the Roman Empire, after Rome and Alexandria, Egypt. Paul doesn't say where he's writing from. But he does mention that after leaving Timothy, he travels on to Macedonia. That's a Roman province in what is now northern Greece, where Philippi and Thessalonica are located. He may be writing from there.

The Sisters Grimké

Angelina Grimké
1805–1879

Sarah Moore Grimké
1792–1873

WOMEN'S LIB 1800s—CHRISTIAN STYLE

Southern Quaker sisters Angelina and Sarah Grimké wanted to do what they could to rally Americans against slavery. But when they started addressing mixed crowds of men and women, they were told they had gone too far.

Women aren't supposed to teach men.

Worse, the sisters took it upon themselves to teach ministers. They did this by writing an essay called "An Epistle to the Clergy of the Southern States."

Northern ministers came to the rescue of their southern colleagues. In a pastoral letter written in 1837, a council of Massachusetts ministers denounced all women preachers and reformers, whether or not the ladies had good intentions.

The sisters Grimké responded two ways:
- They added another cause to their portfolio: women's rights.
- And big sister Sarah wrote a formal reply:

"*I am persuaded that when the minds of men and women become emancipated from the thralldom of superstition and 'traditions of men,' the sentiments contained in the Pastoral Letter will be recurred to with as much astonishment as the opinions of Cotton Mather and other distinguished men of his day, on the subject of witchcraft. . . .*

"*The Lord Jesus defines the duties of his followers in his Sermon on the Mount. He lays down grand principles by which they should be governed, without any reference to sex or condition: 'Ye are the light of the world. . . .'*

"*Whatever is right for man to do, is right for woman. . . .*

"*Thine in the bonds of womanhood,*
SARAH M. GRIMKÉ"

Paul implies that Christians can spot fakes by watching them chase the money. The dust that these frauds kick up in their frantic run causes nothing but trouble in the church.

Paul tells Timothy to live and teach the opposite of the money-hungry Christians. God's people, Paul says, "should be rich in good works and generous to those in need, always being ready to share with others. By doing this they will be storing up their treasure as a good foundation for the future so that they may experience true life" (6:18–19).

PAUL'S PUZZLING worship advice

I do not let women teach men or have authority over them.

1 TIMOTHY 2:12

Chauvinist to the bone—or so it seems—Paul zeroes in on what he expects of women in worship services in the church at Ephesus:
- modest clothing;
- no garish jewelry or elaborate hair styles; and
- silence.

The advice of this bachelor seems extraordinary—dramatically out of sync with the tolerance he shows when he starts dishing out his tips for healthy worship services.

He begins innocently enough by urging Timothy to have Christians pray for everyone, including political leaders of the day. That means Emperor Nero, who, by the time Paul writes this letter, has already executed his own mother, his wife, and a brother-in-law.

By praying for such leaders, Paul says, "we can live peaceful and quiet lives marked by godliness and dignity" (1 Timothy 2:2). More important, this allows the church to keep spreading the good news about Jesus, since God "wants everyone to be saved and to understand the truth" (1 Timothy 2:4). Even Nero.

Peace is an important theme for Paul. He's constantly telling church members to live at peace with one another. Here, too, he tells Timothy that he wants people to pray together "free from anger and controversy."

Oddly, the next thing out of his mouth is perhaps the most controversial, divisive teaching in all of his letters.

It's easy to understand Paul's advice about dressing modestly. Women in this culture have an earned reputation for going to the temple—whatever temple that might be—dressed in their finest. One historian, Herodotus, described women going to a temple "in their best clothes, as if they were headed to a festival." But Paul doesn't want Christian women calling attention to themselves, as if they're trolling a red carpet on their way to the Oscars.

It's understandable, too, that Paul prohibits braided hair—for the same reason. Women of the day have recently started imitating ladies of the emperor's court, who, to an unfortunate extent, are no ladies at all. Paul has no problems with braids. In today's culture he might think they're cute, especially on little girls. But in his culture, this kind of raised hairdo apparently raised eyebrows.

But why would he order women to take a low profile in church—almost a no profile? He says much the same thing in a letter to another church: "Women should be silent during the church meetings. It is not proper for them to speak" (1 Corinthians 14:34).

What's especially perplexing about this is that elsewhere Paul compliments women leaders in the church: Phoebe, Lydia, Euodia, Syntyche, Junia, and Priscilla—the woman who enlightened the famous preacher Apollos with her insights about Jesus.

Junia, according to some Bible translations, held the church's top office. She wasn't just one of many apostles; she was one of the "very important apostles" (Romans 16:7 NCV). Other translations turn the meaning inside out, saying she was "highly respected among the apostles."

Scholars offer their guesses about why Paul tells women in Ephesus and Corinth to take a submissive role in church worship services.

Protecting marriage. He is actually telling the women not to publicly argue with their husbands about matters of faith. In this male-dominated society, Paul doesn't want the women humiliating their husbands.

Targeting two troubled churches. Some say Paul is addressing just these two churches, where women may be stirring up trouble. In other churches where the sexes are getting along fine, Paul doesn't order the women to back off.

Saying what he means. Some insist that Paul means exactly what he says—and that it's sound advice for all cultures in all times. Some scholars call this the complementarian view, though many women don't consider it a compliment. The theory here is that though men and women are equal, they have different roles in society. And men are the church leaders.

CHECKLIST for hiring church leaders

An elder must. . . .exercise self-control, live wisely, and have a good reputation.

1 TIMOTHY 3:2

Paul gives Timothy advice about what to look for in the church leaders he appoints.

There are two types of officials Paul talks about.

The first—a top leader in the local church—is called by some Bible translations an elder. Other Bibles call him an overseer or an official. These are the guardians or shepherds of the congregational flock.

The second type of leader is sometimes called a deacon, servant, or church officer. These might compare with volunteer workers and elected officials in the local church today.

Paul's checklist for both leaders is similar, with the exception that elders should be able to teach.

Qualifications from chapters 3 and 5:

Pastoral staff		
Above reproach	Enjoys having guests in his home	Not quarrelsome
Faithful to his wife	Able to teach	Not money-hungry
Self-controlled	Not a heavy drinker	Obedient, respectful children
Makes wise choices	Not violent	Not a new Christian
Good reputation	Gentle	Admired by non-Christians

Church workers, elected officers		
Well respected	Not dishonest about money	Passes evaluation by church leaders
Lives with integrity	Committed to the faith	Faithful to his wife
Not a heavy drinker	Lives with a clear conscience	Manages children and household well

One common question about this list is why Paul—a single guy—insists that married church leaders in both groups need to keep their families on a short leash.

Or as Paul puts it, "He must manage his own family well, having children who respect and obey him. For if a man cannot manage his own household, how can he take care of God's church?" (1 Timothy 3:4–5).

Conventional wisdom is that the pastor's kids are often among the most troubled in the church. Conventional wisdom also explains why: It's because the pastor is away from home too much.

Some Bible experts say that if Paul were writing for today's culture—and especially if he had kids of his own—he'd cut the church leaders some slack. But in Paul's day, when men ruled, the family was more of a reflection of the household leader than it is in our day when kids and parents often don't even eat together.

Paul also gives some practical advice for Timothy, as a church leader.

- Treat older men with respect, talking to them "as you would to your own father" (1 Timothy 5:1).
- Treat younger men like your brothers.
- Treat women like your mother or your sister, depending on their age.
- Take care of helpless people like widows who have no one else to look after them.
- Take your time selecting church leaders.
- Make sure the ministers are paid well. "Those who work deserve their pay!" (1 Timothy 5:18).
- Don't listen to an accusation against a minister unless it is confirmed by two or three witnesses.

Who wrote the letters to Timothy and Titus?

The Bible gives Paul credit for writing three letters to his former missionary colleagues—two letters to Timothy and one to Titus. Bible experts call them the Pastoral Letters. This short trilogy is a tight pack of advice on how to pastor a church.

Early church leaders included these letters in the Bible because they believed Paul wrote them. But many Bible experts today say the letters don't sound like Paul. They argue that one of Paul's students wrote the letters on his behalf—a common practice in ancient times.

A few key points and counterpoints in the debate:

The writing style and word choices are wrong. Paul didn't write like that.

Counterpoint: Paul, like others of his day, probably used professional writers and others to help him polish the writing—though he signed off on the content. The pro helping Paul with Romans actually added his own PS: "I, Tertius, the one writing this letter for Paul, send my greetings, too, as one of the Lord's followers" (Romans 16:22).

Paul uses key words differently in these letters. "Faith" becomes a substitute word for Christianity, though in Paul's other letters it means trust in Jesus.

Counterpoint: This could reflect the work of the professional writers helping Paul. Or it could reflect Paul's changing use of words over the nearly two decades he wrote such letters. Paul probably wrote these Pastoral Letters during his last years of ministry.

Some key ideas are missing. One big example: Jewish laws are obsolete now that the Holy Spirit has come to guide us.

Counterpoint: Paul is writing to a couple of colleagues who traveled with him, heard many of his sermons, and know the theological basics.

2 TIMOTHY

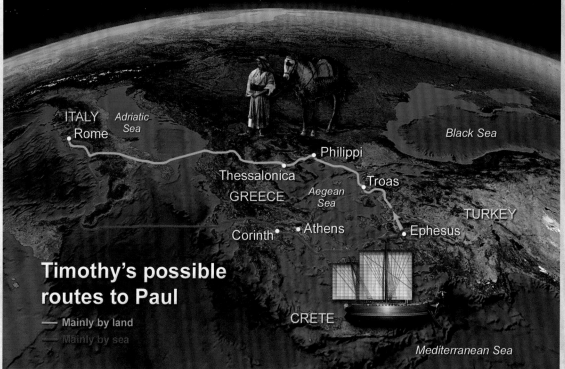

ITALY
Rome

Adriatic Sea

Black Sea

Philippi

Thessalonica

Troas

GREECE

Aegean Sea

TURKEY

Corinth

Athens

Ephesus

Timothy's possible routes to Paul

—— Mainly by land
—— Mainly by sea

CRETE

Mediterranean Sea

Come quickly. Writing from prison in Rome—and expecting execution soon—Paul asks Timothy to leave the church in Ephesus right away and come to him. With favorable winds, Timothy could have sailed the 1,000 miles in a couple of weeks. By land it could have taken a month or two, even traveling on the Roman Empire's stone-paved roads: the Egnatian Way across Greece and the Appian Way through Italy.

PAUL'S LAST WORDS

It feels a bit intrusive to read this intimate letter. It's too personal.

It's like leaning down and listening in on a dying father whispering a few last words to his son. These are the last surviving words of Paul, most scholars say. He's a prisoner in Rome. And he knows he's about to die in an execution for the crime of practicing an outlawed faith.

So the old bachelor writes one last letter to a young man he loves like a son: Timothy, pastor of the church in Ephesus.

There are just two main things Paul wants to say. One is a final piece of advice. The other is a last request. Both of these would make perfect sense to any hospice worker who has helped take care of the dying:

- Don't be afraid.
- Come and stay with me.

Paul knows that the persecution he's facing may spread like a fire throughout the Roman Empire, hurting Christians everywhere—especially leaders like Timothy. He doesn't want Timothy to give in to fear and to give up on the faith.

"Timothy, my dear son, be strong through the grace that God gives you in Christ Jesus," Paul writes. "Always remember that Jesus Christ. . .was raised from the dead. This is the Good News I preach" (2 Timothy 2:1, 8). Paul adds that this eternal life is for everyone who remains faithful to Christ.

Like many people about to die, Paul doesn't want to die alone. He wants those he loves most to be with him. So he asks Timothy to come quickly to Rome.

MAIN POINT:

"Never be ashamed to tell others about our Lord. . . . With the strength God gives you, be ready to suffer with me for the sake of the Good News" (2 Timothy 1:8).

WRITER:

"This letter is from Paul. . . . I am writing to Timothy, my dear son" (2 Timothy 1:1–2). Scholars debate this. See "Who Wrote the Letters to Timothy and Titus?" page 445.

DATE:

Most Bible experts say Paul probably wrote this letter shortly before the Romans executed him in about AD 67.

LOCATION:

Paul writes from his prison in Rome to his closest friend, Timothy, pastor of the church in Ephesus about 1,000 miles away.

TIMOTHY, JUST THE FACTS

Born: Lystra, in what is now Turkey

Mother: Eunice, a Jew

Father: Non-Jew

Joins Paul: About AD 49, during Paul's second missionary trip

Early ministry: Troubleshooter, delivering Paul's messages and solving problems at churches in Thessalonica and Corinth

Late ministry: Pastor of church in Ephesus

Receives Paul's last letter: About AD 67

Final years: Early church leaders say he became bishop at Ephesus; martyred in AD 97.

NO fear

God has not given us a spirit of fear and timidity, but of power. . . .
Don't be afraid of suffering for the Lord.

2 TIMOTHY 1:7; 4:5

Paul and Timothy have been close colleagues for almost 20 years. They linked up on Paul's second missionary trip, when Paul revisited Timothy's hometown of Lystra.

The son of a Jewish mother and a non-Jewish father, Timothy turns out to be a fine addition to Paul's ministry team. A child of both cultures, Timothy is especially equipped to build bridges of understanding between Jews and non-Jews.

In fact, it's on Timothy's first expedition that Paul starts using him as a church trouble-shooter—to carry Paul's letters and help solve problems in various churches. Timothy took Paul's messages to the second coming–obsessed church at Thessalonica and to the bickering church at Corinth. And when teachers with warped ideas started bugging the church at Ephesus, Paul appointed Timothy as the pastor, leaving him to stay there and work out the bugs.

Now, in the waning hours of his 30-year ministry, Paul writes Timothy a letter from prison. Paul gets reflective about their long partnership—even a bit nostalgic: "I remember your genuine faith, for you share the faith that first filled your grandmother Lois and your mother, Eunice" (2 Timothy 1:5).

Now Paul turns to his last words of advice for Timothy. Paul tells the young minister to keep on spreading the good news about Jesus—no matter what.

Easier said than done—especially if Bible experts are right when they set the year at about AD 67. Two-thirds of Rome had burned to the ground three years earlier. Nero, according to some ancient accounts, blamed the Christians—and then launched the first of many persecutions of the Christians.

But even in such a hostile setting, Paul tells his young colleague, "Never be ashamed to tell others about our Lord. And don't be ashamed of me, either, even though I'm in prison for him. With the strength God gives you, be ready to suffer with me for the sake of the Good News" (2 Timothy 1:8).

Suffering isn't Paul's last word, though. He quotes part of what may have been an early creed or maybe the lyrics of a Christian song.

If we die with him,
> *we will also live with him.*
If we endure hardship,
> *we will reign with him* (2 Timothy 2:11–12).

With this in mind, Paul tells Timothy to stay focused on the ministry. "Run from anything that stimulates youthful lusts. Instead, pursue righteous living, faithfulness, love, and peace. . . . Gently instruct those who oppose the truth. Perhaps God will change those people's hearts" (2 Timothy 2:22, 25).

Paul's dungeon. A short walk from the Coliseum in Rome, Mamertine Prison was the last residence of Paul and Peter. So say early Christian writers. Prisoners were dropped into the dungeon through a hole in the prison floor—the only way in or out. This stone-cold room might explain why Paul asks Timothy to bring him a coat. A shrine displaying an upside-down cross serves as a reminder that church leaders said Peter was crucified upside down.

"THE TIME of my death is near"

I have fought the good fight, I have finished the race, and I have remained faithful. And now the prize awaits me—the crown of righteousness.

2 TIMOTHY 4:7–8

Paul spends a lot of time in jail—some scholars estimate the better part of a decade. Four of those years are on a single charge described in Acts: causing a riot. He waits for trial two years at Caesarea followed by two more in Rome.

Making good use of his time in jail, Paul writes. Often he writes about what he'll do when he's released: "Prepare a guest room for me, for I am hoping that God will answer your prayers and let me return to you soon" (Philemon 22).

But not this time. He expects to die.

"You should know this, Timothy, that in the last days there will be very difficult times" (2 Timothy 3:1). Paul goes on to describe not just the sinful people of his day, but sinful people of any era in history: unforgiving, unloving, and with no self-control.

Paul and other New Testament writers often speak of their era as the "last days." We've now had about 2,000 years of last days. That's roughly equal to the time between Abraham and Jesus—beginning at God's first covenant agreement with humanity, through Abraham, and reaching to the start of his second covenant, through Jesus. Many Bible experts say the "last days" represents humanity's final era, however long God chooses to allow it to continue.

But for Paul, these are literally the last days: "My life has already been poured out as an offering to God" (2 Timothy 4:6). Most of his colleagues have left him. He has sent some on assignment. But others, he says, have abandoned him. The only one left is Luke, the Gentile physician thought to have written the Gospel of Luke, as well as Paul's story in the book of Acts.

"Timothy, please come as soon as you can," Paul writes. "Do your best to get here before winter" (2 Timothy 4:9, 21).

Paul asks Timothy to bring Mark, who had traveled with Paul and Barnabas on the first missionary trip almost 20 years earlier. Paul also asks for the coat he left in Troas and for his books and papers—probably to help him pass what is left of his time.

Paul's mention of Troas suggests that Timothy might have traveled by land and sea. He could have walked north to Troas and caught a ship to the port at Neapolis, near Philippi. From there he would have traveled westward across Greece on the Roman road called the Egnatian Way. A second ship would have carried him across a narrow strip of the Adriatic Sea into Italy. From there he would have traveled up the Appian Way to Rome and Paul.

The Bible never says if Timothy made the 1,000-mile trip or if he reached Paul in time. It would have taken Timothy about two months, walking 20 miles a day (common at the time) and resting on the Sabbath. Traveling by horseback or wagon could have cut this time in half. Sailing from Ephesus to Rome could have taken about two weeks, with favorable winds.

Early church writers said the Romans beheaded Paul—the quick death permitted for Roman citizens such as Paul. This execution, tradition says, took place at mile marker 3 on the Ostian Way on the outskirts of Rome. Christians built a chapel there in the AD 400s, after Rome adopted Christianity as the empire's religion. Above the chapel ruins stands a fitting memorial for the church planter. It's a church: Saint Paul of the Three Fountains.

Thumbs down. Emperor Nero delivers the death sentence. In AD 64 he begins widespread persecution of Christians—many of whom are slaughtered in arenas by gladiators and wild animals. Paul probably died during this period of intense persecution. Church leaders said the Romans beheaded him.

TITUS

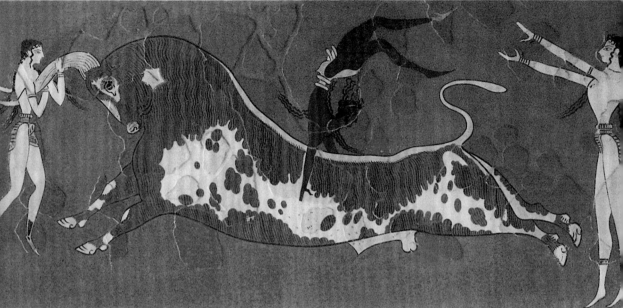

Bull jumping. Grabbing the bull by the horns, a jumper vaults over the bull's back. It's just a guess, but historians say bull jumping may have been an acrobatic sport during Crete's cultural heyday. That was back when Minoans ruled, 1,500 years before Paul. Eventually, Crete's culture took a dive. By Paul's day, Cretans were better known for slinging the bull: "Liars all," as one of their own writers described them. Paul agreed.

HOW TO PASTOR A CONGREGATION OF SCUM

A photocopier might have saved Paul from having to write this letter. He could simply have sent Titus a copy of 1 Timothy, erasing Timothy's name and writing in Titus's name. The two letters are just about that similar.

Paul would have added a PS for Titus, though. For this one-liner is unique to Titus's letter: "The people of Crete are all liars, cruel animals, and lazy gluttons."

Actually, these aren't Paul's words. He's quoting a Crete writer talking about his own island people. But Paul—in what sounds like prejudice gone wild—adds a nod of agreement: "This is true" (Titus 1:13).

The story behind this is mystifying. It seems that Paul writes this letter some time after the events in Acts. This assumes he was released from prison in Rome and continued his missionary travels. He and Titus end up on the small island of Crete, where they start several churches.

Paul then moves on to other missionary fields. But he leaves Titus behind on a short-term assignment. Titus's job is to organize the churches, appoint leaders, and continue teaching the people about Christianity.

Paul must assume Titus's job will be tough since the island people are descended from mercenaries, pirates, and swindlers. This might be why Paul says what he does about the people. Maybe he wants Titus to realize that any slow progress that might take place isn't his fault.

Though the Cretans may be spiritually sick, Paul knows they're just the kind of people who need Jesus most.

TOUGH love

Even one of their own men, a prophet from Crete, has said about them, "The people of Crete are all liars, cruel animals, and lazy gluttons." This is true. So reprimand them sternly.

TITUS 1:12–13

After writing an extended greeting that's typical in letters of the day, Paul reminds Titus that he's on the island of Crete to "complete our work there and appoint elders in each town" (Titus 1:5).

Then Paul gives Titus much the same job description and advice he writes in his first letter to Timothy, who is pastoring the church in Ephesus.

At the top of Titus's to-do list is finding pastors for each of the churches scattered around the island. It's actually a bit funny to read Paul's description of what kind of people Titus should look for. From among the island's inventory of "liars, cruel brutes, and lazy gluttons," Titus needs to find men who "live a blameless life" (Titus 1:6).

Perhaps it would have been easier to find such men in the time of Abraham to

MAIN POINT:
"Promote the kind of living that reflects wholesome teaching" (Titus 2:1).

WRITER:
"This letter is from Paul. . . . I am writing to Titus, my true son in the faith that we share" (Titus 1:1, 4). Scholars debate this. See "Who Wrote the Letters to Timothy and Titus?" page 445.

DATE:
It's uncertain when Paul writes this letter. Most Bible experts say it's after the events in Acts. They say Paul probably won his court case in Rome in about AD 62 and went back to his travels. He probably wrote this letter about the same time he wrote 1 Timothy: around AD 63, or maybe a couple of years later.

LOCATION:
Paul is writing to Titus, who is selecting leaders for new churches on the island of Crete about 100 miles south of Greece. Stretching some 150 miles east to west and 35 miles north to south, Crete is about the size of Rhode Island. Paul says he's sending a replacement for Titus. And he asks Titus to meet him at Nicopolis. There are several cities by that name. Perhaps Paul is referring to the port town in western Greece.

Rome
Adriatic Sea
ITALY
GREECE
Nicopolis
Aegean Sea
Corinth
Athens
Ephesus
Black Sea
TURKEY
Thera volcano eruption
CYPRUS
CRETE
Mediterranean Sea
ISRAEL
Jerusalem
EGYPT

Titus' Mission Field

Moses—1,500 to 2,000 years earlier. That's when the island flourished under the rule of the Minoans, a name that comes from their legendary ruler, Minos. The people produced such wonderful architecture, statues, pottery, paintings, and metalwork that mainland Greeks came to the island to study the art and architecture.

Tragically, the elegant Minoan civilization collapsed by about the 1200s BC—for mysterious reasons. Perhaps earthquakes destroyed the infrastructure. Or maybe society crumbled gradually from the lingering effects of a tidal wave spawned centuries earlier by the eruption of a volcano on nearby Thera. The wave could have wiped out important Minoan cities, as well as the fleet, which harbored on the northern shores. Invaders might be to blame, too.

This culturally gifted island descends into a culturally deprived hideout for mercenaries and pirates. And it becomes a port of last resort for traders on their way to somewhere else. Jews on the island eventually ask the Romans to restore calm—which they do by conquering the island in 67 BC.

But old habits die hard—and it apparently takes more than a century. For even by Paul's day, Cretans are still drawing harsh criticism.

Paul has given Timothy a checklist for the kind of church leaders to appoint in Ephesus. Now he gives Titus a similar one. Cretan pastors should

- be faithful to their wives;
- have well-behaved children;

- not be arrogant or quick-tempered;
- not be heavy drinkers, violent, or dishonest;
- enjoy having guests in their homes; and
- be able to teach others about the Christian lifestyle.

Paul also offers some advice about tradition-loving Jews who live on the island. They insist that Christians observe the Jewish laws, including the rite of circumcision. These are the same people Paul talks about in chapter 3—people who brag about their Jewish pedigree.

"They must be silenced," Paul says, "because they are turning whole families away from the truth by their false teaching" (Titus 1:11).

If Titus can do that, he'll be doing what Paul himself hasn't been able to do anywhere, as far as the Bible reports. Before the century's end, Judaism will make a formal break with Christianity, which had started as a Messiah movement within the Jewish religion. Jews who believe that Jesus is the Messiah will be excommunicated from the synagogues.

Paul's advice for dealing with Jewish Christians in Crete is that Titus shouldn't waste time arguing with them. "Give a first and second warning. After that, have nothing more to do with them" (Titus 3:10).

WHAT a Christian looks like

We should live in this evil world with wisdom, righteousness, and devotion to God.

TITUS 2:12

Paul offers Titus some age-appropriate, circumstances-appropriate advice.

Older men. Paul tells Titus to teach them self-control and patience so they'll make wise choices and earn the respect that younger people give them. And since others look up to them, they of all people need to understand the Christian faith.

Older women. They shouldn't bad-mouth people or drink too much. And they should become mentors, teaching young women how to be good wives and mothers.

Young men. They should learn from Titus's example of what it means to be kind and helpful toward others.

Slaves. They should try their best to please their masters. (For more on this, see "Masters and Slaves," page 414.)

Roman citizens. "Remind the believers to submit to the government and its officers. They should be obedient, always ready to do what is good" (Titus 3:1). Paul wants Christianity to become one of the shining lights in the Roman Empire—a spiritual power for good in an evil world.

"I want you to insist on these teachings so that all who trust in God will devote themselves to doing good. These teachings are good and beneficial for everyone" (Titus 3:8).

CRETE

Phoenix

Fair Havens

Wintering in Phoenix. Saint Paul's Beach in the bay at right commemorates the winter that should have been. Sailing to Rome, Paul hoped to winter in balmy Phoenix, Crete, just beyond this bay. The captain had refused to anchor at their earlier port in Fair Havens. Bad decision. A typhoon intercepted the ship and pummeled it 600 miles west before running it aground.

CRETE CRITICS

It's a beautiful island laced with warm beaches and trimmed with majestic mountains. No need to choose between beach and mountain—not when you can have both. That's why tourism is Crete's biggest moneymaker.

People today say wonderful things about the land and the hospitable people who live there.

But folks in Bible times weren't nearly so complimentary:

"The people of Crete are all liars, evil brutes, and lazy gluttons."
—Epimenides
Cretan prophet, 600s BC

"Kretizo."
—Ancient verb form of "Cretan." It means "lie," as in "You lied to me!" The nation's most infamous lie was its claim to having land sacred enough for the tomb of Zeus, chief god of Greece.

"Cretans are always liars. A tomb, O Lord, Cretans built for you. But you did not die, for you are forever."
—Callimachus
Cretan poet, 200s BC, Hymn to Zeus

"All of his soldiers abandoned him except for the Cretans, who followed him not out of good will, but because they were as devoted to his riches as bees to their honeycombs."
—Plutarch
Greek historian, AD 100s, reporting the story of an evil king, The Life of Aemilius

"He was trying to play the Cretan with a Cretan."
—Polybius
Greek historian, 100s BC, writing about a would-be king trying to cheat a Cretan, The Histories.
It was like an amateur crook trying to swindle a pro. The newbie didn't have a prayer.

PHILEMON

A FAVOR FROM A CHRISTIAN SLAVE OWNER

In Paul's shortest surviving letter—only one chapter—he asks a Christian slave owner named Philemon (fi-LEE-muhn) to show mercy to a runaway slave named Onesimus (oh-NESS-uh-muhs).

Philemon isn't just a Christian. He's a Christian leader. A congregation meets in his home. Christians typically meet in homes because they don't have church buildings. They don't start building churches for another 300 years—that's how long it takes Rome to legalize Christianity.

Paul is writing "in these chains for preaching the Good News" (Philemon 13). He doesn't say where he is. Perhaps he's in Rome or Ephesus or one of the many other cities where he spent time in jail.

Many Bible experts guess Rome. That's because during Paul's two-year house arrest there, while waiting for his trial, he has unusual freedom. He "welcomed all who visited him, boldly proclaiming the Kingdom of God and teaching about the Lord Jesus Christ. And no one tried to stop him" (Acts 28:30–31).

Perhaps it's here that he meets Onesimus, Philemon's runaway slave. Wherever the meeting takes place, Paul converts Onesimus and convinces him to go back to his master. If Paul could go with him to plead in person with the slave master to forgive the runaway, he most likely would. But he can't. So Paul writes this letter asking Philemon to do him a big favor.

It's not just a plea for Philemon to forgive Onesimus. It's a not-so-subtle hint for Philemon to free the slave and send him back to Paul.

Slave labor. Dressed in the humble clothes of a slave, a Roman worker in a pottery shop carries a tray of merchandise, perhaps to set it out for display. Some historians estimate that one in three people living in the Roman Empire were slaves.

GIFT OF persuasion

I am confident as I write this letter that you will do what I ask and even more!

PHILEMON 21

Paul knows how to apply pressure to nudge people in the right direction. His letter to Philemon is probably the best example of this.

In several other letters, Paul teaches that slaves should do all they can to please their masters. Now that he meets and converts a runaway to Christianity, he shows his consistency. He advises the slave, Onesimus, to go back to his master.

But Paul sends him back with a letter—one that shows what Paul thinks about slavery.

Bucking conventional wisdom, Paul considers slaves equal to everyone else—at least in the eyes of God and God's people. Paul doesn't become a political activist who stirs up an abolitionist movement to abolish slavery throughout the Roman Empire. He digs deeper than surface behavior. Instead, he urges Christians to treat one another with love. He probably realizes that when Christians start doing this, masters will become servants and slaves will become free.

MAIN POINT:

Paul asks a church leader named Philemon to welcome home a runaway slave: Onesimus.

WRITER:

Paul writes this letter to Philemon, a Christian slave owner who hosts church meetings in his home.

DATE:

It's uncertain when Paul writes this letter because it's uncertain where he is at the time. He says he's in prison. But where? Many guess he wrote this letter during his two-year arrest in Rome, which started in about AD 60.

LOCATION:

Onesimus is a runaway slave from Colosse, a city in what is now western Turkey. He is converted under Paul's ministry, but it's uncertain where. Many Bible experts speculate that it's in Rome, during Paul's two years of house arrest, since he was allowed to preach during that time. Others call attention to the fact that the distance between Colosse and Rome is more than 1,000 miles, requiring a ship for part of the journey. So Rome seems out of reach for a runaway slave, unless he stole some money. Another possibility is Ephesus, a one-week, 120-mile walk west of Colosse.

Yet Paul is anything but gentle in this letter. He's doing just about everything possible to convince Philemon to show kindness to Onesimus. His persuasion tactics range from offering compliments to making veiled threats.

Paul's persuasive statement	Reading between the lines
"I am writing to Philemon. . .and to the church that meets in your house" (1–2).	"If you refuse to do what I'm about to ask, I hope the Christians in your church will talk some sense into you."
"I keep hearing about your faith in the Lord Jesus and your love for all of God's people" (5).	"I hear that you love all people, including slaves."
"I am praying that you will put into action the generosity that comes from your faith" (6).	"If you don't do what I'm about to ask, you're not acting like a Christian."
"I am boldly asking a favor of you. I could demand it in the name of Christ because it is the right thing for you to do. But because of our love, I prefer simply to ask you" (8–9).	"I'm an apostle—your boss. I could order you to do what I'm about to ask. And if you don't, I just might."
"I became his father in the faith while here in prison" (10).	"Treat Onesimus like he's my own son."
"I wanted to keep him here with me. . .and he would have helped me on your behalf. But I didn't want to do anything without your consent" (13–14).	"Give your consent. Send him back to me."
"He is no longer like a slave to you. He is more than a slave, for he is a beloved brother" (16).	"He's not just my son. He's your brother. Which, by the way, makes you my son, as well. So call me Dad, and do what I say."
"If you consider me your partner, welcome him as you would welcome me" (17).	"If you don't, you're no partner of mine."
"If he has wronged you in any way or owes you anything, charge it to me. . . . I won't mention that you owe me your very soul!" (18–19).	"Okay, I mentioned it. So how could you possibly charge me anything when you owe me everything? Didn't Jesus tell a parable about this kind of hypocrisy?" (It's the parable of the unforgiving debtor, Matthew 18.)
"I am confident as I write this letter that you will do what I ask and even more!" (21).	"And if you don't, you'll be sorry."
"Prepare a guest room for me, for I am hoping that God will answer your prayers and let me return to you soon" (22).	"If you don't do as I ask, you'll have some explaining to do when I come to town."

The Bible doesn't tell us how things turned out or if Paul ever made it to Colosse. But about 50 years later, a church leader named Ignatius wrote a letter to the church leader at neighboring Ephesus: Bishop Onesimus.

Perhaps he was the very same slave who became famous in this region, as Christian leaders started passing Paul's letters from one church to another.

SLAVE-EATING EELS

A cruel slave master, Vedius Pollio of Rome, stocked a pool with vicious, sharp-toothed moray eels—so he could recycle bad slaves into fish bait.

Moray eel

While entertaining the emperor Augustus one day, Pollio became livid at one of his slaves for accidentally breaking a crystal goblet. At once, Pollio ordered the slave to be fed to the eels.

The slave dropped to his knees before the emperor and pled for his life. Augustus tried to convince Pollio to overlook the man's mistake. But Pollio refused. So Augustus asked Pollio to bring him every goblet in the house. Augustus then ordered all of them smashed.

Pollio could no longer kill the slave for breaking one goblet accidentally when the emperor broke all the rest on purpose.

—Source: Dio Cassius (about AD 150–235), *Roman History*

Emperor Augustus
(63 BC–AD 14)

Rome • ITALY
Adriatic Sea
GREECE
Aegean Sea
Corinth • • Athens
Ephesus •
TURKEY
• Colosse
Black Sea
Mediterranean Sea

Onesimus, Slave on the Run from Colosse

Running to where? The runaway slave Onesimus leaves his master's home in Colosse, perhaps with some money and supplies he has stolen. He later meets Paul, who converts him to Christianity. Paul may have been under arrest as far away as Rome or as close as Ephesus.

HEBREWS

THE SYNAGOGUE IS NO PLACE FOR A JEW

Good Jews belong in church.

That's the bottom line in this letter—which, at 13 chapters, is the New Testament's longest sustained argument on a single topic.

The background to the letter is anyone's guess. Most Bible experts say the book is written mainly to Christians who are Jews by race. This would help explain how the book got its name, since "Hebrew" is an ancient term for the Jewish people.

Scholars reading between the lines also guess that some of these Jewish Christians are giving up on Christianity and going back to their old-time religion. These scholars speculate that it's because of the increasing persecution Christians are facing.

If this letter is written in the AD mid-60s, as many Bible experts propose, Emperor Nero has just unleashed a world of hurt on Christians who are practicing their outlawed religion. He blames them for setting fire to Rome in AD 64. By this time, tradition-minded Jews have already been persecuting Christians for more than 30 years. So the hardship has already been getting old. And now it's getting worse.

Sabbath at the synagogue. In a portrait from the late 1800s, Jews gather at their synagogue during the holiest day on the Jewish calendar: Yom Kippur. Also called the Day of Atonement, this is when Jews atone for sins committed during the past year. The writer of Hebrews argues that Judaism, with its emphasis on tradition, rules, and rituals, is now obsolete—replaced by Christianity.

To escape it, some Jewish Christians have apparently quit the church and gone back to their local synagogue. And others are considering doing the same.

Big mistake, according to the writer of Hebrews.

There's nothing to go back to. God's agreement with Abraham, which set the Jews apart as his chosen people, has expired—just as the Jewish Bible said it would. God had promised to make a new covenant.

The writer's thesis is that Christianity is not only God's planned replacement for Judaism—it's new *and* improved. And the writer drives this thesis home with three big points:

- Jesus is better than any of the revered Jewish heroes, including Moses and even the heavenly angels.
- Jesus is better than the high priest—the spiritual leader of the Jews.
- Jesus' sacrifice is better than animal sacrifices.

MAIN POINT:

The law-abiding Jewish religion is obsolete: "When God speaks of a 'new' covenant, it means he has made the first one obsolete. It is now out of date" (Hebrews 8:13).

WRITER:

The book doesn't name the writer.

Many early church leaders—following the lead of Augustine in the AD 300s—said Paul wrote it. But most scholars today doubt it for many reasons:

- The Hebrews writer says he learned the good news of salvation from ministers Jesus personally sent out (Hebrews 2:3). But Paul said he didn't get his message secondhand. He's one of those ministers the writer is referring to—someone personally commissioned by Jesus.
- Hebrews is a smooth-flowing essay, while Paul's letters are choppy, with abrupt transitions.
- Hebrews is a literary standout, written in the most polished Greek of the New Testament.

- The writer quotes only from the Greek version of the Old Testament, instead of the Hebrew original that Paul knew well.

DATE:

Many Bible experts guess that the book was written during a six-year window of opportunity—after Emperor Nero started persecuting Christians in AD 64, but before AD 70. It was in AD 70 that the Romans tore down the Jerusalem temple, ending the Jewish system of worshipping God by offering animal sacrifices. This is probably something the writer would have mentioned, since the book's main point is that the Jewish religion is obsolete. But there's no mention of it.

LOCATION:

Hebrews reads like an open letter to Christians—especially Jewish Christians—scattered all over the Roman Empire. But some scholars say it could have been directed to Jewish Christians in Rome.

The first person on record to quote Hebrews was the church leader Clement of Rome, writing a letter in about AD 97.

JESUS, a better hero

Jesus deserves far more glory than Moses.

HEBREWS 3:3

Christianity revolves around its namesake: Christ. That word *Christ* is actually a title describing Jesus as the Messiah: Jesus Christ. So instead of Jesus, Ph.D., it's Jesus, Messiah. The writer of Hebrews knows how critical it is for Jewish Christians to accept Jesus as the Messiah whom the prophets said would come to save Israel and the world.

Jews have to be fully convinced of this, because Christianity radically changes the Jewish religion. It changes their worship practices, the way they seek forgiveness, and even the way they approach God. Everything changes with Jesus.

But in a religion in which traditions and rituals are treated as holy—and have been for well over a thousand years—these sacred practices die hard.

But die they must. Christianity, says the Hebrews writer, is the next step in God's plan of salvation. And it's a step the prophets predicted. They said the covenant, or agreement, God made with the Jews would be replaced. That old agreement required Jews to observe the laws and worship rituals God gave Moses. "But this is the new covenant I will make with the people of Israel. . . . I will put my instructions deep within them, and I will write them on their hearts" (Jeremiah 31:33; quoted in Hebrews 8:10).

"When God speaks of a 'new' covenant," the Hebrews writer explains, "it means he has

One last prayer. Entertainment for Roman crowds and fresh meat for wild animals, Christians huddle together for prayer. Surrounding them are human torches—a technique the Roman emperor Nero is said to have used once to light the evening entertainment. The crowds reacted with disgust, perhaps at the smell. Nero started persecuting Christians in AD 64, apparently after accusing them of setting fire to Rome. Because of the persecution, some Christians abandoned the faith.

made the first one obsolete. It is now out of date and will soon disappear" (Hebrews 8:13).

Jesus' arrival marks the beginning of this new covenant. But about 30 years after the start of Christianity, some Jewish Christians are beginning to have their doubts—especially now that the Romans have joined the tradition-minded Jews in persecuting Christians.

So the writer of Hebrews appeals to the Jewish Bible, traditions, and widespread Jewish beliefs to make his case that the new covenant is here and that it's better than the old one.

Angels. Jews of the day believe that angels are revered beings holy enough to stand in the presence of God. But the writer of Hebrews says Jesus is better.

Quoting Psalm 2:7 and 110:1, the writer says, "God never said to any angel what he said to Jesus: 'You are my Son.' . . . 'Sit in the place of honor at my right hand' " (Hebrews 1:5, 13).

Angels actually worship Jesus. This, too, was predicted—by none other than Moses. The writer quotes a song of Moses that many Jews of the day think refers to the Messiah: "Rejoice with him, you heavens, and let all of God's angels worship him" (Deuteronomy 32:43; quoted in Hebrews 1:6). The "him" refers to the Messiah.

Moses. A bit like an angel on earth, Moses was able to stand in the presence of God: "The LORD would speak to Moses face to face, as one speaks to a friend" (Exodus 33:11). Moses also delivered God's laws to the Israelites—every one of the worship rituals, kosher laws, and religious traditions that they followed.

But just as Jesus is better than the angels, he is better than Moses, too.

CHRISTIANITY: OUTLAW RELIGION

Romans outlawed many troublesome religions—and Christianity qualified.

It wasn't that Christians tried to stir up trouble. They were a peace-loving people. But some of their teachings riled the Jews and fed the rumor mill.

Riled Jews

Observant Jews hated Christianity because Christians taught that

- God has a Son who is also divine, though the Jewish Bible says there is only one God.
- Now that the Messiah—Jesus—has come, Jewish laws are obsolete. Faith in Jesus is the way to salvation.

The Romans outlawed Christianity partly because of the violent response it provoked among the Jews. In the early decades of Christianity, most Christians were Jews who worshipped in synagogues with other Jews. The difference is that Jewish Christians, unlike traditional Jews, believed that the promised Messiah had come, and his name was Jesus.

Arguments between the two groups erupted into loud debates, riots, arrests, trials for blasphemy, executions, and sometimes murder. In AD 49, the bickering apparently grew so intense in Rome that Emperor Claudius ordered all Jews expelled from the capital. They returned after he died five years later.

Rumor mill

Romans were also troubled by rumors that Christians practiced the following:

- **Cannibalism.** That rumor stemmed from a misunderstanding of the Lord's Supper, in which Christians ate bread and drank wine as a way of remembering the Crucifixion. Broken bread represented Jesus' broken body. Wine represented his blood.
- **Incest.** Christians called other Christians "brothers" and "sisters." And they greeted one another with a kiss on the cheek, typical in Middle Eastern culture.
- **Treason.** Christians worshipped "Jesus as Lord." They refused to worship the emperor.

In the long haul, Christian perseverance won. The Roman emperor Constantine legalized Christianity in AD 313. And 10 years later it became the Roman Empire's official religion.

JESUS, a better priest

We have a great High Priest who has entered heaven, Jesus the Son of God. . . . This High Priest of ours understands our weaknesses, for he faced all of the same testings we do, yet he did not sin.

HEBREWS 4:14–15

The high priest is the Jewish nation's spiritual leader. He's an advocate who represents the people before God. This priest is the only human being allowed to enter the holiest room in the Jewish worship center: the Holy of Holies. This is the room where Jews once kept the gold-covered chest that held the original 10 Commandments. The chest, called the Ark of the Covenant, is gone by this time. Babylonian invaders from what is now Iraq probably carried it off when they sacked Jerusalem 600 years earlier.

But the sacred room still exists in the Jerusalem temple of the writer's day. The high priest goes in there only one day a year: on the Day of Atonement (Yom Kippur). There, he sprinkles blood from a sacrificed animal to atone for his sins during the past year, as well as for the sins of the entire nation.

The day sacrifices end. Roman soldiers storm into the Jerusalem temple courtyard in AD 70, crushing Jewish rebels making a last stand at their holiest site. After the battle, the temple is dismantled and never rebuilt. Without a temple, the priesthood dies and animal sacrifices end. The Jews replace sacrifices with prayer, as many believe was predicted:

- "Accept our good sacrifices of praise instead of bulls" (Hosea 14:2 CEV).
- "Accept my prayer as incense offered to you, and my upraised hands as an evening offering" (Psalm 141:2).

The writer of Hebrews says Jesus is a more effective advocate for the people than any high priest.

- Jesus ministers in heaven's temple in the very presence of God, not in a man-made building.
- And unlike other high priests, Jesus never sinned.

The writer says Jesus is even a better priest than the mysterious Melchizedek—who was considered a spiritual superior to Abraham, father of the Jewish religion. Abraham gave offerings to this priest. Melchizedek, as revered as he was in the Jewish faith, died—like all other priests. "But because Jesus lives forever, his priesthood lasts forever" (Hebrews 7:24).

Quoting Psalm 110:4, the Hebrews writer says a psalmist predicted this eternal priesthood: "The LORD has taken an oath and will not break his vow: 'You are a priest forever' " (Hebrews 7:21).

JESUS, a better sacrifice

God's will was for us to be made holy by the sacrifice of the body of Jesus Christ, once for all time.

HEBREWS 10:10

In the days of Moses, God made an agreement with the Jewish people. God would protect and bless them if they obeyed him. But God knew there would be times when they disobeyed. So he established a sacrificial system that would remind them how serious sin is but that would also allow them to receive forgiveness.

In the eyes of a holy God, sin is a capital offense. It requires the death penalty. But God allows the Jews to sacrifice defect-free animals as substitutes. The animals die in place of the sinners. "Life is in the blood, and I have given you the blood of animals to sacrifice in place of your own" (Leviticus 17:11 CEV).

The trouble with animal sacrifices was that they didn't seem to change the spirit of most worshippers. The people kept sinning. So instead of providing the people with relief from their guilt, "those sacrifices actually reminded them of their sins year after year" (Hebrews 10:3).

Jesus' sacrifice is different. "By his one sacrifice he has forever set free from sin the people he brings to God" (Hebrews 10:14 CEV).

No more sacrifices. No more reminders of sin. No more slavery to sin.

Instead, freedom.

Freedom from mind-numbing rituals. Freedom from guilt. And freedom to serve God and to receive instant forgiveness whenever requested—because the sacrifice has already been made.

FAITH IS what God wants, not rituals

It was their faith that made our ancestors pleasing to God.
HEBREWS 11:2 CEV

The Jewish religion in Bible times includes a heavy dose of ritual.

Jews live by the laws and the rituals that Moses delivered from God. There are sacrificial rituals to express sorrow for sin and praise for God. There are bathing rituals to wash away defilement, such as a menstrual period or a wet dream, or even for accidentally touching a non-Jew. There are religious holidays and sacred festivals to observe, such as the Passover meal that Jews eat each spring to remember how God freed their ancestors from Egyptian slavery.

The writer of Hebrews knows all this. But he takes his readers back in history to a time before the law. He wants to remind them that faith is more important to God than rituals.

- Noah had enough faith in God to obey him and build a boat.
- Abraham obeyed God by leaving his homeland in what is now Iraq and moving to what is now Israel. Abraham was also willing to sacrifice his son Isaac, though God didn't require him to go through with it.
- Isaac, Jacob, and Joseph—Abraham's son, grandson, and great-grandson—all showed their faith in God by obeying him.
- Moses obeyed God by going to Egypt and demanding the release of God's enslaved people.

To these famous names, the writer adds a who's who of other Jewish heroes—all of whom are praised not for observing the right rituals but for obeying God.

The point the writer is making is a lot like the one that the prophet Samuel made when he scolded King Saul for thinking a sacrifice ritual would make up for disobedience. "Listen! Obedience is better than sacrifice" (1 Samuel 15:22).

Rituals don't make up for insincere repentance. A Jewish poet puts it this way: "The sacrifice you desire is a broken spirit. You will not reject a broken and repentant heart, O God" (Psalm 51:17).

It never has been rituals that save people. Again the writer quotes the Jewish Bible, this time the prophet Habakkuk: "The person who is right with me [God] will live by trusting in me" (Hebrews 10:38 NCV).

That's the definition of faith—trusting in the invisible God. "Faith is the confidence that what we hope for will actually happen; it gives us assurance about things we cannot see" (Hebrews 11:1).

With this in mind, the writer closes his letter with one last plea. "Remember your leaders who taught you the word of God. Think of all the good that has come from their lives, and follow the example of their faith. Jesus Christ is the same yesterday, today, and forever" (Hebrews 13:7–8).

JAMES

DO-NOTHING CHRISTIANS ARE FRAUDS

Rich and talking. In double danger, as far as James is concerned, a couple of Romans engage in two activities that draw serious warnings. They surround themselves with opulence. And they open their mouths. James, probably the brother of Jesus, warns that wealth can consume us like a fire—and that an uncontrolled tongue is just as incendiary.

This short letter reads a bit like a collection of random Post-it notes from a frustrated pastor. He's upset that some folks in his congregation talk a fine religion but won't put muscle to their words.

So every time he sees it happen, he writes a note about it and tacks it to his office wall. Before long, his walls are pasted with dozens of notes. So he takes them down and copies them all onto a scroll—in no particular order. Then he sends the scroll out as a letter, circulating among churches throughout the region. He's apparently assuming other pastors are having the same problems.

The Old Testament book of Proverbs is patched together in much the same way. It's a collection of wise sayings from elderly men, intended for young men. The difference is that the sayings in Proverbs are usually shorter: one-liners and two-liners. James has some of these, too. But most of what James has to say comes in short-burst paragraphs—a paragraph or two on each topic.

His notes aren't completely random. There's a main idea connecting them: Christianity isn't just a way of thinking; it's a way of living.

That means people of faith should be easy to spot. People reveal they are Christians not by what they think or say. They reveal it by what they do.

What exactly do Christians do?

The letter of James works nicely as a checklist. Three biggies on the list:

- Take control of your tongue, and guard what you say.
- Don't give preferential treatment to rich people.
- Treat hardship as a good thing, an opportunity to mature spiritually.

MAIN POINT:

"Can't you see that faith without good deeds is useless?" (James 2:20).

WRITER:

"This letter is from James" (James 1:1). But which James? Two are famous enough to write an open letter to the church and identify themselves only by their name:
- The apostle James. He was one of Jesus' closest friends, along with his brother John. Herod Agrippa executed James in about AD 44.
- James the brother of Jesus. He led the Jerusalem church. He was executed by local Jews just before the AD 66–70 Jewish war for independence, according to Josephus, a first-century Jewish historian. Since the early centuries, most Bible experts have said the brother of Jesus probably wrote this letter. He led the first church council meeting, reported in Acts 15, and he became widely recognized as leader of the Christian movement among Jews.

DATE:

It's uncertain when James wrote this letter. There are two main theories:
- Middle to late AD 40s, which would make it the oldest book in the New Testament. James still sees the Jewish law as a good thing, and he mentions worshipping in the synagogue—both of which were more common in the first two decades after Jesus.
- Early AD 60s, after traditional Jews start persecuting Jewish Christians. James encourages his readers to remember that "when your faith is tested, your endurance has a chance to grow" (James 1:3).

LOCATION:

If the brother of Jesus is doing the writing, he probably does so from his ministry headquarters in Jerusalem. He writes to "Jewish believers scattered abroad" (James 1:1).

SUFFERING can be a good thing

When troubles come your way, consider it an opportunity for great joy. For you know that when your faith is tested, your endurance has a chance to grow.

JAMES 1:2–3

Jewish Christians are facing tough times. Tradition-minded Jews are persecuting them as heretics—members of a breakaway Jewish cult that degrades God by calling Jesus God's Son.

Also, Jewish Christians where James lives, in Jerusalem, are facing financial troubles. In the late AD 50s, Paul collects "an offering for the poor among the believers in Jerusalem" (Romans 15:26). Perhaps other Jewish Christians around the Roman Empire are feeling the money drought, as well. It could be part of an orchestrated effort by traditional Jews to make life miserable for the Jewish followers of Jesus.

James spins this suffering in a strange direction. Suffering is not a downward spiral, he says. Instead, it lifts us up. It makes us stronger. It builds our muscles of faith, giving us the extra endurance we'll need in tougher times ahead.

"For examples of patience in suffering, dear brothers and sisters, look at the prophets who spoke in the name of the Lord," James writes. "You know about Job, a man of great endurance" (James 5:10–11). James doesn't want his fellow believers to think that God is behind this suffering—or behind anything that would tempt people to leave the Christian faith. The original Greek word for "testing" or "trial"—which James uses to describe the suffering—is the same word for "temptation."

"Do not say, 'God is tempting me.'. . . He never tempts anyone else. Temptation comes from our own desires, which entice us and drag us away. These desires give birth to sinful actions" (James 1:13–15).

In the face of persecution, a strong survival instinct can overpower a person's faith. But James says that Christians interested in eternal survival should remember this: "God blesses those who patiently endure testing and temptation. Afterward they will receive the crown of life that God has promised to those who love him" (James 1:12).

TREAT THE POOR like they're rich

Hasn't God chosen the poor in this world to be rich in faith? Aren't they the ones who will inherit the Kingdom he promised to those who love him? But you dishonor the poor!

JAMES 2:5–6

James is quoting his brother Jesus, who said in the Sermon on the Mount: "God blesses those who are poor and realize their need for him, for the Kingdom of Heaven is theirs" (Matthew 5:3).

But like today, people in Bible times often give preferential treatment to rich folks while ignoring the poor. It happens even in the church—with some biblical support, shaky though it is.

Some Christians raised in the Jewish tradition were taught that God blesses good people with good things: health, wealth, and fame. And they believe that God punishes bad people with bad things: disease, poverty, and shame. People in James's day get these exaggerated ideas from passages like this: "The blessing of the LORD makes a person rich" (Proverbs 10:22).

Tell it to Job sitting in the ashes.

For a stretch of time, he lost nearly everything: his health, wealth, and family. In fact, many Bible experts say his story is in the Bible to correct the presumption that wealth is God's way of blessing us and that poverty is God's way of punishing us. God won't be squeezed into a mold that restrictive.

But the correction intended by Job's story didn't seem to take. That's why Jesus' disciples were shocked when Jesus said it's almost impossible for rich people to make it into heaven. Thoroughly indoctrinated in the teaching that rich people are among God's most blessed, the disciples replied, "Then who in the world can be saved?" (Matthew 19:25).

James has noticed that even in the church rich people are getting special attention, such as the best seats in the house. He attacks this practice in two ways.

- He reminds Christians that rich people are generally the biggest sinners on the planet—often getting rich by exploiting others.

"Isn't it the rich who oppress you and drag you into court? Aren't they the ones who slander Jesus Christ. . . ?" (James 2:6–7).

James even warns the rich directly, "This treasure you have accumulated will stand as evidence against you on the day of judgment. For listen! Hear the cries of the field workers whom you have cheated of their pay. . . . You have spent your years on earth in luxury, satisfying your every desire. You have fattened yourselves for the day of slaughter" (James 5:3–5).

- He reminds Christians to love all their neighbors, rich and poor.

"It is good when you obey the royal law as found in the Scriptures: 'Love your neighbor as yourself.' But if you favor some people over others, you are committing a sin" (James 2:8–9).

Prayer power. Tattered prayer book in hand, a Jewish woman prays at the holiest Jewish site on earth: Jerusalem's Western Wall near where the ancient Jewish temple once stood. It's time well spent, according to James: "The earnest prayer of a righteous person has great power and produces wonderful results" (James 5:16).

BE a do-gooder

What good is it, dear brothers and sisters, if you say you have faith but don't show it by your actions? Can that kind of faith save anyone?

JAMES 2:14

James points to demons to make a compelling case that belief isn't enough to save us: "You say you have faith, for you believe that there is one God. Good for you! Even the demons believe this, and they tremble in terror. How foolish! Can't you see that faith without good deeds is useless?" (James 2:19–20).

The apostle Paul seems to say just the opposite—that faith is all we need:

"This Good News tells us how God makes us right in his sight. This is accomplished from start to finish by faith. As the Scriptures say, 'It is through faith that a righteous person has life' " (Romans 1:17).

Martin Luther, the Roman Catholic priest whose protests against corruption in the Catholic Church jump-started the Protestant movement in the 1500s, not only sided with Paul; he once said the book of James should be ripped out of the Bible. It doesn't belong. Bad theology. He called James a "letter of straw." That's like comparing it to the house of straw built by one of the Three Little Pigs. The wolf blew that house down. And as far as Luther was concerned, the theology of James was just as feeble.

Yet many Bible experts say there's really no substantial clash between James, Paul, and Luther. It just looks like a train wreck because the three men hit the topic from different directions.

- James is reacting to Christians who don't want to practice what they preach. So he emphasizes the need to put faith into action.
- Paul is often reacting to extremist Jewish Christians who insist that anyone who wants to be saved—including non-Jews—has to observe all the Jewish customs, such as eating only kosher food. So Paul emphasizes that salvation is God's gift to us and that all we have to do is accept this gift and trust God for our salvation.
- Martin Luther is reacting to his own sense of inadequacy—driven by his desire to earn salvation by being a better person. This inadequacy is fed by church leaders of his day who teach that people are saved by doing what the church tells them to do. So Luther is elated to discover in Paul's writings that he can stop trying to earn his salvation.

Paul and Luther both agree with James that faith leads to good deeds. Paul says, "May he [God] give you the power to accomplish all the good things your faith prompts you to do" (2 Thessalonians 1:11). And Luther—a man of action who translated the Bible into German and wrote commentaries and hymns such as "A Mighty Fortress Is Our God"—later in life retracted his criticism of James's letter.

James isn't saying that Christians have to follow a bunch of strict rules to make it into heaven. He's saying that our faith in God changes us from the inside out. We become God's children. And we start acting like it. We don't keep on acting like the devil.

James gives an example. If we come across someone who needs warm clothes and a hot meal, a genuine Christian won't blow off the person by saying, "Good-bye and have a good day; stay warm and eat well" (James 2:16). A real Christian would help. Paul would. And so would Martin Luther.

WATCH your mouth

The tongue is a flame. . . . It can set your whole life on fire.

JAMES 3:6

James uses captivating word pictures to remind Christians of the power in a tongue, though it's just a tiny part of our body—a little more than a tenth of a pound.
- A faint spark can start a huge forest fire.
- A little rudder can steer a massive ship, even into a headwind.
- A five-inch metal bar called a bit can turn a one-ton horse.

The tiny tongue is much the same. It's just a little muscle, but it can do big things—some bad. It can set our life on fire. It can steer us into a furious storm. And it can turn us in directions we'd rather not go.

James implies that it's impossible to completely control what we say: "People can tame all kinds of animals, birds, reptiles, and fish, but no one can tame the tongue" (James 3:7–8).

Yet James clearly believes that Christians should have at least some control over their brainless tongues: "If you claim to be religious but don't control your tongue, you are fooling yourself, and your religion is worthless" (James 1:26).

So as powerful as the tongue is, Christians can and should be able to harness that power and use it for good—at least most of the time.

James gives an example: "Don't speak evil against each other" (James 4:11). He's referring to harsh and unfair criticism—the kind of back-stabbing judgments people often pass along in gossip. There's certainly a time and place for the tough chore of confronting fellow Christians about their sinful behavior. But even that should be done in a spirit of love, in the hope of helping them.

ONCE SAVED, always saved?

My dear brothers and sisters, if someone among you wanders away from the truth and is brought back, you can be sure that whoever brings the sinner back will save that person from death and bring about the forgiveness of many sins.

JAMES 5:19–20

Some Christians teach that once people accept Jesus as their Savior, they have the key to heaven. The doctrine is called "eternal security." It means that no matter what sins they commit afterward, their home in heaven is secure.

Many Presbyterians, Baptists, and Lutherans teach this. They draw their conclusion from Bible passages like these:

- "My sheep listen to my voice; I know them, and they follow me. I give them eternal life, and they will never perish. No one can snatch them away from me" (John 10:27–28).

- "We have been born again. . . . Now we live with great expectation, and we have a priceless inheritance—an inheritance that is kept in heaven for you, pure and undefiled, beyond the reach of change and decay. And through your faith, God is protecting you by his power until you receive this salvation" (1 Peter 1:3–5).

Other church groups, such as United Methodists, Nazarenes, and the Salvation Army, offer a different take on the matter.

They teach that Christians can abandon their faith. In other words, they would agree that no power can snatch Jesus' sheep from the flock. But they'd add that the sheep have the free will to walk away from the flock.

Christians from this theological camp draw their conclusion from passages such as the one above, from James 5. They also point to another New Testament writer who talks about how difficult it is to "to bring back to repentance those who were once enlightened—those who have experienced the good things of heaven and shared in the Holy Spirit, who have tasted the goodness of the word of God and the power of the age to come—and who then turn away from God" (Hebrews 6:4–6).

Each of these two groups responds with different theories about how to interpret these verses. For example, some pro–eternal security Christians would say the backsliders were never genuine believers in the first place. And some would say the backsliding is only temporary.

But many Christians in both groups would agree that anyone who really wants the eternal life that God offers can have it. That's because both the desire and the gift come from God.

Chosen forever. "Eternal life is foreordained for some, eternal damnation for others," wrote John Calvin. He's the theological father of church groups such as some Presbyterian and Baptist denominations. The people God has chose for heaven, Calvin said, are going to end up in heaven. Other scholars argue that God gave people free will to accept or reject salvation—and that, "He does not want anyone to be destroyed, but wants everyone to repent" (2 Peter 3:9).

1 PETER

HOW TO SURVIVE RELIGIOUS DISCRIMINATION

It's a mystery why the apostle Peter would write a letter like this.

He sounds a lot like a supreme church leader. Maybe even the first pope—which is exactly how the Roman Catholic Church describes him.

For one thing, he's addressing far-flung churches scattered over nearly a quarter of a million square miles—most of modern-day Turkey. That's odd for the following reasons:

- There's no hint that Peter knows any of these people. He doesn't mention any by name.
- They seem non-Jewish, though Peter's ministry seems tipped toward Jewish Christians living in what is now Israel. Paul is the Gentile missionary specialist.
- They live on Paul's turf, in a part of the world where Paul plants congregations.

Some Bible experts speculate the answer to why Peter writes this letter might be as simple as this: Peter is visiting the church in Rome when he gets word that Christians in Turkey are having a hard time with some type of persecution.

Maybe the trouble comes from locals. Perhaps they don't like the changes they're seeing in their neighbors who have abandoned the village gods and the pagan customs in favor of Jesus and Christian behavior. That's a widespread view among Bible experts today.

Or maybe the Christians are facing persecution from Jews, just as Paul did wherever he went. And perhaps the Romans are involved.

These are just guesses, since Peter never says where the trouble comes from.

What Peter does say is that Jesus suffered all the way to the grave—and

Keeper of the church. "I will give you the keys of the Kingdom of Heaven," Jesus once told Peter (Matthew 16:19). With this statement, say some Bible experts, Jesus put the man who had led the 12 disciples in charge of leading the church.

that Christians should be prepared to do the same. But in the meantime, Peter urges believers to live like Christians, obeying God and submitting to everyone in authority over them.

MAIN POINT:

"If you suffer for doing what is right, God will reward you for it" (1 Peter 3:14).

WRITER:

"This letter is from Peter, an apostle of Jesus Christ" (1 Peter 1:1). Some Bible experts challenge this claim, since Peter was a mere fisherman and this letter is written in polished Greek. But Peter, like many people in this era of limited literacy, may have called on the help of a professional writer—or at least someone with more education than he has. In fact, Peter admits he's writing "with the help of Silas" (1 Peter 5:12). Church leaders referring to 1 Peter in the AD 90s and 100s consistently identify Peter as the author.

DATE:

Peter probably writes this letter in the AD 60s. Many Bible experts say he likely writes it before the persecution that starts in AD 64. On the night of July 18, 64, a fire breaks out that destroys two-thirds of Rome. Emperor Nero blames Christians and starts arresting and killing them. Other scholars say the persecution mentioned in the letter might suggest Peter wrote it during Nero's four years of persecution—after the fire but before Nero's suicide in AD 68.

LOCATION:

Peter says he's writing from a "sister church here in Babylon" (1 Peter 5:13). Perhaps he's talking about the city of Babylon on the outskirts of modern-day Baghdad. It was once capital of the Babylonian Empire. But most Bible experts guess that Peter is talking about Rome. Jews gave Rome this unflattering nickname because, like the Babylonians 600 years earlier, the Romans invaded and exploited the Jewish homeland. The similarities grow in AD 70 when the Romans, like the Babylonians, destroy Jerusalem and level the temple. Peter addresses his letter to Christians in what is now Turkey, in the Roman provinces of "Pontus, Galatia, Cappadocia, Asia, and Bithynia" (1 Peter 1:1).

Black Sea

Bithynia, Pontus

Galatia

TURKEY

Asia

Cappadocia

Ephesus

Antioch in Pisidia
Iconium

Colosse

Lystra

Derbe

Mediterranean Sea

CYPRUS

LIVE like outsiders

Live as God's obedient children. Don't slip back into your old ways of living.

1 PETER 1:14

Peter describes his readers with a bizarre phrase. Though they're in their own hometowns, he says they're "people who are living as foreigners" (1 Peter 1:1).

It almost sounds as if he's talking about unwelcome outsiders who speak a different language and practice a different culture. Instead, he's talking about locals who change into people whom their neighbors no longer recognize. Christianity produces a change that is this radical. Peter describes it as being "born again" (1 Peter 1:3).

Peter is writing mostly to non-Jewish people who once worshipped a gallery of gods, probably including ones popular in their hometowns. These people had joined in the local parties and festivals that honored the gods.

But no more.

They have converted to Christianity. Now they worship only the Lord. They stay away from drunken parties thrown in the name of idols and mythological gods. And in the process, they become social dropouts.

Peter understands what's happening. He knows that it's tough living on the fringe of society. So he encourages the young Christians—essentially reminding them that living on the outskirts like this will guarantee them a home in a pearl-gated community for the rest of eternity.

"There is wonderful joy ahead," Peter says, "even though you have to endure many trials for a little while" (1 Peter 1:6).

In the meantime, Peter says, they should continue living as earth's "temporary residents and foreigners" (1 Peter 2:11). By doing this, they'll show that they're citizens of heaven.

Forget the fancy hairdo. Roman high society loves the big-hair look, captured in this funeral sculpture from the early AD 100s. Peter advises women not to worry about "fancy hairstyles, expensive jewelry, or beautiful clothes. You should clothe yourselves instead with the beauty that comes from within" (1 Peter 3:3–4).

- "You must be holy in everything you do, just as God who chose you is holy" (1 Peter 1:15).

This probably doesn't mean they're to be morally perfect, never making a mistake. People and temple objects in Bible times are declared holy when they are completely devoted to God—meaning they can't be used for anything else. Humans will make mistakes in judgment from time to time. But for people devoted to God, this will be the exception instead of the rule.

- "Love each other deeply with all your heart" (1 Peter 1:22).
- "Get rid of all evil behavior. Be done with all deceit, hypocrisy, jealousy, and all unkind speech" (1 Peter 2:1).
- "Keep a humble attitude" (1 Peter 3:8).
- "Don't repay evil for evil. Don't retaliate with insults when people insult you. Instead, pay them back with a blessing" (1 Peter 3:9).

SUBMIT to people in charge

For the Lord's sake, respect all human authority.

1 PETER 2:13

Peter gives much the same advice that Paul did in letters he wrote to a pair of churches in the same area: Ephesus and Colosse. Most Bible experts say Paul was probably in Rome from about AD 60 to 62 awaiting trial when he wrote those two letters. Perhaps Peter visits him there, hears what's happening in Turkey, and decides to add his advice in a separate letter to all churches in the region. Silas, the man who helps Peter write this letter, is also one of Paul's associate ministers. So that's another possible source of information for Peter.

Peter, like Paul, says Christians should submit to people in authority. Instead of being instigators and troublemakers, Christians should be easy to get along with.

Citizens must respect the authority of the head of state. Emperor Nero is probably running the Roman Empire at the time, reigning from AD 54 to 68. This makes Peter's advice especially jarring. For during the last four years of Nero's depraved life, he orders Christians in Rome arrested and killed in the arenas.

Peter's reasoning is that the best way to silence critics of Christianity is to live honorable lives.

"You who are slaves must accept the authority of your masters with all respect" (1 Peter 2:18). Anything but an abolitionist, Peter says slaves should obey their masters "not only if they are kind and reasonable, but even if they are cruel." Peter reminds Christian slaves that Jesus suffered unfairly, too.

Wives should accept the authority of their husbands. This includes women married to non-Christians. In this case, Peter tells the women, "Your godly lives will speak to them without any words. They will be won over by observing your pure and reverent lives" (1 Peter 3:1–2).

Also like Paul, Peter tells women not to worry about fancy hairdos and expensive jewelry. "Clothe yourselves instead with the beauty that comes from within," Peter says, "the unfading beauty of a gentle and quiet spirit, which is so precious to God. This is how the holy women of old made themselves beautiful" (1 Peter 3:4–5).

"Husbands must give honor to your wives. . . . She is your equal partner" (1 Peter 3:7). Actually, in most cultures of the day throughout the vast Roman Empire, the wife is no more of a partner than a slave is. She's the man's property. She can't possibly be equal.

She's not as strong. And in many cases she's not as educated. Boys generally get the education, if teachers are available in town. Girls usually learn at home from their mothers—the academically blind leading the blind.

But Peter, like Paul, sets the stage for a quiet gender revolution. For when attitudes change, actions follow.

EXPECT suffering

Don't be surprised at the fiery trials you are going through. . . . Instead, be very glad—for these trials make you partners with Christ in his suffering.

1 PETER 4:12–13

Peter doesn't say what kind of "fiery trials" the Christians are facing. Many Bible experts say they're probably not the kind that landed Christians in arenas, facing wild animals and gladiators. That's because the experts say Peter probably wrote this letter before Emperor Nero starting doing that sort of thing to Christians.

The book of Acts and several other New Testament books give us a peek at the kinds of unjust persecution Christians faced during the church's first decades:

- insults,
- threats,
- economic discrimination,
- arrest,
- beatings,
- lawsuits,
- fines,
- confiscation of property,
- jail time,
- mob attacks, and
- execution.

Peter reminds the Christians in Turkey that Jesus suffered unfairly, too. "He never sinned, but he died for sinners to bring you safely home to God. He suffered physical death, but he was raised to life in the Spirit" (1 Peter 3:18).

Peter says Christians can expect suffering. He even implies they might be killed.

Coming across as a hardcore optimist, Peter says that whatever they suffer because of their faith, Christians should approach that suffering with a positive attitude.

And here's what Peter says is upbeat about the suffering:

- Critics are calling them Christians. "Praise God for the privilege of being called by his name!" (1 Peter 4:16).
- In suffering, Christians become "partners with Christ in his suffering" (1 Peter 4:13).
- "God will reward you for it" (1 Peter 3:14).
- As partners with Jesus, they "will have the wonderful joy of seeing his glory when it is revealed to all the world" (1 Peter 4:13).

PETER, THE FIRST POPE?

Many Christians say it's no mistake that 1 Peter sounds so authoritative—as though it's coming from the church's supreme leader.

That's because it is, at least as far as most Roman Catholics are concerned.

The Catholic Church teaches that before Jesus left the planet, he put Peter in charge of the church—as the first pope, a title known in the first century as "bishop of Rome." Later titles included "vicar of Christ," "successor to the prince of the apostles," and "supreme pontiff of the universal church." Whatever the title, it soon became two jobs in one: bishop of Rome and leader of the entire Christian church.

That's why popes, after nearly 2,000 years, still live at the Vatican in Rome.

Catholics teach that as the first pope, Peter spoke for God. They base this teaching on something Jesus told Peter shortly before the Crucifixion.

"You are Peter (which means 'rock'), and upon this rock I will build my church, and all the powers of hell will not conquer it. And I will give you the keys of the Kingdom of Heaven. Whatever you forbid on earth will be forbidden in heaven, and whatever you permit on earth will be permitted in heaven" (Matthew 16:18–19).

But many Protestants don't come away from these verses ready to call Peter the pope—or, for that matter, ready to give anyone else the title of God's spokesperson on planet Earth.

They see Jesus predicting that Peter's leadership will help launch the church. That's what happened when Peter preached the Pentecost sermon in Jerusalem a few weeks after the Resurrection. More than 3,000 Jews converted. As for the matter of what's allowed and not allowed on earth, many Protestant Bible experts say Jesus is simply giving Peter the authority to discipline church members as needed.

Saint Peter's Basilica. Tourists in Rome wander through the church where the pope ministers. It's a church named after the apostle whom Roman Catholics say was the first pope.

2 PETER

LAST WORDS OF PETER

On the brink of death, Peter writes an open letter to Christians everywhere.
"I know that I'm to die soon; the Master has made that quite clear to me. And so I am especially eager that you have all this down in black and white so that after I die, you'll have it for ready reference" (2 Peter 1:14–15 THE MESSAGE).

There are three main pieces of advice Peter wants to leave as his legacy.

Keep growing in the faith. "Supplement your faith with a generous provision of moral excellence, and moral excellence with knowledge, and knowledge with self-control, and self-control with patient endurance, and patient endurance with godliness, and godliness with brotherly affection, and brotherly affection with love for everyone" (2 Peter 1:5–7).

Don't let false teachers lure you away from God. "They are doomed to blackest darkness" (2 Peter 2:17).

Don't get frustrated by Christ's delay in coming back. Jesus will return when the time is right, Peter says. "And so, dear friends, while you are waiting for these things to happen, make every effort to be found living peaceful lives that are pure and blameless in his sight" (2 Peter 3:14).

Apostle crucified. Peter is nailed to a cross in Rome. Early church leaders consistently report that Peter died a martyr's death in Rome. One historian, Eusebius, said Emperor Nero ordered him crucified. And *Acts of Peter*, a book written in the AD 100s, adds that Peter felt unworthy to be crucified like Jesus—so he asked to hang upside down. But this book with many tall tales—such as Peter giving a long lecture from the cross—wasn't widely circulated.

MAIN POINT:

Peter urges Christians not to be fooled by evil people posing as ministers who "cleverly teach destructive heresies.... They will make up clever lies to get hold of your money. But God condemned them long ago, and their destruction will not be delayed" (2 Peter 2:1, 3).

WRITER:

"This letter is from Simon Peter, a slave and apostle of Jesus Christ" (2 Peter 1:1).

Many Bible experts say the letter is more likely written by one of Peter's students, decades after Peter died—attempting to apply Peter's ideas to new situations. This was a common practice done in tribute to a teacher.

Two key reasons for suggesting Peter wasn't the writer:
•   The letter seems to address problems that don't surface until the end of the first century and into the second century.
•   It seems to classify Paul's writings as "Scripture" (2 Peter 3:16)—which is a bit early since Paul is still alive.

Bible experts who say Peter wrote the letter argue that Paul's letters had been circulating for 15 years or more—long enough for Peter to recognize their authority. And the problems the letter addresses may be early seedling shoots of heresies that blossom later.

DATE:

If Peter wrote this letter, he probably did so shortly before he died. Church leaders said the Romans executed Peter and Paul during Emperor Nero's wave of Christian persecution, from AD 64 to 68. If a fan of Peter's ideas wrote this letter, it could have come decades later. Many Bible experts say it fits the AD 80s and 90s, when false teachers started exploiting the fact that Jesus still hadn't returned.

LOCATION:

Peter doesn't say where he's writing from or to whom. He may be writing from Rome. Church leaders say the Romans executed him there. And Peter does say, "Our Lord Jesus Christ has shown me that I must soon leave this earthly life" (2 Peter 1:14). Perhaps he's writing to Christians in Turkey, as he did in his first letter. He describes this as "my second letter to you" (2 Peter 3:1).

FRAUD ministers ahead

There were also false prophets in Israel, just as there will be false teachers among you.

2 PETER 2:1

Peter starts his letter by encouraging Christians to keep growing in the faith. If they work hard at obeying God, Peter promises, they "will never fall away. Then God will give you a grand entrance into the eternal Kingdom of our Lord and Savior Jesus

Christ" (2 Peter 1:10–11).

Next, Peter warns the believers about a group of fake ministers who will entice many people away from the genuine faith.

Bible experts would love to know exactly which "false teachers" Peter has in mind. He doesn't reveal enough about their teachings to identify any particular group. He spends more time talking about their depraved lifestyle and their selfish motives.

These fake ministers

- teach destructive heresies (2:1);
- deny the Master, meaning perhaps that they deny Jesus is God's Son (2:1);
- practice shameful immorality and "twisted sexual desire," perhaps adultery and homosexuality (2:2, 10, 14);
- trick people out of money (2:3);
- make fun of the supernatural (2:10);
- eat with Christians as one of them (2:13);
- brag about themselves (2:18); and
- promise freedom, perhaps from rules of morality (2:19).

Some Bible experts guess that Peter may be talking about one of two religious philosophies: Gnosticism (NOSS-tah-CIZ-um) or Epicureanism (EP-ah-CURE-ee-an-is-um).

Gnosticism doesn't emerge as a full-blown heresy until the AD 100s. But some seeds may have been growing long before that. Gnostics—who originally call themselves Christians—teach that the body and the physical world have little to do with the spirit or spiritual life.

This means that people can do whatever they please, and it won't affect their spirituality. Secret knowledge is what saves people, Gnostics teach. And the Gnostics say they're the ones with the knowledge—the way to personal divinity through an inner search. That's how they get their name. The Greek word for "knowledge" is *gnosis*. Some Gnostics see themselves as children of God just as much as Jesus is. And they teach that people can do what Jesus did on earth if they can find the inner deity that Jesus found.

A modern religion that acknowledges its roots in Gnosticism is Unity School of Christianity.

Epicureans teach that people should seek pleasure above everything else—favoring intellectual pleasure above sensual pleasures.

The Greek philosopher Epicurus, founder of the philosophy, said people are happiest when they overcome their fear of gods, death, and punishment in an afterlife. So he taught that there's nothing to fear. He said that gods don't affect our lives and that there is no afterlife or judgment.

Peter may not have either group in mind. Perhaps he's drawing on a mismatched collection of heresies he has seen during three decades of ministry. Or maybe he's adding his observations to a warning he heard earlier from Jesus: "Don't let anyone mislead you, for many will come in my name. . . . False messiahs and false prophets will rise up and perform great signs and wonders so as to deceive, if possible, even God's chosen ones" (Matthew 24:4–5, 24).

War in heaven. The archangel Michael leads his celestial army in crushing a coup attempt by Satan. "The ancient serpent called the devil" gets tossed out of heaven, along with all his angels.

ANGELS in hell

God did not spare even the angels who sinned. He threw them into hell, in gloomy pits of darkness, where they are being held until the day of judgment.

2 PETER 2:4

Using an extreme example, Peter assures his Christian readers that "false teachers" are doomed because of their sins. God will punish them as surely as he exiled his own angels into hell.

The Greek word Peter uses for "hell" isn't the typical word used elsewhere in the Bible. Peter uses the word *Tartarus*. And this is the only time it shows up in the Bible. Tartarus is a place of punishment in Greek stories. Deep in the underworld, it's where the gods locked up their enemies.

Bible experts are left guessing about the story behind the fallen angels. Peter could be referring to one of several scenes from the Bible.

• "I saw Satan fall from heaven like lightning!" Jesus once told his disciples (Luke 10:18). Ancient Jewish writings said Satan and his demons once lived in heaven but rebelled and were thrown out.

• "There was war in heaven," wrote John, describing one of his visions. "Michael and his angels fought against the dragon and his angels. And the dragon lost the battle, and he and his angels were forced out of heaven. This great dragon—the ancient serpent called the devil, or Satan, the one deceiving the whole world—was thrown down to the earth with all his angels" (Revelation 12:7–9).

• "The sons of God saw the beautiful women and took any they wanted as their wives. . . . Giant Nephilites lived on the earth, for whenever the sons of God had intercourse with women, they gave birth to children who became the heroes and famous warriors of ancient times" (Genesis 6:2, 4). "Sons of God" is a phrase that can refer to angels. But it can refer to humans, as well.

SECOND coming on hold

In the last days scoffers will come, mocking the truth and following their own desires. They will say, "What happened to the promise that Jesus is coming again?"

2 PETER 3:3–4

If Peter's doing the writing, Christians have been waiting about 35 years for Jesus to make good on the promise his apostles gave: "Remember, the Lord is coming soon". (Philippians 4:5). And if a follower of Peter is doing the writing near the end of the century, Christians have been waiting 50 years or more.

Peter's explanation for the delay wouldn't win any awards for logic.

"The Lord isn't really being slow about his promise, as some people think. No, he is being patient for your sake. He does not want anyone to be destroyed, but wants everyone to repent" (2 Peter 3:9).

Bible experts are mystified by this explanation. Some offer theories, but the ideas are complex, meandering, and every bit as perplexing as Peter's original statement. We're just going to have to wait out this mystery—which seems appropriate since the point Peter is trying to make is about patience.

God isn't late, Peter's saying. He's patient. God is waiting for the right time. That's the point behind Peter's vexing explanation.

This patience of God is like nothing a human can understand. "The length of our days is seventy years—or eighty, if we have the strength. . .they quickly pass, and we fly away" (Psalm 90:10 NIV).

So to us, a few decades could seem like an eternity. But for God, who has existed since before physical time began, "a day is like a thousand years. . .and a thousand years is like a day" (2 Peter 3:8). That's a quote from the same Jewish song about the shortness of human life—a song that also praises the timeless eternity of God: "For you, a thousand years are as a passing day" (Psalm 90:4).

This isn't mere poetry—a fancy way of redefining "soon" to give the apostles an escape clause from their promise about the second coming. Time in the spiritual dimension may be this radically compressed. Perhaps the closest we can come to getting a sense of spirit time is when we take a look over our shoulder at where we've been in decades past. Some powerful events, even though removed half a century or more, can seem as joyful or painful as they were when we first experienced them. A war veteran may weep when speaking of a friend who died in battle long ago. The emotion is freshly preserved in the old soldier's spirit. A half century ago can seem just a moment ago—even for a human.

Don't worry about the timing of Jesus' return, Peter says, because "the day of the Lord will come as unexpectedly as a thief" (2 Peter 3:10).

Christians aren't in the business of waiting. We're in the business of obeying God. "Since this is what you have to look forward to," Peter says, "do your very best to be found living at your best, in purity and peace" (2 Peter 3:14 THE MESSAGE).

Birth of the Universe

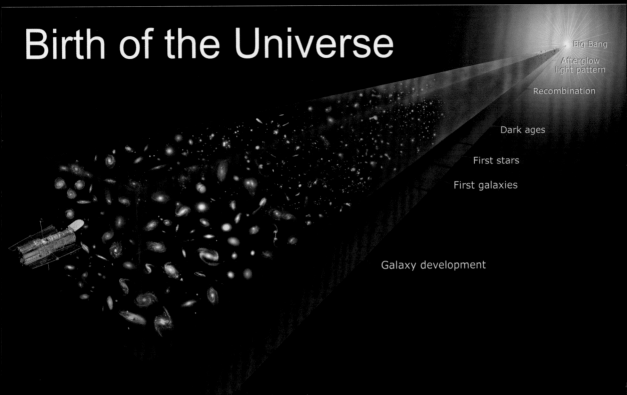

Big Bang

Afterglow
light pattern

Recombination

Dark ages

First stars

First galaxies

Galaxy development

Galaxy clusters

WHEN GOD TURNS OUT THE LIGHTS

About 14 billion years ago the universe began with a bang, most astrophysicists agree—a massive explosion of creative power. Of course, many Christians would argue that God was the "creative power." Some believe he used evolution over eons of time to create the universe we live in, while others disagree, insisting that God made the universe just a few thousand years ago.

However or whenever God created the universe—Big Bang or not—the apostle Peter hints that it will end with a bang: "The heavens will pass away with a terrible noise, and the very elements themselves will disappear in fire. . . . On that day, he [God] will set the heavens on fire, and the elements will melt away in the flames. But we are looking forward to the new heavens and new earth he has promised, a world filled with God's righteousness" (2 Peter 3:10–13).

Peter, however, may be speaking more as a poet than a scientist.

Astrophysicists debate how the universe will end.

Big Rip. Some guess the Big Bang will end with a Big Rip as the ever-expanding universe stretches thin—with all stars and planets moving out of sight of each other. Eventually everything rips apart as the universe spreads—stars, rocks, and eventually even the tiniest particles. All that's left is vast, dark nothingness.

Big Crunch. Others guess we're headed to a Big Crunch, after gravity eventually reverses the expansion and the universe collapses back onto itself. This compressed ball might then explode into another Big Bang—recycling the universe.

There are many other theories, as well.

Before any of this happens, scientists predict, planet Earth will either freeze or fry.

In several billion years, the sun is expected to swell into a red giant before finally shrinking into a white dwarf that pumps out just a fraction of the heat that our sun produces today. The transformation will involve cycles of expansion and contraction. If the sun contracts first, shrinking by about 20 percent, this could release earth into a higher, freezing orbit. But if the sun expands first, it could swallow the earth with "the heavens on fire."

1 JOHN

ANTICHRISTS ARE COMING AND GOING

There's trouble in the church—unlike any yet reported in the New Testament.

This is a new generation with new problems. Most of the first-generation Christians have died, leaving the future of Christianity in the hands of their children.

If this short letter is any indication, Christians are past the big debate of Paul's day. Back then, Jews were trying to convince Christians to observe Jewish laws, such as circumcising eight-day-old boys or eating only kosher food. Jews did this because many of them saw Christianity as just another branch of the Jewish religion, since most Christians were Jews by race.

But by the time 1 John is written, perhaps several decades after Paul died, Jews have finally accepted that Christianity is a distinctly different religion. So they have excommunicated Jews who practice Christianity. Debate over. The two sides agree to disagree.

But new debates flare up inside the church.

At some local churches there's a mass exodus, with split-off groups forming their own congregations. But the new churches aren't Christian at all. The anonymous writer of this letter, presumed to be John the disciple of Jesus, calls these breakaway folks antichrists—because they're against Christ.

Based on what John says, these splinter congregations seem to have dreamed up some strange ideas about Jesus.

- He wasn't really God's Son any more than we are all God's children.
- He was either a spirit being all along or a man who morphed into a spirit being. Either way he only pretended to have a physical body.
- As a spirit, he couldn't have died for us. He only pretended to die.

These bizarre ideas apparently lead to some crazy life

Son of a god. In a painting from John's century, the ancient superhero Hercules poses with a queen. Greek mythology says Hercules, son of Zeus the chief god, was born after Zeus disguised himself as the husband of a beautiful human and had sex with her. Greek philosophers insisted that spirit beings couldn't really become human—that they could only appear human. John's letter seems to target Christians who say the same thing about Jesus—that he was a spirit being who only appeared human.

application. One of the craziest is to presume that the physical world doesn't matter when it comes to spirituality. And that spiritual people can do anything they want: Speak hateful words. Commit adultery. Drink till they drop. None of these things matter to people who say they can ascend from physical existence to a higher plane of spirituality.

It's not just hogwash as far as John is concerned. It's poison. And it's killing people forever—robbing them of the gift of eternal life.

MAIN POINT:

"I am writing these things to warn you about those who want to lead you astray. But you have received the Holy Spirit, and he lives within you, so you don't need anyone to teach you what is true" (1 John 2:26–27).

WRITER:

The writer doesn't identify himself except to say, "We saw him [Jesus] with our own eyes and touched him with our own hands" (1 John 1:1). Since at least the early AD 100s, church leaders have attributed this letter to one of Jesus' closest disciples: John the brother of James.

The writing style and phrasing are incredibly similar to those used the Gospel of John. Both, for example, describe Jesus as the "Word" (John 1:1; 1 John 1:1), *Logos* in Greek. It's a term that Greek philosophers used to describe the mysterious principle behind the universe—the eternal force that drives everything.

DATE:

John lived to become an elderly man, probably dying in the late AD 90s. Based on the heresies he writes about, and the fact that he calls his readers "my dear children," (1 John 2:1), most Bible experts say he likely wrote this letter late in life—perhaps in the AD 80s or 90s.

LOCATION:

John probably writes from Ephesus on Turkey's west coast, addressing churches in the region. Church leaders say John moved from the Jewish homeland to Ephesus. The book of Revelation, also commonly attributed to John, addresses some of those churches by name and shows they have similar problems with the false teachers John writes about in 1 John. (See map of seven churches of Revelation, page 501.

HOW TO SPOT a genuine Christian

If someone claims, "I know God," but doesn't obey God's commandments, that person is a liar and is not living in the truth.

1 JOHN 2:4

Splinter groups have left the church, taking with them a warped view of Christianity—which they spread around as though it's the genuine religion.

"These people left our churches," John writes to the faithful Christians who remain, "but they never really belonged with us;

otherwise they would have stayed with us. When they left, it proved that they did not belong with us" (1 John 2:19).

"These people" may be the beginnings of a heresy that grows strong enough to challenge traditional Christianity in the AD 100s and 200s: Gnosticism. Based on their writings—many of which have survived, such as the *Gospel of Thomas*—they don't think of themselves as heretics. They think of themselves as people who have an inside scoop on spiritual matters—secret knowledge. That's how they get their name. *Gno* in Greek has the same root word as *kno* in English, referring to "knowledge." These are people who think they're in the know.

One widespread "secret" insight among Gnostics actually seems to come from an ancient Greek idea: that everything physical is evil and everything spiritual is good.

But that assumption among Christians leads to some strange conclusions—and behavior.

- God is not evil. So God the Son could not have come to earth as a physical being. This means Jesus didn't shed his blood for our sins. He didn't die. And he didn't rise from the dead. It only looked that way.
- Since we're physical, we can't possibly live good lives no matter how hard we try.

Because of these presumptions, some Gnostics separate their spirituality from their physical lives, as though the two are disconnected and unrelated. These Gnostics teach that it doesn't matter how we live on earth. So they live like the devil, chasing money, sex, and power.

John seems to address these people when he argues that authentic Christians obey God's laws of morality by treating others with love and by resisting selfish temptations.

"The world offers only a craving for physical pleasure, a craving for everything we see, and pride in our achievements and possessions. These are not from the Father, but are from this world. And this world is fading away. . . . But anyone who does what pleases God will live forever" (1 John 2:16–17).

The false teachers also seem to deny the existence of sin—at least as it relates to their spirituality. Though their physical bodies are evil, they admit, they insist that they're spiritually perfect. Their secret knowledge secures them, they say.

John begs to differ. "If we claim we have no sin, we are only fooling ourselves and not living in the truth. But if we confess our sins to him, he is faithful and just to forgive us our sins and to cleanse us from all wickedness" (1 John 1:8–9).

THE Antichrist

You have heard that the Antichrist is coming, and already many such antichrists have appeared.

1 JOHN 2:18

Here's a surprise for many Christians. There's no "Antichrist" in Revelation—or in any other Bible book about the end times.

John is the only Bible writer to use the word. And he uses it only in the short letters of 1 and 2 John, usually to describe heretics who teach lies about Jesus: "So who is lying here? It's the person who denies that Jesus is the Divine Christ, that's who. This is what makes an antichrist: denying the Father, denying the Son" (1 John 2:22 THE MESSAGE).

But who is the Antichrist whom John says "you have heard. . .is coming"?

The Bible doesn't say. But Bible students make educated guesses:

- **One of many end-time deceivers Jesus spoke about.** "False messiahs and false prophets will rise up and perform great signs and wonders so as to deceive, if possible, even God's chosen ones" (Matthew 24:24).
- **A mysterious "man of lawlessness" who calls himself God.** "That day [of Christ's return] will not come until there is a great rebellion against God and the man of lawlessness is revealed—the one who brings destruction. He will exalt himself and defy everything that people call god and every object of worship. He will even sit in the temple of God, claiming that he himself is God" (2 Thessalonians 2:3–4).
- **One of the two beasts mentioned in Revelation.** "The beast was allowed to wage war against God's holy people and to conquer them. And he was given authority to rule over every tribe and people and language and nation. And all the people who belong to this world worshiped the beast" (Revelation 13:7–8).

By the early Middle Ages in the AD 600s–1000s, some Bible scholars say, preachers started merging these disconnected ideas into one combo portrait of the Antichrist. And later ministers added colorful details that came from who knows where.

THE LAST HOUR

The last hour is here.
1 JOHN 2:18

About 17 million hours ago John writes that the last hour is here.

By "last hour," John isn't talking about the world's last few months or years. So say most Bible experts. He's talking about the last stage in God's plan to save human beings from sin—the era launched by the coming of the Messiah.

God starts his plan of salvation with one righteous man, Abraham. And from Abraham, God establishes a righteous nation: Israel. God entrusted Israel with guidelines for holy living and with a commission: "You will be a light to guide the nations" (Isaiah 42:6). But Israel fails its mission. So God sends his Son, Jesus, to complete this mission by showing people how to live as citizens of God's kingdom and by sending out disciples to "go and make disciples of all the nations" (Matthew 28:19).

The "last hour" begins and ends with Jesus—his coming and his coming again.

HOW TO SPOT an antichrist

If a person. . .acknowledges that Jesus Christ came in a real body, that person has the Spirit of God. But if someone. . .does not acknowledge the truth about Jesus, that person is not from God. Such a person has the spirit of the Antichrist.

1 JOHN 4:2–3

John knows that the heresy at work could undermine the most basic teachings of Christianity: that God's Son came to earth as a flesh-and-blood human being who offered his life as a sacrifice for the sins of the world.

So John urges Christians to "remain faithful to what you have been taught from the beginning" (1 John 2:24)—from apostles like himself who personally knew Jesus and who "saw him with our own eyes and touched him with our own hands" (1 John 1:1).

People who reject this basic teaching, John says, are antichrists: enemies of Christ.

In Old Testament times, there were a lot of fake prophets. And Moses gave the Israelites a tip for spotting them: "If the prophet speaks in the LORD's name but his prediction does not happen or come true, you will know that the LORD did not give that message" (Deuteronomy 18:22).

John says much the same about fake teachers in the church. He gives Christians some tips for spotting them. False teachers include anyone who

- says Jesus is not the Messiah (1 John 2:22);
- denies the deity of the Father and the Son (1 John 2:22);
- denies that Jesus is God's Son (1 John 2:23);
- denies that Jesus came in a real body (1 John 4:2);
- hates a Christian brother or sister (1 John 4:20); and
- makes a practice of sinning (1 John 5:18).

WHAT SINS lead to death?

All wicked actions are sin, but not every sin leads to death.

1 JOHN 5:17

This short sentence is just a passing note in John's letter, but Bible experts can't pass it up. They want to know what sins can kill us and what sins only wound us.

Many Roman Catholics distinguish between these two kinds of sin.

There are "mortal sins"—serious sins such as murder or adultery, which Catholics say will keep unrepentant people out of heaven.

And there are "venial sins"—less serious sins, such as failure to pray every day, which require only penance: prayers or time in purgatory before entering heaven.

But some Protestant Bible experts wonder if John was talking about sins that can kill us physically. If a man raped a woman, Jewish law said that "the man must die" (Deuteronomy 22:24).

Other experts say John may have been thinking of unconfessed sin as the "sin that leads to death." So the sinner misses out on the gift John was talking about a few sentences earlier: eternal life. Still others wonder if John, given the context of his letter, thought that the fatal sin is teaching heresy, or perhaps the stubborn refusal to treat others with love and respect.

Whatever sin John is thinking about, he assures his readers that all sins can be forgiven—even the mysterious sin that leads to death. "If we confess our sins to him, he is faithful and just to forgive us our sins and to cleanse us from all wickedness" (1 John 1:9).

A MONK'S VIEW OF ANTICHRIST

During end-time fever near the turn of the first millennium, in about AD 950, a French monk named Adso offered a few insights about the Antichrist. They came in a letter to the French queen Gerbera, who had asked him about the mysterious figure. A few excerpts:

- "The Antichrist will be born from the Jewish people....At the very beginning of his conception the devil will enter his mother's womb...just as the Holy Spirit came into the mother of our Lord Jesus Christ."
- "He will come to Jerusalem and...will kill all the Christians he cannot convert."
- "He will circumcise himself and say to the Jews, 'I am the Christ promised to you.' "
- "The Antichrist will be killed on the Mount of Olives."
- "The Lord will grant former believers 40 days to do penance because they were led astray by the Antichrist."

How the monk knew all this, he didn't say.

But everything that many Bible scholars today say they know with certainty about the Antichrist comes from the few fleeting references they find in the letters of John.

Devilish tag team. Satan whispers instructions to the Antichrist, a mysterious figure whose title shows up in only a few, fleeting references in John's short letters. But for more than a thousand years, some Christians have speculated that he's the beast of Revelation who gains world-dominating power with the devil's help and who performs miracles that fool many into believing he's a god.

2 JOHN

DON'T WELCOME HERETICS

This letter reads like 1 John condensed—five chapters shrunk to 13 verses.

But it's not just a *Reader's Digest* version of 1 John, intended for a fast-paced crowd. It's a separate, more personal letter on the same general topic probably intended for a single congregation.

First John doesn't have the typical greeting and closing of an ancient letter, which makes it sound about as personal as an essay. Second John, on the other hand, has both a warm greeting and a personable closing, with a promise to visit soon.

John makes the same two main points he covered in his first letter:

- Obey God's laws, such as loving one another, "just as you heard from the beginning" (2 John 6). As opposed to a new gospel they were getting from other church leaders.
- Don't be duped into believing false teachers who are worming their way into churches and convincing many people that Jesus didn't have a physical body. "Such a person is a deceiver and an antichrist" (2 John 7).

These false teachers may be the pioneers of a heresy that threatens to overpower the church in the AD 100s and 200s: Gnosticism. Many Gnostics in these early centuries—people who consider themselves Christian—teach that Jesus was actually a spirit being who only appeared human. So he didn't really die for our sins and rise from the dead.

These people also disconnect spirituality from behavior, arguing that physical beings can't be good no matter how hard they try. So they stop trying. Salvation, as far as they are concerned, comes from secret knowledge about the spiritual world—not from faith in the sacrificial death of Jesus and from living a life that pleases God.

"If anyone comes to your meeting and does not teach the truth about Christ, don't invite that person into your home or give any kind of encour-

The church as a lady. "To the chosen lady and her children." That's the puzzling address John gives in his short letter. Most Bible experts say it's an affectionate way of referring to one local church and its members, the "children."

agement. Anyone who encourages such people becomes a partner in their evil work" (2 John 10–11).

John isn't telling these Christians to give every sinner the cold shoulder. After all, Jesus came to help sinners, arguing that "healthy people don't need a doctor—sick people do" (Matthew 9:12). But Jesus didn't have much patience with religious frauds—self-absorbed priests and scholars leading the Jewish people away from God. "What sorrow awaits you teachers of religious law and you Pharisees. Hypocrites! For you are like whitewashed tombs—beautiful on the outside but filled on the inside with dead people's bones and all sorts of impurity" (Matthew 23:27).

MAIN POINT:

"I am writing to remind you, dear friends, that we should love one another" (2 John 5).

WRITER:

"This letter is from John, the elder" (2 John 1). Actually, the writer doesn't identify himself as John. But all the ancient Greek copies of this letter include John's name in the title. Early church leaders said the apostle John is the author.

"Elder" is a word that often refers to the leader of a local church—the pastor. But it can also refer to an apostle. The apostle Peter wrote, "I, too, am an elder" (1 Peter 5:1).

DATE:

Since the letter reads like a short version of 1 John, it may have been written about the same time. That would likely put it late in the apostle John's life, perhaps in the AD 80s or 90s.

LOCATION:

"I am writing to the chosen lady and to her children" (2 John 1). That's all the hint we get about the location. Church leaders in the AD 100s said the apostle John moved to Ephesus on the west coast of Turkey. Though the letter of 1 John seems to address churches throughout the region, 2 John may address one particular church, which John calls "the chosen lady" and "her children."

Some Bible experts, however, say John may have been writing to a particular family, led by a woman. Yet most scholars say he was speaking metaphorically, addressing a local church as a lady. That fits a pattern. The Bible also calls the church the "pure bride" of Christ (2 Corinthians 11:2). And it lovingly refers to the nation of Israel as a "woman" (Isaiah 54:1).

3 JOHN

Warm welcome. Glass raised high in a toast of hospitality, a Samaritan in Israel welcomes his guests to a meal. Jesus once praised a good Samaritan for helping an injured traveler. In Bible times, people traveling throughout the rugged Middle East depended on the compassion and hospitality of others. That's why the apostle John gets so upset with a pastor who runs off Christian travelers.

SHOW HOSPITALITY TO TRAVELING CHRISTIANS

The apostle John has a gripe about a control-freak pastor with bad manners.

The pastor is a fellow named Diotrephes. He "loves to be the leader" (3 John 9). He refuses to submit to John's authority or to read John's letters to the congregation. And he makes "evil accusations" about John.

That's bad-mannered enough. But there's more.

Diotrephes doesn't even show the manners of a pagan. Hospitality toward strangers is expected in the ancient Middle East. It's the basic minimum in this hot and arid region—where a cup of water, a plate of food, and shelter from the night can mean the difference between life and death for travelers. Hospitality is still the custom in many Middle Eastern areas.

Diotrephes refuses to show the slightest hospitality to Christian teachers passing through. And he orders church members to follow his example. If they don't, "he puts them out of the church" (3 John 10).

Why would Diotrephes do such a thing? Probably because he considers the outsiders a threat to his authority, most Bible experts say.

John gets word of Diotrephes' bad manners, perhaps from the Christian travelers themselves—some of whom John may have sent out among the churches. So John writes this letter to a man named Gaius, perhaps someone in Diotrephes' church or in another church nearby. John apparently sends it by a courier named Demetrius.

John compliments Gaius for bucking the bad-manner trend by welcoming Christian teachers.

"Please continue providing for such teachers in a manner that pleases God. For they are traveling for the Lord, and they accept nothing from people who are not believers. So we ourselves should support them so that we can be their partners as they teach the truth" (3 John 6–8).

John says he has more that he wants to talk about, but he hopes to do it in person when he visits. He promises, too, that when he comes he'll deal with Diotrephes.

MAIN POINT:

"You are being faithful to God when you care for the traveling teachers who pass through" (3 John 5).

WRITER:

"This letter is from John, the elder" (3 John 1). As in 2 John, the writer doesn't actually identify himself as John. He simply calls himself "the elder." But all the ancient Greek copies of this letter include John's name in the title. Early church leaders said the apostle John wrote all three letters—1, 2, and 3 John—along with the Gospel of John. "Elder" often refers to the leader of a local church—the pastor. But it can also refer to an apostle.

DATE:

It may have been written about the same time many Bible experts say 1 and 2 John were written: late in John's life, perhaps in the AD 80s or 90s.

LOCATION:

John says he's writing to his friend Gaius. But he doesn't say where he's writing from or where Gaius lives. Church leaders in the AD 100s said the apostle John moved to Ephesus on Turkey's west coast. Since 1 John seems to address churches throughout the region, many Bible experts guess that Gaius lived in the region, too.

JUDE

WHY NOT SIN, SINCE WE'RE ALREADY FORGIVEN?

Heretics passing themselves off as Christian scholars start marketing an alternative brand of the faith. "Christianity Lite" might describe it.

These "ungodly people," as Jude calls them, make several big mistakes.

- They have "denied our only Master and Lord, Jesus Christ" (Jude 4). Perhaps they're arguing that Jesus wasn't really divine.
- They're "saying that God's marvelous grace allows us to live immoral lives" (Jude 4).
- They practice what they preach. They "live immoral lives, defy authority, and scoff at supernatural beings. . .living only to satisfy their desires. They brag loudly about themselves, and they flatter others to get what they want" (Jude 8, 16).

Down with sin. For those who think sin is okay with God, Jude reminds them of Korah—an arrogant man who led a rebellion against Moses. "The earth opened its mouth and swallowed the [rebel] men, along with their households and all their followers" (Numbers 16:32).

Who are these heretics? One popular guess among Bible history experts is that they're the pioneers of a movement that builds to peak force in the next two centuries, competing with traditional Christianity: Gnosticism.

Gnostics teach that secret knowledge is what saves us. They also teach that the physical world is evil and the spiritual world is good—so we can't live good lives no matter how hard we try. For this reason, many of them don't bother trying. (For more about Gnosticism, see "Fraud Ministers Ahead," page 481.)

For anyone who thinks sin is okay with God, Jude offers a short lesson in history. He draws from the Jewish Bible. He also draws from other popular Jewish stories that never made it into the Bible, apparently because he thinks they'll serve as good examples of what he's talking about.

Israel. For persistently sinning, in spite of warnings from the prophets, Israel gets erased from the world map. God's chosen people get exiled for about 50 years into Babylon, modern-day Iraq.

Rebel angels. Angels step out of line and get punished for it. They "left the place where they belonged" (Jude 6). This might refer to a rebellion in heaven, led by Satan. But it could also refer to when "the sons of God [possibly angels] saw the beautiful women and took any they wanted as their wives" (Genesis 6:2).

Archangel Michael. He avoids the sinful act of scoffing at even the vilest of supernatural beings: Satan. Instead, he leaves that to God, saying, "The Lord rebuke you!" (Jude 9). This story about Michael and Satan fighting over the body of Moses appears in a Jewish book called *Testament of Moses*, possibly written in Jude's century.

Sodom and Gomorrah. These are the twin sin cities that God seared off the planet, "wiping out all the people and every bit of vegetation" (Genesis 19:25).

Cain. For murdering his brother, Cain is exiled from his homeland and condemned to become "a homeless wanderer on the earth" (Genesis 4:12).

Balaam. He was a non-Jewish prophet for hire. Israelites "killed Balaam" (Numbers 31:8).

Korah. He led a coup against Moses, but the ground swallowed him "alive into the grave" (Numbers 16:33).

Point made. God hates sin.

Jude tells his readers to encourage each other to hold on to the true faith. And he urges them to show mercy toward those whose faith is wavering—probably those attracted to the false teachings.

MAIN POINT:

Don't believe false teachers in the church who say it's okay to sin. God punishes sinners. History is full of proof.

WRITER:

"This letter is from Jude. . .a brother of James" (Jude 1). Jude is probably a brother of Jesus, too. Jesus had four brothers: "James, Joseph, Simon, and Judas" (Matthew 13:55). Jude is a nickname for Judas. And though there are several Judes in the Bible, there's only one with a brother named James.

DATE:

Bible experts guess Jude wrote this letter in the middle of the first century, perhaps in the AD 60s. That's partly because Jude and 2 Peter seem to have been written about the same time. They share a lot of phrases and ideas: false teachers who say it's okay to sin, angels getting punished, Sodom and Gomorrah getting destroyed.

LOCATION:

Jude's brother James leads the church in Jerusalem. But Jude may have written from his Nazareth hometown. Or perhaps he wrote from Jesus' ministry headquarters in nearby Capernaum, which was also Peter's hometown.

REVELATION

Heaven, out of this world. Helix nebula, 690 light-years from earth, looks like the gateway to a brighter world. But the glow is actually from gases of a dying star. The heaven of scripture, many say, has nothing to do with the physical universe. There's no galactic address. Heaven lies in a spiritual dimension.

GOOD-BYE, FLESH AND BLOOD

The end isn't near. It's here—in a vision of the future.

The physical dimension is gone. It's replaced by something that sounds a bit like a super-physical dimension, blending the best of both worlds—physical and spiritual.

A mysterious man named John sees these cosmic changes unfold in a series of visions, which he carefully records—as instructed: "Write in a book everything you see" (Revelation 1:11).

John sees plenty. In spirit, he's transported to heaven, where celestial beings are worshipping God. There he sees someone he describes as "a Lamb that looked as if it had been slaughtered" (Revelation 5:6). This Lamb—presumed to be Jesus—starts to open a scroll. As the Lamb breaks seven seals so he can unroll the scroll, each snapping seal seems to open a window allowing John to see a future disaster.

There is war, famine, and disease—which wipe out a fourth of humanity. Christians are martyred for their religion. A massive earthquake convulses the planet, and falling stars pummel Earth into a new stone age, forcing people to hide in caves.

John sees happy events, too. Gathered in heaven are the martyred people of God, "too great to count, from every nation" (Revelation 7:9). Satan and his followers are pitched into a lake of fire. And God's home becomes the eternal home of everyone who has loved him. This is a place of heavenly bliss, with no room for "death or sorrow or crying or pain" (Revelation 21:4).

Written in a genre famous for extreme symbolism and code words, Revelation mystifies most Bible experts. Yet the big idea behind the book easily muscles through the symbols: God and goodness win. Satan and evil lose.

MAIN POINT:

God defeats Satan and all the forces of evil. People who love God live with him forever.

WRITER:

"This letter is from John" (Revelation 1:4). But which John? He describes himself only as a servant of Jesus.

Apostle John, say some Bible experts, pointing to one of Jesus' closest disciples. They cite early church leaders who agree, such as Irenaeus writing in the AD 100s. One reason for supporting the apostle John as the author: Most early church leaders took this position.

John the Elder, say others, referring to an otherwise unknown spiritual leader.

They cite early church leaders, too, such as Papias, who also lived in the AD 100s. One reason for supporting John the Elder: though John mentions "the twelve apostles of the Lamb" (Revelation 21:14), he doesn't identify himself as one of them.

DATE:

Scholars generally crowd around one of two decades. Both fit John's description of troubled times when Christians are being persecuted. The AD 60s are preferred by some experts. The Roman emperor Nero persecuted Christians in Rome from AD 64 to 68. The AD 90s are preferred by most. The Roman emperor Domitian persecuted Christians for not worshipping him as a god. He reigned from AD 81 to 96.

LOCATION:

John is writing from exile on the tiny "island of Patmos for preaching the word of God" (Revelation 1:9). Forty miles off Turkey's west coast, Patmos serves as a Roman prison island.

John addresses his letter "to the seven churches in the province of Asia" (Revelation 1:4). Not Asia as we know it today, but as Romans knew it. Romans divided their empire into provinces and called western Turkey "Asia." The list of seven churches begins with the west coast city where church leaders said the apostle John lived: Ephesus, followed by Smyrna, Pergamum, Thyatira, Sardis, Philadelphia, and Laodicea.

A MESSAGE for Christians

"Write in a book everything you see, and send it to the seven churches in the cities of Ephesus, Smyrna, Pergamum, Thyatira, Sardis, Philadelphia, and Laodicea."

REVELATION 1:11

Exiled on an ancient version of Alcatraz, John begins to have visions of the future. He's on the small island of Patmos, which Romans used as a penal colony. John is there for "preaching the word of God and for my testimony about Jesus" (Revelation 1:9).

The visions begin while he's worshipping on a Sunday, "the Lord's day." Behind him a booming voice tells him to write down everything he's about to see and to send it to seven churches in what is now western Turkey.

John turns to see who's talking. It's someone "like the Son of Man." That was Jesus' favorite way of describing himself.

Jesus tells John to begin the book of visions with seven short letters—one letter for each of the seven churches. Though the letters address specific concerns in those churches, the number seven leads some Bible experts to suggest that the letters are intended as an evaluation tool for all churches. "Seven" is a code in Jewish writings. It symbolizes fullness, completion—in this case, perhaps, the entire Christian church. The symbol comes from Creation. God created the world in six days and rested on the seventh when all the work was done.

APOCALYPSE: A STYLE OF WRITING

There's one big clue to solving the mysteries of Revelation. It's understanding the genre in which it's written.

There are many literary genres in the Bible: poetry, fictional morality stories, and nonfiction, to name a trio.

John wrote in a genre called *apocalyptic* (uh-POC-uh-LIP-tick). The name is from the Greek word *apokalypsis*, which means "revelation"—as in "revealing secret information." That's where Revelation gets its name—from the book's first word in the original Greek version. English translations call the book "a revelation [*apokalypsis*] from Jesus Christ" (Revelation 1:1).

Apocalyptic lit:
- Usually points to the end times.
- Paints bizarre word pictures and uses code words, often to hide its message from hostile outsiders. That's because the message often delivers bad news about the outsiders, who might retaliate if they knew what was being said about them. So the coded message is a way of protecting the message and the messenger.
- Is often written during a time of oppression,

when coded messages are necessary.
- Often pits the forces of good against forces of evil, such as God against Satan.
- Shows the good guys winning—at least in the Bible's apocalyptic writings. But they win only after good people suffer through hard times.

Besides Revelation, there are two other Bible books with a heavy dose of apocalyptic messages. One is Ezekiel, written when the prophet Ezekiel was exiled in what is now Iraq. Another is Daniel, written by the prophet Daniel after he was exiled to Iraq and Iran.

Some historians say this style of writing started about the time of Moses, with a prophet named Zoroaster. He lived in what is now Iran. He taught that an evil god was at war with a good god. Zoroaster said that the good god created humanity as his allies and that they will be resurrected to live forever once evil is finally defeated.

However the style began, several Bible writers embraced the genre and used it to give their readers hope in tough times.

SATAN'S THRONE

Tourists explore the reconstructed Great Altar of Pergamum—perhaps the very object John had in mind when he spoke of "Satan's throne." In John's day, archaeologists say, people came here to sacrifice animals to pagan gods such as Zeus and Athena. Sculptures at the altar show Greek gods fighting a race of giants—supposedly descended from the offspring of gods mating with humans. Writing from exile on the island of Patmos, John tells the people of Pergamum, "I know that you live in the city where Satan has his throne" (Revelation 2:13).

The messages for the churches:

Ephesus. "You don't love me or each other as you did at first!" (Revelation 2:4). This leading church in the Roman Empire's third largest city has endured persecution and resisted efforts of heretics to distort the gospel teachings. But they've lost some of their spiritual passion. Perhaps kind deeds are becoming too rare.

Smyrna. There's nothing but praise and encouragement for this church. Christians here are poor. Perhaps it's from persecution: getting fired and getting their businesses boycotted. But Jesus reminds them that they are rich in spiritual treasure that will last beyond the "second death." That's judgment day, when sinners are thrown into the "lake of fire" (Revelation 20:14).

Pergamum. This church has tolerated an obscure group of heretics known as Nicolaitans. The heretics apparently teach Christians to get along with their neighbors in two ways:

- eat the same meat, which is sacrificed to idols and then sold in the marketplace; and
- take part in festivals that involve sex rituals, such as the springtime feast honoring Aphrodite, goddess of love.

Thyatira. Jesus dittos his message to Pergamum. Christians at Thyatira have grown in the faith. But a woman in the church apparently is teaching the Nicolaitan brand of warped Christianity. Jesus compares her to the evil queen Jezebel who, hundreds of years earlier, tried to turn Israel into a country that worshipped Baal, chief god of the Canaanites.

Sardis. "You have a reputation for being alive—but you are dead. Wake up!" (Revelation 3:1–2). Yet Jesus says some believers there have their names written in "the Book of Life" (Revelation 3:5). This book is probably a metaphor, meaning the Sardis Christians are citizens in the spiritual kingdom of God.

Philadelphia. Like the message for Smyrna, there's only good news for Philadelphia—no critique. This is apparently a small congregation of "little strength" (Revelation 3:8). Jesus says he has opened a door for them—perhaps a reference to the closed door they got from the Jews. At the Jewish Council of Jamnia in about AD 90, Jews agreed to excommunicate from the synagogue any Jews who said Jesus was the promised Messiah. Philadelphia Christians might not be welcome in the local synagogue, but they're welcome in heaven.

Laodicea. Jesus uses three word pictures that are perfect for Laodicea's halfhearted yet cocky Christians.

- *"Since you are like lukewarm water, neither hot nor cold, I will spit you out of my mouth!"* (Revelation 3:16). Laodiceans get their water from an aqueduct that taps into hot mineral springs five miles south. By the time the water reaches Laodicea, it's lukewarm.
- *"You say, 'I am rich. I have everything I want. I don't need a thing!' And you don't realize that you are wretched and miserable and poor"* (Revelation 3:17). This image tracks with what the city did after a devastating earthquake in AD 60. Wealthy Laodicea became the only city in the region to refuse disaster relief from Rome.
- *"Buy medicine for your eyes, so that you will be able to see"* (Revelation 3:18 CEV). Laodicea is famous for health care, especially eye care. They have a medical school in the city, along with natural chemicals they use to make eye ointment.

SEVEN SEALS of doom

I saw the Lamb open the first of the seven seals. . . . Then I saw a white horse. Its rider carried a bow.

REVELATION 6:1–2 CEV

After taking divine dictation for the seven letters, John is ushered in spirit to God's heavenly throne room to see "what must happen" (Revelation 4:1). God glimmers in a spray of light that resembles the colors of precious jewels, while celestial beings worship him.

Joining in the worship are 24 elders, honored with their own thrones surrounding God's throne. It's unclear who these double dozen are. Some Bible experts say they are saintly human souls, such as the 12 apostles with 12 Old Testament patriarchs—or perhaps 24 representatives of Israel's priesthood. Temple worship involved 24 rotating teams of priests. Others speculate that the elders are heavenly beings, partly because Revelation seems to refer to the elders and the saints as two separate groups.

God holds a scroll that's bound closed with seven seals. In all of heaven and earth, only one person is worthy of breaking the seals for God the Father. It's God the Son. John describes him with coded language that Jewish Christians would recognize.

- "The Lion of the tribe of Judah, the heir to David's throne" (Revelation 5:5). This is a reference to the Messiah, who Old Testament prophets said would come from both the tribe of Judah and King David's family.
- "A Lamb that looked as if it had been slaughtered" (Revelation 5:6). This refers to Jesus dying as a sacrifice for the sins of humanity.

Each time the Lamb breaks open a seal, disasters strike.

Seals 1–4 unleash the four horsemen of the apocalypse.

First comes a power-hungry rider on a white horse. This rider seems like an Alexander the Great or a Napoleon—someone bent on world domination and ready to use force to get it.

Second comes a war-hungry rider on a red horse.

Third comes a rider on a black horse, bringing famine.

And last comes a rider on a gray horse. The rider's name is Death. This rider and his accomplice, Hades—a symbol for the destination of those who die—are authorized to kill a fourth of the world's population by using violence, famine, plagues, and wild animals.

All four of these scenarios play out in John's century, some scholars say. Romans control much of the civilized world. Yet persistent rebellion along with recurring famines and outbreaks of disease keep the Romans grappling to maintain control of their Mediterranean empire.

Seal 5 reveals a group of martyrs in heaven asking when God will avenge their deaths. Each martyr gets a white robe and is told to wait a little longer—that judgment day is coming.

Off and on, depending on the emperor of the moment, the Romans continue to persecute and kill Christians for practicing their outlawed religion. Wild animals in Rome's Coliseum will eat Bishop Ignatius in AD 110. On his way to Rome, the bishop writes a letter about what he is facing: "Fire and cross and battles with wild beasts. . .let these come upon me, only let me reach Jesus."

Seal 6 rocks civilization back to the stone age, sending even top rulers running for cover to caves. A massive quake shakes the planet. Stars crash to the ground. Mountains collapse. Islands sink. The sun goes dark. And the moon shines red. These images are from Old Testament prophecies about what judgment day will be like for sinners. One of many examples: "The earth quakes. . . . The sun and moon grow dark, and the stars no longer shine" (Joel 2:10).

Whether these images are literal or figurative is anyone's guess. But many say they're probably metaphors of disaster since the apocalyptic style of writing dishes out heavy doses of symbolism.

Before the last seal is opened, angels wait at the four corners of the earth and hold back the winds of disaster. They are told to wait until the servants of God are marked: 144,000 of them—12,000 from each of the 12

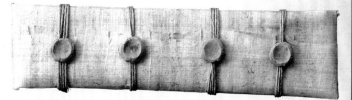

Signed, sealed, and delivered. To ensure privacy, letters and scrolls were rolled up, tied with string, and sealed with small plugs of wet clay or warm wax embedded onto the string. For added security, the writer pressed a personal design into the soft plugs—often from a signet ring. The plugs dried hard. Anyone reading the letter had to first break the seals and remove the string. The document here has four seals, but the scroll John saw had seven.

original tribes of Israel. Scholars debate what 144,000 symbolizes. Among the many guesses: martyrs from all times; Christians who will become martyrs during some future persecution; all the Jewish Christians; or all true believers, representing the New Israel.

Seal 7 silences heaven. It's the calm before the storm. The moment of awe before God unleashes the full force of his judgment on sin.

One by one, seven angels blow trumpets that release fresh waves of disaster. Hail and fire destroy a third of earth's plant life. A fiery mountain thrown into the sea destroys a third of the ocean life. A star falls, poisoning a third of the fresh water. A third of the stars lose their glow. Another star falls, opening a deep tunnel in the earth and releasing deadly creatures. Angels of death kill a third of the world's remaining people.

TAG TEAM beasts

I saw a beast rising up out of the sea. . . . Then I saw another beast come up out of the earth.

REVELATION 13:1, 11

Satan—code-named "Dragon"—links up with two evil allies to form an unholy trinity.

Before the beasts arrive, Satan tries to steal a woman's newborn son. This is probably a reference to the birth of Jesus. Clues: The son "was to rule all nations" and was snatched from Satan and "caught up to God and to his throne" (Revelation 12:5). Unsuccessful, Satan "declared war against the rest of her children—all who keep God's commandments and maintain their testimony for Jesus" (Revelation 12:17).

John sees two beasts.

Beast 1: from the sea
The first beast is the one predicted earlier. It kills two prophets who have completed their ministry: "The beast that comes up out of the bottomless pit will declare war against them, and he will conquer them and kill them" (Revelation 11:7). In chapter 13 this beast is described as coming from "the sea." But both places of origin are the same: the pit (the Abyss) and the sea (the depths).

The sea beast, whoever or whatever it is, has seven heads and ten horns. An angel reveals what the heads and horns symbolize.

Seven heads. "The seven heads of the beast represent the seven hills where the woman [the Great Prostitute of Babylon] rules. They also represent seven kings. Five kings have already fallen, the sixth now reigns, and the seventh is yet to come" (Revelation 17:9–10).

Many Bible experts say John is referring to the Roman Empire. Rome is famous throughout the ancient world as the city built on seven hills. And "Babylon" is a code name for Rome. Both empires conquered the Jewish homeland, occupied the land, and decimated Jerusalem.

There's another clue that points to Rome. Anyone from Rome who came to western Turkey—John's target audience—usually arrived from "the sea," by ship.

Many experts also say the seven kings associated with these seven hills represent the full range of emperors—147 of them spanning almost four centuries. "Seven" is a symbol of completion.

One of these seven "heads" recovers from a mortal wound, which sounds a bit like an evil counterpoint to Jesus' resurrection. The description tracks with a first-century urban legend about Nero, which was similar to stories about Elvis: His death was staged and he's coming back. A year after Nero died, a look-alike slave in what is now western Turkey said he was Nero. Many believed him until a governor in the area executed him. A second fake Nero appeared in AD 80, gathering a following. So did a third man a decade later.

Ten horns. His ten horns are "ten kings who have not yet risen to power. They will be appointed to their kingdoms for one brief moment to reign with the beast" (Revelation 17:12).

These may be "client" kings who ruled at the pleasure of Rome. Herod the Great was such a king. The Romans put him in power over the Jewish homeland and kept him there because he remained loyal to Rome.

Beast 2: from the earth

This beast is often associated with the Antichrist. "Let the one with understanding solve the meaning of the number of the beast, for it is the number of a man. His number is 666" (Revelation 13:18).

Actually, the number is 616 in some ancient editions of the Bible.

There's good reason for the discrepancy, say many Bible scholars. The letters of the Hebrew language—the native language of the Jews—have numerical equivalents. Like A=1 and B=2.

It just so happens that the Hebrew letters for "Nero Caesar," the emperor's name as it appeared on Roman coins, tally up to 666. But that's only when the letters are transliterated into Hebrew from Greek, the language in which John wrote. The letters tally to 616 when transliterated from Latin, the language of the Romans.

Transliteration works like this: Pronounce the words in Greek or Latin. Then select the corresponding letters that produce these sounds in Hebrew. When we take the transliteration one step further, into English, we end up with two possible names:

- Neron Caesar, when starting with Greek.
- Nero Caesar, when starting with Latin.

The English-version tally of the numerical equivalents looks as follows. The bold letters show the numerical equivalents from Hebrew. Light letters show no value because they weren't used in the writing. People writing in Hebrew generally used just the consonants—as an ancient shorthand.

GREEK VERSION

50		200	6	50	100		60		200	=666
N	*e*	**r**	**o**	**n**	**C**	*a*	*e*	**s**	*a*	**r**

LATIN VERSION

50		200	6	100		60		200	=616
N	*e*	**r**	**o**	**C**	*a*	*e*	**s**	*a*	**r**

This doesn't solve the mystery for many Christians. They still wonder if John could have been talking about some other Nero-like tyrant, perhaps a powerful end-time figure opposed to Christianity—an antichrist.

Most Bible scholars say they can't be sure. Some say they wonder if even the people of John's day knew who he was talking about.

MARK of the beast

[The beast] required everyone—small and great, rich and poor, free and slave—to be given a mark on the right hand or on the forehead. And no one could buy or sell anything without that mark.

REVELATION 13:16–17

Some end-time specialists today have worried about an upgrade on the computer swipe: the people swipe. They speculate that a world bank will conduct business transactions by scanning tattooed codes or tiny chips located on hands or foreheads.

But most Bible experts say that's probably taking a too-literal reading from this genre of writing, which is rich in symbolism.

John may have been expecting his readers to see this mark of the beast as the flip side of a mark God required of his own people. God once told the Jews to wear their religion on their hands and foreheads.

The law given by Moses is what distinguished the Jews as God's chosen people. And God said of these laws, "Tie them to your hands and wear them on your forehead as reminders" (Deuteronomy 6:8).

God was probably speaking metaphorically, telling the Jews to keep the laws near and dear—learn them and obey them. Yet some Orthodox Jews today wear tiny black boxes strapped to their hands and foreheads. Inside the boxes are excerpts from their Bible.

Because of this Old Testament connection, which would have been familiar to most of John's readers, many Bible experts say John's reference to the mark of the beast shouldn't be taken literally.

The mark may mean that people will be pressured to show their loyalty to an evil leader by conforming to the ungodly culture around them—something Christians of John's day understand all too well. They're expected to worship the emperor, take part in local festivals honoring Roman gods, and eat meat sacrificed to idols—just like all other good citizens of the empire do. If they don't, they can be treated as outcasts. Their social lives can suffer. So can their finances. It even costs many Christians their lives.

Mark of God. An Orthodox Jew wears the mark of God strapped to his hand and forehead: boxes holding key Bible verses written on tiny scrolls. These boxes tell the world that this man worships the God of the Jews. Some Bible experts wonder if the mark of the beast—also worn on the hand or forehead—is a symbolic counterpoint, a way of saying that everyone has to choose whom they will serve. And that some will not choose God.

ARMAGEDDON and judgment day

I saw the dead, both great and small, standing before God's throne. . . .
And all were judged according to their deeds.

REVELATION 20:12–13

John sees more plagues. He sees sores breaking out on "everyone who had the mark of the beast and who worshiped his statue" (Revelation 16:2). And in one of his most famous visions, he sees "all the rulers of the world. . .gather. . .for battle against the Lord on that great judgment day of God the Almighty" (Revelation 16:14).

The battlefield: a mysterious place John calls Armageddon.

There's no such place mentioned anywhere else in the Bible. But one location sounds very much like it: *Har Megiddo*, "mountain of Megiddo." It overlooks the largest valley in Israel—the Jezreel Valley, where more than 30 major battles have been fought. It's a triangle about 20 miles by 20 miles by 12 miles. Napoleon called it the world's most perfect battlefield.

The battle of Armageddon doesn't seem to involve Christians fighting non-Christians. Instead, it's heaven's army fighting an earthly army led by Satan, the beast, and a false prophet. Leading the celestial army is a rider on a white horse. "He wore a robe dipped in blood, and his title was the Word of God" (Revelation 19:13). This coded phrasing points to Jesus, who shed his blood on a cross. Also, the Gospel of John describes Jesus as "the Word" who was with God and who was God (John 1:1).

The heavenly warriors, some Bible experts say, aren't angels. Instead, they're martyred Christians wearing the same "pure white linen" as the martyrs who had gathered for the "wedding feast of the Lamb" (Revelation 19:7).

In fact, the battle is described as another feast—this one for vultures. "Come! Gather together for the great banquet God has prepared," an angel says, calling the vultures. "Come and eat the flesh of kings, generals, and strong warriors; of horses and their riders; and of all humanity, both free and slave, small and great" (Revelation 19:17–18).

Jesus wins the battle. As predicted in John's earlier visions, "Babylon"—code name for the Roman Empire—falls. Bible experts debate whether or not this is a literal war. If so, it might refer to the collapse of the Roman Empire, or to a future battle, or to both. If it's not about a literal war, some scholars suggest it might be a symbolic way of saying that the persecution of Christians will lead to Rome's downfall. For it's an army of martyrs that wins the day.

The beast and the false prophet get pitched into a lake of fire. Satan, however, ends up locked in a bottomless pit where he stays for "a thousand years" (Revelation 20:2). It's hard to say if this is a literal thousand years. From God's perspective in the spiritual dimension—the same dimension in which John experiences this vision—"a thousand years is like a day" (2 Peter 3:8).

Satan is released for a time to deceive earth's leaders. He gathers another army "called Gog and Magog" (Revelation 20:8).

The prophet Ezekiel predicted this battle about seven centuries before John. In Ezekiel 38, Gog is the ruler of Magog. And he amasses an international coalition to attack Israel.

Many scholars speculate that "Gog" is a name derived from King Gyges of Lydia, a region in what is now western Turkey—home of three of the cities John addresses: Sardis, Thyatira, and Philadelphia. Gyges ruled in the 600s BC, a century before Ezekiel. Assyrians called him Gugi, a name that may have evolved into Gog. "Magog" may come from *mat Gugi*, meaning "land of Gog."

Whoever these soldiers are, and wherever they came from, they end up toast. God destroys them with fire from heaven.

Satan gets tossed into the lake of fire, joining the beast and the false prophet. There they are "tormented day and night forever and ever" (Revelation 20:10). The same doom awaits all human beings throughout history whose names don't show up in the Book of Life. God condemns them to "the second death." The first death is physical and temporary, apparently limited to the physical dimension. But the second death is spiritual and eternal.

Surprisingly, there's no indication that God's people are judged. Judgment day is for the sinners.

WHEN IS JESUS COMING BACK?

Bible students have many theories about when Jesus is coming back. Some of these theories spin around the mysterious thousand years of peace on earth, when John says Satan will be locked up in a bottomless pit.

Pre-millenium. Jesus will come back to launch the thousand years of peace and to rule earth from Jerusalem.

Post-millenium. Jesus will return after the thousand years of peace to take his followers to heaven. Many call this exodus into heaven the rapture. "The Christians who have died will rise from their graves. Then, together with them, we who are still alive and remain on the earth will be caught up in the clouds to meet the Lord in the air. Then we will be with the Lord forever" (1 Thessalonians 4:16–17).

A-millenium. We're living in the thousand years now. Through the church, Jesus is bringing peace to the world.

Pan-millenium. More of a joke among scholars than a theory, the idea here is that everything will pan out in the end. In the meantime, there are only two things we can know for certain about the second coming: Jesus will come back, but we don't know when. "I will come as unexpectedly as a thief!" (Revelation 16:15).

Other theories spin around "the great tribulation" (Revelation 7:14). Some Bible experts say Jesus will come before a terrible end-time persecution of Christians. Some say after. Some say during. Still others say the tribulation John is talking about is the Roman persecution of Christians and that it has nothing to do with the second coming.

HEAVEN at last

Then I saw a new heaven and a new earth, for the old heaven and the old earth had disappeared.

REVELATION 21:1

In John's last vision—the climax of the entire Bible—he sees what he calls "the new Jerusalem, coming down from God out of heaven" (Revelation 21:2).

To many Bible students, this sounds like heaven on earth—but new and improved, since the first heaven and earth have disappeared. Also gone: death, sorrow, crying, and pain— "gone forever" (Revelation 21:4).

Others see this descent of Jerusalem as a description of heaven itself. They see John drawing from a famous scene in the Prophets: "Look! I am creating new heavens and a new earth. . . . I will create Jerusalem as a place of happiness. . . . And the sound of weeping and crying will be heard in it no more" (Isaiah 65:17–19).

Wherever this place is, and whatever it is—physical, spiritual, or both—it's the eternal home of God and his people.

HELL: ETERNAL TORTURE?

Hell's a puzzler. Even for top Bible scholars. There are three reasons they often mention.

The word "hell" isn't in the Bible.

When "hell" shows up in English Bibles, it's almost always translating the word Gehenna, the name of a valley just outside Jerusalem's city walls. Jews used to kill people in this valley—children included—as sacrifices to idols. Since this kind of idolatry is what led God to exile Jews from their homeland in 586 BC, the valley apparently became a reminder of the punishment and a symbol of God's judgment.

The Bible has clashing descriptions of where souls will be punished.

Jesus talked about "the unquenchable fires of hell [Gehenna]" (Mark 9:43). But Peter spoke of God sending angels "into hell, in gloomy pits of darkness" (2 Peter 2:4). Firelight dispels darkness. So how can there be both firelight and darkness?

Eternal torture doesn't sound like something God would do.

God is love. Even when he punishes, he has a redemptive goal: to help people. He uses punishment to correct people—to turn them away from sin and the destruction it causes. But what good can come from throwing souls into "the fiery lake" where they are "tormented day and night forever and ever" (Revelation 20:10)?

Perplexed over what to make of hell, Bible scholars offer theories like these.

- **It's a real place.** People who end up in hell will suffer forever in flames. Sure, God is love. But he's holy, too. He can't overlook sin. But he can and does warn people about where sin leads. If they choose to follow that path, it's their choice—not his.
- **There's no physical fire.** There's just the torment of being forever separated from God.
- **Fire symbolizes annihilation.** Sinners won't suffer endlessly. They'll be destroyed. It's the destruction, not the suffering, that lasts forever.
- **God will keep sinners alive forever—not to punish them, but to allow reconciliation.** How else could it be true, some scholars ask, that "God reconciled everything to himself. He made peace with everything in heaven and on earth by means of Christ's blood on the cross" (Colossians 1:20)?

Touring hell. The ghost of the Roman poet Virgil, left, leads Dante on a terrifying tour of hell. The Italian nobleman Dante Alighieri, in the late 1200s, wrote a poem about the fictional journey: *The Divine Comedy.* His tale inspired generations of artists to capture the scenes on canvas. In Dante's version of hell, demons dump sinners into designated zones. Angry souls land in the zone of wrath where they fight each other forever.

SNAPSHOTS OF HEAVEN

John describes heaven.

It's a cube, 1,400 miles in every direction. Many scholars say we should read this as a code. The holiest spot on earth was a cube. It was a room in the Jerusalem temple where the Jews kept their most sacred object: the ark of the covenant, a gold-plated chest that held the original 10 Commandments. Only the high priest could go inside this holy room, which stretched a mere 30 feet in each direction. What John sees is unimaginably greater than even the holiest spot on earth.

It's decorated in jewels and treasure. Walls of jeweled jasper. A dozen gates, each made of one massive pearl. Streets of gold so pure they look like glass.

It glows with the light of God's glory. "The city has no need of sun or moon, for the glory of God illuminates the city, and the Lamb is its light" (Revelation 21:23). Throughout the Bible, celestial beings are often described as glowing. Shortly before his crucifixion, Jesus appears to momentarily transfigure into his heavenly form: "The appearance of his face was transformed, and his clothes became dazzling white" (Luke 9:29).

Again, Bible students aren't sure how literally to take John's description of the holy city. Some say they intend to walk on streets of gold. Others say John is trying to describe a non-physical place to physics-bound earthlings who have no frame of reference for comparison. So he picks out some of the most mundane features in this celestial city—walls, streets, and gates—and he reports that even these boring objects are better than the greatest treasures on earth.

NEW Eden

Then the angel showed me a river with the water of life, clear as crystal, flowing from the throne of God and of the Lamb. It flowed down the center of the main street. On each side of the river grew a tree of life.

REVELATION 22:1–2

"In the beginning God created the heavens and the earth" (Genesis 1:1). Then in a paradise called Eden, God placed the first human beings: Adam and Eve. God nourished Eden with a river. And he offered Adam and Eve a future forever, provided by fruit from the tree of life. At least that's what some Bible experts say the tree was doing in Eden.

But the first humans broke the one and only rule God gave them. They ate from a forbidden tree. This disobedience somehow contaminated God's creation, introducing sin and death into the cosmic equation. The rest of the Bible—from Genesis to Revelation—is the story of God working his plan to undo the damage.

John, in his final vision, sees the end of that story. And it looks very much like the beginning. A pure river flows from the throne of God. Trees of life sprout up along both sides of the river.

Paradise lost has now been found. It's better than ever. And it's forever and ever.

Having seen the future, John has just one request: "Come, Lord Jesus!" (Revelation 22:20).

INDEXES

KEY TO SUBJECT/TOPIC INDEX
bold numbers: featured
regular numbers: mentioned
color numbers: image

ART RESOURCES

Old Testament
8, Saint Peter, S/AR.

Genesis
10, New star forming, NASA; JPL-Caltech, R. Hurt (SSC); 14, Gerard, Francois, Psyche and Amor, 1798, Louvre, Paris, France, EL/AR; 16, Prism, Ashmolean Museum; 17 top, 3D profile of Mt. Ararat, NASA Jet Propulsion Laboratory; 17 bottom, Map of the Middle East, RC/GSI; 17 map art right, Noah's Ark, Edward Hicks/WM; 17 map art left, Eve, Lucien Levy-Dhurmer/WM; 17 map art bottom, Camel caravan, Norman McDonald/Saudi Aramco World/PADIA; 18, Chemicals drying in Dead Sea, Albatross; 18 map art, Dead Sea, NASA/Earth Observatory; 21, Rachel, William Whitaker; 24, Joseph, Overseer of Pharaoh's Granaries, 1874 (oil on panel), Alma-Tadema, Sir Lawrence (1836–1912)/© Dahesh Museum of Art, New York, USA/BAL.

Exodus
27, Slaves leaving Egypt, TYN; 29, Making mud bricks, Joe McDonald/Corbis; 30, The Finding of Moses by Pharaoh's Daughter, 1904, Alma-Tadema, Sir Lawrence (1836–1912)/Private Collection/BAL; 32, Locusts over pyramids, Juan Medina/Reuters/Corbis; 34, Relief of royal family of Amenophis IV Akhenaton offering a sacrifice to Aton, the sun god, Egyptian Museum, Cairo, Egypt, EL/AR; 35, Map of Sinai, NASA/WW; 35 map art, Exodus travelers, LC/DR; 38, Hebrews worship bull at Mt. Sinai, TYN; 40, Tabernacle replica, ZR; 41, Priests, AKG/Peter Connolly.

Leviticus
42, Zurbaran, Francisco de, Agnus Dei (Lamb of God), Museo del Prado, Madrid, Spain, S/AR; 45, Jews talking at fish market, BA; 47, Samaritans cooking over Passover sacrifices, Dean Conger/Corbis.

Numbers
48, Goodall, Frederick, Early Morning in the Wilderness of Shur, Guildhall Art Gallery, London, Great Britain, HIP/AR; 49, Map on a satellite photo, NASA/WW; 49 map art, Exodus travelers, LC/DR; 50, Israelites and the bronze snake pole, TYN; 52, Man riding donkey, LC; 53, Painting of Mt. Sinai with St. Catherine's Monastery, LC/DR.

Deuteronomy
54, Walking toward the Jordan River Valley, LC/DR; 56, Code of Hammurabi, BM; 57, Jew in prayer shawl, BA; 58, Michelangelo Buonarroti, Moses, S. Pietro in Vincoli, Rome, Italy, S/AR; 60 top right, Tissot, James Jacques Joseph, Moses Sees the Promised Land from Afar, The Jewish Museum, New York, NY, U.S.A., JM/AR; 60 bottom left, Tissot, James Jacques Joseph, Moses and Joshua in the Tabernacle, The Jewish Museum, New York, NY, U.S.A., JM/AR.

Joshua
61, Battle scene, National Geographic/Tom Lovell; 63, Woman representing Rachel, William Whitaker; 64, Crossing the Jordan, LC/DR; 65, Cliffs of Jordan, LC/Frank and Frances Carpenter; 66, Jericho mound, ZR; 67, Map of Joshua's battle sites, CH; 68, Sun standing still during battle, TYN; 69, Map of twelve tribes and cities of refuge, RC/GSI.

Judges
71, Samson grinding at mill, Carl Bloch/Statens Museum for Kunst; 74, Mount Tabor, Albatross; 75, Camel rider, LC/MPC; 77, Delilah holding Samson's hair, Kirk Richards.

Ruth
79, Bedouin woman, LC/MPC; 81, Map of Naomi's journey, CH; 81 map art, Ruth and Naomi, William Blake/WM; 82, Bethlehem widow, SM; 83, Jewish bride and groom with head covering, Owen Franken/Corbis.

1 Samuel
84, Boy with donkey, Owen Franken/Corbis; 89, Tissot, James Jacques Joseph, The Idol Broken Down Before the Ark, The Jewish Museum, New York, NY, U.S.A., JM/AR; 90, David kills Goliath, TYN; 92, Aerial of En-gedi region, Bibleplaces.com/Todd Bolen; 92 map art left, Map of En-gedi, RC/GSI; 92 map art right, En-gedi waterfall, Richard T. Nowitz/Corbis; 93, Statue of dog, Rodrigo/WM.

2 Samuel
94, Mola, Pier-Francesco, Oriental warrior holding a bow, Louvre, Paris, France, EL/AR; 95, Stone fragment: "House of David", ZR; 96, Map of David's Kingdom, RC/GSI; 96 map art, David's Jerusalem, ZR; 98, Robed woman as Bathsheba bathing, William Whitaker.

1 Kings
101, Poussin, Nicolas, Judgment of Solomon, Louvre, Paris, France, EL/AR; 104, Painting of Solomon's temple, Peter V. Bianchi/National Geographic; 105, Man and his harem, Bettmann/Corbis; 106, Map of divided nation of Israel, RC/GSI; 106 map art, Tinette/WM; 107, Moabite stone, BM; 108, Elijah statue on Mt. Carmel, SM.

2 Kings
110, Hayez, Francesco, The Destruction of the Temple of Jerusalem, Accademia, Venice, Italy, Cameraphoto Arte, Venice/AR; 112, Jehu, King of Israel, prostrating himself before King Shalmaneser III of Assyria, British Museum, London, Great Britain, EL/AR; 114, Assyrian warriors impaling Jewish prisoners after conquering Jewish fortress of Lachish, British Museum, London, Great Britain, EL/AR; 115, Hezekiah's Tunnel, ZR; 116, Sennacherib's prism, Israel Museum (IDAM), Jerusalem, Israel, EL/AR; 117, Map of route to Babylon exile, NASA/MODIS; 117 map art, Elamite prisoners led into exile by an Assyrian soldier, Israel Museum (IDAM), Jerusalem, Israel, EL/AR.

1 Chronicles
118, Old scribe writing onto a scroll, BA; 122, Ark of the Covenant, Bill Latta.

2 Chronicles
124, Cutaway of Solomon's temple, TYN; 126, Map of Sheba, NASA/MODIS; 126 map art, Woman from Yemen, LC/Pascal Sebah; 128 left, Cyrus Cylinder, British Museum, London, Great Britain, HIP/AR; 128 right, Persian warrior, BM.

Ezra
130, Camel caravan, LC/MPC; 132, Map of route home from Babylonian exile, NASA/MODIS; 132 map art, Travelers, LC/DR.

Nehemiah
135, Worker repairing model, Greg Schneider; 136 top, Gold cup decorated with winged lion, Archaeological Museum, Teheran, Iran, S/AR; 136 bottom, Serving a drink, British Museum, London, Great Britain, EL/AR; 138, Model of Jerusalem walls, Leen Ritmeyer.

Esther
140, Esther and the king, Peter V. Bianchi/National Geographic; 141, Map of Persian Empire, NASA/JPL/NIMA; 141 map art, Lion, Marie-Lan Nguyen/WM; 142, The Court of the Harem (oil on canvas), Girard, Albert (1839–1920)/© Towneley Hall Art Gallery and Museum, Burnley, Lancashire/BAL; 146, Persians in battle, Museo Archeologico Nazionale, Naples, Italy, Alinari/AR.

Job
147, Bonnat, Leon, Job, Musee Bonnat, Bayonne, France, RMN/AR; 150,

Person with shingles, Lester V. Bergman/Corbis; **151**, Blake, William, Job Rebuked by His Friends, The Pierpont Morgan Library, New York, NY, U.S.A., The Pierpont Morgan Library/AR; **152**, Creation scene, NASA/JPL-Caltech.

Psalms
154, Actor portraying David with harp, Dave Bartruff/Corbis; **156**, Camel rider at sunset, Tony Craddock/Corbis; **161**, Painting of travelers going to Jerusalem, LC/DR; **162**, Qumran cave, SM; **162** map art, Satellite map, NASA.

Proverbs
163, Three men of Minsk, BA; **165**, Mummy mask of Amenemope, Sandro Vannini/Corbis; **166**, Nausicaa, Leighton, Frederic (1830–96)/Private Collection, Photo © Christie's Images/BAL; **168**, Farmer plowing, LC/Frank and Frances Carpenter.

Ecclesiastes
170, Orator or a philosopher, Museo Archeologico Nazionale, Naples, Italy, EL/AR; **171**, Pearce, Charles Sprague, Lamentations Over the Death of the First-Born of Egypt, Smithsonian American Art Museum, Washington, DC, U.S.A., SAAM/AR; **173**, Painting of woman with wine, William Bouguereau/Thebrid/WM; **174**, Babylonian epic of Gilgamesh describing the deeds of the legendary hero who sought eternal life, Israel Museum (IDAM), Jerusalem, Israel, EL/AR.

Song of Solomon
175, Dinet, Etienne, Slave of Love and Light of Eyes, Musee d'Orsay, Paris, France, RMN/AR; **176**, St. Bernard of Clairveau, The Granger Collection, NY; **179**, Autumn Mandrake, from the 'Hortus Eystettensis' by Basil Besler (1561–1629) pub. 1613 (hand coloured engraving), German School, (17th century)/Private Collection, The Stapleton Collection/BAL; **180**, Cupid with Arrow, William Bouguereau/Thebrid/WM; **181**, Egyptian couple, BM.

Isaiah
182, Angel and Isaiah, Benjamin West, Isaiah's Lips Anointed with Fire; **183**, Isaiah scroll, John C. Trever, PhD./The Dead Sea Scroll Foundation, Inc./Corbis; **184**, Gallery of prophets, LC/John Singer Sargent; **186**, Map of Prophets, RC/GSI; **188**, Mantegna, Andrea, Dead Christ, Pinacoteca di Brera, Milan, Italy, S/AR; **190**, Deep impact, © Topham/The Image Works; **192**, Map of doomed countries and Assyrian and Babylonian empires, RC/GSI.

Jeremiah
195, Scribe in Louvre, BM; **200**, Potter working at wheel, Tor Eigeland/Saudi Aramco World/PADIS; **201** left, Lachish letter on broken pottery, ZR; **201** right, Baruch seal, ZR; **203**, Rachel weeping, Stephen Gjertson.

Lamentations
205, The Daughters of Judah in Babylon, Schmalz, Herbert Gustave (1856–1935)/Private Collection, Photo © Christie's Images/BAL; **207**, Portrait on casket, BM; **208**, Man praying at Western Wall, SM.

Ezekiel
211, Human anatomy sketch, Unites States National Library of Medicine/Artist, Jan Wandelaar/Anatomist, Bernhard Siegfried Albinus; **212**, Mark with lion, BM; **214**, Ezekiel at death of his wife, Philadelphia Museum of Art/Corbis; **215**, Sketch of Sabbatai Zevi, SM; **216**, Map "Bad News for Judah's Neighbors," NASA/WW; **219**, Michelangelo Buonarroti, The Sistine Chapel; ceiling frescos after restoration. The Prophet Ezekiel, Sistine Chapel, Vatican Palace, Vatican State, EL/AR.

Daniel
220, Map of Daniel's route to Babylon and Babylonian Empire, NASA/WW; **220** map art, Officer conducts 2 Judeans to the king, British Museum, London, Great Britain, EL/AR; **224**, Rembrandt Harmensz van Rijn, Belshazzar's Feast, National Gallery, London, Great Britain, AR; **225**, Daniel in the lion's den, TYN; **227**, Alexander the Great attacking Persians, H. M. Herget/National Geographic; **228**, Snake, U.S. Fish and Wildlife Service

Hosea
229, Prostitute, AKG; **230**, Baal holding club and blooming spear, BM; **232**, Jezreel Valley, SM; **233**, Map of Judah, Israel, and Jezreel Valley, RC/GSI; **234**, Temple priestess, William Bouguereau/Thebrid/WM.

Joel
236, Locusts with tourists, Juan Medina/Reuters/Corbis; **238** top, Locust egg pods, LC/MPC; **238** middle first, Burning locusts, LC/MPC; **238** middle second, Poisoning locusts, LC/MPC; **238** middle third, Pit trap for locusts, LC/MPC; **238** bottom left, Stomping locusts, LC/MPC; **238** bottom right, Locust eating, LC/MPC; **240**, Greek soldier.

Amos
243, Beggar family, LC; **245**, Map of prophecies against Israel's neighbors,

NASA/WW; **247**, Egyptian plumbline, The Granger Collection; NY.

Obadiah
249, Petra entrance, SM; **250**, Painting of Petra's temple, LC/DR; **252**, Map of Edom, RC/GSI; **252** map art, Camel rider, LC/Detroit Photographic Company.

Jonah
253, Whale swallows Jonah, TYN; **255**, Map of Jonah's route, NASA/JPL/NIMA; **255** map art top, Statue of whale in Joppa, SM; **255** map art bottom, Phoenician ship model, ZR; **258**, Nineveh, Stapleton Collection/Corbis.

Micah
259, Farmer with wooden plow and plowshare, Roger Wood/Corbis; **261**, Chart art of prophecies for 700s BC, LC/John Singer Sargent; **262**, Map of Micah's day, RC/GSI; **262** map art, Micah, The Yorck Project/WM/Artist, Giovanni Battista Tiepolo; **264**, Woman at the well in Bethlehem, LC/MPC.

Nahum
265, Map of Assyrian Empire, NASA/WW; **265** map art, Assyrian dignitary, BM; **266**, Tablet with part of the Babylonian Chronicle, British Museum, London, Great Britain, EL/AR; **267**, Bridgman, Frederick Arthur, Entertainment of an Assyrian King, Private Collection, AR; **269** top, Warriors carrying heads of enemies and throwing them on a heap, British Museum, London, Great Britain, EL/AR; **269** bottom, Stone panel from the Southwest Palace of King Sennacherib Nineveh, British Museum, London, Great Britain, EL/AR.

Habakkuk
270, Martin Luther nailing 95 theses to church door, AKG; **272** left, Ishtar priest, BM; **272** right, Ishtar mold and figurine, The Granger Collection: NY; **273**, Habakkuk commentary from Dead Sea Scrolls, LC/MPC.

Zephaniah
274, Line art of prophet with hooded robe, LC/John Singer Sargent; **276**, "No fear" photo of flood surrounding house, Les Stone/Sygma/Corbis. **278**, Map of doomed cities, RC/GSI.

Haggai
280, Woman farming with mattock, David Turnley/Corbis; **282**, Western Wall and Dome of the Rock, Albatross; **283**, Art of temple construction, TYN.

Zechariah
285, Thayer, Abbott Handerson, Angel, Smithsonian American Art Museum, Washington, DC, U.S.A., SAAM/AR; **288**, Musician with lyre, 1878, Josephson, Ernst (1851–1906)/© Nationalmuseum, Stockholm, Sweden, BAL; **290**, Jesus riding donkey, TYN.

Malachi
291, Bull, Raymond Gehman/National Geographic; **294**, Cheerful giver in church, SM/Thomas Worth/C.S. Reinhart/Harper's Weekly; **295**, Circumcision ritual, BA.

Apocrypha
296, Alexandria library in watercolor, Michael Grimsdale/Saudi Aramco World/PADIA.

New Testament
298, Church council meeting, 1880: The Beginning of Church Dissidence in Russia, 1880, Kivshenko, Aleksei Danilovich (1851–95)/Central Naval Museum, St. Petersburg, Russia, BAL.

Matthew
300, The Wise Men Journeying to Bethlehem, illustration for 'The Life of Christ,' c. 1886–94, Tissot, James Jacques Joseph (1836–1902)/Brooklyn Museum of Art, New York, USA, BAL; **302**, Map of the world of Jesus and the wise men, RC/GSI/NASA/WW; **302** map art top left, Mary holding Jesus, William-Adolphe Bouguereau/WM/Stevertigo; **302** map art bottom left, Detailed map, RC/GSI/NASA/WW; **302** map art right, Men on camels, LC/MPC; **304**, Chart of Saturn, Jupiter, and Pisces, Catherine Thompson and Ashley Schrock/Barbour; **304** chart art, Saturn and Jupiter, NASA/Hubble Space Telescope; **304** chart art bottom right, Pisces constellation, NASA; **305**, Bethlehem massacre of children, AKG; **307**, Mount of Beatitudes, SM; **309**, Fish mosaic at Tabgha, SM; **310**, Statue of Jesus and Peter at Church of Primacy, SM; **311**, Aerial of Church of Transfiguration on Mt. Tabor, Albatross; **315**, Jesus carries cross, BM.

Mark
317, Fishermen in boat, LC/MPC; **322** top, Perfume and herbs, John Feeney/Saudi Arabia World/PADIA; **322** middle, Mustard seeds, David Turner; **322** bottom, Wheat stalks and grain, Agricultural Research Service Information, US Dept. of Agriculture/Scott Bauer; **324**, Jesus healing a man, Patrick Devonas; **327**, Jerusalem Temple, AKG; **329**, Window in The Church of the Lord Wept, SM; **330**, Dead Jesus on slab, Patrick Devonas.